SOUTHERN LITERARY CULTURE

Dedicated to the many reference librarians and the members of their staffs who made this book possible, especially to Mrs. Patricia Salomon, Bowling Green State University, who believes that people are more important than numbers.

SOUTHERN LITERARY CULTURE

A BIBLIOGRAPHY OF MASTERS' AND DOCTORS' THESES

REVISED AND ENLARGED EDITION

Compiled and Edited by
O. B. EMERSON
and MARION C. MICHAEL

THE UNIVERSITY OF ALABAMA PRESS
University, Alabama

This study was prepared under
the auspicies of the Society for the
Study of Southern Literature and
with a grant from the
National Endowment for the Humanities

Library of Congress Cataloging in Publication Data

Emerson, O. B.
  Southern literary culture.

  Edition published in 1955 by C. H. Cantrell and W. R.
Patrick.
    1. American literature--Southern States--History and
criticism--Bibliography.   2. Dissertations, Academic--
Bibliography.   I. Michael, Marion C., joint author.
II. Cantrell, Clyde Hull. Southern literary culture.
III. Title.
Z1251.S7C3   1979   [PS261]   016.810'9'975   78-10771
ISBN 0-8173-9514-8

CONTENTS

Introduction / xi

Part One: INDIVIDUAL WRITERS

Andy Adams / 1
James Agee / 1
James Lane Allen / 2
William Hervey Allen / 3
Ewing Allison / 3
Washington Allston / 3
Harriette Arnow / 3
Henry Austin / 4
Mary Hunter Austin / 4
Dora Aydelotte / 4
Thomas Bacon / 4
George William Bagby / 4
Temple Bailey / 4
Karle Wilson Baker / 4
Joseph Glover Baldwin / 4
Nancy Huston Banks / 4
James Barbour / 5
William Barksdale / 5
John Barth / 5
Katherine Belleman / 5
John Barry Benefield / 6
William Beverley / 6
Theodore G. Bilbo / 6
John Peale Bishop / 6
Hugo L. Black / 6
James Blair / 6
Richard Bland / 6
Albert Taylor Bledsoe / 7
John Henry Boner / 7
Gail Borden / 7
Jonathan Boucher / 7
James Boyd / 7
Virginia Frazer Boyle / 7
Roark Bradford / 7
William Cowper Brann / 7
Cleanth Brooks / 8
Alexander Brown / 8
Joseph E. Brown / 8
William G. Brown / 8
William Wells Brown / 8
Philip Alexander Bruce / 8
Robert Wilton Burton / 9
Sigman Byrd / 9
William Byrd / 9
James Branch Cabell / 9
Joseph Carrington Cabell / 11
George Washington Cable / 11
Erskine Caldwell / 13

John C. Calhoun / 14
George Henry Calvert / 14
Charles Campbell / 14
John Archibald Campbell / 14
Truman Capote / 15
Hodding Carter / 15
Peter Cartwright / 15
William Alexander Caruthers / 16
George Washington Carver / 16
Wilbur Joseph Cash / 16
Madison Cawein / 16
Katherine Hopkins Chapman / 16
Charles Waddell Chesnutt / 17
Thomas Holley Chivers / 17
Kate Chopin / 17
Jeremiah Clemens / 18
Samuel L. Clemens (Mark Twain)
  / 18
Irvin S. Cobb / 34
Thomas R.R. Cobb / 35
Edward Louis Cochran / 35
Zitella Cocke / 35
Oscar Branch Colquitt / 35
Moncure Conway / 35
Ebenezer Cook / 35
John Esten Cooke / 35
Philip Pendleton Cooke / 35
Thomas Cooper / 36
James Andrew Corcoran / 36
John Cotton / 36
David Crockett / 36
Grace Noll Crowell / 36
Jabez Lamar Monroe Curry / 36
Robert Lewis Dabney / 36
Josephus Daniels / 37
Olive Tilford Dargan / 37
Donald Davidson / 37
William Lee Davidson / 37
Maria Thompson Daviess / 37
Jefferson Davis / 37
Mary Evelyn Moore Davis / 37
Robert Means Davis / 38
Varina Howell Davis / 38
Francis Warrington Dawson / 38
George Bannerman Dealey / 38
James D.B. De Bow / 38
Sidonie De La Houssaye / 38
Charles De Morse / 38

Cabeza de Vaca / 38
Thomas Roderick Dew / 39
James Dickey / 39
Harris Dickson / 39
Thomas Dixon / 39
J. Frank Dobie / 39
William E. Dodd / 39
Sarah Anne Dorsey / 40
Frederick Douglass / 40
William Allen Dromgoole / 40
Harry Stillwell Edwards / 40
George Cary Eggleston / 40
Sarah Burnwell Elliot / 40
Stephen Elliott / 40
William Elliott / 40
Ralph Ellison / 41
Loula Grace Erdman / 41
William C. Falkner / 71
John Faulkner / 41
William Faulkner / 41
Mary McNeill Fenollosa / 71
Jim Ferguson / 71
George Fitzhugh / 71
John Gould Fletcher / 71
Shelby Foote 72
Jesse Hill Ford / 72
John Salmon Ford / 72
John Forsyth / 72
Alcee Fortier / 72
John Fox, Jr. / 73
John C. Fremont / 73
Alice French (Octave Thanet) / 73
Virginia French / 73
Lucy Furman / 73
Christopher Gadsden / 73
Joseph Gales, Sr. / 74
Charles Etienne Arthur Gayarré
    / 74
Robert Wilson Gibbes / 74
Basil Lanneau Gildersleeve / 74
Caroline Howard Gilman / 74
Francis Walker Gilmer / 74
Ellen Glasgow / 74
Carter Glass / 80
Caroline Gordon / 80
Francis Robert Goulding / 81
Henry W. Grady / 81
Shirley Ann Grau / 81
William John Grayson / 81
Duff Green / 82
Paul Green / 82
Frances Nimmo Greene / 83
Hugh Blair Grigsby / 83
Frank Grimes / 83

Sarah Grimké / 83
Reuben Post Halleck / 83
James Henry Hammond / 83
Will N. Harben / 83
Isaac Harby / 84
William Joseph Hardee / 84
Frances E.W. Harper / 84
Robert Goodloe Harper / 84
Corra Harris / 84
George Washington Harris / 84
Joel Chandler Harris / 85
Constance Cary Harrison / 86
Atticus Greene Haygood / 87
Paul Hamilton Hayne / 87
William Hamilton Hayne / 87
William Shakespeare Hays / 87
Lafacadio Hearn / 87
Lillian Hellman / 89
Hinton Rowan Helper / 90
Patrick Henry / 90
Caroline Lee Hentz / 90
Hilary Abner Herbert / 91
John Hill Hewitt / 91
DuBose Heyward / 91
Walter Barnard Hill / 91
William W. Holden / 91
George Frederick Holmes / 91
Johnson Jones Hooper / 92
George Moses Horton / 92
Sam Houston / 92
R.B.C. Howell / 92
Langston Hughes / 92
Kermit Hunter / 93
Robert Hancock Hunter / 93
R.M.T. Hunter / 93
Zora Neale Hurston / 93
Joseph Holt Ingraham / 93
James Iredell / 93
Henry Rootes Jackson / 93
Cecilia Viets Jamison / 93
Randall Jarrell / 93
Thomas Jefferson / 94
James Weldon Johnson / 97
Lyndon Baines Johnson / 97
Siddie Joe Johnson / 97
Annie Fellows Johnston / 97
Mary Johnston / 97
Richard Malcolm Johnston / 98
William Preston Johnston / 98
Charles Colcock Jones, Jr. / 98
John Beauchamp Jones / 98
Madison Jones / 98
Helen Adams Keller / 98
Frances Anne Kemble 98

James Lawson Kemper / 99
Amos Kendall / 99
George Wilkins Kendall / 99
John P. Kennedy / 99
Francis Scott Key / 100
Frances Parkinson Keyes / 100
Joseph Buckner Killebrew / 100
Aline Kilmer / 100
Grace Elizabeth King / 100
Martin Luther King, Jr. / 100
Frederick Henry Koch / 101
Harry Harrison Kroll / 101
Joseph Wood Krutch / 101
Lucius Q.C. Lamar / 101
Mirabeau B. Lamar / 101
John Mercer Langston / 101
Edwin Lanham / 102
Clifford Anderson Lanier / 102
Sidney Lanier / 102
Richard Henry Lee / 106
Robert E. Lee / 106
Hugh Swinton Legaré / 106
Octavia Walton Levert / 106
Alfred Henry Lewis / 107
Francis Lieber / 107
Clinton Lockhart / 107
John A. Lomax / 107
Huey P. Long / 107
John Benjamin Long / 107
Augustus Baldwin Longstreet / 107
Robert Loveman / 107
Grace Lumpkin / 107
Andrew Nelson Lytle / 108
James Madison / 108
Julia Magruder / 108
Walter Malone / 108
Basil Manly II / 109
Elliott Crayton McCants / 109
Louisa C. McCord / 109
Carson McCullers / 109
Katherine Sherwood Bonner
  McDowell (Sherwood Bonner)
  / 112
John B. McFerrin / 112
Randal William McGavock / 112
Ralph McGill / 112
Carlyle McKinley / 112
John Charles McNeill / 112
Alexander Beaufort Meek / 113
Adah Issacs Menken / 113
Henry Louis Mencken / 113
Dr. Alfred Mercier / 114
Thomas Merton / 114
George Milburn / 114
William Henry Milburn / 114

Heather Ross Miller / 114
Lucian Minor / 114
Margaret Mitchell / 114
Andrew Jackson Montague / 115
Idora McClellan Moore / 115
John Trotwood Moore / 115
Merrill Moore / 115
Patrick D. Moreland / 115
Edgar Young Mullins / 115
William Munford / 115
Mary Noailles Murfree
  (Charles Egbert Craddock)
  / 116
A.O.P. Nicholson / 116
Charles Fenton Mercer Noland
  / 116
Adolph S. Ochs / 117
Flannery O'Connor / 117
Williamson Simpson Oldham / 121
F.L. Olmsted / 121
John Page / 121
Thomas Nelson Page / 121
Walter Hines Page / 122
Benjamin Morgan Palmer / 122
John Williamson Palmer / 122
Samuel Minturn Peck
Walker Percy / 122
William Alexander Percy / 122
George Sessions Perry / 123
Robert Peter / 123
Julia Mood Peterkin / 123
Charles Joseph Peterson / 123
James Louis Petigru / 124
Francis W. Pickens / 124
Albert Pike / 124
Clarence Hamilton Poe / 124
Edgar Allan Poe / 124
Edward Alfred Pollard / 140
Katherine Anne Porter / 140
William S. Porter
  (O. Henry) / 144
John Pory / 145
William Louis Poteat / 145
Reuben Marmaduke Potter / 145
George D. Prentice / 145
Margaret Junkin Preston / 146
Reynolds Price / 146
Louise Clarke Pyrnelle / 146
J.G.M. Ramsey / 146
James Ryder Randall / 146
John Randolph / 146
Ryland Randolph / 146
Thomas Jefferson Randolph / 146
John Crowe Ransom / 146
Marjorie Kinnan Rawlings / 148

[vii]

Opie Pope Read / 149
Byron Herbert Reece / 149
Lizette Woodworth Reese / 149
Clara Reyes
  (Walther Gray) / 149
Robert Barnwell Rhett / 149
Alice Hegan Rice / 149
Cale Young Rice / 150
Lynn Riggs / 150
Spencer Roan
  (Algernon Sidney) / 150
Elizabeth Madox Roberts / 150
Will Rogers / 151
Anne Royall / 151
Irwin Russell / 151
Mildred Lewis Rutherford / 152
Fr. Abram Joseph Ryan / 152
Joseph Salyards / 152
George Sandys / 152
Herbert Ravenel Sass / 153
Lyle Saxon / 153
Dorothy Scarborough / 153
Evelyn Scott / 153
Sequoyah / 153
William Gilmore Simms / 153
Charles A. Siringo / 157
Ashbel Smith / 157
Charles Henry Smith / 157
  (Bill Arp) / 157
Dollilee Davis Smith / 157
Francis Hopkinson Smith / 158
Mrs. E.D.E.N. Southworth / 158
Laurence Stallings / 158
Mrs. Mary Newton Stanard / 158
Frank L. Stanton / 158
Alexander Hamilton Stephens
  / 159
William Henry Stiles / 159
James Still / 159
William Stith / 159
James Street / 159
Thomas S. Stribling / 159
David Hunter Strother
  (Porte Crayon) / 160
William Styron / 160
Jesse Stuart / 161
Ruth McEnery Stuart / 162
Alexander Edwin Sweet / 162
John Banister Tabb / 162
Allen Tate / 163
Peter Taylor / 163
Mary Virginia Terhune
  (Marion Harland) / 164
Alexander Watkins Terrell / 164
Charles Testut / 164

Augustus Thomas / 164
John R. Thompson / 164
Maurice Thompson / 164
William Tappan Thompson / 164
James Henley Thornwell / 164
Thomas Bangs Thorpe / 165
Francis Orray Ticknor / 165
Frances Christine Fisher Tiernan
  (Christian Reed) / 165
Henry Timrod / 165
Robert A. Toombs / 166
Jean Toomer / 166
Albion Winegar Tourgée / 166
William Barret Travis / 166
William Peterfield Trent / 166
William Henry Trescot / 166
Amélia Rives Troubetzkoy
  (Amélie Rives) / 166
George W. Truett / 167
George Tucker / 167
Nathaniel Beverly Tucker / 167
St. George Tucker / 167
William Orrie Tuggle / 167
Joseph Addison Turner / 167
Julia Strudwich Tutwiler / 167
Joseph Rogers Underwood / 168
Abel Parker Upshur / 168
James K. Vardaman / 168
Judge Félix Voorhies / 168
John Donald Wade / 168
Robert J. Walker / 168
Robert Sparks Walker / 168
George C. Wallace / 168
Robert Walsh / 168
Jeanette R.H. Walworth / 169
Rufus Waples / 169
Benjamin B. Warfield / 169
Catharine Anne Warfield / 169
Robert Penn Warren / 169
Booker Taliaferro Washington
  / 174
Thomas E. Watson / 174
Henry Watterson / 174
Charles Wilkins Webber / 175
Mason Locke Weems
  (Parson Weems) / 175
Eudora Welty / 175
Richard Henry Wilde / 177
James Wilkinson / 177
Espy Williams / 177
Tennessee Williams / 178
Augusta Jane Evans Wilson / 185
William Winans / 185
William Wirt / 185
Thomas Wolfe / 186

Richard Wright / 195
William L. Yancey / 196
Frank Yerby / 196
Martha Young / 196
Stark Young / 196

Part Two: CULTURAL, HISTORICAL, AND
SOCIAL BACKGROUNDS OF SOUTHERN LITERATURE

General / 199
Ballads, Folklore, Music, and the Folk Tradition / 226
Education / 238
History of Theater / 244
Libraries and Lyceums / 251
Onomastic Studies / 253
Southern Language, Speech, Oratory, and Dialect / 254
Southern Culture through Others' Eyes / 265

Part Three: LITERATURE

Studies that Include the South / 269
Studies Restricted to Southern Literary Topics and
     Southern Writers / 334
Bibliographies and Checklists / 364
Comparative Studies / 371
Newspapers and Periodicals / 377
Original Works Written at Southern Universities / 392

Acknowledgments / 395

INTRODUCTION

The first volume of *Southern Literary Culture: A Bibliography of Masters' and Doctors' Theses*, compiled and edited by Clyde H. Cantrell and Walton R. Patrick, was published in 1955. The preparation of the volume had begun in 1948 with the endorsement of the American Committee of the South-Atlantic Modern Language Association, chaired by Herman E. Spivey. In 1969, with the endorsement and full support of the Society for the Study of Southern Literature, we began the work necessary to revise and update *Southern Literary Culture*.

The aim of the editors of the first volume of *Southern Literary Culture* was to list the title of every masters' thesis and every doctors' dissertation bearing on Southern literature and its cultural and historical backgrounds written in any graduate school in the United States up through the summer of 1948. Our compilation includes the titles in Cantrell and Patrick's volume and extends the list of titles through the winter of 1969. As work on the revision became known, we received lists of titles that reached into 1970. These we have also included. Further, we have included titles of theses and dissertations accepted at foreign universities. We are grateful for the help which Professor James Hart, University of British Columbia, gave us in locating titles of theses and dissertations accepted at universities in the British Commonwealth. And we have relied heavily upon Lawrence F. McNamee's *Dissertations in English and American Literature: Theses accepted by American, British, and German Universities, 1865-1964* (1968) and James L. Woodress' *Dissertations in American Literature, 1891-1966* (1968) to list those accepted at other foreign universities.

Further, in addition to consulting all available bibliographies of theses and dissertations, including graduate announcements, we directly solicited from over 300 graduate schools lists of titles for possible inclusion. Our solicitation, perhaps at times, became harrassment, especially when we found it necessary to ask for clarification of a title or for an annotation. It is impossible to detail in the limited space of these introductory comments the generous help which reference librarians, library assistants, department chairmen, and others, all of whom are listed in the acknowledgments, gave us in the preparation of this book. Two examples must suffice. After we sent out our initial letters requesting aid in locating titles, Mrs. Antoinette Ciolli, Director of Special Collections Division at Brooklyn College (CUNY), quickly responded that she would assist us. Then with the help of Mrs. Sylvia Bernstein, College Administrative Assistant, Mrs. Ciolli provided us with 141 typewritten pages of titles, many of which were pertinent to our work. Ohio University was at the time in the process of microfilming all file cards for dissertations and theses, and, after the microfilming had been completed, gave us the entire collection of file cards for examination.

The geographical scope of this bibliography consists of the states of Alabama, Arkansas, Florida, Georgia, Kentucky, Louisiana, Maryland, Mississippi, North Carolina, Oklahoma, South Carolina, Tennessee, Texas, Virginia, and the District of Columbia. Like the original editors, we resolved the problem of classifying a writer as Southern on the basis of where he flourished as a writer. For this reason, like Cantrell and Patrick, we have excluded Conrad Aiken, but have included writers such as Hervey Allen, Alice French, and Thomas Merton. The first volume of *Southern Literary Culture* did not include Mark Twain. Following the lead of *A Bibliographical Guide to the Study of Southern Literature*, edited by Lewis Rubin, Jr., we decided to include Twain in this revised edition. The nature of our research, however, prevented our making an exhaustive search for theses and dissertations written on Twain before 1948. In all instances of deciding whether a writer should be classified as Southern, we have leaned toward inclusiveness rather than toward exclusiveness. Hopefully, our decisions will not appear arbitrary.

The 1955 volume of *Southern Literary Culture* includes 2529 titles and lists the titles alphabetically by the last name of the author of the thesis or dissertation. This revised volume includes approximately 8000 titles. One significant indication of this increase is the fact that the 1955 volume of *Southern Literary Culture* lists 45 theses or dissertations that deal with William Faulkner. This revised volume lists over 600 theses or dissertations written exclusively on Faulkner, and the number of theses and dissertations that include him increases this number to approximately 1000. Confronted with the tremendous increase in the number of titles to be listed, we decided that a new format for *Southern Literary Culture* was necessary.

In all instances in this revised volume, our concern has been with providing a useful and convenient research source for the student of Southern literature. Therefore, in listing titles, we have, as far as possible, focused on the individual writer. Part One, therefore, lists the writers alphabetically and gives, where it is available, the dates of their lives. As we collected titles, we confronted many difficulties in deciding upon the categories under which we should list titles, especially those in Part Two and Part Three. Obviously, some of the titles overlap; and in some instances the decisions which we made for listing a particular title are, like pass interference, judgment calls and will not be to everyone's liking. Although we believe that the various categories are self-explanatory, some specific comment about them is necessary to provide convenience for the researcher who will use this book.

Because we have attempted to focus as much as possible upon individual Southern writers, a title such as "The Short Story Sequence in Modern English Literature: James Joyce and William Faulkner" has been listed under "William Faulkner." However, we have provided a separate category for comparative studies where appear such titles as "Camus' Adaptation of Faulkner's *Requiem for a Nun*." Titles that are restricted to but that include several Southern writers--for example, "The Critic as Artist: A Study of the Critical and Creative Work of John Crowe Ransom, Allen Tate and Robert Penn Warren"--also, obviously, had to appear in a separate section to avoid duplication in the listing of a title. In the section headed "Studies that Include the South" appear those titles that reach across the geographical scope which we had

[xii]

established for Southern literature but which are not, strictly speaking, comparative. For instance, Mary Sue Carlock's dissertation "I Celebrate Myself, and Sing Myself: Character-Types in Early American Autobiographies, 1840-1870" includes both Southern and Northern autobiographies. Therefore, it appears under "Studies that Include the South" with the Southern writers of autobiography being listed alphabetically in the annotation. With the innovations in graduate programs, some universities--Brigham Young and Pennsylvania State, particularly--have accepted a series of papers on different subjects, in lieu of a study focused on one subject, for the M.A. or Ph.D. Therefore under "Edgar Allan Poe" will appear a title such as "Those Ravens and Cats of Mr. Poe; Myth, Eliot, and *The Elder Statesman*; and 'Pas de Deux' and 'Curtain Call,' Two Original Short Stories." In the format which we have adopted, we have attempted in the initial citation to give full information about a title, avoiding extensive abbreviations of names of schools. Further, one aim in establishing our categories for listing titles was to avoid the necessity for cross indices. Too often, we believe, extensive abbreviations, with tables to explain them, and intricate systems of cross references create the conditions of impossible acrostics. Since all annotations in Part Two and Part Three list the Southern writers in alphabetical order, it is a relatively simple matter for the researcher to locate those titles that include any writer in whom he is interested. Finally, we have updated the names of all schools as they appeared in Cantrell and Patrick's volume and have made minor revision of their annotations to suit our revised format.

In publishing this bibliography, we make no claim to definitiveness. In some instances, we were unable to provide annotations for titles. Further, the difficulties of this kind of research dictated that we would miss some titles that should be included. Since a bibliography is out of date even before it is published, we have determined, with the support of the Society for the Study of Southern Literature, to prepare five-year supplements of *Southern Literary Culture*. Work on the first supplement is already underway and, hopefully, will be published within one year of the appearance of this volume.

As we view this work as a whole and look forward to the supplements, we must concur with Cantrell and Patrick's statement in 1955 that "one can hardly do other than to view with admiration the substantial contribution graduate students have already made to Southern Literary Culture."

O. B. EMERSON

MARION C. MICHAEL

SOUTHERN LITERARY CULTURE

PART I
INDIVIDUAL WRITERS

ANDY ADAMS (1859-1935)

Foss, John H. The Value of Andy Adams as a Depictor of Life
on the Cattle Trails of Texas. Duke Univ., 1953. Thesis:
English.
Henry, Jean S.J. Andy Adams. Texas Christian Univ., 1938.
Thesis: English.

JAMES AGEE (1909-1955)

Barson, Alfred T. James Agee: A Study of Artistic Conscious-
ness. Univ. of Massachusetts, 1969. Dissertation:
English.
Behar, Jack. James Agee, the World of His Work. Ohio State
Univ., 1963. Dissertation: English.
Bourn, Ruth E. James Agee: The Man and His Work. Lamar
Univ., 1963. Thesis: English.
Broughton, Panthea R. The Autonomy Credo in the Fiction of
James Agee. Univ. of Alabama, 1963. Thesis: English.
Coffee, Caryl J. Theme, Character and Symbol in the Major
Writings of James Agee. Sacramento State College, 1963.
Thesis: English.
Finlay, Edward R., Jr. James Agee and Religion. Univ. of
South Carolina, 1967. Thesis: English.
Goar, Thomas T. *A Death in the Family/All the Way Home*:
Agee's Novel, Mosel's Play, Reisman's Screenplay. Univ.
of Texas (Austin), 1966. Thesis: English.
Hayne, Kathleen M. An Analysis of the Imagery of James Agee's
A Death in the Family. Iowa State Teachers College,
1965. Thesis: English.
Kramer, Victor A. James Agee's "dissonant prologue": A
Study of *Let Us Now Praise Famous Men*. Univ. of Texas
(Austin), 1963. Thesis: English.
_____. Agee: A Study of the Poetry, Prose, and Unpublished
Manuscripts. Univ. of Texas (Austin), 1969. Dissertation:
English.
Macklin, F.A. Disguised as a Child: A Study of James Agee.
Villanova Univ., 1963. Thesis: English.
Mayo, Charles W. James Agee: His Literary Life and Work.
George Peabody College, 1969. Dissertation: English.
McCay, Mary A. The Scenarios of James Agee. Boston College,
1966. Thesis: English.
Monsees, Katherine A. James Agee and the Iridescence of Life.
Cornell Univ., 1960. Thesis: English.
Ohlin, Peter H. James Agee: A Critical Study. Univ. of New
Mexico, 1964. Dissertation: English.
Perry, John. James Agee and American Romantic Tradition.
Temple Univ., 1968. Dissertation: English.
Pollard, Patrick H. A Critical Study of James Agee's *A Death
in the Family*. Univ. of Texas (Austin), 1963. Thesis:
English.

Powell, Grayson C. A Critical Interpretation of James Agee's
    The Morning Watch. Univ. of North Carolina (Chapel Hill),
    1967. Thesis: English.
Runyon, Bryce F., Jr. James Agee: His Art and Message.
    Columbia Univ., 1951. Thesis: English.
Seib, Kenneth A. Promise and Fulfillment: A Study of James
    Agee. Univ. of Pittsburgh, 1966. Dissertation: English.
Swoboda, Robert J. James Agee's New Prose. Kansas State
    Teachers College, 1964. Thesis: English.
Thomas, Martha J. James Agee: A Bio-Bibliography. Univ. of
    Tennessee, 1967. Thesis: English.
Winkler, Marjorie M. The Significance of Religion in the
    Writings of James Agee. Brooklyn College, 1969. Thesis:
    English.
Woodill, Dale P. The Comic Element in the Works of James
    Agee. Univ. of Tennessee, 1963. Thesis: English.

JAMES LANE ALLEN (1849-1925)

Bailey, Goldie E. The Blue Grass Region of Kentucky as
    Revealed through the Writings of James Lane Allen.
    Columbia Univ., 1931. Thesis: English.
Bradley, Eustace U. Kentucky Literature and James Lane Allen.
    Columbia Univ., 1919. Thesis: English.
Haynes, Kenneth N. Sentimentalism in James Lane Allen.
    Tufts Univ., 1935. Thesis: English.
Holmes, J.W. James Lane Allen: His Literary Theories.
    Univ. of Pittsburgh, 1931. Thesis: English.
Hunter, Lucy E. James Lane Allen; the Man and His Works.
    Univ. of Kansas, 1927. Thesis: English.
Ivey, Bessie B. The Kentucky Novels of James Lane Allen.
    Western Kentucky Univ., 1935. Thesis: English.
Ivey, Burnett S. What James Lane Allen Has to Say for Himself.
    Columbia Univ., 1923. Thesis: English.
Jennings, Ellen L. James Lane Allen's Theories and Practices
    in Fiction. Univ. of Virginia, 1927. Thesis: English.
McCready, John D. The Collected Works of James Lane Allen.
    Columbia Univ., 1923. Thesis: English.
McFadden, Elizabeth H. A Study of the Short Stories of James
    Lane Allen. Univ. of Kansas, 1934. Thesis: English.
Purvis, George G. A Study of Nature in Two Novels of James
    Lane Allen. Texas Christian Univ., 1967. Thesis:
    English.
Tucker, Ruth E. Kentucky as Portrayed in the Fiction of James
    Lane Allen. George Peabody College, 1930. Thesis:
    English.
Wells, Pauline. A Study of the Technique of James Lane Allen's
    Fiction. Miami Univ. (Ohio), 1943. Thesis: English.
White, Rata R. The Interrelationship of the Life and Work of
    James Lane Allen. Ohio State Univ., 1942. Thesis:
    English.

WILLIAM HERVEY ALLEN (1889-1949)

Evans, Nancy C. The Use Made of Vincent Nolte's *Fifty Years in Both Hemispheres* (1854) and Captain Theodore Canot's *Adventures of an African Slaver* (1854) in Hervey Allen's *Anthony Adverse* (1933). Univ. of Kentucky, 1939. Thesis: English.

EWING ALLISON (1853-1932)

Shutt, Mary J. Young Ewing Allison. Western Kentucky Univ., 1936. Thesis: English.

WASHINGTON ALLSTON (1779-1843)

Bartlett, Mabel R. Washington Allston as Critic. Boston Univ., 1960. Dissertation: Fine Arts.
Goodin, Nadine K. A Critical Reevaluation of Washington Allston's *Monaldi*. Univ. of Louisville, 1969. Thesis: English.
Gordenstein, Arnold S. Washington Allston and the Psychology of Federalism. Harvard Univ., 1957. Dissertation: History.
Lewis, Judith L. The Writings of Washington Allston. Columbia Univ., 1961. Thesis: English.
Murphy, Phillip J. The Writings and Literary Contacts of Washington Allston. Univ. of North Carolina (Chapel Hill), 1950. Thesis: English.
Quattlebaum, Marvin. Washington Allston. Univ. of South Carolina, 1932. Thesis: English.
Winston, George P. Washington Allston as a Man of Letters. Syracuse Univ., 1955. Dissertation: English.

JOSEPH ALTSHELER (1862-1919)

Demaree, Ona B. Joseph Altsheler: His Contribution to American Fiction for Boys. Univ. of Louisville, 1938. Thesis: English.

HARRIETTE ARNOW (1908-   )

Armstrong, Mary S. A Lexical Study of the Vocabulary of Harriette Arnow's Regional Novel, *Hunter's Horn*. Univ. of Virginia, 1952. Thesis: English.
Dominick, Doris S. A Lexical Study of the Vocabulary of a Part of Harriette Arnow's Regional Novel, *Hunter's Horn*. Univ. of Virginia, 1955. Thesis: English.
Unrue, John C. The Major Novels of Harriette Arnow: A Study of *Hunter's Horn* and *The Dollmaker*. Marshall Univ., 1965. Thesis: English.

[3]

HENRY AUSTIN (1782-1852)

Hogan, William R. The Life and Letters of Henry Austin, 1782-1852. Univ. of Texas (Austin), 1932. Thesis: History.

MARY HUNTER AUSTIN (1868-1934)

McClanaham, Muriel H. Aspects of Southern Regionalism in the Prose Works of M.H. Austin. Univ. of Pittsburgh, 1940. Dissertation: English.

Wynn, Dudley T. A Critical Study of the Writings of M.H. Austin, 1868-1934. New York Univ., 1940. Dissertation: English.

DORA AYDELOTTE (1878-1968)

Winn, Mary K. Oklahoma Folk Speech in the Novels of Dora Aydelotte. Univ. of Tulsa, 1948. Thesis: English.

THOMAS BACON (1700-1768)

Deibert, W.E.E. Thomas Bacon, Priest of the Establishment: The Life, Thought, and World of a Maryland Clergyman. Univ. of Maryland, 1966. Thesis: History.

GEORGE WILLIAM BAGBY (1828-1883)

King, J.L. Dr. George William Bagby: A Study in Virginian Literature, 1850-1880. Columbia Univ., 1927. Dissertation: English.

TEMPLE BAILEY (1869-1953)

Pierce, Rachel. A Study of Temple Bailey's Method of Visualization in *The Blue Window*. Sam Houston State Univ., 1940. Thesis: English.

KARLE WILSON BAKER (1878-1960)

Harper, Wilma. Karle Wilson Baker: Poet. Sam Houston State Univ., 1942. Thesis: English.

Luker, Winnie D. Karle Wilson Baker, Local Colorist of Texas. Stephen F. Austin State Univ., 1943. Thesis: English.

JOSEPH GLOVER BALDWIN (1815-1864)

Harvey, Samuel C. The Life and Times of Joseph Glover Baldwin. Auburn Univ., 1929. Thesis: English.

Stewart, Samuel B. Joseph Glover Baldwin. Vanderbilt Univ., 1942. Dissertation: English.

NANCY HUSTON BANKS (1849-1934)

Hines, Velma L. Nancy Huston Banks: Her Life and Works. Western Kentucky Univ., 1933. Thesis: English.

[4]

JAMES BARBOUR (1775-1842)

Lowery, Charles D.   James Barbour: A Politician and Planter
     of Ante-Bellum Virginia.   Univ. of Virginia, 1966.
     Dissertation: History.

WILLIAM BARKSDALE (1821-1863)

McKee, James W., Jr.   William Barksdale: The Intrepid
     Mississippian.   Mississippi State Univ., 1966.   Disser-
     tation: English.

JOHN BARTH (1930-   )

Chiasson, Sharon D.   A Survey of John Barth's Narrative Art,
     With Emphasis on *Giles Goat-Boy*.   Lamar Univ., 1969.
     Thesis: English.
Clark, Mary L.   John Barth: From Anti-Hero to Hero.   Temple
     Univ., 1967.   Thesis: English.
Hicks, Walter J.   John Barth's Early Novels.   Univ. of North
     Carolina (Chapel Hill), 1967.   Thesis: English.
Hunt, Sandra A.   John Barth: The Novel of Fiction.   Univ. of
     North Carolina (Chapel Hill), 1969.   Thesis: English.
Lambert, Beverly.   Rake, Saint, and Cynic: John Barth's
     Masks.   Georgia State Univ., 1969.   Thesis: English.
Leonard, Lionel R.   A Study of John Barth's *Giles Goat-Boy*
     as an "Anatomy."   Chico State College, 1968.   Thesis:
     English.
Spackey, James A.   Inhuman Comedy: The Nihilism of John Barth.
     Kent State Univ., 1968.   Thesis: English.
Tatham, Campbell.   The Novels of John Barth: An Introduction.
     Univ. of Wisconsin, 1968.   Dissertation: English.
Wells, Daniel A.   John Barth and Attitudes Toward Reality.
     Duke Univ., 1969.   Thesis: English.

KATHERINE BELLAMANN (-1965)

Deevers, LaVerne B.   An Edition of "Aunt Easter's Stories":
     An Unpublished Collection of Folk Stories by Katherine
     Bellamann.   Mississippi College, 1963.   Thesis: English.
Herring, Robert H.   An Edition of *The Slave Bells of Glenallen*:
     An Unpublished Novel by Katherine Bellamann.   Mississippi
     College, 1961.   Thesis: English.
Ray, Tommy J.   An Edition of the Sonnets of Katherine Bellamann.
     Mississippi College, 1961.   Thesis: English.
Shuffield, Sherron S.   An Edition of Katherine Bellamann's
     Children's Verses.   Mississippi College, 1963.   Thesis:
     English.

JOHN BARRY BENEFIELD (1880-   )

Bolin, Elizabeth. John Barry Benefield: A Study. East Texas
    State Univ., 1941. Thesis: English.
Gantt, Georgia. Barry Benefield: His Life and Works. George
    Peabody College, 1930. Thesis: English.

WILLIAM BEVERLEY (1698-1756)

Carson, Jane D. William Beverley and Beverley Manor. Univ.
    of Virginia, 1937. Thesis: History.

THEODORE G. BILBO (1877-1932)

Balsamo, Larry T. Theodore G. Bilbo and Mississippi Politics,
    1877-1932. Univ. of Missouri (Columbia), 1967.
    Dissertation: History.
Doler, Thurston E. Theodore G. Bilbo's Rhetoric of Racial
    Relations. Univ. of Oregon, 1968. Dissertation: Speech.

JOHN PEALE BISHOP (1892-1944)

Begnal, Michael H. "The Lion in the Lute": The Poetry of
    John Peale Bishop. Pennsylvania State Univ., 1963.
    Thesis: English.
Bier, Jesse. A Critical Biography of J.P. Bishop. Princeton
    Univ., 1956. Dissertation: English.
Crawford, Marguerite. John Peale Bishop: A Critical Appraisal.
    Vanderbilt Univ., 1956. Thesis: English.
Moore, Stephen C. Variations on a Theme: The Poetry and
    Criticism of John Peale Bishop. Univ. of Michigan, 1963.
    Dissertation: English.
Ward, Robert J. Irony in the Poetry and Prose of John Peale
    Bishop. Univ. of Akron, 1951. Thesis: English.

HUGO LAFAYETTE BLACK (1886-1971)

Berman, Daniel M. The Political Philosophy of Hugo L. Black.
    Rutgers Univ., 1957. Dissertation: Political Science.

JAMES BLAIR (1655-1743)

Mohler, Samuel R. Commissary James Blair, Churchman, Educator,
    and Politician of Colonial Virginia. Univ. of Chicago,
    1941. Dissertation: History.
Walter, Donna J. Imagery in the Sermons of James Blair.
    Univ. of Tennessee, 1967. Thesis: English.

RICHARD BLAND (1710-1776)

Daetweiler, Robert C. Richard Bland: Conservator of Self-
    Government in Eighteenth Century Virginia. Univ. of
    Washington, 1968. Dissertation: History.
Smith, Helen S. Richard Bland, the Antiquary. Univ. of
    Virginia, 1937. Thesis: History.

ALBERT TAYLOR BLEDSOE (1809-1877)

Bennett, John B. Albert Taylor Bledsoe: Social and Religious
Controversialist of the Old South. Duke Univ., 1942.
Dissertation: Religion.

JOHN HENRY BONER (1845-1903)

Simmons, Alma J. John Henry Boner, North Carolina Poet. Duke
Univ., 1939. Thesis: English.
Williams, Mabel. John Henry Boner. Columbia Univ., 1928.
Thesis: English.

GAIL BORDEN (1801-1874)

Frantz, Joe B. Infinite Pursuit: The Story of Gail Borden.
Univ. of Texas (Austin), 1948. Dissertation: History.

JONATHAN BOUCHER (1738-1804)

Zimmer, Anne Y. Jonathan Boucher: Moderate Loyalist and
Public Man. Wayne State Univ., 1966. Dissertation:
History.

JAMES BOYD (1888-1944)

Stevens, Charles H. James Boyd's Use of History in *Drums*.
Univ. of North Carolina (Chapel Hill), 1955. Thesis:
English.
Whisnant, David E. James Boyd, 1888-1944, A Literary Biography.
Duke Univ., 1965. Dissertation: English.

VIRGINIA FRAZER BOYLE (1863-1938)

Gallman, Mary N. A Critical Biography of Virginia Frazer
Boyle. Univ. of North Carolina (Chapel Hill), 1942.
Thesis: English.

ROARK BRADFORD (1896-1948)

Adams, Marjorie. Roark Bradford's Negro Characters. Univ.
of Texas (Austin), 1948. Thesis: English.
Durrett, Ruth L. Roark Bradford's Portrayal of the Negro.
Louisiana State Univ., 1950. Thesis: English.
Folsom, Sarah B. Roark Bradford: His Life and Works. Auburn
Univ., 1941. Thesis: English.
Richardson, Rupert N., Jr. Roark Bradford: An Analysis of
His Works and Technique. Univ. of Texas (Austin), 1941.
Thesis: English.

WILLIAM COWPER BRANN (1855-1898)

Randolph, John. The Apostle of the Devil: A Critical Biography
of William Cowper Brann. Vanderbilt Univ., 1939.
Dissertation: English.

[7]

Whitaker, John R. W.C. Brann: His Life and Influence in
Texas. Univ. of Texas (Austin), 1938. [The author has
traced Brann's life in some detail from the point of his
arrival in Texas. In addition, the reaction of people and
the press to his crusade against social evils is indicated.
Material for study includes the *Iconoclast* and Brann's
other published works, newspaper files and memories of
friends.]

CLEANTH BROOKS (1906-   )

Hart, Sr. Mary J., I.H.M. Cleanth Brooks and the Formalist
Approach to Metaphysical and Moral Values in Literature.
Univ. of Southern California, 1963. Dissertation: English.
Itnyre, Terry. Cleanth Brooks: His Theory of Poetry. Iowa
State Teachers College, 1959. Thesis: English.
Prowse, Walter F. The Poetic Theory of Cleanth Brooks. Morris
Harvey College, 1948. Thesis: English.
Schubert, Leland W. The Application of the Critical Principles
of Cleanth Brooks to Romantic Poetry. John Carroll Univ.,
1970. Thesis: English.
Tassin, Anthony G., O.S.B. The Phoenix and the Urn: The
Literary Theory and Criticism of Cleanth Brooks.
Louisiana State Univ., 1966. Dissertation: English.

ALEXANDER BROWN (1843-1906)

Harvey, Marvin E. Alexander Brown and the Renaissance of
Virginia History. College of William and Mary, 1947.
Thesis: History.

JOSEPH E. BROWN (1821-1894)

Roberts, Derrell C. Joseph E. Brown and the New South. Univ.
of Georgia, 1958. Dissertation: History.

WILLIAM G. BROWN (1868-1913)

Chalker, Robert P. William G. Brown, Southern Critic and
Man of Letters. Duke Univ., 1936. Thesis: History.

WILLIAM WELLS BROWN (1816-1884)

Guy, Mattye B. A Biography of William Wells Brown. Hampton
Institute, 1948. Thesis: English.

PHILIP ALEXANDER BRUCE (1856-1933)

Simm, Lyman M., Jr. Philip Alexander Bruce: His Life and
Works. Univ. of Virginia, 1966. Dissertation: History.

ROBERT WILTON BURTON (1848-1917)

Stewart, Gladys Steadham. Robert Wilton Burton: A Biographical Sketch Including a Selection of His Writing. Auburn Univ., 1932. Thesis: English.

SIGMAN BYRD (1909-   )

Lester, Beckie B. Sigman Byrd: A Study. East Texas State Univ., 1942. Thesis: English.

WILLIAM BYRD (1674-1744)

Abbott, Daniel C. A Study of William Byrd's Song Collections of 1588, 1589, and 1611 with Special Emphasis on the Role of the First Singing Part and One Word Painting. Brown Univ., 1958. Thesis: Music.

Beatty, Richmond C. William Byrd of Westover. Vanderbilt Univ., 1932. Dissertation: English.

Boren, Dorothy J. William Byrd of Virginia: Gentleman of Letters. Texas Christian Univ., 1963. Thesis: English.

Connell, Harold G. The Five-Part Madrigals of William Byrd. Brigham Young Univ., 1959. Thesis: Music.

McEwen, Ruth E. The Vocabulary of William Byrd's *A Journey to the Land of Eden*. Univ. of Virginia, 1933. Thesis: English.

McQueen, W.B., Jr. The Literary Background of Colonel William Byrd. Univ. of North Carolina (Chapel Hill), 1932. Thesis: English.

Millar, Albert E., Jr. Spiritual Autobiography in Selected Writings of Sewall, Edwards, Byrd, Woolman, and Franklin: A Comparison of Technique and Content. Univ. of Delaware, 1968. Dissertation: English.

North, N.C. A Study of William Byrd's *Journal*, His *History of the Dividing Line*. Univ. of North Carolina (Chapel Hill), 1935. Thesis: English.

Robertson, Henry A., Jr. A Critical Analysis of William Byrd II and His Literary Technique in *The History of the Dividing Line* and *The Secret History of the Line*. Univ. of Delaware, 1966. Dissertation: English.

JAMES BRANCH CABELL (1879-1958)

Arons, Peter L. The Romanticism of James Branch Cabell. Yale Univ., 1964. Dissertation: English.

Bardin, Henry J. III. The Development of Certain Unities in the Early Levels of Composition of Cabell's *Jurgen*. Univ. of Virginia, 1959. Thesis: English.

Bellamy, John E. James Branch Cabell: A Critical Consideration of His Reputation. Univ. of Illinois, 1954. Dissertation: English.

Canary, Robert H. The Cabellian Landscape: A Study of the Novels of James Branch Cabell. Univ. of Chicago, 1963. Dissertation: English.

Davis, Charles L. "The Biography of Dom Manuel": A Study
of the Art of James Branch Cabell. Univ. of Virginia,
1926. Thesis: English.
Duke, Jean M. James Branch Cabell's Library: A Catalogue.
Univ. of Iowa, 1968. Dissertation: English.
Gay, William T. A Study of the Works of James Branch Cabell.
Univ. of Alabama, 1928. Thesis: English.
Gibson, Lary H. The Disenchanted Garden: A Study of the
Major Fiction of James Branch Cabell's "The Biography of
the Life of Manuel." Univ. of Oregon, 1965. Dissertation:
English.
Gray, Charles F. The Theory of Literature of James Branch
Cabell. Univ. of Florida, 1966. Dissertation: English.
Halbmeier, E.V. An Informative Index to the "Biography of
Manuel" of James Branch Cabell. New York Univ., 1935.
Thesis: English.
Henderlite, Claude E.V. James Branch Cabell's Philosophy of
Romance. Univ. of Washington, 1925. Thesis: English.
Hodgson, Mary F.B. James Branch Cabell, Allegorist. Univ. of
Delaware, 1968. Thesis: English.
Homer, K.C. James Branch Cabell: An Interpretation. McGill
Univ., 1945. Thesis: English.
Huebsch, George V. The Literary Philosophy and Artistic
Method of James Branch Cabell. Marquette Univ., 1939.
Thesis: English.
Jernigan, J.J. James Branch Cabell's Working-Code of Romance.
Univ. of Mississippi, 1949. Thesis: English.
Lovejoy, Cecyl L.B. The Cabellian Romance. Univ. of
Washington, 1928. Thesis: English.
Mayne, John A. The Revisions of James Branch Cabell.
Pennsylvania State Univ., 1951. Thesis: English.
McGowan, Arthur E. The Development of James Branch Cabell's
Dream World. Univ. of Southern California, 1950. Thesis:
English.
Owens, Betsy K. James Branch Cabell as a Critic of American
Literature Between 1920 and 1930. Univ. of Tennessee,
1964. Thesis: English.
Palmer, Joseph H. The Influences of Chivalry and Gallantry
Upon James Branch Cabell. Univ. of Kentucky, 1928.
Thesis: English.
Revelise, Max. Cabell the Allegorist. Univ. of South Carolina,
1942. Thesis: English.
Rothe, Charles E. James Branch Cabell: Romantic Realist.
Univ. of Texas (Austin), 1937. Thesis: English.
Rothman, Julius L. James Branch Cabell, Satirist. Columbia
Univ., 1947. Thesis: English.
_____. A Glossarial Index to "The Biography of the Life of
Manuel." Columbia Univ., 1954. Dissertation: English.
Rugg, Hazel E. Relationships Observed in the Novels of James
Branch Cabell and Sinclair Lewis. Ohio State Univ., 1932.
Thesis: English.
Scott, Gwendolyn. James Branch Cabell: A Rediscovery. East
Texas State Univ., 1940. Thesis: English.
Shea, Jerome P. Cabell's Three-Fold Nightmare. Colorado
State Univ., 1966. Thesis: English.

Smith, Nelson J. III. Jesting Pilate: A Critical Study of
the Fictional World of James Branch Cabell. Indiana
Univ., 1965. Dissertation: English.
Stevenson, Ruth M. Cabell's Rational Morality as Expressed
Through the Dream-Vision Technique in *Jurgen*. Univ.
of Richmond, 1962. Thesis: English.
Stone, Donald O. The Questing Spirit of James Cabell: The
Evolution of a Theme. Florida State Univ., 1969.
Dissertation: English.
Sullivan, Francis W. A Dictionary of Mythological Allusions
in Certain Selected Novels of James Branch Cabell. Univ.
of South Dakota, 1950. Thesis: English.
Tarrant, D.S.G. James Branch Cabell: A Study of His Devel-
opment as a Literary Artist and of His Relationship to
His Era and Contemporaries. Univ. of London, 1956.
Thesis: English.
Villareal, Jesse J. The Idea of Creative Evolution in James
Branch Cabell. Univ. of Texas (Austin), 1937. Thesis:
English.
Wells, Arvin R. Jesting Moses. A Study in Cabellian Comedy.
Univ. of Michigan, 1959. Dissertation: English.

JOSEPH CARRINGTON CABELL (1778-1856)

Tanner, Carol M. Joseph Carrington Cabell, 1778-1856. Univ.
of Virginia, 1948. Dissertation: History. [Argues that
the years spent working with Thomas Jefferson to give to
the state of Virginia a great university were the most
important ones in Cabell's life.]

GEORGE WASHINGTON CABLE (1844-1925)

Altman, Jean. The Literary Reputation of George Washington
Cable, 1879-1900. Duke Univ., 1951. Thesis: English.
Arnaud, Henri A. L'Element Francais dans L'Oeuvre de Georges
Washington Cable. Louisiana State Univ., 1936. Thesis:
English.
Asbani, Muneer. The Potential Drama in the Works of George
Washington Cable. Bowling Green State Univ., 1969.
Thesis: English.
Bacoats, Irene B.C. Race Problems in the Fiction of George
Washington Cable. Univ. of Iowa, 1943. Thesis: English.
Berthelot, Mary C. Cable's Creoles From a New Angle. Louisiana
State Univ., 1928. Thesis: English.
Bonfoey, Winifred L. George W. Cable's Treatment of the Negro.
Duke Univ., 1937. Thesis: English.
Brandwein, Lillian. Cable and the Quadroons. Columbia Univ.,
1966. Thesis: English.
Bradford, Mildred B. The Prostituted Art of George W. Cable.
Univ. of Texas (El Paso), 1970. Thesis: English.
Brubaker, Bill R. George W. Cable: The Writer as Social
Conscious. Southern Illinois Univ. (Carbondale), 1956.
Thesis: English.

Butcher, Charles P. George Washington Cable as a Social
    Critic: 1887-1907. Columbia Univ., 1956. Dissertation:
    English.
Cleman, John L. A Study of Atmosphere in Three Works by
    George Washington Cable. Washington State Univ., 1967.
    Thesis: English.   *
Cooper, Virginia. George Washington Cable. Southern Methodist
    Univ., 1925. Thesis: English.
De Motte, Grace M. The Creoles in the Romances of George
    Washington Cable. Univ. of Oklahoma, 1925. Thesis:
    English.
Donnelly, Willie M. George Washington Cable as a Critic of
    the South. North Texas State Univ., 1949. Thesis:
    English.
Downey, Thomas H. George Washington Cable. Louisiana State
    Univ., 1930. Thesis: English.
Drake, Carol S. George Washington Cable's Treatment of the
    Creole in His Early Works. Baylor Univ., 1970. Thesis:
    English.
Ekstrom, Kjell. George Washington Cable: A Study of His Early
    Life and Work. Upsala College, 1950. Dissertation:
    English.
Farnham, Mary D. A Study of George W. Cable's Writings on
    the Negro Question, 1875-1885. Univ. of North Carolina
    (Chapel Hill), 1962. Thesis: English.
Friedl, Ute. Die Erziehung des Lokalkolorits in den Werken
    von S.O. Jewett, G.W. Cable, und F. Bret Harte. Graz,
    1953. Dissertation: English.
Frotscher, Lydia E. George Cable and His Louisiana Studies.
    Tulane Univ., 1907. Thesis: English.
Gordon, Robert G. The Fiction of George W. Cable. Columbia
    Univ., 1952. Thesis: English.
Gregg, Dorothy. A Linguistic Study of G.W. Cable's Novel
    The Grandissimes. Univ. of Kansas, 1930. Thesis:
    English.
Heissenbuttel, Ernest G. George Washington Cable: The History
    of His Literary Reputation. Columbia Univ., 1930. Thesis:
    English.
. Hodge, Dorothy F. Miscegenation in the Works of George W.
    Cable. Sacramento State College, 1962. Thesis: English.
Hood, Carolyn G. George Washington Cable and His New Orleans
    Contemporaries. Univ. of South Carolina, 1941. Thesis:
    English.
Juhan, Norma D. A Critical Study of George Washington Cable's
    Fiction. Univ. of Georgia, 1940. Thesis: English.
Kendrick, Juanita. George W. Cable's Concern with Social
    Problems in His Fiction. Louisiana State Univ., 1943.
    Thesis: English.
Lane, Tommy D. Cable's Southerners. Texas Christian Univ.,
    1967. Thesis: English.
Lipani, David J. George W. Cable: Movement into Realism.
    Bowling Green State Univ., 1968. Thesis: English.

Luke, Paul R. A Study in Black and White: Evidences of
    Social Criticism in the Fiction of George W. Cable
    Between the Years 1879 and 1894. Columbia Univ., 1952.
    Thesis: English.
McInnis, James E. Cable's Mulattoes. Univ. of Wyoming,
    1960. Thesis: English.
Moon, Theodore L. Plot and Characters: The Key to Cable's
    Decline. McNeese State Univ., 1967. Thesis: English.
Nix, Rosary V. Creole vs. Cable, or Creoles of Louisiana
    and George Washington Cable. Columbia Univ., 1937.
    Thesis: English.
Pace, Billy J. Imagery in the Novels of George W. Cable.
    Univ. of North Carolina (Chapel Hill), 1965. Thesis:
    English.
Pallez, Mildred A. Cable's Treatment of the Creoles. Fordham
    Univ., 1939. Thesis: English.
Predmore, Richard L. George Washington Cable, Realist or
    Romanticist? Univ. of Virginia, 1967. Thesis: English.
Pugh, Griffith T. George Washington Cable: A Critical
    Biography. Vanderbilt Univ., 1944. Dissertation:
    English.
Roach, Mary L. George W. Cable's Deflected Literary Career.
    Univ. of Texas (El Paso), 1963. Thesis: English.
Sandford, Herman P. The Moral Vision of George Washington
    Cable. Univ. of Arkansas, 1968. Dissertation: English.
Scarboro, Louise. George W. Cable's New Orleans with Special
    Reference to *Old Creole Days* and *The Grandissimes.* Duke
    Univ., 1944. Thesis: English.
Shillcutt, Doris J. George Washington Cable: Artist or
    Reformer? Trinity Univ. (Texas), 1964. Thesis: English.
Smith, Anna B. Creole Men in the Works of G.W. Cable. George
    Peabody College, 1936. Thesis: English.
Suetterlin, Etta M. George Washington Cable's Contribution
    to the Local Color Movement. Univ. of Missouri, 1934.
    Thesis: English.
Van Horn, Ivil N. George Washington Cable as a Critic of
    His Own Society. Southwest Texas State Univ., 1968.
    Thesis: English.
Walston, Rosa L. George W. Cable: A Critical Study. Duke
    Univ., 1931. Dissertation: English.
Wilkins, Joyce F. Violence in the Major Fiction of George W.
    Cable. Duke Univ., 1966. Thesis: English.
Wilson, S.W. Creole Tropes: A Study of the Functions and
    Biographical Significance of George Washington Cable's
    Imagery. Univ. of Mississippi, 1955. Thesis: English.
Wingo, Eleanor R. George Washington Cable and the Race
    Question: His Writings and Their Reception. Univ. of
    Texas (Austin), 1946. Thesis: English.

ERSKINE CALDWELL (1903-   )

Brodersen, Jens. The World of Jeeter Lester. Duke Univ., 1961.
    Thesis: English.
Burke, Hatton W. The South of Erskine Caldwell. Vanderbilt
    Univ., 1952. Thesis: English.

Cross, Carlyle. Erskine Caldwell as a Southern Writer.
Univ. of Georgia, 1963. Dissertation: English.
Deschenes, Louise. Erskine Caldwell, Writer of the South.
Univ. of Montreal, 1961. Thesis: English.
Fennell, Cornelia E. Some Naturalistic Patterns of Erskine
Caldwell. North Carolina College (Durham), 1952.
Thesis: English.
Golle, Guenter. Sprach und Stil bei Erskine Caldwell. Jena,
1961. Dissertation: English.
Rosenthal, Gisela. Erskine Caldwell: Wesen und Grenzen
seiner Kunst. Humboldt Universität (East Berlin), 1952.
Dissertation: English.
Scheffel, Werner. Die Darstellung der Weissen Anteilpächter
in den Romanen und Kurzgeschichten Erskine Caldwells.
Jena, 1962. Dissertation: English.
Shartip, Alfred S. Social Criticism in the Fiction of Erskine
Caldwell. Columbia Univ., 1950. Thesis: English.
Speer, Michael D. The Contribution of Journalism to the
Creative Writing of John Dos Passos and Erskine Caldwell.
Univ. of Tulsa, 1967. Thesis: English.
Stewart, Mrs. Sally A.S. Caldwell's Treatment of the Southern
Tenant Farmer. Southwest Texas State Univ., 1950.
Thesis: English.
Tcheng, Victoria P. The "Poor Whites" in Erskine Caldwell's
Works. Columbia Univ., 1956. Thesis: English.

JOHN C. CALHOUN (1782-1850)

Currie, Laura. The Symbolism of John C. Calhoun. Univ. of
California (Riverside), 1964. Thesis: History.
Hammett, Julius E. Opinions of John Caldwell Calhoun as
Revealed by His Private Letters and Public Life. Wofford
College, 1944. Thesis: English.
Robbins, Wiley B. The Public Life of John C. Calhoun.
Jacksonville State Univ., 1967. Thesis: History.

GEORGE HENRY CALVERT (1803-1889)

Everson, Ida G. George Henry Calvert, American Literary
Pioneer. Columbia Univ., 1943. Dissertation: English.

CHARLES CAMPBELL (1807-1876)

Cryer, William H. Charles Campbell: Early Life and Works
(1807-1847). College of William and Mary, 1947. Thesis:
History.

JOHN ARCHIBALD CAMPBELL (1811-1889)

Mann, Justine S. The Political and Constitutional Thought of
John Archibald Campbell. Univ. of Alabama, 1966.
Dissertation: Political Science.

TRUMAN CAPOTE (1924-   )

Blair, Mary H. Truman Capote and the Nonfiction Novel.
    San Francisco State College, 1966. Thesis: English.
Bucco, Martin. The Method in Truman Capote's Madness.
    Columbia Univ., 1957. Thesis: English.
Clayton, Glenn N., Jr. Truman Capote: Evil and Innocence.
    North Texas State Univ., 1968. Thesis: English.
Cullen, E.L. Use of the Traditional Gothic Properties in
    the Writings of Truman Capote. Univ. of Florida, 1963.
    Thesis: English.
Dapollonia, James A. A Production Study of Truman Capote's
    The Grass Harp. Bowling Green State Univ., 1968.
    Thesis: Speech.
Frey, Sharen N. A Study of Truman Capote's Personality as
    Reflected in His Writing. Washington State Univ., 1967.
    Thesis: English.
Gerety, Robert. Truman Capote and the Delta School. Hunter
    College, 1958. Thesis: English.
Goad, Craig M. Form as Content in the Works of Truman Capote.
    Kansas State Teachers College, 1966. Thesis: English.
Gdub, Lester S. The Fiction of Truman Capote: A Study in
    Psychological Insight. San Francisco State College, 1961.
    Thesis: English.
Love, Wanda F. Truman Capote: Elements of Gothic Myth and
    a Basic Dramatic Movement in the Early Stories. Southwest
    Texas State Univ., 1968. Thesis: English.
Moore, James K. Truman Capote's Fiction: Encounters with
    Evil. Univ. of North Carolina (Chapel Hill), 1964.
    Thesis: English.
Ronaldson, Walker Y., Jr. The Reflection of Love: The
    Fictional World of Truman Capote. Tulane Univ., 1965.
    Thesis: English.
Taylor, Richard L. The Frozen Palace: The Gothic Mood in
    Truman Capote's Other Voices, Other Rooms. Univ. of
    Louisville, 1964. Thesis: English.
Vintschger, Franz E. The Searching Adolescent: A Study of
    Character in Truman Capote. Boston College, 1966.
    Thesis: English.
Watson, Estelle M. The Three Phases of Love: Truman Capote's
    Other Voices, Other Rooms as a Search for Love. Tulane
    Univ., 1968. Thesis: English.

HODDING CARTER (1907-   )

Ingram, Lawrence F. Hodding Carter Rebels. Southeastern
    Louisiana Univ., 1968. Thesis: History.

PETER CARTWRIGHT (1785-1872)

Agnew, Theodore L. Peter Cartwright and His Times: The
    First Fifty Years, 1785-1835. Harvard Univ., 1953.
    Dissertation: History.

Taylor, Auvella L. The Autobiography of Peter Cartwright and
the Humor of the Old Southwest. Vanderbilt Univ., 1961.
Thesis: English.

WILLIAM ALEXANDER CARUTHERS (1802-1846)

Cole, Henry O. William Alexander Caruthers. Vanderbilt
Univ., 1931. Thesis: English.
Davis, Curtis C. Chronicler of the Cavaliers: The Career
and Opinions of William Alexander Caruthers, M.D.
(1802-1846). Duke Univ., 1947. Dissertation: English.
Hendrix, James F. An Analysis of Three Novels by William
Alexander Caruthers. Univ. of South Carolina, 1969.
Thesis: English.

GEORGE WASHINGTON CARVER (1864?-1943)

Hughes, Mary L. Life and Work of Dr. George Washington Carver.
Southern Methodist Univ., 1941. Thesis: Education.

WILBUR JOSEPH CASH (1901-1941)

Moss, Bobby G. Wilbur Joseph Cash, Critic of the South.
Univ. of Virginia, 1966. Thesis: History.

MADISON CAWEIN (1865-1914)

Davis, Frank J. Madison Cawein and His Poetry. Univ. of
Virginia, 1935. Thesis: English.
Ferguson, Donald E. An Appraisal of the Life and Work of
Madison Cawein. Ohio State Univ., 1934. Thesis: English.
Harrison, Richard C. Studies in the Poetry of Madison Cawein.
Univ. of Texas (Austin), 1917. Thesis: English.
Hollis, Ellis W., Jr. The Life, Works, and the Religious
Concepts of Madison Julius Cawein. Duke Univ., 1960.
Thesis: English.
King, Julia C. Some Aspects of the Poetry of Madison Cawein.
Univ. of Louisville, 1916. Thesis: English.
Shea, Sr. Victoria. Madison Cawein as a Nature Poet.
Marquette Univ., 1931. Thesis: English.
Swank, Albert L. Madison Cawein, a Poet of Kentucky. Univ.
of Pittsburgh, 1933. Thesis: English.
Tyree, Mabel I. The Arthurian Legend as Treated by Four
American Poets: James Russell Lowell, Richard Hovey,
Madison Cawein, Edwin Arlington Robinson. Univ. of
Kentucky, 1938. Thesis: English.

KATHERINE HOPKINS CHAPMAN (1870-1930)

Barker, Neutena. The Life and Fiction of Katherine Hopkins
Chapman. George Peabody College, 1932. Thesis: English.

CHARLES WADDELL CHESNUTT (1858-1932)

Foster, Charles W. The Representation of Negro Dialect in
Charles W. Chesnutt's *The Conjure Woman*. Univ. of
Alabama, 1968. Dissertation: Linguistics.
Hubert, Julia M. *The Marrow of Tradition*: Studies in the
Fiction of Charles W. Chesnutt. Ohio State Univ., 1948.
Thesis: English.
Jones, Norma R. Black Identity in the Major Works of Charles
Waddell Chesnutt. Bowling Green State Univ., 1970.
Thesis: English.
Mason, Cynthia R. Charles W. Chesnutt: His Life and Works.
Howard Univ., 1947. Thesis: English.
Mellinger, Virginia H. Charles Waddell Chesnutt: A Tran-
sitional Figure in Negro Literature. Columbia Univ.,
1955. Thesis: English.
Render, Sylvia L. Eagle with Clipped Wings: Form and Feeling
in the Fiction of Charles Waddell Chesnutt. George Peabody
College, 1962. Dissertation: English.
Ramsey, William M. Character Stereotype in the Novels of
Charles Waddell Chesnutt. Univ. of North Carolina (Chapel
Hill), 1969. Thesis: English.

THOMAS HOLLEY CHIVERS (1809-1858)

Barton, Lewis R. The Literary Reputation of Thomas Holley
Chivers. Univ. of North Carolina (Chapel Hill), 1963.
Thesis: English.
Walker, William E. A Critical Study of Thomas Holley Chivers.
Columbia Univ., 1948. Thesis: English.
Watts, Charles H., II. Thomas Holley Chivers: His Literary
Career and His Poetry. Brown Univ., 1953. Dissertation:
English.
Wilson, Edna A. Thomas Holley Chivers, M.D.: a Forgotten
Romantic Poet of Georgia (1809-1858). Auburn Univ.,
1941. Thesis: English.

KATE CHOPIN (1851-1904)

Bradshaw, Margaret A. Kate Chopin: *The Awakening*. Columbia
Univ., 1960. Thesis: English.
Jordan, Merle M. Kate Chopin: Social Critic. Univ. of Texas
(Austin), 1959. Thesis: English.
Pitman, Sally C. The New Woman in Selected Fiction of Kate
Chopin. Louisiana State Univ., 1969. Thesis: English.
Rankin, Daniel S. Kate Chopin and Her Creole Stories. Univ.
of Pennsylvania, 1932. Dissertation: English.
Shedd, Patricia T. The Fiction of Kate Chopin. Queens College,
1968. Thesis: English.
Taggart, Amy E. Mrs. Kate O'Flaherty Chopin: Her Life and
Her Writing. Tulane Univ., 1928. Thesis: English.

JEREMIAH CLEMENS (1814-1865)

Bedsole, Vergil L. The Life of Jeremiah Clemens. Univ. of
    Alabama, 1934. Thesis: History.
Drummond, Clyde. Biography of Jeremiah Clemens: A Personal,
    Political, Military and Literary Sketch of His Life.
    Auburn Univ., 1932. Thesis: English.

SAMUEL L. CLEMENS (1835-1910)
(MARK TWAIN)

Abernethy, Francis E. Mark Twain's Literary Judgments.
    Louisiana State Univ., 1953. Thesis: English.
Ackley, Raymond P. Mark Twain and Social Darwinism. San
    Diego State College, 1968. Thesis: English.
Adams, Gloria J. Mark Twain's *Pudd'nhead Wilson*: An Historical
    and Critical Study. Univ. of Texas (Austin), 1964.
    Thesis: English.
Adelsberg, Lester S. *Huckleberry Finn* as Twainian Significance.
    Univ. of Iowa, 1965. Thesis: English.
Albritton, Merilyn L. Mark Twain's Pessimism: A Review of
    the Criticism from 1920 to the Present. Univ. of Georgia,
    1969. Thesis: English.
Aldridge, Rebecca B. Mark Twain and Biblican Fundamentalism
    after 1880. Duke Univ., 1964. Thesis: English.
Alsen, Eberhard R. Tragedy and Comedy: Form and Structure in
    the Short Fiction of Henry James and Mark Twain. Indiana
    Univ., 1964. Thesis: English.
Altenbernd, August L. The Influence of European Travel on
    the Political and Social Outlook of Henry Adams, William
    Dean Howells, and Mark Twain. Ohio State Univ., 1954.
    Dissertation: English.
Andres, James M. John, Jane, and Orion Clemens: Their
    Influence on Mark Twain's Art. John Carroll Univ., 1969.
    Thesis: English.
Andrews, Kenneth R. Mark Twain's Hartford. Univ. of Illinois,
    1948. Dissertation: English.
Angle, Edwin F. The Question of Mark Twain's Genius. Ohio
    Univ., 1939. Thesis: English.
Armstrong, LeRoy W. Mark Twain's Technique of Dichotomy:
    The Meaning of "Doubleness" in Three Novels. Georgia
    State Univ., 1969. Thesis: English.
Arthur, Charles S. Mark Twain's *Joan of Arc*: A Literary
    Analysis. Univ. of Maryland, 1966. Thesis: English.
Asmundsson, Doris R. Mark Twain's Treatment of Joan of Arc.
    Columbia Univ., 1958. Thesis: English.
Aspiz, Harold. Mark Twain's Reading: A Critical Study.
    Univ. of California (Los Angeles), 1950. Dissertation:
    English.
Asselineau, Roger M. The Literary Reputation of Mark Twain,
    1910-1950. Paris, 1953. Dissertation: English.
Bader, Judith F. The Dominant Character in Mark Twain's Major
    Fiction. Indiana Univ., 1969. Dissertation: English.
Baender, Paul E. Mark Twain's Transcendent Figure. Univ. of
    California (Berkeley), 1957. Dissertation: English.

Baetzhold, Howard G. Mark Twain's Attitudes toward England.
Univ. of Wisconsin, 1953. Dissertation: English.
Bailey, Mary M. Mark Twain and the Fine Arts. Univ. of
Pittsburgh, 1938. Dissertation: English.
Baldwin, Marilyn A. An Edition of W.D. Howells' *My Mark Twain*:
Introduction and Notes. Rutgers Univ., 1963.
Dissertation: English.
Bali, Om P. William Dean Howells on Mark Twain: American,
Artist, Humorist, and Humanitarian. Miami Univ. (Ohio),
1969. Thesis: English.
Barlet, Sr. Mary D. Mark Twain, Historian of American Mores:
A Critical Study of *Roughing It*, *The Gilded Age* and
The Adventures of Tom Sawyer. Canisius College, 1952.
Thesis: English.
Bass, Jeanne H. Mark Twain's Representation of the American
West. North Texas State Univ., 1953. Thesis: English.
Bates, Allan C. Mark Twain and the Mississippi River. Univ.
of Chicago, 1968. Dissertation: English.
Beal, Barbara M. The Significance of Bernard DeVoto on the
Interpretation of Mark Twain. Univ. of Arizona, 1960.
Thesis: English.
Beard, Elaine L. Determinism in *Pudd'nhead Wilson*. Univ. of
Virginia, 1965. Thesis: English.
Bell, Bonita L. Three Studies in English: Interpretations
of *Pearl*; Order in *Paradise Lost*; Mark Twain and Europe.
Pennsylvania State Univ., 1968. Thesis: English.
Bell, Marvin C. Mark Twain and His American Critics. Texas
Christian Univ., 1951. Thesis: English.
Bellamy, Gladys C. Mark Twain as a Literary Artist. Univ. of
Oklahoma, 1947. Dissertation: English.
Bellar, Hilliard I. The Style of *Huckleberry Finn*: A
Statistical Study. Brooklyn College, 1959. Thesis:
English.
Benson, Ivan. The Western Development of Mark Twain. Univ.
of Southern California, 1937. Dissertation: English.
Berry, Marcia E. Metamorphosis in Mark Twain: A Study in
Three Archetypes. Univ. of Tulsa, 1966. Thesis: English.
Bicknese, Guenther. Mark Twain und Die Tradition Der Alten
Welt. Marburg, 1953. Dissertation: English.
Bie, Wendy A. Dual Identity in Selected Novels of Mark Twain.
Univ. of Idaho, 1968. Thesis: English.
Blackman, Carolyn M. Three Studies in English: Donne's
Mannerist Conceits; "Andrea del Sarto"; *Huckleberry Finn*.
Pennsylvania State Univ., 1968. Thesis: English.
Blecha, Louis J. *Adventures of Huckleberry Finn*: A Study of
Comic *Mythos* and Characters. Univ. of Kansas, 1967.
Thesis: English.
Blues, Thomas O. The Individual and the Community in the
Works of Mark Twain. Univ. of Iowa, 1966. Dissertation:
English.
Bonham, Virginia L. The Ambiguity and Innocence in Mark
Twain's Novels. Univ. of Kansas, 1966. Thesis: English.
Bonham, William D. *The Mysterious Stranger*: Adaptation and
Presentation of Narrative Prose in Group Oral Reading Form.
Southern Illinois Univ. (Carbondale), 1962. Thesis: Speech.

Bousquet, Elizabeth. The Twain Tradition: Sherwood Anderson, Ernest Hemingway, Stephen Crane. Montreal, 1968. Thesis: English.

Bowman, Larry B. Mark Twain. The Paradoxical Influence of Calvinism. Univ. of Wyoming, 1971. Thesis: English.

Bradley, Ruth M. The Making of Mark Twain's *Personal Recollections of Joan of Arc*. Univ. of California (Los Angeles), 1970. Dissertation: English.

Branch, Edgar M. The Literary Development of Mark Twain, 1852-1865. Univ. of Iowa, 1941. Dissertation: English.

Brashear, Minnie M. Formative Influences in the Mind and Writing of Mark Twain. Univ. of North Carolina (Chapel Hill), 1930. Dissertation: English.

Bredeson, Robert C. Mark Twain's Landscapes: A Study in Changing Literary Conventions. Univ. of Minnesota, 1963. Dissertation: English.

Brengelman, Frederick H. Mark Twain's Social Views. Dana College, 1948. Thesis: English.

Briggs, Warren M. Gulliver's Travels on the Mississippi River: A Question of Mark Twain's Satyre and Jonathan Swift's Humour. Columbia Univ., 1954. Thesis: English.

Browdwin, Stanley. Mark Twain and the Fall of Man. Columbia Univ., 1967. Dissertation: English.

Brown, Anthony E. Rhetorical Devices Effecting Humor in the Works of Mark Twain. Univ. of South Carolina, 1962. Thesis: English.

Bunker, Robert M. The Idea of Failure in Henry Adams, Charles Sanders Pierce, and Mark Twain. Univ. of New Mexico, 1955. Dissertation: English.

Bunn, James W. Mark Twain and Religion: The Foundation of His Faith. Columbia Univ., 1966. Thesis: English.

Burhans, Clinton S., Jr. The Inconsistent Mark Twain and the American Democratic Faith. Univ. of Wisconsin, 1962. Dissertation: English.

Burnam, Thomas B. Mark Twain and the Gilded Age. Univ. of Idaho, 1937. Thesis: English.

_____. Mark Twain and the Machine. Univ. of Washington, 1950. Dissertation: English.

Buxton, Teresa. A Study of the Relationship of William Dean Howells and Samuel Langhorne Clemens. Bucknell Univ., 1930. Dissertation: English.

Cameron, Thomas D. Mark Twain's Views of Formal Education. North Texas State Univ., 1966. Thesis: English.

Caplan, Eleanor D. The Ambivalence of Howells' Critical Reception of Twain. Univ. of Massachusetts, 1966. Thesis: English.

Capps, Mikie L. The Conscience and the Dream: An Analysis of the Influence of Mark Twain's Determinism on Characterization and Thematic Unity in *Huckleberry Finn*. Texas A & M Univ., 1965. Thesis: English.

Carter, Paul J., Jr. The Social and Political Ideas of Mark Twain. Univ. of Cincinnati, 1939. Dissertation: English.

Chambers, Nettie J. Repetitions in the Most Popular Works of Mark Twain. North Texas State Univ., 1949. Thesis: English.

[20]

Christensen, Elise. The Contribution of Mark Twain to Modern
Religious Thought. Univ. of Arizona, 1939. Thesis:
English.
Churchman, Charles J. Mark Twain's Treatment of Southern Life.
Univ. of Virginia, 1957. Thesis: English.
Clark, William G. Superstitions in the Works of Mark Twain.
State Univ. of Iowa, 1949. Thesis: English.
Clark, William S. An Analysis of Mark Twain's Style. Univ.
of Denver, 1960. Dissertation: English.
Coburn, Mark D. The Progress of Twain's Pilgrims. Stanford
Univ., 1969. Dissertation: English.
Coffee, Jessie. Mark Twain's Gospel as Expressed in *Pudd'nhead
Wilson*. Sacramento State College, 1961. Thesis: English.
Coffeen, Rebecca L. Deterministic Symbols in Mark Twain's
Later Fragments. West Georgia College, 1968. Thesis:
English.
Coleman, Philip Y. Mark Twain's Desperate Naturalism. Univ.
of Illinois, 1964. Dissertation: English.
Conner, Marie. Aunt Polly: The Failure of Mark Twain's Women.
C.W. Post College of Long Island Univ., 1966. Thesis:
English.
Cooper-Smith, Marilyn. Some Similarities and Differences in
Great Expectations and *Adventures of Huckleberry Finn*.
Southern Connecticut State College, 1967. Thesis: English.
Courtney, Lee F. The Boggs-Sherburn Episode: A Digression in
Huckleberry Finn. Texas A & M Univ., 1964. Thesis:
English.
Covici, Pascal, Jr. Humor as Form: A Study of Structure in
Mark Twain's Works. Radcliffe College, 1955. Dissertation:
English.
Cox, James M. Mark Twain: A Study in Nostalgia. Univ. of
Indiana, 1955. Dissertation: English.
Crossman, Lester G. The Humor of Mark Twain. Saskatchewan,
1946. Thesis: English.
_____. Samuel Clemens in Search of Mark Twain: A Study of
Clemens's Changing Conception of His Role as a Writer.
Univ. of Washington, 1957. Dissertation: English.
Cummings, Sherwood P. Mark Twain and Science. Univ. of
Wisconsin, 1951. Dissertation: English.
Danielson, Jeanette C. Mark Twain's Attitude Toward Women
as Reflected in Selected Works. Bowling Green State
Univ., 1962. Thesis: English.
da Ponte, Durant. American Periodical Criticism of Mark Twain,
1869-1917. Univ. of Maryland, 1953. Dissertation:
English.
Davidson, Janice G. Mark Twain's London Lectures, 1873.
Univ. of Maryland, 1968. Thesis: Speech.
Davidson, W.E. Mark Twain and Conscience. Univ. of Missouri,
1940. Dissertation: English.
Davis, Billy A. Mark Twain and Medievalism: Twain's View
of the Middle Ages and of Medieval Influences in Recent
Times. Stanford Univ., 1949. Thesis: English.
Davis, John H. Mark Twain and the Dream Progression. Auburn
Univ., 1970. Thesis: English.

Davis, Helen C. Clemens--Kipling: A Comparative Study of Social Concepts. Florida State Univ., 1949. Thesis: English.

Davitz, Lois J.L. Washington, D.C., as Seen Through the Eyes of Mark Twain, Henry Adams, John Dos Passos. Columbia Univ., 1949. Thesis: English.

Day, Patrick J. Mark Twain's Views of Religion and Their Effect on His Art. John Carroll Univ., 1969. Thesis: English.

De Falco, Joseph M. Ritual Journey in *Huckleberry Finn*. Univ. of Florida, 1958. Thesis: English.

De Gregory, James R. The Development of the Critical Estimates of *Huckleberry Finn*. John Carroll Univ., 1966. Thesis: English.

Delaney, Paul W. Young Satan as Mark Twain's View of Christ: A New Reading of *The Mysterious Stranger*. Emory Univ., 1969. Thesis: English.

Denniston, Constance. The Romance--Parody: A Study in Melville, Twain, Purdy, and Heller. Kansas State Teachers College, 1965. Thesis: English.

De Nyse, Diane R. J. Ross Browne and Mark Twain: The Question of Literary Influence. Univ. of Wyoming, 1965. Thesis: English.

Dickenson, Leon T. Mark Twain's *Innocents Abroad*: Its Origins, Composition, and Popularity. Univ. of Chicago, 1945. Dissertation: English.

Donner, Stanley T. The Speaking and Reading of Mark Twain. Northwestern Univ., 1947. Dissertation: Speech.

Dubin, Harold N. *The Adventures of Huckleberry Finn*, by Mark Twain, and *The Catcher in the Rye*, by J.D. Salinger: Two Studies in Fiction of the Adolescent in Society. Columbia Univ., 1958. Thesis: English.

Dry, Bernice S. Expressed Opinions of Mark Twain on Government and Politicians. Northeast Missouri State College, 1959. Thesis: English.

Duke, Keith E. A Contribution to the History of Trans-continental Travel in the Middle of the Nineteenth Century: Mark Twain's *Roughing It*. Bordeaux, 1950. Dissertation: English.

Durrigl, Karl. Die Abweichungen von Standard English in *The Adventures of Tom Sawyer* von Mark Twain. Vienna, 1923. Dissertation: English.

Duskis, Henry. The Journalistic Endeavors of Mark Twain from 1868 to 1890. Univ. of Southern California, 1952. Thesis: English.

Edwards, Corliss J., Jr. Pessimism and Determinism in the Later Writings of Mark Twain. Univ. of Georgia, 1960. Thesis: English.

Ellinger, Ruth N. Mark Twain's Hannibal, 1839-1853. Washington Univ. (St. Louis), 1953. Thesis: English.

Emberson, Frances G. The Vocabulary of Samuel Langhorne Clemens from 1852 to 1884. Univ. of Missouri, 1932. Dissertation: English.

Ensor, Allison R., Jr. Mark Twain and the Bible. Indiana Univ., 1965. Dissertation: English.

Erickson, Mary D. Huckleberry Finn: Realist vs. Romanticist. Montana State Univ., 1961. Thesis: English.

Ervin, Jean C. Mark Twain: Speechmaker. Univ. of Missouri, 1950. Dissertation: Speech.

Ewing, Lora M. A Justification of the Ending of *Adventures of Huckleberry Finn*. Univ. of Massachusetts, 1965. Thesis: English.

Fallwell, Marshall L., Jr. Mark Twain's Fable of Vindication: The Mississippi Trilogy. Vanderbilt Univ., 1967. Thesis: English.

Fava, Thomas D. The Biographical and Environmental Factors Which Influenced Mark Twain's Writing of *The Adventures of Huckleberry Finn* and *A Connecticut Yankee in King Arthur's Court*. Niagara Univ., 1967. Thesis: English.

Fawley, John S. Neither, Nor: A Study of the Role of the Innocent and the Hero in the Writings of Mark Twain. De Pauw Univ., 1967. Thesis: English.

Feinstein, George W. Mark Twain's Literary Opinions. Univ. of Iowa, 1945. Dissertation: English.

Feinstein, Herbert C.V. Mark Twain's Lawsuits. Univ. of California (Berkeley), 1968. Dissertation: English.

Ferguson, John P. Tom and Huck: Two Aspects of Conflict Within Sam Clemens. Columbia Univ., 1958. Thesis: English.

Finck, June A. The Evolution of Mark Twain's *Pudd'nhead Wilson* and *Those Extraordinary Twins*. Queens College (N.Y.), 1955. Thesis: English.

Fischer, Douglas. Mark Twain as Southerner. Univ. of Arizona, 1966. Thesis: English.

Flood, Verle D. The Sociological Basis of Mark Twain's Pessimism: 1863-1889. State Univ. of Iowa, 1950 Thesis: English.

Flowers, Frank C. Mark Twain's Theories of Morality. Louisiana State Univ., 1941. Dissertation: English.

Ford, Jeanne M.D. The Treatment of Human Cruelty in the Novels of Mark Twain. North Texas State Univ., 1956. Thesis: English.

Ford, Marian M. Mark Twain's Determinism in His Later Works. State Univ. of Iowa, 1950. Thesis: English.

Ford, Thomas W. An Historical and Critical Examination of Mark Twain's *Pudd'nhead Wilson*. Univ. of Texas (Austin), 1951. Thesis: English.

Foster, Charles W. A Structural and Thematic Comparison of *Huckleberry Finn* and *The Catcher in the Rye*. East Tennessee State Univ., 1963. Thesis: English.

Fowler, Sharlene. Recurring Patterns and Episodes in Mark Twain's Work. Louisiana State Univ., 1969. Thesis: English.

Frame, Lois C. Mark Twain as Conscious Artist. Univ. of Virginia, 1967. Thesis: English.

Frantz, Ray W., Jr. The Place of Folklore in the Creative Art of Mark Twain. Univ. of Illinois, 1956. Dissertation: Folklore.

French, Bryant M. A Critical Study of Twain's *The Gilded Age*.
Univ. of Southern California, 1961. Dissertation: English.
Fried, Martin B. The Composition. Sources and Popularity of
Mark Twain's *Roughing It*. Univ. of Chicago, 1951.
Dissertation: English.
Fuller, Lawrence B. The Influence of Melodrama in Several
Novels of Mark Twain. Columbia Univ., 1963. Thesis:
English.
Gaetano, Theodora A. "The Exquisite Misery of Uncertainty":
A Reappraisal of Mark Twain's *Life on the Mississippi*.
Columbia Univ., 1964. Thesis: English.
Gainer, Ruby J. Realism in the Novels of Mark Twain. Atlanta
Univ., 1953. Thesis: English.
Gardner, Gwendolyn C. Mark Twain as a Political Satirist.
North Texas State Univ., 1953. Thesis: English.
Gardner, Joseph H. Dickens in America: Mark Twain, Howells,
James, and Norris. Univ. of California (Berkeley), 1969.
Dissertation: English.
Gaudek, Ida. Personliches in den Werken Mark Twains. Vienna,
1938. Dissertation: English.
Gervais, Ronald J. Mark Twain and the Fall into the Moral
Sense. Univ. of Oregon, 1969. Dissertation: English.
Gibson, Judith C. New England's Personal and Critical
Reception of Mark Twain, 1871-1891. Univ. of North
Carolina (Chapel Hill), 1961. Thesis: English.
Gibson, William M. William Dean Howells and Mark Twain, Anti-
Imperialists. Univ. of Chicago, 1940. Dissertation:
English.
Gilkey, Robert. Mark Twain Voyageur et Son Image de L'Europe.
Paris, 1951. Dissertation: English.
Gillespie, V. The Moral Philosophy of Mark Twain. Univ. of
Mississippi, 1952. Thesis: English.
Glorioso, Joseph A. Mark Twain and His Literary Art as Shaped
by the Lecture Circuit. John Carroll Univ., 1969. Thesis:
English.
Goff, Ida E. Mark Twain and the Dreyfus Case. Washington Univ.
(St. Louis), 1950. Thesis: English.
Gold, John D. The Writing and Editing of Mark Twain's *Christian
Science*, Part I. Univ. of North Carolina (Chapel Hill),
1965. Thesis: English.
Goold, Edgar H., Jr. Mark Twain's Literary Theories and
Opinion. Univ. of North Carolina (Chapel Hill), 1949.
Dissertation: English.
Goold, Martha L. The Literary and Personal Relationships of
Bret Harte and Mark Twain. Univ. of North Carolina (Chapel
Hill), 1948. Thesis: English.
Gordon, Joseph T. A Comparison of the Social and Political
Thought of Mark Twain and Henry Adams. Pennsylvania State
Univ., 1967. Dissertation: English.
Greenagel, Frank L. The Irony of Mark Twain: An Analysis of
a Rhetorical Strategy. Univ. of Minnesota, 1965.
·Dissertation: English.
Grimes, Mary M. Joan of Arc as Personal Ideal and Literary
Symbol in the Life and Writings of Samuel L. Clemens.
North Texas State Univ., 1958. Thesis: English.

Grimm, Clyde L., Jr. Mark Twain: The Unreconstructed Temperament. Univ. of Illinois, 1963. Dissertation: English.

Gustafson, Danny D. Patterns of Romantic Comedy and Satire in Mark Twain's *The Prince and the Pauper* and *A Connecticut Yankee in King Arthur's Court*. Univ. of Nebraska, 1968. Dissertation: English.

Haig, Sara L. Mark Twain's American Idealism. Univ. of Virginia, 1960. Thesis: English.

Hall, Mary E. Mark Twain's Treatment of the Negro in *Huckleberry Finn* and *Pudd'nhead Wilson*. Virginia State College, 1969. Thesis: English.

Hammock, Herman. Mark Twain: The Mysterious Stranger. East Tennessee State Univ., 1965. Thesis: English.

Hankinson, Marilyn C. The Influence of the Mississippi River on Mark Twain and How It Pervaded His Writing. Drake Univ., 1965. Thesis: English.

Harrell, Don. Patterns of Escape in Mark Twain's Fiction. Vanderbilt Univ., 1968. Dissertation: English.

Hartley, Peter E. Myth and Meaning in *Huckleberry Finn*: A Heuristic Analysis. Univ. of Colorado, 1965. Thesis: English.

Hastings, Grace A. A Study of the Oral Interpretation Techniques of Charles Dickens, Mark Twain, and Robert Frost. Bowling Green State Univ., 1964. Thesis: Speech.

Hausman, S.J. A Study of Mark Twain's Attitude Toward Women as Reflected in His Writings. Univ. of Tulsa, 1953. Thesis: English.

Havens, Charles B. Mark Twain's Use of Native American Humor in his Principal Literary Works. Vanderbilt Univ., 1954. Dissertation: English.

Hawkins, Charles E. Mark Twain and the South. Vanderbilt Univ., 1949. Thesis: English.

Hays, John Q. The Serious Elements in the Writings of Mark Twain. Univ. of California (Berkeley), 1942. Dissertation: English.

Heimerl, Catherine D. A Study of *Huckleberry Finn*'s Controversial Ending. Villanova Univ., 1968. Thesis: English.

Hemminghaus, Edgar H. Mark Twain in Germany. Columbia Univ., 1939. Dissertation: German.

Herrick, Michael J. Mark Twain's Indictment of Slavery: *Huckleberry Finn* and *Pudd'nhead Wilson*. John Carroll Univ., 1965. Thesis: English.

Hill, Hamlin L. The American Publishing Company and the Writings of Mark Twain, 1867-1880. Univ. of Chicago, 1959. Dissertation: English.

Hoegel, Rolf K. Literary Use of the River in Mark Twain. Southern Illinois Univ. (Carbondale), 1956. Thesis: English.

Hoffman, Dorothy. Mark Twain and the Double. Tufts Univ., 1966. Thesis: English.

Holt, James L. Mark Twain and the Negro. Texas Tech Univ., 1967. Thesis: English.

Hord, Larry D. Mark Twain's Despair: A Comparison of the Deterministic Ideas of the Old Man in *What is Man?* and Satan in *The Mysterious Stranger*. Texas A & M Univ., 1964. Thesis: English.

Horne, Linda S. Mark Twain's Treatment of Slavery in *Huckleberry Finn*, *A Connecticut Yankee in King Arthur's Court*, and *Pudd'nhead Wilson*. Univ. of Texas (Austin), 1964. Thesis: English.

Hoyt. Charles L. *Pudd'nhead Wilson* and *A Double-Barreled Detective Story*: Mark Twain's Vision of the Detective Story. Univ. of Massachusetts, 1969. Thesis: English.

Humphrey, Stella O. The Development of Mark Twain's Religious Views. Baylor Univ., 1951. Thesis: English.

James, Joseph G. Religion and Morality as Themes in *Tom Sawyer*, *Huckleberry Finn*, and *Pudd'nhead Wilson*. Univ. of Georgia, 1966. Thesis: English.

Jensen, Franklin L. Mark Twain as a Literary Critic. Kansas State Teachers College, 1961. Thesis: English.

Johansson, Kurt L. Voice in *Huckleberry Finn*. Cornell Univ., 1965. Thesis: English.

Jones, Alexander E. Mark Twain and Religion. Univ. of Minnesota, 1950. Dissertation: English.

Jones, Lucylle C. Mark Twain as a Literary Critic. North Texas State Univ., 1953. Thesis: English.

Jones, Tandy A. Nathaniel Hawthorne, Mark Twain and Carl Sandburg as Writers for Children. Duke Univ., 1957. Thesis: English.

Jurich, Joseph. Mark Twain's *Joan of Arc*: Origins, Purposes, and Accomplishment. Univ. of Illinois, 1962. Dissertation: English.

Kelley, Sr. Marie W. Joan of Arc in Shakespeare, Twain, and Shaw. Duquesne Univ., 1966. Thesis: English.

Kephart, Eva H. Paradox of Mark Twain: A Study of the Conflicting Ideas in Twain's Late Years; A Thesis. North-East Missouri State College, 1959. Thesis: English.

Kiichli, Gertrude C. The Theatrical Adventures of Mark Twain, Playwright. Univ. of California (Los Angeles), 1963. Thesis: Theater Arts.

Kinnibrew, Mary A. Mistaken Identity in Mark Twain's Major Fiction. Rice Univ., 1964. Thesis: English.

Klaus, Rosemarie. Mark Twain: Der Kritiker Reiner Zeit. Berlin (Humboldt), 1955. Dissertation: English.

Koch, Stephen. "The Last Dream of Freedom": A Study of Mark Twain's "The Great Dark." Columbia Univ., 1964. Thesis: English.

Kolb, Harold H., Jr. The Illusion of Life: American Realism as a Literary Form in the Writings of Mark Twain, Henry James, and W.D. Howells in the Mid-1880's. Indiana Univ., 1968. Dissertation: English.

Kreuter, Kent. The Literary Response to Science, Technology and Industrialism: Studies in the Thought of Hawthorne, Melville, Whitman, and Twain. Univ. of Wisconsin, 1963. Dissertation: English.

[26]

Kunst, Arthur E. Twenty-Four Versions of *Huckleberry Finn*:
  Studies in Translation. Indiana Univ., 1961. Disser-
  tation: Comparative Literature.
Leavell, Frank H. Mark Twain's Thought as Revealed in His
  Travel Books. Baylor Univ., 1953. Thesis: English.
Lennon, Edward J., Jr. Mark Twain: The Speaker. Univ. of
  Wisconsin, 1952. Dissertation: Speech/Drama.
Lieberman, Herbert H. *Huckleberry Finn*: A Biblical Inter-
  pretation. Columbia Univ., 1957. Thesis: English.
Lingle, Gladys H. Mark Twain: His Religious Background and
  Its Influence on His Pessimism. Southern Illinois Univ.
  (Carbondale), 1962. Thesis: English.
Low, David H. Offspring of the Frontier: Mark Twain and
  Roughing It. Columbia Univ., 1953. Thesis: English.
Lowenherz, Robert J. Mark Twain and William Dean Howells:
  A Literary Relationship. New York Univ., 1954.
  Dissertation: English.
Loweth, Margaret G. Three Studies in English: Chaucer's
  Women; T.W. Robertson; Mark Twain in Conflict.
  Pennsylvania State Univ., 1969. Thesis: English.
Luck, Susan G. Patterns of Diminutive Imagery in Selected
  Works of Jonathan Swift and Mark Twain. Bowling Green
  State Univ., 1968. Thesis: English.
Lynn, Sr. Mary, I.H.M. Mark Twain's *Innocents Abroad* and
  the Tradition of American Travel Literature. Villanova
  Univ., 1963. Thesis: English.
Lyon, James C. A Study of Mark Twain's Developing Use of
  Irony and His Growth as a Satirist as Evidenced in His
  Short Stories. Northern Illinois Univ., 1966. Thesis:
  English.
Madigan, John J., III. Mark Twain and the Romantic Tradition:
  An Analysis of the Mississippi Trilogy. Univ. of
  Virginia, 1969. Thesis: English.
Magady, Nola L. The Disloyal Patriot: The Political Mark
  Twain. Kansas State Teachers College, 1968. Thesis:
  English.
Maloney, Francis J. Mark Twain: The Heir to Southwest Humor.
  Univ. of Portland, 1955. Thesis: English.
Marshall, Josephine A. The Publishing Venture of Mark Twain.
  Ohio Univ., 1948. Thesis: English.
Matsumoto, Tomone. *The Adventures of Huckleberry Finn* in
  Japanese: Problems of Linguistics and Culture. Univ. of
  Texas (El Paso), 1969. Thesis: English.
McClung, Daniel H. Mark Twain's Use of the Bible in "The
  Man That Corrupted Hadleyburg," "Extracts from Captain
  Stormfield's Visit to Heaven," *Personal Recollections of
  Joan of Arc*, and "The Mysterious Stranger." Univ. of
  Redlands, 1965. Thesis: English.
McCormack, Ann K. Mark Twain and Contemporary Humorists.
  John Carroll Univ., 1969. Thesis: English.
McGlockton, Yvonne E. Humor in the Early Works of Mark Twain.
  Atlanta Univ., 1963. Thesis: English.
McKinney, Brian C. The Monomyth and Mark Twain's Novels.
  San Francisco State College, 1967. Thesis: English.

McMahan, Elizabeth E. Mark Twain and the "Damned Human Race."
A Study of Samuel L. Clemens' Indictment of Humanity.
Univ. of Houston, 1962. Thesis: English.

McNamara, Eugene J. Mark Twain's Theory and Practice of Fiction,
*The Adventures of Tom Sawyer, Adventures of Huckleberry
Finn, The Tragedy of Pudd'nhead Wilson.* Northwestern Univ.,
1964. Dissertation: English.

McQuitty, Robert A. Mark Twain and Literary Naturalism. Texas
Christian Univ., 1963. Thesis: English.

Mello, Edward C. Mark Twain's Writing on Oral Interpretation.
North Texas State Univ., 1965. Thesis: Speech and Drama.

Menke, Pamela G. Mark Twain and the Forms of Escape: Childhood
as Theme in Nineteenth Century American Literature. Univ.
of North Carolina (Chapel Hill), 1966. Thesis: English.

Minnehan, Hallena B. Mark Twain's Portrayal of Life in the
Mississippi Valley. Univ. of Texas (Austin), 1967.
Thesis: English.

Moehle, Guenther. Das Europbild Mark Twains. Grundlagen und
Bildungselemente. Irving, Hawthorne, Mark Twain. Bonn,
1940. Dissertation: English.

Moldenhauer, Joseph. Innocence and Experience: A Thematic
Study in the Works of Mark Twain. Columbia Univ., 1957.
Thesis: English.

Molter, Leticia S.R. A Study of the Social Criticism in the
Essays of Mark Twain. Univ. of Pittsburgh, 1969.
Dissertation: English.

Moore, Robert H. The Use of "Nigger" in Mark Twain's *Adventures
of Huckleberry Finn.* Univ. of North Carolina (Chapel Hill),
1964. Thesis: English.

Moore, William E. Mark Twain's Techniques of Humor. George
Peabody College, 1947. Dissertation: English.

Morgan, Ann D. Mark Twain's "Symbolic Sad Initiation." East
Tennessee State Univ., 1969. Thesis: English.

Morgan, Elizabeth A. The Importance of Caricature in the
Artistry of Mark Twain. Univ. of North Carolina (Chapel
Hill), 1966. Thesis: English.

Morton, Paul S. Representative Criticism of *Huckleberry Finn*:
1884-1932. Washington Univ. (St. Louis), 1950. Thesis:
English.

Mosely, Nellie L. A Vision of Humanity: Mark Twain's Use of
Satiric Narrators. Duke Univ., 1967. Thesis: English.

Motola, Gabriel. Mark Twain and the Detective. New York Univ.,
1969. Dissertation: English.

Mott, Bertram L., Jr. The Residual Calvinism of Mark Twain:
Its Evidence in His Post-1892 Work. Univ. of Pennsylvania,
1968. Dissertation: English.

Murray, James. Mark Twain's *A Connecticut Yankee in King
Arthur's Court*: A Critical Study. Univ. of Texas (Austin),
1955. Thesis: English.

Myers, Joseph W. The Royal Image and the Theme of the Prince-
Pauper Contrast in the Works of Mark Twain. Univ. of
California (Berkeley), 1966. Dissertation: English.

Neidlinger, S.L. The Presentation of Slavery in Three of Mark
Twain's Novels. Indiana State Univ., 1969. Thesis: English.

Nelley, William F. Mark Twain and Aristocracy. West Texas
    State Univ., 1969. Thesis: English.
Neubauer, Heinz. Amerikanische Goldgräeberliteratur (Bret
    Harte, Mark Twain, Jack London). Griefswald, 1936.
    Dissertation: English.
Neuner, Maria. Mark Twain and the South. Kent State Univ.,
    1964. Thesis: English.
Newmar, Patricia W. The Critical Journey of Huckleberry Finn.
    Mississippi State Univ., 1969. Thesis: English.
Odle, Zelma R. Plot Structure in the Novels of Mark Twain.
    North Texas State Univ., 1949. Thesis: English.
Oglesby, Ethel A. A Historical and Critical Study of Mark
    Twain's The Adventures of Tom Sawyer. Univ. of Texas
    (Austin), 1958. Thesis: English.
Packer, James E. Mark Twain's Attitude Toward the Negro
    Problem. Texas Christian Univ., 1960. Thesis: English.
Park, Ulna F. Mark Twain and the Image of the South. Univ.
    of Wisconsin, 1970. Dissertation: English.
Parman, Michael J. Commentary on the Virginia City Newspaper
    Career and Personal Life of Mark Twain by His Contemporaries.
    Univ. of Nevada (Reno), 1968. Thesis: Journalism.
Paswuier-Doumer, Marie C. Mark Twain and the Mississippi River.
    Cornell Univ., 1955. Thesis: English.
Peabody, Henry W. The Degeneration of a Character: Tom Sawyer
    in Four Works. Univ. of Georgia, 1968. Thesis: English.
Pearson, Thomas A. An Analysis of The Adventures of Huckleberry
    Finn for Oral Interpretation. Baylor Univ., 1955. Thesis:
    Speech.
Perri, Josephine M. Mark Twain, Ironic Surveyor of American
    Life. St. John's Univ. [N.Y.], 1951. Thesis: English.
Pfeiffer, Benjamin. Religious, Moral, and Social Ideas in
    the Works of Mark Twain. Univ. of Nebraska, 1964.
    Dissertation: English.
Phelps, Arthur T. Some Historical and Religious Aspects of
    the Treatments of Joan of Arc by Mark Twain and George
    Bernard Shaw. Canisius College, 1940. Thesis: English.
Pierotti, Alfred. Comedy in Huckleberry Finn. Univ. of
    Dallas, 1969. Thesis: English.
Pollock, George W. Mark Twain's Views of Racial Minorities
    in America. Baylor Univ., 1966. Thesis: English.
Pousson, John D. Critical Attitudes Toward Mark Twain's
    Huckleberry Finn. Louisiana State Univ., 1960. Thesis:
    English.
Pozychki, Mary A. The Adventures of Huckleberry Finn--Portrait
    of America: A Study of the Critical Analysis of Mark
    Twain from 1884 to the 1960's. Villanova Univ., 1966.
    Thesis: English.
Proctor, Kenneth R. The Negro in the Works of Mark Twain.
    East Carolina Univ., 1964. Thesis: English.
Raphael, Carolyn B. Twain's Connecticut Yankee: The Problem
    of Satire and Characterization. Queens College, 1965.
    Thesis: English.
Rarn, Holten W. Mark Twain and Nineteenth Century Scientific
    Thought. San Diego State College, 1950. Thesis: English.

[29]

Ratcliffe, Robert R. The Writing, Publication, and Reception of *The Mysterious Stranger*. Univ. of North Carolina (Chapel Hill), 1960. Thesis: English.

Reagan, Fred C. A Comparison of the Religious Philosophies of Mark Twain and Huckleberry Finn. Eastern New Mexico Univ., 1962. Thesis: English.

Reckford, Philip J. Some Aspects of Mark Twain's Code. Univ. of North Carolina (Chapel Hill), 1965. Thesis: English.

Rees, Robert A. Mark Twain and the Bible: Characters Who Use the Bible and Biblical Characters. Univ. of Wisconsin, 1966. Dissertation: English.

Regan, Robert C. The Unpromising Hero in the Writings of Mark Twain. Univ. of California (Berkeley), 1965. Dissertation: English.

Roberson, Robert E. Mark Twain, Satirist and Critic of the Human Race. Emory Univ., 1940. Thesis: English.

Robinson, Vivian U. Social Criticism in the Novels of Mark Twain. Atlanta Univ., 1963. Thesis: English.

Rodney, Robert M. Mark Twain in England: A Study of the English Criticism of and Attitude toward Mark Twain, 1867-1940. Univ. of Wisconsin, 1946. Dissertation: English.

Rogers, Franklin R. The Role of Literary Burlesque in the Development of Mark Twain's Structural Patterns, 1855-1885. Univ. of California (Berkeley), 1958. Dissertation: English.

Rogers, Janie F. Representations of the Mother-Son Relations in the Major Novels of Samuel Clemens. North Texas State Univ., 1968. Thesis: English.

Rosa, Alfred F. Mark Twain's Use of the Technique and Theme of Appearance and Reality. Univ. of Massachusetts, 1966. Thesis: English.

Rosen, Nathan. The Two Worlds of Mark Twain: A Study of His Major Novels. Columbia Univ., 1949. Thesis: English.

Rowlette, Robert O. Mark Twain's *Pudd'nhead Wilson*: Its Themes and Their Development. Univ. of Kansas, 1967. Dissertation: English.

Ruesch, Robert. Mark Twain and the Negro. Hofstra Univ., 1970. Thesis: Humanities.

Rulon, Curt M. The Dialects in *Huckleberry Finn*. Univ. of Iowa, 1967. Dissertation: Linguistics.

Russell, James. The Genesis, Sources and Reputation of Mark Twain's *A Connecticut Yankee in King Arthur's Court*. Univ. of Chicago, 1966. Dissertation: English.

Russell, James G. Mark Twain: His Quest for Soul. Slippery Rock State College, 1969. Thesis: Education.

St. Pierre, Jean M. The Worlds of Hannibal, Dawson's Landing, and Eseldorf: A Study of Illusion and Reality in the Works of Mark Twain. Columbia Univ., 1961. Thesis: English.

Salomom, Roger B. Mark Twain's Conceptions of History. Univ. of California (Berkeley), 1957. Dissertation: English.

Sandberg, James S. The Celebration of Boyhood by Mark Twain and His Midwestern Contemporaries. Stanford Univ., 1949. Thesis: English.

Sargent, Marjorie. Mark Twain's Concern for Justice as seen in *The Adventures of Huckleberry Finn* and *The Mysterious Stranger*. Univ. of Denver, 1970. Thesis: English.

Sbaratta, Philip. Three Studies in English: Robin Hood Legend; An Unpublished Letter of Henley; Twainian Ambivalence. Pennsylvania State Univ., 1967. Thesis: English.

Schieber, Alois J. Autobiographies of American Novelists: Twain, Howells, James, Adams, and Garland. Univ. of Wisconsin, 1957. Dissertation: English.

Schiffman, Michael. Mark Twain's Humor and *The Innocents Abroad*. Columbia Univ., 1966. Thesis: English.

Schmidt, Paul S. Samuel Clemens's Technique as a Humorist, 1857-1872. Univ. of Minnesota, 1951. Dissertation: English.

Scott, Arthur L. Mark Twain as a Critic of Europe. Univ. of Michigan, 1948. Dissertation: English.

Scott, Emmy L.M. Mark Twain's *Roughing It*: An Historical and Critical Analysis. Univ. of Texas (Austin), 1964. Thesis: English.

Scott, Harold P. Mark Twain's Theory of Humor: An Analysis of the Laughable in Literature. Univ. of Michigan, 1917. Dissertation: English.

Scott, Hazelyn D. Mark Twain's Treatment of the Negro. Atlanta Univ., 1955. Thesis: English.

Shane, Marion L. Spiritual Poverty in Selected Works of Four American Novelists: Mark Twain, Crane, Fitzgerald, Dreiser. Syracuse Univ., 1953. Dissertation: English.

Sharpe, Johnnie L.M. The Evolution of Pessimism in the Works of Mark Twain. Atlanta Univ., 1968. Thesis: English.

Shell, Peggy T. The Evolution of a Cynic: The Philosophy of Mark Twain. Northeast Louisiana Univ., 1968. Thesis: English.

Shipman, Elsa B. The Pessimism of Mark Twain. Ohio Univ., 1945. Thesis: English.

Singleton, Marvin K. The Medievalism of Mark Twain. Duke Univ., 1957. Thesis: English.

Sipple, Margaret N. Mark Twain and the Mysterious Stranger. Univ. of Wisconsin, 1968. Dissertation: English.

Sisk, Sr. Mary E. Mark Twain's *The Mysterious Stranger*: A Study in Pessimism. Duquesne Univ., 1958. Thesis: English.

Skaggs, Peggy D. Folklore in *Huckleberry Finn*. Texas A & M Univ., 1965. Thesis: English.

Smalley, Webster L. The Critical Reception of Mark Twain in England: 1870-1910. Columbia Univ., 1948. Thesis: English.

Smith, J.H. The Expressed Opinions of Mark Twain on Heredity and Environment. Univ. of Wisconsin, 1955. Dissertation: English.

Speeks, Ida M. Humor in Selected Travel Books by Mark Twain. Duke Univ., 1961. Thesis: English.

Spengemann, William C. The Meaning of Innocence in the Works of Samuel Clemens. Stanford Univ., 1961. Dissertation: English.

Stampleman, Jed R. Mark Twain: The Development of the Crowd as à Character. Univ. of Massachusetts, 1966. Thesis: English.

Stappenbeck, Herbert L. Mark Twain and the American Indians. Univ. of Texas (Austin), 1958. Thesis: English.

Startt, William. A Survey of the Early Criticism of *The Adventures of Huckleberry Finn* (1884-1910). Univ. of Maryland, 1963. Thesis: English.

Startzmen, Patricia K. A Comparison of the Determinism of Mark Twain and Theodore Dreiser. Texas A & M Univ., 1968. Thesis: English.

Steinbrink, Jeffrey C. A Consideration of Innocence in *Adventures of Huckleberry Finn*. Univ. of North Carolina (Chapel Hill), 1968. Thesis: English.

Stevenson, Dwight W. Samuel Langhorne Clemens as a Literary Artist: A Study of His Use of the Novella Form. Univ. of Michigan, 1965. Dissertation: English.

Stevenson, Sam D. The Authentic Mark Twain. Texas Christian Univ., 1970. Thesis: English.

Stone, Albert E., Jr. Mark Twain's Children. Yale Univ., 1957. Dissertation: English.

Stockdale, William A. How Calvinism and Deism Influenced Mark Twain. Univ. of Kansas, 1950. Thesis: English.

Stordahl, Linn M. Mark Twain and the Frontier Spirit. Colorado State Univ., 1966. Thesis: English.

Stovall, Stella S. A Critical Study of Mark Twain's *Roughing It*. Baylor Univ., 1951. Thesis: English.

Struhs, William H. Mark Twain's Theory of Humor. State Univ. of Iowa, 1949. Thesis: English.

Stumbo, Richard R. The Literary Reputation of Mark Twain in America, 1885-1910. Univ. of Kansas, 1965. Thesis: English.

Sutrina, John J. Literary Criticism Contained in the Works of Mark Twain. Montana State Univ., 1951. Thesis: English.

Tanner, P.A. The Uses of Wonder and Naivety in American Literature With Special Reference to Mark Twain and the Development of the Vernacular Child Narrator. Cambridge Univ. (Kings), 1965. Dissertation: English.

Tarzinski, George. Mark Twain's Contempt for Mankind as It Is Reflected in *The Adventures of Huckleberry Finn*, *A Connecticut Yankee in King Arthur's Court*, and *The Mysterious Stranger*. Univ. of Dayton, 1970. Thesis: English.

Taylor, John F. Mark Twain and the Woman. Columbia Univ., 1950. Thesis: English.

Tenney, Thomas A. Mark Twain in 1910: A Study of His Popular and Critical Standing at the End of His Career. Columbia Univ., 1965. Thesis: English.

Therrell, Katheryne. Folklore in the River Novels of Mark Twain. East Texas State Univ., 1966. Thesis: English.

Thoeni, S.M. Literary Theory and Practice of Mark Twain. College of the Holy Names, 1966. Thesis: English.

Thomas, Niles B. A Study of the Determinism of Mark Twain: Selected Novels, 1885-1910, and *What Is Man?* Auburn Univ., 1969. Thesis: English.

Thompson, Elizabeth J. Major Trends in Mark Twain Criticism. Mississippi State Univ., 1966. Thesis: English.

Thomson, David T., Jr. Deception in *The Adventures of Huckleberry Finn*. Univ. of Florida, 1966. Thesis: English.

Tomlinson, Katie L. Mark Twain's Portrait of the Negro as Compared with Selected Fiction of His Time. Kansas State Teachers College, 1964. Thesis: English.

Toole, Ross W. Mark Twain's and Charles Dudley Warner's *The Gilded Age*: An Historical and Critical Study. Univ. of Texas (Austin), 1951. Thesis: English.

Tozer, Eliot F. Mark Twain, Comedian. Columbia Univ., 1949. Thesis: English.

Truitt, Dona W. Conscience in the Writings of Mark Twain. Northeast Missouri State Univ., 1967. Thesis: English.

Tucker, Carolyn H. Mark Twain's Attitudes Toward the Concept of Free Will: A Study of Selected Works. Bowling Green State Univ., 1961. Thesis: English.

Tuckey, John S. Mark Twain as a Satirist. Univ. of Notre Dame, 1953. Dissertation: English.

Turner, Margery B. Mark Twain at Mid-Century, 1950-1961. A Synthesis of Critical Views Fifty Years After His Death. Univ. of Nebraska (Omaha), 1961. Thesis: English.

Tyler, Ronald T. Mark Twain's Mythic Vision: An Affirmation of Man's Possibilities. Univ. of Nevada (Reno), 1970. Thesis: English.

Vetterli, Clarence H. The Evolution of Mark Twain's Political and Social Philosophy. Univ. of Southern California, 1950. Thesis: English.

Vogelback, Arthur L. The Literary Reputation of Mark Twain in America, 1869-85. Univ. of Chicago, 1938. Dissertation: English.

Wager, Willis J. A Critical Edition of the Morgan Manuscript of Mark Twain's *Life on the Mississippi*. New York Univ., 1942. Dissertation: English.

Wagner, Gerard. Mark Twain, Political Orator. Indiana Univ. [Date Unknown]. Dissertation: Speech.

Wallace, Robert D. An Analytical-Historical Study of the Factors Contributing to the Success of Mark Twain as an Oral Interpretor. Univ. of Southern California, 1962. Dissertation: Speech.

Ward, Fadwa E.T. The Influence of Virginia City on Mark Twain's Writings from 1862-1872. Baylor Univ., 1968. Thesis: English.

Ward, Marilyn K. Huck's Maturation Through Inner Conflict. Univ. of Rhode Island, 1969. Thesis: English.

Ware, Mary J. A Study of Mark Twain's *Roughing It*. Univ. of Texas (Austin), 1968. Thesis: English.

Watkins, E.M. Mark Twain's Religion. Northeast Missouri State Univ., 1967. Thesis: English.

Watson, Romer D. Mark Twain's Mature Attitude Towards Southern Society. Univ. of North Carolina (Chapel Hill), 1967. Thesis: English.

Webb, Guelford P. A Historical and Critical Analysis of Mark Twain's *The Prince and the Pauper*. Univ. of Texas (Austin), 1951. Thesis: English.

Werge, Thomas A. The Persistence of Adam: Puritan Concerns
and Conflicts in Melville and Mark Twain. Cornell Univ.,
1967. Dissertation: English.
West, Ralph E., Jr. Heart Versus Reason in *The Mysterious
Stranger*: A Theme Continued from *Huckleberry Finn*. Univ.
of Virginia, 1966. Thesis: English.
Wexler, Janet S. The Critics on Mark Twain's Pessimism:
1900-1947. Univ. of Maryland, 1953. Thesis: English.
Whorton, Mary T. Mark Twain and the Naturalism of Stephen
Crane. Northeast Missouri State Univ., 1965. Thesis:
English.
Wiggins, Robert A. Mark Twain's Novels: Principles and
Practice of Realism. Univ. of California (Berkeley),
1953. Dissertation: English.
Williams, James D. The Genesis, Composition, Publication and
Reception of Mark Twain's *A Connecticut Yankee*. New York
Univ., 1961. Dissertation: English.
Williams, Patricia W. The Unity of Moral Vision in *Huckleberry
Finn* and *The Catcher in the Rye*. Texas A & M Univ., 1966.
Thesis: English.
Woods, June S. Mark Twain and the Rebel Angel. Western State
College of Colorado, 1965. Thesis: English.
Worrell, Jack E. A Study of Social Satire in Representative
Novels of Mark Twain. Univ. of Houston, 1960. Thesis:
English.
Wright, Homer L. Mark Twain, A Historian of Missouri.
Washington Univ. (St. Louis), 1939. Thesis: English.
Young, Mary A. The Phelps Episode in *Huckleberry Finn*. Emory
Univ., 1959. Thesis: English.
Young, Philip. Ernest Hemingway and *Huckleberry Finn*: A Study
in Continuity. Univ. of Iowa, 1948. Dissertation: English.
Young, Sara L. Mark Twain's Biography: From Panegyric to
Synthesis. Univ. of Louisville, 1968. Thesis: English.
Zuckerman, Frances. Strained Laughter: A Study of Mark Twain's
Pudd'nhead Wilson. Columbia Univ., 1964. Thesis: English.
Zuckert, Michael P. An Introduction to Mark Twain and His *A
Connecticut Yankee in King Arthur's Court*. Univ. of
Chicago, 1967. Thesis: English.
Zurich, Joseph G. Mark Twain's *Joan of Arc*: Origins, Purposes,
and Accomplishment. Univ. of Illinois, 1963. Dissertation:
English.

IRVIN S. COBB (1876-1944)

Burkhalter, Berry L. A Rhetorical Study of Irvin S. Cobb.
Murray State Univ., 1967. Thesis: English.
Halpern, Beulah R. The Place of Irvin S. Cobb in the Devel-
opment of the American Short Story. Univ. of Texas (Austin),
1938. Thesis: English.
Logsdon, Katherine. Irvin S. Cobb and His Judge Priest Stories.
Western Kentucky Univ., 1936. Thesis: English.
Pickard, Lessie D. An Appreciation of the Life and Writings of
Irvin S. Cobb. George Peabody College, 1938. Thesis:
English.

THOMAS R.R. COBB (1823-1862)

McCash, William B. Thomas R.R. Cobb: A Biography. Univ. of
Georgia, 1968. Dissertation: History.

EDWARD LOUIS COCHRAN (1899-   )

Taylor, H.L. Louis Cochran: Mississippi Novelist. Fort
Hays Kansas State College, 1965. Thesis: English.

ZITELLA COCKE (1831-1929)

Eborn, Mary L. An Appreciation of the Life and Writings of
Zitella Cocke. George Peabody College, 1931. Thesis:
English.

OSCAR BRANCH COLQUITT (1861-1940)

Huckaby, George P. Oscar Branch Colquitt: A Political Biography.
Univ. of Texas (Austin), 1946. Dissertation: History.

MONCURE CONWAY (1832-1907)

Burtis, Mary E. Moncure Conway, 1832-1907. Columbia Univ.,
1952. Dissertation: English.
Campbell, Philip S. Moncure Daniel Conway. Duke Univ., 1941.
Thesis: English.

EBENEZER COOK[E] (1670?-post 1732)

Pole, James T. Ebenezer Cook: *The Sot-Weed Factor. An Edition.*
Columbia Univ., 1931. Thesis: English.

JOHN ESTEN COOKE (1830-1886)

Beaty, John O. John Esten Cooke, Virginian. Columbia Univ.,
1922. Dissertation: English.
Bratton, Mary J.J. John Esten Cooke: The Young Writer and the
Old South, 1830-1861. Univ. of North Carolina (Chapel
Hill), 1969. Dissertation: History.
Freeman, Walter C. The Old Dominion Novels of John Esten Cooke.
Miami Univ. (Ohio), 1948. Thesis: English.
Johnson, Emma B. John Esten Cooke and the Civil War. Duke
Univ., 1943. Thesis: English.
Riley, John A. John Esten Cooke: A Comparative Study of His
Non-Fiction Writings on the Civil War. Univ. of Georgia,
1967. Dissertation: English.
Walker, William E. John Esten Cooke: A Critical Biography.
Vanderbilt Univ., 1957. Dissertation: English.

PHILIP PENDLETON COOKE (1816-1850)

Allen, John D. Philip Pendleton Cooke: A Critical and
Biographical Study. Vanderbilt Univ., 1938. Dissertation:
English.

Thompson, May A. Philip Pendleton Cooke. Columbia Univ.,
     1923. Thesis: English.

THOMAS COOPER (1759-1839)

Malone, Dumas. The Public Life and Writings of Thomas Cooper,
     1783-1839. Yale Univ., 1923. Dissertation: History.

JAMES ANDREW CORCORAN (1820-1889)

Lowman, Sr. Mary M. James Andrew Corcoran: Editor, Theologian,
     Scholar (1820-1889). St. Louis Univ., 1958. Dissertation:
     History.

JOHN COTTON (c.1643-post 1680)

Rosenmeier, Jesper. The Image of Christ: The Typology of
     John Cotton. Harvard Univ., 1957. Dissertation: History.

DAVID CROCKETT (1786-1836)

Arpad, Joseph. David Crockett, An Original: Legendary
     Eccentricity and Early American Character. Duke Univ.,
     1969. Dissertation: English.
Catron, Anna G. The Public Career of David Crockett. Univ.
     of Tennessee, 1955. Thesis: History.
Crockett, Frank Q. A Study of the Politics of "The Honourable
     David Crockett, M.C." Univ. of Mississippi, 1930. Thesis:
     History.
Dowell, Ruth B. The Congressional Career of David Crockett.
     Columbia Univ., 1925. Thesis: Political Science.
Gates, Margaret H. Fact and Fiction in the Early Biographies
     of David Crockett. Univ. of Illinois, 1929. Thesis:
     English.
Shackford, James A. The Autobiography of David Crockett,
     Annotated. Vanderbilt Univ., 1948. Dissertation:
     English.

GRACE NOLL CROWELL (1877-1969)

Fuller, Myra S. A Study of the Poetry of Grace Noll Crowell.
     East Texas State Univ., 1937. Thesis: English.
Robinson, Lillie. Religious Implications in Grace Noll
     Crowell's Poetry. Hardin-Simmons Univ., 1950. Thesis:
     English.

JABEZ LAMAR MONROE CURRY (1825-1903)

Peck, Richard C. Jabez Lamar Monroe Curry, Educational Crusader.
     George Peabody College, 1942. Dissertation: English.

ROBERT LEWIS DABNEY (1787-1825)

Lewis, Frank B. Robert Lewis Dabney: Southern Presbyterian
     Apologist. Duke Univ., 1946. Dissertation: Religion.

JOSEPHUS DANIELS (1862-1948)

Morrison, Joseph L. Josephus Daniels as "Tar Heel Editor,"
1894-1913. Duke Univ., 1961. Dissertation: History.

OLIVE TILFORD DARGAN (1869-1968)

Love, Catherine. Mrs. Olive Tilford Dargan. Univ. of South
Carolina, 1919. Thesis: English.

DONALD DAVIDSON (1893-1968)

Freeze, Leslie H. The Poetry of Donald Davidson. Univ. of
Kansas, 1964. Thesis: English.
Glass, John V. The Theme of Tradition in the Poetry of Donald
Davidson. Univ. of Georgia, 1967. Thesis: English.
Gower, Dona S. Donald Davidson and the Tall Men: Toward a
Definition of the Public Poet. Vanderbilt Univ., 1967.
Thesis: English.
Williams, Joseph. Donald Davidson, Agrarian and Poet. Univ.
of South Carolina, 1957. Thesis: English.

WILLIAM LEE DAVIDSON (1746-1781)

Davidson, Chalmers G. The Life and Letters of General William
Lee Davidson. Harvard Univ., 1942. Dissertation: History.

MARIA THOMPSON DAVIESS (1872-1924)

Ashley, Anne. Harpeth Valley in the Fiction of Maria Thompson
Daviess. George Peabody College, 1935. Thesis: English.

JEFFERSON DAVIS (1808-1889)

Daniel, Arthur G. Jefferson Davis and the Confederate Governors.
North Texas State Univ., 1959. Thesis: History.
Krause, Richard A. An Investigation of the Literary Treatment
of Jefferson Davis during the Past Century. Stetson Univ.,
1963. Thesis: History.
Mallonée, Frank B. The Political Thought of Jefferson Davis.
Emory Univ., 1966. Dissertation: Political Science.
Mann, Kenneth E. An Analysis of the Speech Style of Jefferson
Davis. Brigham Young Univ., 1966. Thesis: Public Address.
Pohl, James W. Jefferson Davis and His Command Problem. North
Texas State Univ., 1955. Thesis: History.

MARY EVELYN MOORE DAVIS (1852-1902)

Ingram, Lilly P. Mrs. Mollie Evelyn Moore Davis: A Biographical
and Critical Study. Univ. of Mississippi, 1930. Thesis:
English.
Wilkinson, Clyde W. The Broadening Stream: The Life and
Literary Career of Mollie E. Moore Davis. Univ. of
Illinois, 1947. Dissertation: English.

ROBERT MEANS DAVIS (1849-1904)

Leonard, Mary A. Robert Means Davis, 1849-1904: A Study of
    His Life and Services as Journalist, Educator, and
    Publicist. Univ. of South Carolina, 1926. Thesis: English.

VARINA HOWELL DAVIS (1826-1906)

Deuschle, Marie. An Estimate of the Character and Career of
    Varina Howell Davis. Southern Methodist Univ., 1938.
    Thesis: History.

FRANCIS WARRINGTON DAWSON (1840-1889)

Logan, S.F. Francis W. Dawson, 1840-1889: South Carolina
    Editor. Duke Univ., 1947. Thesis: History.
Williams, Charles Braxton. Francis Warrington Dawson: Editor
    of *The News and Courier* (Newspaper of Charleston, S.C.).
    Univ. of South Carolina, 1926. Thesis: English.

GEORGE BANNERMAN DEALEY (1859-1946)

Sharpe, Ernest A. Dealey of Dallas. Univ. of Texas (Austin),
    1941. Thesis: Journalism.

JAMES D.B. DE BOW (1820-1867)

Sanders, Robert H. Some Aspects of James D.B. De Bow and His
    Review. Univ. of Alabama, 1950. Thesis: Journalism.
Skipper, Ottis C. J.D.B. De Bow, Editor and Publicist. Harvard
    Univ., 1942. Dissertation: History.

SIDONIE DE LA HOUSSAYE (1820-1894)

Perret, Joseph J. A Critical Study of the Life and Writings of
    Sidonie De La Houssaye with Special Emphasis on the
    Unpublished Works. Louisiana State Univ., 1966. Disser-
    tation: English.
Savoie, Velma. The Life and Writings of Madame Sidonie de la
    Houssaye. Louisiana State Univ., 1936. Thesis: Romance
    Languages.

CHARLES DeMORSE (1816-1887)

Wallace, Ernest. Charles DeMorse: Pioneer Editor and Statesman.
    Univ. of Texas (Austin), 1942. Dissertation: History.

CABEZA DE VACA (c.1490-c.1557)

Campbell, Thelma. Cabeza de Vaca, the First Historian of Texas.
    Columbia Univ., 1933. Thesis: Romance Languages and
    Literature.

THOMAS RODERICK DEW (1802-1846)

Mansfield, Stephen S. Thomas Roderick Dew: Defender of the
    Southern Faith. Univ. of Virginia, 1968. Dissertation:
    History.

JAMES DICKEY (1923-   )

Hodge, Marion. Meat and Illusion: An Interpretive Analysis
    of James Dickey's Poetry. East Tennessee State Univ.,
    1970. Thesis: English.
Korsborn, Winnifred L. The Religious Element in the Early
    Poetry of James Dickey. Eastern Washington State College,
    1970. Thesis: English.
Sekula, Jeffrey C. The Techniques of Transformation in the
    Poetry of James Dickey. Univ. of Tennessee, 1968.
    Thesis: English.

HARRIS DICKSON (1868-   )

Newman, Daisy. The Negro in the Writings of Harris Dickson.
    George Peabody College, 1938. Thesis: English.

THOMAS DIXON (1864-1946)

Cook, Raymond A. Thomas Dixon: His Books and His Career.
    Emory Univ., 1953. Dissertation: English.
Harris, Max F. The Ideas of Thomas Dixon on Race Relations.
    Univ. of North Carolina (Chapel Hill), 1949. Thesis:
    History.
Lutz, Sr. M.A., O.S.F. Thomas Dixon's Contribution to American
    Literature with Special Reference to the Original Manuscript
    of *The Root of Evil*. St. Bonaventure Univ., 1948. Thesis:
    English.
Minton, Lucile. A Study of Thomas Dixon, Southerner. Univ.
    of Georgia, 1938. Thesis: English.
St. Clair, Jane. A Study of the Novels of Thomas Dixon.
    Louisiana State Univ., 1952. Thesis: English.
Sheldrew, James W. *The Birth of a Nation*: Romantic or
    Democratic? Auburn Univ., 1968. Thesis: Speech.
Wright, James Z. Thomas Dixon: The Mind of a Southern Apologist.
    George Peabody College, 1966. Dissertation: History.

J. FRANK DOBIE (1888-1964)

Pinkham, Sibyl V. The Life and Work of J. Frank Dobie. George
    Peabody College, 1933. Thesis: English.

WILLIAM E. DODD (1869-1940)

Ware, Lowry P. The Academic Career of William E. Dodd. Univ.
    of South Carolina, 1956. Dissertation: History.

SARAH ANNE DORSEY (1829-1879)

Billingsley, Allie W. Sarah Anne Dorsey: A Critical and
    Biographical Study. Univ. of Mississippi, 1929. Thesis:
    English.
Lewis, Charlotte E. Sarah Anne Dorsey: A Critical Estimate.
    Louisiana State Univ., 1940. Thesis: English.

FREDERICK DOUGLASS (1817-1895)

Knickerbocker, Lydia S. Frederick Douglass, Father of the
    Protest Movement. Southern Methodist Univ., 1966.
    Thesis: History.

WILLIAM ALLEN DROMGOOLE (1860-1934)

King, Anna M. Will Allen Dromgoole: A Writer of Tennessee Life.
    George Peabody College, 1930. Thesis: English.

HARRY STILLWELL EDWARDS (1855-1938)

Fain, Elethia. Harry Stillwell Edwards as a Writer of Local
    Color Short Stories. Univ. of Georgia, 1941. Thesis:
    English.
Looney, Grace G. Harry S. Edwards. George Peabody College,
    1930. Thesis: English.
Toole, Lila E. What Is Harry Stillwell Edwards' Contribution
    to Southern Literature? Mercer Univ., 1928. Thesis:
    English.

GEORGE CARY EGGLESTON (1839-1911)

Abee, Florence E. Virginia Life in the Novels of George Cary
    Eggleston. Duke Univ., 1938. Thesis: English.
Callison, Louise E. George Cary Eggleston: A Biography and
    Critical Study. Case Western Reserve Univ., 1969.
    Dissertation: Biography.

SARAH BURNWELL ELLIOT (1848-1928)

Flowers, Charles V. The Fiction of Sarah Burnwell Elliot.
    Univ. of Tennessee, 1950. Thesis: English.

STEPHEN ELLIOTT (1806-1866)

Davis, Virgil S. Stephen Elliott: A Southern Bishop in Peace
    and War. Univ. of Georgia, 1964. Dissertation: History.

WILLIAM ELLIOTT (1788-1863)

Skardon, B.N. William Elliott, Planter-Writer of Ante-Bellum
    South Carolina. Univ. of Florida, 1964. Thesis: English.

RALPH ELLISON (1914-   )

Baumgaertner, Jill P. The Quest for Visibility in Ralph
    Ellison's *Invisible Man*, John Steinbeck's *The Grapes of
    Wrath*, and Norman Mailer's *The Naked and the Dead*. Drake
    Univ., 1969. Thesis: English.
Collins, A.P. The Work of Ralph Ellison: An Introduction.
    Manchester, 1967. Thesis: English.
Cowsky, David L. Blindness and Distorted Vision Symbolism in
    the *Invisible Man* by Ralph Ellison. Bowling Green State
    Univ., 1966. Thesis: English.
Fischer, Russell G. *Invisible Man* as Symbolic History. San
    Francisco State College, 1970. Thesis: English.
Hux, Samuel H. American Myth and Existential Vision: The
    Indigenous Existentialism of Mailer, Bellow, Styron, and
    Ellison. Univ. of Connecticut, 1965. Dissertation:
    English.
Lourie, Richard M. Shadows of Invisibility: A Comparative
    Study of Herman Melville's *Benito Cereno* and Ralph Ellison's
    Invisible Man. Columbia Univ., 1960. Thesis: English.
Polsgrove, Carol C. Aspects of the Grotesque in Ralph Ellison's
    Invisible Man. Univ. of Louisville, 1969. Thesis: English.
Turngren, John A. Ralph Ellison's *Invisible Man*. Claremont
    Graduate School, 1966. Thesis: English.
Webb, Mary H. The Structure of *Invisible Man*. Univ. of Florida,
    1967. Thesis: English.
Weisman, Jack E. II. The Mask of the Artist: Social, Ritual,
    Stereotype, and the Blues in Ralph Ellison's *Invisible Man*.
    Univ. of Virginia, 1966. Thesis: English.

LOULA GRACE ERDMAN (? -   )

Brown, Loyce L. Television Dramatization of an Adaptation of
    the Book, *Separate Star*, by Loula Grace Erdman. West
    Texas State Univ., 1957. Thesis: Speech.

JOHN FAULKNER (1901-1963)

King, Dicki L. John Faulkner and the Folk Humor Tradition.
    Midwestern Univ., 1966. Thesis: English.

WILLIAM FAULKNER (1897-1962)

Abadie, Margaret M. William Faulkner's Dynamism, Romanticism,
    Bergsonism, and "The Bear." Tulane Univ., 1963. Thesis:
    English.
Abbott, Horace P. The Mind and "The Old Meat": Vision and
    the Verities in Faulkner's Ethic. Toronto, 1964.
    Thesis: English.
Abbott, Priscilla A. Family Relationships in Faulkner's Novels:
    Microcosm of the South's Degeneration. Texas Christian
    Univ., 1966. Thesis: English.
Adamowski, Thomas H. The Dickens World and Yoknapatawpha
    County: A Study of Character and Society in Dickens and
    Faulkner. Indiana Univ., 1969. Dissertation: English.

[41]

Albritton, Sue P. Faulkner's Lost Women of the Aristocracy.
    Univ. of Mississippi, 1968. Thesis: English.
Aldridge Henry B. The Function of Imagery in the Narratives
    of William Faulkner's *Absalom, Absalom!* Univ. of North
    Carolina (Chapel Hill), 1968. Thesis: English.
Alexander, Esther M. A Critical Analysis of the Roles of
    Lucas Beauchamp in William Faulkner's *Go Down, Moses* and
    Intruder on the Dust. Univ. of North Carolina (Chapel
    Hill), 1962. Thesis: English.
Allen, Ada E.H. Faulkner's Little Old Ladies. Univ. of
    Florida, 1967. Thesis: English.
Allen, Annette C. Form as Meaning in William Faulkner's *The
    Sound and the Fury* and *Absalom, Absalom!* Southern Methodist
    Univ., 1970. Thesis: English.
Allen, Billups S. Faulkner's Soldiers. Univ. of Mississippi,
    1968. Thesis: English.
Allen, Judson B. Rightness Beyond Morality: The Intelligible
    Form of *The Sound and the Fury.* Vanderbilt Univ., 1954.
    Thesis: English.
Amer, Marilyn. William Faulkner's Uses of the Old Testament.
    Univ. of Denver, 1965. Thesis: English.
Anderson, Janet C.S. Classical Allusions in the Works of
    William Faulkner. Univ. of Maryland, 1969. Thesis:
    English.
Anderson, Jean M. William Faulkner as Moralist: *A Fable*
    Univ. of the Pacific, 1959. Thesis: English.
Anderson, Katherine T. Search For Values in Faulkner's Trilogy.
    Univ. of Denver, 1966. Thesis: English.
Andrews, Katherine I. William Faulkner and the Southern Ideal
    of Womanhood. Univ. of Miami (Coral Gables), 1967.
    Thesis: English.
Applewhite, James W., Jr. Benjy's Perception of Value in *The
    Sound and the Fury.* Duke Univ., 1960. Thesis: English.
Arant, Fairlie. The South of William Faulkner as Seen in
    Absalom, Absalom! Columbia Univ., 1961. Thesis: English.
Archer, Lewis F. Coleridge's Definition of the Poet and the
    Works of Herman Melville and William Faulkner. Drew Univ.,
    1967. Dissertation: English.
Arkin, Barbara A. Agrarianism in the Works of William Faulkner.
    Univ. of Denver, 1967. Thesis: English.
Arpe, Jane C. Gavin Stevens--Faulkner's Trying Man. Lehigh
    Univ., 1964. Thesis: English.
Austin, Gloria J. The Role of the Negro in William Faulkner's
    Yoknapatawpa County Novels. Middle Tennessee State Univ.,
    1970. Thesis: English.
Aycook, Charles B. The Homeless Future: A Study of Time in
    the Novels of William Faulkner. East Carolina Univ.,
    1961. Thesis: English.
Baacke, Margareta. William Faulkners Menschen: Charakter-
    darstellung der Weissen aus Yoknapatawpha County. Marburg,
    1953. Dissertation: English.
Backman, Melvin A. The Pilgrimage of William Faulkner: A Study
    of Faulkner's Fiction, 1929-1942. Columbia Univ., 1960.
    Dissertation: English.

Balkman, Betty A. The Role of Women in the Work of William Faulkner. North Texas State Univ., 1968. Thesis: English.

Barbour, Brian M. Faulkner's Decline. Kent State Univ., 1969. Dissertation: English.

Bardwell, Barbara J. Reflections of the Code of Chivalry in Faulkner's Fiction. Mississippi College, 1967. Thesis: English.

Barnett, Bill M. Relationship of Point of View and Theme in Three Novels of William Faulkner. Auburn Univ., 1960. Thesis: English.

Barth, Mary K. The Study of Loneliness in the Novels and Short Stories of William Faulkner. State Univ. of New York (Buffalo), 1955. Thesis: English.

Battaglia, Francis J. Faulkner's Prose: A Study in Rhetoric as a Key to Style. Duke Univ., 1964. Thesis: English.

Baum, Anna C.B. Caddy Compson as Heroine of *The Sound and The Fury*. Emory Univ., 1961. Thesis: English.

Beauchamp, Gorman L. Archetypes in William Faulkner's "The Bear." Univ. of Houston, 1966. Thesis: English.

Bedell, Barbara. Alienation in the Early Works of Faulkner, 1929-1932. C.W. Post College of Long Island Univ., 1970. Thesis: English.

Bell, H.H., Jr. Lucius Priest and Ike McCaslin: A Comparative Study of Their Initiation into Manhood. Univ. of Maryland, 1965. Thesis: English.

Bellomy, Joyce. Christ Figures in the Novels of William Faulkner. Univ. of Texas (Austin), 1958. Thesis: English.

Benazon, Michael. Yoknapatawpha County: The Macrocosm of William Faulkner. Toronto Univ., 1960. Thesis: English.

Bennett, Myrtalee A. The Endurance Theme in William Faulkner's Major Novels. Hardin-Simmons Univ., 1968. Thesis: English.

Benton, Robert R. The Unity of *Go Down, Moses*: A Study of Faulkner's Revisions. Univ. of North Carolina (Chapel Hill), 1963. Thesis: English.

Berger, Stanley E. Cash Bundren and the Funeral Journey in Faulkner's *As I Lay Dying*. Univ. of New Hampshire, 1969. Thesis: English.

Berner, Robert L. The Theme of Responsibility in the Later Fiction of William Faulkner. Univ. of Washington, 1960. Dissertation: English.

Bethel, Patricia R. The Narrative Technique of William Faulkner. Villanova Univ., 1961. Thesis: English.

Blackburn, Brenda. The Development and Use of Archetypal Patterns in the Work of Faulkner. Kansas State Teachers College, 1969. Thesis: English.

Blanchard, Jo A. Five Major Themes in the Fiction of William Faulkner. East Tennessee State Univ., 1966. Thesis: English.

Blissard, Thomasina. The Role of the Negro in William Faulkner's Yoknapatawpha Series. Vanderbilt Univ., 1948. Thesis: English.

Boeckman, Frances B. A Study of the Evil Influences of William Faulkner's Female Characters. Mississippi College, 1967. Thesis: English.

Bonham, Ronald A. Unreality as Inhumanity: Faulkner's Ike McCaslin and the Failure of Humanism. Manitoba, 1967. Thesis: English.

Bostian, Frieda A. A Study of William Faulkner's *As I Lay Dying*. Univ. of North Carolina (Chapel Hill), 1966. Thesis: English.

Bosworth, Kirk L. A Study of Characterization in *A Fable*. Univ. of Vermont, 1970. Thesis: English.

Bower, Richard. William Faulkner's Reputation in France, 1931-1950. Hunter College, 1966. Thesis: English.

Boyd, Mary J. Faulkner's Primitives and the Timeless Values. Hunter College, 1967. Thesis: English.

Bozdech, James O. An Analysis of Time in the Early Novels of William Faulkner. Univ. of Dayton, 1966. Thesis: English.

Bradford, Melvin E.A. Faulkner's Doctrine of Nature: A Study of the "Endurance" Theme in the Yoknapatawpha Fiction. Vanderbilt Univ., 1968. Dissertation: English.

Bradley, Helena M. "A High and Delicate Art": A Study of William Faulkner's Tall Tales. Occidental College, 1967. Thesis: English.

Brady, Emily K. The Literary Faulkner: His Indebtedness to Conrad, Lawrence, Hemingway, and Other Modern Novelists. Brown Univ., 1962. Dissertation: English.

Brady, Sr. Mary H. Racism in *Light in August*. St. Louis Univ., 1967. Thesis: English.

Bramlett, Judith G. Gothic Elements in the Novels of William Faulkner. Sam Houston State Univ., 1963. Thesis: English.

Branam, Harold F. Faulkner's Icons: The Earth Mother Figures. Temple Univ., 1967. Thesis: English.

Brewer, William D. Faulkner in New Orleans. Univ. of Virginia, 1968. Thesis: English.

Brodsky, Louis D. Man and Nature: A Study of Animal Imagery in *As I Lay Dying*, *Old Man*, and "The Bear." Washington Univ. (St. Louis), 1967. Thesis: English.

Brogunier, Joseph E. The Jefferson Urn: Faulkner's Literary Sources and Influences. Univ. of Minnesota, 1969. Dissertation: English.

Brown, Jewell L.W. Faulkner's Preachers. Univ. of Texas (Austin). Thesis: English.

Brown, William R. William Faulkner's Use of the Material of Abnormal Psychology in Characterization. Univ. of Arkansas, 1965. Dissertation: English.

Bruccoli, Arlyn F. The Focus of William Faulkner's *Absalom, Absalom!* Univ. of Virginia, 1959. Thesis: English.

Brylowski, Walter M. Man's Enduring Chronicle: A Study of Myth in the Novels of William Faulkner. Michigan State Univ., 1964. Dissertation: English.

Buice, Joe C. An Evaluation of William Faulkner's *Requiem for a Nun*. Univ. of Texas (Austin), 1963. Thesis: English.

Burch, Betty A. An Analysis of Language Patterning and Its Literary Uses in William Faulkner's *The Sound and the Fury*. DePaul Univ., 1967. Thesis: English.

[44]

Burch, Bradley A. William Faulkner: The Man, the Mind, and the Dust. Columbia Univ., 1949. Thesis: English.

Burnett, Theda D.D. The Aesthetic Unity of William Faulkner. McNeese State Univ., 1968. Thesis: English.

Burns, Stuart L. A Comparative Analysis of the Waste Land Theme in T.S. Eliot and William Faulkner. Drake Univ., 1960. Thesis: English.

Butler, Eugenia W. William Faulkner's Rhetoric of Negation. Univ. of Georgia, 1967. Thesis: English.

Byrne, Sr. Mary E. From Tradition to Technique: Development of Character in Joyce and Faulkner. Univ. of Southern Mississippi, 1968. Dissertation: English.

Cain, Roy E. The Social Hierarchy of the South in the Works of William Faulkner. North Texas State Univ., 1954. Thesis: English.

Callen, Shirley P. Bergsonian Dynamism in the Writings of William Faulkner. Tulane Univ., 1962. Dissertation: English.

Calloway, Elizabeth T. Man's Search for Meaning: A Study of Faulkner's Heroes. Southern Methodist Univ., 1967. Thesis: English.

Carey, Glenn O. The Humor in William Faulkner's Fiction. Pennsylvania State Univ., 1949. Thesis: English.

_____. William Faulkner: Critic of Society. Univ. of Illinois, 1962. Dissertation: English.

Carnes, Frank F. On the Aesthetics of Faulkner's Fiction. Vanderbilt Univ., 1968. Dissertation: English.

Carter, Bernice B. Justice and Retribution in the Novels of William Faulkner. Univ. of Houston, 1967. Thesis: English.

Carter, Stephen L. A Study of Similarities in Emerson and Faulkner. West Texas State Univ., 1968. Thesis: English.

Cate, Judy E. Down the Long Corridor: A Study of Child Characters in Faulkner's Fiction. Univ. of Tennessee, 1966. Thesis: English.

Chappell, Charles M. The Defeat of the Indian in Faulkner's Wilderness. Emory Univ., 1965. Thesis: English.

Cherry, Joyce L. The Evolution of Faulkner's Attitude Toward the Negro: A Study of His Major Fiction. Atlanta Univ., 1969. Thesis: English.

Chiarilli, Anthony L. From *The Sound and the Fury* to *Absalom, Absalom!*: The Inception of the Faulknerian Techniques. Oakland Univ., 1968. Thesis: English.

Chisholm, William S. Sentence Patterns in *The Sound and the Fury*. Univ. of Michigan, 1964. Dissertation: English.

Christadler, Martin. Nature und Geschichte im Werk von William Faulkner. Tuebingen, 1960. Dissertation: English.

Christy, Wallace M. Myth and Method in William Faulkner's *As I Lay Dying*. Brown Univ., 1968. Thesis: American Civilization.

Clemmer, James H., Jr. William Faulkner and the Southern Gentleman. Univ. of Tennessee, 1963. Thesis: English.

Clinton, Patricia P. The Duality of Ratliff in Faulkner's *The Hamlet*. Western Washington State College, 1969. Thesis: English.

Clune, Sr. Marie P., I.N.J.M. The Theme of Isolation in the Work of
William Faulkner. Villanova Univ., 1965. Thesis: English.
Coffee, Jessie A. Faulkner's Un-Christlike Christians: Biblical
Allusions in the Novels. Univ. of Nevada (Reno), 1971. Thesis:
English.
Cok, Georgette W. The Faulknerian Woman: A Study. Dalhousie
Univ., 1966. Thesis: English.
Coleman, Clara R. Faulkner's Snopeses, 1929-1939. Univ. of North
Carolina (Chapel Hill), 1964. Thesis: English.
Coleman, Irwin W. The Negro Problem in William Faulkner's
Yoknapatawpha Series. Univ. of Texas (Austin), 1956. Thesis:
English.
Collins, Mary S. William Faulkner as a Gothic Writer: An
Examination of the Snopes Trilogy. Wake Forest Univ., 1967.
Thesis: English.
Colson, Theodore L. The Characters of Hawthorne and Faulkner:
A Typology of Sinners. Univ. of Michigan, 1967. Disser-
tation: English.
Confessore, Ralph J., S.J. Suicide in the Novels of William
Faulkner: The Definitive Gesture. Fordham Univ., 1965.
Thesis: English.
Considine, Raymond H. A Man Who Endures: A Study of the
Character of Jason Compson in Faulkner's *The Sound and the
Fury*. Lehigh Univ., 1968. Thesis: English.
Cooper, Richard A. An Interpretation of Faulkner's *Pylon*. Univ.
of North Carolina (Chapel Hill), 1968. Thesis: English.
Corder, Jimmie W. The Enduring "Was": William Faulkner's
Treatment of Time. Texas Christian Univ., 1954. Thesis:
English.
Core, George. Faulkner's Comic Vision: The Snopes Trilogy.
Vanderbilt Univ., 1960. Thesis: English.
Coslow, Mary A. Churches, Universities, and Courts in Faulkner's
Novels. Duke Univ., 1958. Thesis: English.
Cowdy, I.F. The Relation of Form to Meaning in the Work of
William Faulkner. Manchester, 1958. Thesis: English.
Cox, Clyde. William Faulkner's *Sanctuaries*: A Comparison. City
College of New York, 1967. Thesis: English.
Craib, Roderick H. William Faulkner's South: The Creation of a
Region. Columbia Univ., 1949. Thesis: English.
Craig-Rogow, Norma. William Faulkner and Dylan Thomas: An
Imaginary Conversation. Univ. of Miami (Coral Gables), 1969.
Thesis: English. [The words they speak are their own,
quotations culled from . . . any source in which the two speak
in their own "voice."]
Creighton, Joanne V. *Dubliners* and *Go Down, Moses*: The Short
Story Composite. Univ. of Michigan, 1969. Dissertation:
English.
Curto, Josephine J. An Analysis of Faulkner's Major Techniques of
Comedy. Florida State Univ., 1969. Dissertation: English.
Daly, Charles E. The Problem of Incest in Five Faulkner Novels.
Univ. of Virginia, 1967. Thesis: English.
Dance, Daryl C. An Analysis of William Faulkner's *Light in August*.
Virginia State College, 1963. Thesis: English.

Dardis, Thomas A. William Faulkner: The Double Legend. Columbia Univ., 1952. Thesis: English.

Davis, Dorothy A.S. The Tragic Vision of Hawthorne and Faulkner. Mississippi College, 1963. Thesis: English.

Davis, Lloyd M. Empathy in Faulkner's *As I Lay Dying*. Vanderbilt Univ., 1954. Thesis: English.

Daehofe, Winfield A. The Realism, Romanticism and Irony of William Faulkner. Univ. of Minnesota, 1936. Thesis: English.

Dean, Harry N. Study of the Horse and the Mule in William Faulkner's Fiction. Univ. of Tennessee, 1969. Thesis: English.

DeCuir, Jene J. The Poetry of *The Sound and the Fury*. Tulane Univ., 1968. Thesis: English.

Deeter, Gary D. The Ambivalent Affirmation: A Study of Faulkner's Christian Symbolism. Kansas State Teachers College, 1966. Thesis: English.

Dembo, Lawrence S. William Faulkner: The Symbolic Action of Sin and Redemption. Columbia Univ., 1952. Thesis: English.

Dennis, Stephen N. The Making of *Sartoris*: A Description and Discussion of the Manuscript and Composite Typescript of William Faulkner's Third Novel. Cornell Univ., 1969. Dissertation: English.

De Roller, Joseph M. The Paradox of Joe Christmas: A Study of Faulkner's *Light in August*. Lehigh Univ., 1967. Thesis: English.

Dessommes, Carolyn. William Faulkner's Gavin Stevens. Univ. of Dallas, 1968. Thesis: English.

Dew, Marian N. A Study of William Faulkner's *Requiem for a Nun*. Univ. of North Carolina (Chapel Hill), 1962. Thesis: English.

Dew, Ozella E.B. Structure and Theme in Faulkner's *Go Down, Moses* Stories. Univ. of Texas (Austin), 1965. Thesis: English.

Dick, Brenda. Abnormality in the Novels of William Faulkner. Columbia Univ., 1949. Thesis: English.

Dike, Donald A. The World of Faulkner's Imagination. Syracuse Univ., 1954. Dissertation: English.

Dillard, Richard H.W. The Theme of Victory Through Defeat in Works by Faulkner, Steinbeck, and Hemingway. Univ. of Virginia, 1959. Thesis: English.

Dirksen, Sherland. William Faulkner's Snopes Family: A Study of Materialistic Power. Kansas State Teachers College, 1961. Thesis: English.

Ditsky, John M. Land-Nostalgia in the Novels of Faulkner, Cather, and Steinbeck. New York Univ., 1967. Dissertation: English.

Donelan, Shirley B. Language as Related to Style in William Faulkner's "Old Man." Ball State Univ., 1964. Thesis: English.

Dorsch, Robert L. An Interpretation of the Central Themes in the Work of William Faulkner. Kansas State Teachers College, 1959. Thesis: English.

Doster, William C. William Faulkner and the Negro. Univ. of Florida, 1955. Dissertation: English.

Dowell, Bobby R. Faulkner's Comic Spirit. Univ. of Denver, 1962. Dissertation: English.
Draper, Lowell A. William Faulkner's Tense Shifts: A Study of the Relation Between William Faulkner's Tense Shifts and His Time Themes. Fresno State College, 1964. Thesis: English.
Duckworth, Phyllis H. Faulkner's Older Women: An Analysis. Univ. of Virginia, 1966. Thesis: English.
Dudley, Michael D. *Light in August*: A Study of Loneliness and Rigidity of Spirit. Univ. of Mississippi, 1969. Thesis: English.
Ealy, Marguerite B. Snopes Learning: Faulkner's Trilogy, *The Hamlet, The Town, The Mansion*. Univ. of Akron, 1969. Thesis: English.
Edbon, Priscilla A. Faulkner's Colonels: Reality and Fiction. Univ. of Maryland, 1969. Thesis: English.
Eberly, Ralph D. Immediacy, Suspense, and Meaning in William Faulkner's *The Sound and the Fury*: An Experiment in Critical Analysis. Univ. of Michigan, 1953. Dissertation: English.
Eklin, Stanley L. Religious Themes and Symbolism in the Novels of William Faulkner. Univ. of Illinois, 1961. Dissertation: English.
Ellis, Janet B. An Analysis of Parallel-Narrative Structure in the Novels of William Faulkner. Northern Illinois Univ., 1966. Thesis: English.
Emerson, O.B. The Literary Reputation of William Faulkner in America. Vanderbilt Univ., 1962. Dissertation: English.
English, Dorothy. The Poet's Voice: A Study of Christianity in William Faulkner's Novels: *Absalom, Absalom!, Light in August*, and *The Sound and the Fury*. Univ. of Texas (El Paso), 1966.
Everett, Maxine S. Folklore in William Faulkner's Yoknapatawpha Fiction. Texas Tech Univ., 1961. Thesis: English.
Everett, Walter K. A Comprehensive Dictionary of William Faulkner's Characters. Mississippi College, 1962. Thesis: English.
Ewell, Barbara N. To Move in Time: A Study of the Structure of Faulkner's *As I Lay Dying, Light in August*, and *Absalom, Absalom!* Florida State Univ., 1969. Dissertation: English.
Fadiman, Regina K. Faulkner's *Light in August*: Sources and Revisions. Univ. of California (Los Angeles), 1970. Dissertation: English.
Farley, Pamela. Three Studies in English: Lyly's *Sapho* and *Phao*; Pope and *The Dunciad*; Faulkner's *Old Man*. Pennsylvania State Univ., 1967. Thesis: English.
Farnham, James F. They Who Endure and Prevail: Characters of William Faulkner. Case Western Reserve Univ., 1962. Dissertation: English.
Fatherree, D.J. A Vessel of Honor: The Role of Yeomanry in Faulkner's Yoknapatawpha Fiction. Univ. of Dallas, 1968. Thesis: English.
Faught, Patsy K. Metamorphosis: William Faulkner's Incorporation of Short Stories into Longer Narratives. North Texas State Univ., 1961. Thesis: English.

[48]

Fazio, Rocco R. The Fury and the Design: Realms of Being and
    Knowing in Four Novels of William Faulkner. Univ. of
    Rochester, 1964. Dissertation: English.
Field, Bettye. William Faulkner and the Humor of the Old
    Southwest. Vanderbilt Univ., 1952. Thesis: English.
Fireash, Martha S. "Go Slow, Now": An Evaluation of Faulkner's
    Attitudes toward Equality. Univ. of Houston, 1968. Thesis:
    English.
Fireman, Judith K. The Rhetoric of *Absalom, Absalom!* Columbia
    Univ., 1966. Thesis: English.
Fisher, Arnold. The Shape of Morality in the Novels of William
    Faulkner. Columbia Univ., 1954. Thesis: English.
Fitch, Betty A. William Faulkner's Use of the Negro as a
    Fictional Pivot. North Carolina College (Durham), 1963.
    Thesis: English.
Fitzgerald, Barbara G. Humor and Its Function in Faulkner's
    Funniest Novels. Univ. of Georgia, 1969. Thesis:
    English.
Fitzgerald, Sr. Joseph M., S.M. The Short Story Sequence in
    Modern English Literature: James Joyce and William Faulkner.
    Lone Mountain College, 1965. Thesis: English.
Fitzgerald, Pauline M. The Purple within Faulkner's Gro-
    tesqueries. Univ. of Mississippi, 1969. Thesis: English.
Folsom, Gordon R. Folk Narrators of Yoknapatawpha County:
    Suggestions for a Re-Interpretation of William Faulkner.
    Univ. of New Hampshire, 1951. Thesis: English.
Forbus, Jere K. The Function of Game Imagery in Faulkner's
    Sartoris Myth. Univ. of Massachusetts, 1969. Thesis:
    English.
Ford, Oliver J. Elements of Marlowe's *Doctor Faustus* in
    Faulkner's *The Rievers*. Tulane Univ., 1968. Thesis:
    English.
Forgey, Susan M. William Faulkner's Use of Commentator-
    Narrator Characters: V.K. Ratliff and Gavin Stevens.
    Univ. of Colorado, 1966. Thesis: English.
Fourier, Ruth G. The "Prufrock" Theme in the Novels of William
    Faulkner. Univ. of South Carolina, 1948. Thesis: English.
Fowlks, Bessie. A Study of William Faulkner's Literary
    Reputation in the United States, 1926-1952. North Carolina
    College (Durham), 1955. Thesis: English.
Frame, Garry. William Faulkner and Sherwood Anderson: A Study
    of a Literary Relationship. Univ. of British Columbia,
    1968. Thesis: English.
Franklin, Rosemary F. Clairvoyance, Vision, and Imagination in
    the Fiction of William Faulkner. Emory Univ., 1968.
    Dissertation: English.
Freeman, Gordon Q. William Faulkner's Treatment of the Negro.
    Duke Univ., 1955. Thesis: English.
French, LaVon. Faulkner's Saintly Characters. Drake Univ., 1970.
    Thesis: English.
Friedland, Ronald L. The Tragic Hero in William Faulkner.
    Columbia Univ., 1960. Thesis: English.
Friend, George L. Levels of Matruity: The Theme of Striving in
    the Novels of William Faulkner. Univ. of Illinois, 1964.
    Dissertation: English.

[49]

Friend, Robert III. Humor in Jason's Section of William
Faulkner's *The Sound and the Fury*. Univ. of North Carolina
(Chapel Hill), 1963. Thesis: English.
Friesen, Menno M. A Comparison of the Use of Spatio-Temporal
Order in the Novels of Thomas Hardy and William Faulkner.
Kansas State Teachers College, 1958. Thesis: English.
Fulkerson, Sara J. The Evolution of the "The Bear" from "Lion":
William Faulkner's Revisions. Georgetown Univ., 1968.
Thesis: English.
Funk, Margaret A. A Guide to the Fiction of William Faulkner.
Washington Univ. (St. Louis), 1949. Thesis: English.
Galbraith, Margaret E. Faulkner's Trilogy: Technique as
Approach to Theme. Univ. of British Columbia, 1962.
Thesis: English.
Gardner, Margaret J. Faulkner's Theme of Suffering. Drake
Univ., 1964. Thesis: English.
Gasque, Thomas J. A Character Study of Faulkner's Mink Snopes.
Emory Univ., 1962. Thesis: English.
Gate, Judy E. Down the Long Corridor: A Study of Child
Characters in Faulkner's Fiction. Univ. of Tennessee,
1966. Thesis: English.
Georger, Audrey J. Faulkner's Innocents. St. Louis Univ.,
1967. Thesis: English.
Gescheider, Margaret N. William Faulkner's Gavin Stevens in
the Snopes Trilogy. Univ. of Virginia, 1964. Thesis:
English.
Giardini, Patricia S. An Introduction to the Study of *The
Sound and the Fury* by William Faulkner. Owens College,
1967. Thesis: English.
Gibson, Margaret F. Short Stories into Novels: The Unifying
Elements in Faulkner's *Go Down, Moses* and *The Unvanquished*.
Univ. of Virginia, 1967. Thesis: English.
Gilliland, Joe D. Sin and Redemption in Faulkner. Univ. of
Texas (Austin), 1955. Thesis: English.
Glenn, Barbara M. Humor in the Works of William Faulkner.
Virginia State College, 1965. Thesis: English.
Gold, Joseph. The Single Vision: A Study of the Philosophy
and the Forms of Its Presentation in the Works of William
Faulkner. Univ. of Wisconsin, 1959. Dissertation:
English.
Goodman, Gerald T. The War Fiction of William Faulkner.
Miami Univ. (Ohio), 1966. Thesis: English.
Goren, Leyla M. William Faulkner: An International Novelist.
Harvard Univ., 1963. Dissertation: American Civilization.
Gourley, Dan M. The Unity of *Go Down, Moses*. Univ. of Texas
(Austin), 1966. Thesis: English.
Gowan, Richard D. The Structure and Purpose of the Benjy
Section of *The Sound and the Fury* by William Faulkner.
Univ. of South Dakota, 1958. Thesis: English.
Graves, John A. Techniques in the Fiction of William Faulkner.
Columbia Univ., 1948. Thesis: English.
Gray, Betty J.W. The Role of Women in Four Faulkner Novels.
Univ. of Northern Iowa, 1966. Thesis: English.

Gray, Carol R. The Tragic Possibilities of William Faulkner's
  Absalom, Absalom! Eastern Illinois Univ., 1967. Thesis:
  English.
Gray, Charles F. Interpenetrated Images of Time and Eternity
  in William Faulkner's *The Sound and the Fury.* Univ. of
  Florida, 1958. Thesis: English.
Greer, Dorothy D. The Negro as a Gauge of Moral Character as
  Shown in Selected Fiction of William Faulkner. Kansas
  State Teachers College, 1959. Thesis: English.
Green, Sally M. The Female in the Novels of William Faulkner:
  A "Gynecological Demonology." Brown Univ., 1964.
  Thesis: English.
Greet, Thomas Y. The Southern Legend in Yoknapatawpha Fiction
  of William Faulkner. Univ. of North Carolina (Chapel Hill),
  1950. Thesis: English.
Gregg, Alvin L. A Critical Analysis of William Faulkner's
  "The Bear." Texas Tech. Univ., 1957. Thesis: English.
_____. Style and Dialect in *Light in August* and Other Works
  by William Faulkner. Univ. of Texas (Austin), 1969.
  Dissertation: English.
Gregory, Charles T. Darkness to Appall: Destructive Designs
  and Patterns in Some Characters of William Faulkner.
  Columbia Univ., 1968. Dissertation: English.
Griffin, Ernest G. William Faulkner and the Tragic Ritual.
  Columbia Univ., 1951. Thesis: English.
Groman, George L. William Faulkner and the Changing Social
  Structure of the South. Columbia Univ., 1951. Thesis:
  English.
Groppe, John D. The Predatory Females of William Faulkner:
  A Study of *Mosquitoes, Sanctuary,* and *The Wild Palms.*
  Columbia Univ., 1960. Thesis: English.
Gross, Ellen S. An Analysis of the Role of the Negro in
  Faulkner. Hofstra Univ., 1966. Thesis: Humanities.
Grossi, Joseph L. The Function of William Faulkner's
  Sartorises. Univ. of Rhode Island, 1967. Thesis: English.
Grosskurth, Phyllis M. A Study of Snopesism in the Novels of
  William Faulkner. Ottawa, 1960. Thesis: English.
Grossman, Martha. Structure, Narrative and Imagery in William
  Faulkner's *Light in August.* Queens College (N.Y.), 1965.
  Thesis: English.
Grover, Elizabeth B. Puritanism in Faulkner's *Light in August.*
  Temple Univ., 1966. Thesis: English.
Guetti, James L., Jr. The Failure of the Imagination: A Study
  of Melville, Conrad, and Faulkner. Cornell Univ., 1964.
  Dissertation: English.
Guirard, Gregory W. "The Bear" as a Composite of William
  Faulkner's Major Themes. Louisiana State Univ., 1964.
  Thesis: English.
Gullet, David. Faulkner's Metaphysic of Time in *Light in August.*
  Brown Univ., 1970. Thesis: English.
Hafner, John H. William Faulkner's Narrators. Univ. of
  Wisconsin, 1969. Dissertation: English.
Hall, Eugene J. William Faulkner: Character as Theme and
  Structure. Columbia Univ., 1952. Thesis: English.

Hall, Patsy A. Faulkner's *The Sound and the Fury*. Univ. of Texas (Austin), 1958. Thesis: English.

Hall, Peggy C. William Faulkner's Use of Mirror Imagery as a Structural Device. Barry College, 1968. Thesis: English.

Halsell, Robert J. The Thematic Value of Faulkner's Yoknapatawpha County Heroines. Northeast Louisiana Univ., 1968. Thesis: English.

Hamblin, Bobby W. Faulkner's Suspense: A Study in Literary Technique. Univ. of Mississippi, 1965. Thesis: English.

Hammond, Alexander L. The Tragic Conflict in William Faulkner's Major Works. Univ. of Redlands, 1966. Thesis: English.

Hardy, Thomas W. Two Unifying Devices in Faulkner's *The Hamlet*. Univ. of North Carolina (Chapel Hill), 1968. Thesis: English.

Harris, Jeanette G. Faulkner's Portrayal of the Negro. East Texas State Univ., 1957. Thesis: English.

Hartsell, Anne D. The Snopes Clan in William Faulkner's Fiction. East Tennessee State Univ., 1963. Thesis: English.

Harwick, Robert D. Humor in the Novels of William Faulkner. Univ. of Nebraska, 1965. Dissertation: English.

Hashimoto, Hiroshi. William Faulkner's Moral Vision in the Yoknapatawpha Saga. Stetson Univ., 1964. Thesis: English.

Hawkins, E.O., Jr. A Handbook of Yoknapatawpha. Univ. of Arkansas, 1961. Dissertation: English.

Haworth, Roberta. Yoknapatawpha County: Faulkner's Battleground for Modern Man. Univ. of Arizona, 1968. Thesis: English.

Hayes, Darwin L. Form and Content in *The Sound and the Fury*: A Study in Faulkner's "Old Verities." Brigham Young Univ., 1964. Thesis: English.

Hebaisha, Hoda A. Faulkner's Revisions in "The Bear." Columbia Univ., 1960. Thesis: English.

Hefner, Lonnie D. The Concept of Love in Novels of William Faulkner. Univ. of Texas (Austin), 1955. Thesis: English.

Heimer, Jackson W. William Faulkner and the Contemporary Social Scene, (1920-1950). Univ. of Kentucky, 1952. Thesis: English.

Heineman, Fredrik J. Quentin Compson and Southern Guilt. Univ. of Delaware, 1966. Thesis: English.

Henderson, Charles G. Faulkner's Snopses: The Genesis and Growth of a Symbol. Univ. of Delaware, 1967. Thesis: English.

Henderson, Gretchen K. Tragic Elements in the Works of William Faulkner. Univ. of Wyoming, 1959. Thesis: English.

Henss, Herbert. William Faulkner's *Sartoris* Als Literarisches Kunstwerk. Mainz, 1964. Dissertation: English.

Hepburn, Kenneth W. *Soldier's Pay* to *The Sound and the Fury*: Development of the Poetic in Early Novels of William Faulkner. Univ. of Washington, 1968. Dissertation: English.

Herman, Amy B. William Faulkner: An Interpreter of Human History. Univ. of Denver, 1969. Thesis: English.

Herman, Myron S. "To Endure and Prevail": The Optimism of *The Sound and the Fury*, *Sanctuary*, *As I Lay Dying*, and *Light in August*. Tulane Univ., 1965. Thesis: English.

Higgins, William R. William Faulkner's Endurance and *Arete*.
    Tulane Univ., 1959. Thesis: English.
Hilfer, Anthony C. William Faulkner and Jacobean Drama: A
    Comparison. Columbia Univ., 1960. Thesis: English.
Hill, Harriet B. *As I Lay Dying*: Its Critical Reception in
    France and the U.S. Compared. Univ. of North Carolina
    (Chapel Hill), 1962. Thesis: English.
Hill, James A. The Narrative Technique of William Faulkner.
    Univ. of Texas (Austin), 1947. Thesis: English.
Hill, Larry L. The Development of Time in Faulkner's Early
    Novels. San Francisco State College, 1966. Thesis:
    English.
Hilliard, Lewis J. A View of Faulkner's Women. Southern
    Illinois Univ. (Carbondale), 1959. Thesis: English.
Hinchliffe, A.P. Symbolism in the American Novel, 1850-1950:
    An Examination of the Findings of Recent Literary Critics
    in Respect of the Novels of Hawthorne, Melville, James,
    Hemingway, and Faulkner. Manchester, 1963. Dissertation:
    English.
Hinteregger, Gerald. Das Land und die Menschen in William
    Faulkner's Erzahlen den werken. Graz, 1953. Dissertation:
    English.
Hoadley, Frank M. The World View of William Faulkner. Univ.
    of Oklahoma, 1955. Dissertation: English.
Hofamann, Albert G., Jr. Faulkner's Conflicting Galaxies:
    A Study in Literary Polarity. Pennsylvania Univ., 1951.
    Dissertation: English.
Holmes, Edward M. Faulkner's Twice-Told Tales: His Re-Use
    of His Material. Brown Univ., 1962. Dissertation:
    English.
Hopkins, Gertrude M. The Secret Cause: A Study of Pursuit
    and Flight in William Faulkner's Early Work. Univ. of
    Maryland, 1969. Thesis: English.
Hornback, Vernon T., Jr. William Faulkner and the Terror of
    History: Myth, History, and Moral Freedom in the
    Yoknapatawpha Cycle. St. Louis Univ., 1963. Dissertation:
    English.
Hubbard, Minnie G. Parallels to Calvinism in the Works of
    William Faulkner. Fort Hays Kansas State College, 1961.
    Thesis: English.
Huffstetter, Emily S. The Adolescent in Yoknapatawpha.
    West Georgia College, 1969. Thesis: English.
Hull, Leon C. William Faulkner's *A Fable*: Christ Again and
    Everyman. Univ. of Rhode Island, 1969. Thesis: English.
Hunt, John W., Jr. William Faulkner's Rendering of Modern
    Experience: A Theological Analysis. Univ. of Chicago,
    1961. Dissertation: Religion.
Hupp, Ellen K. William Faulkner: The Primitive Initiation Rite.
    Univ. of Texas (Austin), 1966. Thesis: English.
Hutchinson, James W. Faulkner's Humor: Its Nature and Uses.
    Univ. of Virginia, 1966. Thesis: English.
Hutchinson, Julia A. *Go Down, Moses, Intruder in the Dust,
    The Reivers*: Faulkner's Interracial McCaslins in their
    Changing South. Auburn Univ., 1970. Thesis: English.

Ingold, David E. *The Sound and the Fury* and Southern Romanticism. Univ. of North Carolina (Chapel Hill), 1969. Thesis: English.

Ingram, Bettie P. William Faulkner's *Light in August*: A Study. North Carolina College (Durham), 1964. Thesis: English.

Israel, Charles M. The Initiation of Isaac McCaslin as a Modern Hero in William Faulkner's "The Bear." Emory Univ., 1969. Thesis: English.

Jacobskind, Barbara R. The Early Reception of William Faulkner, 1924-1939. Brown Univ., 1967. Thesis: English.

Jaeger, Ernest. Myth and Legend in *As I Lay Dying*. Lehigh Univ., 1970. Thesis: English.

James, Sharon. The Theme of *Go Down, Moses*. Arkansas State Univ., 1966. Thesis: English.

Jeffrey, Mildred M. *Absalom, Absalom!* and William Faulkner. Adelphia Univ., 1962. Thesis: English.

Jewell, Richard B. William Faulkner's Use of Extrasensory Perception in Three Novels. Univ. of Florida, 1969. Thesis: English.

Jividen, Phyllis D. William Faulkner and the Double View. Ohio Univ., 1963. Thesis: English.

Jobes, Lavon M. William Faulkner: The Sins and the Curse. Univ. of Nebraska (Omaha), 1961. Thesis: English.

Jodrie, Beulah V. An Approach to the Christ Figures of Melville and Faulkner. Brown Univ., 1965. Thesis: English.

Johnson, Barbara A. Snopesism: A Study of the Snopeses in the Writings of William Faulkner. West Texas State Univ., 1969. Thesis: English.

Johnson, Patricia A. Women in the Fiction of William Faulkner. Wake Forest Univ., 1969. Thesis: English.

Johnson, Thomas P. Yoknapatawpha County: The Land and the People as Used in the Writing of William Faulkner. Columbia Univ., 1949. Thesis: English.

Joiner, Marilyn A. The Role of the Negro in Faulkner's Novels. Queen's (Ontario), 1967. Thesis: English.

Jones, Elizabeth K. Faulkner's Construction of Four Snopes Characters. Univ. of Houston, 1966. Thesis: English.

Jones, Mary J. Four Themes in Faulkner: The Land, the Design, the Past, and the Negro. Univ. of Houston, 1964. Thesis: English.

Jones, Miriam C. The Faulknerian Truth of Twinship. Univ. of South Carolina, 1967. Thesis: English.

Jones, Ray T. The Christ Figure in Three Modern Novels: William Faulkner. West Texas State Univ., 1965. Thesis: English.

Julian, Jane D. Faulkner's Man in Action: The Effective Word. Tulane Univ., 1969. Thesis: English.

Junkin, Lorraine S. William Faulkner's Use of Stream of Consciousness. Shippensburg State College, 1966. Thesis: Education.

Kaimowitz, Benita R. The Crack in the Urn: A Study of Women in the Writings of William Faulkner. Sarah Lawrence College, 1966. Thesis: English.

Kartiganer, Donald M. The Individual and the Community: Values in the Novels of William Faulkner. Brown Univ., 1964. Dissertation: English.

Kathe, Sr. Mary G., R.S.M. William Faulkner: Alienation in Yoknapatawha County. Saint Joseph College (Connecticut), 1967. Thesis: English.

Kauffman, Donald G. Repetition in *As I Lay Dying*. Univ. of Maryland, 1967. Thesis: English.

Kay, Shirley L. The Moral Order of William Faulkner. South Dakota State Univ., 1958. Thesis: English.

Kearney, J.A. The Theme of Doom in the Novels of William Faulkner. York Univ., 1969. Thesis: English.

Keefer, Truman F. The Critical Reaction to the Novels of William Faulkner as Expressed in Reviews Published in American Periodicals up to 1952. Duke Univ., 1953. Thesis: English.

Keegan, Barbara J. Gavin Stevens in the Faulkner Novels. Univ. of Virginia, 1966. Thesis: English.

Kelley, Jane P. The Heroism of Thomas Sutpen in William Faulkner's *Absalom, Absalom!* Emory Univ., 1962. Thesis: English.

Kermenl, Leyla M. William Faulkner: An International Novelist. Harvard Univ., 1963. Dissertation: American Civilization.

Kerr, Patricia L. Faulkner's View of the Moral and Social Dissolution of the South. Eastern Illinois Univ., 1969. Thesis: English.

Kinoian, Vartkis. Analysis of *Absalom, Absalom!* An Approach to the Structure of William Faulkner's Major Novels. Columbia Univ., 1957. Thesis: English.

Kirk, Robert W. An Index and Encyclopedia of the Characters in the Fictional Works of William Faulkner. Univ. of Southern California, 1959. Dissertation: English.

Knox, Robert H. William Faulkner's *Absalom, Absalom!* Harvard Univ., 1959. Dissertation: English.

Kohn, Richard S. Existentialism and the Death Motif in Yoknapatawpha County. Univ. of Vermont, 1966. Thesis: English.

Krajci, Carol L. The Theme of Responsibility in William Faulkner's *The Sound and the Fury* and *As I Lay Dying*. Pennsylvania State Univ., 1961. Thesis: English.

Kroner, Jacob L. William Faulkner's Ideology as Expressed in his Writing. Columbia Univ., 1949. Thesis: English.

Krumm, Helen. William Faulkner's Negroes: A Standard by Which to Judge White Society. Sacramento State College, 1969. Thesis: English.

Kupka, Joseph E. Justification for Violence in William Faulkner's Novels. Kent State Univ., 1967. Thesis: English.

Kurtz, Ralph F. William Faulkner and Ernest Hemingway Depict the "Lost Generation." Indiana Univ. of Pennsylvania, 1966. Thesis: Education.

La France, Marston. Faulkner's Myth: The Town and County. Cornell Univ., 1955. Thesis: English.

Lamar, Lewis W. Faulkner's Use of Nature. Auburn Univ., 1968. Thesis: English.

[55]

Lanceley, Jana K.C. Faulkner's Use of Myth In Three Novels:
A Critique of the Criticism. Texas Tech. Univ., 1969.
Thesis: English.

Landes, James E. The Evolution of a Style: A Stylo-linguistic
Study of William Faulkner. San Francisco State College,
1970. Thesis: English.

Lang, Eleanor M. The Function of Christian Symbolism in
William Faulkner. Lehigh Univ., 1964. Thesis: English.

Lasseter, Victor K. Love and Money in William Faulkner's Snopes
Trilogy. Florida State Univ., 1963. Thesis: English.

Lawson, Deanna H. Faulkner's Women. Middle Tennessee State
Univ., 1968. Thesis: English.

Lawson, Richard A. Patterns of Initiation in William Faulkner's
Go Down, Moses. Tulane Univ., 1966. Dissertation: English.

Leach, Frances H. A Statistical Analysis of Selected Factors
of William Faulkner's Language Style in The Sound and The
Fury. Indiana Univ. of Pennsylvania, 1964. Thesis:
Education.

Lehrman, Barbara J. An Interpretation and Reevaluation of
Dilsey. Lehigh Univ., 1969. Thesis: English.

Leonard, Karen K.B. The Negro in the Fiction of William Faulkner.
Southern Methodist Univ., 1967. Thesis: English.

Le Parte, Patricia L. Definition of the Situation: Its
Importance in Theme Development and Character Portrayal
in Faulkner's The Sound and the Fury and As I Lay Dying.
Univ. of Rhode Island, 1967. Thesis: English.

Levins, Lynn G. The Four Narrative Perspectives in Absalom,
Absalom! Univ. of North Carolina (Chapel Hill), 1966.
Thesis: English.

Levit, Donald J. William Faulkner's The Hamlet: Its Revisions
and Structure. Univ. of Chicago, 1968. Dissertation:
English.

Lewis, Clifford L. Artistic Vision and Historical Reflection:
A Comparison Between William Faulkner's Intruder in the Dust
and James U. Silver's The Closed Society. State Univ. of
New York (Buffalo), 1965. Thesis: American Studies.

Lewis, Margaret D. Racial Attitudes in Three Works by William
Faulkner: Go Down, Moses, Light in August, and Absalom,
Absalom! Temple Univ., 1968. Thesis: English.

Libby, Anthony P. Chronicles of Children: William Faulkner's
Short Fiction. Stanford Univ., 1969. Dissertation:
English.

Lidums, Susan B. The Theme of Endurance in Faulkner's
Yoknapatawpha Novels. Univ. of Portland, 1970. Thesis:
English.

Ligon, Linda C. From Poetry to Prose: The Metamorphosis of
Faulkner's Art. Oklahoma State Univ., 1966. Thesis:
English.

Lilly, Paul R., Jr. Silence and the Impeccable Language: A
Study of William Faulkner's Philosophy of Language.
Fordham Univ., 1971. Dissertation: English.

Livingston, Travis L. Variations in Faulkner's Style As
Related to His Themes. Hardin-Simmons Univ., 1961.
Thesis: English.

Locey, Margaret L. William Faulkner on Race: A Southern
    Artist Confronts His Heritage. San Francisco State College,
    1970. Thesis: English.
Lock, Joyce. The Search for Self-Identity in William Faulkner's
    Light in August. Eastern Illinois Univ., 1970. Thesis:
    English.
Lockwood, Isabel A. A Critique of the Theory of Archetypes
    and an Application to Faulkner's *As I Lay Dying*. Univ.
    of North Carolina (Chapel Hill), 1962. Thesis: English.
Lohner, Edgar. Thematik. Symbolik und Technik im Werk William
    Faulkners. Bonn, 1951. Dissertation: English.
Lojek, Helen H. Faulkner's Use of History in *Absalom, Absalom!*
    Univ. of North Carolina (Chapel Hill), 1969. Thesis:
    English.
Long, Pierre. Imagery in the Prologue of Faulkner's *Mosquitoes*.
    Univ. of Illinois (Chicago Circle), 1970. Thesis: English.
Longley, John L., Jr. The Problem of Evil in Three Novels of
    William Faulkner. Univ. of Tennessee, 1949. Thesis:
    English.
_____. Faulkner's Tragic Heroes. New York Univ., 1957.
    Dissertation: English.
Lord, Maryanne F. An Experiment in Linguistic Analysis of the
    Prose Style of William Faulkner. Univ. of Houston, 1965.
    Thesis: English.
Loughrey, The Rev. Thomas F. Values and Love in the Fiction
    of William Faulkner. Univ. of Notre Dame, 1962.
    Dissertation: English.
Lowderbaugh, Thomas E. Thematic Unity in the Novels of the
    Snopes Trilogy. Univ. of Maryland, 1967. Thesis: English.
Lowrey, Perrin H. The Critical Reception of William Faulkner's
    Work in the United States, 1926-1950. Univ. of Chicago,
    1956. Dissertation: English.
Lufkin, Agnes B. A Study of the Element of Humor in the Work
    of William Faulkner. Southern Methodist Univ., 1967.
    Thesis: English.
Lyons, Eugene. V.K. Ratliff and the Unity of William Faulkner's
    Snopes Trilogy. Univ. of Virginia, 1966. Thesis: English.
Magruder, William T. Character Identities in William Faulkner's
    A Fable. Univ. of Mississippi, 1963. Thesis: English.
Mahaffey, Ethel D.W. The Snopes Metaphor in the Works of
    William Faulkner. Mississippi College, 1963. Thesis:
    English.
Malin, Irving M. William Faulkner: An Interpretation.
    Stanford Univ., 1958. Dissertation: English.
Marion, Jeff D., Jr. The Unified Design: *Light in August* as a
    Comedy. Univ. of Tennessee, 1966. Thesis: English.
Marks, Margaret L. Religious Characters in Selected Novels of
    William Faulkner. Duke Univ., 1968. Thesis: English.
Marshall, Jean S. Thematic Imagery in William Faulkner's
    Absalom, Absalom! Brigham Young Univ., 1969. Dissertation:
    English.
Martin, Edward A. William Faulkner's Proper Study: An Essay
    on the Positive Directive in Faulkner's Writing. Columbia
    Univ., 1952. Thesis: English.

[57]

Mascitelli, David W. Faulkner's Characters of Sensibility.
Duke Univ., 1968. Dissertation: English.
Massey, Tom M. Faulkner's Females: The Thematic Function of
Women in the Yoknapatawpha Cycle. Univ. of Nevada, 1969.
Dissertation: English.
Matteson, Linda M. Faulkner's Adolescents. Univ. of Vermont,
1970. Thesis: English.
Matthews, Rex O. William Faulkner: A Study in Technique. Univ.
of Washington, 1948. Thesis: English.
Maurer, Barbara S. Thematic Development in the Works of William
Faulkner. Univ. of Louisville, 1962. Thesis: English.
McClung, James W. *As I Lay Dying* and *Light in August*: Counter-
point in Perspective and Counterpoint in Plot. Tulane
Univ., 1965. Thesis: English.
McCorquodale, Marjorie K. William Faulkner and Existentialism.
Univ. of Texas (Austin), 1956. Dissertation: English.
McDonald, John. William Faulkner and the Old Southwestern Yarn
Spinners. Univ. of Miami (Coral Gables), 1954. Thesis:
English.
McFadden, Nancy. Faulkner's Women in the Structure of His
Yoknapatawpha World, 1929-1936. Univ. of North Carolina
(Chapel Hill), 1959. Thesis: English.
McHaney, Thomas L. The Image of the Railroad in the Novels of
William Faulkner, 1926-1942. Univ. of North Carolina
(Chapel Hill), 1962. Thesis: English.
_____. William Faulkner's *The Wild Palms*: A Textual and Critical
Study. Univ. of South Carolina, 1969. Dissertation:
English.
McKee, Margaret B. William Faulkner: A Study of Evil. Vanderbilt
Univ., 1960. Thesis: English.
McLaughlin, Carrol D. Religion in Yoknapatawpha County. Univ.
of Denver, 1962. Dissertation: English.
McNames, Donna G. Functions of Gothicism in William Faulkner's
Trilogy. Chico State College, 1969. Thesis: English.
Meeks, Elizabeth L. A Contextual Approach to the Teaching of
Two Novels by William Faulkner at College Level. Univ. of
Houston, 1965. Dissertation: English.
Mellard, James M. Humor in Faulkner's Novels: Its Development,
Forms, and Function. Univ. of Texas (Austin), 1964.
Dissertation: English.
Meltabarger, Beverly A. Rules and Circumstances: The Young
Protagonist and the Social Codes in Faulkner's Fiction.
Univ. of British Columbia, 1967. Thesis: English.
Meriwether, James B. The Place of *The Unvanquished* in William
Faulkner's Yoknapatawpha Series. Princeton Univ., 1958.
Dissertation: English.
Milano, Joan. Essays in Criticism: Shakespeare and Dryden;
The Novels of William Golding; William Faulkner's *A Fable*.
Pennsylvania State Univ., 1967. Thesis: English.
Millard, Sr. Miriam J., I.H.M. Aspects of William Faulkner's
Religious Themes in Three Major Novels. Villanova Univ.,
1962. Thesis: English.
Millgate, E.J. Short Stories Into Novels: A Textual and Critical
Study of Some Aspects of Faulkner's Literary Method. Leeds,
1963. Thesis: English.

Miner, Ward L. The World of William Faulkner. Univ. of
    Pennsylvania, 1951. Dissertation: American Civilization.
Mirabelli, Eugene, Jr. The Apprenticeship of William Faulkner:
    The Early Short Stories and the First Three Novels.
    Harvard Univ., 1964. Dissertation: English.
Monaghan, D.M. The Socio-Political Implications of Faulkner's
    Treatment of His Negro Characters. Leeds, 1969. Thesis:
    English.
Monroe, Ursula R. Female Characters in William Faulkner's Novels
    and Short Stories. Colorado College, 1953. Thesis: English.
Moreland, Agnes L. A Study of Faulkner's Presentation of Some
    Problems that Relate to Negroes. Columbia Univ., 1960.
    Dissertation: English.
Morabito, Richard A. The Theme of the Initiation of Youth into
    Manhood in Robert Ruark's The Old Man and the Boy: A
    Comparison with John Steinbeck's The Red Pony, William
    Faulkner's The Bear, and Ernest Hemingway's In Our Time.
    Univ. of North Carolina (Chapel Hill), 1967. Thesis: English.
Morris, A.B. The Anticonventionalism of William Faulkner. Boston
    Univ., 1941. Thesis: English.
Moseley, Francis S. Statement of Time in William Faulkner. C.W.
    Post College of Long Island Univ., 1968. Thesis: English.
Mullen, R.J. The Novels of William Faulkner. Liverpool, 1969.
    Thesis: English.
Murdock, Marilan. The Individual and the Family: A Study of
    Conflict and Union in Selected Novels of William Faulkner.
    Columbia Univ., 1965. Thesis: English.
Murphy, Kathleen A. Three Studies in English: Shakespeare's
    Troilus and Cressida; Tennyson's Idylls; and Faulkner's
    Fiction. Pennsylvania State Univ., 1965. Thesis: English.
Murphy, Mary G. William Faulkner and Human Freedom. John Carroll
    Univ., 1964. Thesis: English.
Nagy, Carolyn E. The World of Nature in Some Typical Stories
    of William Faulkner. Columbia Univ., 1955. Thesis: English.
Nail, John M. The Relation of Theme and Characterization to
    Structure in Light in August. Tulane Univ., 1961. Thesis:
    English.
Neeb, Bob F. Obsessed Heroes in the Novels of William Faulkner.
    Texas Tech Univ., 1967. Thesis: English.
Nelson, Francis W. William Faulkner: Critic of the Decadent
    South. Columbia Univ., 1949. Thesis: English.
Nemser, William J. Early Faulkner Criticism. Columbia Univ.,
    1952. Thesis: English.
Nesselhof, John M. The Negro in the Prose of William Faulkner.
    Univ. of Kansas, 1950. Thesis: English.
Newman, Jules. The Religion of William Faulkner: An Inquiry
    into the Calvinist Mind. Columbia Univ., 1953. Thesis:
    English.
Nicholas, Roberta J. Love and a Power Struggle in William
    Faulkner's Wild Palms. Univ. of Maryland, 1967. Thesis:
    English.
Nichols, Nicholas P. The Poor Whites in the Works of William
    Faulkner. Columbia Univ., 1956. Thesis: English.
Nigliazzo, Marc A. The Indians in the Works of William Faulkner.
    Texas A & M Univ., 1967. Thesis: English.

Nolting-Hauff, Lore. Sprachstil und Weltbild bei William Faulkner. Freiburg, 1958. Dissertation: English.

Ntege, Lubuana. The Violations of Negro-White Relationship in William Faulkner's Works. Univ. of Denver, 1962. Thesis: English.

O'Brien, Matthew C. William Faulkner and the Civil War. Univ. of Maryland, 1968. Thesis: English.

Oldenburg, Egbert W. William Faulkner's Early Experiments with Narrative Techniques. Univ. of Michigan, 1966. Dissertation: English.

Olds, Rosemary. The Southern Lady: Her Role in the Yoknapatawpha Chronicle. Univ. of Denver, 1964. Thesis: English.

Olsen, Frederick B. Faulkner's Dramatic Psychology. Indiana Univ. (Bloomington), 1954. Thesis: English.

Orlansky, Claire B. The Impact of 19th Century Scientific Thought on Tennyson, Dreiser, and Faulkner. Univ. of Utah, 1967. Thesis: English.

Overly, Dorothy N. The Problem of Character in the Development of Theme in the Novels and Short Stories of William Faulkner. Univ. of Chicago, 1950. Dissertation: English.

Owen, David E. A Giant's Gesture: Religious Implications in the Work of William Faulkner. Pennsylvania State Univ., 1956. Thesis: English.

Page, Felicia A. An Analysis of William Faulkner's Portrayal of Negro Characters. Iowa State Teachers College, 1961. Thesis: English.

Page, Ralph S. William Faulkner and the Grotesque. Univ. of Houston, 1963. Thesis: English.

Page, Sally R. Woman in the Works of William Faulkner. Duke Univ., 1969. Dissertation: English.

Park, William J. Harmony in Discord: A Study of Faulkner's *Light in August*. Columbia Univ., 1954. Thesis: English.

Parker, Margaret M. William Faulkner: Symbolic Prophet. Texas Christian Univ., 1961. Thesis: English.

Parr, Carolyn A.M. William Faulkner: His Use of the Christ Symbol. Vanderbilt Univ., 1960. Thesis: English.

Parrisle, Katherine E. Temple Drake and Her Sisters: A Study of William Faulkner's Women Characters. Univ. of Tennessee, 1963. Thesis: English.

Pastore, Philip E. The Structure and Meaning of William Faulkner's *A Fable*. Univ. of Florida, 1969. Dissertation: English.

Pate, Frances W. Order Out of Disorder: The Theme of *The Sound and the Fury*. Vanderbilt Univ., 1961. Thesis: English.

_____. Names of Characters in Faulkner's Mississippi. Emory Univ., 1969. Dissertation: English.

Payne, David M. Thomas Sutpen: Modern Tragic Hero. Seton Hall Univ., 1967. Thesis: English.

Pearce, Jon R. The Double Vision of William Faulkner. Toronto, 1963. Thesis: English.

Pearce, Richard A. William Faulkner: A Study in Time, the Self, and the Novel. Columbia Univ., 1957. Thesis: English.

Pebworth, Ted-Larry. Emerson and Faulkner: Some Problems of the Romantic Artist in America. Tulane Univ., 1958. Thesis: English.

Pena, Ruth. The Religion of William Faulkner. The Vestiges of Christianity in Ralph Waldo Emerson. Univ. of Texas (El Paso), 1970. Thesis: English.

Penny, Beverly J. Regional Guilt and Shame in Selected Novels of Hawthorne and Faulkner. Louisiana State Univ., 1966. Thesis: English.

Perlin, Charlotte W. A Maturing Gavin Stevens: The Story of Growth in Faulkner's Trilogy. Univ. of Miami (Coral Gables), 1967. Thesis: English.

Petesch, Donald A. Theme and Characterization in Faulkner's Snopes Trilogy. Univ. of Texas (Austin), 1968. Dissertation: English.

Peterson, Richard F. Time as Character in the Fiction of James Joyce and William Faulkner. Kent State Univ., 1969. Dissertation: English.

Pfaff, Charlotte. Requiem for a Nun: Faulkner's Contrapuntal Vision of Man. Univ. of Dallas, 1968. Thesis: English.

Pfaff, James. 'The Poor Sons of Bitches': The Conclusion of *The Mansion* of the Unity of Faulkner's Snopes. Univ. of Dallas, 1969. Thesis: English.

Pham Van Lan, The Rev. Augustine. William Faulkner: Criticism in Catholic Periodicals. John Carroll Univ., 1964. Thesis: English.

Phillips, Mary J. The Sources and Uses of Faulkner's Mythology in *As I Lay Dying* as Influenced by *The Waste Land* and *Ulysses*. Univ. of North Carolina (Chapel Hill), 1960. Thesis: English.

Phillips, Ruth V. Humor in William Faulkner's Novels Based on the Yoknapatawpha Tradition. Univ. of Wyoming, 1965. Thesis: English.

Pilkington, James P. The Place of *Sanctuary* in Faulkner's Scheme of Novels. Vanderbilt Univ., 1946. Thesis: English.

Pinsley, Stanley. The Embrace of a Chimera: The Dying World of William Faulkner. Columbia Univ., 1956. Thesis: English.

Player, Raleigh P., Jr. The Negro Character in the Fiction of William Faulkner. Univ. of Michigan, 1965. Dissertation: English.

Ploegstra, Henry A. William Faulkner's *Go Down, Moses*: Its Sources, Revisions, and Structure. Univ. of Chicago, 1966. Dissertation: English.

Poe, M. The Price of Cain: A Study in the Use of Violence by William Faulkner. Brooklyn College, 1967. Thesis: English.

Polek, F.J. Time and Identity in the Novels of William Faulkner. Univ. of Southern California, 1968. Dissertation: English.

Polk, Noel E. Existential Isolation in the Works of William Faulkner: A Thematic Study of *As I Lay Dying*, *Light in August*, and *The Mansion*. Mississippi College, 1966. Thesis: English.

Pollard, Rebecca A.H. The Negro as Victim in William Faulkner's Fiction. Univ. of Texas (Austin), 1967. Thesis: English.

Pollock, Agnes S. The Current of Time in the Novels of William Faulkner. Univ. of California (Los Angeles), 1965. Dissertation: English.

Porterfield, Christopher. Faulkner's Snopes Trilogy: A Study of *The Hamlet*, *The Town*, and *The Mansion*. Columbia Univ., 1965. Thesis: English.

Poston, Thomas H. Structural Techniques and Patterns in William Faulkner's *The Sound and the Fury*. Univ. of Maryland, 1969. Thesis: English.

Powell, Cash. The Use of the Comic by William Faulkner: Analyzed with Some Reference to Henri Bergson. Miami Univ. (Ohio), 1957. Thesis: English.

Powell, Irma A. Man in His Struggle: Structure, Technique, and Theme in Faulkner's Snopes Trilogy. Florida State Univ., 1969. Dissertation: English.

Poxson, David M. The Critical Reception of William Faulkner in America. Michigan State Univ., 1948. Thesis: English.

Pratt, William C., Jr. William Faulkner's *The Sound and the Fury*: A Study in Point of View. Vanderbilt Univ., 1951. Thesis: English.

Presley, Margie. An Anlaysis of Elements of Style in William Faulkner and Ernest Hemingway. East Tennessee State Univ., 1969. Thesis: English.

Prince, Jeffrey R. Chronology and Structure in *Absalom, Absalom!* Univ. of Virginia, 1966. Thesis: English.

Privette, Belle F. Symbolic Use of Setting in the Works of William Faulkner. Univ. of Virginia, 1966. Thesis: English.

Pyland, Joel L. The Decay of Faulkner's Aristocracy. North Texas State Univ., 1962. Thesis: English.

Ramsey, William C. A Critical Interpretation of William Faulkner's *The Unvanquished*. Univ. of North Carolina (Chapel Hill), 1967. Thesis: English.

Rasco, Kay. The Yoknapatawpha Woman. Univ. of Mississippi, 1953. Thesis: English.

Rau, Suzanne G. "Snopesism" in Faulkner's Trilogy. Univ. of Rhode Island, 1966. Thesis: English.

Rectenwald, Robert P. Faulkner's Presentation of Time in *The Sound and the Fury*. Univ. of North Carolina (Chapel Hill), 1963. Thesis: English.

Redemius, Joan C. The Development of Gavin Stevens from 1930 to 1950 in the Stories and Novels of William Faulkner. Hofstra Univ., 1970. Thesis: English.

Reirdon, Suzanne R. Caddy, the Tragic Figure in *The Sound and the Fury*. Texas Christian Univ., 1969. Thesis: English.

Reiser, John. Faulkner's Storyteller: An Analysis of the Narrative Voice in Selected Short Stories by William Faulkner. Montreal, 1968. Thesis: English.

Reiss, Marilyn. A Descriptive Bibliography of William Faulkner's Short Stories. Columbia Univ., 1949. Thesis: English.

Reynolds, Joseph H., Jr. The Growing Optimism of William Faulkner. Vanderbilt Univ., 1953. Thesis: English.

Richards, Margaret W. A Comparison of Degeneracy and Regeneration: Hawthorne's *The House of the Seven Gables* and Faulkner's *Absalom, Absalom!* Hardin-Simmons Univ., 1970. Thesis: English.

Richardson, Harold E. William Faulkner: From Past to Self-Discovery: A Study of His Life and Work Through *Sartoris* (1929). Univ. of Southern California, 1963. Dissertation: English.

[62]

Richardson, Kenneth E. Quest for Faith: A Study of Destructive and Creative Force in the Novels of William Faulkner. Claremont Graduate School, 1962. Dissertation: English.

Richardson, Mary S. Temporal Conflict and Spiritual Dilemma in Three Novels by William Faulkner. Univ. of Houston, 1959. Thesis: English.

Richey, Dauthor J. A Study of Sibling Relationships in Selected Writings of William Faulkner. Bowling Green State Univ., 1965. Thesis: English.

Ridley, Norma. The Revisions of William Faulkner's Go Down, Moses. Univ. of Arkansas, 1955. Thesis: English.

Rigel, Mary A.E. Social Relationships in William Faulkner's Works. Kent State Univ., 1951. Thesis: English.

Rinaldi, Nicholas M. Game-Consciousness and Game-Metaphor in the Work of William Faulkner. Fordham Univ., 1963. Dissertation: English.

Riskin, Myra J. Faulkner's South: Myth and History in the Novel. Univ. of California (Berkeley), 1968. Dissertation: English.

Roberts, James L. William Faulkner: A Thematic Study. State Univ. of Iowa, 1957. Dissertation: English.

Roberts, M.J. The Role of the Negro in Faulkner's Fiction. Bristol, 1969. Thesis: English.

Rocchio, Anthony M. Faulkner's Outrage. Univ. of Rhode Island, 1967. Thesis: English.

Rodnon, Stewart. William Faulkner and the Negro. Brooklyn College, 1952. Thesis: English.

————. Sports, Sporting Codes, and Sportsmanship in the Work of Ring Lardner, James T. Farrell, Ernest Hemingway, and William Faulkner. New York Univ., 1961. Dissertation: English.

Roerecke, Howard H. William Faulkner's Jason Compson: A Major Portrayal of Malice Without Motive. Columbia Univ., 1958. Thesis: English.

Rogers, Rebecca N. An Index and Concordance to the Characters of William Faulkner. Univ. of Mississippi, 1964. Thesis: English.

Rohrberger, Mary H. William Faulkner's Fiction. Tulane Univ., 1952. Thesis: English.

Romano, Anthony Z. Humor and the Perceptions of the Narrators in Faulkner's The Town. Univ. of Delaware, 1970. Thesis: English.

Ross, Maude C. Moral Values of the American Woman as Presented in Three Major American Authors: Hawthorne, James, Faulkner. Univ. of Texas (Austin), 1964. Dissertation: English.

Roth, Russell F. William Faulkner: An Experiment in Existential Reading. Univ. of Minnesota, 1948. Thesis: English.

Rother, Carole A. Motifs of Alienation in William Faulkner's As I Lay Dying. McGill Univ., 1965. Thesis: English.

Rubel, Warren G. The Structural Function of the Christ Figure in the Fiction of William Faulkner. Univ. of Arkansas, 1964. Dissertation: English.

Rudnick, Lois P. The Grail and the Urn: A Study of William Faulkner's Women Characters. Tufts Univ., 1968. Thesis: English.

Ruffin, Paul D. Faulkner's Dark Hero, Flem Snopes. Mississippi State Univ., 1968. Thesis: English.

[63]

Ruland, Vernon. Descent into Hell: William Faulkner and a
    Theology of Death. Univ. of Chicago, 1967. Dissertation:
    Theology.
Ryan, John H. The Second Fall of Man: A Study of the Anti-Hero
    in William Faulkner's *The Sound and the Fury*, *Pylon*, *Sartoris*,
    and *Light in August*. Brown Univ., 1967. Thesis: English.
Sample, Dorothy J. The Wilderness Theme in *Go Down, Moses*.
    Louisiana State Univ., 1966. Thesis: English.
Sather, Margarette T. A Study on the Theme of Negro Endurance
    in the Writings of William Faulkner. Univ. of Louisville,
    1966. Thesis: English.
Sayles, Rhuehama L. Source and Symbolism in William Faulkner's
    "The Bear." John Carroll Univ., 1969. Thesis: English.
Schaff, Jay B. A Critical Analysis of William Faulkner's *The
    Sound and the Fury*; and, William Faulkner: An Annotated
    Bibliography. Roosevelt Univ., 1953. Thesis: English.
Schendler, Sylvan. William Faulkner's *A Fable*. Northwestern
    Univ., 1956. Dissertation: English.
Schultz, William J. Motion in Yoknapatawpha County: Theme and
    Point of View in the Novels of William Faulkner. Kansas
    State Univ., 1968. Dissertation: English.
Schwartz, Elizabeth B. *Light in August*: The Individual in the
    Community. Carnegie-Mellon Univ., 1966. Thesis: English.
Scott, Mack H. III. *All Our Yesterdays*: The Vital Statistics
    of Yoknapatawpha County. Vanderbilt Univ., 1963. Thesis:
    English.
Searfin, Sr. Joan M., F.S.E. Faulkner's Use of the Classics.
    Univ. of Notre Dame, 1968. Dissertation: English.
Serebnick, Judith. William Faulkner: A Southerner's Growth
    Toward Universality. Pennsylvania State Univ., 1954.
    Thesis: English.
Seymour, Betty J. The Individual and the Problem of Self-
    Definition in Faulkner: Isolation and Gesture in *Light in
    August*, *The Sound and the Fury*, *Absalom, Absalom!* and
    As I Lay Dying. Univ. of Richmond, 1967. Thesis: English.
Shanaghan, Father Malachy M. A Critical Analysis of the Fictional
    Techniques of William Faulkner. Univ. of Notre Dame, 1960.
    Dissertation: English.
Shapiro, Barbara C. A Pollen of Ideas: A Comparative Study of
    William Faulkner and James Joyce. American Univ., 1969.
    Thesis: English.
Sharp, Etta R. Symbolism in Five Novels by William Faulkner.
    East Tennessee State Univ., 1957. Thesis: English.
Shell, Janet C. Classical Allusions in the Works of William
    Faulkner. Univ. of Maryland, 1968. Thesis: English.
Shelton, Frank. Three Aspects of Blackness: Faulkner's *Sanctuary*,
    Light in August, *Absalom, Absalom!* Columbia Univ., 1963.
    Thesis: English.
Sheperd, Edna R.S. *A Fable*: William Faulkner's Handwriting on the
    Wall; An Interpretation and Handbook for Students. Mississippi
    College, 1966. Thesis: English.
Sherman, Edward F. The South's Jurisprudence of William Faulkner.
    Univ. of Texas (El Paso), 1966. Thesis: English.
Sherman, Thomas. These Thirteen: The Structures of the Yoknapata-
    pha Stories. Emory Univ., 1957. Thesis: English.

[64]

Shively, Diana L. Myths and Realities: Poor-Whites in the Fiction of William Faulkner. Kent State Univ., 1967. Thesis: English.

Shumaker, Harvey W. A Quarter Century of *The Sound and the Fury*: A Survey of Faulkner Criticism. Kent State Univ., 1964. Thesis: English.

Sidney, George R. Faulkner in Hollywood: A Study of His Career as a Scenarist. Univ. of New Mexico, 1959. Dissertation: English.

Silverman, Yvonne. The Hour Before the Dawn: A Study of William Faulkner's Treatment of the Negro. Columbia Univ., 1954. Thesis: English.

Simmen, Edward R. *The Sound and the Fury* and *As I Lay Dying*: A Comparison. Univ. of Texas (Austin), 1959. Thesis: English.

Simons, Madeleine A. An Introduction to William Faulkner's Art. Univ. of Miami (Ohio), 1947. Thesis: English.

Simpson, Hassell A. William Faulkner's Negroes: A Study in Changing Attitudes. Florida State Univ., 1957. Thesis: English.

_____. The Short Stories of William Faulkner. Florida State Univ., 1962. Dissertation: English.

Slabey, Robert M. William Faulkner's "The Waste Land" Phase. Univ. of Notre Dame, 1961. Dissertation: English.

Slatoff, Walter J. Emphases and Modes of Organization in the Fiction of William Faulkner: A Study in Patterns of Rhetoric and Perception. Univ. of Michigan, 1956. Dissertation: English.

Slaughter, Catherine R. Some Aspects of Transcendentalism in William Faulkner's Story "The Bear." "Death Comes for the Archbishop"--A Study in Style. A Comparison of "Lycidas" and "Thyrsis" in Terms of Dr. Johnson's Criticism of "Lycidas." Brigham Young Univ., 1960. Thesis: English.

Sleeth, Irene L. The Main Trends in the Criticism of William Faulkner. Univ. of North Carolina (Chapel Hill), 1957. Thesis: Library Science.

Smith, Grace H. Faulkner's Flem Snopes in *The Hamlet*. Univ. of Texas (Austin), 1964. Thesis: English.

Smith, J.H. William Faulkner's Sartoris and Snopes: A Study in Tradition and Anti-Tradition. Univ. of Mississippi, 1957. Thesis: English.

Smith, Kearney I. The Function of Food and Shoe Imagery in Unifying *Light in August*. Univ. of North Carolina (Chapel Hill), 1968. Thesis: English.

Smith, Mary E. Faulkner's Myth. Univ. of Rhode Island, 1957. Thesis: English.

Smith, Paul. William Faulkner's *The Sound and the Fury*: An Explication and Evaluation. Univ. of Rochester, 1951. Thesis: English.

Smithers, Betty J. The Christ Figure in William Faulkner's Novels. Univ. of Idaho, 1955. Thesis: English.

Solomon, Alice F. Faulkner's Mulattoes and the South. Univ. of Wyoming, 1970. Thesis: English.

Solomon, Linda N. William Faulkner as an American Humorist. Columbia Univ., 1965. Thesis: English.

[65]

Speer, Ralph H. The Biblical Concept of Struggle between Spirit and Flesh in Eight Novels by William Faulkner. Drake Univ., 1970. Thesis: English.

Springer, Cecil L. The Problem of Humanity in Faulkner's Yoknapatawpha Stories. Texas Tech Univ., 1961. Thesis: English.

Stack, Mildred R. The Frontier Tradition in *The Hamlet* and Selected Stories by William Faulkner. Univ. of Texas (Austin), 1962. Thesis: English.

Stahr, Alden. Flem Snopes, the Epitome of Evil in Faulkner's Trilogy. Lehigh Univ., 1965. Thesis: English.

Stanton, Brian E. Theme, Characterization, and Imagery in William Faulkner's *Light in August*. Brigham Young Univ., 1966. Thesis: English.

Steege, Martin T. Battling the "reducto absurdum"; Quentin Compson as a Hamlet Figure. Bowling Green State Univ., 1967. Thesis: English.

Stein, Randolph E. The World Outside Yoknapatawpha: A Study of Five Novels by William Faulkner. Ohio Univ., 1965. Dissertation: English.

Steinberg, Aaron. Faulkner and the Negro. New York Univ., 1963. Dissertation: English.

Steinberg, Ronnie A. Archetypal Symbols in William Faulkner's *Light in August*: The Adventure of the Hero. Univ. of Miami (Coral Gables), 1966. Thesis: English.

Stevens, Patsy A. The Tragic Lives of the Yoknapatawpha Women. West Texas State Univ., 1969. Thesis: English.

Stevens, Ronald D. V.K. Ratliff of Faulkner's Snopes Trilogy: The Spokesman for Faulkner? Kent State Univ., 1967. Thesis: English.

Stevens, Sandra K. Structural and Thematic Aspects of Humor in Faulkner's Trilogy. Univ. of Tennessee, 1964. Thesis: English.

Stewart, George G. The Southern Yeomanry in the Faulknerian Myth. Tulane Univ., 1960. Thesis: English.

Stone, Sheila W. The Sense of Sense in Faulkner. Mississippi College, 1967. Thesis: English.

Stoneback, Harry R. Faulkner's Use of Dialect. Univ. of Hawaii, 1966. Thesis: English.

Stratiff, Frank M. Three Studies in English: *King Lear*; Wordsworth and Coleridge; *The Sound and the Fury*. Pennsylvania State Univ., 1967. Thesis: English.

Strother, Bonnie L. The Role of the Negro in the Implied Solution to Slavery as Seen by William Faulkner. Univ. of South Carolina, 1962. Thesis: English.

Stuart, James E., Jr. William Faulkner Among the Critics 1962-1967. Samford Univ., 1969. Thesis: English.

Stutman, Suzanne. Faulkner's Woman: Promise and Peril. Temple Univ., 1965. Thesis: English.

Sullivan, William J. Studies on James, Dreiser, and Faulkner. Univ. of Utah, 1966. Thesis: English.

Sullivan, William P. William Faulkner and the Community. Columbia Univ., 1961. Dissertation: English.

Sulton, George W. Primitivism in the Fiction of William Faulkner. Univ. of Mississippi, 1967. Dissertation: English.

Sutton, Thomas. Myth and the Short Stories of William Faulkner. Atlanta Univ., 1952. Thesis: English.

Swiggart, Charles P. Time and Structure in the Novels of William Faulkner. Yale Univ., 1954. Dissertation: English.

Swink, Helen M. The Oral Tradition in Yoknapatawpha County. Univ. of Virginia, 1969. Dissertation: English.

Tanner, Jimmie E. The Twentieth Century Impressionistic Novel: Conrad and Faulkner. Univ. of Oklahoma, 1964. Dissertation: English.

Taylor, Evelyn R. A Comparative Study of Hawthorne and Faulkner. Drake Univ., 1960. Thesis: English.

Taylor, Robert G. The History of the Aristocrats of William Faulkner's Yoknapatawpha County. East Texas State Univ., 1961. Thesis: English.

Taylor, Robert N. Redemption in *Light in August*: A Study of Gail Hightower. Lehigh Univ., 1966. Thesis: English.

Taylor, Walter F., Jr. The Role of the Negro in William Faulkner's Fiction. Emory Univ., 1964. Dissertation: English.

Terry, Eleanor F. Representative Children in William Faulkner's Fiction. Mississippi College, 1965. Thesis: English.

Theriault, William D. Faulkner's Four-Dimensional World. Univ. of Denver, 1970. Thesis: English.

Thetford, James W., Jr. William Faulkner: A Critical Estimate. Vanderbilt Univ., 1935. Thesis: English.

Thomas, Nell H. The Negroes in William Faulkner. Univ. of Mississippi, 1952. Thesis: English.

Thrower, Linda G. William Faulkner and the Negro. Jacksonville State Univ., 1968. Thesis: English.

Tidwell, Patricia L. Isolation and the Community in the Works of Nathaniel Hawthorne and William Faulkner. Midwestern Univ., 1970. Thesis: English.

Tillman, Daniel S. William Faulkner's Use of the Bible in *Absalom, Absalom!* Sacramento State College, 1970. Thesis: English.

Tilson, Minot L. The Unity of *Go Down, Moses*. Temple Univ., 1965. Thesis: English.

Tinsley, N.L. A Critical Analysis of the Unity in the Long Fiction of William Faulkner. Stetson Univ., 1952. Thesis: English.

Tippens, Dora M. Ambivalent Characters in the Novels of William Faulkner: A Study of Development and Change. Kent State Univ., 1967. Thesis: English.

Toal, Phyllis A. An Inquiry into the Myth of Cosmic Pessimism Considering Its Implications and Conclusions in Selected Works of William Faulkner. Brown Univ., 1960. Thesis: English.

Todd, June F. William Faulkner: The Yoknapatawpha Novels and the Nobel Prize Speech. Southern Illinois Univ. (Carbondale), 1954. Thesis: English.

Tomarken, Carol J. Tradition and Process of Personal Identity in the "The Bear," *Light in August* and *Absalom, Absalom!* Toronto, 1966. Thesis: English.

Travis, Mildred K. Woman as Nature: Major Women in Faulkner's Novels. Mississippi State Univ., 1962. Thesis: English.

Tremblay, William A. William Faulkner's Myth of the South in the Snopes Trilogy. Clark Univ., 1962. Thesis: English.

Tritschler, Donald H. Whorls of Form in Faulkner's Fiction. Northwestern Univ., 1957. Dissertation: English.

Troy, Anne. A Study of Selected Faulknerian Negro Women. Univ. of Northern Iowa (Cedar Falls), 1968. Thesis: English.

Trummer, Joseph F. A Portrait of the Artist in Motion: A Study of the Artist-Surrogates in the Novels of William Faulkner. Purdue Univ., 1968. Dissertation: English.

Tumlinson, Mary S. The Development of Gavin Stevens: A Survey of Critical Opinion. Mississippi State Univ., 1968. Thesis: English.

Udy, Robert W. The Comic Dimension of *The Sound and the Fury*. Univ. of Florida, 1963. Thesis: English.

Ulery, Pamela A. Faulkner's *Sanctuary* and *Requiem for a Nun*: Songs of Innocence and Experience. Cornell Univ., 1963. Dissertation: English.

Underwood, June O. Three Studies in English: Quarles' *Emblems*; Emerson and Carlyle; and Faulkner's *The Reivers*. Pennsylvania State Univ., 1966. Thesis: English.

Uzzell, Minter. William Faulkner, His Message and His Methods. Univ. of Tulsa, 1952. Thesis: English.

Valenstein, Time and Its Furniture: A Study of the Content of Faulkner's Novels from *Soldiers' Pay* through *The Wild Palms*. Claremont Graduate School, 1967. Thesis: English.

Van Savage, Jean. Black Shadow or White Salvation; a Study of Negro Character and Race Relationships in Faulkner. Seton Hall Univ., 1964. Thesis: English.

Vaughn, Sue C. William Faulkner's Use of Judaic-Christian Tradition in Six Major Works. Eastern New Mexico Univ., 1969. Thesis: English.

Vickery, Olga W. The Novels of William Faulkner: Patterns of Perspective. Univ. of Wisconsin, 1954. Dissertation: English.

Vinson, Audrey J.L. The Affirmation of Depravity: Symbols of Moral Surrender in the Fiction of William Faulkner. Wesleyan Univ., 1969. Certificate of Advanced Study Essay.

Vitale, Lois L. Faulkner's Women: A Study of the Destructive Agents in Their Lives. Southern Connecticut State College, 1967. Thesis: English.

Vogt, Kathleen M. Toward a Definition of the Hero: A Study of Two Major Characters in the Work of William Faulkner. Bowling Green State Univ., 1958. Thesis: English.

Voth, Ruth A. William Faulkner and the Gothic Tradition. Univ. of Maryland, 1958. Thesis: English.

Voyles, James R. Quest for Identity: A Study of the Adolescent Character in the Novels of William Faulkner. Univ. of Louisville, 1964. Thesis: English.

Wagstaff, Lyle. An Interpretation of William Faulkner. Univ. of Utah, 1940. Thesis: English.

Walker, Don D. Anderson, Hemingway, Faulkner: Three Studies in Mytho-Symbolism in American Literature. Univ. of Utah, 1947. Thesis: English.

Wall, Carey G. Faulkner's Rhetoric. Stanford Univ., 1964. Dissertation: English.

Wallace, Alline A. Faulkner of Oxford: The Town as Background
    in His Works. Sam Houston State Univ., 1958. Thesis:
    English.
Ward, John C. Some Uses of Humor in Faulkner's Novels. Univ. of
    Virginia, 1967. Thesis: English.
Ward, Wilber H. William Faulkner's Attitude Toward Machinery in
    the Yoknapatawpha County Novels. Univ. of Tennessee, 1968.
    Thesis: English.
Warders, Donald F. Character Consciousness of God in Faulkner's
    Novels. Univ. of Kansas, 1961. Thesis: English.
Warren, Joyce W. William Faulkner: A Comparison with James Joyce.
    Brown Univ., 1960. Thesis: English.
Warren, Leland E. William Faulkner's Gavin Stevens: Moral Center
    in the New Society. Univ. of Georgia, 1968. Thesis: English.
Watson, Arlene E. Yoknapatawpha Redmen: Faulkner's Indians.
    Purdue Univ., 1965. Thesis: English.
Watson, Betty L.E. A Study of Women Character-Types in Novels of
    William Faulkner. Univ. of Houston, 1958. Thesis: English.
Watson, James G. "The Snopes Dilemma": Morality and Amorality
    in Faulkner's Snopes Trilogy. Univ. of Pittsburgh, 1968.
    Dissertation: English.
Watson, Samuel D., Jr. Innocence and Dimensions of Justice of
    Faulkner's *Absalom, Absalom!* Univ. of Virginia, 1966.
    Thesis: English.
Webb, Mary L. Faulkner's Use of Imagery in *Absalom, Absalom!*
    Louisiana State Univ., 1963. Thesis: English.
Webster, Grant T. A Study of the Snopes Clan in the Works of
    William Faulkner. Columbia Univ., 1958. Thesis: English.
Weems, Benjamin F. III. Problems of Perspective: The Point of
    View of the Narrator in the Novels of William Faulkner and
    Virginia Woolf. Columbia Univ., 1956. Thesis: English.
Welch, Sally M. Faulkner's Comic Vision. Austin Peay State
    Univ., 1970. Thesis: English.
Weldon, Jane P. The Heroism of Thomas Sutpen in William Faulkner's
    Absalom, Absalom! Emory Univ., 1963. Thesis: English.
Wells, Andrea A. William Faulkner's Snopes Family. Univ. of
    Florida, 1964. Thesis: English.
Werner, Mary J. Faulkner's Use of Irony as a Unifying Device in
    Light in August. Univ. of Dayton, 1966. Thesis: English.
Werts, Mattie R. Twentieth Century Time Concept in the Work of
    William Faulkner. Kansas State Teachers College, 1957.
    Thesis: English.
Weston, Eunice G. Symbolism in the Short Stories of William
    Faulkner. Atlanta Univ., 1952. Thesis: English.
Weymer, Velda. Freudian Structure of *The Sound and the Fury.*
    Queens College (N.Y.), 1968. Thesis: English.
Wheeler, Sara P. Chronology in *Light in August.* Emory Univ.,
    1968. Thesis: English.
Whiteside, George A. A Study of William Faulkner's *A Fable.*
    Columbia Univ., 1959. Thesis: English.
Wigley, Joseph A. An Analysis of the Imagery of William Faulkner's
    Absalom, Absalom! Northwestern Univ., 1956. Dissertation:
    English.
Wiley, William J. William Faulkner's Yoknapatawpha Characters.
    Univ. of Texas (Austin), 1952. Thesis: English.

[69]

Williams, James O. A Study of William Faulkner's Moral Philosophy.
Univ. of Denver, 1958. Thesis: English.

Williams, Kay. A Study of the Calvinist and New Humanist Philosophies as the Basis of Faulkner's *Light in August*. Univ.
of Mississippi, 1967. Thesis: English.

Williams, M.C. Faulkner's "Dead Humor." Univ. of Florida, 1965.
Thesis: English.

Williams, Mary M.W. The Critical Reputation of William Faulkner's
Novel *Sanctuary*, 1931-1965. North Carolina College (Durham),
1966. Thesis: English.

Willis, Virginia S. Man and the Machine in Four Faulkner Novels.
East Tennessee State Univ., 1968. Thesis: English.

Wilson, Bob G. The White Society's Mythical Concept of the Negro
in Novels of William Faulkner. Sam Houston State Univ.,
1970. Thesis: English.

Wilson, Charmayne. Theme and Technique in Faulkner's *The Sound
and the Fury* and *Light in August*. Texas Tech Univ., 1963.
Thesis: English.

Wilson, Herman O. A Study of the Humor in the Fiction of William
Faulkner. Univ. of Southern California, 1955. Dissertation:
English.

Wilson, Leon A. Faulkner's Fiction in Motion: Short Story into
Novel. Univ. of Georgia, 1967. Thesis: English.

Winkel, Carol A.G. The *I-Thou* Theme in Faulkner's Yoknapatawpha
Chronicle. Texas Christian Univ., 1965. Thesis: English.

Witherington, Paul. William Faulkner's *Light in August*: A
Critical Analysis. Univ. of Texas (Austin), 1960. Thesis:
English.

Wood, Dorothy F. A Study of William Faulkner's Use of the Negro
as a Symbol. Chico State College, 1955. Thesis: English.

Woodward, Charles L. The Spirit and Letter of the Law in William
Faulkner's Yoknapatawpha County. Univ. of Nebraska (Omaha),
1966. Thesis: English.

Wright, Jerry T. Negro Dialect in Selected Novels of William
Faulkner. East Tennessee State Univ., 1969. Thesis:
English.

Wright, Ray G. Humility and Pride: Pharisaism in the Writings
of William Faulkner. Univ. of Houston, 1967. Thesis:
English.

Wynn, Leila D. The Decline of Faulkner's Art. Univ. of Texas
(Austin), 1955. Thesis: English.

Yerby, Janet. A Theotorical Analysis of Selected Addresses by
William Faulkner. Bowling Green State Univ., 1963. Thesis:
Speech.

Yonce, Margaret J. Man's Relation to Nature: A Criterion of
Character in Faulkner. Univ. of Georgia, 1967. Thesis:
English.

Yonge, George A. Echoes of Existentialism in the Novels of
William Faulkner. Hardin-Simmons Univ., 1967. Thesis:
English.

Young, Ann M. William Faulkner's Use of Mirror Imagery as a
Structural Device. Clemson Univ., 1969. Thesis: English.

Young, Janick M. A Fourfold Study of Tom Horn's *The Shallow Grass*
and Selected Novels by William Faulkner. West Texas State
Univ., 1969. Thesis: English.

Young, Sau H. Cultural Tensions in William Faulkner and Hawaiian Myth. Ohio State Univ., 1951. Thesis: English.
Youngblood, Alyce L. The "Pebble's Watery Echo": The Theme of Moral Responsibility in Four Early Faulkner Novels. West Texas State Univ., 1970. Thesis: English.
Zink, Karl E. William Faulkner: Studies in Form and Idea. Univ. of Washington, 1953. Dissertation: English.

WILLIAM C. FALKNER (1825-1889)

Duclos, Donald P. Son of Sorrow! The Life, Works and Influence of Colonel William C. Faulkner, 1825-1889. Univ. of Michigan, 1962. Dissertation: English.
Owen, Virginia R. W.C. Faulkner: A Critical and Biographical Study. Univ. of Mississippi, 1930. Thesis: English.
Puryear, Joan C. Life and Legend of Colonel W.C. Faulkner as a Source for Colonel John Sartoris. Florida State Univ., 1969. Thesis: English.

MARY McNEILL FENOLLOSA (1865-1954)

Grimmett, Floy. Mary McNeill Fenollosa: A Sketch of Her Life and Work. Auburn Univ., 1939. Thesis: English.

JIM FERGUSON (1871-1944)

Keever, Jack E. Jim Ferguson and the Press, 1913-1917. Univ. of Texas (Austin), 1965. Thesis: Journalism.

GEORGE FITZHUGH (1806-1881)

Baldwin, Mary F. The Social Theories of George Fitzhugh. Univ. of Texas (Austin), 1933. Thesis: History.
Brooks, F.J. George Fitzhugh: A Study in Antebellum Southern Thought. Univ. of Chicago, 1937. Thesis: History.
Echart, L.H. The Political Theory of George Fitzhugh. Southern Methodist Univ., 1948. Thesis: Government.
Elliott, Diane D. George Fitzhugh and Authoritarianism. Southern Methodist Univ., 1969. Thesis: History.

JOHN GOULD FLETCHER (1886-1950)

Darling, Oliver H. John Gould Fletcher, Impressionist Poet: Some Aspects of His Poetry Prior to 1914. Columbia Univ., 1951. Thesis: English.
Douglass, Thomas E. The Correspondence of John Gould Fletcher: A Catalogue (Appendix Bound Separately). Univ. of Arkansas, 1965. Dissertation: English.
Fletcher, Amine W. John Gould Fletcher, Imagist Poet. Columbia Univ., 1920. Thesis: English.
Haun, Frederic E. The Allusive Method of John Gould Fletcher: An Analysis. Vanderbilt Univ., 1946. Thesis: English.

McMartin, Christina M. A Study of the Poetry of John Gould
    Fletcher. Occidental College, 1945. Thesis: English.
Moffett, James M. A Name, Works, and Selected Subjects Index
    of the Correspondence of John Gould Fletcher for Corres-
    pondents "L" Through "Z." Univ. of Arkansas, 1968.
    Dissertation: English.
Osborne, William R. The Poetry of John Gould Fletcher: A Critical
    Analysis. George Peabody College, 1955. Dissertation:
    English.
Peters, Oliver L. A Name, Works, and Selected Subjects Index of
    the Correspondence of John Gould Fletcher for Correspondents
    "A" Through "K." Univ. of Arkansas, 1965. Dissertation:
    English.
Piercey, Mary A. John Gould Fletcher. Univ. of Texas (Austin),
    1941. Thesis: English.
Stephens, Edna B. The Oriental Influence in John Gould Fletcher's
    Poetry. Univ. of Arkansas, 1961. Dissertation: English.
Yen, Barbara Y. The Oriental Background of John Gould Fletcher's
    Poetry. Columbia Univ., 1939. Thesis: English.
Zur, Bernard P. John Gould Fletcher, Poet: Theory and Practice.
    Northwestern Univ., 1958. Dissertation: English.

SHELBY FOOTE (1916-   )

Butler, Bonnie B.W. Isolation and Sterility as Themes in the
    Four Related Novels of Shelby Foote. Mississippi State
    Univ., 1968. Thesis: English.
Sudduth, Katherine A. The Small Town in the Fiction of Shelby
    Foote. Mississippi State Univ., 1968. Thesis: English.

JESSE HILL FORD (1928-   )

Clark, Anderson A. Violence in the Fiction of Jesse Hill Ford.
    Vanderbilt Univ., 1970. Thesis: English.

JOHN SALMON FORD (1815-1897)

Laroche, Clarence J. Rip Ford: Frontier Journalist. Univ. of
    Texas (Austin), 1942. Thesis: Journalism.

JOHN FORSYTH (1812-1877)

Chesnutt, David R. John Forsyth: A Southern Partisan (1865-1867).
    Auburn Univ., 1967. Thesis: History.
Olliff, Donathon C. John Forsyth's Ministership to Mexico,
    1856-1859. Auburn Univ., 1966. Thesis: History.

ALCEE FORTIER (1856-1914)

Keaty, Lucille. The Works of Alcee Fortier. Louisiana State
    Univ., 1929. Thesis: English.

JOHN FOX, JR. (1863-1919)

Brame, Walter H. The Life and Longer Stories of John Fox, Jr.
George Peabody College, 1933. Thesis: English.
Herndon, Jerry A. Kentucky as It Appears in the Works of John
Fox, Jr. Duke Univ., 1964. Thesis: English.
Kruger, Arthur N. The Life and Works of John Fox, Jr. Louisiana
State Univ., 1941. Dissertation: English.
Osborn, Scott C. A Study and Contrast of the Kentucky Mountaineer
and the Blue Grass Aristocrat in the Works of John Fox, Jr.
Univ. of Kentucky, 1939. Thesis: English.
Page, Ruth E. John Fox, Jr., and His Mountain Folk. Univ. of
Texas (Austin), 1938. Thesis: English.
Sheeran, Joseph A. John Fox, Jr.: A Critical Appreciation.
Catholic Univ., 1939. Thesis: English.
Stout, Glen W. A Critical Evaluation of the Fictional Works of
John Fox, Jr. Columbia Univ., 1961. Thesis: English.

JOHN C. FREMONT (1813-1890)

Shannon, Mary. John C. Fremont: A Study of the Controversial
Points in his Career. Marquette Univ., 1934. Thesis:
History.

ALICE FRENCH (OCTAVE THANET) (1850-1934)

Martin, Theodore K. The Social Philosophy of Alice French.
Louisiana State Univ., 1941. Thesis: English.
McMichael, George L. Minor Figure: A Biography of Octave
Thanet--Alice French. Northwestern Univ., 1949. Dissertation:
English.
Sewell, Rebecca. Alice French: The "Octave Thanet" of Literature.
Southern Methodist Univ., 1934. Thesis: English.

VIRGINIA FRENCH (1825-1881)

Lewis, Virginia. Virginia French: A Critical Biography.
Vanderbilt Univ., 1940. Dissertation: English.
Peck, Virginia L. Life and Works of L. Virginia French.
Vanderbilt Univ., 1940. Dissertation: English.

LUCY FURMAN (1869?-1958)

Browning, Robert L. A Study of the Humor in the Early Works of
Lucy Furman. Univ. of Louisville, 1961. Thesis: English.
Landrum, Louise M. A Study of Kentucky Mountain Dialect Based
on Lucy Furman's *Quare Women*. Univ. of Kentucky, 1930.
Thesis: English.
Neal, Julia. Lucy Furman, Life and Works. Western Kentucky Univ.,
1933. Thesis: English.

CHRISTOPHER GADSDEN (1785-1852)

Potts, James L. Christopher Gadsden and the American Revolution.
George Peabody College, 1958. Dissertation: History.

JOSEPH GALES, SR. (1761-1841)

Martin, Santford, Jr. Joseph Gales, Sr., and the Raleigh *Register*.
Wake Forest Univ., 1948. Thesis: English.

CHARLES ETIENNE ARTHUR GAYARRÉ (1805-1895)

Duchein, Mary S. Research on Etienne Arthur Gayarré. Louisiana
State Univ., 1934. Thesis: Romance Languages.
Lund, Mary I. Charles Gayarré as a Man of Letters. Tulane Univ.,
1943. Thesis: English.
Saucier, Earl N. Charles Gayarré, the Creole Historian. George
Peabody College, 1934. Dissertation: English.
Socola, Edward. C.E.A. Gayarré. A Biography. Univ. of
Pennsylvania, 1954. Dissertation: English.

ROBERT WILSON GIBBES (1809-1866)

Childs, Arney R. Dr. Robert Wilson Gibbes: 1809-1866. Univ. of
South Carolina, 1925. Thesis: History.

BASIL LANNEAU GILDERSLEEVE (1831-1924)

Garant, Geraldine. Basil Lanneau Gildersleeve, the American
Scholar. Vanderbilt Univ., 1942. Thesis: English.

CAROLINE HOWARD GILMAN (1794-1888)

Walsh, Mary K. Caroline Howard Gilman. Duke Univ., 1941.
Thesis: English.

FRANCIS WALKER GILMER (1790-1826)

David, Richard B. The Life, Letters and Essays of Francis W.
Gilmer: A Study in Virginia Literary Culture in the First
Quarter of the Nineteenth Century. Univ. of Virginia, 1936.
Dissertation: English.

ELLEN GLASGOW (1874-1945)

Aldridge, Margaret. Traditionalism in the Novels of Edith Wharton,
Ellen Glasgow, and Willa Cather as Controlled by Their
Personalities. Univ. of the Pacific, 1956. Thesis: English.
Ashley, Serena B. An Evaluation of *The Sheltered Life* by Ellen
Glasgow. Univ. of Connecticut, 1951. Thesis: English.
Aspray, Ruth M. Ellen Glasgow and the New South. Univ. of
Washington, 1927. Thesis: English.
Atkins, Dorothy W. Ellen Glasgow: Novelist of Change. Ohio
State Univ., 1942. Thesis: English.
Bates, Rudolph D. Changing Views: A Study of Ellen Glasgow's
Fluctuating Philosophy. Univ. of South Carolina, 1966.
Dissertation: English.
Beaumont, Lulu A. Ellen Glasgow: Social Historian. San
Francisco State College, 1963. Thesis: English.

Becker, Allen. Ellen Glasgow: Her Novels and Their Place in
     the Development of Southern Fiction. Johns Hopkins Univ.,
     1956. Dissertation: English.
Berg, Gertrude (Gabriel, Mother M., R.S.H.M.). Ellen Glasgow:
     Versatile Fictionist. St. John's Univ. (N.Y.), 1960.
     Thesis: English.
Blanco, Sr. Margaret C. Ellen Glasgow: Her Contribution to the
     Novel of Manners. St. John's Univ. (N.Y.), 1948. Thesis:
     English.
Bressler, Maybelle J. A Critical Study of the Published Novels
     of Ellen Glasgow. Univ. of Nebraska, 1965. Dissertation:
     English.
Briney, Martha M. Ellen Glasgow: Social Critic. Michigan State
     Univ., 1956. Dissertation: English.
Brown, Ann E. A Comparison-Contrast Study of the Land as Force
     in Willa Cather's O Pioneers! and Ellen Glasgow's Barren
     Ground. Bowling Green State Univ., 1963. Thesis: English.
Burkett, Eva M. Virginia Life as Portrayed by Ellen Glasgow.
     George Peabody College, 1930. Thesis: English.
Burns, James T., Jr. Three Main Themes in the Works of Ellen
     Glasgow. Columbia Univ., 1951. Thesis: English.
Bushman, Claudia L. Old Values and New: The Heroines of Ellen
     Glasgow, Edith Wharton,and Willa Cather. Brigham Young
     Univ., 1963. Thesis: English.
Butts, Barbara. Ellen Glasgow and the New South. Univ. of
     Mississippi, 1941. Thesis: English.
Carter, Alice B. The Repetitions in Ellen Glasgow's Novels.
     Univ. of South Carolina, 1933. Thesis: English.
Cartrell, Francesca W. The Part That the Negro Played in the
     Novels of Ellen Glasgow. Univ. of Florida, 1951. Thesis:
     English.
Chalk, Nancy E. The Early Naturalism of Ellen Glasgow. Univ. of
     Texas (Austin), 1967. Thesis: English.
Clements, Margie P. Ellen Glasgow and the Victorian Morality in
     the South. College of William and Mary, 1930. Thesis:
     English.
Collier, Fay. Ellen Glasgow's Methods of Visualization in Vein of
     Iron. Sam Houston State Univ., 1941. Thesis: English.
Copelin, Pauline S. Symbolism in the Later Novels of Ellen
     Glasgow. Midwestern Univ., 1953. Thesis: English.
Dann, Lois M. The Novels of Ellen Glasgow. Columbia Univ., 1946.
     Thesis: English.
Davis, Mary L.S. Patterns and Changes in Family Life in Ellen
     Glasgow's Novels. Mississippi State Univ., 1967. Thesis:
     English.
Derrig, P.A., C.M. Ellen Glasgow's Role in American Literature:
     A Re-Interpretation. St. John's Univ., 1963. Dissertation:
     English.
Dillard, Richard H.W. Pragmatic Realism: A Biography of Ellen
     Glasgow's Novels. Univ. of Virginia, 1965. Dissertation:
     English.
Dolan, Patricia A. Willa Cather and Ellen Glasgow: Interpreters
     of the American Past. Univ. of Illinois, 1948. Thesis:
     English.

Dunn, Norma E. Ellen Glasgow's Search for Truth. Univ. of
    Pennsylvania, 1968. Dissertation: English.
Edwards, Ava L. Women and Girls in Nine Recent Novels by Ellen
    Glasgow. George Peabody College, 1933. Thesis: English.
Edwards, Herbert W. A Study of Values in Selected Published
    Prose of Ellen Glasgow. New York Univ., 1960. Dissertation:
    English.
Finnell, Flora. Social Philosophy of Ellen Glasgow. Hunter
    College, 1941. Thesis: English.
Flomerfelt, Oriene. The Negro in the Novels of Ellen Glasgow.
    Univ. of Missouri, 1945. Thesis: English.
Foors, Curtis E. Ellen Glasgow: An Analysis of "Literary
    Realism." Univ. of Virginia, 1969. Thesis: English.
Galloway, Nancy G. Ellen Glasgow and the New South. Univ. of
    Oklahoma, 1964. Thesis: English.
Garson, Helen. Local Color in the Work of Ellen Glasgow. Univ.
    of Georgia, 1947. Thesis: English.
Gatlin, Judith T. Ellen Glasgow's Artistry. Univ. of Iowa,
    1969. Dissertation: English.
Gilborn, Alice C.W. Ellen Glasgow: Between Two Worlds. Univ.
    of Delaware, 1968. Thesis: English.
Glendon, Patricia E. An Analysis of Three Important Themes in
    Seven of Ellen Glasgow's Novels. Univ. of Rhode Island,
    1961. Thesis: English.
Good, Ruth. The Southern Woman in Ellen Glasgow's Novels. Univ.
    of North Carolina (Chapel Hill), 1950. Thesis: English.
Gore, Luther Y. Ellen Glasgow's *Beyond Defeat*, a Critical
    Edition. Volume One: Editor's Introduction. Volume Two:
    The Text of *Beyond Defeat*. Univ. of Virginia, 1964.
    Dissertation: English.
Gorham, Joann E. The Literary Reputation of Ellen Glasgow in
    America. Columbia Univ., 1948. Thesis: English.
Greene, Alice W. Ellen Glasgow: Reflections of Experience in
    the Major Novels. Queens College (N.Y.), 1964. Thesis:
    English.
Gregory, Laura B. Miss Glasgow and Social Readjustment. Univ.
    of South Carolina, 1932. Thesis: English.
Guilmartin, A.J. Clarification of Ellen Glasgow's Perspectives.
    Boston Univ., 1947. Thesis: English.
Hagler, Sandra L.A. Symbolism in Three Novels by Ellen Glasgow.
    Texas Woman's Univ., 1970. Thesis: English.
Hall, Henry M. The Novels of Ellen Glasgow: A History of
    Manners. Univ. of Idaho, 1950. Thesis: English.
Hartmann, John L. Age and Change in Four Glasgow Novels.
    Mississippi State Univ., 1959. Thesis: English.
Harvey, Helen. The Validity of the Depiction of the Depression
    in Ellen Glasgow's Novels. Indiana Univ. of Pennsylvania,
    1965. Thesis: English.
Hauss, Mary A. Virginia Life in the Novels of Ellen Glasgow.
    Duke Univ., 1931. Thesis: English.
Havel, Lillian K. Political, Economic, and Social Transition in
    Virginia Following the Civil War as Shown in Ellen Glasgow's
    Novels. Univ. of Nebraska, 1947. Thesis: English.

Hill, Belle M. The Flight from Love Motif in the Novels of
    Ellen Glasgow, with Special Emphasis on: *The Descendant,
    Virginia, Barren Ground, The Romantic Comedians, Vein of
    Iron, In This Our Life*. Univ. of Virginia, 1958. Thesis:
    English.
Holladay, Pauline. A Comparison of the Women in the Novels of
    Willa Cather with those in the Novels of Ellen Glasgow.
    Univ. of Mississippi, 1955. Thesis: English.
Houghton, Everett A. Ellen Glasgow as a Critical Historian of
    the South. Miami Univ. (Ohio), 1944. Thesis: English.
Howard, David C. Ellen Glasgow's South, as Presented in Her Last
    Six Novels. Duke Univ., 1963. Thesis: English.
Jacobs, Pansy E. The Economic, Social and Religious Life of the
    People of Virginia as Seen in the Country Novels of Ellen
    Glasgow. Virginia State College, 1953. Thesis: English.
Jessup, Josephine L. Faith of our Feminists: Edith Wharton,
    Ellen Glasgow, Willa Cather. Vanderbilt Univ., 1948.
    Dissertation: English.
Johnson, Albert L., Jr. Ellen Glasgow's Social Criticism of
    the South Before and After the Civil War. Univ. of South
    Carolina, 1969. Thesis: English.
Joiner, Sarah B. The Women Characters in Ellen Glasgow's Novels.
    Duke Univ., 1941. Thesis: English.
Julian, Elizabeth A. A Study of the Feminine Characters in the
    Novels of Ellen Glasgow. Univ. of Mississippi, 1962.
    Thesis: English.
Kammer, Joseph A. (Brother David Ottmar, F.M.S.). A Study of the
    "Good People" of Virginia, Particularly as Interpreted by
    Ellen Glasgow. St. John's Univ., 1954. Thesis:
Kelly, William W. Struggle for Recognition: A Study of the
    Literary Reputation of Ellen Glasgow. Duke Univ., 1957.
    Dissertation: English.
King, Margaret F. John Phillips Marquand and Ellen Glasgow:
    The Individual in a Traditional Society. Univ. of North
    Carolina (Chapel Hill), 1969. Thesis: English.
Kreider, Thomas M. Ellen Glasgow: Southern Opponent to the
    Philistine. Univ. of Cincinnati, 1952. Dissertation:
    English.
Kump, Br. Lucius M., F.S.C. Realism of Ellen Glasgow. Loyola
    Univ. (Chicago), 1948. Thesis: English.
Le Hew, Anne R. The Rebel Motif in the Novels of Ellen Glasgow,
    with Emphasis upon *Barren Ground, Vein of Iron,* and
    They Stooped to Folly. Univ. of Virginia, 1955. Thesis:
    English.
Lemon, Gertrude. Ellen Glasgow: A Study of her Philosophy of
    Character. Kansas State Teachers College, 1953. Thesis:
    English.
Levy, Amelia R. Ellen Glasgow's Lost Generations. Univ. of
    Texas (El Paso), 1956. Thesis: English.
Mantor, Ruth. Fortitude in Ellen Glasgow. Univ. of Texas
    (Austin), 1948. Thesis: English.
Marimon, Rosa B. Some Distinguishing Characteristics of Ellen
    Glasgow's Novels. Univ. of Utah, 1937. Thesis: English.
Mayo, Betsy B. The Virginia Woman of the New South as Shown
    in the Novels of Ellen Glasgow. Southern Methodist Univ.,

[77]

1940. Thesis: English.

McCollum, Kay R. The Feminine Psyches in Ellen Glasgow's Novels. Drake Univ., 1968. Thesis: English.

McCollum, Nancy M. Ellen Glasgow: Virginia Satirist. Univ. of Georgia, 1964. Thesis: English.

McLennand, Marie C.S. Ellen Glasgow's Theories of Fiction. Univ. of Pittsburgh, 1947. Thesis: English.

Meinecke, Rosa. A Study of the Men and the Women of Ellen Glasgow. Sam Houston State Univ., 1953. Thesis: English.

Mendoza, Helen N. The Past in Ellen Glasgow. Univ. of Minnesota, 1966. Dissertation: English.

Meyer, Edgar V. The Art of Ellen Glasgow. Univ. of Denver, 1955. Dissertation: English.

Mitchell, Mary E. Idealism and Realism in the Novels of Ellen Glasgow. Univ. of Texas (El Paso), 1964. Thesis: English.

Moake, Frank B. The Problems of Characterization in the Novels of Ellen Glasgow. Univ. of Illinois, 1957. Dissertation: English.

Moore, Clara W. Ellen Glasgow's Method of Characterization in *Barren Ground*. Sam Houston State Univ., 1939. Thesis: English.

Murphy, Denis M. Vein of Ambivalence: Structural, Stylistic, and Personal Dualisms in Ellen Glasgow's Major Novels. Princeton Univ., 1969. Dissertation: English.

Meyer, Elizabeth G. The Social Situation of Women in the Novels of Ellen Glasgow. Brown Univ., 1947. Thesis: English.

Norred, Barbara A. A Study of the Middle Class Character in the Novels of Ellen Glasgow. Univ. of Mississippi, 1958. Thesis: English.

Oaks, Mildred R. The Virginia Gentlewoman: A Study of Ellen Glasgow's Development in the Realistic Treatment of a Social Type. Temple Univ., 1939. Thesis: Education.

O'Donnell, Sheryl R. Moral Responsibility in the Novel of Ellen Glasgow: A Thematic Study. John Carroll Univ., 1965. Thesis: English.

Oppenheim, Abe. Some Studies in Ellen Glasgow's Concept of Fortitude. Columbia Univ., 1961. Thesis: English.

Patterson, Daniel W. Ellen Glasgow's Use of Virginia History. Univ. of North Carolina (Chapel Hill), 1959. Dissertation: English.

Patterson, Mary K.J. Ellen Glasgow: Social Historian. Wofford College, 1939. Thesis: English.

Pedrick, Aleta I.M. A Continual Becoming: Ellen Glasgow's Maturing Art in Her Trilogy on Manners: *The Romantic Comedians*, *They Stooped to Folly*, and *The Sheltered Life*. American Univ., 1969. Thesis: English.

Phelps, Sylvia E. The Novels of Ellen Glasgow. Univ. of Delaware, 1940. Thesis: English.

Porter, Dorothy M. Description in Ellen Glasgow's Novels. Univ. of Nebraska, 1925. Thesis: English.

Porter, Maud D. Lack of Dramatic Art in Ellen Glasgow's Novels. Univ. of Nebraska, 1927. Thesis: English.

Prichard, Virginia. Religion in the First Nine Novels of Ellen Glasgow. Duke Univ., 1954. Thesis: English.

Quesenbery, William D., Jr. Ellen Glasgow's Isolation, with a Definitive Critical Bibliography of Primary and Secondary Sources. Columbia Univ., 1957. Thesis: English.

Raitt, Mildred D. Ellen Glasgow and Her Virginia Tradition. Columbia Univ., 1955. Thesis: English.

Ramsey, Edna J. The social Concepts of Ellen Glasgow as Shown in the Treatment of Characters. Univ. of Oklahoma, 1942. Thesis: English.

Raper, Julius R., Jr. Ellen Glasgow and Darwinism, 1873-1906. Northwestern Univ., 1966. Dissertation: English.

Rayburn, Harriet K. The Cultural Relations of the South as Discussed in the Novels of Ellen Glasgow: A Thesis. Whittier College, 1950. Thesis: English.

Reeves, Ruth. "Father, I Have Written a Book": A Study of Characterization in Ellen Glasgow's Novels. Univ. of Houston, 1948. Thesis: English.

Richards, Marion K. The Development of Ellen Glasgow as a Novelist. Columbia Univ., 1961. Dissertation: English.

Riker, Joyce R.P. The Major Women Characters in Ellen Glasgow's Novels: The Southern Belle and the "New Woman." Univ. of Houston, 1968. Thesis: English.

Ringheim, Barbara J. Ellen Glasgow's Interpretation of Human Action and Ethics as Reflected in Her Novels and Essays. Stanford Univ., 1948. Thesis: English.

Rosenthal, Yvette C. Ellen Glasgow as a Realist. Univ. of Texas (Austin), 1936. Thesis: English.

Rouse, Hubert B. Studies in the Works of Ellen Glasgow. Univ. of Illinois, 1942. Dissertation: English.

Santas, Joan F. Ellen Glasgow's American Dream. Cornell Univ., 1963. Dissertation: English.

Sawyer, Ione Z. The Use of Social Background in the Novels of Ellen Glasgow. Univ. of Southern California, 1940. Thesis: English.

Shafer, Mary H. Ellen Glasgow's Ironic Portraits. Univ. of Wyoming, 1945. Thesis: English.

Shelton, John K. Ellen Glasgow: The Progress of Her Novels. Miami Univ. (Ohio), 1960. Thesis: English.

Smart, Catherine. Ellen Glasgow's Interpretation of the South. Univ. of North Carolina (Chapel Hill), 1948. Thesis: History.

Stalnaker, Susan L. Major Male Characters in the Novels of Ellen Glasgow. West Virginia Univ., 1969. Thesis: English.

Stevens, Lucile. Miss Glasgow's Treatment of Virginia Scenes and People. Univ. of Kansas, 1933. Thesis: English.

Talbot, Gloria A. Tradition and Rebellion in Ellen Glasgow's Novels. Duke Univ., 1957. Thesis: English.

Thomas, J.J. Ellen Glasgow. Ein Beitrag zum Studium des Traditionalismus in der Amerikanischen Erzählenden Literatur des 20. Jahrhunderts. Köln, 1952. Dissertation: English.

Virgin, Elizabeth A. Ellen Glasgow's Concept of the Undaunted Woman. Univ. of Georgia, 1959. Thesis: English.

Wagner, Charlotte A. Two Frontiers: A Study in the Major Novels of Ellen Glasgow and Willa Cather. Columbia Univ., 1953. Thesis: English.

Walden, Mary. Ellen Glasgow and Social Democracy. Texas A. and I
  Univ., 1943. Thesis: English.
Walker, Adeline N. Ellen Glasgow's South. Vanderbilt Univ.,
  1951. Thesis: English.
Wehmeier, Helga. Die Widerspiegelung und Entwicklung der
  Ökonomischen und Geistigen Struktur des Amerikanischen
  Staates Virginia von 1850 bis 1930 in den Romanen von Ellen
  Glasgow. Humboldt Universität (East Berlin), 1952.
  Dissertation: English.
Wetmore, Adeline B. The *Vein of Iron* in Ellen Glasgow. Boston
  Univ., 1940. Thesis: English.
White, Imogene R. Ellen Glasgow, Virginia Rebel. North Texas
  State Univ., 1956. Thesis: English.
White, James E., Jr. Symbols in the Novels of Ellen Glasgow.
  Boston Univ., 1964. Dissertation: English.
Wilkins, Ruth J. Ellen Glasgow's Virginia: The Background of
  Her Novels. Univ. of Richmond, 1951. Thesis: English.
Williams, Ena L.W. The Novels of Ellen Glasgow. Univ. of
  Miami (Coral Gables), 1964. Thesis: English
Woodham, Louise K. Ellen Glasgow: A Portrayer of the Southern
  People. Birmingham-Southern College, 1936. Thesis:
  English.
Worley, Harriet C. Ellen Glasgow: Author or Character? The
  Autobiographical Element in Miss Glasgow's Later Novels.
  Univ. of Tennessee, 1964. Thesis: English.
Worley, Veronica. Parallels in Ellen Glasgow's Portrayal of
  Women. North East Louisiana Univ., 1966. Thesis: English.
Zakitis, Eva Y. Ellen Glasgow: The Tragedy of Every Women as
  It Was Lately Enacted in the Commonwealth of Virginia.
  Univ. of Georgia, 1960. Thesis: English.

CARTER GLASS (1858-1946)

Goolrick, Chester B., Jr. Carter Glass: Wilson's Apostle. Univ.
  of Virginia, 1950. Thesis: History.
Poindexter, Harry E. From Copy Desk to Congress: The Pre-
  Congressional Career of Carter Glass. Univ. of Virginia,
  1966. Dissertation: History.

CAROLINE GORDON (1895-   )

Arnold, Christina W. Caroline Gordon, Agrarian Novelist. Hardin-
  Simmons Univ., 1964. Thesis: English.
Brown, Jane A. A Road to Damascus: A Study of God and Man in the
  Works of Caroline Gordon. Cornell Univ., 1955. Thesis:
  English.
Brown, Samuel A. Caroline Gordon and the Impressionist Novel.
  Vanderbilt Univ., 1958. Dissertation: English.
Griffis, Marcia. The Sense of Order in Caroline Gordon's Early
  Novels. Mississippi State Univ., 1967. Thesis: English.
Martin, Carter W. A Critical Study of Caroline Gordon's Collected
  ·Short Stories, *The Forest of the South*. Vanderbilt Univ.,
  1958. Thesis: English.
Mayo, Dorothy H. The Novels of Caroline Gordon. Vanderbilt Univ.,
  1953. Thesis: English.

Perry, Lora P. Carolyn Gordon: A Critical Evaluation of Her
    Novels. Birmingham-Southern College, 1960. Thesis:
    English.
Rawlings, Margaret G. Caroline Gordon's Theory and Use of
    Point of View. Univ. of North Carolina (Chapel Hill),
    1964. Thesis: English.
Rocks, James E. The Mind and Art of Caroline Gordon. Duke Univ.,
    1966. Dissertation: English.
Scharff, Sr. M.L.B. Caroline Gordon, Biographer of the South.
    Villanova Univ., 1940. Thesis: English.
Webb, Sr. Mary E. Theory and Practice of Point of View in the
    Fiction of Caroline Gordon. Univ. of Portland, 1964.
    Thesis: English.
Wise, Kenneth K. The Art of Caroline Gordon and the Religious
    Theme in Her Novels. Columbia Univ., 1960. Thesis:
    English.

FRANCIS ROBERT GOULDING (1810-1881)

Macon, Alethea J. Francis Robert Goulding, Georgia Author. Univ.
    of Georgia, 1925. Thesis: English.

HENRY W. GRADY (1850-1889)

Bauer, Marvin G. Henry W. Grady: Spokesman of the New South.
    Univ. of Wisconsin, 1937. Dissertation: Economics.
Nixon, Raymond B. Henry W. Grady: Journalistic Leader in Public
    Affairs. Univ. of Minnesota, 1942. Dissertation: Jour-
    nalism.
_____. Henry Woodfin Grady and the Atlanta *Constitution*. Univ.
    of Wisconsin, 1934. Thesis: Journalism.
Terrell, Russell F. A Study of the Early Journalistic Writings
    of Henry W. Grady. George Peabody College, 1926.
    Dissertation: English.

SHIRLEY ANN GRAU (1929-   )

Gusick, Diana. The Alienated, Hypersensitive Characters in the
    Fiction of Shirley Ann Grau. Hofstra Univ., 1969. Thesis:
    English.
Tate, Dorothy L. The Structural Implications of the Theme of
    Violence in Shirley Ann Grau's *The Keepers of the House*.
    Appalachian State Univ., 1969. Thesis: English.

WILLIAM JOHN GRAYSON (1788-1863)

Bass, Robert D. The Autobiography of William J. Grayson, Edited,
    with an Introduction. Univ. of South Carolina, 1933.
    Dissertation: English.
Jarrett, Thomas D. William J. Grayson's *The Hireling and the
    Slave*: A Study of Ideas, Form, Reception, and Editions.
    Univ. of Chicago, 1947. Dissertation: English.

DUFF GREEN (1791-1875)

Nelson, Gale H. The Political Activities of Duff Green during
the Jackson Period. Univ. of Texas (Austin), 1941. Thesis:
History.

PAUL GREEN (1894-   )

Anderson, Ruth W. Paul Green: A Study of His Life, His Writings,
and His Portrayal of 'the Negro. Birmingham-Southern College,
1937. Thesis: English.
Ashely, Oscar R. The Negro Character in the Plays of Paul Green.
George Peabody College, 1942. Thesis: English.
Coe, Berenice. Paul Green, the American Dramatist. Southern
Methodist Univ., 1944. Thesis: English.
Cox, Louise H. Paul Green's *Negro Folk Plays*: A Criticism.
Univ. of Texas (Austin), 1949. Thesis: English.
Creighton, Ruth. Paul Green and His Drama. Univ. of South
Carolina, 1929. Thesis: English.
Devin, Philip L., Jr. Form and Structure in Paul Green's
Tragedies. Indiana Univ., 1967. Dissertation: Theater.
Eaton, Gregory S. Paul Green: The Emergence of Symphonic Drama
from Selected Early Plays. Univ. of Washington, 1967.
Thesis: English.
Groff, Edward B. Paul Green: A Critical Study of America's
Leading Folk Dramatist. Univ. of Kansas, 1957. Disser-
tation: English.
Haynes, Lucy T. Paul Green's People, Victims of Heritage.
Hardin-Simmons Univ., 1950. Thesis: English.
Just, Ethel H. Negro American Folk Plays of Paul Green with
Special Reference to Their Sociological Value. Boston
Univ., 1936. Thesis: English.
Kavanaugh, John M. A Study of Paul Green's Negro Plays.
Louisiana State Univ., 1937. Thesis: English.
Linney, Daniel A. Social Problems in the Plays of Paul Green.
Univ. of North Carolina (Chapel Hill), 1964. Thesis:
Dramatic Art.
Middleton, Frances S. Paul Green's South: A Land of Contrasts.
North Texas State Univ., 1955. Thesis: English.
Owens, Henry G. The Social Thought and Criticism of Paul Green.
New York Univ., 1946. Dissertation: English.
Paine, John R. The Plays of Paul Green. Occidental College,
1938. Thesis: English.
Pearce, Howard D. The Plays of Paul Green: Their Growth from
Literary and Folk Traditions. Florida State Univ., 1967.
Dissertation: English.
Penny, Robert L. The Treatment of the Negro in the Drama of
Paul Green. Univ. of North Carolina (Chapel Hill), 1960.
Thesis: English.
Power, Helen L. The Development of the Folk Drama in North
Carolina with Special Reference to the Plays of Paul Green.
Univ. of Southern California, 1945. Thesis: English.
Pritchard, Arthur S. Paul Green's Early Plays on Negro Life.
Texas Christian Univ., 1966. Thesis: English.

Redd, LaVerne M. The Plays of Paul Green: A Study of Technique. Fisk Univ., 1936. Thesis: English.

Rourke, Margaret E. Paul Green, Folkwriter. Univ. of Illinois, 1934. Thesis: English.

Seale, Maurie L. Southern Negroes Presented by Paul Green in Seven of His Folk Plays. Sam Houston State Univ., 1954. Thesis: English.

Smith, Dolores A. The Symphonic Drama of Paul Green. Univ. of Tennessee, 1961. Thesis: English.

Treat, Donald R. Paul Green's Concept of Symphonic Drama and Its Application to His Outdoor Plays. Univ. of Denver, 1963. Dissertation: Theater.

FRANCES NIMMO GREENE (-1937)

Rockett, Anita. An Appreciation of the Literary Work of Frances Nimmo Greene. George Peabody College, 1926. Thesis: English.

HUGH BLAIR GRIGSBY (1806-1881)

Bigelow, Alden G. Hugh Blair Grigsby: Historian and Antiquarian. Univ. of Virginia, 1957. Dissertation: History.

FRANK GRIMES (1891-1961)

Adams, Donald P. Frank Grimes, 1891-1961: Historical Study of the Life and Works of the Editor of *The Abilene Reporter-News*. Univ. of Texas (Austin), 1968. Thesis: Journalism.

CHARLOTTE FORTEN GRIMKE (   )

Lewis, Thelma S. The Civil War Diaries of Charlotte Forten Grimkè. Northwestern Univ., 1946. Thesis: English. [Kept while Mrs. Grimkè resided in Fort Royal, South Carolina, 1862-1864]

REUBEN POST HALLECK (1859-1936)

Bowling, Patricia K. Reuben Post Halleck: A Biography. Univ. of Louisville, 1968. Thesis: Education.

JAMES HENRY HAMMOND (1807-1864)

Tucker, Robert C. James Henry Hammond, South Carolinian. Univ. of North Carolina (Chapel Hill), 1958. Dissertation: History.

WILL N. HARBEN (1858-1919)

Johnson, Rose B. Will N. Harben, Georgia Novelist. Univ. of Georgia, 1925. Thesis: English.

Mercer, Julia. North Georgia Life in the Fiction of Will N. Harben. Duke Univ., 1938. Thesis: English.

ISAAC HARBY (1788-1828)

Moise, L.C. Isaac Harby. Univ. of South Carolina, 1930. Thesis:
    English.

WILLIAM JOSEPH HARDEE (1815-1873)

Hughes, Nathaniel C., Jr. William Joseph Hardee, C.S.A., 1861-
    1865. Univ. of North Carolina (Chapel Hill), 1959. Disser-
    tation: History.

FRANCES E.W. HARPER (1825-1911)

Clark, James W., Jr. Frances Ellen Watkins Harper, 1825-1911:
    A Literary Biography. Duke Univ., 1967. Thesis: English.
Daniel, Theodora W. The Poems of Frances E.W. Harper, Edited
    with a Biographical and Critical Introduction and Bibli-
    ography. Howard Univ., 1937. Thesis: English.

ROBERT GOODLOE HARPER (1765-1825)

Cox, Joseph W. Robert Goodloe Harper: The Evolution of a
    Southern Federalist Congressman. Univ. of Maryland, 1967.
    Dissertation: History.

CORRA HARRIS (1869-1935)

Blackstock, Walter, Jr. Corra Harris: An Analytical Study of
    Her Novels. Vanderbilt Univ., 1944. Thesis: English.
Dobbins, C.G. Corra Harris: Her Life and Work. Columbia Univ.,
    1931. Thesis: English.
Johnson, A.W. A Critical Biography of Corra Harris. Univ. of
    North Carolina (Chapel Hill), 1940. Thesis: English.
Mundy, Beverly J. The Philosopher of the Heart, Corra White
    Harris: The Circuit Rider's Wife's Philosophy of Man.
    Univ. of South Carolina, 1967. Thesis: English.
Reeves, Ruby C. Corra Harris, Her Life and Works. Univ. of
    Georgia, 1937. Thesis: English.

GEORGE WASHINGTON HARRIS (1814-1869)

Black, William P. Sut Lovingood as Seen by George Washington
    Harris. Duke Univ., 1966. Thesis: English.
Boykin, Carol. A Study of the Phonology, Morphology, and
    Vocabulary of George Washington Harris' Sut Lovingood Yarns.
    Univ. of Tennessee, 1966. Thesis: English.
Crouch, Howard G. George Washington Harris: Southwestern
    Humorist and Creator of Sut Lovingood, "A Nat'ral born
    durn'd fool." Radford College, 1965. Thesis: English.
Day, Donald. Life and Works of George W. Harris. Univ. of
    Chicago, 1942. Dissertation: English.
Gentry, Robert B., Jr. The Animal Motif in the Sut Lovingood
    Yarns. Univ. of Tennessee, 1967. Thesis: English.
Heflin, John J., Jr. George Washington Harris ("Sut Lovingood"):

A Biographical and Critical Study. Vanderbilt Univ., 1934.
Thesis: English.
Inge, Milton T. A Study of the Sut Lovingood Yarns and Other
Writings of George Washington Harris. Vanderbilt Univ.,
1960. Thesis: English.
_____. The Uncollected Writings of George Washington Harris:
An Annotated Edition. Vanderbilt Univ., 1964. Dissertation:
English.
Latta, Charles M. Reason in Fooldom: George Washington Harris'
Sut Lovingood. Univ. of Louisville, 1967. Thesis: English.
Plater, Ormonde. Narrative Folklore in the Works of George
Washington Harris. Tulane Univ., 1969. Dissertation:
English.

JOEL CHANDLER HARRIS (1848-1908)

Barnes, Madeleine. Joel Chandler Harris' *Nights with Uncle Remus*:
The Question of Origin. Univ. of Kansas, 1965. Thesis:
English.
Brookes, Stella B. Folklore in the Writings of Joel Chandler
Harris. Cornell Univ., 1946. Dissertation: English.
Calder, Norman D. A Historical Interpretation of the Uncle
Remus Stories. Univ. of Utah, 1967. Thesis: English.
Cousins, Paul M. Joel Chandler Harris: A Study in the Culture
of the South, 1848-1908. Columbia Univ., 1966. Disser-
tation: English.
Dance, Willis L. Georgia Life in the Stories of Joel Chandler
Harris. Duke Univ., 1933. Thesis: English.
Ellison, Rhoda C. Joel Chandler Harris. Columbia Univ., 1929.
Thesis: English.
Fisher, Alice M. Studies in Uncle Remus. Colorado College, 1933.
Thesis: English.
Green, Sue B. A Bibliography of Joel Chandler Harris. Emory
Univ., 1939. Thesis: English.
Griffis, Deane P. The Negro as Intermediary of Reconciliation in
the Writings of Joel Chandler Harris. Tulane Univ., 1951.
Thesis: English.
Henderson, Mary M. Folklore in the Uncle Remus Stories. Univ.
of South Carolina, 1932. Thesis: English.
Herndon, Jerry A. Social Comment in the Writings of Joel Chandler
Harris. Duke Univ., 1966. Dissertation: English.
Ives, Sumner A. The Negro Dialect of the Uncle Remus Stories.
Univ. of Texas (Austin), 1950. Dissertation: English.
Johnson, Charles W.M. An Annotated Checklist of Joel Chandler
Harris Manuscripts in the Memorial Collection of the Emory
University Library. Emory Univ., 1934. Dissertation:
English.
Johnson, Susan E. Joel Chandler Harris without "Uncle Remus."
(A Critical Study of Joel Chandler Harris as a Writer of
the Mountaineer and the Georgia Cracker during the Confederate
War and the Reconstruction Period.). Univ. of Georgia, 1943.
Thesis: English.
Jones, Robert L. (Mrs.). Uncle Remus: A Study of the Slave Negro.
Southern Methodist Univ., 1924. Thesis: English.

Kelly, Kathleen E. The Uncle Remus Stories: A Portrayal of the
Plantation Negro. Duke Univ., 1946. Thesis: Education.
Lavin, Elizabeth I. A Survey of the Criticism on Joel Chandler
Harris. St. John's Univ. (N.Y.), 1940. Thesis: English.
Lowery, John H. Joel Chandler Harris: His Journalistic Rise to
Literary Fame. Univ. of Georgia, 1965. Thesis: English.
McKneely, Lewis M. Analysis of the Local Color Elements in the
Novels of Joel Chandler Harris. Emory Univ., 1943. Thesis:
English.
McLeod, Agnes A. Joel Chandler Harris. Columbia Univ., 1914.
Thesis: English.
Noll, Irene. The Types of Poor Whites in the Stories of Joel
Chandler Harris. Univ. of Kansas, 1934. Thesis: English.
Norwood, Lila R. A Literary History of Joel Chandler Harris's
Uncle Remus. Univ. of Texas (Austin), 1944. Thesis:
English.
Ray, Charles A. A Study of Realism in the Writings of Joel
Chandler Harris. Univ. of Southern California, 1952.
Dissertation: English.
Sellers, Bettie M. Beyond Uncle Remus: A Study of Some of Joel
Chandler Harris' Negro Characters. Univ. of Georgia, 1966.
Thesis: English.
Stevens, Annie W. An Inquiry into the Sources of the Beast Tales
of Joel Chandler Harris. Columbia Univ., 1921. Thesis:
English.
Strother, Louise M. Joel Chandler Harris. Univ. of Georgia, 1936.
Thesis: English.
Taylor, Celia B. Cherokee and Creek Folklore Elements in the
Uncle Remus Stories: A Comparison of the Tales by Joel
Chandler Harris and Legends of the Southeast. Auburn Univ.,
1959. Thesis: English.
Taylor, Sr. Marie C. The Development of the Literary Personality
and the Inspiration of the Work of Joel Chandler Harris.
Villanova Univ., 1945. Thesis: English.
Tubb, Hilda. Characteristics of Negroes and Animals in the Uncle
Remus Stories. George Peabody College, 1925. Thesis:
English.
Underwood, J.K. J.C. Harris' Portrayal of Negro Life after the
War. George Peabody College, 1931. Thesis: English.
Walton, David A. A Study of Compensation in Uncle Remus: His
Songs and Sayings. Bowling Green State Univ., 1966.
Thesis: English.
Washburn, B.E. The Uncle Remus Stories. Univ. of North Carolina
(Chapel Hill), 1909. Thesis: English.
Whitten, N.M. A Study of the Fiction of Joel Chandler Harris.
Univ. of Mississippi, 1959. Thesis: English.
Wiggins, Robert L. Joel Chandler Harris, The Formative Years.
Univ. of Virginia, 1915. Dissertation: English.
Williamson, May. Joel Chandler Harris. Oglethorpe Univ., 1937.
Thesis: English.

CONSTANCE CARY HARRISON (1843-1920)

Hartness, Edna B. Plantation Life in Virginia as Revealed in Mrs.
Burton Harrison's Fiction. Duke Univ., 1939. Thesis: English.

ATTICUS GREENE HAYGOOD (1839-1896)

Howie, Naomi. Atticus Greene Haygood: Christian Educator and
    Humanitarian. Duke Univ., 1939. Thesis: Religion.
Mann, Harol W. The Life and Times of Atticus Greene Haygood.
    Duke Univ., 1962. Dissertation: History.
Smith, Marion L. Atticus Greene Haygood: Christian Educator.
    Yale Univ., 1928. Dissertation: Education.

PAUL HAMILTON HAYNE (1830-1886)

Arant, Frances. Paul Hamilton Hayne: A Study. Columbia Univ.,
    1927. Thesis: English.
Gibson, Harvey T. The Early Poetry of Paul Hamilton Hayne, 1848-
    1865. Duke Univ., 1935. Thesis: English.
Hardendorff, Victor H. Paul Hamilton Hayne and the North. Duke
    Univ., 1942. Thesis: English.
Johnson, Tezzie O. Paul Hamilton Hayne: A Representative Southern
    Poet. Univ. of Texas (Austin), 1943. Thesis: English.
Parks, Lillian L. An Appraisal of Paul Hamilton Hayne's Sonnets
    in the American Sonnet Tradition. Univ. of North Carolina
    (Chapel Hill), 1947. Thesis: English.
Plyler, Conrad A. Paul Hamilton Hayne: A Man of Letters. Wofford
    College, 1935. Thesis: English.
Rodgers, Elena. The Life and Poetry of Paul Hamilton Hayne.
    Louisiana State Univ., 1937. Thesis: English.

WILLIAM HAMILTON HAYNE (1856-1929)

Tolbert, Dorothy J. Life and Poetry of William Hamilton Hayne.
    Wofford College, 1930. Thesis: English.

WILLIAM SHAKESPEARE HAYS (1837-1907)

Grise, George C. Will S. Hays, His Life and Works. George Peabody
    College, 1947. Thesis: English.

LAFACADIO HEARN (1850-1904)

Bass, Ray. Lafcadio Hearn: His Life and His Literary Thought.
    Univ. of Mississippi, 1946. Thesis: English.
Briessen, Fritz van. Stil und Form bei Lafcadio Hearn. Giessen,
    1937. Dissertation: English.
Chekenian, Iris. Lafcadio Hearn: Commentator on Nineteenth-
    Century English Literature. Duke Univ., 1951. Thesis:
    English.
Clark, Christopher T. The Bohemian as Moralist: The Paradox of
    Lafcadio Hearn. Georgetown Univ., 1966. Thesis: English.
Cohn, Meyer. Lafcadio Hearn. Columbia Univ., 1916. Thesis:
    English.
Collins, Henry H. Lafcadio Hearn and Japan. Columbia Univ., 1917.
    Thesis: English.
Cortale, Frank. A Context for Some of Lafcadio Hearn's Views on
    Japanese Life and Folkways. Brooklyn College, 1962. Thesis:
    English.

Coyne, Robert. Lafcadio Hearn's Criticism of English Literature. Florida State Univ., 1969. Dissertation: English.

Derrickson, Howard S. Biographies of Lafcadio Hearn. Washington Univ. (St. Louis), 1942. Thesis: English.

Dorough, Charles D. The Life and Mind of Lafcadio Hearn. Univ. of Texas (Austin), 1936. Thesis: English.

Frost, Orcutt W., Jr. The Early Life of Lafcadio Hearn. Univ. of Illinois, 1954. Dissertation: English.

Garig, Aminie R. Lafcadio Hearn: The Man and His Works. Louisiana State Univ., 1929. Thesis: English.

Gaulding, Roxie G. Lafcadio Hearn in New Orleans. Duke Univ., 1939. Thesis: English.

Gowdy, Robert C. The Theme of Ghosts in the Writings of Lafacadio Hearn. Louisiana State Univ., 1964. Thesis: English.

Green, Innes E. The Treatment of Death in the Writings of Lafcadio Hearn. Northeast Louisiana Univ., 1966. Thesis: English.

Gross, S.W. Some Aspects of the Orientalism of Lafcadio Hearn. Brooklyn College, 1942. Thesis: English.

Hamlin, Mary A. Southern Regionalism in the Writings of Lafcadio Hearn. George Peabody College, 1942. Thesis: English.

Jordan, Gerald M. The Literary Criticism of Lafcadio Hearn, Based on Lectures Given at the University of Tokyo during 1896-1902. Univ. of Southern California, 1948. Thesis: English.

Kiley, George B. The Social Attitudes of Lafcadio Hearn. Univ. of Pittsburgh, 1947. Thesis: English.

Lawless, Ray M. Lafcadio Hearn, Critic of American Life and Letters. Univ. of Chicago, 1940. Dissertation: English.

Liptzin, Solomon. Lafcadio Hearn, the Teacher. Columbia Univ., 1922. Thesis: English.

McAdow, Margaret A. A Descriptive Bibliography of the Writings of Lafcadio Hearn (1850-1904). Texas Christian Univ., 1966. Thesis: English.

McKinnon, William T. The Life and Work of Lafcadio Hearn. Univ. of South Carolina, 1926. Thesis: English.

Mestayer, Myrtle. Lafcadio Hearn in New Orleans. Louisiana State Univ., Thesis: English.

Morrison, Robert F. The Growth of the Mind and Art of Lafcadio Hearn. Univ. of Wisconsin, 1941. Dissertation: English.

Nelson, Bonnie. A Study of Lafcadio Hearn's Understanding of Beauty. Columbia Univ., 1963. Thesis: English.

Nomura, Hanji. Lafcadio Hearn and his Interpretation of Japan. Stanford Univ., 1915. Thesis: English.

Patterson, Vernon K. Lafcadio Hearn: The Teacher in Japan. Univ. of Southern California, 1946. Thesis: English.

Pierce, Berta M. Lafcadio Hearn in Louisiana. George Peabody College, 1928. Thesis: English.

Pleasants, Martha G. Lafcadio Hearn: His Life and Work. Tulane Univ., 1905. Thesis: English.

Ravetch, P.H. Lafcadio Hearn's Appraisal of Japanese Life and Culture. Brooklyn College, 1948. Thesis: English.

Ray, Marguerite M. Verbal Artistry in the Writings of Lafcadio Hearn. Vanderbilt Univ., 1950. Thesis: English.

Russell, Carol S. Lafcadio Hearn in Japan: His Life, Critics, Lectures, Fairy Tales. Univ. of Texas (Austin), 1958. Thesis: English.
Suzuki, Kazudo. A Critical Study of the Sources of Lafcadio Hearn's Japanese Folk Tales. Univ. of Southern California, 1941. Thesis: English.
Swanson, Kathryn. A Study of the Development of Lafcadio Hearn's Style. Univ. of Minnesota, 1928. Thesis: English.
Tuttle, Allen E. Lafcadio Hearn and Herbert Spencer. Northwestern Univ., 1950. Dissertation: English.
Vincent, Mary L. Lafcadio Hearn and Late Romanticism. Univ. of Minnesota, 1967. Dissertation: English.
Ward, Allie M. Lafcadio Hearn: Interpreter of Japanese Life. Univ. of Oklahoma, 1939. Thesis: English.
Wertheim, Martha H. Definite and Precise Use of Color in Selected Writings of Lafcadio Hearn. Bowling Green State Univ., 1955. Thesis: English.
Wilkes, Anita E. Lafcadio Hearn: Orientalist. Columbia Univ., 1937. Thesis: English.
Wright, Bertram C. Lafcadio Hearn: Interpreter of English Literature. Univ. of Texas (El Paso), 1962. Thesis: English. [Hearn's lectures on English literature to his students at the Imperial University, Tokyo, 1896-1902, explaining to the Oriental that which seems exotic in western literature]
Wulf, Ingeborg. Das Japanbild Lafcadio Hearns. Freie Universität (West Berlin), 1951. Dissertation: English.
Young, Dorothy T. Lafcadio Hearn's Tokyo Lectures. Columbia Univ., 1943. Thesis: English.
Yu, Beongcheon. An Ape of Gods: A Study of Lafcadio Hearn. Brown Univ., 1958. Dissertation: English.

LILLIAN HELLMAN (1905-   )

Ackley, Meredith E. The Plays of Lillian Hellman. Univ. of Pennsylvania, 1969. Dissertation: English.
Brockington, John. A Critical Analysis of the Plays of Lillian Hellman. Yale Univ., 1962. Dissertation: Drama.
Brown, Kent R. Lillian Hellman and Her Critics. Univ. of California (Santa Barbara), 1967. Thesis: Dramatic Art.
Dessler, Harold. Lillian Hellman: An Evaluation. Univ. of North Carolina (Chapel Hill), 1948. Thesis: English.
Haller, Charles D. The Concept of Moral Failure in the Eight Original Plays of Lillian Hellman. Tulane Univ., 1967. Dissertation: Theater.
Hines, John H. The Intermissions as Essential Dramatic Units in Well Constructed Realistic Plays, as Illustrated in the Dramas of Lillian Hellman. Tufts Univ., 1963. Thesis: Drama.
Kalaher, Lucille F. The Theme of Evasive Idealism in the Plays of Lillian Hellman. Univ. of Wyoming, 1964. Thesis: English.
Keller, Alvin J. Form and Content in the Plays of Lillian Hellman: A Structural Analysis. Stanford Univ., 1965. Dissertation: English.
Lederer, Katherine G. The Critical Reaction to the Dramatic Works of Lillian Hellman. Univ. of Arkansas, 1967. Dissertation: English.

Lee, Flora M.S. The Forces of Evil in the Plays of Lillian Hellman. Hardin-Simmons Univ., 1951. Thesis: English.

Parrish, James A. A Study of the Plays of Lillian Hellman. Florida State Univ., 1949. Thesis: English.

Robertson, Helen E. Lillian Hellman and the Psychology of Evil. Univ. of Texas (Austin), 1964. Thesis: English.

Schemerhorn, Leora H. Lillian Hellman: Craftsman, Moralist, Thinker. Stetson Univ., 1966. Thesis: English.

Shropshire, Anne W. The Plays of Lillian Hellman: A Study in Contemporary Drama. Univ. of Kentucky, 1946. Thesis: English.

Triesch, Manfred. Lillian Hellman: Eine Analyse und Wuerdigung. Frankfurt, 1964. Dissertation: English.

Whitesides, Glenn E. Lillian Hellman: A Biographical and Critical Study. Florida State Univ., 1968. Dissertation: English.

HINTON ROWAN HELPER (1829-1909)

Cardoso, Joaquin J. The Treason of Belief: A Critical Study of Hinton Rowan Helper of North Carolina. Lehigh Univ., 1959. Thesis: History.

_____. Hinton Rowan Helper: A Nineteenth Century Pilgrimage. Univ. of Wisconsin, 1967. Dissertation: History.

Wall, James W. Hinton Rowan Helper and The Impending Crisis. Univ. of North Carolina (Chapel Hill), 1949. Thesis: History.

PATRICK HENRY (1736-1799)

Kneller, George R. Opposition to the Constitution: An Appraisal of Three Speeches of Patrick Henry at the Virginia Convention of 1788. Bowling Green State Univ., 1967. Thesis: Speech.

Mallory, Louis A. Patrick Henry: Orator of the American Revolution. Univ. of Wisconsin, 1939. Dissertation: English.

CAROLINE LEE HENTZ (1800-1856)

Berdan, Alan. Caroline Lee Hentz: Northern Defender of Southern Tradition. St. John's Univ. (N.Y.), 1948. Thesis: English.

Carter, Maude. A Study of Caroline Lee Hentz, Sentimentalist of the Fifties. Duke Univ., 1942. Thesis: English.

Enloe, Mildred. A Criticism of Mrs. Caroline Lee Hentz. Auburn Univ., 1936. Thesis: English.

Hardy, Evelyn. Mrs. Caroline Lee Hentz: A Woman of Her Time. Auburn Univ., 1935. Thesis: English.

Moran, Neva R. Caroline Lee Hentz; an Early Southern Novelist: A Study of the Life and Works of Mrs. Caroline Lee Hentz. Birmingham-Southern College, 1937. Thesis: English.

Whichard, Lindsay R. Caroline Lee Hentz, Pro-Slavery Propagandist. Univ. of North Carolina (Chapel Hill), 1951. Thesis: English.

Zimmerman, John J. The Novels of Caroline Lee Hentz. Univ. of Florida, 1949. Thesis: English.

HILARY ABNER HERBERT (1834-1919)

Hammett, Hugh B. Hilard Abner Herbert: A Southerner Returns to the Union. Univ. of Virginia, 1969. Dissertation: History.

JOHN HILL HEWITT (1801-1890)

Alexander, Marianne E. John Hill Hewitt--A Shadow on the Wall: A Study of the Reflections and Contributions of a Nineteenth Century Composer, Editor, and Poet. Univ. of Maryland, 1964. Thesis: English.
Huggins, Coy E. John Hill Hewitt: Bard of the Confederacy. Florida State Univ., 1964. Dissertation: Music.

DUBOSE HEYWARD (1885-1940)

Bailey, Rosalie V. DuBose Heyward: Poet, Novelist, Playwright. Duke Univ., 1941. Thesis: English.
Creighton, Nannie E. DuBose Heyward and His Contribution to Literature. Univ. of South Carolina, 1933. Thesis: English.
Cooper, John W. A Comparative Study of *Porgy*, the Novel, *Porgy*, the Play, and *Porgy and Bess*, the Folk Opera. Columbia Univ., 1950. Thesis: English.
Crammond, Dorothy W. DuBose Heyward's Treatment of the Negro in the Play *Porgy*. Univ. of North Carolina, 1964. Thesis: Dramatic Art.
Durham, Francis M. DuBose Heyward: The Southerner as Artist: A Critical and Biographical Study. Columbia Univ., 1953. Dissertation: English.
Macfie, Anne E. The Representation of Aristocrats in the Novels of DuBose Heyward. Univ. of North Carolina (Chapel Hill), 1958. Thesis: English.
Whitesides, Glenn E. DuBose Heyward and the Mediums of *Porgy*. Florida State Univ., 1960. Thesis: English.

WALTER BARNARD HILL (1851-1905)

Mathis, Mary K. Walter Barnard Hill: Constructive Southern American. Georgia Southern College, 1969. Thesis: History.

WILLIAM W. HOLDEN (1818-1892)

Folk, Edgar E. W.W. Holden, Civil War Editor. Columbia Univ., 1931. Thesis: Journalism.
_____. William W. Holden, Political Journalist, Editor of The North Carolina *Standard*, 1843-1865. George Peabody College, 1934. Dissertation: English.

GEORGE FREDERICK HOLMES (1820-1897)

Betts, Leonidas. George Frederick Holmes: A Critical Biography of a Nineteenth Century Southern Educator. Duke Univ., 1966. Dissertation: English-Education.

[91]

JOHNSON JONES HOOPER (1815-1862)

Kelley, Marion. The Life and Writings of Johnson Jones Hooper.
    Auburn Univ., 1934. Thesis: English.
Smith, Howard W. Johnson Jones Hooper: A Critical Study.
    Vanderbilt Univ., 1963. Thesis: English.
_____. An Annotated Edition of Hooper's *Some Adventures of
    Captain Simon Suggs*. Vanderbilt Univ., 1965. Dissertation:
    English.
Tuggle, Thomas T. Folklore in the Humorous Works of Johnson Jones
    Hooper. Univ. of Georgia, 1968. Thesis: English.

GEORGE MOSES HORTON (1798(?)-Ca. 1880)

Lakin, Mattie T.T. The Life of George Moses Horton. North Carolina
    College (Durham), 1951. Thesis: English.

SAM HOUSTON (1793-1863)

Doegey, Lorayne M. Sam Houston: Southern Spokesman for the Cause
    of Union. Southern Illinois Univ. (Carbondale), 1968.
    Dissertation: Speech.
Friend, Lierena B. The Great Designer: Sam Houston in the American
    Political Scene. Univ. of Texas (Austin), 1951. Dissertation:
    History.
Mitchell, Yetta G. An Evaluation of Sam Houston's Oratory. Univ.
    of Southern California, 1945. Thesis: Speech.
Rosson, Dorothy M. A Biography of Sam Houston for Use in High
    School Language Arts Classes. Univ. of Texas (Austin), 1961.
    Thesis: Education.

R.B.C. HOWELL (1801-1868)

Spain, Rufus B. R.B.C. Howell, Tennessee Baptist, 1801-1868.
    Vanderbilt Univ., 1948. Thesis: History.

LANGSTON HUGHES (1920-1960)

Dickinson, Donald C. A Bio-Bibliography of Langston Hughes, 1920-
    1960. Univ. of Michigan, 1964. Dissertation: Library
    Science.
Emanuel, James A. The Short Stories of Langston Hughes. Columbia
    Univ., 1962. Dissertation: English.
Hill, Eloise H. Langston Hughes: Versatile Spokesman for His
    Race. Northeast Missouri State College, 1957. Thesis:
    English.
Russell, Mildred P. Race Consciousness of Langston Hughes as
    Portrayed in His Writings. East Texas State Univ., 1949.
    Thesis: English.
Zeidman, Nathalie. The Image of the Negro through the Eyes of
    Langston Hughes. Roosevelt Univ., 1962. Thesis: English.

KERMIT HUNTER (1910-   )

Rogers, Lawrence B. The Influence of Kermit Hunter on American
    Outdoor Drama. East Tennessee State Univ., 1960. Thesis:
    English.

ROBERT HANCOCK HUNTER (1813-1902)

Eanes, Evelyn L. The Orthography and Phonology of *The Narrative
    of Robert Hancock Hunter*: A Study in the Origins of Texas
    Speech. Univ. of Texas (Austin), 1939. Thesis: English.

R.M.T. HUNTER (1809-1887)

Fisher, John E. Statesman of the Lost Cause: The Career of
    R.M.T. Hunter, 1859-87. Univ. of Virginia, 1966. Thesis:
    History.

ZORA NEALE HURSTON (1901(?)-1960)

Brown, Judith B. Point of View in Zora Neale Hurston's Florida
    Novels. Univ. of Florida, 1969. Thesis: English.
Pastor, Maria D. Social Overtones in the Works of Zora Neale
    Hurston. Univ. of Florida, 1959. Thesis: History.
Turner, Kenneth W. Negro Collectors of Negro Folklore: A Study
    of J. Mason Brewer and Zora Neale Hurston. East Texas State
    Univ., 1964. Thesis: English.

JOSEPH HOLT INGRAHAM (1809-1860)

French, Warren G. Joseph Holt Ingraham, Southern Romancer, 1809-
    1860. Univ. of Texas (Austin), 1948. Thesis: English.
Turnipseed, James O. Joseph Holt Ingraham: His Life and Works.
    Auburn Univ., 1938. Thesis: English.

JAMES IREDELL (1751-1799)

Herndon, Nettis S. James Iredell. Duke Univ., 1944. Dissertation:
    English.

HENRY ROOTES JACKSON (1820-1898)

Mack, Kent E. The Early Life of Henry Rootes Jackson. Univ. of
    Georgia, 1939. Thesis: English.

CECILIA VIETS JAMISON (1837-1909)

Brown, Harper G. Mrs. Cecilia Viets Jamison: A Critical and
    Biographical Study. Tulane Univ., 1931. Thesis: English.

RANDALL JARRELL (1914-1965)

Aronson, Paula E. The Antiwar Poetry of Randall Jarrell. Sacramento
    State College, 1969. Thesis: English.

Cline, Hermina J. Randall Jarrell: An Evaluation and Inter-
pretation. Samford Univ., 1969. Thesis: English.
Durrell, John B. The Difficult Resolution in the Poetry of Randall
Jarrell. Univ. of Virginia, 1962. Thesis: English.
Eisiminger, Sterling K. The Poetry of Randall Jarrell: A Study of
Its Critical Acceptance and the Poet's Development of His
Major Themes and Motifs. Auburn Univ., 1968. Thesis: English.
Fisher, Nancy M. Fantasy and Reality in the Poetry of Randall
Jarrell. Univ. of Tennessee, 1969. Dissertation: English.
Gillikin, Dure J. Conventions in Randall Jarrell's War Poems. Univ.
of North Carolina (Chapel Hill), 1958. Thesis: English.
Hayden, John P. The Poetic Language of Randall Jarrell. Univ. of
Portland, 1964. Thesis: English.
Honeycutt, Laura B. Randall Jarrell: A Study of His World, His
War, His Woods. East Tennessee State Univ., 1969. Thesis:
English.
Hughes, Betty S. The Dream Motif in the Poetic Works of Randall
Jarrell. Lamar Univ., 1966. Thesis: English.
Killgallon, Donald A. The Literary Criticism of Randall Jarrell.
Univ. of Maryland, 1966. Thesis: English.
Leidig, Daniel G., Jr. Jarrell as Critic. Vanderbilt Univ., 1954.
Thesis: English.
Schwartz, John M. An Introduction to the Poems of Randall Jarrell.
Univ. of California (Los Angeles), 1969. Dissertation:
English.
Torres, F.B., F.S.C. Randall Jarrell: A Critical Study. Villanova
Univ., 1961. Thesis: English.
Vardamis, Alex A. Randall Jarrell: Poem and *Marchen*. Columbia
Univ., 1967. Thesis: English.

THOMAS JEFFERSON (1743-1826)

Adams, Dickinson W. Jefferson's Politics of Morality: The Purpose
and Meaning of His Extracts from the Evangelists: "The
Philosophy of Jesus Nazareth" and "The Life and Morals of
Jesus of Nazareth." Brown Univ., 1970. Dissertation: American
Civilization.
Adams, Mary P. Jefferson's Military Policy with Special Reference
to the Frontiers, 1805-1809. Univ. of Virginia, 1958.
Dissertation: History.
Arnold, Malcolm H. Thomas Jefferson--a Pioneer in Anglo-Saxon.
Univ. of Virginia, 1915. Dissertation: English.
Bär, Max. Thomas Jefferson, eine Engwicklungsgeschichte seiner
demokratischen Ideen. Erlangen, 1951. Dissertation: English.
Brewer, Paul W. Jefferson's Administration of Patronage: New
York, 1801-1804. Univ. of Virginia, 1968. Thesis: History.
Bridges, David L. A Historical Study of Thomas Jefferson. North
Texas State Univ., 1958. Thesis: History.
Brooks, Joan L. Jefferson and Bryant: The Embargoes. Univ. of
Virginia, 1966. Thesis: English.
Brown, Edward A. An Investigation of the Attitudes Expressed by
Richmond's Press toward Thomas Jefferson in the Presidential
Elections of 1800, 1804, and 1808. Univ. of Richmond, 1964.
Thesis: History.

Carey, Alma P. Thomas Jefferson's Ideal University: Dream and Actuality. Univ. of Texas (Austin), 1937. Thesis: Education.

Carey, Paul M. Jefferson and Slavery. Univ. of Virginia, 1952. Thesis: History.

Ciolli, Antoinette. Thomas Jefferson as a Man of Science. Brooklyn College, 1940. Thesis: History.

Colbourn, Harold T. The Saxon Heritage: Thomas Jefferson Looks at English History. Johns Hopkins Univ., 1953. Dissertation: History.

Coleman, John. The Concept of Equality as Held by Thomas Jefferson. Univ. of Pittsburgh, 1934. Dissertation: Philosophy.

Cragan, Thomas M. Thomas Jefferson's Early Attitudes toward Manufacturing, Agriculture, and Commerce. Univ. of Tennessee, 1965. Dissertation: History.

Crenshaw, Frank S. Minor Architectural Designs of Thomas Jefferson. The Executed and Non-executed Residential Designs and Executed Non-residential Designs. Univ. of Virginia, 1961. Thesis: History.

Dodd, William E. Thomas Jefferson's Ruckkehr zur Politik 1796. Leipzig, 1900. Dissertation: English.

Eubanks, Seaford W. A Vocabulary Study of Thomas Jefferson's *Notes on Virginia*. Univ. of Missouri, 1940. Thesis: English.

Floyd, Mildred D. Thomas Jefferson and the Louisiana Purchase. Atlanta Univ., 1951. Thesis: History.

Hall, Richard. Jefferson and the Physiocrats. Univ. of Virginia, 1950. Thesis: Rural Social Economics.

Hanchette, William F., Jr. Politics and the Judiciary under Jefferson. Univ. of California (Berkeley), 1949. Thesis: History.

Harrold, Frances L. Thomas Jefferson and the Commonwealth of Virginia: A Study in Constitutional Thought. Bryn Mawr College, 1960. Dissertation: History.

Hash, Ronald J. Slavery on Thomas Jefferson's Plantations. Millersville State College, 1969. Thesis: Social Science.

Heslep, Robert D. The Views of Jefferson and Dewey as Bases for Clarifying the Role of Education in an American Democratic State. Univ. of Chicago, 1963. Dissertation: Education.

Huegli, Jon M. Jeffersonian Rhetoric: Persistent Witness to Democratic Republicanism. Indiana Univ., 1967. Thesis: Speech and Theater.

Johnson, Luciana. Thomas Jefferson and the Beginning of the Republican Party (1790-1792). Univ. of California (Riverside), 1956. Thesis: History.

Johnson, Peggy A. "Diamonds in a Dunghill": The Gospel According to Thomas Jefferson. Univ. of California (Riverside), 1967. Thesis: History.

Jones, Paul W. Jefferson and the *National Gazette*. Bowling Green State Univ., 1961. Thesis: History.

Koch, Adrienne. The Philosophy of Thomas Jefferson. Columbia Univ., 1944. Dissertation: Philosophy.

Lacy, Alexander B., Jr. Jefferson and Congress: Congressional Method and Politics, 1801-1809. Univ. of Virginia, 1964. Dissertation: Political Science.

Levy, Richard. The First Inaugural Address of Thomas Jefferson: The Founding of the American Republic. Univ. of Chicago, 1966. Thesis: Political Science.

Lindley, Thomas F., Jr. The Philosophical Presuppositions of Thomas Jefferson's Social Theories. Boston Univ., 1952. Dissertation: Philosophy.

Lokensgard, Hjalmar O. Aristocratic Elements in Jefferson's Educational Plan. Univ. of Iowa, 1932. Thesis: English.

Long, Everett L. Jefferson and Congress: A Study of the Jeffersonian Legislative System, 1801-1809. Univ. of Missouri, 1966. Dissertation: History.

Martin, Edwin. Thomas Jefferson and the Idea of Progress. Univ. of Wisconsin, 1942. Dissertation: English.

Moffat, Alexander D. A Defense of the New World: Jefferson's *Notes on Virginia* and Some 18th Century Theories of American Degeneracy. Southern Methodist Univ., 1966. Thesis: History.

Montgomery, Henry C. Thomas Jefferson and the Classical Tradition. Univ. of Illinois, 1946. Dissertation: History.

Mumper, James A. The Jefferson Image in the Federalist Mind, 1801-1809: Jefferson's Administration from the Federalist Point of View. Univ. of Virginia, 1966. Dissertation: History.

Nolan, Carolyn G. Thomas Jefferson: Gentleman Musician. Univ. of Virginia, 1967. Thesis: Music.

Norton, Paul F. Latrobe, Jefferson, and the National Capitol. Princeton Univ., 1952. Dissertation: Fine Arts.

Osborn, Robert W. Portrait of a Revolutionary: Thomas Jefferson and the Coming of the American Revolution. Fort Hays Kansas State College, 1969. Thesis: History.

Peden, William H. Thomas Jefferson: Book Collector. Univ. of Virginia, 1942. Dissertation: English.

Peterson, Merrill D. The Jefferson Image in the American Mind, 1826-1861. Harvard Univ., 1950. Dissertation: American Studies.

Pulley, Judith P. Thomas Jefferson at the Court of Versailles: An American *Philosophe* and the Coming of the French Revolution. Univ. of Virginia, 1966. Dissertation: History.

Rogers, Robert, Jr. Thomas Jefferson's Leadership of the Republican Party, January, 1797 to June, 1798. Univ. of California (Berkeley), 1953. Thesis: History.

Smith, Doris N. Thomas Jefferson's Proposals Concerning Public Education of an Educated Electorate. Bowling Green State Univ., 1962. Thesis: History.

Serpell, Jean K. Thomas Jefferson: His Relationship with France. Stetson Univ., 1957. Thesis: History.

Todd, Terry E. Thomas Jefferson and the Founding of the University of Virginia. Univ. of California (Riverside), 1965. Thesis: History.

Trainor, Sister M.R., C.S.J. Thomas Jefferson on Freedom of Conscience. St. John's Univ. (N.Y.), 1966. Dissertation: Philosophy.

Williams, Edward K. Jefferson's Theories of Language. Univ. of Wyoming, 1948. Thesis: English.

Williams, Kenneth R. The Ethics of Thomas Jefferson. Boston Univ., 1962. Dissertation: Philosophy.

JAMES WELDON JOHNSON (1871-1938)

Barksdale, Howard R. James Weldon Johnson as a Man of Letters.
    Fisk Univ., 1936. Thesis: English.
Clark, Peter W. A Study of the Poetry of James Weldon Johnson.
    Xavier Univ. (New Orleans), 1942. Thesis: English.
Crawford, Lucille H. The Musical Activities of James Weldon
    Johnson. Fisk Univ., 1941. Thesis: Music.
Eisenberg, Bernard. James Weldon Johnson and the National
    Association for the Advancement of Colored People, 1916-1934.
    Columbia Univ., 1968. Dissertation: History.
Gilbert, Louise. James Weldon Johnson, Citizen, Diplomat, Author.
    Sam Houston State Univ., 1951. Thesis: History.
Tate, Ernest C. The Social Implications of the Writings and the
    Career of James Weldon Johnson. New York Univ., 1959.
    Dissertation: English.

LYNDON BAINES JOHNSON (1908-1973)

Connelly, Fred M., Jr. A Rhetorical Analysis of Selected Speeches
    of Lyndon Baines Johnson on the War in Vietnam. Ohio State
    Univ., 1967. Dissertation: Speech.
Delson, Jane. Ethos or "Image" in Contemporary Political Persua-
    sion, with Particular Reference to Lyndon B. Johnson, 1964.
    Univ. of California (Los Angeles), 1967. Dissertation:
    Political Science.
Hall, Robert N. A Rhetorical Analysis of Selected Speeches of
    Senator Lyndon B. Johnson, 1955-1961. Univ. of Michigan,
    1963. Dissertation: Speech.

SIDDIE JOE JOHNSON (1905-   )

Nicholson, Mabel C. Siddie Joe Johnson: Her Contribution to
    Literature. East Texas State Univ., 1950. Thesis: English.

ANNIE FELLOWS JOHNSTON (1863-1931)

Wilson, Gladys. Annie Fellows Johnston and the Little Colonel
    Books. Western Kentucky Univ., 1936. Thesis: English.

MARY JOHNSTON (1870-1936)

Chapman, Mary E. Mary Johnston from Virginia to America. Longwood
    College, 1966. Thesis: English.
Conson, Virginia J. The Virginia History in the Historical Novels
    of Mary Johnston. George Peabody College, 1936. Thesis:
    English.
Edelmann, Louise L. Virginia Life in the Novels of Mary Johnston.
    Duke Univ., 1943. Thesis: English.
McCown, William F. Mary Johnston: The First Phase. Birmingham-
    Southern College, 1960. Thesis: English.
Patterson, Dorothya R. Mary Johnston as a Novelist. Southern
    Methodist Univ., 1941. Thesis: English.

Young, Claire S. Development of American Life as Shown in Mary
    Johnston's Novels. George Peabody College, 1932. Thesis:
    English.

RICHARD MALCOLM JOHNSTON (1822-1898)

Brinson, Lessie B. (Mrs. Fred) Richard Malcolm Johnston: Georgia
    Author. Univ. of Georgia, 1927. Thesis: English.
Dyar, Pat M. Schools and Teachers of Richard Malcolm Johnston.
    Univ. of Georgia, 1940. Thesis: English.
Eyler, Clement M. Richard Malcolm Johnston and His "Dukesborough
    Tales." Columbia Univ., 1926. Thesis: English.
Hendricks, Edna. Richard Malcolm Johnston. Univ. of Georgia, 1936.
    Thesis: English.
Martin, Minerva. Richard Malcolm Johnston, a Local Colorist.
    Louisiana State Univ., 1937. Thesis: English.
Pittman, Frances E.H. Middle Georgia Life in the Fiction of
    Richard Malcolm Johnston. Duke Univ., 1941. Thesis: English.
Tumulty, C.M., Michael J. The Virtue of Honesty as Reflected in
    the Life and Works of Richard Malcolm Johnston. St. John's
    Univ. (N.Y.), 1956. Thesis: English.
Wood, James W. Richard Malcolm Johnston. Univ. of South Carolina,
    1931. Thesis: English.

WILLIAM PRESTON JOHNSTON (1831-1899)

Shaw, Arthur M. The Life and Works of William Preston Johnston.
    Louisiana State Univ., 1941. Dissertation: English.

CHARLES COLCOCK JONES, JR. (1831-1893)

Moore, Hamilton F. Charles Colcock Jones, Jr.: Romanticist.
    Univ. of Georgia, 1935. Thesis: English.

JOHN BEAUCHAMP JONES (1810-1866)

Brockman, Clark. John Beauchamp Jones. Univ. of South Carolina,
    1937. Thesis: English.

MADISON JONES (1925-   )

Helbert, Aubrey F. The Agrarian Vision of Madison Jones. Hardin-
    Simmons Univ., 1969. Thesis: English.

HELEN ADAMS KELLER (1880-1968)

Collins, Louise H. Helen Adams Keller: Her Life and Work. Auburn
    Univ., 1949. Thesis: English.

FRANCES ANNE KEMBLE (1809-1893)

Driver, Leota S. Fannie Kemble Butler. Vanderbilt Univ., 1931.
    Dissertation: English.
Hymel, Margret C. Fanny Kemble: Dramatic Reader. Louisiana State
    Univ., 1942. Thesis: Speech.

JAMES LAWSON KEMPER (1823-1865)

Jones, Robert R. Conservative Virginian: The Post-War Career
    of Governor James Lawson Kemper. Univ. of Virginia, 1964.
    Dissertation: History.
_____. Forgotten Virginian: The Early Life and Career of James
    Lawson Kemper, 1823-1865. Univ. of Virginia, 1961. Thesis:
    History.

AMOS KENDALL (1789-1869)

Daniels, James D. Amos Kendall: Cabinet Politician, 1829-1841.
    Univ. of North Carolina (Chapel Hill), 1968. Dissertation:
    History.
Lam, Kenneth F. Amos Kendall in Kentucky. Western Kentucky Univ.,
    1936. Thesis: History.
Marshall, Lynn L. The Early Career of Amos Kendall: The Making
    of a Jacksonian. Univ. of Southern California, 1962. Disser-
    tation: History.

GEORGE WILKINS KENDALL (1809-1867)

Bode, Gilbert R. The Life and Time of George Wilkins Kendall.
    Univ. of Texas (Austin), 1932. Thesis: History.
Copeland, Fayette. Kendall of the *Picayune*. Louisiana State Univ.,
    1945. Dissertation: History.

JOHN PENDLETON KENNEDY (1795-1870)

Adams, Christopher A. Study of the Life and Works of John Pendleton
    Kennedy. Trinity Univ. (Texas), 1940. Thesis: English.
Bohner, Charles H. John Pendleton Kennedy, Novelist and Nationalist.
    Univ. of Pennsylvania, 1957. Dissertation: English.
Boyer, Innes. The Note Book of John Pendleton Kennedy. Columbia
    Univ., 1935. Thesis: English.
Callahan, Br. Francis P., F.S.C. John Pendleton Kennedy, Novelist
    (1795-1870). Villanova Univ., 1943. Thesis: English.
Gwathmey, Edward M. A Literary Biography of John Pendleton Kennedy.
    Univ. of Virginia, 1926. Dissertation: English.
Harrison, Thomas D. The Novels of John Pendleton Kennedy, 1832-
    1840. Emory Univ., 1948. Thesis: English.
Jackson, Katie L. John Pendleton Kennedy as an Interpreter of
    Southern Life and History. Univ. of Texas (Austin), 1940.
    Thesis: English.
Kean, William A. Factors that Limited the Literary Productivity
    of John P. Kennedy. Columbia Univ., 1952. Thesis: English.
Lewis, Dimples. A Critical Study of the Literary Works of John
    Pendleton Kennedy. Univ. of Georgia, 1940. Thesis: English.
Moore, Rosa A.T. Kennedy's *Swallow Barn*, 1832 and 1851: A Study
    of Textual Variants. Univ. of Virginia, 1959. Thesis:
    English.
Osborne, William S. John Pendleton Kennedy: A Study of his
    Literary Career. Columbia Univ., 1960. Dissertation:
    English.

Pretzer, Wallace L. Eighteenth Century Literary Conventions in
    the Fictional Style of John Pendleton Kennedy. Univ. of
    Michigan, 1963. Dissertation: English.
Timlin, Thomas D. Romanticism in the Novels of John Pendleton
    Kennedy. St. John's Univ. (N.Y.), 1958. Thesis: English.
Tobiasson, Loran J. The Tradition of the Sketch as Seen in
    Irving's *Sketch Book* and *Bracebridge Hall*, Longfellow's
    Outre-Mer, and Kennedy's *Swallow Barn*. Brigham Young Univ.,
    1968. Dissertation: English.

FRANCIS SCOTT KEY (1778-1843)

Barcus, Annie E. Francis Scott Key. Columbia Univ., 1924. Thesis:
    English.

FRANCES PARKINSON KEYES (1885-1970)

Perich, Nancy L. Louisiana Novels of Frances Parkinson Keyes.
    Texas Christian Univ., 1967. Thesis: English.

JOSEPH BUCKNER KILLEBREW (1840-1906)

Smith, Samuel B. Joseph Buckner Killebrew and The New South
    Movement in Tennessee. Vanderbilt Univ., 1962. Dissertation:
    History.

ALINE KILMER (1888-1941)

Loveless, Mildred M. A Study of the Writings of Aline Kilmer.
    George Peabody College, 1930. Thesis: English.

GRACE ELIZABETH KING (1851-1932)

Hughes, Katherine E. Grace Elizabeth King: A Study in Local
    Color. Univ. of Texas (Austin), 1951. Thesis: English.
Jastremski, Sarah L. Grace King. Louisiana State Univ., 1929.
    Thesis: English.
Jones, Eunice E. The Short Stories of Grace Elizabeth King. Univ.
    of Kansas, 1936. Thesis: English.
Lester, Mrs. Lawrence T., Jr. Grace King. South Carolina, 1924.
    Thesis: English.

MARTIN LUTHER KING, JR. (1929-1968)

Carpenter, Joseph. The Leadership Philosophy of Dr. Martin Luther
    King, Jr.: Its Educational Implications. Marquette Univ.,
    1970. Dissertation: Sociology.
Grice, Nurline H. The Influence of Black Power on the Rhetorical
    Practices of Dr. Martin Luther King. Miami Univ. (Ohio),
    1968. Thesis: Speech.
Reeder, James D. Two Views of Civil Disobedience: Henry David
    Thoreau and Martin Luther King, Jr. Morehead State Univ.,
    1970. Thesis: English.

Smith, Donald H. Martin Luther King, Jr.: Rhetorician of Revolt.
    Univ. of Wisconsin, 1964. Dissertation: Speech.
Walton, Hanes, Jr. The Political Philosophy of Martin Luther
    King, Jr. Howard Univ., 1967. Dissertation: Political
    Science.
Warren, Mervyn A. A Rhetorical Study of the Preaching of Doctor
    Martin Luther King, Jr., Pastor and Pulpit Orator. Michigan
    State Univ., 1966.

FREDERICK HENRY KOCH (1877-1944)

Hagan, John P. Frederick Henry Koch and the American Folk Drama.
    Indiana Univ., 1969. Dissertation: Theater.

HARRY HARRISON KROLL (1888-1967)

Satterwhite, Joseph N. Harry Harrison Kroll and the New South.
    Vanderbilt Univ., 1950. Thesis: English.

JOSEPH WOOD KRUTCH (1893-1970)

Bauer, Judith A. Nature, Human Nature, and the Machine: A Study
    of Selected Writings of Joseph Wood Krutch. Bowling Green
    State Univ., 1969. Thesis: American Studies.
Green, Gordon C. An Analytical Study of the Dramatic Criticism
    of Joseph Wood Krutch as Published in the *Nation*, 1924-1952.
    Univ. of Southern California, 1959. Dissertation: Speech
    and Drama.
Green, Joseph G. Joseph Wood Krutch, Critic of the Drama. Indiana
    Univ., 1965. Dissertation: Speech and Drama.
Prizeman, Herbert H. Joseph Wood Krutch and The Human Image in
    Modern American Drama. Tulane Univ., 1969. Dissertation:
    Theater.

LUCIUS Q.C. LAMAR (1825-1893)

Murphy, James B. L.Q.C. Lamar: Pragmatic Patriot. Louisiana
    State Univ., 1968. Dissertation: History.
Reeves, Harry R. Lucius Q.C. Lamar as a Representative of Southern
    Literary Culture. Louisiana State Univ., 1938. Thesis:
    English.

MIRABEAU B. LAMAR (1798-1859)

Reese, Ruth S. Mirabeau B. Lamar, Father of Texas Education. Univ.
    of Texas (Austin), 1933. Thesis: Education.

JOHN MERCER LANGSTON (1829-1897)

Cheek, William F. III. Forgotten Prophet: The Life of John
    Mercer Langston. Univ. of Virginia, 1961. Dissertation:
    History.

EDWIN LANHAM (1904-   )

McGuire, Dorothy M. Edwin Lanham, Texas Novelist. East Texas
    State Univ., 1949. Thesis: English.

CLIFFORD ANDERSON LANIER (1844-1908)

Jones, David M. Clifford Anderson Lanier: The Man and His
    Literary Work. Univ. of Georgia, 1953. Thesis: English.

SIDNEY LANIER (1842-1881)

Abernethy, Cecil E. A Critical Edition of Sidney Lanier's *Tiger-
    Lilies*. Vanderbilt Univ., 1941. Dissertation: English.
Anderson, Denis M., Rev., O.F.M. Sidney Lanier and His Conception
    of Versification. St. Bonaventure Univ., 1947. Thesis:
    English.
Atkinson, Eleanor M. A Study of the Poetic Art of Sidney Lanier.
    Univ. of Texas (Austin), 1928. Thesis: English.
Belton, James E. The Reading Done by Sidney Lanier. Univ. of
    Illinois, 1937. Thesis: English.
Bergbauer, Sr. Corda M., O.S.F. Elements of English Romanticism
    in Sidney Lanier. Villanova Univ., 1963. Thesis: English.
Blitch, Lila M. Sidney Lanier: Artist, Critic, and Human Being.
    Univ. of Maryland, 1935. Thesis: English.
Brown, P.E. A Study of Sidney Lanier's Verse Technique. Univ. of
    Chicago, 1921. Thesis: English.
Bryan, W.F. Sidney Lanier's Poems: A Study in Style and Content.
    Univ. of North Carolina (Chapel Hill), 1908. Thesis: English.
Burnett, Gussie A. Study of Lanier's Poetic Art. Hardin-Simmons
    Univ., 1928. Thesis: English.
Cabaniss, Jelks H. Sidney Lanier: The Man and His Poetry. Univ.
    of Alabama, 1907. Thesis: English.
Capon, Reginald L. The Literary Critical Ideas of Sidney Lanier.
    Boston Univ., 1936. Thesis: English.
Coker, Lavinia C. A Study of Sidney Lanier's Attitude Toward
    Human Limitations. Univ. of South Carolina, 1933. Thesis:
    English.
Conrath, Mary C. The Poetic Technique of Sidney Lanier. Stetson
    Univ., 1933. Thesis: English.
Cox, Alice B. Sidney Lanier as a Nature Poet. Columbia Univ.,
    1910. Thesis: English.
Credo, Ethel. The Use of Figures of Speech in Lanier's Longer
    Poems. Univ. of Texas (Austin), 1938. Thesis: English.
Davis, J.R. The Treatment of Nature in the Poetry of Sidney Lanier.
    North Texas State Univ., 1938. Thesis: English.
DeBellis, Jack A. Sidney Lanier and the Morality of Feeling. Univ.
    of California (Los Angeles), 1964. Dissertation: English.
Earnest, Elizabeth. Sidney Lanier. George Washington Univ., 1923.
    Thesis: English.
Edwards, John S. Sidney Lanier: His Life and Work in Music.
    Univ. of Georgia, 1967. Thesis: English.
Egleston, Louise A. Sidney Lanier as a Critic and Interpreter of
    American Life. Univ. of North Carolina (Chapel Hill), 1931.
    Thesis: English.

Elliott, Winifred M.K. The Adam Image and the Christ Image in the Poetry of Sidney Lanier. Texas Christian Univ., 1963. Thesis: English.

Fesmire, William S. Contours of Lanier Criticism: A Study of the Critical Reputation of Sidney Lanier. Mississippi State Univ., 1965. Thesis: English.

Fife, Herzl. A Critique of the Prosody of Sidney Lanier. New York Univ., 1933. Thesis: English.

Fitzpatrick, Grace M. Sidney Lanier: A Study in the Development of Literary Craftsmanship. St. John's Univ. (N.Y.), 1940. Thesis: English.

Forsythe, Gladys M. Sidney Lanier the Man. Univ. of Maryland, 1928. Thesis: English.

Galbraith, Evelyn M.D. The Poetry of Sidney Lanier: A Study in Diction and Imagery. Univ. of Missouri, 1948. Thesis: English.

Garnett, Anna M. Sidney Lanier's Theory of Verse. Colorado College, 1946. Thesis: English.

Glover, Erman W. The Literary Reputation of Sidney Lanier's "The Centennial Meditation of Columbia." Univ. of North Carolina (Chapel Hill), 1964. Thesis: English.

Gourdin, Virginia B. Conflicts in the Poetry of Sidney Lanier. Univ. of South Carolina, 1951. Thesis: English.

Graham, Philip E. Sidney Lanier's Thought in Relation to that of His Age. Univ. of Chicago, 1927. Dissertation: English.

Griswold, Frances C. Sidney Lanier: His Theories of Verse in Relation to His Practice. Univ. of Illinois, 1927. Thesis: English.

Gummow, Willette A. A Study of Imagery in Lanier's Poetry. Univ. of Southern California, 1948. Thesis: English.

Hallbrook, Mamie S. A Study of the Music of Sidney Lanier's Poetry. George Peabody College, 1931. Thesis: English.

Hand, Miriam F. Sidney Lanier as Critic of Literature. Univ. of Georgia, 1959. Thesis: English.

Hanley, Evelyn A. Music and Prosody: An Analysis of Lanier's Verse. New York Univ., 1937. Thesis: English.

Havens, Elmer A. Sidney Lanier's Concept and Use of Nature. Univ. of Wisconsin, 1965. Dissertation: English.

Heath, Marguerite T. Sidney Lanier: A Study of Certain Phases of His Thinking. East Texas State Univ., 1951. Thesis: English.

Henderson, Irene S. Sidney Lanier's Imagery. Southwestern Univ., 1938. Thesis: English.

Hoffman, Mary E. Sidney Lanier. Ohio State Univ., 1931. Thesis: English.

Hollister, Cora. Sidney Lanier as a Critic of Literature. New York Univ., 1932. Thesis: English.

Hoover, Edna M. Studies in the Criticism of the Works of Sidney Lanier and the Development of his Reputation. Duke Univ., 1949. Thesis: English.

Housman, Anna B. Sidney Lanier as a Citizen of the World. Columbia Univ., 1925. Thesis: English.

Howard Chester J. A Study of the Religion of Sidney Lanier. Texas Christian Univ., 1962. Thesis: English.

_____. Sidney Lanier in 1967. Texas Christian Univ., 1968.
Dissertation: English.

Jestes, Dallas A. Sidney Lanier: A Critic of His Time. Columbia
Univ., 1952. Thesis: English.

Jones, Nancy J. Three American Nature Poets--Emerson, Lanier,
Whittier. Columbia Univ., 1945. Thesis: English.

Kerr, Carl A. Sidney Lanier As Poet: A Study in the "Intermittent
Mist of Defect." Ohio State Univ., 1951. Thesis: English.

King, Mildred B. Sidney Lanier's Social Philosophy as Revealed
in His Works. Univ. of Arizona, 1941. Thesis: English.

Knoll, Margaret F. The Poetry of Sidney Lanier. Pennsylvania
State Univ., 1933. Thesis: English.

Kramer, Rosella C. Sidney Lanier's Theory and Practice of Poetry.
Columbia Univ., 1926. Thesis: English.

Lipschitz, Louis. Sidney Lanier: His Place in American Literature.
New York Univ., 1931. Thesis: English.

McCaskill, Agnes S. Sidney Lanier. Oglethorpe Univ., 1936.
Thesis: English.

McCorvey, Eleanor P. The Poetry of Sidney Lanier. Univ. of
Alabama, 1906. Thesis: English.

McDowell, Edward A. Sidney Lanier as a Literary Critic.
Vanderbilt Univ., 1950. Thesis: English.

McGrath, Sr. Catharine M. An Appreciation of the Poetry of Sidney
Lanier. Villanova Univ., 1948. Thesis: English.

Marsh, Alice M. Love in Search of a Word: A Romantic Biography
of Sidney Lanier. Southwestern Univ., 1929. Thesis: English.

Maynard, Amanda J. A Study of Whitman's and Lanier's Poems of
the Sea. Univ. of North Carolina (Chapel Hill), 1959.
Thesis: English.

Miles, John W. The Influence of Music on the Poetry of Sidney
Lanier. Atlanta Univ., 1958. Thesis: English.

Mitchell, Ruth D. A Study of Smoky Mountain Regional Speech as
Used in Lanier's _Tiger-Lilies_. Univ. of South Carolina, 1963.
Thesis: English.

Moore, Lelia Z. Religious Element in Sidney Lanier's Works. Univ.
of Kansas, 1924. Thesis: English.

Morris, Alton C. A Study of the Nature Element in the Works of
Sidney Lanier. Univ. of Florida, 1928. Thesis: English.

Muldoon, Sr. Reparata M. Sidney Lanier: Self-Revealed. St.
Bonaventure Univ., 1960. Thesis: English.

Niessner, Gertrude. Sidney Lanier als Lyriker und seine metrischen
Theorien. Vienna, 1939. Dissertation: English.

O'Dowd, Sara C. An Appraisal of Sidney Lanier's _Science of English
Verse_. Iowa State Teachers College, 1964. Thesis: English.

Olson, Ruth H. The Poetry of Sidney Lanier. Univ. of Nebraska,
1935. Thesis: English.

Owings, Ralph S. Sidney Lanier: A Man of His Times. Wofford
College, 1935. Thesis: Education.

Pearce, Eva F. The Influence of Music on the Literary Career of
Sidney Lanier. Columbia Univ., 1913. Thesis: English.

Perry, Margaret E. Sidney Lanier: A Transitional Figure in
American Literature. Univ. of Alabama, 1939. Thesis: English.

Phillips, Ruth C. The Religion of Sidney Lanier. Univ. of
Tennessee, 1969. Thesis: English.

Preston, Miriam. The Correspondence of Sidney Lanier with Northern Authors. Vanderbilt Univ., 1952. Thesis: English.

Priddy, Jewell C. The Southern Scene as Reflected in the Works of Sidney Lanier. Univ. of Southern California, 1945. Thesis: English.

Pullen, Sr. M.C. Imagery of Sidney Lanier. Catholic Univ., 1940. Thesis: English.

Ribbens, Dennis N. The Reading Interests of Thoreau, Hawthorne, and Lanier. Univ. of Wisconsin, 1969. Dissertation: English.

Ritchey, Liane M. Sidney Lanier's Two Springs: Music and Poetry. Iowa State Teachers College, 1965. Thesis: English.

Schiller, Rose L. A Study of Sidney Lanier As Critic. Brooklyn College, 1949. Thesis: English.

Seals, Thomas D. Lanier as a Metrist. Columbia Univ., 1918. Thesis: English.

Ser, Cary D. Sidney Lanier's Major Poems. Univ. of Florida, 1966. Thesis: English.

Shaw, Edwin Page. An Application of Sidney Lanier's Theories of Poetic Composition to His Poem, "The Symphony." East Carolina Univ., 1964. Thesis: English.

Shields, Margaret V. A Concordance of Sidney Lanier's Poems Excluding the Dialect and Unrevised Early Poems. Duke Univ., 1938. Thesis: English.

Simonton, Carol H. Sidney Lanier: Critic of Society. Northeast Louisiana Univ., 1968. Thesis: English.

Smith, Jessie D. Illustrative Material for a Study of Lanier's Poems. George Peabody College, 1927. Thesis: English.

Smith, Leland C. The Literary Reputation of Sidney Lanier. Univ. of North Carolina (Chapel Hill), 1946. Thesis: English.

Steele, Joy H. The South in the Works of Sidney Lanier. Clemson Univ., 1968. Thesis: English.

Stone, Ruby. Musical Influence on the Poetry and Prosody of Sidney Lanier. Vanderbilt Univ., 1967. Thesis: English.

Strain, Jennie. Sidney Lanier and His Poetry. Univ. of Washington, 1930. Thesis: English.

Strickland, Anna B. Bible and Mystical Elements in the Works of Sidney Lanier. George Peabody College, 1935. Thesis: English.

Tillman, Ruth J. A Study of Sidney Lanier's Criticism of George Eliot's Works. North Carolina College at Durham, 1953. Thesis: English.

Todd, Edgeley W. Sidney Lanier's Theory of Poetry and Its Sources. Northwestern Univ., 1947. Dissertation: English.

Tomlinson, David O. Sidney Lanier Agrarianism. Univ. of North Carolina (Chapel Hill), 1969. Thesis: English.

Uppman, Ingegerd M. Old-world Influences on the Poems of Sidney Lanier. Stanford Univ., 1921. Thesis: English.

Watkins, Hortense. A Study of the Religious Concepts of Sidney Lanier. Southern Methodist Univ., 1947. Thesis: English.

Weaver, Lester. Sidney Lanier, The New Southerner. George Peabody College, 1917. Thesis: English.

Weed, Marguerite. The Ethical and Religious Beliefs of Sidney Lanier. Columbia Univ., 1932. Thesis: English.

Wheeler, Harold P. Lanier's Conception of the Poet. Duke Univ.,
    1929. Thesis: English.
Whitaker, George W., Jr. Sidney Lanier as a Critic of His Times.
    Univ. of South Carolina, 1947. Thesis: English.
Willcockson, Ruth. The Rhythmical Principles and Practices of
    Sidney Lanier. Univ. of Chicago, 1928. Thesis: English.
Wilsey, Collin M. Certain Influences of Contemporary Science upon
    the Critical Theory and Practice of Sidney Lanier. Univ. of
    Southern California, 1942. Thesis: English.
Woods, J.S. A Critical Study of The Nature Imagery of Sidney
    Lanier's Poetry. Georgia Southern College, 1966. Thesis:
    English.

RICHARD HENRY LEE (1732-1794)

Bowers, Paul C., Jr. Richard Henry Lee and The Continental
    Congress: 1774-1779. Duke Univ., 1965. Dissertation:
    History.
Coulston, J. The Philosophy of Richard Henry Lee. Univ. of
    Chicago, 1929. Thesis: History.

ROBERT E. LEE (1807-1870)

Adams, Francis R., Jr. An Annotated Edition of The Personal Letters
    of Robert E. Lee, April, 1855-April, 1861. Univ. of Maryland,
    1955. Dissertation: History.
Tribble, Edward J. A Historiographical Study of The Literature
    Pertaining to Robert E. Lee and The Battle of Gettysburg.
    Stetson Univ., 1968. Thesis: History.
West, Mabel A. General Robert E. Lee in Biography, Novel and
    Verse. Columbia Univ., 1932. Thesis: English.

HUGH SWINTON LEGARÉ (1797-1843)

Christophersen, Merrill G. A Rhetorical Study of Hugh Swinton
    Legaré: South Carolina Unionist. Univ. of Florida, 1954.
    Dissertation: Speech.
Coates, K.D. Hugh Swinton Legaré, Literary Critic. Univ. of
    North Carolina (Chapel Hill), 1932. Thesis: English.
Powell, Elizabeth. Romantic and Classical Elements in the Works
    of Hugh Swinton Legaré. Univ. of Georgia, 1954. Thesis:
    English.
Rhea, Linda. Hugh Swinton Legaré: An Apogee of Charleston.
    Vanderbilt Univ., 1933. Dissertation: English.
Willis, Larry J. The Character and Literary Style of Hugh Swinton
    Legaré. Univ. of South Carolina, 1928. Thesis: English.

OCTAVIA WALTON LEVERT (1810-1877)

Jeter, Myrtle K. Life and Critical Estimate of Madame Octavia
    Walton Levert. Auburn Univ., 1928. Thesis: English.
Stephens, Corinne C. Madame Octavia Walton Levert. Univ. of
    Georgia, 1940. Thesis: English.

ALFRED HENRY LEWIS (c.1858-1914)

Turner, Tressa. Life and Works of Alfred Henry Lewis. Univ. of
Texas (Austin), 1936. Thesis: English.

FRANCIS LIEBER (1800-1872)

Berry, Hester. Francis Lieber as a Teacher and Political Writer
in the South Carolina College. Univ. of South Carolina, 1943.
Thesis: English.

CLINTON LOCKHART (1858-1951)

Hinrichs, Fay-Bond. Clinton Lockhart: Cultural and Religious
Pioneer. Texas Christian Univ., 1939. Thesis: English.

JOHN A. LOMAX (1872-1948)

Ross, Maude E.H. The Early Years of John A. Lomax. Univ. of Texas
(Austin), 1953. Thesis: English.

HUEY P. LONG (1893-1935)

Bormann, Ernest G. A Rhetorical Analysis of The National Radio
Broadcasts of Senator Huey P. Long. State Univ. of Iowa,
1953. Dissertation: Speech.

JOHN BENJAMIN LONG (1843-1924)

Moore, Sue E. The Life of John Benjamin Long. Univ. of Texas
(Austin), 1924. Thesis: History.

AUGUSTUS BALDWIN LONGSTREET (1790-1870)

Altschul, Debra. Augustus Baldwin Longstreet: Manners and Morals
in Southwestern Folk Humor. Columbia Univ., 1960. Thesis:
English.
Wade, John D. Augustus Baldwin Longstreet. Columbia Univ., 1923.
Dissertation: English.
Zula, Marian I. Augustus Baldwin Longstreet, Humorist. Univ. of
South Carolina, 1940. Thesis: English.

ROBERT LOVEMAN (1864-1924)

Friedman, Helen A. Robert Loveman: Belated Romanticist. Univ.
of Alabama, 1932. Thesis: English.
Sorrells, Daniel J. Robert Loveman, Man and Poet. Univ. of
Georgia, 1937. Thesis: English.
Towson, Frances H. Robert Loveman, Georgia Author. Univ. of
Georgia, 1928. Thesis: English.

GRACE LUMPKIN (   )

Smith, Gerald Y. Grace Lumpkin: Her Life and Works. Oglethorpe
Univ., 1938. Thesis: English.

ANDREW NELSON LYTLE (1902-   )

Fair, Henrietta S. The Technique of Andrew Nelson Lytle's *The Velvet Horn*. Vanderbilt Univ., 1964. Thesis: English.
Fears, Rubel G. Agrarianism in The Works of Andrew Lytle. Mississippi State Univ., 1969. Thesis: English.
Glaze, Myrtle L. Andrew Nelson Lytle: An Agrarian Writer. Birmingham-Southern College, 1963. Thesis: English.
Harvey, Mary A. Andrew Nelson Lytle: A Critical Study of His Southern Novels and Short Stories. Vanderbilt Univ., 1960. Thesis: English.
Hoskins, John S. III. The Problem of Good and Evil in the Novels of Andrew Nelson Lytle. Vanderbilt Univ., 1947. Thesis: English.
Pemberton, James M. Archetypal Symbolism in Andrew Nelson Lytle's *The Velvet Horn*. Univ. of Tennessee, 1966. Thesis: English.
Waltz, Nell F. The Novels of Andrew Nelson Lytle. Vanderbilt Univ., 1960. Thesis: English.

JAMES MADISON (1751-1836)

Dewey, Donald O. The Sage of Montpelier: James Madison's Constitutional and Political Thought, 1817-1836. Univ. of Chicago, 1960. Dissertation: History.
Ingalls, Arthur. The Dual Sovereignty Theory of James Madison. Southern Methodist Univ., 1949. Thesis: Government.
Katz, Arthur B. James Madison--Consistent Constitutionalist. Brooklyn College, 1960. Thesis: History.
Ketcham, Ralph L. The Mind of James Madison. Syracuse Univ., 1956. Dissertation: History.
Lutz, Donald S. James Madison As a Conflict Theorist: The Madison Model Extended. Indiana Univ., 1969. Dissertation: Political Science.
Pilgrim, Wilma J. A Defense of the Constitution: Alexander Hamilton, James Madison and Publius. Univ. of Chicago, 1963. Thesis: History.
Potter, Sandra P. The Religious Philosophy of James Madison. Hardin-Simmons Univ., 1969. Thesis: History.
Traphell, Robert N. James Madison and Religious Liberty. Univ. of Texas (Austin), 1968. Thesis: History.
Vanderoef, John S. The Political Thought of James Madison. Princeton Univ., 1968. Dissertation: Political Science.

JULIA MAGRUDER (1854-1907)

Graham, Alice A. Julia Magruder, 1854-1907. George Washington Univ., 1934. Thesis: English.

WALTER MALONE (1866-1915)

Corban, Ruth. The Life and Literary Works of Walter Malone. Univ. of Mississippi, 1930. Thesis: English.
Stith, Mary E. Walter Malone, Jurist, Poet, Man. George Peabody College, 1927. Thesis: English.

BASIL MANLY, II (1825-1892)

Dickey, Rex H. Basil Manly II, Educator and Apostle of Southern
    Rights. Auburn Univ., 1967. Thesis: History.

ELLIOTT CRAYTON McCANTS (1865-1953)

Busch, Bruce L.M. Elliott Crayton McCants, South Carolina Author.
    Duke Univ., 1947. Thesis: English.

LOUISA C. McCORD (1810-1879)

Fraser, Jessie M. Louisa C. McCord. Univ. of South Carolina,
    1919. Thesis: English.

CARSON McCULLERS (1917-1967)

Barkowsky, Edward R. The Theme of Spiritual Isolation in The
    Major Works of Carson McCullers prior to 1962. Texas Tech
    Univ., 1968. Thesis: English.
Barnett, Gene A. The Tragic Theme of Carson McCullers. Univ. of
    Oklahoma, 1953. Thesis: English.
Bozarth, Rona S. Some Paradoxical Elements in The Fiction of
    Carson McCullers. Western Kentucky Univ., 1970. Thesis:
    English.
Brown, Joanne. Clean As A Pig: A Study of Irony and Paradox in
    The Major Works of Carson McCullers. Drake Univ., 1969.
    Thesis: English.
Brown, Peggy. Characters As Symbols in The Fiction of Carson
    McCullers. Eastern New Mexico Univ., 1965. Thesis: English.
Burnside, Patricia. Carson McCullers: A Study in Disillusionment.
    Univ. of Texas (El Paso), 1967. Thesis: English.
Byrd, Thomas L., Jr. The Dual Angel: A Study of Values in The
    Novels of Carson McCullers. Brown Univ., 1960. Thesis:
    English.
Byrne, Sue B. The Link in The Chain Called Love: A Study of The
    Novels of Carson McCullers. Tulane Univ., 1969. Thesis:
    English.
Cary, Elizabeth E. A Production Book for *The Member of the Wedding*.
    Kansas State Univ., 1966. Thesis: English.
Cover, Josephine E.M. Carson McCullers: A Song of Loneliness
    and Love. Lamar Univ., 1969. Thesis: English.
Daniel, John W. Carson McCullers' View of Love. Wake Forest
    Univ., 1967. Thesis: English.
Davis, Beulah. The Adolescent Characters In The Novels of Carson
    McCullers: Symbols of the Loneliness of The Human Condition.
    East Tennessee State Univ., 1970. Thesis: English.
Dickson, William W. Character Types and Development in the Fiction
    of Carson McCullers. Duke Univ., 1968. Thesis: English.
Few, Elizabeth V. (Mrs. Thornton Penfield). The Theme of Alienation
    in Selected Works of Carson McCullers. Duke Univ., 1962.
    Thesis: English.
Flowers, Mack O. *Reflections in A Golden Eye*, Adapted from the
    Novel by Carson McCullers. San Francisco State College, 1962.
    Thesis: Drama.

[109]

Forbes, James M., Jr. The Two Worlds: Theme and Its Unity in the Novels of Carson McCullers. Vanderbilt Univ., 1965. Thesis: English.

Frazier, Adelaide H. A Consideration of Imagery in Carson McCullers' *The Ballad of the Sad Cafe*. Northeast Louisiana Univ., 1969. Thesis: English.

Frosch, Jesse F. The Many Facets of Love in the Novels of Carson McCullers. Univ. of Georgia, 1966. Thesis: English.

Goldstein, Lee N. The Art of Fiction: A Study of Carson McCullers. American Univ., 1963. Thesis: English.

Gralin, Suzanne. The Function of The Grotesque, Abnormal, and Adolescent Characters in the Fiction of Carson McCullers. Univ. of Tennessee, 1961. Thesis: English.

Hamon, Mary S. The Use of the Child as a Literary Device by Henry James and Carson McCullers. Univ. of Texas (Austin), 1964. Thesis: English.

Hansen, Mildred P. The World of Love in Five Novels of Carson McCullers. Sacramento State College, 1969. Thesis: English.

Hartmann, Ruth A. Carson McCullers: The Relation of Isolation to Love. Univ. of Texas (Austin), 1965. Thesis: English.

Hatley, Mary L. The Implementation of Theme in the Novels and Novellas of Carson McCullers. Univ. of North Carolina (Chapel Hill), 1965. Thesis: English.

Henderson, Gloria A.M. The Theme of the Adolescent's Search for Self-Realization in the Prose Fiction of Carson McCullers. Vanderbilt Univ., 1968. Thesis: English.

Hollenback, Robert F. The Challenge of Form in Carson McCullers' *The Heart is a Lonely Hunter*. Lehigh Univ., 1969. Thesis: English.

Hull, Anne T. Carson McCullers and The Hazard of Human Existence. Univ. of Massachusetts, 1961. Thesis: English.

Ishler, Margaret F. The Lonely World of Carson McCullers. Pennsylvania State Univ., 1961. Thesis: English.

Jaskol, Helen S. Characterization in the Novels of Carson McCullers as Seen Through the Dialogue. Ohio State Univ., 1952. Thesis: English.

Kendall, Donald. Carson McCullers: The Sense of Dread. Columbia Univ., 1961. Thesis: English.

Kilby, Emily R. An Examination of the Stylistic Techniques Employed in The Novels of Carson McCullers. Bowling Green State Univ., 1970. Thesis: English.

Kilp, Carlo R. *The Heart Is a Lonely Hunter*: A Study. Univ. of Texas (Austin), 1958. Thesis: English.

Kirk, Dorothy J. The World of Carson McCullers. Univ. of North Carolina (Greensboro), 1969. Thesis: English.

Kopit, Stanford. Love in the Novels of Carson McCullers. Long Island Univ., 1970. Thesis: English.

Lemley, Raymond E. A Study of Alienation In the Novels of Carson McCullers. Iowa State Teachers College, 1965. Thesis: English.

Lerner, Linda. The Failure of Love In the Novels of Carson McCullers. Brooklyn College, 1969. Thesis: English.

Lowe, Margaret A. Isolation in the Works of Carson McCullers and Stephen Crane. Brigham Young Univ., 1968. Dissertation: English.

Martin, Virginia A. A Discussion of the Works of Carson McCullers. Columbia Univ., 1954. Thesis: English.

Mayer, Ruth S. The Kitchen Versus the Cafe: Symbolism in the Novels of Carson McCullers. City College of New York, 1968. Thesis: English.

McCarthy, Lawrence J. Carson McCullers: Her Fiction, 1936-1960. Florida State Univ., 1961. Thesis: English.

Miles, Betty L. A General Critical Study of the Works of Carson McCullers. Univ. of Louisville, 1964. Thesis: English.

Naples, Terry C. The World of Carson McCullers. Wagner College, 1970. Thesis: English.

Newton, Daniel R. Carson McCullers' Utilization of Character in Developing the Theme of Human Loneliness. Univ. of South Carolina, 1954. Thesis: English.

Olson, Charles. The Uses of The Grotesque in the Novels of Carson McCullers. Midwestern Univ., 1964. Thesis: English.

Person, Clara L. Carson McCullers: Her Adaptation of the Grotesque. Univ. of Wyoming, 1960. Thesis: English.

Reese, Regina. The Quest for Identity in the Novels of Carson McCullers. Univ. of Mississippi, 1969. Thesis: English.

Rodenberger, Molcie L. A Study of Techniques of Characterization in the Work of Carson McCullers. Texas A & M Univ., 1967. Thesis: English.

Santoro, William D. Carson McCullers: Classics from the South. Columbia Univ., 1955. Thesis: English.

Schmersahl, Curt W. Carson McCullers' Definition of Love and Alienation in Her Novels. McNeese State Univ., 1968. Thesis: English.

Scott, Mary E. Everyman through the Eyes of Carson McCullers. Miami Univ. (Ohio), 1969. Thesis: English.

Smith, Christopher M. Carson McCullers' *The Heart Is a Lonely Hunter*. Isolation and Self-Fulfillment. Univ. of North Carolina (Greensboro), 1969. Thesis: English.

Smith, Kyle A. The Isolated Individual in the Novels of Carson McCullers. North Texas State Univ., 1965. Thesis: English.

Smith, Simeon M., Jr. Carson McCullers: A Critical Introduction. Univ. of Pennsylvania, 1964. Dissertation: English.

Stoll, Rae H. Character as Symbol in the Novels of Carson McCullers. Southern Methodist Univ., 1966. Thesis: English.

Stone, Bonnie V. Alienation, Love, and Community in the Novels and Plays of Carson McCullers: A Critique. Duke Univ., 1967. Thesis: English.

Sullivan, Margaret S. Carson McCullers: An Analysis of Four Major Works. Auburn Univ., 1961. Thesis: English.

_____. Carson McCullers, 1917-1947: The Conversion of Experience. Duke Univ., 1966. Dissertation: English.

Thompson, Bernita L. The Theme of Love in the Six Major Works of Carson McCullers. Univ. of South Dakota, 1965. Thesis: English.

Tucker, William M. Structural and Thematic Unity in the Novels of Carson McCullers. Vanderbilt Univ., 1956. Thesis: English.

Walker, John D. Thematic Unity in the Novels and Stories of Carson McCullers. Univ. of Texas (Austin), 1956. Thesis: English.

Weber, Ellen. Carson McCullers: A Study of Her Developments in the Use of Imagery. City College of New York, 1969. Thesis: English.

Whitton, Steven J. The Grotesque as Symbol for the Theme of Loneliness in the Novels of Carson McCullers. Samford Univ., 1969. Thesis: English.

Wiley, Edward B. Carson McCullers: The Necessity of Futility of Illusions. Murray State Univ., 1969. Thesis: English.

KATHERINE SHERWOOD BONNER McDOWELL (1849-1883)
(SHERWOOD BONNER)

Burger, Nash K., Jr. Katherine Sherwood Bonner: A Study in the Development of a Southern Literature. Univ. of Virginia, 1935. Thesis: English.

Frank, William L. Katherine Sherwood Bonner McDowell: A Critical Biography. Northwestern Univ., 1964. Dissertation: English.

Gilligan, Dorothy L. Life and Works of Sherwood Bonner. George Washington Univ., 1930. Thesis: English.

JOHN B. McFERRIN (1807-1887)

Stowe, William M. John B. McFerrin, Editorial Controversialist, 1840-1858. Duke Univ., 1935. Bachelor of Divinity.

RANDAL WILLIAM McGAVOCK (1826-1863)

Allan, Jack. The Diary of Randal William McGavock 1852-1862: An Interpretation of a Period. George Peabody College, 1941. Dissertation: Education.

RALPH McGILL (1898-1969)

Burks, Altonette T. The Negro as Reflected in Some of the Writings of Ralph McGill. Atlanta Univ., 1965. Thesis: History.

Logue, Calvin M. A Rhetorical Analysis of The Speech Theory and Practice of Ralph McGill. Louisiana State Univ., 1967. Dissertation: Speech.

Murray, Mary E.P. The South and Ralph McGill. Emory Univ., 1965. Thesis: History.

CARLYLE McKINLEY (1847-1904)

McCullough, John W. Carlyle McKinley. Univ. of Georgia, 1941. Thesis: English.

JOHN CHARLES McNEILL (1874-1907)

Idol, Elizabeth V. The Life and Works of John Charles McNeill. Columbia Univ., 1927. Thesis: English.

Polk, Alice M. John Charles McNeill: A Poet of North Carolina. Duke Univ., 1942. Thesis: English.

Smith, Mary L. John Charles McNeill. Columbia Univ., 1917. Thesis: English.

ALEXANDER BEAUFORT MEEK (1814-1865)

Gillis, Margaret H. Alexander B. Meek, Pioneer Man of Letters.
Columbia Univ., 1926. Thesis: English.
Madison, Blaine M. The Life and Works of Alexander Beaufort
Meek. Duke Univ., 1933. Thesis: English.

ADAH ISSACS MENKEN (1835-1868)

Davis, Kate W. Adah Isaacs Menken: Her Life and Poetry in America.
Southern Methodist Univ., 1944. Thesis: English.
Leach, Catherine. Adah Isaacs Menken: The Biography of an
American Actress. Louisiana State Univ., 1937. Thesis:
English.
Riback, William H. The Life and Works of Adah Isaacs Menken.
Northwestern Univ., 1933. Thesis: English.

HENRY LOUIS MENCKEN (1880-1956)

Atwell, Br. James S. Two Studies in Twentieth Century American
Literature: Eclipse and Emergence: H.L. Mencken's "Dark
Years" and the Advent of His Second Career and J.F. Powers'
Morce D'Urban: Religious Satire and Prophetic Theme.
Univ. of Maryland, 1968. Thesis: English.
Brown, Barbara I. The Political Thought of H.L. Mencken,
Inception--1923. Johns Hopkins Univ., 1966. Thesis: English.
Donnolly, Eugene F. (Br. Kieran Matthew, F.M.S.). Henry Louis
Mencken, Defender of Theodore Dreiser. St. John's Univ.
(N.Y.), 1954. Thesis: English.
Cooper, Sharon T. H.L. Mencken's Social Criticism in *The American
Mercury*. Univ. of Texas (Austin), 1967. Thesis: English.
Coslick, Robert D. Decline of H.L. Mencken: 1925-1940. Kent
State Univ., 1963. Thesis: English.
Evitts, William J. H.L. Mencken and the South in the 1920's. Univ.
of Virginia, 1966. Thesis: History.
Gillis, Adolph. H.L. Mencken as Critic. Columbia Univ., 1928.
Thesis: English.
Hickman, William. Influence of Attitude Toward Religion upon the
Writings of H.L. Mencken. Univ. of Pittsburgh, 1963.
Dissertation: English.
Kramoris, Ivan J. The Principles of Literary Criticism of H.L.
Mencken. Marquette Univ., 1938. Thesis: English.
Morelli, Patrick A. H.L. Mencken: His Literary and Personal
Relationships with Percival Pollard and James Huneker. Duke
Univ., 1969. Thesis: English.
Nolte, William H. The Literary Criticism of H.L. Mencken. Univ.
of Illinois, 1959. Dissertation: English.
O'Brien, Br. Adrian P. A Critical Study of the Editorials of
Henry Louis Mencken in *The American Mercury* From January 1924
to December 1933. St. John's Univ. (N.Y.), 1959. Dissertation:
English.
Pickett, Roy G. H.L. Mencken's Rhetorical Battle. Univ. of Iowa,
1960. Dissertation: English.

Remley, David A. The Correspondence of H.L. Mencken and Upton
    Sinclair: An Illustration of How Not To Agree. Indiana
    Univ., 1967. Dissertation: English.
Shuford, Cecil E. An Evaluation of the Influence of H.L. Mencken
    and *The American Mercury* upon American Thought. Northwestern
    Univ., 1929. Thesis: Journalism.
Simpson, Herbert M. Mencken and Nathan. Univ. of Maryland, 1965.
    Dissertation: English.
Stenerson, Douglas C. A Genetic History of the Prejudices of
    H.L. Mencken. Univ. of Minnesota, 1961. Dissertation:
    English.
Thoma, George N. A Study of the Rhetoric of H.L. Mencken's Essays,
    1917-1927. Univ. of Chicago, 1958. Dissertation: English.
Wagner, Kenyon L. O Thee I Sing: H.L. Mencken and the *American
    Mercury*, 1925-1933: A Study of H.L. Mencken's Idea On
    Literature, Politics, Democracy, and Religion. Eastern New
    Mexico Univ., 1963. Thesis: English.

DR. ALFRED MERCIER (1816-1894)

La Croix, Rena M. Dr. Alfred Mercier: The Man and His Works.
    Louisiana State Univ., 1929. Thesis: English.

THOMAS MERTON (1915-1968)

Flaherty, Luke. Mystery and Unity as Anagogical Vision in Thomas
    Merton's *Cables to the Ice*: A Critical Explication. Univ.
    of Louisville, 1969. Thesis: English.

GEORGE MILBURN (1906-   )

Rackleff, Julia M. Oklahoma Folk Speech in the Novels and Short
    Stories of George Milburn. Univ. of Tulsa, 1949. Thesis:
    English.

WILLIAM HENRY MILBURN (1823-1903)

McLeod, John F., Jr. The Life of William Henry Milburn, The Blind
    Man Eloquent. Auburn Univ., 1936. Thesis: English.

HEATHER ROSS MILLER (1939-   )

Wenger, Doris A. Heather Ross Miller's Use of Dreams to Elucidate
    the Search for Identity. Univ. of North Carolina (Chapel Hill),
    1968. Thesis: English.

LUCIAN MINOR (1802-1858)

McKean, James N. Lucian Minor: Cosmopolitan Virginia Gentleman
    of the Old School. College of William and Mary, 1948.
    Thesis: History.

MARGARET MITCHELL (1900-1949)

Anderson, Reta M. *Gone With the Wind*: An Evaluation. Vanderbilt
    Univ., 1956. Thesis: English.

[114]

Bearden, Ethel M. Margaret Mitchell and Her Place in Atlanta. Duke Univ., 1957. Thesis: English.

Chandler, Judith Y. The Language Structures of Epic as Seen in *Gone With the Wind* and *Water of Life*. Morehead State Univ., 1970. Thesis: English.

Cheney, Merlin G. *Vanity Fair* and *Gone With the Wind*: A Critical Comparison. Brigham Young Univ., 1966. Thesis: English.

Verdross, Dorothea. Die Darstellung der Verhältnisse des Südens der Vereinigten Staaten zur Zeit des Bürgerkrieges und der Rekonstruktionszeit in Margaret Mitchell's *Gone With the Wind*. Innsbruck, 1946. Dissertation: English.

ANDREW JACKSON MONTAGUE (1862-1937)

Larsen, William E. Governor Andrew Jackson Montague of Virginia, 1862-1937: The Making of a Southern Progressive. Univ. of Virginia, 1961. Dissertation: History.

IDORA McCLELLAN MOORE (1843-1929)
(BETSY HAMILTON)

McCain, Louise B. Idora McClellan Moore: A Biographical Sketch including Selections of Her Writings. Auburn Univ., 1934. Thesis: English.

JOHN TROTWOOD MOORE (1858-1929)

Green, C.B. John Trotwood Moore: A Tennessee Man of Letters. Duke Univ., 1953. Dissertation: English.

Walker, Bessie M. Life and Works of John Trotwood Moore. George Peabody College, 1929. Thesis: English.

MERRILL MOORE (1903-1957)

Trantham, Mary A. Merrill Moore: A Study of Some Representative Sonnets. Vanderbilt Univ., 1952. Thesis: English.

PATRICK D. MORELAND (1897-   )

Nobles, Jennie P. The Poetry of Patrick D. Moreland. East Texas State Univ., 1940. Thesis: English.

EDGAR YOUNG MULLINS (1860-1928)

Spears, Julius H. The Christology of Edgar Young Mullins. Duke Univ., 1945. Thesis: Religion.

WILLIAM MUNFORD (1775-1825)

Purcell, Ralph E. William Munford: A Biographical and Critical Study. Duke Univ., 1941. Thesis: English.

MARY NOAILLES MURFREE (1850-1922)
(CHARLES EGBERT CRADDOCK)

Byrd, Eva M. The Life and Writings of Mary Noailles Murfree.
    Univ. of Tennessee, 1937. Thesis: English.
Cousins, Paul M. Charles Egbert Craddock. Columbia Univ., 1920.
    Thesis: English.
Curtis, J.L. The Dialect Writing of Charles Egbert Craddock in the
    Light of the Author's Background. Univ. of North Carolina
    (Chapel Hill), 1942. Thesis: English.
Harris, Isabella D. Charles Egbert Craddock as an Interpreter of
    Mountain Life. Duke Univ., 1933. Thesis: English.
Johnson, E.G. Mary Noailles Murfree as a Writer of Local Color
    Fiction. Univ. of Mississippi, 1961. Thesis: English.
Magee, Mary V. Charles Egbert Craddock and Her Background.
    Louisiana State Univ., 1935. Thesis: English.
Mooney, Mary S. An Intimate Study of Mary Noailles Murfree,
    Charles Egbert Craddock. George Peabody College, 1928.
    Thesis: English.
Ogle, Gladys L. Mary Noailles Murfree (Pseudonym: Charles Egbert
    Craddock). Columbia Univ., 1924. Thesis: English.
Parks, Edd W. Charles Egbert Craddock (Mary Noailles Murfree):
    A Study of Local Color in the South. Vanderbilt Univ., 1933.
    Dissertation: English.
Reichert, Alfred. Charles Egbert Craddock and Die Amerikanische
    Short Story. Leipzig, 1912. Dissertation: English.
Sherman, Marian C. The Local Color Motif in The Writings of Mary
    Noailles Murfree (Charles Egbert Craddock). Ohio State Univ.,
    1944. Thesis: English.
Spencer, E.B. Collected Reminiscences of Mary N. Murfree. George
    Peabody College, 1928. Thesis: English.
Swink, Lottie H. The Literary Reputation of Charles Egbert Craddock
    with an Annotated Selected Bibliography of Craddock Criticism
    from 1884 to June, 1968. Univ. of North Carolina (Chapel Hill),
    1968. Thesis: English.
Trouy, Fr. Lucien, O.F.M. Charles Egbert Craddock and the Southern
    Mountains and Mountaineers. Catholic Univ., 1932. Thesis:
    English.
Welsh, Clara I. An Evaluation of the Writings of Mary Noailles
    Murfree. Univ. of Pittsburgh, 1930. Thesis: English.
Wilkerson, Isabelle J. A Compilation of the Proverbial Expressions
    in the Works of Charles Egbert Craddock. Univ. of Tennessee,
    1963. Thesis: English.

A.O.P. NICHOLSON (1808-1876)

Clark, Patricia P.P. A.O.P. Nicholson of Tennessee: Editor,
    Statesman, and Jurist. Univ. of Tennessee, 1965. Thesis:
    History.

CHARLES FENTON MERCER NOLAND (1810-1858)

Milner, Joseph O. Charles Fenton Mercer Noland: Early Southwestern
    Humorist. Univ. of North Carolina (Chapel Hill), 1964.
    Thesis: English.

ADOLPH S. OCHS (1858-1935)

Hinkel, J.V. The Contribution of Adolph S. Ochs to Journalism.
    Columbia Univ., 1931. Thesis: Journalism.

FLANNERY O'CONNOR (1925-1964)

Adelman, Selma S. A Study of the Fiction of Flannery O'Connor.
    Trinity Univ. (Texas), 1963. Thesis: English.
Aderholt, Martha J. Flannery O'Connor's Thematic Use of Family
    Relationships. Univ. of Tennessee, 1969. Thesis: English.
Aiken, David H. New Testament Character Types in Selected Short
    Fiction of Flannery O'Connor. Univ. of Georgia, 1969.
    Thesis: English.
Archer, Patricia F. Determinism in the Fiction of Flannery
    O'Connor. Texas A & M Univ., 1970. Thesis: English.
Asala, Frederick J., Jr. Flannery O'Connor: An Interpretive Study.
    Brown Univ., 1967. Dissertation: English.
Balcer, Joan. Flannery O'Connor's Christian Insight Revealed by
    Style and Content. Aquinas College, 1966. Thesis: English.
Blackwell, Annie L. The Artistry of Flannery O'Connor. Florida
    State Univ., 1966. Dissertation: English.
Blanton, William H. The Two Modes of Vision in Flannery O'Connor's
    Short Fiction. Univ. of North Carolina (Chapel Hill), 1969.
    Thesis: English.
Boyer, Ken B. The Grotesque in Flannery O'Connor's Fiction. St.
    Louis Univ., 1967. Thesis: English.
Brewster, Rudolph A. The Literary Devices in the Writings of
    Flannery O'Connor. East Texas State Univ., 1968. Dissertation:
    English.
Brittain, Joan T. Symbols of Violence: Flannery O'Connor's
    Structure of Reality. Univ. of Louisville, 1967. Thesis:
    English.
Browning, Preston M., Jr. Flannery O'Connor and the Grotesque
    Recovery of the Holy. Univ. of Chicago, 1969. Dissertation:
    Divinity.
Bruce, Duane F. The Regional and Religious Dimensions of Flannery
    O'Connor's Fiction. Univ. of North Carolina (Chapel Hill),
    1967. Thesis: English.
Burns, Thomas S. Southern Evangelism and Flannery O'Connor. Univ.
    of Georgia, 1967. Thesis: English.
Bush, George D. An Author Looks at Her Work: An Approach to
    Flannery O'Connor. Univ. of Tennessee, 1966. Thesis:
    English.
Chandler, Tommie A. Ironic Redemption: A Study of Flannery
    O'Connor's Fiction. Emory Univ., 1964. Thesis: English.
Cherry, Charles L. Theme, Structure and Symbol in Flannery
    O'Connor's *The Violent Bear It Away*. Univ. of North Carolina
    (Chapel Hill), 1966. Thesis: English.
Connolly, Janet M. The Fiction of Flannery O'Connor. Columbia
    Univ., 1966. Dissertation: English.
Coulbourn, Mildred E. Flannery O'Connor's "Displaced Persons."
    Duke Univ., 1967. Thesis: English.

Delafield, Carter. Flannery O'Connor: Prophet and Evangelist.
    Univ. of North Carolina (Greensboro), 1966. Thesis: English.
Demouy, Jane K. Damascus Road: Epiphany and Theme in the Works
    of Flannery O'Connor. Univ. of Maryland, 1967. Thesis:
    English.
Dinneen, Patricia M. Flannery O'Connor: Realist of Distances.
    Pennsylvania State Univ., 1967. Dissertation: English.
Dreyer, Ladonna J. The Truth Shall Make You Free: Flannery
    O'Connor's Ideology as Presented in her Prose. West Texas
    State Univ., 1969. Thesis: English.
Dula, Martha A. The State of Man as It Is Portrayed in Flannery
    O'Connor's *Wise Blood*. Univ. of North Carolina (Chapel Hill),
    1967. Thesis: English.
Dunn, Sr. Francis M., P.B.V.M. Functions and Implications of
    Setting in the Fiction of Flannery O'Connor. Catholic Univ.
    of America, 1966. Dissertation: English.
Elkins, Sharon J. Redemption and Associated Themes in Flannery
    O'Connor's Fiction. Tulane Univ., 1964. Thesis: English.
Floerchinger, Sharon M. The Rat-gray and The Wooden Leg: The
    Meaning of the Grotesque in Flannery O'Connor. Wichita State
    Univ., 1966. Thesis: English.
Fuller, Donald C. The Relation of Idea and Reality in the Works of
    Flannery O'Connor. Univ. of Georgia, 1967. Thesis: English.
Gafford, Charlotte K. The Fiction of Flannery O'Connor.
    Birmingham-Southern College, 1962. Thesis: English.
Gattuso, Josephine F. The Fictive World of Flannery O'Connor.
    Columbia Univ., 1968. Dissertation: English.
Gerber, Leslie E. Flannery O'Connor and the Fugitives: A Matter
    of the City. Emory Univ., 1967. Thesis: Political Science.
Gibbs, Jeanne M. Beyond the Absurd: Right and Wrong in the
    Fiction of Flannery O'Connor. Moorhead State College, 1969.
    Thesis: English.
Gillikin, Sandra A. The Face of Evil: A Study of Irony in
    Flannery O'Connor's *The Violent Bear It Away*. East Carolina
    Univ., 1968. Thesis: English.
Gregory, Donald L. An Internal Analysis of the Fiction of Flannery
    O'Connor. Ohio State Univ., 1967. Dissertation: English.
Griffin, Joan R. Flannery O'Connor and the Development of the
    Grotesque in American Literature. South Dakota State Univ.,
    1970. Thesis: English.
Guilka, Mother Therese E. Flannery O'Connor's Violent World.
    Boston College, 1966. Thesis: English.
Hart, Gary V. The Eucharistic Symbol and the Concept of Grace in
    the Works of Flannery O'Connor. Pepperdine College, 1969.
    Thesis: English.
Herbkersman, Gretchen A. Matrices of Paradox: The Style of
    Flannery O'Connor's Short Stories. San Francisco State
    College, 1968. Thesis: English.
Holloway, Phyllis. The Power of Shock: A Study of the Central
    Figures in Flannery O'Connor's Fiction. East Tennessee State
    Univ., 1969. Thesis: English.
Hook, Wilma G. The World of Flannery O'Connor: The Grotesque
    Pilgrimage. Central Michigan Univ., 1967. Thesis: English.

Huff, Carol A.C. Flannery O'Connor and the Technique of Charac-
    terization. Texas Christian Univ., 1968. Thesis: English.
Hurlburt, Ronald E. The Functions of the Child Characters in the
    Fiction of Flannery O'Connor. Murray State Univ., 1968.
    Thesis: English.
Julienne, Marietta L. Confrontation and Redemption in Flannery
    O'Connor's *A Good Man Is Hard to Find*. Univ. of North Carolina
    (Chapel Hill), 1969. Thesis: English.
Keane, Sr. Melinda. Structural Irony in Flannery O'Connor:
    Instruments of the Writer's Vision. Loyola Univ. (Chicago),
    1969. Dissertation: English.
Kerr, Robert L. Flannery O'Connor: Realist of Distances. Duke
    Univ., 1966. Thesis: English.
Lavin, Mary J.W. Image and Reality: A Study of the Complete Works
    of Flannery O'Connor. John Carroll Univ., 1962. Thesis:
    English.
La Vois, Caroline F. The Theme of Death in the Works of Flannery
    O'Connor. Sam Houston State Univ., 1969. Thesis: English.
Lukas, Dorothy A. The Dual Function of the Grotesque in Flannery
    O'Connor. Pennsylvania State Univ., 1967. Thesis: English.
Lynn, Denise D. A Study of Certain Aspects of the Fiction of
    Graham Greene and Flannery O'Connor. Iowa State Teachers
    College, 1963. Thesis: English.
Marlowe, Jeanne A. A Comparison of Religious Themes in the Fiction
    of Graham Greene and Flannery O'Connor. Bowling Green State
    Univ., 1969. Thesis: English.
Maroney, Janet M. The Grotesque in Flannery O'Connor. Columbia
    Univ., 1962. Thesis: English.
Marschel, Jacqueline A. The Figure of Innocence in Flannery
    O'Connor. St. Louis Univ., 1967. Thesis: English.
Martin, Carter W. The Convergence of Actualities: Themes in the
    Fiction of Flannery O'Connor. Vanderbilt Univ., 1967.
    Dissertation: English.
Mayer, David R., S.V.D. Flannery O'Connor's Treatment of Grace and
    Baptism in *The Violent Bear It Away*. Georgetown Univ., 1970.
    Thesis: English.
McCullagh, James C. Flannery O'Connor's Theology Viewed through
    the Haze of the Grotesque. Lehigh Univ., 1970. Thesis:
    English.
McGrath, Mary A. A Study of the Mystery, the Fact, and the
    Unexpected in the Writings of Flannery O'Connor. Univ. of
    Dayton, 1966. Thesis: English.
Moore, Lofton S. Flannery O'Connor: A Descriptive Analysis of
    Her Fiction. Univ. of Idaho, 1966. Thesis: English.
Morley, Irene. The Unknown Self in Flannery O'Connor's Novels.
    Columbia Univ., 1966. Thesis: English.
Muller, Gilbert H. Flannery O'Connor and the Catholic Grotesque.
    Stanford Univ., 1967. Dissertation: English.
Murphy, Brenda C. Flannery O'Connor: A Searing Vision. Wagner
    College, 1968. Thesis: English.
Newman, Georgia A. Flannery O'Connor: Annotated Bibliography of
    Secondary Sources. Florida State Univ., 1970. Thesis:
    English.

Newman, William S. Flannery O'Connor's Distinctive Use of Place in Her Novels and Short Stories. Univ. of Tennessee, 1965. Thesis: English.

Oliver, LaTrelle B. Physical Markings in O'Connor Country. Flannery O'Connor's Use of Concrete Particulars from Her Region. Duke Univ., 1968. Thesis: English.

Ouzts, Cuyler E. Flannery O'Connor's Use of the Grotesque. Texas Christian Univ., 1968. Thesis: English.

Peacock, Claire R. A Vision of Reality: Characterization in the Novels and Short Stories of Flannery O'Connor. Vanderbilt Univ., 1963. Thesis: English.

Perrin, Elaine. The Unique Achievement of Flannery O'Connor. Texas Tech Univ., 1969. Thesis: English.

Pritchard, Alice S. Violence in Flannery O'Connor's Fiction. Univ. of Maryland, 1967. Thesis: English.

Rainey, Carol A. Narrative Distance in the Short Stories of Flannery O'Connor. Univ. of Cincinnati, 1967. Thesis: English.

Regin, Patsy K., R.S.C.J. Paradox in the Works of Flannery O'Connor. Lone Mountain College, 1970. Thesis: English.

Riley, Eleanor M. The Fiction and the Aesthetic Principles of Flannery O'Connor: A Study in Theory and Practice. Creighton Univ., 1967. Thesis: English.

Robinson, Margaret. Flannery O'Connor's Terrifying Vision. Drake Univ., 1970. Thesis: English.

Rocky, Donald J., Jr. The Achievement of Flannery O'Connor: Her System of Thought, Her Fictional Techniques, and an Explication of Her Thought and Techniques in *The Violent Bear It Away*. Loyola Univ. (Chicago), 1968. Dissertation: English.

Scalia, Linda F. The Theological Vision of Flannery O'Connor in *Everything that Rises Must Converge*. Northeast Louisiana Univ., 1968. Thesis: English.

Schroeder, Vanessa M. Flannery O'Connor and the Moral Tragedy of Modern Society. California State College (Hayward), 1970. Thesis: English.

Short, Donald A. The Concrete is her Medium: The Fiction of Flannery O'Connor. Univ. of Pittsburgh, 1969. Dissertation: English.

Smith, Margaret M. Redemption in the Works of Flannery O'Connor. Sam Houston State College, 1962. Thesis: English.

Smith, Rupert L. Flannery O'Connor in the Context of the Southern Literary Tradition. Wake Forest Univ., 1963. Thesis: English.

Smith, Suzanne W. Backwoods Odyssey: Flannery O'Connor's *The Violent Bear It Away*. Univ. of Virginia, 1968. Thesis: English.

Stephens, Martha T. An Introduction to the Work of Flannery O'Connor. Indiana State Univ., 1968. Dissertation: English.

Stumbo, Carol. The Technique of the Grotesque in the Writings of Flannery O'Connor. Morehead State Univ., 1968. Thesis: English.

Tucker, Mary F. Redemptive Violence in the Short Stories of Flannery O'Connor. Saint Joseph College, 1969. Thesis: English.

Ward, Sr. Mary B. Children in the Fiction of Flannery O'Connor. Georgetown Univ., 1967. Thesis: English.

Warren, F.E. God's Pursuit of Man in the Fiction of Flannery
O'Connor. Kansas State Teachers College, 1967. Thesis:
English.
Watson, William E., Jr. The Cost of Agony: The Revelation of
Grace through Violence in the Writings of Flannery O'Connor.
Southern Methodist Univ., 1970. Thesis: English.
Wiseman, William J. Idiots Clapping in Church: The Fiction of
Flannery O'Connor. Univ. of Tulsa, 1968. Thesis: English.
Wood, Ralph C. The Scandal of Redemption: Religious Meaning in the
Novels of Flannery O'Connor. East Texas State Univ., 1965.
Thesis: English.
Yerger, Norval R. Patterns of Imagery in Flannery O'Connor's *The
Violent Bear It Away*. Univ. of Virginia, 1966. Thesis:
English.
York, Beth M. An Ax for the Frozen Sea within Us: Flannery
O'Connor's Prose. West Texas State Univ., 1965. Thesis:
English.

WILLIAMSON SIMPSON OLDHAM (1813-1868)

King, Alma D. The Political Career of Williamson Simpson Oldham.
Univ. of Texas (Austin), 1929. Thesis: History.

F.L. OLMSTED (1822-1903)

Mitchell, Broadus. F.L. Olmsted: A Critic of the Old South. Johns
Hopkins Univ., 1924. Dissertation: History.
Pearce, Bessie M. Frederick Lam Olmsted: His Life and Work. Univ.
of Texas (Austin), 1949. Thesis: English.

JOHN PAGE (1744-1808)

Tanner, Carol M. John Page of Rosewell. Univ. of Virginia, 1944.
Thesis: History.

THOMAS NELSON PAGE (1853-1922)

Abernathy, Robert. The Southern Planter Portrayed in the Fiction
of Thomas Nelson Page. George Peabody College, 1933. Thesis:
English.
Allibritten, Geraldine. The Conception of the Southern Aristocracy
in the Fiction of Thomas Nelson Page. Univ. of Kansas, 1933.
Thesis: English.
Bittinger, Mary S. The Historical Validity of Representative Short
Stories of Thomas Nelson Page. Vanderbilt Univ., 1945.
Thesis: English.
Bridgers, Frank E., Jr. Thomas Nelson Page's Treatment of Southern
Plantation Life. Duke Univ., 1933. Thesis: English.
Craver, Sadie B. Thomas Nelson Page. Southern Methodist Univ.,
1944. Thesis: English.
Davis, Mary M. Children in T.N. Page's Stories of Children.
George Peabody College, 1931. Thesis: English.
Holman, Harriet R. The Literary Career of Thomas Nelson Page,
1884-1910. Duke Univ., 1948. Dissertation: English.

Howard, Helen E. The Negro in the Fiction of T.N. Page. George
    Peabody College, 1932. Thesis: English.
McFadin, Maude A. Thomas Nelson Page as a Short Story Writer.
    Univ. of Kansas, 1935. Thesis: English.
Smith, Mrs. L.H. Thomas Nelson Page: The Literary Interpreter of
    Ole Virginia (1850-1880). Auburn Univ., 1936. Thesis:
    English.

WALTER HINES PAGE (1855-1918)

Bennett, Caroline. Walter Hines Page: Political Thinking, 1900
    to 1913. Columbia Univ., 1934. Thesis: History.
Boswell, George W. Walter Hines Page as a Southerner. Vanderbilt
    Univ., 1940. Thesis: English.
Cox, Mary J. Walter Hines Page: Journalist, Reformer, Statesman.
    Southern Methodist Univ., 1925. Thesis: English.
Gregory, Ross M. The Ambassadorship of Walter (Hines) Page.
    Indiana Univ., 1964. Dissertation: History.
Holt, Mildred E. Walter Hines Page: A Study of His Influence on
    Our Entry Into World War I. Vanderbilt Univ., 1946. Thesis:
    History.
Kihl, Mary R. A Failure of Ambassadorial Diplomacy: The Case of
    Page and Spring Rice. Pennsylvania State Univ., 1968.
    Dissertation: History.
Minor, Olive. Walter Hines Page's Reconstruction Policy with the
    Atlantic Monthly. Columbia Univ., 1934. Thesis: English.
Weaver, Frederick H. Walter H. Page and the Progressive Mood.
    Duke Univ., 1968. Dissertation: History.

BENJAMIN MORGAN PALMER (1818-1892)

Hickey, Doralyn J. Benjamin Morgan Palmer: Churchman of the Old
    South. Duke Univ., 1962. Dissertation: Religion.

JOHN WILLIAMSON PALMER (1825-1906)

Switzer, Leona D. The Life and Works of John Williamson Palmer.
    Columbia Univ., 1940. Thesis: English.

SAMUEL MINTURN PECK (1854-1938)

Whitaker, Isola B. A Study of the Poetry of Samuel Minturn Peck.
    George Peabody College, 1929. Thesis: English.

WALKER PERCY (1917-   )

Kent, Margaret L. The Novels of Walker Percy. Univ. of North
    Carolina (Chapel Hill), 1969. Thesis: English.

WILLIAM ALEXANDER PERCY (1885-1942)

Dickey, Benjamin W. William Alexander Percy: An Alien Spirit in
    the Twentieth Century. Auburn Univ., 1951. Thesis: English.

Malone, Carol. William Alexander Percy: Knight to His People, Ishmael to Himself, and Poet to the World. Univ. of Mississippi, 1964. Thesis: English.

Peacock, Kathleen M. William Alexander Percy: A Study in Southern Conservatism. Birmingham-Southern College, 1958. Thesis: English.

Spalding, Billups P. William Alexander Percy, His Philosophy of Life as Reflected in his Poetry. Univ. of Georgia, 1957. Thesis: English.

Talley, May R. A Study of the Poems of William Alexander Percy. East Texas State Univ., 1939. Thesis: English.

Ware, Hester S. A Study of the Life and Works of William Alexander Percy. Mississippi State Univ., 1950. Thesis: History.

Windham, Hudean. A Study of W.A. Percy's Life and Poetry. George Peabody College, 1939. Thesis: English.

GEORGE SESSIONS PERRY (1910-1956)

Cowser, Robert G. A Biographical and Critical Interpretation of George Sessions Perry (1910-1956). Texas Christian Univ., 1965. Dissertation: English.

Hairston, Maxine E.C. The Development of George Sessions Perry as a Writer of Rural Texas. Univ. of Texas (Austin), 1968. Dissertation: English.

Webb, Christine B. George Sessions Perry, a Successful Failure. Univ. of Texas (El Paso), 1970. Thesis: English.

ROBERT PETER (1805-1894)

Wright, John D., Jr. Robert Peter and Early Science in Kentucky. Columbia Univ., 1955. Dissertation: History.

JULIA MOOD PETERKIN (1880-1961)

Comer, Nannette H. Julia Mood Peterkin: Delineator of the Gullah Negro and his Life. Univ. of Mississippi, 1967. Thesis: English.

Henry, Louis L. Julia Peterkin: A Biographical and Critical Study. Florida State Univ., 1965. Dissertation: English.

Jordan, Mary R. The Prose Fiction of Julia Peterkin: A Study of Technique. Fisk Univ., 1936. Thesis: English.

Maddox, Marilyn P. The Life and Works of Julia Mood Peterkin. Univ. of Georgia, 1956. Thesis: English.

Moore, Laura L. The Life and Fiction Writings of Julia Peterkin. George Peabody College, 1930. Thesis: English.

Morrow, Lenna V. Folklore in the Writing of Julia Peterkin. Univ. of South Carolina, 1963. Thesis: English.

Wells, Betty J. Regionalism and Fictional Art in the Writings of Julia Mood Peterkin. Vanderbilt Univ., 1963. Thesis: English.

CHARLES JOSEPH PETERSON (1819-1887)

Presturich, L.A. Charles Jacobs Peterson, Editor and Friend of Lowell and Poe. Columbia Univ., 1939. Thesis: English.

JAMES LOUIS PETIGRU (1789-1863)

Campbell, Julius G. James Louis Petigru: A Rhetorical Study.
    Univ. of South Carolina, 1961. Dissertation: English.

FRANCIS W. PICKENS (1805-1869)

Edmunds, John B., Jr. Francis Wilkinson Pickens: A Political
    Biography. Univ. of South Carolina, 1967. Dissertation:
    History.

ALBERT PIKE (1809-1891)

Brown, Walter L. Albert Pike, Arkansan, 1809-1847. Univ. of Texas
    (Austin), 1950. Thesis: History.
_____. Albert Pike, 1809-1891. Univ. of Texas (Austin), 1955.
    Dissertation: History.
Kidd, Custer. Life of Albert Pike, with an Introcution to His
    Poetry. Southern Methodist Univ., 1927. Thesis: English.
Nitsche, Mrs. Willard G. Albert Pike's Service to the Confederacy.
    Univ. of Texas (Austin), 1927. Thesis: History.
Riley, Susan B. The Life and Works of Albert Pike to 1860. George
    Peabody College, 1934. Dissertation: English.
Yarnell, Dorothy A. A Life of Albert Pike. Columbia Univ., 1924.
    Thesis: English.

CLARENCE HAMILTON POE (1881-1964)

Cote, Joseph A. Clarence Hamilton Poe: The Formative Years, 1899-
    1917. East Carolina Univ., 1969. Thesis: History.

EDGAR ALLAN POE (1809-1849)

Adair, Margaret C.C. Literary Techniques and Death Symbolism in
    Selected Short Stories of Edgar Allan Poe. Northeast
    Louisiana Univ., 1968. Thesis: Education.
Albright, Thelma. Poe's Interest in Contemporary Affairs. Duke
    Univ., 1937. Thesis: English.
Alexander, A.S. The Changing Character of the Increasing Interest
    in Edgar Allan Poe. Univ. of Oregon, 1928. Thesis: English.
Alexander, Jean A. Affidavits of Genius. French Essays on Poe,
    From Forgue to Valery. Univ. of Washington, 1961. Disser-
    tation: English.
Allan, Carlisle V. The Military Services of Edgar Allan Poe.
    Columbia Univ., 1925. Thesis: English.
Allen, M.L. Edgar Allan Poe and the British Magazine Tradition.
    Birmingham [England], 1965. Dissertation: English.
Allen, Ruth C. Edgar Allan Poe's Doctrine of the Single Effect.
    Duke Univ., 1936. Thesis: English.
Alloway, Ruby V. Poe's Methods of Developing Atmosphere in his
    Short Stories. Univ. of South Dakota, 1954. Thesis:
    English.
Alterton, Margaret. Origins of Poe's Critical Principles. Univ. of
    Iowa, 1922. Dissertation: English.

Andra, Carl E. Those Ravens and Cats of Mr. Poe; Myth, Eliot, and *The Elder Statesman*; and "Pas de Deux" and "Curtain Call," Two Original Short Stories. Brigham Young Univ., 1964. Thesis: English.

Antosca, Francis E. *Tamerlane* to *Eureka*: The Evolution of Poe's Cosmic Myth. Univ. of Rhode Island, 1970. Thesis: English.

Arhippainan, Laila H. An Analysis of the Development of Poe's Poetic Technique. Kent State Univ., 1964. Thesis: English.

Arnold, John W. The Poe Perplex: A Guide to the Tales. Univ. of Massachusetts, 1967. Dissertation: English.

Ayala, Esperanza. Edgar Allan Poe's Place in Literature. Texas A & I Univ., 1943. Thesis: English.

Baab, Thomas H. Social and Political Commentary in the Works of Edgar Allan Poe. Columbia Univ., 1952. Thesis: English.

Bailey, Patricia R. Poe and Griswold. Columbia Univ., 1948. Thesis: English.

Baird, Ruth C. The Modernity of Edgar Allan Poe's Criticism. Vanderbilt Univ., 1943. Thesis: English.

Ballard, Ruby T. Poe as a Critic. Baylor Univ., 1948. Thesis: English.

Bancroft, Anne D. Poe's Theory of Poetry and the Doctrine of Art for Art's Sake. Stanford Univ., 1927. Thesis: English.

Barclay, Lynden H.W. The Characteristic Qualities of the Mind of Edgar Allan Poe as Revealed in His Short Stories. Queen's [Canada], 1934. Thesis: English.

Barefoot, Spencer W. Sources of Poe's Tales. Univ. of Oklahoma, 1931. Thesis: English.

Barnett, Donald E. Poe's Ideal Woman: A Composite Portrait with Variations. Univ. of Georgia, 1952. Thesis: English.

Barshay, Robert H. Three Studies in English: Milton's *Paradise Lost*; Joyce's *Ulysses*; and Poe and the English Aesthetic. Pennsylvania State Univ., 1967. Thesis: English.

Bass, William W. Edgar Allan Poe as Critic of Southern Writers and Literature. Univ. of North Carolina (Chapel Hill), 1954. Dissertation: English.

Bayless, Joy. Rufus Wilmot Griswold, Poe's Literary Executor. Columbia Univ., 1940. Dissertation: English.

Beard, D.B. Poe" Toward the Dramatic Ideal. Univ. of North Dakota, 1962. Thesis: English.

Berces, Frances A. Poe, Opium, and Imagination. Wake Forest Univ., 1967. Thesis: English.

Bierly, Charles E. *Eureka* and the Drama of The Self: A Study of the Relationship Between Poe's Cosmology and his Fiction. Univ. of Washington, 1957. Dissertation: English.

Binder, Sr. M.C. Studien zur Charakterisierungstechnik in Kurzgeschichten W. Irvings, E.A. Poes, und Nathaniel Hawthornes. Graz, 1950. Dissertation: English.

Bittner, William. Poe's *Tales of the Folio Club*: A Critical and Descriptive Edition. Univ. of Pennsylvania, 1948. Dissertation: English.

Bjurman, Gunnar. Edgar Allan Poe. Ein Litteraturhistorisch Studie. Lund, 1916. Dissertation: English.

Body, Lois M. The Influence of the Gothic Novel on the Works of Edgar Allan Poe. Univ. of Illinois, 1941. Thesis: English.

Boje, Louise M. Notes on Poe's Criticisms in *Burton's Gentleman's Magazine*. Columbia Univ., 1924. Thesis: English.

Bondurant, Agnes M. Poe's Richmond. Duke Univ., 1941. Thesis: English.

Bonner, Thomas, Jr. A Study of "The Bells" of Edgar Allan Poe. Tulane Univ., 1968. Thesis: English.

Borenstein, Lisa. Edgar Allan Poe's Vision. McGill, 1967. Thesis: English.

Boussoulas, Nicolas I. La Peur et l'Univers dans l'Oeuvre d'Edgar Poe. Paris, 1950. Dissertation: English.

Bowles, Lester. Irving's Influence on Poe. Southern Methodist Univ., 1936. Thesis: English.

Bradfield, Elizabeth. A Study of Poe's Narrative Art. Univ. of Texas (Austin), 1933. Thesis: English.

Braswell, John W. Poe as a Critic. Duke Univ., 1931. Thesis: English.

Brodie, Bernard. Poe as an Artist. Temple Univ., 1926. Thesis: Education.

Brody, Paul. Poe's *Eureka*. Brooklyn College, 1954. Thesis: English.

Brooks, Curtis M. Poe's Defense of the Creative Imagination. Univ. of Virginia, 1966. Thesis: English.

Brown, Marion F. Poe in France. Columbia Univ., 1914. Thesis: English.

Brown, Ruth. Unpublished Correspondence of Poe. Hunter College, 1936. Thesis: English.

Browne, Robert E. Art and Artifice in the Poetry of Poe. Columbia Univ., 1964. Thesis: English.

Bryant, Anne. Poe and *Godey's Lady's Book*. Duke Univ., 1940. Thesis: English.

Budde, Nelda. The Reading of Edgar Allan Poe. Univ. of Kansas, 1946. Thesis: English.

Budick, Emily. Meditating between the Human and the Ideal: Philosophy and Art in the Tales of Edgar Allan Poe. Cornell Univ., 1970. Thesis: English.

Burbank, Blanche. Edgar Allan Poe's Literary Criticisms of Women Writers. Univ. of Texas (Austin), 1937. Thesis: English.

Burnette, Bernard J. Poe's *Narrative of A. Gordon Pym*: A Work Divided. Florida State Univ., 1969. Thesis: English.

Butler, Susan P. Elements of Mysticism in the Work of Poe. Southwest Texas State Univ., 1927. Thesis: English.

Cain, Henry E. James Clarence Mangan and the Poe-Mangan Question. Catholic Univ., 1929. Dissertation: English.

Calcott, Emily S. The Influence of Isaac Disraeli on Edgar A. Poe. Univ. of Virginia, 1931. Dissertation: English.

Caldwell, Henry H. The Other Poe. Columbia Univ., 1921. Thesis: English.

Callaghan, Barry J.M. An Investigation into the Narrative Technique of *The Narrative of A. Gordon Pym* by E.A. Poe. Toronto, 1963. Thesis: English.

Carmean, Hillis. The Methods of Poe and Coleridge in Attaining a Weird, Uncanny Effect. Stetson Univ., 1926. Thesis: English.

Carpenter, W.C. Some Mental Aspects of Edgar Allan Poe. Univ. of Maryland, 1935. Thesis: Psychology.

[126]

Carrere, Bertrand. Degenerescence et Dipsomanie d'Edgar Poe. Toulouse, 1908. Dissertation: Medicine.

Casabian, Edward K. The Use of Setting in the Selected Prose Tales of Edgar Allan Poe. Iowa State Teachers College, 1966. Thesis: English.

Casale, Ottavio M. Edgar Allan Poe and Transcendentalism: Conflict and Affinity. Univ. of Michigan, 1965. Dissertation: English.

Caspari, Heinz. Edgar Allan Poes Verhaeltnis zum Okkultismus. Freiburg, 1922. Dissertation: English.

Cate, Julian O. Edgar Allan Poe and the Romance Languages. Univ. of Texas (Austin), 1937. Thesis: English.

Cauthen, Irby B., Jr. A Descriptive Bibliography of Criticism of Edgar Allan Poe, 1827-1941. Univ. of Virginia, 1942. Thesis: English.

Chamberlain, Florence C. The Nature and Use of the Death Theme and Motif in Edgar Allan Poe's Works. Drake Univ., 1961. Thesis: English.

Chambers, John K. The Growth and Development of Edgar Allan Poe's Concept of Originality in Art. Queen's [Canada], 1963. Thesis: English.

Cherry, Kenneth H. Poe's Sound Effects: Alliteration, Assonance, and Consonance. Univ. of Tennessee, 1966. Thesis: English.

Clanton, Doris E.D. Edgar Allan Poe's Reputation in the Twentieth Century as a Short Story Writer. Auburn Univ., 1959. Thesis: English.

Cole, Cacy A. Poe and Emerson: The Development of Their Poetic Theories. Southern Methodist Univ., 1954. Thesis: English.

Conway, John D. Evil and Poe: A Study of "The House of Usher." Illinois State Univ., 1965. Thesis: English.

Cooper, Ruth. Byron's Influence on the Poetry of Poe. Univ. of Alabama, 1937. Thesis: English.

Cox, Fay. *Graham's Magazine* and Edgar Allan Poe. Duke Univ., 1931. Thesis: English.

Crowder, Ashby B., Jr. Poe as a Critic of Women Writers. Univ. of Tennessee, 1966. Thesis: English.

Culhane, Mary J. Thoreau, Melville, Poe, and the Romantic Quest. Univ. of Minnesota, 1945. Dissertation: English.

Cullen, John C. III. Charles Brockden Brown's Major Novels and the Fiction of Edgar Allan Poe. Univ. of Virginia, 1966. Thesis: English.

Currie, Elizabeth L. A Study of the Influence of Women upon Edgar Allan Poe. Cornell Univ., 1940. Thesis: English.

Dameron, John L. Edgar Allan Poe in the Mid-Twentieth Century: His Literary Reputation in England and America 1928-1960 and a Bibliography of Poe Criticism 1942-1960. Univ. of Tennessee, 1962. Dissertation: English.

Davis, Georgia M. Investigations since 1909 Concerning the Biography of Edgar Allan Poe. Univ. of Colorado, 1929. Thesis: English.

Day, Douglas T. III. *The Narrative of Arthur Gordon Pym*: A Review of Recent Criticism. Univ. of Virginia, 1959. Thesis: English.

Deaton, Frances W. Poe's Tendencies as a Writer of Fiction as Shown in His Early Tales. Northwestern Univ., 1928. Thesis: English.

DeFato, Grace R. The Critical Reception of Edgar Allan Poe's *Narrative of Arthur Gordon Pym*. Columbia Univ., 1960. Thesis: English.

Dickinson, Lucy E. Byron and Poe: A Comparison and a Study of Byron's Influence Upon Poe. Auburn Univ., 1941. Thesis: English.

Dix, William S., Jr. The Gothic Element in the Short Stories of Edgar Allan Poe. Univ. of Virginia, 1932. Thesis: English.

Dolbee, Cora. Poe's Place in Southern Criticism. Univ. of Kansas, 1911. Thesis: English.

Dorich, Bernadine. Edgar Allan Poe: The Isolated Search for Identity. Kent State Univ., 1968. Thesis: English.

Doyle, John R., Jr. Poe's Debt to Byron, Coleridge, Moore, and Shelley: A Study of Influences in the Development of a Poet's Art. Univ. of Virginia, 1937. Thesis: English.

Duboise, Novella E. A Study of Some Parallel Ideas Found in the Literary Works of Edgar Allan Poe and Robinson Jeffers in the Light of Scientific Progress. Univ. of Kentucky, 1942. Thesis: English.

Earle, Ethel J. Poe's Philosophy of Literary Composition as Exemplified in His Poems. Boston Univ., 1932. Thesis: English.

Easley, John B. The Critical Reception of Edgar Allan Poe 1927-1952. Univ. of North Carolina (Chapel Hill), 1956. Thesis: English.

Eaton, Ariel. Poe's Use of Phrenology. Univ. of Virginia, 1964. Thesis: English.

Eikleberry, Doris L. Poe's Criticism in the Light of Recent Studies. Univ. of Illinois, 1947. Thesis: English.

Eisenman, Mayette B. Edgar Allan Poe and the South. New York Univ., 1949. Thesis: English.

English, Carroll N. Mythological Allusions in Poe's Tales and Poems. Univ. of Texas (Austin), 1936. Thesis: English.

Espy, Robert B. The Poe-Osgood Affair: A Study of the Relations of Edgar Allan Poe and Frances Sargent Osgood. Washington and Lee Univ., 1941. Thesis: English.

Evans, Elizabeth. The Narrator in Three Tales by Edgar Allan Poe. Univ. of North Carolina (Chapel Hill), 1960. Thesis: English.

Faris, Paul P. The Poetry of Edgar Allan Poe: A Study in Diction. Univ. of Missouri, 1928. Thesis: English.

Feazel, Delmar D. Poe's Literary Borrowings. Southern Illinois Univ. (Carbondale), 1950. Thesis: English.

Feinstein, George W. "The Raven," a Drama in Prologue and Five Acts. Univ. of North Dakota, 1937. Thesis: English.

Fiat, Suzanne J. Edgar Allan Poe, Poet of Ecstasy. Kansas State Teachers College, 1953. Thesis: English.

Figliozzi, Dominic W. Edgar Allan Poe, Dramatist. St. John's Univ. (Minnesota), 1950. Thesis: English.

Fioke, Clarence J. A Study of the Prose Poems of Edgar Allan Poe. Tulane Univ., 1965. Thesis: English.

Fisher, Benjamin F. Gothic Techniques in Poe's Short Stories. Duke Univ., 1969. Dissertation: English.

Flannery, Peggy A.S. Edgar Allan Poe in Anthologies of American Literature, 1849-1899. Duke Univ., 1945. Thesis: English.

Flowers, Frank C. Poe and the Problem of God. Louisiana State
    Univ., 1939. Thesis: English.
Fort, J.C., Jr. Satire in the Works of Edgar Allan Poe. Vanderbilt
    Univ., 1939. Thesis: English.
Fox, Hugh B. Poe and Cosmology: The God-Universe Relationship in
    a Romantic Context. Univ. of Illinois, 1958. Dissertation:
    English.
Frank, Frederick S. Perverse Pilgrimage: The Role of the Gothic
    in the Works of Charles Brockden Brown, Edgar Allan Poe,
    Nathaniel Hawthorne. Rutgers Univ., 1968. Dissertation:
    English.
Fred, Raymond M. Mural Representing Edgar Allan Poe and His Work.
    Univ. of North Dakota, 1947. Thesis: Art.
Freeman, Jennie Y. A Study of the Criticism of Edgar Allan Poe.
    Columbia Univ., 1907. Thesis: English.
Gage, James D. Edgar Allan Poe's Criticism of the Novel. Western
    Kentucky Univ., 1968. Thesis: English.
Gaillard, Dawson F.D. Edgar Allan Poe's Three Tales of Poetic
    Vision: An Interpretation Based on Poe's Use of Ritual and
    Myth. Tulane Univ., 1965. Thesis: English.
Gay, Pauline M. The Tell-Tale Cane: Death of Edgar Allan Poe.
    Univ. of Texas (El Paso), 1967. Thesis: English.
Gillen, Madeline M. Personal Incidents and Theories in the Poetry
    of Edgar Allan Poe. Boston Univ., 1940. Thesis: English.
Gilliam, Carroll L. Poe's Revisions as Related to His Poetic
    Theories. Univ. of South Carolina, 1950. Thesis: English.
Glimp, Isie T. Women in the Life of Edgar Allan Poe. St. Mary's
    Univ. (San Antonio), 1944. Thesis: English.
Goldberg, Milton J. The Literary Reputation of Edgar Allan Poe in
    England to 1880. New York Univ., 1940. Thesis: English.
Goldzung, Valerie J. The Theory and Practice of Annihilation:
    Themes and Images in the Works of Edgar Allan Poe. Univ. of
    Massachusetts, 1966. Thesis: English.
Goodrich, Stephen F. Poe and God: A Descent into Unity. Columbia
    Univ., 1956. Thesis: English.
Gottschalk, Hans W. The Imagery of Poe's Poems and Tales: A
    Chronological Interpretive Study. State Univ. of Iowa, 1949.
    Dissertation: English.
Grennan, Sr. Mary J. A Comparison of the Poetic Theories of Emerson
    and Poe. Univ. of Notre Dame, 1957. Thesis: English.
Griffith, Alice M. A Survey of the Critical Opinion Concerning the
    Effect of Edgar Allan Poe's Life upon His Literary Work. Univ.
    of Richmond, 1952. Thesis: English.
Griggs, Earl L. Notes on Edgar Allan Poe's Pinakidia. Columbia
    Univ., 1923. Thesis: English.
Guilds, John C. Poe's Mother and Foster-Mother: An Interpretative
    Study. Duke Univ., 1949. Thesis: English.
Hall, Thomas. Science and Pseudo-Science in Poe's Works. North
    Texas State Univ., 1938. Thesis: English.
Halliburton, David G. The Grotesque in American Literature: Poe,
    Hawthorne, and Melville. Univ. of California (Riverside),
    1966. Dissertation: English.
Hambury, Thomas B. The Setting as Expressive of the State of Mind
    of the Main Character in Six Works by Edgar Allan Poe. Tulane
    Univ., 1968. Thesis: English.

Hancock, Arthur S. Emerson, Lowell, Poe and Whitman, on the Functions of Poetry. Columbia Univ., 1923. Thesis: English.

Haney, Lois. Dramatic and Stylistic Devices in Poe's Stories of the Grotesque: An Analysis. Southwest Texas State Univ., 1968. Thesis: English.

Hanks, Lacola L. The Narrative Art of Edgar Allan Poe. North Texas State Univ., 1939. Thesis: English.

Hart, Charles W. Poe's Humor in the *Tales of the Folio Club*. Catholic Univ., 1935. Thesis: English.

Harwood, Sprigg. Sources of Poe's Tales. Southern Methodist Univ., 1940. Thesis: English.

Haverstick, Iola S. The Two Voyages of Arthur Gordon Pym. Columbia Univ., 1965. Thesis: English.

Hawkes, Helen S. Poe's Use of Gothic Romance in His Prose Tales. Univ. of Idaho, 1928. Thesis: English.

Hawkins, Patricia W. The Supernatural and Uncanny Aspects of Hawthorne and Poe. San Francisco State College, 1968. Thesis: English.

Hayden, Richard A. Edgar Allan Poe's Concept of Beauty. Tulane Univ., 1965. Thesis: English.

Heazlett, Helen J. Poe and the British. Univ. of Pittsburgh, 1924. Thesis: English.

Heckman, Franklin J. Edgar Allan Poe--the Critic. Pennsylvania State Univ., 1926. Thesis: English.

Heitzman, Mary B. Hawthorne's Use of Sin in *The Scarlet Letter*; Thoreau's "Hut" as a Symbol of His Ideas and Attitudes Expressed in *Walden*; The Spirit of Perverseness in the Tales of Edgar Allan Poe. Morehead State College, 1966. Thesis: English.

Helfers, Melvin C. The Military Career of Edgar Allan Poe. Duke Univ., 1949. Thesis: English.

Hensley, Virgil W. Edgar Allan Poe as Critic in Theory and Practice. Univ. of Tulsa, 1965. Thesis: English.

Herring, Louise L. Poe's Habits of Composition. Univ. of Texas (Austin), 1937. Thesis: English.

Highum, Clayton D. Poe's Consistency of Practice in the Short Story. Iowa State Teachers College, 1961. Thesis: English.

Hill, Johnsie C. American Criticism of Poe, 1909-1937. Duke Univ., 1938. Thesis: English.

Hill, Nellie. Edgar Allan Poe as a Critic. Univ. of Arkansas, 1932. Thesis: English.

Hippe, Fritz. Edgar Allan Poes Lyrick in Deutschland. Muenster, 1913. Dissertation: English.

Holden, Mrs. R.E. Poe as a Novelist. Ohio Univ., 1933. Thesis: English.

Holt, Jerry G. Poe's Existential Predicament: A Study of His Minor Tales. Univ. of Oklahoma, 1967. Thesis: English.

Holub, Peter F. Poe's Rhythmical Creation of Beauty. Univ. of Pittsburgh, 1948. Thesis: English.

Honeycutt, Julian B. Edgar Allan Poe's Attitude Toward the Immortality of the Soul. Louisiana State Univ., 1920 Thesis: English.

Hoole, William S. Edgar Poe and his Times. Wofford College, 1931. Thesis: English.

Hornung, Willard R. Edgar Allan Poe's Treatment of Women in His Writings. Wofford College, 1949. Thesis: English.

Howell, Ruby. Poe's Influence on Rossetti. Louisiana State Univ., 1929. Thesis: English.

Hubbell, Harold B. Edgar Allan Poe's Use of Source Material in Three Sea Tales. Columbia Univ., 1948. Thesis: English.

Hudson, Ruth L. Poe's Craftmanship in the Short Story. Univ. of Virginia, 1935. Dissertation: English.

Hughes, James M. The Dialectic of Death in Poe, Dickinson, Emerson and Whitman. Univ. of Pennsylvania, 1969. Dissertation: English.

Hull, William D. II. A Canon of the Reviews of Edgar Allan Poe in *The Southern Literary Messenger* and *Burton's Gentleman's Magazine*. Univ. of Virginia, 1940. Thesis: English.

_____. A Canon of the Critical Works of Edgar Allan Poe with a Study of Poe as Editor and Reviewer. Univ. of Virginia, 1941. Dissertation: English.

Hutcherson, Dudley R. One Hundred Years of Poe: A Study of Edgar Allan Poe in American and English Criticism, 1827-1927. Univ. of Virginia, 1936. Dissertation: English.

Hutter, Rebecca T. The Devices of Edgar Allan Poe as Seen in *The Narrative of Arthur Gordon Pym* and other Tales. Memphis State Univ., 1963. Thesis: English.

Hyneman, Esther. A Bibliography of Poe Criticism. Columbia Univ., 1962. Thesis: English.

Hyneman, Esther F. The Contemporaneous Reputation of Edgar Allan Poe with Annotated Bibliography of Poe Criticism: 1827-1967. Columbia Univ., 1968. Dissertation: English.

Inlow, Richard M. The Contemporaneity of Poe's Criticism. Vanderbilt Univ., 1956. Thesis: English.

Jack, June S. Edgar Allan Poe: His Influence on Children's Creative Writing. Iowa State Teachers College, 1961. Thesis: English.

Jackson, David K., Jr. Poe and the Southern Literary Messenger. Duke Univ., 1930. Thesis: English.

Jacobs, Robert D. Eighteenth Century Aesthetics in the Literary Theory and Practice of E.A. Poe. Johns Hopkins Univ., 1948. Thesis: English.

_____. Poe's Heritage from Jefferson's Virginia. Johns Hopkins Univ., 1953. Dissertation: English.

Jeffrey, David K. Rationality, Reality, and Intuition in Edgar Allan Poe. Univ. of Virginia, 1966. Thesis: English.

Jenkin, Leonard. States of Consciousness in the Writings of Edgar Allan Poe. Columbia Univ., 1964. Thesis: English.

Johnson, Falk S. Edgar Allan Poe as a Critic of Poetry. Wake Forest Univ., 1936. Thesis: English.

Johnson, George R. Style and Effect in the Short Stories of Edgar Allan Poe. Miami Univ. (Ohio), 1968. Thesis: English.

Johnstone, Lilla. Edgar Allan Poe's Approach to Death. Univ. of Virginia, 1968. Thesis: English.

Jones, Dan P. The Language of Poe's Vision: The Significance of *Eureka* in Relation to the Fictional and Poetic Works of Edgar Allan Poe. Univ. of Texas (Austin), 1964. Thesis: English.

Just, Walter. Die Romantische Bewegung in der Amerikanischen Literatur: Brown, Poe, Hawthorne: Ein Beitrag zur Geschichte der Romantik. Munster, 1910. Dissertation: English.

Kafka, Karl A. Edgar Allan Poe as Judge of America in the *Southern Literary Messenger*. Brooklyn College, 1937. Thesis: English.

Kelly, George E. The Aesthetic Theories of Edgar Allan Poe: An Analytical Study of his Literary Criticism. State Univ. of Iowa, 1953. Dissertation: English.

Kelly, Herbert L. Four of Poe's Women and the Contemporary Magazine Heroine. San Diego State College, 1965. Thesis: English.

Kelly, Sr. M.O., I.H.M. The Mechanics of the Grotesque and Arabesque in the Works of Edgar Allan Poe. Duquesne Univ., 1946. Thesis: English.

Kelly, Ruth. The Influence of Thomas de Quincey on Edgar Allan Poe. Univ. of Southern California, 1938. Thesis: English.

Kelley, Rhoda A. The Reputation of Edgar Allan Poe in America, 1875-1909. Duke Univ., 1937. Thesis: English.

Kennedy, Ralph C., Jr. The Poems and Short Stories of Edgar Allan Poe: Their Composition, Publication, and Reception. Univ. of Arkansas, 1961. Dissertation: English.

Ketterer, D. Edgar Allan Poe. Sussex, 1969. Dissertation: English.

King, Joanne. Edgar Allan Poe, Master and Victim. Montreal, 1949. Thesis: English.

Kirby, Robert R. A Study of Repetition and Self-Plagiarism in Poe's Reviews. Univ. of North Carolina (Chapel Hill), 1958. Thesis: English.

Kirkland, James W. Narrative Procedure in "The Fall of the House of Usher." Univ. of Florida, 1966. Thesis: English.

Knight, Mary R. The Reputation of Edgar Allan Poe in England, 1875-1900. Duke Univ., 1943. Thesis: English.

Koch, Mary L. *The Marginalia* as a Reflection of Poe's Interests in History, Science, the Arts, Philosophy, and Literature. Univ. of Texas (Austin), 1962. Thesis: English.

Kremenliev, Elva B. The Literary Uses of Astronomy in the Writings of Edgar Allan Poe. Univ. of California (Los Angeles), 1963. Dissertation: English.

Krisel, Stuart V. An Examination of Poe's Theory and Practice of Poetry. Brown Univ., 1961. Thesis: English.

Künelt, Harro. Edgar Allan Poe und Dante Gabriel Rosetti. Innsbruck, 1948. Dissertation: English.

Lake, Philip A. Intellectual Aristocracy: The Aim of Poe's Journalism. Univ. of Dayton, 1949. Thesis: English.

Lauvrière, Emile. Un Génie morbide: La vie d'Edgar Allan Poe. Paris, 1904. Dissertation: English.

Laverty, Carroll D. Science and Pseudo-Science in the Writings of Edgar Allan Poe. Duke Univ., 1951. Dissertation: English.

Lazar, Beverly B. Edgar Allan Poe's Theories of Prose Fiction. Univ. of Tennessee, 1964. Thesis: English.

Leerhoff, Dick A. An Examination of the Dramatic Criticism of Edgar Allan Poe. Univ. of South Dakota, 1968. Thesis: English.

Lerner, Arthur. Psychoanalytically Oriented Criticism of Three American Poets: Poe, Whitman, and Aiken. Univ. of Southern California, 1968. Dissertation: English.

Levine, Stuart G. "The Proper Spirit": A Study of the Prose Fiction of Edgar Poe. Brown Univ., 1958. Dissertation: English.

Levy, David. The Counterfeit Revelation; A Study of the Junction
of Life, Death and Eternity in the Works of Edgar Allan Poe.
Montreal, 1966. Thesis: English.
Lewis, Ruby P. A Study of Imagery in the Poems of Edgar Allan Poe.
Univ. of Southern California, 1947. Thesis: English.
Ligon, John F. On Desperate Seas: A Study of Poe's Imaginary
Journeys. Univ. of Washington, 1961. Dissertation: English.
Linville, Jane J. A Study of Some of the Literary and Legendary
Sources of Poe's "Gold Bug." Columbia Univ., 1947. Thesis:
English.
Little, Sally V.A. An Analysis of the Angle of Narration in the
Tales of Edgar Allan Poe. Univ. of Houston, 1957. Thesis:
English.
Long, Travis B. Poe's Relationship with Editors and Publishers.
Tulane Univ., 1964. Thesis: English.
Lubbers, Klaus. Die Todesszene und Ihre Funktion im Kurtz-
geschichtenwerk von Edgar Allan Poe. Mainz, 1961. Disser-
tation: English.
Lubell, Albert J. Edgar Allan Poe, Critic and Reviewer. New York
Univ., 1951. Dissertation: English.
Lyon, Joette E. Edgar Allan Poe, Frontiersman of the Short Story.
Duquesne Univ., 1936. Thesis: English.
Mabbott, Thomas O. New Light on Poe. Columbia Univ., 1921.
Thesis: English.
_____. *Politian*, an Unfinished Tragedy by Edgar A. Poe. Columbia
Univ., 1923. Dissertation: English.
Madden, Emily M. Perceptible Consequences of Sin in Hawthorne and
Poe. Virginia State College, 1958. Thesis: English.
Mallard, Joy H. A Bibliographical Study of Selected Poems of
Edgar Allan Poe. Univ. of Georgia, 1967. Thesis: English.
Marshall, Carol E. Edgar Allan Poe's Philosophy of Man and the
Universe. Univ. of Virginia, 1943. Thesis: English.
Martin, Princess. Poe's Use of Landscape. North Texas State
Univ., 1942. Thesis: English.
Mascitelli, David W. Poe as Critic of American Literature. Duke
Univ., 1962. Thesis: English.
Massello, William. Edgar Allan Poe and Modern Science. Univ. of
Texas (El Paso), 1965. Thesis: English.
Maxwell, Mignonne C. The Gothic Influence on Edgar Allan Poe's
Short Stories. Mississippi College, 1967. Thesis: English.
Mazow, Julia. The Fugitive Character in Selected Works of Edgar
Allan Poe. Univ. of Houston, 1969. Thesis: English.
McAndrew, William. The Fugitive Vision of Edgar Allan Poe. Tufts
Univ., 1966. Thesis: English.
McAuley, Patricia H. The French Reception of Poe's *Arthur Gordon
Pym*. Memphis State Univ., 1966. Thesis: English.
McCluney, Anne. Edgar Allan Poe as a Precursor of Surrealism.
Southern Methodist Univ., 1961. Thesis: English.
McElroy, Maurine D. Auditory Imagery in Poe's Poetry. Hardin-
Simmons Univ., 1941. Thesis: English.
McGinty, Barbara W. A Dictionary of Proper Names in the Short
Stories of Edgar Allan Poe. Tulane Univ., 1968. Thesis:
English.
McNahan, Dean W. Edgar Allan Poe and the Theme of the Fall.
Pennsylvania State Univ., 1968. Dissertation: English.

[133]

McNair, Hallie. The Reputation of Edgar Allan Poe in America, 1849-1875. Duke Univ., 1932. Thesis: English.

McPherson, Maud E. The Genius of Edgar Allan Poe as Manifested in His Tales. George Washington Univ., 1905. Thesis: English.

McWhorter, Marjorie A. Poe and the Terror of Soul. Columbia Univ., 1952. Thesis: English.

Meaux, Mary A. Emerson and Poe: A Beginning Approach to Their Relationship. Tulane Univ., 1966. Thesis: English.

Meister, John G.H. Poe's *Eureka*: A Study of Its Ideas, Sources, and Its Relationship to His Work. Univ. of Pennsylvania, 1948. Thesis: English.

_____. The Descent of the Irrelative Ode: The Metaphysics and Cosmology of Edgar Allan Poe's *Eureka*. Univ. of Pennsylvania, 1969. Dissertation: English.

Menascé, Ester. Edgar Allan Poe and the Poetry of Night: The Fallen Archangel and the Terror of the Soul. Columbia Univ., 1957. Thesis: English.

Menz, Lotte. Die Sinnlichen Elemente bei Edgar Allan Poe und ihrer Einfluss auf Technik und Stil des Dichters. Marburg, 1916. Dissertation: English.

Mexxanotte, John J. Significance of Myth Making in Poe's Poetry. Southern Connecticut State College, 1965. Thesis: English.

Meyers, Bruce K. The Anti-Bellum Magazine and Edgar Allan Poe. Kent State Univ., 1967. Thesis: English.

Miller, Arthur M. The Influence of Edgar Allan Poe on Ambrose Bierce. Stanford Univ., 1932. Thesis: English.

Miller, Helen F. A Partial Study of Sources for the Works of Edgar Allan Poe. Ohio State Univ., 1931. Thesis: English.

Miller, John C. Poe's English Biographer: John Henry Ingram, A Biographical Account and Study of His Contributions to Poe Scholarship. Univ. of Virginia, 1954. Dissertation: English.

Miller, Newton E., Jr. A Study of Poe's Use of Imaginary and Extraordinary Voyages. Univ. of Texas (Austin), 1940. Thesis: English.

Mixon, Gloria A. Gothicism in the Short Stories of Edgar Allan Poe. Atlanta Univ., 1956. Thesis: English.

Monahan, Dean W. Edgar Allan Poe and the Theme of the Fall. Pennsylvania State Univ., 1968. Dissertation: English.

Montesi, Richard L. Representative Critical Comments on the Artistic Views of Edgar Allan Poe. Iowa State Teachers College, 1960. Thesis: English.

Mooney, Stephen L. Poe's Grand Design: A Study of Theme and Unity in the Tales. Univ. of Tennessee, 1960. Dissertation: English.

Moran, Catharine R. Edgar Allan Poe. George Washington Univ., 1920. Thesis: English.

Morris, Elizabeth G. Science Fiction in the Tales of Edgar Allan Poe. Univ. of South Carolina, 1948. Thesis: English.

Morris, George D. James Fenimore Cooper et Edgar Poe d'après la critique francise du dixneuvième siècle. Paris, 1942. Dissertation: English.

Morrison, Carolyn P. Poe's Major Biographers in English. (a Comparative Study) Vanderbilt Univ., 1950. Thesis: English.

Moss, Richard F. The Transcendental Vision of Hawthorne, Poe, and Melville, as Seen in Some of Their Short Stories. Univ. of Massachusetts, 1959. Thesis: English.

Moss, Sidney P. Poe's Literary Battles. Univ. of Illinois, 1954. Dissertation: English.

Motchenback, Frank W. Edgar Allan Poe's "Prisoner" Theme. Univ. of Texas (El Paso), 1965. Thesis: English.

Murphy, Winnie A. The Literary Relations of Poe with Bryant, Hawthorne, and Lowell. Univ. of North Carolina (Chapel Hill), 1937. Thesis: English.

Murray, Lynn M. The Shaping of an Image: Nineteenth and Twentieth Century Criticism of Edgar Allan Poe. John Carroll Univ., 1963. Thesis: English.

Nakamura, Junichi. Edgar Allan Poe's Relations with New England Writers. Duke Univ., 1938. Thesis: English.

Nave, Barbara. Edgar Allan Poe, Literateur. Iowa State Teachers College, 1961. Thesis: English.

Neal, Sharon B. Edgar Allan Poe and the Shadow that Haunted Him. Univ. of Texas (El Paso), 1969. Thesis: English.

Nelson, Sydney L. The Sources of Poe's Later Tales (1841-1849). New York Univ., 1942. Thesis: English.

Newlin, Paul A. The Uncanny in the Supernatural Short Fiction of Poe, Hawthorne and James. Univ. of California (Los Angeles), 1967. Dissertation: English.

Nixon, Gloria A. Gothicism in the Short Stories of Edgar Allan Poe. Atlanta Univ., 1956. Thesis: English.

Nogues, Valerie W. A Study of the Gothic Elements in the Tales of Edgar Allan Poe. Baylor Univ., 1970. Thesis: American Studies.

Novack, Aaron. The Imagery of Edgar Allan Poe. Brooklyn College, 1941. Thesis: English.

Null, Stephanie. Literary Allusion in Poe's Tales. Univ. of Massachusetts, 1969. Thesis: English.

O'Brien, John J. A Study of the Poetry of James Clarence Mangan, With Special Reference to Edgar Allan Poe and the Symbolist Movement. Catholic Univ., 1907. Dissertation: English.

O'Brien, Patricia. The Development of Poe's Concept of Unity: A Study of His Literary Criticism and "Tales of Ratiocination." Toronto, 1960. Thesis: English.

Oldenburg, Grace M. Coleridge and Poe. Univ. of Maryland, 1933. Thesis: English.

Oliver, Eleanor. Poe and Mrs. Browning. Columbia Univ., 1927. Thesis: English.

Orr, Sr. M.S.M. Mental Mechanisms in Edgar Allan Poe. Catholic Univ., 1934. Thesis: English.

Ostrom, John W. A Critical Edition of the Letters of Edgar Allan Poe. Univ. of Virginia, 1947. Dissertation: English.

Ott, Catherine R. A Study of Edgar Allan Poe's Use of the Dominant Will To Live in His Prose Fiction. Univ. of Rhode Island, 1965. Thesis: English.

Packenham, Howard E. Poe's Literary Theories and Their Application in His Creative Work. Univ. of Idaho, 1933. Thesis: English.

Pappas, Guy M. A Dream within a Dream: A Study of the Women in the Tales of Edgar Allan Poe. Kent State Univ., 1964. Thesis: English.

[135]

Partridge, Claire E. Religious Tendencies of Edgar Allan Poe.
Boston Univ., 1931. Thesis: English.

Patten, Lawrence. Poe's Treatment of Terror in Fiction. Univ. of
North Carolina (Chapel Hill), 1940. Thesis: English.

Payne, Velma. Poe's Influence in English Literature. Univ. of
Texas (Austin), 1929. Thesis: English.

Peach, Susie. The Influence of the Gothic on Poe's Prose Tales.
Univ. of Alabama, 1935. Thesis: English.

Penner, John T. Edgar Allan Poe and the *Broadway Journal*.
Columbia Univ., 1965. Thesis: English.

Percival, Mary M. Poe's Editorship of the *Southern Literary
Messenger*. Columbia Univ., 1926. Thesis: English.

Perlman, Helen D. Edgar Allan Poe: His Use of Source Material in
the Stories of 1840. New York Univ., 1942. Thesis: English.

Peschka, Corinne M. E.A. Poe and the Hippies. Univ. of Texas
(El Paso), 1970. Thesis: English.

Peterson, Dewayne A. Poe's Grotesque Humor: A Study of the
Grotesque Effects in his Humorous Tales. Duke Univ., 1962.
Dissertation: English.

Petit, Georges. Etude Medico-Psychologique sur Edgar Poe. Lyon,
1906. Dissertation: Medicine.

Pezold, Nedra M. The Journey of the Mind toward Beauty as Seen in
Poe's "MS Found in a Bottle" and "A Descent into the
Maelstrom." Tulane Univ., 1969. Thesis: English.

Phillips, Elizabeth. Edgar Allan Poe: The American Context. Univ.
of Pennsylvania, 1957. Dissertation: English.

Pohler, Lola E. Poe's Sense of His Own Worth: A Study of Pride
and Humiliation. Univ. of Texas (Austin), 1941. Thesis:
English.

Poindexter, John. The Gothic Tradition in Poe. Vanderbilt Univ.,
1948. Thesis: English.

Pollak, Simon. Edgar Poe, un Génie Toxicomane. Paris, 1928.
Dissertation: Medicine.

Pugh, Anna E. The Ways in Which Edgar Allan Poe Has Used Conno-
tative Material and Expressions. Univ. of Florida, 1931.
Thesis: English.

Purcell, I.M. Actual Place in Poe's Prose. Duquesne Univ., 1942.
Thesis: English.

Randle, Flo A. A Study of Destructive Forces in the Tales of
Edgar Allan Poe. Univ. of Texas (Austin), 1962. Thesis:
English.

Rans, G. The Origin and History of the Idea of Corruption in
American Writing, and Its Expression in James Fenimore Cooper,
Edgar Allan Poe and Ralph Waldo Emerson. Leeds, 1964.
Dissertation: English.

Rasco, Edna E. The Technique of Effect: A Study of Poe's Narrative
Method. North Texas State Univ., 1941. Thesis: English.

Reece, James B. The *Broadway Journal* with Special Reference to Poe.
Duke Univ., 1949. Thesis: English.

————. Poe and the New York Literati. A Study of the "Literati"
Sketches and of Poe's Relations with the New York Writers.
Duke Univ., 1954. Dissertation: English.

Reilly, John E. Poe in Imaginative Literature: A Study of American
Drama, Fiction, and Poetry Devoted to Edgar Allan Poe or His
Works. Univ. of Virginia, 1965. Dissertation: English.

Richey, Evlyn B. An Interpretation of Edgar Allan Poe's "The Fall of the House of Usher." Northwestern Univ., 1937. Thesis: Speech.

Ridings, Robert. Three Studies in English: Donne's "Evaporations of Wit"; Hopkins' "The Starlight Night"; Poe's Imaginary Voyage. Pennsylvania State Univ., 1969. Thesis: English.

Riess, Lynda A. The Philosophy of Edgar Allan Poe in *Eureka*. Baylor Univ., 1967. Thesis: English.

Robertson, James A. The American Short Story's Four Pioneers: Irving, Hawthorne, Poe and Harte. Acadia (Canada), 1948. Thesis: English.

Robinson, Carolyn K. The Significance of Astronomical Phenomena in the Writings of Edgar Allan Poe. Drake Univ., 1968. Thesis: English.

Roland, Albert. Edgar Allan Poe: A Study in Poetic Technique. Univ. of Kansas, 1951. Thesis: English.

Rosenblatt, William F., Jr. The Aesthetic Theory and Practice of Edgar Allan Poe. Vanderbilt Univ., 1932. Thesis: Philosophy.

Ruska, Margaret K.M. Edgar Allan Poe, Frustrated Dramatist. Univ. of Texas (Austin), 1965. Thesis: English.

Sadock, Jeffrey J. "The Haunted Palace": The Figure of the Dying Heroine in Edgar Allan Poe. Tufts Univ., 1966. Thesis: English.

St. Armand, Barton L. In the American Manner: An Inquiry into the Aesthetics of Emily Dickinson and Edgar Allan Poe. Brown Univ., 1968. Dissertation: English.

St. Germain, Arthur R. Reason and Emotion in Edgar Allan Poe. Montreal, 1953. Thesis: English.

Salzberg, Joel. The Grotesque as Moral Aesthetic: A Study of the Tales of Edgar Allan Poe. Univ. of Oklahoma, 1967. Dissertation: English.

Sanford, Marie C. Trends in Poe Criticism, 1849-1930. Tulane Univ., 1967. Thesis: English.

Scheurman, John W. Present Status of Poe as Literary Critic. Univ. of Wyoming, 1952. Thesis: English.

Schlichenmaier, Carol. The Poetic Theory of Emerson, Poe, and T.S. Eliot. Univ. of Miami (Coral Gables), 1963. Thesis: English.

Schneider, Josephine M. French Criticism of Poe, Especially Since 1900. Univ. of South Carolina, 1929. Thesis: Romance Languages.

Schuhmann, Kuno. Die Erzählende Prosa Edgar Allan Poe. Ein Beitrag zu einer Gattungsgeschichte der Amerikanischen Short Story. Frankfurt, 1957. Dissertation: English.

Sears, Vera M. The Philosophy of Edgar Allan Poe. Univ. of Oklahoma, 1936. Thesis: Philosophy.

Seawell, Elizabeth. Poe's Interest in Contemporary Affairs. Columbia Univ., 1928. Thesis: English.

Seigler, Milledge B. Gothicism in Poe's Short Stories. Duke Univ., 1936. Thesis: English.

Sexton, Richard J. The Minor Criticism of Edgar Allan Poe. Fordham Univ., 1935. Thesis: English.

Shih, Chung-wen. Poe and Mrs. Sara Helen Whitman. Duke Univ., 1949. Thesis: English.

Shuck, Emerson C. Poe and Science. Ohio State Univ., 1940. Thesis: English.

Siebel, Paul. Der Einflusz Samuel Taylor Coleridges auf Edgar Allan Poe. Munster, 1924. Dissertation: English.

Silvia, Barbara J. Poe: Short Story Author and Critic. Univ. of Rhode Island, 1964. Thesis: English.

Simpson, Helen. Edgar Allan Poe's Doctrine of Effect. Southern Methodist Univ., 1936. Thesis: English.

Simpson, Mary H. A History of the Criticism of Edgar Allan Poe. Vanderbilt Univ., 1938. Thesis: English.

Skaggs, Calvin L. Narrative Point of View in Edgar Allan Poe's Criticism and Fiction. Duke Univ., 1966. Dissertation: English.

Sloane, David E.E. Early Nineteenth-Century Medicine in Poe's Short Stories. Duke Univ., 1966. Thesis: English.

Smith, Carl Y. The Vocabulary of E.A. Poe. George Peabody College, 1939. Thesis: English.

Smith, Charlotte J. The Narrative Point of View in Edgar Allan Poe's Short Stories. Univ. of Georgia, 1969. Thesis: English.

Smith, Mary E. Imagery in the Poetry of Edgar Allan Poe. Univ. of Oklahoma, 1937. Thesis: English.

Smith, Sarah F. Poe and Anderson. A Study in the Tradition of the Short Story. Auburn Univ., 1949. Thesis: English.

Snider, Harry C. An Edition of the Poems in Poe's Last Collection Based Largely on His Own Critical Principles. Univ. of Michigan, 1963. Dissertation: English.

Snyder, Lulu N. A Study of Edgar Allan Poe's "Fall of the House of Usher." Columbia Univ., 1926. Thesis: English.

Speake, Margery M. The Development of the Poe Biography before Woodberry. Columbia Univ., 1928. Thesis: English.

Spear, Dorothy A. Edgar Allan Poe in Germany. Columbia Univ., 1913. Thesis: English.

Stauffer, Donald B. Prose Style in the Fiction of Edgar A. Poe. Indiana Univ., 1963. Dissertation: English.

Steen, Gladys E. Poe's Indebtedness to the Periodicals of His Time. Univ. of Texas (Austin), 1931. Thesis: English.

Stewart, Robert A. Textual Notes for the Tales of Edgar Allan Poe, Virginia Edition, Vols. II to VI. Univ. of Virginia, 1901. Dissertation: English.

Stovall, Jennie. Fantastic Effects in Poe's stories: A Study of the Use of the Supernatural. Univ. of Texas (Austin), 1937. Thesis: English.

Strange, Arthur F. The World of Edgar Poe. Columbia Univ., 1959. Thesis: English.

Stroer, Ernst. Edgar Allan Poe's Lyrick. Vienna, 1910. Dissertation: English.

Struggles, Eva. Edgar Allan Poe as a Critic. Columbia Univ., 1918. Thesis: English.

Stutzman, Dorles C. The Development of Edgar Allan Poe as a Short Story Writer. Univ. of Illinois, 1933. Thesis: English.

Sullivan, Joseph L. Methods of Humor in Poe's Prose Tales. Univ. of Rhode Island, 1965. Thesis: English.

Teefy, Martha H. The Technique of Disintegration in Selected Tales of Poe. Virginia Polytechnic Institute, 1969. Thesis: English.

Tewell, Dan J. A Dissertation of Poe's Literary Principles as Illustrated by His Prose Narratives. Kansas State College (Pittsburgh), 1935. Thesis: English.

Theurer, Lydia A. A Study of the Literary Criticism of Edgar Allan Poe. Stetson Univ., 1942. Thesis: English.

Thompson, Gary R. Poe's Romantic Irony: A Study of the Gothic Tales in a Romantic Context. Univ. of Southern California, 1967. Dissertation: English.

Thomas, Glen R. Consistency in Psychoanalytic Approaches to Literary Criticism: Evaluation of Eighteen Studies of Six Works By Hawthorne, Poe and James. American Univ., 1964. Thesis: English.

Thornton, Edythe C. Poe as Theoretical and Practicing Critic. Vanderbilt Univ., 1940. Thesis: English.

Tollerson, Jo A. The Feminine Protagonist in Edgar Allan Poe's Short Stories. Univ. of Georgia, 1966. Thesis: English.

Trimble, Louise M. A Study of the Works of Edgar Allan Poe for the Secondary Schools. Columbia Univ., 1903. Thesis: Education.

Truscello, Samuel J. A Study of Poe's Mental and Physical Health. Kent State Univ., 1954. Thesis: English.

Vann, Jerry D. The Obsessed Man in the Tales of Edgar Allan Poe. Texas Christian Univ., 1960. Thesis: English.

Varnado, Seaborn L. The Numinous in the Work of Edgar Allan Poe. Fordham Univ., 1965. Dissertation: English.

Varner, John G. Poe and Mrs. Whitman: A Study of the Documents of Sarah Helen Whitman. Univ. of Virginia, 1932. Thesis: English.

Vaughan, Joseph L. The Literary Opinions of Edgar Allan Poe. Univ. of Virginia, 1940. Dissertation: English.

Veters, Anna J. Some Notes on the Sources of Poe. Tulane Univ., 1915. Thesis: German.

Voorhees, Virginia D. The History of Opinion in America Regarding the Life of Edgar Allan Poe. Univ. of Kansas, 1943. Thesis: English.

Walker, I.M. A Study of Edgar Allan Poe. Nottingham, 1963. Dissertation: English.

Walton, Gerald W. Edgar Allan Poe as a Literary Critic. Univ. of Mississippi, 1959. Thesis: English.

Waterman, Jennifer. The Relationship between Poe's Developing Theory and Personal Taste, and the Creations and Revisions of the Poetry. Carleton (Canada), 1967. Thesis: English.

Waters, Charles M. The Influence of Poe's Journalism on His Art and Criticism. Univ. of Tennessee, 1952. Thesis: English.

West, Dale H. Poe's Early Reception in England. Univ. of Southern California, 1956. Thesis: English.

Whipple, William. A Study of Edgar Allan Poe's Satiric Patterns. Northwestern Univ., 1951. Dissertation: English.

Whisnant, David E. Edgar Allan Poe's Study of Science. Duke Univ., 1962. Thesis: English.

White, M.E. Influence of Coleridge on Poe. State Univ. of New
    York (Fredonia), 1940. Thesis: English.
Whitman, Max. A Study of Poe's "Marie Roget." Columbia Univ.,
    1932. Thesis: English.
Widger, Howard D.F. The Reading of Edgar Allan Poe with Special
    Reference to Its Effect upon His Writing. Univ. of Illinois,
    1930. Thesis: English.
Wiggins, Genevieve. Humor and Satire in Poe's *Tales of the Folio
    Club*. Vanderbilt Univ., 1950. Thesis: English.
Wilder, Emmett J. *Eureka*: Poe's Climactic Dream. Louisiana State
    Univ., 1964. Thesis: English.
Wiley, Virginia. The Interior Settings of Edgar Allan Poe's Short
    Stories. Duke Univ., 1946. Thesis: English.
Wilkins, Margaret B. The Ironies in the Criticisms of Edgar Allan
    Poe's Life and Work. Iowa State Teachers College, 1964.
    Thesis: English.
Williams, John R. Poe's Treatment of the Macabre. Southern
    Methodist Univ., 1947. Thesis: English.
Willis, L.H. The Soul as Medium of Poe's Criticism of Life.
    Sheffield (England), 1966. Thesis: English.
Wills, O.L. Edgar Allan Poe: Themes of Guilt. Miami Univ. (Ohio),
    1963. Thesis: English.
Wilson, Katherine E. Satire in Poe's works. Univ. of North Carolina
    (Chapel Hill), 1924. Thesis: English.
Wiltshire, Evelyn. Influence of Nineteenth Century English Poetry
    on E.A. Poe. Yale Univ., 1939. Thesis: English.
Wolff, Anne L. Tod und Unsterblichkeit das Leitmotiv von Edgar Allan
    Poe. Humboldt (East Berlin), 1937. Dissertation: English.
Wood, Marie L. An Autobiographical Interpretation of the Poems of
    Edgar Allan Poe. Univ. of Texas (Austin), 1951. Thesis:
    English.
Woods, Carrie S.B. The Narrator in Poe's Tales of Horror. Texas
    Woman's Univ., 1965. Thesis: English.
Wranek, William H., Jr. The Psychology of Poe. Univ. of Virginia,
    1926. Thesis: English.
Wuletich, Sybil. Poe: The Rationale of the Uncanny. Ohio State
    Univ., 1961. Dissertation: English.
Yanover, Jules. The Gothic Image of Poe and Hawthorne. Iowa State
    Teachers College, 1964. Thesis: English.
Young, Sallie S.M. Edgar Allan Poe in Relation to His Times. North
    Texas State Univ., 1940. Thesis: English.
Zimmerman, Michael P. A Study of *Eureka*: Poe's Last Testament.
    Columbia Univ., 1960. Thesis: English.

EDWARD ALFRED POLLARD (1831-1872)

Cunningham, H.H. Edward Alfred Pollard: Historian and Critic of
    the Confederacy. Univ. of North Carolina (Chapel Hill), 1940.
    Thesis: History.

KATHERINE ANNE PORTER (1894-   )

Adams, Robert H. The Significance of Point of View in Katherine
    Anne Porter's *Ship of Fools*. Univ. of Southern California,
    1965. Dissertation: English.

Ashmore, Doris B. Katherine Anne Porter: Theme and Image in Her
    Short Stories. Florida State Univ., 1958. Thesis: English.
Bass, Royce G. The Theme of Initiation in Katherine Anne Porter:
    Acceptance and Rejection. Midwestern Univ., 1969. Thesis:
    English.
Bauer, Shirley A. An Annotated Bibliography: Criticism of the
    Works of Katherine Anne Porter. Univ. of Maryland, 1969.
    Thesis: English.
Befus, Alice B. Thematic Considerations in the Genesis of
    Katherine Anne Porter's Ship of Fools. Univ. of Wyoming,
    1968. Thesis: English.
Bingham, Elizabeth A. The Religious Theme in Katherine Anne
    Porter's Ship of Fools. Univ. of North Carolina (Chapel Hill),
    1963. Thesis: English.
Bolduc, Sr. Louise. A Study of the Life and Works of Katherine
    Anne Porter, Outstanding Stylist, American Writer. Montreal,
    1955. Thesis: English.
Brewer, Jennifer S.L. Studies in Katherine Anne Porter: The
    Metaphysical Design. Vanderbilt Univ., 1963. Thesis:
    English.
Brewton, Constance D. Miranda's Quest: Katherine Anne Porter's
    Portrayal of Woman. Univ. of Dallas, 1969. Thesis: English.
Cech, Eugene J. Exiles in Time: A Study in Katherine Anne Porter's
    Sense of the Past. Univ. of California (Riverside), 1957.
    Thesis: English.
Clampitt, Thelma F. An Examination of Characters in Fiction of
    Katherine Anne Porter. Iowa State Teachers College, 1960.
    Thesis: English.
Council, Mary J. The Collected Fiction of Katherine Anne Porter: A
    Doubter's World in Miniature. Univ. of Texas (El Paso), 1957.
    Thesis: English.
Dempsey, Dewey W. National Types in the Fiction of Katherine Anne
    Porter. Univ. of South Carolina, 1969. Thesis: English.
Denley, Rosemary R. Katherine Anne Porter's Apprehension of
    Catastrophe: A Study of Ship of Fools. Univ. of Mississippi,
    1966. Thesis: English.
Engle, Marjorie S. A Comparative Study of Familial Structure in
    Katherine Anne Porter's Ship of Fools and "Miranda" Stories.
    Bowling Green State Univ., 1966. Thesis: English.
Ewing, Mary D.C. Regionalism in the Short Works of Katherine Anne
    Porter. Texas Christian Univ., 1965. Thesis: English.
Ferguson, Susan M. Katherine Anne Porter's Fiction: Man in a
    Falling World. North Texas State Univ., 1968. Thesis:
    English.
Finklestein, Adele D. Katherine Anne Porter. Columbia Univ., 1947.
    Thesis: English.
Frumin, Leslie. A Critical Edition of Katherine Anne Porter's Pale
    Horse, Pale Rider. Queens College (N.Y.), 1967. Thesis:
    English.
Gacke, Sr. Monica M. Roses Among Brimstone: Katherine Anne Porter's
    "World View" of the Human Condition. Loras College, 1969.
    Thesis: English.
Gessel, Michael A. The Downward Path to Wisdom: A Study of the
    Fiction of Katherine Anne Porter. Roosevelt Univ., 1966.
    Thesis: English.

Gilbert, John H. Katherine Anne Porter: Structural and Thematic
Unity in the Stories of Tradition and Initiation. Vanderbilt
Univ., 1957. Thesis: English.

Goodrick, Evelyn J. Katherine Anne Porter's Characters: The
Vital Company. Kent State Univ., 1965. Thesis: English.

Grau, Carlyn. Major Themes in the Fiction of Katherine Anne
Porter. Texas Tech Univ., 1963. Thesis: English.

Hahamovitch, Lillian. Katherine Anne Porter: Point of View and
Irony. Montreal, 1965. Thesis: English.

Hall, Audrie W. Aspects of the Feminine Mind in the Collected
Short Stories of Katherine Anne Porter. Virginia State
College, 1966. Thesis: English.

Hamer, Gwendolyn. The Narrative Technique of Katherine Anne
Porter. Vanderbilt Univ., 1954. Thesis: English.

Handy, Dierdre C. Family Legend in the Stories of Katherine Anne
Porter. Univ. of Oklahoma, 1953. Thesis: English.

Hanson, Karyn M. Moral Consciousness in Katherine Anne Porter's
Fiction. Moorhead State College, 1969. Thesis: English.

Hennis, Rucker S., Jr. The Critical Reception of the Work of
Katherine Anne Porter. Univ. of North Carolina (Chapel Hill),
1956. Thesis: English.

Hertz, Robert N. Rising Waters: A Study of Katherine Anne Porter.
Cornell Univ., 1964. Dissertation: English.

Hetherington, Joy M. Katherine Anne Porter: Her Search for Truth.
Univ. of Wyoming, 1955. Thesis: English.

Irby, Hazel M. Katherine Anne Porter: Her Contribution to the
American Short Story. Univ. of Texas (Austin), 1951. Thesis:
English.

Kinser, Elizabeth A. Katherine Anne Porter's Disenchanted Women.
Univ. of Tennessee, 1966. Thesis: English.

Krishnamurthi, Matighatta G. Katherine Anne Porter: A Study in
Themes. Univ. of Wisconsin, 1966. Dissertation: English.

Lackey, Horace G. Katherine Anne Porter's Theory of Art as
Revealed in Her Life and Work. Texas Tech Univ., 1966.
Thesis: English.

Lawrence, Donnie G. *Ship of Fools*: A Comparison With Earlier Works
by Katherine Anne Porter. San Francisco State College, 1964.
Thesis: English.

Ledbetter, Nan W.T. The Thumbprint: A Study of People in Katherine
Anne Porter's Fiction. Univ. of Texas (Austin), 1966.
Dissertation: English.

Lowry, Evelyn. Katherine Anne Porter: Ironic Betrayal in "Maria
Concepcion," "He," and "Flowering Judas." Fresno State
College, 1965. Thesis: English.

Maass, Henry E. Mexico and Mexicans in the Fiction of Steinbeck,
Morris, Traven, and Porter. North Texas State Univ., 1966.
Thesis: English.

Marcello, Joanne L. Myth and Symbol as the Cohering Element in
"The Source," "The Witness," "The Circus," "The Old Order,"
"The Last Leaf," "The Grave," "Old Mortality," *Pale Horse,
Pale Rider* by Katherine Anne Porter. Iowa State Teachers
College, 1965. Thesis: English.

McCray, Susan S. Katherine A. Porter's *Ship of Fools*: A Study in
Irony and the Ironic Mode. Univ. of Louisville, 1969. Thesis:
English.

[142]

Murphy, Edward F. Henry James and Katherine Anne Porter: Endless
Relations. Ottawa, 1959. Dissertation: English.
Nance, Brother William L., S.M. The Principle of Rejection: A
Study of the Thematic Unity in the Fiction of Katherine Anne
Porter. Univ. of Notre Dame, 1963. Dissertation: English.
Page, Willie E., Jr. Katherine Anne Porter: A Study in Creative
Concepts. Florida State Univ., 1959. Thesis: English.
Redden, Dorothy S. The Legend of Katherine Anne Porter. Stanford
Univ., 1965. Dissertation: English.
Robbins, Orville M. "True Testimony": The Short Stories of
Katherine Anne Porter. Texas Christian Univ., 1958. Thesis:
English.
Schunk, Gene M. The Function of Caste and Class in Katherine Anne
Porter. Duke Univ., 1962. Thesis: English.
Schwartz, Edward. The Fiction of Katherine Anne Porter. Syracuse
Univ., 1953. Dissertation: English.
Sewell, Joan D. The Theme of Isolation in Stories by Katherine
Anne Porter. Univ. of Houston, 1965. Thesis: English.
Shan, Lily O. A Twentieth Century Guest: The Miranda in Katherine
Anne Porter's Fiction. Cornell Univ., 1956. Thesis: English.
Stalling, Donald L. Katherine Anne Porter: Life and the Literary
Mirror. Texas Christian Univ., 1951. Thesis: English.
Steckman, Eleanore H. The Craft of Katherine Anne Porter.
Pennsylvania State Univ., 1956. Thesis: English.
Swaim, Kathleen M. The Function of Myth in the Fiction of Katherine
Anne Porter. Pennsylvania State Univ., 1958. Thesis: English.
Treitel, Renata M. Miranda's Quest in *Pale Horse, Pale Rider*.
Univ. of Tulsa, 1965. Thesis: English.
Valvoda, Theodore F. The Influence of Katherine Anne Porter's
Literary Theories upon Her Fiction. John Carroll Univ., 1960.
Thesis: English.
Vliet, Vida A.R. The Shape of Meaning: A Study of the Development
of Katherine Anne Porter's Fictional Form. Pennsylvania State
Univ., 1968. Dissertation: English.
Waldrip, Louise D.B. A Bibliography of the Works of Katherine Anne
Porter. Univ. of Texas (Austin), 1967. Dissertation: English.
Walker, Nancy G. A Study of Katherine Anne Porter's Miranda
Stories. Univ. of North Carolina (Chapel Hill), 1968. Thesis:
English.
Walters, Dorothy J. The Theme of Destructive Innocence in the
Modern Novel: Greene, James, Cary, Porter. Oklahoma, 1960.
Dissertation: English.
Welch, Evie A. Some Aspects of Unity in Selected Works of Katherine
Anne Porter. Virginia State College, 1968. Thesis: English.
Whitfield, Shirley M. Katherine Anne Porter and Man's Infirmity.
Emory Univ., 1964. Thesis: English.
Wilson, Florence J. The Narrative Technique of Katherine Anne Porter.
Baylor Univ., 1961. Thesis: English.
Yosha, Lee W. The World of Katherine Anne Porter. Univ. of Michigan,
1961. Dissertation: English.
Zeiss, Todd R. Katherine Anne Porter: Her Literary Reputation.
Univ. of Virginia, 1960. Thesis: English.

WILLIAM S. PORTER (1862-1910)
(O. HENRY)

Beardshear, William M. The Style and Plot Structure of O. Henry's Short Stories. Columbia Univ., 1913. Thesis: English.

Connally, Lucy B. A Study of the Social Background of the Characters in O. Henry's New York Short Stories. North Texas State Univ., 1940. Thesis: English.

Crichlow, Isabel L. O. Henry's Social Attitudes. Univ. of Missouri, 1950. Thesis: English.

Day, Charles S. O. Henry: The Man, His Life, and His Work. Acadia (Canada), 1937. Thesis: English.

Duncan, F.H. Humanism of O. Henry. Univ. of South Dakota, 1921. Thesis: English.

Felker, Violet. A Study of O. Henry's Southeastern Types. Stetson Univ., 1935. Thesis: English.

Harrell, Mary S. O. Henry's Texas Contacts. Univ. of Texas (Austin), 1935. Thesis: English.

Hixon, Carolyn. The Literary Reputation of O. Henry. Auburn Univ., 1951. Thesis: English.

Howell, Dana M. Settings and Characters of O. Henry's Texas Stories. George Peabody College, 1937. Thesis: English.

Huntley, Stephen M. O. Henry: An American Story Teller. Univ. of South Carolina, 1920. Thesis: English.

Kincheloe, Joe L. The Satire of O. Henry. East Tennessee State Univ., 1952. Thesis: English.

Kingman, Daniel C. "The Indian Summer of Dry Valley Johnson": An Opera In Two Acts and Eight Scenes. Michigan State Univ., 1964. Dissertation: Music. [Based on the short story by O. Henry]

Kreiter, Wolfgang. Zur Frage des Realismus in den Short Stories O. Henry. Humboldt Universität (East Berlin), 1956. Dissertation: English.

Long, Eugene H. O. Henry as Seen by the Critics. Baylor Univ., 1931. Thesis: English.

_____. O. Henry: A Biographical Study. Univ. of Pennsylvania, 1942. Dissertation: English.

MacAndrew, James F. A Critical Analysis of the Literary Reputation of O. Henry. Columbia Univ., 1938. Thesis: English.

McCasland, Gurney S. O. Henry In New York: A Biographical and Critical Study. Univ. of Southern California, 1955. Thesis: English.

McDavid, A.G. Texas Trails of O. Henry. Univ. of Colorado, 1927. Thesis: English.

Meadors, Olive G. Types of Characters Portrayed in O. Henry's New York Stories. George Peabody College, 1930. Thesis: English.

Mitchell, Eleen R. The Dramatizations of O. Henry's Short Stories. Auburn Univ., 1965. Thesis: English.

Noack, Heinz. O. Henry Als Mystiker. Humboldt (East Berlin), 1937. Dissertation: English.

Patek, Hertha. O. Henry: Erzählungskunst, Probleme, literarische Stellung. Vienna, 1940. Dissertation: English.

Pike, Cathleen M. O. Henry in North Carolina. George Peabody College, 1938. Thesis: English.

Reed, Dorris I. O'Henry and Henry Lawson: A Comparative Study. Univ. of Texas (Austin), 1959. Thesis: English.

Roddey, Cammie. O. Henry, the Picaroon. Winthrop College, 1945. Thesis: English.

Romulo, Carlos P. O. Henry. Columbia Univ., 1921. Thesis: English.

Scoles, David L. A Study of O. Henry's Southwestern Types. Stetson Univ., 1934. Thesis: English.

Spell, Betty. A Study of the Element of Surprise in O. Henry's Plots. Stetson Univ., 1934. Thesis: English.

Tapp, B.H. The Attitude of O. Henry Toward His Work. George Peabody College, 1929. Thesis: English.

Taylor, Virginia W. The Narrative Art of O. Henry. Univ. of Texas (Austin), 1936. Thesis: English.

Townley, Janice F. O. Henry and the Southern Literary Tradition. Auburn Univ., 1963. Thesis: English.

Tracy, Paul A. A Closer Look at O. Henry's *Rolling Stone*. Univ. of Texas (Austin), 1949. Thesis: Journalism.

Watson, Grace M. O. Henry on the Houston *Post*. Univ. of Texas (Austin), 1934. Thesis: English.

Woodward, Vinola S. O. Henry's Use of the Malapropos and Related Devices. Stetson Univ., 1935. Thesis: English.

Yang, Helen Y.-H. A Study of O. Henry's Social Attitudes as Reflected in His New York Short Stories. Atlanta Univ., 1966. Thesis: English.

Yates, Arminda T. O. Henry's Use of Dialect in Portraying American Character. Hardin-Simmons Univ., 1948. Thesis: English-Education.

JOHN PORY (1572-1635)

Powell, William S. John Pory: His Life, Letters and Work. Univ. of North Carolina (Chapel Hill), 1947. Thesis: English.

WILLIAM LOUIS POTEAT (1856-1938)

Bryan, George M. The Educational, Religious, and Social Thought of William Louis Poteat as Expressed in His Writings, Including Unpublished Notes and Addresses. Wake Forest Univ., 1944. Thesis: Religion.

REUBEN MARMADUKE POTTER (1802-1890)

Leach, James H. The Life of Reuben Marmaduke Potter. Univ. of Texas (Austin), 1939. Thesis: History.

GEORGE D. PRENTICE (1802-1870)

Congleton, Betty C. George D. Prentice and His Editorial Policy in National Politics, 1830-1861. Univ. of Kentucky, 1962. Dissertation: History.

Weldy, Margaret. George Denison Prentice, Editor of the Louisville *Journal*, 1830-1869. Columbia Univ., 1929. Thesis: Journalism.

MARGARET JUNKIN PRESTON (1820-1897)

Grey, John H., Jr. Margaret Junkin Preston, Virginia's Poetess of the Old South. Washington and Lee Univ., 1933. Thesis: English.
Williams, Rose E. Margaret Junkin Preston, Poetess of Virginia (Based Chiefly on the Correspondence with Paul Hamilton Hayne). Duke Univ., 1940. Thesis: English.

REYNOLDS PRICE (1933-   )

Brock, Betty M. A Study of the Novels of Reynolds Price. Hardin-Simmons Univ., 1968. Thesis: English.

LOUISE CLARKE PYRNELLE (1852-1907)

Sample, Sue A. A Study of Louise Clarke Pyrnelle. George Peabody College, 1930. Thesis: English.

J.G.M. RAMSEY (1796-1884)

Eubanks, David L. Dr. J.G.M. Ramsey of East Tennessee: A Career of Public Service. Univ. of Tennessee, 1965. Dissertation: History.

JAMES RYDER RANDALL (1839-1908)

Henry, Ida E. James Ryder Randall and His Poetry. Louisiana State Univ., 1933. Thesis: English.
Tennent, Harriete T. The Life and Poetry of James Ryder Randall. Columbia Univ., 1927. Thesis: English.

JOHN RANDOLPH (1773-1833)

Simmons, Dennis E. John Randolph and States' Rights Movement. Millersville State College, 1967. Thesis: Social Science.
Stokes, William E., Jr. The Early Life of John Randolph of Roanoke, 1773-1794. Univ. of Virginia, 1950. Thesis: History.

RYLAND RANDOLPH (1834-1903)

Ward, Gladys. Life of Ryland Randolph. Univ. of Alabama, 1933. Thesis: History.

THOMAS JEFFERSON RANDOLPH (1798-1875)

Vance, Joseph C. Thomas Jefferson Randolph. Univ. of Virginia, 1957. Dissertation: History.

JOHN CROWE RANSOM (1888-1974)

Allen, Mary E. John Crowe Ransom's Use of Irony in His Poetry from 1917 to 1963. Univ. of North Carolina (Chapel Hill), 1966. Thesis: English.

Ayres, James B.   John Crowe Ransom and the Structure of the Concrete
     Universal. Florida State Univ., 1960. Thesis: English.
Bornhauser, Fred W. Disowned Progeny: The Early Poems of John
     Crowe Ransom. Cornell Univ., 1966. Dissertation: English.
Brooks, Mildred M. John Crowe Ransom: A Bibliography. Vanderbilt
     Univ., 1966. Thesis: English.
Buffington, Robert R. "But What I Wear Is Flesh": John Crowe
     Ransom's Poetry. Vanderbilt Univ., 1967. Dissertation:
     English.
Carleton, Emma L.F. The Use of Irony in the Poetry of John Crowe
     Ransom. Univ. of Oklahoma, 1944. Thesis: English.
Clarke, Donald L. John Crowe Ransom: A Critical Bibliography.
     Texas Christian Univ., 1966. Thesis: English.
Coil, Karen L. The Poetry and Prose of John Crowe Ransom: A
     Progression From Myth to Metaphor. Idaho State Univ., 1968.
     Thesis: English.
Collins, Elizabeth A. The Criticism of John Crowe Ransom. Auburn
     Univ., 1954. Thesis: English.
Davis, Jack M. John Crowe Ransom's Aesthetic of Poetry. Columbia
     Univ., 1954. Thesis: English.
Dillhoefer, Florence R. Some Contrasts in Ransom's Poems. John
     Carroll Univ., 1955. Thesis: English.
Duffy, Donald D., Jr. The Inferential Narrator in the Poetry of
     John Crowe Ransom. Oklahoma State Univ., 1969. Dissertation:
     English.
Elliot, Grey. John Crowe Ransom: A Study of the Literary Strategy
     in his Poems. Univ. of Montana, 1969. Thesis: English.
Ferguson, Charles E. John Crowe Ransom as Southern Poet. Texas
     Christian Univ., 1957. Thesis: English.
Fibley, John W. John Crowe Ransom's Structure, Texture, Theory.
     Millersville State College, 1968. Thesis: English.
Harder, Kelsie B. John Crowe Ransom as Poet, Economist, and Critic.
     Vanderbilt Univ., 1951. Thesis: English.
Harper, Jahaila M. The Fragmented Individual in the Poetry of John
     Crowe Ransom. Old Dominion College, 1969. Thesis: English.
Head, Jane. Myth in the Criticism of John Crowe Ransom. Univ. of
     Georgia, 1962. Thesis: English.
Hendrick, Kingsley M. The Metaphysical Conceits in the Poetic
     Theory and Practice of John Crowe Ransom. Univ. of Alabama,
     1967. Thesis: English.
Hinkel, Robert C. The Development of John Crowe Ransom's Poetry.
     Northwestern Univ., 1967. Dissertation: English.
Knight, Karl F. Diction, Metaphor, and Symbol in the Poetry of
     John Crowe Ransom. Emory Univ., 1962. Dissertation: English.
Linger, Sarah M. Yvor Winters and John Crowe Ransom: A Study of
     a Critical Controversy. Ohio State Univ., 1947. Thesis:
     English.
Magner, James E., Jr. John Crowe Ransom: Critical Principles and
     Preoccupations. Univ. of Pittsburgh, 1966. Dissertation:
     English.
Mills, Gordon H. Myth and Ontology in the Thought of John Crowe
     Ransom. Univ. of Iowa, 1943. Dissertation: English.
Morden, Bettie J. The Critical Theory and Practice of John Crowe
     Ransom. Columbia Univ., 1950. Thesis: English.

Morris, Nancy E. Death and Disintegration in the Poetry of John Crowe Ransom. Univ. of Virginia, 1962. Thesis: English.

Petteys, David F. The Poetry of John Crowe Ransom. Columbia Univ., 1957. Thesis: English.

Reese, Mary M. Three Studies in Poetry: Donne's "Aire and Angels"; *Paradise Lost* in *The Prelude*; and Ransom's "First Travels of Max." Pennsylvania State Univ., 1965. Thesis: English.

Robeson, Helen. John Crowe Ransom, Dualist. Vanderbilt Univ., 1944. Thesis: English.

Sandifer, C.L. Poetic and Religious Theories of John Crowe Ransom Applied to His Poetry. Univ. of Mississippi, 1956. Thesis: English.

Sapp, Linda H. Patterns of Change in Certain of John Crowe Ransom's Selected Poems. Emory Univ., 1964. Thesis: English.

Simmons, Sally M. John Crowe Ransom's Theory of Poetic Meaning. Univ. of Florida, 1961. Thesis: English.

Smothers, Marilyn C. Dualism in John Crowe Ransom's Poems about Lovers. East Tennessee State Univ., 1966. Thesis: English.

Swinden, S.H. (Mrs.) Change and Continuity in the Poetry and Criticism of John Crowe Ransom. Manchester, 1969. Thesis: English.

Thomas, Lou A.S. The Dualisms in John Crowe Ransom's Poetry. McNeese State Univ., 1968. Thesis: English.

Walker, Biron H. John Crowe Ransom: An Interpretation of His Poetry. Univ. of Florida, 1941. Thesis: English.

Wood, Larhylia. The Use of Sound-Devices in the Poetry of John Crowe Ransom. East Tennessee State Univ., 1961. Thesis: English.

MARJORIE KINNAN RAWLINGS (1896-1953)

Furlow, C.T. Folklore Elements in the Florida Writings of Marjorie Kinnan Rawlings. Univ. of Florida, 1963. Thesis: English.

Glenn, Beatrice N. A Study of The Women Characters in Marjorie Kinnan Rawling's Fiction. Birmingham-Southern College, 1955. Thesis: English.

Jenkins, Kathleen B. A Study of a Case in Florida Courts about Marjorie Kinnan Rawling's *Cross Creek*. Florida State Univ., 1966. Thesis: English.

McCutcheon, Mary L. A Lexicographical Study of the North Florida Vocabulary Set Forth in Marjorie Rawlings's *The Yearling*. Univ. of Virginia, 1940. Thesis: English.

McGuire, William J., Jr. A Study of Florida Cracker Dialect Based Chiefly on the Prose Works of Marjorie Kinnan Rawlings. Univ. of Florida, 1939. Thesis: English.

Peck, Joseph R., II. The Fiction-Writing Art of Marjorie Kinnan Rawlings. Univ. of Florida, 1954. Thesis: English.

Slagle, Mary L. The Artistic Uses of Nature in the Fiction of Marjorie Kinnan Rawlings. Univ. of Florida, 1953. Thesis: English.

OPIE POPE READ (1852-1939)

Baird, Reed M. Opie Read (1852-1939): A Study in Popular Culture.
    Univ. of Michigan, 1966. Dissertation: English.
Blackmon, William F., Jr. The Life of Opie Pope Read and an
    Evaluation of His Works. Auburn Univ., 1940. Thesis: English.
Durrett, Willie E. The Life and Works of Opie Read. Louisiana
    State Univ., 1951. Thesis: English.
Ransom, William S. Opie Read (1852-   ). Vanderbilt Univ., 1933.
    Thesis: English.

BYRON HERBERT REECE (1917-1958)

Bledsoe, Eugene. The Fire of Boughs: A Thematic Study of Selected
    Works of Byron Herbert Reece. West Georgia College, 1970.
    Thesis: English.

LIZETTE WOODWORTH REESE (1856-1935)

Cato, Harriet E. Lizette Woodworth Reese, A Conventional Poet in an
    Unconventional Age. Winthrop College, 1937. Thesis: English.
Humphrey, Harold E. The Sonnets of Lizette Woodworth Reese: An
    Examination. Columbia Univ., 1947. Thesis: English.
Klein, L.R.M. Lizette Woodworth Reese, A Biography. Univ. of
    Pennsylvania, 1943. Dissertation: English.
McGinley, Sr. Mary W., S.M. Lizette Woodworth Reese. Villanova
    Univ., 1942. Thesis: English.
Morris, Claire M. The Influence of Emily Dickinson on Four Recent
    Poets: Lizette Woodworth Reese, Sara Teasdale, Elinor Wylie,
    and Edna St. Vincent Millay. Univ. of Southern California,
    1942. Thesis: English.
Simmons, Thelma. A Study of the Poetry of Lizette Woodworth Reese.
    George Peabody College, 1935. Thesis: English.

CLARA REYES (1884-1929)
(WALTHER GRAY)

Schulze, Nolan. *The Compadre* by "Walther Gray" (Clara Reyes). A
    Translation with Critical and Biographical Introduction. Univ.
    of Texas (Austin), 1937. Thesis: German.

ROBERT BARNWELL RHETT (1800-1876)

Perritt, Henry H. Robert Barnwell Rhett: South Carolina Secession
    Spokesman. Univ. of Florida, 1954. Dissertation: Speech.

ALICE HEGAN RICE (1870-1942)

Ellis, Lena C. Alice Hegan Rice. Western Kentucky Univ., 1934.
    Thesis: English.
Webb, Lela. An Analytical Study of The Fiction of Alice Hegan Rice.
    George Peabody College, 1929. Thesis: English.

CALE YOUNG RICE (1872-1943)

Bere, Jenny R. Cale Young Rice: A Study of His Life and Works.
Univ. of Louisville, 1939. Thesis: English.

Berry, Br. C.C. A Comparative Study of The Revised Poetic Dramas
of Cale Young Rice with Other Outstanding American Poetic
Drama. St. John's Univ. (N.Y.), 1949. Dissertation: English.

Spears, Woodridge. Examination and Analysis of the Poetic Dramas
of Cale Young Rice. Univ. of Kentucky, 1946. Thesis:
English.

Wells, Kathryn H. Themes in the Non-dramatic Poetry of Cale Young
Rice. George Peabody College, 1929. Thesis: English.

LYNN RIGGS (1899-1954)

Aughtry, Charles E. Lynn Riggs, Dramatist: A Critical Biography.
Brown Univ., 1959. Dissertation: English.

Moskowitz, Abraham L. An Analysis of the Use of Regional Material
in The Plays of Lynn Riggs. Univ. of Iowa, 1939. Thesis:
Dramatic Art.

Nesbitt, Ilse L. A Study of Dialect in Oklahoma in the Plays of
Lynn Riggs. Univ. of Tulsa, 1948. Thesis: English.

Wilson, Eloise. Lynn Riggs: Oklahoma Dramatist. Univ. of
Pennsylvania, 1957. Dissertation: English.

SPENCER ROAN (1762-1802)
(ALGERNON SIDNEY)

Gelbach, Clyde C. Spencer Roan of Virginia, 1762-1802: A
Judicial Advocate of State-Rights. Univ. of Pittsburgh, 1955.
Dissertation: History.

ELIZABETH MADOX ROBERTS (1886-1941)

Beeler, Andrew J. Elizabeth Madox Roberts: Her Interpretation of
Life. Univ. of Louisville, 1940. Thesis: English.

Bell, Vereen McNeill. A Study of the Critical Reception of the
Works of Elizabeth Madox Roberts. Duke Univ., 1956. Thesis:
English.

Chamberlin, Lorraine E.T. Regional Culture in the Novels of
Elizabeth Madox Roberts. Univ. of Idaho, 1948. Thesis:
English.

Coulter, Linda B. The Later Philosophical Novels of Elizabeth
Madox Roberts. Cornell Univ., 1967. Thesis: English.

Davidson, Louise B. An Analysis of the Novels of Elizabeth Madox
Roberts. Univ. of Tulsa, 1948. Thesis: English.

Denmark, Mary A. Romantic Elements in the Fiction of Elizabeth
Madox Roberts. Emory Univ., 1953. Thesis: English.

Donlan, Anne C. Epic Qualities in the Writings of Elizabeth Madox
Roberts. Boston Univ., 1938. Thesis: English.

Guest, Jessie W. Elizabeth Madox Roberts. East Texas State Univ.,
1944. Thesis: English.

Hawley, Isabel L. Elizabeth Madox Roberts: Her Development As
Self-Conscious Narrative Artist. Univ. of North Carolina
(Chapel Hill), 1969. Dissertation: English.

King, Sr. Maria D.S., I.H.M. Elizabeth Madox Roberts and the
American Regional Novel. Villanova Univ., 1943. Thesis:
English.
Kinnard, Wade T. The Major Ñovels of Elizabeth Madox Roberts.
Univ. of Massachusetts, 1969. Thesis: English.
Mayer, Charles L. Ballad in the Novels of Elizabeth Madox Roberts.
Washington Univ. (St. Louis), 1959. Thesis: English.
Nilles, Mary E. Social Development in Four Novels by Elizabeth
Madox Roberts. Long Island Univ., 1967. Thesis: English.
Rovit, Earl H. Elizabeth Madox Roberts: Her Symbolism and
Philosophic Perspective. Boston Univ., 1957. Dissertation:
English.
Slavick, William H. The Meaning of Elizabeth Madox Roberts. Univ.
of Notre Dame, 1951. Thesis: English.
Spears, Woodbridge. Elizabeth Madox Roberts: A Biographical and
Critical Study. Univ. of Kentucky, 1953. Dissertation:
English.
Steger, Annie P. Kentucky History in the Novels of Elizabeth Madox
Roberts. Vanderbilt Univ., 1957. Thesis: English.
West, Estella N. Kentucky as Pictured in the Writings of Elizabeth
Madox Roberts. George Peabody College, 1934. Thesis: English.
Woodside, Harriette C. Berkeleian Idealism in the Works of
Elizabeth Madox Roberts. East Carolina Univ., 1965. Thesis:
English.

WILL ROGERS (1879-1935)

Alworth, E.P. The Humor of Will Rogers. Univ. of Missouri, 1958.
Dissertation: English.
Siegelin, Helen. A Rhetorical Analysis of the Use of Humor by
Will Rogers, Senior, in Selected Public Performances. Miami
Univ. (Ohio), 1965. Thesis: Speech.
Walker, Lois H. Traditional American Humor and Will Rogers.
Stephen F. Austin State Univ., 1942. Thesis: English.

ANNE ROYALL (1769-1854)

McGeehan, Sr. Frances I. Anne Royall: A Forgotten Journalist.
Catholic Univ., 1934. Thesis: English.
O'Reilly, Sr. Frances T. Anne Royall: Her Observations of Manners
and Men. St. John's Univ. (N.Y.), 1945. Thesis: English.

IRWIN RUSSELL (1853-1879)

Banks, Robert L. Irwin Russell, Pioneer in the Literary Development
of the Negro Character. Univ. of Georgia, 1951. Thesis:
English.
Baskerville, K.T. The Study of the Life and Writing of Irwin Russell.
George Peabody College, 1929. Thesis: English.
Daniels, Will C. The Life and Works of Irwin Russell. Louisiana
State Univ., 1936. Thesis: English.
Nyholm, Jens. Irwin Russell: A Biographical and Critical Study.
George Washington Univ., 1934. Thesis: English.
Rice, Frank M. Irwin Russell, Biography, Criticism, Unpublished
Works. Columbia Univ., 1934. Thesis: English.

Smith, Agnes E. The Life and Literary Reputation of Irwin Russell. Tulane Univ., 1944. Thesis: English.
Tabb, Linda E. The Significance of the Russell Circle in the Literary Development of the South. Columbia Univ., 1930. Thesis: English.
Todd, Hollis B. An Analysis of the Literary Dialect of Irwin Russell and a Comparison With The Spoken Dialect of Certain Native Informants of West Central Mississippi. Louisiana State Univ., 1965. Dissertation: Speech.
Webb, James W. New Biographical Material, Criticism and Uncollected Writings of Irwin Russell. Univ. of North Carolina (Chapel Hill), 1946. Thesis: English.

MILDRED LEWIS RUTHERFORD (1852-1928)

Tuthill, Hazelle B. Mildred Lewis Rutherford. Univ. of South Carolina, 1929. Thesis: Education.
Womack, Margaret A. Mildred Lewis Rutherford, Exponent of Southern Culture. Univ. of Georgia, 1946. Thesis: English.

FR. ABRAM JOSEPH RYAN (1838-1886)

Adams, Robert T. A Study of the Life and Works of the Reverend Abram Joseph Ryan, Poet-Priest of the Confederacy. Louisiana State Univ., 1963. Thesis: English.
Dombrowski, Anthony S. Father Ryan, Poet-Priest of the South. Columbia Univ., 1936. Thesis: English.
Fleming, Sr. Agnes. The Influence of Father Abram Ryan, Civil War Chaplain. Villanova Univ., 1944. Thesis: History.
Freiddell, Robert E. An Intimate Study of the Poet-Priest, Abram Joseph Ryan. George Peabody College, 1930. Thesis: English.

JOSEPH SALYARDS (1808-1885)

Lutz, Carolyn. Joseph Salyards and *Idothea, or, The Divine Image*. Madison College, 1959. Thesis: English.

GEORGE SANDYS (1578-1644)

Barker, Russell H. George Sandys. Univ. of Wisconsin, 1935. Dissertation: English.
Grueninger, Guenther H. George Sandys als Unbersetzer des *Christus Patiens* von Hugo Grotius. Freiburg, 1926. Dissertation: English.
Hunter, Grace E. The Influence of Francis Bacon on the Prose Commentary of *Ovid's Metamorphoses* by George Sandys. Univ. of Iowa, 1949. Dissertation: English.
Ingalls, Beatrice K. George Sandys' Translation of Ovid's *Metamorphoses*. Radcliffe College, 1950. Dissertation: English.
Overly, Floyd F. Preliminary Studies in The Ovidian Mythography of George Sandys. Univ. of Chicago, 1949. Dissertation: English.

Schmutzer, Karl E. George Sandys' Paraphrases on the Psalms and
    the Tradition of Metrical Psalmody: An Annotated Edition of
    Fifty Selected Psalms, with Critical and Biographical
    Introduction. Ohio State Univ., 1956. Dissertation: English.

HERBERT RAVENEL SASS (1884-1958)

Johnson, Grace V. The Contributions of Herbert Ravenel Sass to
    South Carolina Literature With Particular Emphasis on His
    Nature Writings. Univ. of South Carolina, 1964. Thesis:
    English.

LYLE SAXON (1891-1946)

Davis, Daryl W. Lyle Saxon: Twentieth Century Champion of
    Louisiana's Heritage. Midwestern Univ., 1960. Thesis:
    English.

DOROTHY SCARBOROUGH (1877-1935)

Beard, Joyce J. Dorothy Scarborough: Texas Regionalist. Texas
    Christian Univ., 1965. Thesis: English.
Dixon, Arline H. The Development of the Novel Lectures of Dorothy
    Scarborough. Baylor Univ., 1943. Thesis: English.
Heavens, Jean E. Dorothy Scarborough--Fictional Historian. Univ.
    of Texas (El Paso), 1968. Thesis: English.
Kone, Laura R. The Life and the Prose Works of Dorothy Scarborough.
    George Peabody College, 1930. Thesis: English.
Maxwell, Mary R. Short Story Lectures of Dorothy Scarborough.
    Baylor Univ., 1942. Thesis: English.
Middlebrook, Marjorie A. Dorothy Scarborough's Lectures on the
    Technique of Writing the Novel. Baylor Univ., 1941. Thesis:
    English.
Muncy, Elizabeth R. Dorothy Scarborough: A Literary Pioneer.
    Baylor Univ., 1940. Thesis: English.
Truett, Luther J. The Negro Element in the Life and Works of
    Dorothy Scarborough. Baylor Univ., 1967. Thesis: English.
Whitcomb, Virginia R. Dorothy Scarborough: Biography and Criticism.
    Baylor Univ., 1945. Thesis: English.

EVELYN SCOTT (1893-1963)

Welker, Robert L. Evelyn Scott: A Literary Biography. Vanderbilt
    Univ., 1958. Dissertation: English.

SEQUOYAH (c.1770-1843)

Davis, John B. The Life and Work of Sequoyah. George Peabody
    College, 1929. Thesis: English.

WILLIAM GILMORE SIMMS (1806-1870)

Ader, Paul F. A Study of the Border Romances of William Gilmore
    Simms. Univ. of North Carolina (Chapel Hill), 1949. Thesis:
    English.

[153]

Argo, Iris S. Simms and The Elizabethans. Univ. of Georgia,
     1966. Dissertation: English.
Barre, Elizabeth F. A Study of the Indian in William Gilmore
     Simms' Novels and Short Stories. Univ. of South Carolina,
     1941. Thesis: English.
Barton, Roger A. Simms' Literary Coterie. Columbia Univ., 1932.
     Thesis: English.
Belser, William G., Jr. William Gilmore Simms, Maecenas of the Old
     South. Univ. of South Carolina, 1933. Thesis: English.
Bernard, Frances M. Representative Short Stories of William Gilmore
     Simms. Vanderbilt Univ., 1952. Thesis: English.
Brackett, Della L. A Critical Study of the Novels of William
     Gilmore Simms. Univ. of Georgia, 1941. Thesis: English.
Brading, Elinor. The Life and Fiction of William Gilmore Simms.
     Ohio State Univ., 1934. Thesis: English.
Bradley, Viola M. The Contrast of Cooper's *The Last of the Mohicans*
     and Simms' *The Yemassee*. Auburn Univ., 1944. Thesis: English.
Brown, R.C. William Gilmore Simms as a Chronicler of the Southwest
     Border. Univ. of Chicago, 1925. Thesis: English.
Bryan, William A. The Revolutionary Romances of William Gilmore
     Simms. Duke Univ., 1933. Thesis: English.
Bryant, Byron R. The Viewpoint of the Southern Aristocracy as
     Reflected in the Fiction of William Gilmore Simms. Stanford
     Univ., 1947. Thesis: English.
Burns, Alberta O. William Gilmore Simms' *The Scout*: A Dialect
     Study. Univ. of Florida, 1969. Thesis: English.
Bush, Lewis M. William Gilmore Simms and the Conflict of Literary
     Nationalism and Sectionalism. Univ. of Miami (Coral Gables),
     1964. Thesis: English.
Calhoun, Robert F. Indian Characterization in Brown, Cooper, and
     Simms. Univ. of Virginia, 1959. Thesis: English.
Cebull, Edward A. The Authenticity and Treatment of the Historical
     Background in the Revolutionary Romances of William Gilmore
     Simms. Univ. of Montana, 1947. Thesis: English.
Chappell, Mary. Simms and the Sectional Controversy. Vanderbilt
     Univ., 1938. Thesis: English.
Claxton, Jonnie C. William Gilmore Simms as a Literary Editor.
     Univ. of Georgia, 1951. Thesis: English.
Deen, Floyd H. William Gilmore Simms, Novelist, Romanticist and
     Short Prose Fictionist. Indiana Univ. (Bloomington), 1940.
     Dissertation: English.
Early, Sr. M.N., I.H.M. A Critical Survey of the Poetry of William
     Gilmore Simms. Villanova Univ., 1942. Thesis: English.
Farrior, J.E. The Use of Historical Characters by William Gilmore
     Simms in His Romances of the Revolution. Univ. of North
     Carolina (Chapel Hill), 1944. Thesis: English.
Fleming, Elizabeth M. William Gilmore Simms Portrayal of the Negro.
     Duke Univ., 1965. Thesis: English.
Froome, Charles D. William Gilmore Simms' Reply to *Uncle Tom's
     Cabin*. Univ. of Wyoming, 1963. Thesis: English.
Gibbs, John E., Jr. William Gilmore Simms and *The Magnolia*. Duke
     Univ., 1931. Thesis: English.
Gill, Elizabeth L. An Examination of Literary Nationalism in the
     Letters and Selected Criticism of William Gilmore Simms. Univ.
     of Houston, 1968. Thesis: English.

Goddard, Mack A. A Study of the Backwoods Characters in the Novels of William Gilmore Simms. Univ. of Tennessee, 1964. Thesis: English.

Guilds, John C., Jr. Simms as a Magazine Editor, 1825-1845: With Special Reference to His Contributions. Duke Univ., 1954. Dissertation: English.

Hartley, Dan M. The Short Stories of William Gilmore Simms. A Study of the Objective Type of Tale in Contrast to the Subjective Type as Written by Nathaniel Hawthorne. Univ. of Virginia, 1929. Thesis: English.

Heekin, Robert E. William Gilmore Simms, Novelist of Colonial and Revolutionary America. Univ. of Cincinnati, 1940. Thesis: English.

Herbert, Edward T. William Gilmore Simms as Editor and Literary Critic. Univ. of Wisconsin, 1957. Dissertation: English.

Holman, C.H. William Gilmore Simms' Theory And Practice of Historical Fiction. Univ. of North Carolina (Chapel Hill), 1949. Dissertation: English.

Hopkins, Konrad H.V. Carolina Epic: A Critical Study of William Gilmore Simms' Romances of the Revolution. Florida State Univ., 1955. Thesis: English.

Jarrell, Hampton M. W.G. Simms, Realistic Romancer. Duke Univ., 1932. Dissertation: English.

Jones, Martin B. William Gilmore Simms. Univ. of South Carolina, 1924. Thesis: English.

Kane, Katherine C. William Gilmore Simms: A Biographical and Critical Study, 1806-1841. Yale Univ., 1943. Dissertation: English.

Lindsey, Laura B. Historical Verifications of W.G. Simms' Revolutionary War Romances. George Peabody College, 1936. Thesis: English.

Linton, Esta L. A Study of the Revolutionary War Novels of William Gilmore Simms. North Texas State Univ., 1948. Thesis: English.

Lukens, Nancy. The Revolutionary Novels of William Gilmore Simms. Columbia Univ., 1924. Thesis: English.

Natt, Sara. A Study of Character Types in the Prose Fiction of William Gilmore Simms. Univ. of South Carolina, 1962. Dissertation: English.

McDowell, David A. The Place of William Gilmore Simms' Fiction in American Literature: A History of the Criticism from 1833 through 1965. Vanderbilt Univ., 1966. Dissertation: English.

McEachern, Furman E., Jr. European Influences on the Drama of William Gilmore Simms. Univ. of South Carolina, 1953. Thesis: English.

McNeil, Evelyn S. A Study of the Elements of Realism in Some Representative Novels of William Gilmore Simms. Univ. of Houston, 1965. Thesis: English.

Miller, James P. James Fenimore Cooper and William Gilmore Simms: A Contrast in the Treatment of the American Indian. Seton Hall Univ., 1956. Thesis: English.

Mizer, Raymond E. The Short Stories of William Gilmore Simms. Ohio State Univ., 1946. Thesis: English.

Morgan, Charles H. William Gilmore Simms' Theory and Practice of the Historical Romance. Tulane Univ., 1962. Thesis: English.

Morris, J.A. The Stories of William Gilmore Simms. Univ. of North Carolina (Chapel Hill), 1938. Thesis: English.

_____. William Gilmore Simms' Contributions to Magazines, Newspapers, and Annuals. Univ. of North Carolina (Chapel Hill), 1941. Dissertation: English.

Mullen, John C. William Gilmore Simms: The Relation of His Theory to His Practice of Fiction. Auburn Univ., 1948. Thesis: English.

Naething, Arthur E. The Treatment of the American Indian in the Romances of William Gilmore Simms. Trinity Univ. (Texas), 1952. Thesis: English.

Nixon, Nell M. William Gilmore Simms as a Writer of Gullah Dialect. Texas Tech Univ., 1964. Thesis: English.

Orts, Diedrich H. A Study of the Poetry of William Gilmore Simms. Univ. of Texas (Austin), 1940. Thesis: English.

Ott, Eleanor. Certain Aspects of the Southern Frontier as Presented in the Romances of William Gilmore Simms. Auburn Univ., 1931. Thesis: English.

Palmer, Raymond C. The Prose Fiction Theories of William Gilmore Simms. Indiana Univ. (Bloomington), 1947. Dissertation: English.

Paysinger, Margaret. The Theory and Practice of Biography and History in the Writings of William Gilmore Simms. Univ. of North Carolina (Chapel Hill), 1951. Thesis: English.

Popp, Klaus-Juergen. The Revolutionary Romances of William Gilmore Simms. Univ. of Arkansas, 1961. Thesis: English.

_____. Die Stellung William Gilmore Simms: A Study of the Humor in His Fiction and Drama. Giessen, 1965. Dissertation: English.

Ridgely, Joseph V. William Gilmore Simms: The Novelist as Southerner. Johns Hopkins Univ., 1956. Dissertation: English.

Seegers, J.C. The Novels of William Gilmore Simms. Columbia Univ., 1916. Thesis: English.

Shillingsburg, Miriam J. An Edition of William Gilmore Simms' *The Cub of the Panther*. Univ. of South Carolina, 1969. Dissertation: English.

Shillingsburg, Peter L. The Use of Sources in Simms' Biography of Francis Marion. Univ. of South Carolina, 1967. Thesis: English.

Silver, James W. The Back-Country People in the Historical Novels of W.G. Simms. George Peabody College, 1929. Thesis: History.

Simpson, Francis W. William Gilmore Simms and the *Southern Quarterly Review*. Furman Univ., 1946. Thesis: English.

Smith, H.N. Use of Phrenological Ideas in the Prose Fiction of William Gilmore Simms and Harriet Beecher Stowe. Univ. of Texas (Austin), 1942. Thesis: English.

Sullivan, Cecille G. The Indian as Treated by Cooper and Simms. Yale Univ., 1925. Thesis: English.

Tedford, Kathryn S. Knights in Homespun and Border Buccaneers in the Novels of William Gilmore Simms. Univ. of Missouri, 1945. Thesis: English.

Thorne, M.E. Class and Caste in the Novels of William Gilmore
Simms. Smith College, 1944. Thesis: English.
Thorpe, Berenice D. Romance and Realism in the Novels of William
Gilmore Simms. Univ. of Washington, 1925. Thesis: English.
Wakelyn, Jon L. William Gilmore Simms: The Artist as Public Man,
A Political Odyssey, 1830-1860. Rice Univ., 1966. Disser-
tation: History.
Welch, Michael S. Social Purpose in Three Early Novels of William
Gilmore Simms. Univ. of Virginia, 1967. Thesis: English.
Welsh, J.R. Southern Life and Character in the Novels of William
Gilmore Simms. Syracuse Univ., 1941. Thesis: English.
Welsh, John R., Jr. The Mind of William Gilmore Simms, His Social
and Political Thought. Vanderbilt Univ., 1952. Dissertation:
English.
Whaley, Grace W. The Influence of Sir Walter Scott's Novels upon
Those of William Gilmore Simms. Duke Univ., 1929. Thesis:
English.
White, Curtis. William Godwin's *Caleb Williams* and William G.
Simms' *Confession*: A Study in Influence. East Tennessee
State Univ., 1970. Thesis: English.
Wimsatt, Mary A.C. The Comic Sense of William Gilmore Simms: A
Study of the Humor in His Fiction and Drama. Duke Univ.,
1964. Dissertation: English.

CHARLES A. SIRINGO (1855-1928)

Sawey, Orlan L. Charles A. Siringo, Cowboy Chronicler. Univ. of
Texas (Austin), 1947. Thesis: English.

ASHBEL SMITH (1805-1886)

Smither, Harriet. The Diplomatic Service of Ashbel Smith to the
Republic of Texas, 1842-1845. Univ. of Texas (Austin)., 1922.
Thesis: History. [Combines biography and extensive
quotation from Smith's *Journal*]

CHARLES HENRY SMITH (1826-1903)
(BILL ARP)

Christy, Annie M. Charles Henry Smith, Bill Arp: A Biographical
and Critical Study of a Nineteenth Century Georgia Humorist,
Politician, Homely Philosopher. Univ. of Chicago, 1952.
Dissertation: English.
Keppel, Placid, O.S.B. Bill Arp (Charles Henry Smith, 1826-1903),
Southern Humorist. Catholic Univ., 1932. Thesis: English.
Landrum, Louella. Charles Henry Smith (Bill Arp): Georgian
Humorist. Duke Univ., 1938. Thesis: English.
Miller, Verdie F. Bill Arp (Charles Henry Smith), Georgia Author.
Univ. of Georgia, 1927. Thesis: English.

DOLLILEE DAVIS SMITH (1913-   )

Pyeatt, Mattie L. The Human Interest in the Poetry of Dollilee
Davis Smith. Hardin-Simmons Univ., 1950. Thesis: English.

FRANCIS HOPKINSON SMITH (1838-1915)

Deal, Louise S. Thackeray's Influence on Francis Hopkinson Smith.
    Southern Methodist Univ., 1946. Thesis: English.
Saucier, Velma M. The Short Stories and the Novels of Francis
    Hopkinson Smith. Louisiana State Univ., 1943. Thesis:
    English.
White, Courtland Y. III. Francis Hopkinson Smith. Univ. of
    Pennsylvania, 1932. Dissertation: English.

MRS. E.D.E.N. SOUTHWORTH (1819-1899)

Boyle, Regis L. Mrs. E.D.E.N. Southworth, Novelist. Catholic
    Univ., 1938. Dissertation: English.
Mason, James H. Mrs. E.D.E.N. Southworth. George Peabody College,
    1935. Thesis: English.

LAURENCE STALLINGS (1894-   )

Harris, Paul C., Jr. *What Price Glory?* By Maxwell Anderson and
    Laurence Stallings: A Production Book. Stanford Univ., 1951.
    Thesis: Speech and Drama.
Stevens, John C. A Technical Production Book for Maxwell
    Anderson's and Laurence Stalling's *What Price Glory?* Stanford
    Univ., 1951. Thesis: Speech and Drama.

MRS. MARY NEWTON STANARD (1865-1929)

Sydnor, Elizabeth C. Mrs. Mary Newton Stanard, Her Life and Works.
    Columbia Univ., 1923. Thesis: English.

FRANK L. STANTON (1857-1927)

Apamian, Elizabeth H. Frank L. Stanton: His Life, Poetry, and
    Work as a Columnist on the *Atlanta Constitution*. Columbia
    Univ., 1931. Thesis: English.
Hanson, Wyoline. The Georgia Cracker in the Poetry of Frank L.
    Stanton. George Peabody College, 1930. Thesis: English.
Jones, Lucile. Sweet Singer of the South, Frank L. Stanton.
    Oglethorpe Univ., 1939. Thesis: English.
Kendrick, Margaret. Frank L. Stanton. Oglethorpe Univ., 1931.
    Thesis: English.
McKelvain, Isla. The Spirit of the New South as Reflected in the
    Poetry of Frank L. Stanton. George Peabody College, 1922.
    Thesis: English.
Milhous, Mary M. Frank L. Stanton, Southern Lyrist, 1857-1927.
    Univ. of South Carolina, 1928. Thesis: English.
Pullen, Mabel G. A Comparative Study of the Dialect Used in the
    Poems of Frank L. Stanton and James W. Riley. George Peabody
    College, 1925. Thesis: English.

ALEXANDER HAMILTON STEPHENS (1812-1883)

Beck, Nemias B. Alexander H. Stephens, Orator. Univ. of Wisconsin, 1938. Dissertation: English.
Reid, Jasper B., Jr. The Mephistopheles of Southern Politics: A Critical Analysis of Some of the Political Thought of Alexander Hamilton Stephens, Vice-President of the Confederacy. Univ. of Michigan, 1966. Dissertation: History.

WILLIAM HENRY STILES (1809-1865)

Harwell, Christopher L. William Henry Stiles: Georgia Gentleman-Politician. Emory Univ., 1959. Dissertation: History.

JAMES STILL (1906-   )

Craf, Katherine L. The Fiction and Poetry of James Still as a Kentucky Writer. Univ. of Louisville, 1966. Thesis: English.
Walker, Edith C. Folk Elements in the Fiction of James Still. Western Kentucky Univ., 1969. Thesis: English.
Wing, Fred E. James Still: An Inquiry into The Intrinsic Value of The Works of a Regional Writer. Colorado State Univ., 1969. Dissertation: English.

WILLIAM STITH (1707-1755)

Tsuruta, Toshiko. William Stith, Historian of Colonial Virginia. Univ. of Washington, 1957. Dissertation: History.

JAMES STREET (1903-1954)

Jones, William M. A Century of Mississippi History with James Street. Univ. of Mississippi, 1969. Thesis: English.
Smith, Frank M. The Versatility of James Street. Baylor Univ., 1956. Thesis: English.

THOMAS S. STRIBLING (1881-1966)

Beasley, William M. T.S. Stribling and the South. Vanderbilt Univ., 1949. Thesis: English.
Eckley, Wilton E. The Novels of T.S. Stribling: A Socio-Literary Study. Case Western Reserve Univ., 1965. Dissertation: English.
Ferguson, Richard W. T.S. Stribling's South: Aspects of His Southern Novels. North Dakota State Univ., 1963. Thesis: English.
Fuller, R.C. T.S. Stribling. Auburn Univ., 1939. Thesis: English.
Garner, Desda. Intimate Study of Life and Writings of T.S. Stribling. George Peabody College, 1933. Thesis: English.
Jarrett, Thomas D. Novels of T.S. Stribling. Fisk Univ., 1937. Thesis: English.
Leamon, Irma G. Satire in T.S. Stribling's Novels of the South. Univ. of Southern California, 1937. Thesis: English.

Moore, Roberta G. A Study of the Background and of the Mechanics of the Stribling Novels. Ohio Univ., 1938. Thesis: English.

Overholser, Martha E. T.S. Stribling as a Twentieth-Century Local Color Writer of Wayne County, Tennessee. George Peabody College, 1967. Thesis: English.

Overpeck, Evelyn. Thomas Stribling as a Regionalist. Univ. of Arizona, 1944. Thesis: English.

DAVID HUNTER STROTHER (1816-1888)
(PORTE CRAYON)

Costello, Helen (Sr. Joseph Miriam, C.S.J.). The Life and Works of David Hunter Strother--Porte Crayon. St. John's Univ. (N.Y.), 1956. Thesis: English.

Eby, Cecil D., Jr. A Critical Biography of David Hunter Strother (Porte Crayon). Univ. of Pennsylvania, 1958. Dissertation: English.

WILLIAM STYRON (1925-   )

Galloway, David D. The Absurd Hero in Contemporary American Fiction: The Works of John Updike, William Styron, Saul Bellow, and J.D. Salinger. Univ. of Buffalo, 1962. Dissertation: English.

Herrin, Lamar. The Existential Evolution of Character and Theme in the Novels of William Styron. Univ. of Tennessee, 1964. Thesis: English.

Johnson, Kari. William Styron: A Modern Traditionalist. Univ. of Montana, 1968. Thesis: English.

Kaslow, Gloria C. The Christian Vision of William Styron. Univ. of Nebraska (Omaha), 1968. Thesis: English.

Kosen, Waldo A. An Appraisal and Analysis of William Styron's Worth As a Significant Modern Writer. Moorhead State College, 1965. Thesis: English.

Logan, Beverly S. A Study of William Styron's Novella *The Long March*. Wesleyan Univ., 1970. Thesis: English.

Luttrell, William. Tragic and Comic Modes in Twentieth Century American Literature: William Styron and Joseph Heller. Bowling Green State Univ., 1969. Dissertation: English.

Merrill, Charles S. An Appraisal of Structure and Point of View in The Novels of William Styron. North Texas State Univ., 1962. Thesis: English.

Mewshaw, Michael F. War as a Thematic Continuum in the Work of William Styron. Univ. of Virginia, 1967. Thesis: English.

Nigro, Augustine J., Jr. William Styron and The Adamic Tradition. Univ. of Maryland, 1964. Dissertation: English.

Oliver, Jane S. Two Progressions in William Styron's Treatment of Minority Group Characters. Univ. of Tennessee, 1969. Thesis: English.

Peterson, Marilyn L. The Achievement of William Styron. Trinity Univ. (Texas), 1966. Thesis: English.

Ritchie, Adam B. The Fiction of William Styron. Univ. of Virginia, 1961. Thesis: English.

Scott, James B. The Individual and Society: Norman Mailer versus William Styron. Syracuse Univ., 1964. Dissertation: English.
Sklepowich, Edward A. Immersion in the Destructive Element in William Styron's Fiction. Univ. of Virginia, 1967. Thesis: English.
Smith, Ronald A. The Absurd Heroine in the Novels of William Styron. Texas A & M Univ., 1969. Thesis: English.
Thompson, Cynthia J. The Interrelation of Techniques and Meaning in Styron's *Lie Down in Darkness*. Univ. of North Carolina (Chapel Hill), 1960. Thesis: English.

JESSE STUART (1905-   )

Austin, Mary F. Agrarianism in the Works of Jesse Stuart. Texas Christian Univ., 1953. Thesis: English.
Blair, Everetta L. Jesse Stuart: A Survey of His Life and Works. Univ. of South Carolina, 1964. Dissertation: English.
Chappell, Mary J. The Social and Economic Aspects of the Novels of Jesse Stuart. Vanderbilt Univ., 1959. Thesis: English.
Davis, Hestelle R. Regional Elements in the Prose Writing of Jesse Stuart. Miami Univ. (Ohio), 1953. Thesis: English.
Dickinson, Meriwether B. A Lexicographical Study of the Vocabulary of Greenup County, Kentucky, Set Forth in Jesse Stuart's *Beyond Dark Hills*. Univ. of Virginia, 1941. Thesis: English.
Dixon, Mae D. Jesse Stuart and Education. Western Kentucky State College, 1952. Thesis: English.
Jeter, Virginia L. Elements of Local Color in the Prose Fiction of Jesse Stuart. East Tennessee State Univ., 1956. Thesis: English.
Knival, Betty J. The Autobiographies of Jesse Stuart: American Regional Writing in a Changing Society. Univ. of Wyoming, 1964. Thesis: English.
Leavell, Frank H. The Literary Career of Jesse Stuart   Vanderbilt Univ., 1965. Dissertation: English.
LeMaster, Jimmie R. Jesse Stuart: Kentucky's Chronicler-Poet. Bowling Green State Univ., 1970. Dissertation: English.
Littleton, David G. Structures of Dialect in Short Stories and Poetry of Jesse Stuart. Morehead State Univ., 1970. Thesis: English.
McKethan, Flora B. Folklore in the Short Stories of Jesse Stuart. Baylor Univ., 1965. Thesis: English.
McKinney, Edith L. Jesse Stuart's Kentucky. Midwestern Univ., 1959. Thesis: English.
Mitchell, Beulah. A Study of the Life and Works of Jesse Stuart. East Texas State Univ., 1952. Thesis: English.
Pennington, Royce L. Jesse Stuart: His Symbolism and Vision. Univ. of Iowa, 1965. Thesis: English.
Ramey, Lee L. An Inquiry into the Life of Jesse Stuart as Related to his Literary Development and a Critical Study of His Works. Ohio Univ., 1941. Thesis: English.
Rose, Mary G. Jesse Stuart: Pioneer Writer of the Kentucky Hills. George Peabody College, 1938. Thesis: English.
Smith, Lula A. Self-Portrayal in the Writings of Jesse Stuart. Miami Univ. (Ohio), 1962. Thesis: English.

[161]

Taylor, Alfred H.   Jesse Stuart and the Short Story.   Vanderbilt
     Univ., 1949. Thesis: English.
Taylor, Halsey P.   The Short Stories of Jesse Stuart.   Univ. of
     Southern California, 1953. Thesis: English.
Washington, Mary L.   The Folklore of the Cumberlands as Reflected
     in the Writings of Jesse Stuart. Univ. of Pennsylvania, 1960.
     Dissertation: Folklore.

RUTH McENERY STUART (1849-1917)

Fletcher, Mary F.   A Biographical and Critical Study of Ruth
     McEnery Stuart. Univ. of Virginia, 1935. Thesis: English.
_____. A Biographical and Critical Study of Ruth McEnery Stuart.
     Louisiana State Univ., 1955. Dissertation: English.
Howell, I.R.   A Critical Biography of Ruth McEnery Stuart.   Univ.
     of North Carolina (Chapel Hill), 1945. Thesis: English.
Longmire, Kathryn E.   A Biographical and Dialectical Study of
     Ruth McEnery Stuart. Louisiana State Univ., 1935. Thesis:
     English.
Stone, Ophelia.   Ruth McEnery Stuart in Dialect and Folklore.
     Columbia Univ., 1922. Thesis: English.

ALEXANDER EDWIN SWEET (1841-1901)

Speck, Ernest B.   An Analysis of the Humor of Alexander Edwin Sweet
     in His *Texas Siftings*. Univ. of Texas (Austin), 1947.
     Thesis: English.

JOHN BANISTER TABB (1845-1909)

Fidelis, Sr.   An Intimate Study of the Poet-Priest John Banister
     Tabb. George Peabody College, 1928. Thesis: English.
Glenn, Sr. Mary C.   The Poetry of Father Tabb. Univ. of Pittsburgh,
     1926. Thesis: English.
Hale, Sr. M.F.   Tone-quality in the Poetry of Fr. Tabb. Catholic
     Univ., 1944. Thesis: English.
Hettich, The Rev. B.   Imagery in the Poems of Father Tabb. Univ.
     of Notre Dame, 1952. Thesis: English.
Kelley, Sr. Miriam L., S.S.J.   Father Tabb's Contribution to
     American Literature. Villanova Univ., 1938. Thesis:
     English.
Lally, Sr. M.A., B.V.M.   The Imagery of Father Tabb. Catholic
     Univ., 1948. Thesis: English.
Litz, Francis E.A.   A Critical Study of the Life and Works of John
     Banister Tabb. Johns Hopkins Univ., 1921. Dissertation:
     English.
Maher, Sr. M.H., S.C.   A Study of Tone-color in the Poetry of John
     Banister Tabb. Marquette Univ., 1943. Thesis: English.
Simar, Anselm D.   Wit and Humor of Father Tabb. St. Mary's (San
     Antonio), 1942. Thesis: English.
Williams, John J.   A Critical Study of the Poetry of John Banister
     Tabb. Univ. of Georgia, 1966. Dissertation: English.

ALLEN TATE (1899-   )

Brown, Gerald K. Allen Tate and the Traditional Society. Univ.
    of Mississippi, 1968. Thesis: English.
Coltrell, Eileen J. An Analysis and Evaluation of the Poetic
    Theory of Allen Tate. San Francisco State College, 1962.
    Thesis: English.
Darring, Walter L. Allen Tate and the Scientific Spirit. Florida
    State Univ., 1964. Thesis: English.
Eder, Ursula E. The Poetry of Allen Tate. Univ. of Wisconsin,
    1955. Dissertation: English.
George, Melvin R. Tension in Poetry: A Review of the Critical
    Position of Allen Tate. Iowa State Teachers College, 1961.
    Thesis: English.
Gerlach, Lee F. The Poetry and "Strategies" of Allen Tate. Univ.
    of Michigan, 1955. Dissertation: English.
Harrington, Ann P. Allen Tate: The Failure of the Historical Myth.
    Boston College, 1966. Thesis: English.
Hunter, Anne C. Attitudes Toward Tradition in Allen Tate's *The
    Fathers*. Univ. of North Carolina (Chapel Hill), 1964. Thesis:
    English.
Lea, Mary L. Allen Tate's Attitude toward the South. Vanderbilt
    Univ., 1946. Thesis: English.
Mangan, Sandra S. Allen Tate and the American Tradition in Letters.
    John Carroll Univ., 1961. Thesis: English.
Meiner, Roger K. The Last Alternatives: The Poetry and Criticism
    of Allen Tate. Univ. of Denver, 1961. Dissertation: English.
McDonald, James L. The Literary Theory of a Modern Man of Letters:
    The Critical Principles of Allen Tate. Northwestern Univ.,
    1965. Dissertation: English.
O'Connor, Sr. M.C.T., O.S.F. Tension in the Poetry of Allen Tate.
    Villanova Univ., 1961. Thesis: English.
O'Dea, Richard J. To Make The Eye Secure: The Criticism, Fiction,
    and Poetry of Allen Tate. Louisiana State Univ., 1964.
    Dissertation: English.
Skurla, Sr. St. George, C.S.J. The Critical Theories of Allen Tate.
    Univ. of Southern California, 1959. Thesis: English.
Sullivan, Naomi C. Allen Tate: Biographer, Critic and Poet.
    Villanova Univ., 1943. Thesis: English.
Wallace, I.R. Some Aspects of the Work of Allen Tate. Manchester,
    1964. Thesis: English.
Williamson, Alan B. The Epic Impulse in Hart Crane, Allen Tate,
    and Robert Lowell. Harvard Univ., 1969. Dissertation:
    English.

PETER TAYLOR (1917-   )

Brantley, Julia A.R. The Past in the Present: A Major Theme in
    Six Short Stories of Peter Taylor. Vanderbilt Univ., 1965.
    Thesis: English.
Schular, Sr. Cor M., R.S.H.M. The House of Peter Taylor: Vision
    and Structure. Univ. of Notre Dame, 1964. Dissertation:
    English.
Wood, Gerald E. Major and Minor Themes in the Works of Peter Taylor.
    Vanderbilt Univ., 1965. Thesis: English.

MARY VIRGINIA TERHUNE (1830-1922)
(MARION HARLAND)

Wright, Mary H. Mary Virginia Hawes Terhune ("Marion Harland"):
Her Life and Works. George Peabody College, 1934. Dissertation: English.

ALEXANDER WATKINS TERRELL (1827-1912)

Chamberlain, Charles K. Alexander Watkins Terrell, Citizen,
Statesman. Univ. of Texas (Austin), 1956. Dissertation:
History.
Wallis, Mary E. The Life of Alexander Watkins Terrell, 1827-1912.
Univ. of Texas (Austin), 1937. [Bibliography lists literary
pieces in Terrell papers]

CHARLES TESTUT (1818-1892)

Legarde, Marie L. Charles Testut: Critic, Journalist, and Literary
Socialist. Tulane Univ., 1948. Thesis: French.

AUGUSTUS THOMAS (1857-1934)

Bynum, Lucy S. The Economic and Political Ideas of Augustus
Thomas. Univ. of North Carolina (Chapel Hill), 1954. Dissertation: English.

JOHN R. THOMPSON (1823-1873)

Miller, Joseph R. John R. Thompson: His Place in Southern Life
and Literature: A Critical Biography. Univ. of Virginia, 1930.
Dissertation: English.

MAURICE THOMPSON (1844-1901)

Parr, Loys. A Study of Maurice Thompson. Univ. of Texas (Austin),
1933. Thesis: English.

WILLIAM TAPPAN THOMPSON (1812-1882)

Harris, Nancy F. A Phonological Study of the Cracker Dialect of
Georgia as Represented in *Major Jones's Courtship* by William
Tappan Thompson. Columbia Univ., 1965. Thesis: English.
Holbrook, Laura D. Georgia Scenes and Life in the Works of William
Tappan Thompson. Univ. of Georgia, 1967. Thesis: English.
Miller, Henry P. The Life and Works of William Tappan Thompson.
Univ. of Chicago, 1942. Dissertation: English.

JAMES HENLEY THORNWELL (1812-1862)

Baker, Virginia K. James Henley Thornwell, Christian Educator of
the Old South. Duke Univ., 1936. Thesis: Religion.
Garber, Paul L. The Religious Thought of James Henley Thornwell.
Duke Univ., 1939. Dissertation: Philosophy.

THOMAS BANGS THORPE (1815-1878)

Dozier, Richard, Jr. Thomas Bangs Thorpe: Reporter of the Old
Southwest. Duke Univ., 1964. Thesis: English.

Gunnison, Herbert F. Thomas Bangs Thorpe: A Study of Conscience
and Prophetic Symbolism. Univ. of Louisville, 1969. Thesis:
English.

Herron, Virginia F. Thomas Bangs Thorpe and the *Spirit of the
Times*: A Study of American Humor, 1840-1850. Auburn Univ.,
1953. Thesis: English.

Rickels, Milton H. Thomas Bangs Thorpe: His Life and Work.
Louisiana State Univ., 1953. Dissertation: English.

FRANCIS ORRAY TICKNOR (1822-1874)

Cheney, Sarah A. Francis Orray Ticknor. Duke Univ., 1934. Thesis:
English.

Hess, Eugene D. A Study of the Life and Writings of Dr. Francis
Orray Ticknor. Auburn Univ., 1933. Thesis: English.

Rogers, Annie B. Francis Orray Ticknor, Georgia Poet. Univ. of
Georgia, 1928. Thesis: English.

FRANCES CHRISTINE FISHER TIERNAN (1846-1920)
(CHRISTIAN REED)

Becker, Sr. M.M. Christian Reid (Frances Christine Fisher
Tiernan): Some Aspects of Her Literary Style. Catholic
Univ., 1933. Thesis: English.

HENRY TIMROD (1828-1867)

Brigham, Lillian M. Charleston--the Background for Timrod. Univ.
of Texas (Austin), 1935. Thesis: English.

Brockman, Allan A. The Early Sonnet Form of Henry Timrod.
Vanderbilt Univ., 1946. Thesis: English.

Clement, Norma. A Study of Speech in Selected Poems of Henry
Timrod. East Tennessee State Univ., 1968. Thesis: English.

Felder, Herman M. Notes on Timrod. Vanderbilt Univ., 1937.
Thesis: English.

Glasgow, Elizabeth A. Henry Timrod: A Study in Artistic Development. Columbia Univ., 1925. Thesis: English.

Greiner, Donald J. Henry Timrod's Theory of Poetry. Univ. of
Virginia, 1963. Thesis: English.

Harris, James H. A Concordance to the Poems of Henry Timrod.
Louisiana State Univ., 1939. Thesis: English.

Jordan, Martha R. Henry Timrod's Early Poems. Duke Univ., 1935.
Thesis: English.

Keller, Mark A. The Making of a Poet: A Survey of the Critical
Reaction to the Poetry of Henry Timrod, 1860-1966.
Mississippi State Univ., 1966. Thesis: English.

Lewis, Ruby R. Henry Timrod. Columbia Univ., 1923. Thesis:
English.

Love, Frances L. Henry Timrod, Confederate Laureate and Nature
Poet. Columbia Univ., 1931. Thesis: English.

McClimon, Grace L. Henry Timrod as Man and Poet. Wofford
    College, 1935. Thesis: English.
Paty, Sadie. Henry Timrod: A Critical Study. Vanderbilt Univ.,
    1943. Thesis: English.
Thomas, Evelyn J.H. Henry Timrod: Romantic and Rebel. Brigham
    Young Univ., 1955. Thesis: English.
Wilburn, W.B.S. Henry Timrod: Literary Influence and Theories
    of Poetry. Univ. of Mississippi, 1938. Thesis: English.

ROBERT A. TOOMBS (1810-1885)

Lowe, Larry V. A Rhetorical Analysis of the Speaking of Robert A.
    Toombs of Georgia. Michigan State Univ., 1965. Dissertation:
    Speech.

JEAN TOOMER (1894-1967)

Dillard, Mabel M. Jean Toomer: Herald of The Negro Renaissance.
    Ohio State Univ., 1967. Dissertation: English.

ALBION WINEGAR TOURGÉE (1838-1905)

Carey, Thomas F.X. Albion Winegar Tourgée: Altruist or Cynic.
    St. John's Univ. (N.Y.), 1950. Thesis: English.
Dibble, Ray F. Albion W. Tourgée. Columbia Univ., 1921. Disser-
    tation: English.
Gross, Theodore L. Albion W. Tourgée: Reporter of the Recon-
    struction. Columbia Univ., 1960. Dissertation: English.
Hillger, Martin E. Albion W. Tourgée: Critic of Society.
    Indiana Univ., 1959. Dissertation: English.
Zimmerman, Gordon G. The Crusade in Fiction of Albion W. Tourgée
    against Race and Class Prejudice. Bowling Green State Univ.,
    1950. Thesis: English.

WILLIAM BARRET TRAVIS (1809-1836)

Mixon, Ruby. William Barrett Travis, His Life and Letters. Univ.
    of Texas (Austin), 1930. Thesis: History.

WILLIAM PETERFIELD TRENT (1862-1939)

Walker, Franklin T. William Peterfield Trent. A Critical Bio-
    graphy. George Peabody College, 1943. Dissertation: English.

WILLIAM HENRY TRESCOT (1822-1898)

Betts, Rose M. William Henry Trescot. Univ. of South Carolina,
    1929. Thesis: English.

AMÉLIE RIVES TROUBETZKOY (1863-1945)
(AMÉLIE RIVES)

Hungerford, Robert W. An Edition of Amélie Rives Troubetzkoy's
    The Young Elizabeth. Univ. of Richmond, 1969. Thesis:
    English.

GEORGE W. TRUETT (1867-1944)

Boyatt, Bernard C. George W. Truett--Preacher and Public Speaker.
    Univ. of Tennessee, 1952. Thesis: English.

GEORGE TUCKER (1775-1861)

McLean, Robert C. George Tucker: Moral Philosopher and Man of
    Letters. Washington Univ., 1960. Dissertation: English.
Pitner, Maria G. A Study of George Tucker's *The Valley of
    Schenandoah*. Univ. of North Carolina (Chapel Hill), 1966.
    Thesis: English.

NATHANIEL BEVERLY TUCKER (1784-1851)

Goodwin, Noma L. The Published Works of Nathaniel Beverly Tucker,
    1784-1851. Duke Univ., 1947. Thesis: English.
Riley, Denise A. The Life and Thought of Nathaniel Beverly Tucker,
    Gentleman Scholar of Old Virginia. Marquette Univ., 1969.
    Thesis: History.
Turrentine, P.W. The Life and Works of Nathaniel Beverly Tucker,
    1784-1841. Harvard Univ., 1933. Dissertation: English.
Wrobel, Arthur. *The Partisan Leader* as Tract and Romance. Univ.
    of North Carolina (Chapel Hill), 1964. Thesis: English.

ST. GEORGE TUCKER (1752-1827)

Laughlin, Hal. A Critical Edition of St. George Tucker's *The Wheel
    of Fortune*. College of William and Mary, 1960. Thesis:
    English.
Prince, William S. St. George Tucker as a Poet of the Early
    Republic. Yale Univ., 1954. Dissertation: English.

WILLIAM ORRIE TUGGLE (1841-1885)

Fuller, William E. William Orrie Tuggle: Journal of 1880-1882.
    Auburn Univ., 1964. Thesis: English.
Hatfield, Dorothy B. The W.O. Tuggle Manuscript of Creek Indian
    Folktales--Its History and Significance. Auburn Univ., 1960.
    Thesis: English.

JOSEPH ADDISON TURNER (1826-1868)

Corry, Raymond H. Joseph Addison Turner, Southern Planter. Univ.
    of Georgia, 1937. Thesis: English.
Huff, Lawrence. Joseph Addison Turner: A Study in the Culture of
    Antebellum Middle Georgia. Vanderbilt Univ., 1958. Disser-
    tation: English.

JULIA STRUDWICH TUTWILER (1841-1916)

Pitts, Clara L. Julia Strudwich Tutwiler, Alabama Pioneer.
    George Washington Univ., 1942. Dissertation: Education.

JOSEPH ROGERS UNDERWOOD (1791-1876)

Brashear, Ralph W. Joseph Rogers Underwood: A Representative
    Nineteenth Century American. Western Kentucky Univ., 1968.
    Thesis: English.

ABEL PARKER UPSHUR (1790-1844)

Hall, Claude H. Abel Parker Upshur. Univ. of Virginia, 1954.
    Dissertation: History.

JAMES K. VARDAMAN (1861-1930)

Holmes, William F. III. The White Chief: James K. Vardaman in
    Mississippi Politics, 1890-1908. Rice Univ., 1964. Disser-
    tation: History.

JUDGE FÉLIX VOORHIES (1839-1919)

Schertz, Marcelle F. The Plays of Judge Félix Voorhies. Louisiana
    State Univ., 1940. Thesis: Romance Languages.
Tilly, Ruth E. The Life and Writings of Judge Félix Voorhies.
    Louisiana State Univ., 1940. Thesis: Romance Languages.

JOHN DONALD WADE (1892-1963)

Benson, Robert G. John Donald Wade: An Analysis and Evaluation.
    Vanderbilt Univ., 1965. Thesis: English.

ROBERT J. WALKER (1801-1869)

Wolpow, Meyer S. For the Greater Glory of the Union: The Last
    Years of Robert J. Walker (1861-1869). New York Univ., 1960.
    Dissertation: History.

ROBERT SPARKS WALKER (1878-   )

Fisher, Mary B. Robert Sparks Walker, Naturalist and Writer.
    George Peabody College, 1937. Thesis: English.

GEORGE C. WALLACE (1919-   )

Makay, John J. The Speaking of Governor George C. Wallace in the
    1964 Maryland Presidential Primary. Purdue Univ., 1969.
    Dissertation: Speech.
Raspberry, Robert W. The Public Image of George Wallace in the
    1968 Presidential Election. North Texas State Univ., 1969.
    Thesis: Speech and Drama.

ROBERT WALSH (1784-1859)

Kennedy,.Fr. J.E., S.J. Robert Walsh, Journalist. Georgetown
    Univ., 1939. Thesis: History.

JEANETTE R.H. WALWORTH (1837-1918)

Roberts, Orville H.   A Criticism of Jeannette Ritchie Hadermann
    Walworth's Novels. Tulane Univ., 1938. Thesis: English.

RUFUS WAPLES (1825-1902)

Twyman, Robert W.   The Civil War Notes and Letters of Rufus Waples,
    Anti-Slavery Southerner. Univ. of Chicago, 1942. Thesis:
    English.

BENJAMIN B. WARFIELD (1865-1943)

Ausley, Paul K.   A Comparative Study of the Calvanism of Benjamin B.
    Warfield and William Adams Brown. Duke Univ., 1945.
    Bachelor of Divinity.

CATHARINE ANNE WARFIELD (1816-1877)

Smith, Sidney L.   A Critical Study of the Life and Novels of
    Catharine Anne Warfield. Univ. of Mississippi, 1929.
    Thesis: English.

ROBERT PENN WARREN (1905-   )

Aden, William C.   Robert Penn Warren's Novels: The Major Theme.
    Cornell Univ., 1957. Thesis: English.
Alexander, Jeanette.   Robert Penn Warren: Prejudice and the
    Southern Intellectual. Emory Univ., 1971. Thesis: English.
Altgelt, Frederick.   Robert Penn Warren. A Study of Symbolism in
    Night Rider and *World Enough and Time*. Vanderbilt Univ.,
    1954. Thesis: English.
Anderson, Carol E.   Religious, Intellectual, and Political Authority
    in the Fictional Works of Robert Penn Warren. Sam Houston
    State Univ., 1961. Thesis: English.
Bankowsky, Richard J.   A Natural History of Supernaturalism: A
    Study of Three Poems by Robert Penn Warren. Columbia Univ.,
    1954. Thesis: English.
Bennett, John B.   The Iron Beach: A Study of the Poetry of Robert
    Penn Warren. Vanderbilt Univ., 1948. Thesis: English.
Bishoff, Robert E.   Pragmatic Man in Search of Himself: A Study
    of the Novels of Robert Penn Warren. New Mexico Highlands
    Univ., 1966. Thesis: English.
Blank, Susan W.   The Problem of Negro Identity in the Works of
    Robert Penn Warren. Brown Univ., 1968. Thesis: American
    Civilization.
Borchers, Nancy N.   Robert Penn Warren's Novels: The Differences
    within the Framework of the Similarities. Vanderbilt Univ.,
    1958. Thesis: English.
Boyce, Edna C.   A Critical Study of Robert Penn Warren's *Flood*.
    Hardin-Simmons Univ., 1965. Thesis: English.
Brubaker, DeLacy P.   The Theme of the Father in the Novels of
    Robert Penn Warren. Columbia Univ., 1960. Thesis: English.

Byrd, John C. The Troubled Southerner: Robert Penn Warren as a
    Social Critic. Univ. of Arizona, 1966. Thesis: English.
Casper, Leonard. The Lost Sense of Community and the Role of the
    Artist in Robert Penn Warren. Univ. of Wisconsin, 1953.
    Dissertation: English.
Cayton, Robert F. Point of View in the Novels of Robert Penn
    Warren. Ohio Univ., 1968. Dissertation: English.
Chambers, Robert H. III. Robert Penn Warren: His Growth as a
    Writer. Brown Univ., 1969. Dissertation: English.
Church, Ralph B. A Synthesis of the Novels of Robert Penn Warren.
    Columbia Univ., 1951. Thesis: English.
Clark, Marden J. Symbolic Structure in the Novels of Robert Penn
    Warren. Univ. of Washington, 1957. Dissertation: English.
Colbert, William J. Robert Penn Warren: The Enduring Search for
    Self-knowledge. Univ. of Mississippi, 1969. Thesis: English.
Coleman, Thomas E. Form as Function in the Novels of Robert Penn
    Warren. Univ. of Louisville, 1950. Thesis: English.
Conwell, Ina C. Justice in Robert Penn Warren's *World Enough and
    Time*. Emory Univ., 1961. Thesis: English.
Cooke, Martha E. From Fact to Fiction: A Study of Robert Penn
    Warren's *World Enough and Time*. Vanderbilt Univ., 1967.
    Thesis: English.
Coplan, Ruth E. Moral Values in the Novels of Robert Penn Warren.
    Univ. of Virginia, 1957. Thesis: English.
Crick, J.B. R.P. Warren and A Pome of Pure Imagination. Univ. of
    Western Ontario, 1966. Thesis: English.
Dooley, Dennis M. The Awful Responsibility of Time: A Study of
    Warren's Concept of the Hero in Early Novels. Kent State
    Univ., 1966. Thesis: English.
_____. This Collocation of Memories: The Poetic Strategy of
    Robert Penn Warren. Vanderbilt Univ., 1970. Dissertation:
    English.
Duncan, Mary A. The Theme of Justice in Robert Penn Warren's Four
    Major Novels. Mississippi College, 1967. Thesis: English.
Eickhoff, Michael E. *World Enough and Time* and Robert Penn Warren's
    Dialectic of Freedom and Necessity. Univ. of Notre Dame, 1957.
    Thesis: English.
Elkins, Dean R. A Bibliographical and Critical Essay upon the
    Robert Penn Warren Collection at the University of Kentucky
    with A Sample Catalogue. Univ. of Louisville, 1969. Thesis:
    English.
Ellingwood, Frances H. The Importance of the Parent-Child Rela-
    tionship in the Fiction of Robert Penn Warren. Eastern
    Washington State College, 1968. Thesis: English.
Estes, Phoebe B. Robert Penn Warren's Philosophy of Existence: A
    Study of *All the King's Men*. Duke Univ., 1960. Thesis:
    English.
Freeman, Mary G. The Betrayal Theme in Robert Penn Warren's
    Novels. Univ. of Tennessee, 1965. Thesis: English.
Fridy, Wilford E. Robert Penn Warren's Use of Kentucky Materials
    in His Fiction as a Basis for His New Mythos. Univ. of
    Kentucky, 1968. Dissertation: English.
Gentry, Rubye E. A Study of Pride in Some of the Fictional Works
    of Robert Penn Warren. Sam Houston State Univ., 1963.
    Thesis: English.
Godsey, Edwin S. The Development of Tragedy in Four Novels by

Robert Penn Warren. Vanderbilt Univ., 1954. Thesis: English.
Grimshaw, James A. *All the King's Men*: Tragedy or Melodrama?
Texas Tech Univ., 1968. Thesis: English.
Halverstadt, Barbara H. The Culmination of Images in Robert Penn
Warren's *Cave*. Univ. of North Carolina (Chapel Hill), 1967.
Thesis: English.
Harrison, Jane. The Fiction of Robert Penn Warren: A Study in
Technique. Vanderbilt Univ., 1947. Thesis: English.
Helbling, Sr. M.R. Responsibility and the Self in Robert Penn
Warren's *All the King's Men*. Univ. of Notre Dame, 1960.
Thesis: English.
Herring, Henry D. The Environment in Robert Penn Warren's
Fictional South. Duke Univ., 1968. Dissertation: English.
Hill, Michael F. Primitivism in the Novels of Robert Penn Warren.
McNeese State Univ., 1966. Thesis: English.
Hochman, Stanley. Robert Penn Warren: Four in Pursuit of
Definition. Columbia Univ., 1952. Thesis: English.
Hornsby, Samuel G., Jr. The Problem of Evil in the Early Novels
of Robert Penn Warren. Univ. of Georgia, 1966. Thesis:
English.
Huff, Mary N. Robert Penn Warren: A Bibliography. Vanderbilt
Univ., 1969. Thesis: English.
Hynes, Sam L. The Poet as Dramatist: Robert Penn Warren and Some
Predecessors. Columbia Univ., 1948. Thesis: English.
Justus, James H. The Concept of Gesture in the Novels of Robert
Penn Warren. Univ. of Washington, 1961. Dissertation:
English.
Kehl, Delmar G. The Dialectics of Reality in the Fiction of Robert
Penn Warren. Univ. of Southern California, 1967. Disser-
tation: English.
Khairallah, George A. A Study of the Ethical Content of Robert
Penn Warren's *All the King's Men*. Columbia Univ., 1953.
Thesis: English.
Kinnaird, John W. Prometheus, Evil and Humpty Dumpty: The Poetry
and Fiction of Robert Penn Warren. Columbia Univ., 1949.
Thesis: English.
Lane, Calvin W. Narrative Art and History in Robert Penn Warren's
World Enough and Time. Univ. of Michigan, 1956. Disser-
tation: English.
Lankford, Willard P. A Consideration of the Concept of "the
speaking voice"--How It Is Used as a Literary Technique in
All the King's Men. Indiana Univ. of Pennsylvania, 1966.
Thesis: English.
Letherbarrow, Ronald. Pragmatism in Robert Penn Warren's *The Cave*.
State Univ. of N.Y. (Buffalo), 1968. Thesis: American
Studies.
Lewis, Ann H. The Logic of Experience: Robert Penn Warren's Use
of History in *Wilderness*. Emory Univ., 1966. Thesis:
English.
Linenthal, Mark, Jr. Robert Penn Warren and the Southern Agrarians.
Stanford Univ., 1957. Dissertation: English.
Love, Patrick J. The Significance of the Parallels between T.S.
Eliot's "The Waste Land" and Robert Penn Warren's *All the
King's Men*. Texas A & M Univ., 1970. Thesis: English.
Maguire, Merrill A. The Role of the Negro in Robert Penn Warren's
Work. Duke Univ., 1960. Thesis: English.

McDonald, Alma J. Pure and Impure Poetry: Robert Penn Warren's
    Selected Poems, 1923-1943. Univ. of South Carolina, 1962.
    Thesis: English.
McLaughlin, Carol. Out of History into History: The Concept of
    History in the Novels of Robert Penn Warren. Univ. of
    Denver, 1958. Thesis: English.
McNutt, Patricia A. A Critical Analysis of the Women in Robert
    Penn Warren's Novels. East Tennessee State Univ., 1969.
    Thesis: English.
McPherson, David C. Robert Penn Warren and the South. Univ. of
    Texas (Austin), 1962. Thesis: English.
McWalters, Mary E. Archetypal Patterns in Robert Penn Warren's
    All the King's Men. Univ. of Virginia, 1966. Thesis:
    English.
Melis, Mary W. The Quest for Self-definition: A Study of the
    Fictional Writing of Robert Penn Warren. Univ. of Wyoming,
    1960. Thesis: English.
Michaelson, Edith L.E. Self-knowledge and History in Three Novels
    by Robert Penn Warren. Hunter College, 1969. Thesis:
    English.
Moore, Littleton H., Jr. Robert Penn Warren and History: "The
    Big Myth We Live." Emory Univ., 1964. Dissertation: English.
Olson, H.L. The American Negro in Selected Writings of Robert
    Penn Warren. South Dakota State Univ., 1970. Thesis:
    English.
Orta, Marjorie P.H. "Identity," "the unconscious self," and the
    "journey to the west" as Themes in Robert Penn Warren's
    Brother to Dragons. Univ. of Georgia, 1969. Thesis: English.
Poenicke, Klaus. Schöpferische Dialektik: Kunswerk und
    kritische Theorie bei Robert Penn Warren. Freie Universität
    (West Berlin), 1957. Dissertation: English.
Prater, Neal B. Point of View in the Novels of Robert Penn Warren.
    Vanderbilt Univ., 1959. Thesis: English.
Pyne, Gloria D. Robert Penn Warren: Character and Philosophy in
    All the King's Men. San Francisco State College, 1967.
    Thesis: English.
Ransom, John B. III. The Integration of the Individual in the
    Fiction of Robert Penn Warren. Stanford Univ., 1949.
    Thesis: English.
Reaves, Gary R. The Significance of Time in the Novels of Robert
    Penn Warren. Sam Houston State Univ., 1963. Thesis: English.
Reedy, Jerry E. Robert Penn Warren and the Critics: A Study of
    the Criticism of Warren's Novels. Univ. of South Dakota,
    1961. Thesis: English.
Roden, Jerry. Technique and Tragedy in the Novels of Robert Penn
    Warren. Auburn Univ., 1962. Thesis: English.
Ross, Joe C. Robert Penn Warren and the Negro. Vanderbilt Univ.,
    1967. Dissertation: English.
Samuels, Charles T. Robert Penn Warren, the End and the Beginning.
    Univ. of California (Berkeley), 1961. Dissertation: English.
Schmidt, Mary P. Betrayal and Identity in Robert Penn Warren: A
    Study of *Blackberry Winter*, *The Circus in the Attic*, and
    World Enough and Time. Wichita State Univ., 1968. Thesis:
    English.

Scott, Willye B. Robert Penn Warren's View of Man: A Study of
    Modern Novelists' Image of American Experiences. North
    Carolina College (Durham), 1964. Thesis: English.
Shaw, Ann B. Conradian Elements in the Novels of Robert Penn
    Warren. Univ. of Tennessee, 1961. Thesis: English.
Shepherd, Allen G. III. A Critical Study of the Fiction of Robert
    Penn Warren. Univ. of Pennsylvania, 1965. Dissertation:
    English.
Smith, Mildred. The Search: A Study of Robert Penn Warren's
    Protagonists from *Night Rider* to *Brother to Dragons*. South-
    west Texas State Univ., 1965. Thesis: English.
Spicehandler, Daniel. Self-knowledge in the Novels of Robert Penn
    Warren. Columbia Univ., 1953. Thesis: English.
Steadmon, Jerry D. Search for Identity in the Novels of Robert
    Penn Warren. Eastern New Mexico Univ., 1965. Thesis:
    English.
Strandberg, Victor H. Robert Penn Warren as a Poet: A Close
    Analysis of *Selected Poems, Brother to Dragons, Promises* and
    You, Emperors, and Others. Brown Univ., 1962. Dissertation:
    English.
Tillman, Polly M. Robert Penn Warren: Patterns for Fulfillment.
    Mississippi College, 1968. Thesis: English.
Trowbridge, Augustus. A Comparative Study of Imagery in the Works
    of Nathaniel Hawthorne and Robert Penn Warren. Brown Univ.,
    1964. Thesis: English.
Wallace, Margaret. Robert Penn Warren's Dialectic Argument for
    Knowledge. Murray State Univ., 1969. Thesis: English.
Ward, Frank W., III. The Problem of Focus of Narration in *All
    the King's Men*. Texas Christian Univ., 1959. Thesis:
    English.
Webber, Winona L. Old Court and New Court: Justice in Robert Penn
    Warren's Fiction. Duke Univ., 1965. Thesis: English.
Welker, Robert L. The Underlying Philosophy of Robert Penn Warren.
    A Study in the Poetic Attitude. Vanderbilt Univ., 1952.
    Thesis: English.
Whittington, Curtis C., Jr. Dialectic Humanism and the Themes of
    Robert Penn Warren. Vanderbilt Univ., 1955. Thesis: English.
Whyte, Samuel W. Agrarianism and Father Rejection in Three Robert
    Penn Warren Novels. Bowling Green State Univ., 1961. Thesis:
    English.
Williamson, Jerry M. The Patterned Protagonist in Robert Penn
    Warren's Novels. Florida State Univ., 1960. Thesis:
    English.
Wilson, G.R. Comparing and Contrasting Characters as a Device
    in the Development of Robert Penn Warren's Novel, *Wilderness*.
    Indiana Univ. of Pennsylvania, 1967. Thesis: Education.
Wilson, Sara S. Existential Aspects of *All the King's Men*. Univ.
    of Florida, 1967. Thesis: English.
Woods, Linda L. The Language of Robert Penn Warren's Poetry.
    Emory Univ., 1969. Dissertation: English.

BOOKER TALIAFERRO WASHINGTON (1856-1915)

Delaney, Marion A. Dominant Themes in the Oratory of Booker T.
Washington. Univ. of Tennessee, 1968. Thesis: Speech and
Theater.
el-Sayeh, Hussein B. Booker T. Washington: A Study of his
Educational Experiments in Tuskegee Normal and Industrial
Institute. Fresno State College, 1964. Thesis: Education.
Gibbs, Betty J. Booker T. Washington and Industrial Education:
Booker T. Washington Viewed Industrial Education as the Only
Practical Solution to the Economic Problems of the Black
Masses. California State College (Hayward), 1970. Thesis:
History.
Henry, Ephriam M. An Interpretative and Evaluative Analysis of
the Literature Dealing With the Philosophy, Techniques, and
Approaches Employed by Booker T. Washington. Atlanta Univ.,
1950. Thesis: Education.
Olliff, Martha W. Booker Taliaferro Washington: Builder of
Character through Tuskegee Institute. Duke Univ., 1938.
Thesis: Religion.
Pearce, Russell J. Booker T. Washington: A Look at His Views on
Education, Civil Rights and Politics. Long Island Univ.,
1967. Thesis: History.
Pipes, William H. Sources of Booker T. Washington's Effectiveness
as a Public Speaker. Atlanta Univ., 1937. Thesis: English.
Pitts, Willis N. A Critical Study of Booker T. Washington as a
Speech-Maker with an Analysis of Seven Selected Speeches.
Univ. of Michigan, 1952. Dissertation: Speech.
Reed, Ernest E. Educational Philosophy of Booker T. Washington.
Univ. of Cincinnati, 1928. Thesis: Education.

THOMAS E. WATSON (1856-1922)

Cashin, Br. Edward L., F.M.S. Thomas E. Watson and the Catholic
Laymen's Association of Georgia. Fordham Univ., 1962.
Dissertation: History.
Woodward C.V. The Political and Literary Career of Thomas E.
Watson. Univ. of North Carolina (Chapel Hill), 1937.
Dissertation: History.

HENRY WATTERSON (1840-1921)

Kirwan, Patrick S. Henry Watterson and the World War Propaganda.
Univ. of Louisville, 1939. Thesis: History.
Klingbeil, Eulalia. Henry Watterson: The Personal Journalist.
Vanderbilt Univ., 1941. Thesis: English.
Logan, Lena C. Henry Watterson, Border Nationalist, 1840-1877.
Indiana Univ. (Bloomington), 1942. Dissertation: History.
Noel, Lois P. The Contributions of Henry Watterson to the
Journalism and Life of His Time. Northwestern Univ., 1932.
Thesis: Journalism.
Plummer, Leonard N. Political Leadership of Henry Watterson.
Univ. of Wisconsin, 1940. Dissertation: Political Science.
Wall, Joseph F. Henry Watterson: Reconstructed Rebel. Columbia
Univ., 1951. Dissertation: History.

CHARLES WILKINS WEBBER (1819-1856)

Young, Norvel. The Life and Works of Charles Wilkins Webber.
Vanderbilt Univ., 1937. Thesis: English.

MASON LOCKE WEEMS (1759-1825)
(PARSON WEEMS)

Piantanida, Ada M. Parson Weems, an Author, Moralist, and Book
Vendor. Rutgers Univ., 1937. Thesis: History.

EUDORA WELTY (1909-   )

Alford, Dorothy C. Theme, Method, and Tone in the Fiction of
Eudora Welty. Vanderbilt Univ., 1957. Thesis: English.
Appel, Alfred, Jr. The Short Stories of Eudora Welty. Columbia
Univ., 1963. Dissertation: English.
Blackwell, Annie L. Roots versus Yellow Guitars: Symbol and
Meaning in Selected Short Stories by Eudora Welty. Florida
State Univ., 1964. Thesis: English.
Burd, Mellie R. The Progression from Innocence to Experience
in the Novels of Eudora Welty. Univ. of Louisville, 1967.
Thesis: English.
Caire, Fred J. Through the Burning-glass: Some Themes and
Techniques in the Short Stories of Eudora Welty. Fresno
State College, 1967. Thesis: English.
Cashion, Virginia S. The First-Person Narrator in the Stories of
Eudora Welty. Univ. of Tennessee, 1968. Thesis: English.
Cole, Hunter M. Eudora Welty: Literary Critic. Univ. of
Arkansas, 1962. Thesis: English.
Coughlin, Betsey. Mythic Motifs in the Short Fiction of Eudora
Welty. Univ. of Vermont, 1971. Thesis: English.
Davis, Charles E. Eudora Welty's Art of Naming. Emory Univ.,
1969. Dissertation: English.
Dilworth, Barbara. Symbolism in the Short Stories of Eudora
Welty. Univ. of Georgia, 1966. Thesis: English.
Dunlacy, Marjorie F. The Three Modes of Eudora Welty's Fiction.
Texas Christian Univ., 1955. Thesis: English.
Eglitis, Neel H.S. Separateness in the Short Stories of Eudora
Welty. Vanderbilt Univ., 1960. Thesis: English.
Endel, Peggy G. Strange Felicity: A Study of Eudora Welty's
Use of Mythology. Cornell Univ., 1966. Thesis: English.
Folsom, Gordon R. Form and Substance in Eudora Welty. Univ. of
Wisconsin, 1960. Dissertation: English.
Griffith, Albert J., Jr. Eudora Welty's Fiction. Univ. of Texas
(Austin), 1959. Dissertation: English.
Hammons, Darby J. Eudora Welty's Lyrical Unity: Love. Millers-
ville State College, 1967. Thesis: English.
Hill, Neda G. Eudora Welty, Literary Aesthete. Mississippi State
Univ., 1961. Thesis: English.
Hinds, Katherine P. The Life and Works of Eudora Welty. Duke
Univ., 1954. Thesis: English.
Hobbs, Marva E.D. The Fiction of Eudora Welty. Atlanta Univ.,
1964. Thesis: English.

Johnson, Jean D. Ratios among Sensorial, Intellectual, and
    Attitudinal Elements in Eudora Welty's Short Stories.
    Morehead State Univ., 1967. Thesis: English.
Jordan, Leona P. Humor in Work of Eudora Welty. Mississippi
    State Univ., 1958. Thesis: English.
Kellogg, Bernard F. Suggested Themes of Existentialism in the
    Fiction of Eudora Welty. St. Michael's College, 1965.
    Thesis: English.
Kidwell, Barbara C. The Wanderer Characters in the Fiction of
    Eudora Welty. Univ. of Tennessee, 1962. Thesis: English.
Menefee, Helen H. A Study of Eudora Welty's Characters: Universal
    Verity in Localized Situations. Midwestern Univ., 1963.
    Thesis: English.
Miller, Philip. Technique as Reality: The World of Eudora Welty.
    Kansas State Teachers College, 1967. Thesis: English.
Morris, Ruth. An Analysis of Symbol and Image in Representative
    Works by Eudora Welty. Ohio Univ., 1961. Thesis: English.
Opitz, Kurt. Travelers for Love: Neo-Romantic Substance--Finding
    a Form in Eudora Welty's Fiction. Freie Universität (West
    Berlin), 1957. Dissertation: English.
Perry, Ronald L. The Places of the Heart and the Legends of the
    Mind, a Critical Analysis of the Progression in Theme and
    Technique through the First Three Major Works of Eudora Welty.
    Univ. of Miami (Coral Gables), 1954. Thesis: English.
Peterson, Dewayne. The Burden and the Search: A Thematic Study
    of Eudora Welty's Fiction. Duke Univ., 1958. Thesis:
    English.
Petty, Betty S. Theme and Form in Selected Short Stories of
    Eudora Welty. Jacksonville State Univ., 1969. Thesis:
    English.
Polk, Marylynn C. Eudora Welty: An Annotated Bibliography.
    Vanderbilt Univ., 1970. Thesis: English.
Prenshaw, Peggy J.W. A Study of Setting in the Fiction of Eudora
    Welty. Univ. of Texas (Austin), 1970. Dissertation:
    English.
Ragland, Jacqueline M. The Theme of Isolation in the Short Stories
    of Eudora Welty. Baylor Univ., 1970. Thesis: English.
Reiff, Velma B. The Importance of the Guiding Heart in the
    Fiction of Eudora Welty: A Study in Human Relationships.
    Hardin-Simmons Univ., 1964. Thesis: English.
Roper, David D. "Powerhouse": Eudora Welty's Portrait of the
    Artist as Jazz Musician. Lehigh Univ., 1969. Thesis:
    English.
Rosburg, Damon O. Eudora Welty: New World of Fantasy. Univ. of
    Wyoming, 1967. Thesis: English.
Rouse, Sarah A. Place and People in Eudora Welty's Fiction: A
    Portrait of the Deep South. Florida State Univ., 1962.
    Dissertation: English.
Sandhop, Genevieve W. Place in the Short Stories of Eudora Welty.
    Sam Houston State Univ., 1960. Thesis: English.
Saunders, Thomas. Moral Values in the Novels of Eudora Welty.
    Univ. of Pittsburgh, 1954. Dissertation: English.
Scales, Sara M. Family-related Themes in the Fiction of Eudora
    Welty. Mississippi State Univ., 1968. Thesis: English.

Shankman, Sarah R. The Unity of Eudora Welty's *The Golden Apples*. Emory Univ., 1965. Thesis: English.
Stough, Phyllis. Eudora Welty: A Master Craftsman of the American Short Story. Auburn Univ., 1951. Thesis: English.
Stuckey, June M. An Examination of Eudora Welty's *The Golden Apples*. Washington Univ. (St. Louis), 1958. Thesis: English.
Sutton, Kathlene H. The Moment of Revelation in the Short Stories of Eudora Welty. Columbia Univ., 1965. Thesis: English.
Swearingen, Bethany C. Eudora Welty: A Critical Bibliography. Columbia Univ., 1958. Thesis: English.
Thompson, Robert M. Recurrent Symbolic Patterns in Selected Writings of Eudora Welty. Pennsylvania State Univ., 1960. Thesis: English.
Turilli, Edward S. The Basic Themes in The Short Fiction of Eudora Welty. Univ. of Rhode Island, 1968. Thesis: English.
Turner, John C. The Theme of the Unattainable in the Works of Eudora Welty. Univ. of Tennessee, 1965. Thesis: English.
Valentour, Kay B. The Shiny Threads: A Study of Detail Pertinent to Time in the Stories of Eudora Welty. Mississippi College, 1965. Thesis: English.
Vaughn, John D. Studies in the Short Stories of Eudora Welty. Univ. of Texas (Austin), 1961. Thesis: English.
Wild, Rebecca S. Studies in the Shorter Fiction of Elizabeth Bowen and Eudora Welty. Univ. of Michigan, 1965. Dissertation: English.
Williamson, Doris B. Love in the Fiction of Eudora Welty. Southern Methodist Univ., 1968. Thesis: English.
Willis, Patricia R. An Examination of Eudora Welty's Concept of Place. Univ. of Tennessee, 1962. Thesis: English.

RICHARD HENRY WILDE (1789-1847)

Graber, Ralph S. The Fugitive Poems of Richard Henry Wilde with an Introduction. Univ. of Pennsylvania, 1959. Dissertation: English.
Jenkins, Barbara W. Richard Henry Wilde: Some Notes on His Life. Univ. of Georgia, 1940. Thesis: English.
Tucker, Edward L. Richard Henry Wilde: Life and Selected Poems. Univ. of Georgia, 1957. Dissertation: English.

JAMES WILKINSON (1757-1828)

Miller, James B. James Wilkinson as Territorial Governor of Louisiana (1805-1806). Ohio State Univ., 1949. Thesis: English.

ESPY WILLIAMS (1852-1908)

Rickels, Patricia K. The Literary Career of Espy Williams: New Orleans Poet and Playwright. Louisiana State Univ., 1961. Dissertation: English.

Altschuler, David T. The Critical Reputation of Tennessee Williams.
     Univ. of Maine, 1966. Thesis: English.
Asral, Ertem. Tennessee Williams on Stage and Screen. Univ. of
     Pennsylvania, 1961. Dissertation: English.
Atwell, Paul D. Naturalism and Romanticism in Representative
     Selections of the Work of Tennessee Williams. Duke Univ.,
     1965. Thesis: English.
Barton, Catherine. Some Evidence of Alienation in the Life and
     Plays of Tennessee Williams. Iowa State Teachers College,
     1966. Thesis: English.
Beltzer, Lee. The Plays of Eugene O'Neill, Thornton Wilder,
     Arthur Miller and Tennessee Williams on the London Stage,
     1945-1960. Univ. of Wisconsin, 1965. Dissertation:
     Theater.
Berger, Frederick J. Symbolism in the Works of Tennessee Williams.
     Colorado College, 1967. Thesis: English.
Ber Nier, Lou A. Tennessee Williams, Playwright. West Texas
     State Univ., 1957. Thesis: Speech.
Bier, Charles R. Tennessee Williams from Play to Screenplay. Univ.
     of Texas (Austin), 1965. Thesis: English.
Blackmon, Betty A. Tennessee Williams as a Literary Artist.
     Vanderbilt Univ., 1963. Thesis: English.
Blackmon, C.H. Tennessee Williams: The Physical and Spiritual in
     Conflict. Sam Houston State Univ., 1968. Thesis: English.
Boyd, Jo B. Changes in Characterization in Tennessee Williams.
     Univ. of Arkansas, 1962. Thesis: English.
Brannon, Steve. The Fisher King Myth in Tennessee Williams'
     Camino Real. East Tennessee State Univ., 1969. Thesis:
     English.
Cagle, Robert K. A Study of Promotive and Theatrical Techniques
     Common to the Plays of William Saroyan, Tennessee Williams,
     and Arthur Miller. Southern Illinois Univ. (Carbondale),
     1952. Thesis: Speech.
Cardwell, Sally S. Symbolism in the Works of Tennessee Williams.
     West Texas State Univ., 1964. Thesis: English.
Calvery, Catherine A. Illusion in Modern American Drama: A Study
     of Selected Plays by Arthur Miller, Tennessee Williams, and
     Eugene O'Neill. Tulane Univ., 1964. Dissertation: Theater.
Cannon, Margaret H. The Short Stories of Tennessee Williams.
     Univ. of North Carolina (Chapel Hill), 1964. Thesis:
     English.
Caskey, Jefferson D. A Study of the Heroines in Selected Plays
     of Tennessee Williams and Their Attempts at Personality
     Integration. Univ. of Houston, 1966. Thesis: English.
Chomsky, Marvin J. A Technical Production Book of the Play *You
     Touched Me!* by Tennessee Williams and Donald Windham.
     Stanford Univ., 1951. Thesis: Speech and Drama.
Converse, Philip E. A Study in the American Drama: Tennessee
     Williams and Arthur Miller. State Univ. of Iowa, 1950.
     Thesis: English.
Clayton, John S. Themes of Tennessee Williams. Yale Univ., 1960.
     Dissertation: English.

Clements, Richard J. A Psychological Study of the Evolution of Tennessee Williams' Creative Works. San Francisco State College, 1965. Thesis: English.

Clinton, Craig D. The Conflict Between Flesh and Spirit in Five Plays by Tennessee Williams. San Francisco State College, 1969. Thesis: English.

Cohen, Mary D. A Study of the Characters in the Works of Tennessee Williams. Southern Illinois Univ. (Carbondale), 1959. Thesis: English.

Cooper, Wilma S. A Study of One of Tennessee Williams' Fugitive Kind: The Spinster and Her Isolation. Mississippi College, 1967. Thesis: English.

Conaway, James C. A Projected Production of Tennessee Williams' *Suddenly Last Summer* for Arena Presentation. West Virginia Univ., 1967. Thesis: English.

Crockett, James E. The Literary Theory of Tennessee Williams. Our Lady of the Lake College, 1968. Thesis: English.

Cunningham, Dennis M. The Theme of Self-delusion in Selected Works of Major American Playwrights (O'Neill, Williams, Miller, 1940-1960). Villanova Univ., 1961. Thesis: English.

Cunningham, James H.M. The Flaming Bird: A Study of the Works of Tennessee Williams, between 1940-1960. Toronto, 1960. Thesis: English.

Czerwinski, Edward J. Tennessee Williams: His Approach to Truth. Pennsylvania State Univ., 1955. Thesis: English.

Cziok, Vera B. Sacrifice and Atonement in the Plays of Tennessee Williams. St. Cloud College, 1966. Thesis: English.

Davis, Betty G. The Victim and the Victimizer in the Plays of Tennessee Williams. East Carolina Univ., 1970. Thesis: English.

Deigham, William P. Loss of Chastity as a Tragic Condition in Selected Works of Tennessee Williams. John Carroll Univ., 1964. Thesis: English.

DeRose, Maria E. Women in the Plays of Tennessee Williams: Studies in Personal Isolation and Outraged Sensibility. Univ. of Arizona, 1966. Thesis: English.

Dervin, Daniel A. The Spook in the Rain-Forest: An Inquiry into the Plays of Tennessee Williams. Columbia Univ., 1963. Thesis: English.

Dieb, Ronald K. Patterns of Sacrifice in the Plays of Arthur Miller, Tennessee Williams, and Edward Albee. Univ. of Denver, 1969. Dissertation: Theater.

Dillard, Robert L. The Tennessee Williams Hero: An Analytical Survey. Univ. of Missouri, 1965. Dissertation: Theater.

Dobson, Eugene, Jr. The Reception of the Plays of Tennessee Williams in Germany. Univ. of Arkansas, 1967. Dissertation: English.

Doerry, Karl W. Romantic Themes and Characters in the Plays of Tennessee Williams. Univ. of Kansas, 1965. Thesis: English.

Drake, Constance M. The Evolution of Love in Tennessee Williams. Univ. of Rhode Island, 1964. Thesis: English.

Edge, Clifford C. The Dramatic Technique of Tennessee Williams. Sam Houston State Univ., 1955. Thesis: English.

Ellen, Rose A. The Mother Symbol in Tennessee Williams' Dramatic Works. John Carroll Univ., 1961. Thesis: English.

[179]

Ellison, Jerome. God on Broadway: Deity as Reflected in the Work of Seven Playwrights Prominent in the Twentieth Century American Commercial Theater: O'Neill, Wilder, MacLeish, Williams, Miller, Albee, Chayefski. South Connecticut State College, 1966. Thesis: English.

England, Donald G. The Importance of the Past in the Plays of Tennessee Williams. Univ. of Texas (Austin), 1964. Thesis: English.

Fedder, Norman J. The Influence of D.H. Lawrence on Tennessee Williams. New York Univ., 1962. Dissertation: English.

Ferrell, James M. A Study of the Principal Women Characters in the Published Plays of Tennessee Williams. East Carolina Univ., 1964. Thesis: English.

Fisher, William J. Trends in Post-Depression American Drama. A Study of William Saroyan, Tennessee Williams, Irwin Shaw, Arthur Miller. New York Univ., 1952. Dissertation: English.

Flanagan, Michael G. A Production Study of Tennessee Williams' Camino Real. Bowling Green State Univ., 1964. Thesis: Speech.

Fox, Gary M. Sin and Retribution in the Drama of Tennessee Williams. Mississippi College, 1967. Thesis: English.

Friedrich, Jutta. Individuum und Gesellschaft in den Dramen von Tennessee Williams. Jena, 1963. Dissertation: English.

Fritscher, John J. Love and Death in Tennessee Williams. Loyola Univ. (Chicago), 1968. Dissertation: English.

Garner, Nathan C. A Proposed Production of Tennessee Williams' The Glass Menagerie. Univ. of North Carolina (Chapel Hill), 1966. Thesis: Dramatic Art.

Garvin, Mary A. Time and Tennessee Williams: A Study of the Playwright's Manipulation of Chronological Time for Dramatic Effect and as a Basic Theme for His Plays. Univ. of South Carolina, 1967. Thesis: English.

Gelia, Charles, Jr. A Study of the Representative Plays of Four Contemporary Playwrights, Eugene O'Neill, Maxwell Anderson, Tennessee Williams, and Arthur Miller, in the Light of a Theory of Tragedy. Canisius College, 1951. Thesis: English.

Ginanni, Francis R. Tennessee Williams' Revisions of The Glass Menagerie. Univ. of Virginia, 1964. Thesis: English.

Glenn, James A. An Evaluation of the Works of Tennessee Williams. Xavier Univ. (Ohio), 1953. Thesis: English.

Gray, Allen B. Characteristic Symbolism in Four Representative Plays by Tennessee Williams. Sacramento State College, 1960. Thesis: English.

Groah, Betty J. Three Recurrent Elements Found in the Three-Act Plays of Tennessee Williams. Ohio Univ., 1955. Thesis: English.

Gunn, Drewey W. A Study of the Southern Neurotic Women in Three Plays by Tennessee Williams. Univ. of North Carolina (Chapel Hill), 1962. Thesis: English.

Hagans, Addie S. The Role of the Southern Woman in Six Selected Plays by Tennessee Williams. North Carolina College (Durham), 1969. Thesis: English.

Hagge, Helmut P. The Plastic Theatre of Tennessee Williams. Univ. of Texas (Austin), 1966. Thesis: English.

Hammouda, Abdul-Aziz Abdul-Salam. The Ogre's Country: A Study of
the South in Tennessee Williams. Cornell Univ., 1965.
Thesis: English.

Hannah, Barbara S. Tennessee Williams: Poet-Dramatist. Univ. of
North Carolina (Chapel Hill), 1965. Thesis: Dramatic Art.

Harry, Orvelle S. Tennessee Williams: A Study of the Plays and
Short Stories Published to 1950. State Univ. of New York
(Buffalo), 1951. Thesis: English.

Hayes, James A., Rev. S.S.J. Tennessee Williams: Poet of the
Damned. St. Bonaventure Univ., 1961. Thesis: English.

Heys, Joan A. The Night of the Iguana by Tennessee Williams: A
Creative Thesis in Design. Miami Univ. (Ohio), 1968. Thesis:
Speech-Theater.

Hindman, Ira, Jr. Tennessee Williams' The Night of the Iguana: A
Departure from Negativism. Stetson Univ., 1965. Thesis:
English.

Humphreys, Don. The Theme of Loneliness, Frustration and Rejection
in the Women of Tennessee Williams' First Major Play.
Trinity Univ. (Texas), 1966. Thesis: English.

Hurley, Paul J. Tennessee Williams: Critic of American Society.
Duke Univ., 1962. Dissertation: English.

Isaac, Dan. Form and Meaning in the Major Plays of Tennessee
Williams. Univ. of Chicago, 1968. Dissertation: English.

Jackson, Esther M. The Emergence of A Characteristic Contemporary
Form in the American Drama of Tennessee Williams. Ohio State
Univ., 1958. Dissertation: Theater.

Juneja, M.M. Vision and Form in the Drama of Tennessee Williams
and Arthur Miller. Leicester, 1968. Dissertation: English.

Kaplan, Barry H. A Creative Project Camino Real by Tennessee
Williams. Adelphi Univ., 1967. Thesis: English.

Keating, Elizabeth W. Tennessee Williams and the Critical Climate
to 1964. San Diego College for Women, 1966. Thesis:
English.

Kent, Susan. Isolation--the Tragedy of Modern Man: T.S. Eliot
and Tennessee Williams. Columbia Univ., 1958. Thesis:
English.

Kindle, Betty B. Falsity in Man: Tennessee Williams' Vision of
Tragedy. North Texas State Univ., 1956. Thesis: English.

King, Barbara K. Tennessee Williams: A Study in the Evolution of
Structure. Univ. of Colorado, 1967. Thesis: English.

Kinney, Jeanne M. The Eros Figure in Selected Plays of Williams
and Inge. John Carroll Univ., 1961. Thesis: English.

Krasnicka, George M., Jr. The Heroic Characters of Tennessee
Williams. Columbia Univ., 1961. Thesis: English.

Laborde, Blanca R. An Analysis and Technical Production of
Tennessee Williams' The Glass Menagerie. Tulane Univ., 1960.
Thesis: Theater.

Laizer, Diane M. An Analysis, Design and Technical Production for
Tennessee Williams' A Streetcar Named Desire. Tulane Univ.,
1967. Thesis: Theater.

Langsam, Paula A. A Study of the Major Character in Selected
Plays of Tennessee Williams. New York Univ., 1966. Dissertation: Theater.

Lee, James R. An Analysis and Prompt Book for Tennessee Williams'
A Streetcar Named Desire. Tulane Univ., 1969. Thesis:
Theater.

Leonard, David R. The Concept of Illusion in the Plays of Tennessee Williams. Univ. of Mississippi, 1969. Thesis: English.

Lester, Frank A. A Study of the Supernatural and the Symbolic in the Works of Tennessee Williams. Univ. of Tennessee, 1956. Thesis: English.

Lewis, Tim G. Major Themes in Plays of Tennessee Williams. Baylor Univ., 1964. Thesis: English.

Little, Sharon K. Tennessee Williams' Reconciliation of Neurosis and Psychosis: An Evolvement of Adjustment through Three Southern Female Characters. East Tennessee State Univ., 1968. Thesis: English.

Luce, Peter H. Tennessee Williams' *Orpheus Descending*: Salvation for the Poetic. Brown Univ., 1963. Thesis: English.

Lutz, John J. A Study of Tennessee Williams' Southern Gentlewomen. Shippensburg State College, 1967. Thesis: Education.

Lyons, Gail S. Recurrent Themes and Symbols in the Plays of Tennessee Williams. Univ. of Florida, 1957. Thesis: English.

MacDonald, Edgar E. Tennessee Williams and the Tragic Tradition. Univ. of Richmond, 1953. Thesis: English.

MacDonald, George B. The Developing Vision of Tennessee Williams. Lehigh Univ., 1964. Thesis: English.

Mason, Irene M. Man's Search for Dignity in the Plays of Tennessee Williams. Univ. of California (Riverside), 1961. Thesis: English.

McManus, Portia A. Tennessee Williams as a Satirist. Univ. of Texas (Austin), 1965. Thesis: English.

McNew, U.H. A Collection of Memorable Heroines from Tennessee Williams. Univ. of Nevada, 1966. Thesis: English.

Miano, Louis S. Tennessee Williams and D.H. Lawrence: A Study of Parallels in Their Lives. Columbia Univ., 1958. Thesis: English.

Mishoe, Billy. The Organic Use of Sets in Tennessee Williams' Plays. Univ. of South Carolina, 1967. Thesis: English.

Moore, Don D. Arthur Miller and Tennessee Williams: Dramatists of Frustration. Vanderbilt Univ., 1957. Thesis: English.

Mordecai, Benjamin. Tennessee Williams in Production. Eastern Michigan Univ., 1968. Thesis: Speech and Dramatic Arts.

Morey, James N. Realism and Idealism: A Study of Symbols, Images, and Themes in the Works of Tennessee Williams. Columbia Univ., 1956. Thesis: English.

Morton, Richard M. Sex as an Instrument of Disillusion and Affirmation in Selected Works of Tennessee Williams. Univ. of South Carolina, 1960. Thesis: English.

Mraz, Doyne J. The Changing Image of Female Characters in the Works of Tennessee Williams. Univ. of Southern California, 1967. Dissertation: Theater.

Mullinax, Paul F. Language Forms in the Plays of Tennessee Williams. West Texas State Univ., 1969. Thesis: English.

Navratil, Carol M. A Production Book of Tennessee Williams' *Cat On A Hot Tin Roof*. Univ. of Maryland, 1964. Thesis: Speech.

Nelson, Thomas A. Symbolic Action and Character in Three Plays of Tennessee Williams: An Analysis. Wichita State Univ., 1962. Thesis: English.

Ochiltree, Fr. Richard S. The Relationship of Catharsis to
     Aesthetic Distance in *A Streetcar Named Desire*. College of
     the Holy Names, 1964. Thesis: English.
O'Connor, Rosemary. Tennessee Williams' Changing Attitude Toward
     Sex in His Plays. St. John's Univ. (N.Y.), 1966. Thesis:
     English.
Pancoast, Carol S. Tennessee Williams: Playwright of the
     Defeated. Duke Univ., 1967. Thesis: English.
Parr, Karen H. Animal Imagery in the Plays of Tennessee Williams.
     Univ. of Alaska, 1966. Thesis: English.
Parver, Michael L. An Analysis and a Production Book of Tennessee
     Williams' *The Glass Menagerie*. Tulane Univ., 1960. Thesis:
     Theater.
Patterson, Nancy M. Patterns of Imagery in the Major Plays of
     Tennessee Williams. Univ. of Arkansas, 1957. Dissertation:
     English.
Pearsall, Elizabeth A. A Comparative Study of the Two Major
     Editions of Tennessee Williams' *The Glass Menagerie*. Univ.
     of North Carolina (Chapel Hill), 1965. Thesis: English.
Pflugrad, Gerald. A Discussion of Love in the Works of Tennessee
     Williams. Chico State College, 1965. Thesis: English.
Pisoni, Michael J. Producing *The Glass Menagerie*. Univ. of
     Washington, 1967. Thesis: English.
Presley, Delma E. The Theological Dimensions of Tennessee Williams:
     A Study of Eight Major Plays. Emory Univ., 1969. Disser-
     tation: English.
Pruitt, Virginia D. Tennessee Williams: The Relationship between
     Three Selected Short Stories and Three Selected Plays. Univ.
     of North Carolina (Chapel Hill), 1966. Thesis: English.
     ["Portrait of a Girl in Glass" and *The Glass Menagerie*; "Desire
     and the Black Masseur," and *Suddenly Last Summer*; "Three Players
     of a Summer Game" and *Cat on a Hot Tin Roof*]
Quillen, R.C. Adapting Selected Plays of Tennessee Williams for
     Television Production. East Tennessee State Univ., 1965.
     Thesis: English.
Quirino, Leonard S. The Darkest Celebrations of Tennessee Williams:
     A Study of *Battle of Angels*, *Orpheus Descending*, *A Streetcar
     Named Desire*, *Camino Real*, *Cat on a Hot Tin Roof* and *Suddenly
     Last Summer*. Brown Univ., 1964. Dissertation: English.
Rackshaw, Richard B. The Drama of Futility in Tennessee Williams.
     Miami Univ. (Ohio), 1962. Thesis: English.
Radosevic, Nancy V. Symbolism and Other Non-Realistic Techniques
     in the Major Plays of Tennessee Williams. Univ. of Kentucky,
     1957. Thesis: English.
Rager, Leora P. An Analysis of the Symbolism of the Staging
     Effects in the Full-length Plays of Tennessee Williams.
     Indiana Univ. of Pennsylvania, 1965. Thesis: Education.
Reck, Tom S. Tennessee Williams: Social Critic of the South.
     Univ. of Houston, 1961. Thesis: English.
_____. The Fiction of Tennessee Williams. Univ. of Texas (Austin),
     1967. Dissertation: English.
Rhoades, John A. Problems for the Scene Designer in Tennessee
     Williams' Plays. Ball State Univ., 1968. Thesis: English.

Richards, Alfred L. A Journey into the Night: The Mythological World of Tennessee Williams. Stetson Univ., 1969. Thesis: English.

Riddick, Ruth M. The Dramatic Development of Tennessee Williams. Univ. of Texas (Austin), 1954. Thesis: English.

Riise, Milton B. A Comparative Study of the Pattern of Human Suffering in the Major Plays of Tennessee Williams. Univ. of South Dakota, 1968. Thesis: English.

Russell, Don. A Production Book of Tennessee Williams' and Donald Windham's "You Touched Me!" Stanford Univ., 1951. Thesis: Speech and Drama.

Russo, Mary C. A Comparative Study of the Directing Problems of Tennessee Williams' *Moony's Kid Don't Cry* in a Stage and a Television Production. Bowling Green State Univ., 1969. Thesis: Speech.

Ruthledge, Jerry W. The Southern Gothic Dramas Of Tennessee Williams. Univ. of Oklahoma, 1966. Thesis: English.

Schweda, Donald N. Morality in the Plays of Tennessee Williams. Univ. of Florida, 1963. Thesis: English.

Simerly, Robert G. Tennessee Williams' Imagery and His Dramatic Theory. Univ. of Tennessee, 1963. Thesis: English.

Slater, Milly H. A Study of Tennessee Williams' Six Major Plays About the South. Tulane Univ., 1959. Thesis: English.

Smith, Harry W., Jr. Mielziner and Williams: A Concept of Style. Tulane Univ., 1965. Dissertation: Theater.
[Tennessee Williams and his scenic designer]

Smith, Henry F. The Persistent Idealism in Tennessee Williams' Major Plays. Adelphi Univ., 1963. Thesis: English.

Smith, Leonidas C. Existential Categories in Eight Plays by Tennessee Williams. Clemson Univ., 1967. Thesis: English.

Somers, Cynthia H. Williams' Neurotic Southern Heroine: A Lament for the Moths. Univ. of South Carolina, 1969. Thesis: English.

Starnes, R.L. Comedy and Tennessee Williams. Yale Univ., 1965. Dissertation: Drama.

Steiner, Robert J. Toward an Integrated Personality: A Study of the Dramas of Tennessee Williams. St. John's Univ. (N.Y.), 1965. Dissertation: English.

Stewart, Judy H. The Abandoned Woman in the Dramas of Tennessee Williams. Morehead State Univ., 1968. Thesis: English.

Strange, Mary M. Negative Saints in the Dramas of Tennessee Williams. Southern Methodist Univ., 1966. Thesis: English.

Sullivan, Michael J.P. "Garland of Roses": An Evaluation of the Major Plays of Tennessee Williams. Univ. of Wyoming, 1967. Thesis: English.

Thompson, Hilary. The Forms of Irony in the Plays of Tennessee Williams. Alberta, 1967. Thesis: English.

Tischler, Nancy M.P. Patterns of Imagery in the Major Plays of Tennessee Williams. Univ. of Arkansas, 1957. Dissertation: English.

Toth, Bill D. The Stories of Tennessee Williams: A Study of Their Thematic Development and Expansion into Full-Length Drama. Chico State College, 1969. Thesis: English.

Tucker, Helen H. *Suddenly, Last Summer*: Modern Morality Play. Stetson Univ., 1962. Thesis: English.

Uka, Kalu. Themes and Characterization in Some Plays of Eugene
    O'Neill and Tennessee Williams. Toronto, 1965. Thesis:
    English.
Van Nieuwenhuize, Paul F. Escape into Illusions of the South in
    Characters of Tennessee Williams. Texas A & M Univ., 1963.
    Thesis: English.
Von Dornum, Jack H. A Critical Study of the Plays of Tennessee
    Williams, 1940-1950. Univ. of Southern California, 1958.
    Thesis: English.
_____. The Major Plays of Tennessee Williams, 1940 to 1960.
    Univ. of Southern California, 1962. Dissertation: English.
Walker, Samuel J., Jr. Tennessee Williams, the Heir Apparent.
    Columbia Univ., 1952. Thesis: English.
Walton, Roxanna G. Tennessee Williams' Heroines: A Role Analysis.
    Pennsylvania State Univ., 1961. Thesis: Theater Arts.
Warren, Clifton L. Tennessee Williams as a Cinematic Writer.
    Indiana Univ. (Bloomington), 1963. Dissertation: English.
Watkins, Ralph F. Sex and a Southern Lady in Tennessee Williams'
    Plays. Columbia Univ., 1954. Thesis: English.
Williams, E.F.G. Feminine Frustration in the Plays of Tennessee
    Williams. Hardin-Simmons Univ., 1968. Thesis: English.
Wilson, Daniel S. Tennessee Williams: Poet of Memory and
    Violence. Columbia Univ., 1949. Thesis: English.
Wilson, Rodney M. A Production Book for *A Streetcar Named Desire*.
    Kansas State Univ., 1966. Thesis: Speech.
Wolf, Morris P. Casanova's Portmanteau: A Study of *Camino Real*
    in Relation to the Other Plays and Stories of Tennessee
    Williams, 1945-1955. Univ. of Georgia, 1959. Dissertation:
    English.

AUGUSTA JANE EVANS WILSON (1835-1909)

Callahan, Ida B.P. Augusta Evans Wilson: An Analytical Study of
    Her Fiction. Vanderbilt Univ., 1943. Thesis: English.
Fidler, William P. The Life and Works of Augusta Evans Wilson.
    Univ. of Chicago, 1947. Dissertation: English.
Munk, Eunice A. The Life and Writings of Augusta Jane Evans
    Wilson. Emory Univ., 1948. Thesis: English.
Phillips, Sidney. The Life and Works of Augusta Evans Wilson.
    Auburn Univ., 1937. Thesis: English.

WILLIAM WINANS (1788-1857)

Holder, Ray. The Autobiography of William Winans. Univ. of
    Mississippi, 1936. Thesis: History.
Kyker, Rex P. William Winans: Minister and Politician of the
    Old South. Univ. of Florida, 1957. Dissertation: Speech.

WILLIAM WIRT (1772-1834)

Burke, Joseph C. William Wirt: Attorney General and Constitutional
    Lawyer. Indiana Univ. (Bloomington), 1965. Dissertation:
    History.
Cauble, Frank P. William Wirt and His Friends: A Study in Southern
    Culture, 1772-1834. Univ. of North Carolina (Chapel Hill),
    1933. Dissertation: English.

THOMAS WOLFE (1900-1938)

Adams, Richard P. Thomas Wolfe and James T. Farrell: A
Comparison in the Autobiographical Method. Univ. of Illinois,
1940. Thesis: English.
Aker, John E. Thomas Wolfe: A Study in a Literary Conflict.
Vanderbilt Univ., 1946. Thesis: English.
Alexander, Rose. The Dissidence of Thomas Wolfe from the American
Way of Life. East Texas State Univ., 1959. Thesis: English.
Baersch, Hans G. Das Epos Thomas Wolfes. Wesen und Gestalt.
Mainz, 1952. Dissertation: English.
Ball, Michael G. An Intrinsic Approach to Thomas Wolfe's Short
Fiction. Western Illinois Univ., 1967. Thesis: English.
Beavers, Martha E.C. The Words of Thomas Wolfe. Texas Tech
Univ., 1956. Thesis: English.
Belaine, Margaret A. Thomas Wolfe, a Romantic Realist: A Study
of His Human Themes and Styles. Montreal, 1964. Thesis:
English.
Blachford, Janet S. Studies in the Novels of Thomas Wolfe.
McGill, 1963. Thesis: English.
Blackwelder, James R. The Dimensions of Literature in *Look
Homeward, Angel*. Emory Univ., 1968. Dissertation: English.
Blake, Pauline. Thomas Wolfe's *Death's Chosen Son*. Univ. of
Wichita, 1957. Thesis: English.
Bodeman, Barbara S. Thomas Wolfe's Romantic Affinity for Germany.
North Texas State Univ., 1966. Thesis: English.
Borzumato, Lawrence P. Four Aspects of the Search for Identity
in Thomas Wolfe's Novels. Univ. of Rhode Island, 1962.
Thesis: English.
Boyer, James D. Wolfe and Ecclesiastes. Millersville State
College, 1968. Thesis: English.
Boyle, Thomas E. Thomas Wolfe's Myth of America. Univ. of
Illinois, 1964. Dissertation: English.
Bryant, James D. Thomas Wolfe and the Jew. Texas Christian
Univ., 1967. Thesis: English.
Brychta, Therese. Thomas Wolfe: A Psychological Study of the
Origin and Development of Major Themes. San Francisco State
College, 1966. Thesis: English.
Bush, Charles K. III. A Comparison of the Youths of Thomas
Wolfe's Eugene Gant and George Webber. Univ. of North Carolina
(Chapel Hill), 1962. Thesis: English.
Campbell, Bernard N. In Character: A Study of Thomas Wolfe.
Southwest Texas State Univ., 1960. Thesis: English.
Cannon, Gerard J. The Singing and the Gold: The Comic Art of
Thomas Wolfe. Columbia Univ., 1955. Thesis: English.
Carlile, R.E. Leitmotif, Modulation, and Chromaticism in Thomas
Wolfe's *Look Homeward, Angel*. Univ. of Florida, 1963.
Thesis: English.
Centi, Paul. Thomas Wolfe: A Study of His Genius. Fordham
Univ., 1950. Thesis: English.
Clayton, Michael V. Thomas Wolfe's *The Hills Beyond*: A Study in
Method and Direction. Univ. of South Carolina, 1969.
Thesis: English.

Clemans, Edna W. A Study of the Structure of the Narratives in the Short Novels of Thomas Wolfe. Univ. of North Carolina (Chapel Hill), 1964. Thesis: English.

Clements, Clyde. Symbolic Patterns in *You Can't Go Home Again*. Bowling Green State Univ., 1961. Thesis: English.

Cole, Joyce M. Thomas Wolfe's Changing Center of Social Consciousness. Univ. of North Carolina (Chapel Hill), 1968. Thesis: English.

Collier, Joseph M. Thomas Wolfe's Spiritual Growth as a Key to His Novels. Univ. of Arizona, 1954. Thesis: English.

Connor, Fran M. The Isolation of Thomas Wolfe. Baylor Univ., 1968. Thesis: English.

Countryman, John R. The German Element in the Writings of Thomas Wolfe. Univ. of Miami (Coral Gables), 1961. Thesis: English.

Daniels, Thomas E. Eliza Gant: Thomas Wolfe's Symbol of 1920's America. Washington Univ. (St. Louis), 1968. Dissertation: English.

Davis, Marlan A. Social Attitudes Expressed in the Novels of Thomas Wolfe. Univ. of South Dakota, 1954. Thesis: English.

Dean, Charles W. Here I Stand: Thomas Wolfe as a Southern Satirist. Univ. of Massachusetts, 1963. Thesis: English.

Delmare, Maxine L. Thomas Wolfe: Another Estimate. Kansas State Teachers College, 1947. Thesis: English.

Donno, Daniel J. The Quest of Thomas Wolfe. Miami Univ. (Ohio), 1947. Thesis: English.

Donohue, Bernard J. The American Critics' View of Thomas Wolfe to 1952. Univ. of Wyoming, 1952. Thesis: English.

Doster, William C. Wolfe and Whitman: A Comparative Study. Univ. of Florida, 1948. Thesis: English.

Dowden, William T. Social Classes in the Work of Thomas Wolfe. Texas A & M Univ., 1968. Thesis: English.

Duffy, Brian F., The Rev. D.F.M. The Short Prose of Thomas Wolfe. St. Bonaventure Univ., 1948. Thesis: English.

Eichelberger, Clayton L. Thomas Wolfe's America: An Expository Evaluation of the Wolfe Novel. Univ. of Texas (Austin), 1956. Dissertation: English.

Ellison, Francis E. The Significance of Character Development in Thomas Wolfe's Early Novels. Univ. of Texas (Austin), 1954. Thesis: English.

Erstling, Julius H. Thomas Wolfe's Knowledge and Use of Milton. Univ. of Florida, 1941. Thesis: English.

Escobedo, Delia N. An Analysis of the Creative Process in Thomas Wolfe. Ohio Univ., 1963. Thesis: English.

Fagan, Lawrence O. A Study of the Concept of Time and Loss in *From Death to Morning* and *The Hills Beyond*. Chico State College, 1957. Thesis: English.

Ferguson, James L. Social Criticism in the Works of Thomas Wolfe. Occidental College, 1954. Thesis: English.

Files, Marilyn. On Symbolism in Wolfe's Tetralogy. Vanderbilt Univ., 1953. Thesis: English.

Fink, Charlotte A. Methods and Devices of Characterization in the Novels of Thomas Wolfe. Univ. of Tennessee, 1945. Thesis: English.

Finney, Frank F. A Critical Examination of the Transition from a Psychological Vision of Life to an Increasingly Christian Awareness of Evil in the Fiction of Thomas Wolfe. Univ. of Oklahoma, 1961. Dissertation: English.

Fleming, Dilmont F. Humor in the Works of Thomas Wolfe. Univ. of Pennsylvania, 1966. Dissertation: English.

Fontaine, Sr. Patricia M., S.S.A. Thomas Wolfe: Search For Identity in America. St. Michael's College, 1968. Thesis: English.

Fortenberry, George E. Thomas Wolfe's Fictional Treatment of the Negro. Texas Christian Univ., 1951. Thesis: English.

Foster, Iva P. The Episode: A Major Fictional Device Used by Thomas Wolfe. Texas Tech Univ., 1970. Thesis: English.

Foster, Ruel E. Thomas Wolfe: A Critical Study. Univ. of Kentucky, 1939. Thesis: English.

Fruehling, George M. Thomas Wolfe's Appraisal of Literature. Columbia Univ., 1950. Thesis: English.

Garrison, Silas H. Asheville People and Places in Thomas Wolfe's *Look Homeward, Angel*. Univ. of South Carolina, 1969. Thesis: English.

Gasnick, Roy M., O.F.M. The Novels of Thomas Wolfe: Fact or Fiction? St. Bonaventure Univ., 1962. Thesis: English.

Gatlin, Jesse C., Jr. The Development of Thomas Wolfe as a Literary Artist. Univ. of Denver, 1961. Dissertation: English.

Geddes, Leonard R. An Analysis of Thomas Wolfe's "The Web of Earth." Univ. of North Carolina (Chapel Hill), 1962. Thesis: English.

Gelfant, Blanche. Urbanization as an Influence on Dreiser, Dos Passos, and Wolfe. Univ. of Wisconsin, 1948. Dissertation: English.

Gendler, Lillian. The Modern Novelist and the Tragic Sense of Life: A Study of Thomas Wolfe. Columbia Univ., 1952. Thesis: English.

George, McChesney. Footsteps in the Desert: Thomas Wolfe and the Pre-existence Myth. Univ. of New Hampshire, 1969. Thesis: English.

Gibbs, Robert C. Thomas Wolfe's Four Years at Chapel Hill: A Study of Biographical Source Material. Univ. of North Carolina (Chapel Hill), 1958. Thesis: Library Science.

Gilbert, John R. Thomas Wolfe: His Development of Social Consciousness. Mississippi State Univ., 1965. Thesis: English.

Gregory, Hoosag K. Lord Byron and Thomas Wolfe: A Comparison of Their Philosophical and Personal Problems. Univ. of Illinois, 1940. Thesis: English.

Green, Mary C. A Study of the Uses of Language in Thomas Wolfe's "A Portrait of Bascom Hawke." Univ. of North Carolina (Chapel Hill), 1969. Thesis: English.

Greene, Terrell E. Thomas Wolfe's Theory of Writing. Columbia Univ., 1949. Thesis: English.

Gromelski, Bradford A. Analysis and Production of *Look Homeward, Angel*. Univ. of Washington, 1967. Thesis: English.

Groves, Elynor P. An Analysis of the Hero in Thomas Wolfe. Atlanta Univ., 1955. Thesis: English.

Guest, Betty J. Sir Thomas Browne and Thomas Wolfe: Parallels in Theme and Style. Southern Methodist Univ., 1968. Thesis: English.

Hallahan, Margaret E. Time and Unity in the Novels of Wolfe. San Diego State College, 1968. Thesis: English.

Halperin, Irving. A Study of Thomas Wolfe's Critics. State Univ. of Iowa, 1950. Thesis: English.

_____. The Basis and Nature of Unity in the Novels of Thomas Wolfe. Washington Univ. (St. Louis), 1957. Dissertation: English.

Hamner, Robert D. Thomas Wolfe: A New Appraisal. Univ. of Texas (Austin), 1966. Thesis: English.

Hanig, David D. The Comic Elements in the Novels of Thomas Wolfe. North Texas State Univ., 1957. Thesis: English.

Harrington, Evea I. Thomas Wolfe: The Theory and Practice of His Characterization. Univ. of Idaho, 1947. Thesis· English.

Harris, William A. Image of the Hero in Thomas Wolfe. East Tennessee State Univ., 1969. Thesis: English.

Harwell, Ann M. Thomas Wolfe: A Critical Survey. Vanderbilt Univ., 1960. Thesis: English.

Harwick, Robert D. Humor in the Novels of Wolfe. Univ. of Nebraska, 1965. Dissertation: English.

Haywood, Jesse H. Thomas Wolfe: The Search for Salvation. Vanderbilt Univ., 1953. Thesis: English.

Hermiz, Thomas. A Critical Analysis of the *Ubi Sunt* and Loneliness Motifs in Thomas Wolfe's *Look Homeward, Angel* and *Of Time and the River*. Univ. of Rhode Island, 1963. Thesis: English.

Hodge, Elizabeth A. A Study of Thomas Wolfe's *Look Homeward, Angel*. Univ. of Texas (Austin), 1949. Thesis: English.

Hogan, Frances V. Thomas Wolfe: Whale in a Strait-Jacket. Columbia Univ., 1940. Thesis: English.

Hollingsworth, Marian E. The Search for a Father in the Novels of Thomas Wolfe. Univ. of North Carolina, 1957. Thesis: English.

Houck, Alberta L. Thomas Wolfe's Reading. Univ. of South Dakota, 1954. Thesis: English.

Howard, Shelley. *By a Mountain Rock*: Thomas Wolfe, Dramatist. Univ. of North Carolina (Chapel Hill), 1964. Thesis: English.

Howell, Betty C. Symbolism in the Works of Thomas Wolfe. Florida State Univ., 1954. Thesis: English.

Huntley, Reid D. Thomas Wolfe's Idea of the Imagination: Similarities to the Views of The Nineteenth Century English Romantic Poets and Critics. Univ. of North Carolina (Chapel Hill), 1969. Dissertation: English.

Hurt, Lester E. A House Divided: A Study of Theme in Thomas Wolfe's Novels. Univ. of Minnesota, 1956. Dissertation: English.

Idol, John L., Jr. Thomas Wolfe's Satire: A Study of Objects, Motives, and Artistry. Univ. of Arkansas, 1965. Dissertation: English.

James, Gary F. The Web and the Rock Imagery in the Novels of Thomas Wolfe. Sam Houston State Univ., 1968. Thesis: English.

Johnson, George W. Thomas Wolfe, the Groping Weaver. Columbia Univ., 1953. Thesis: English.

Johnson, Stanley L. A Critical Study of the Works of Thomas Wolfe. Univ. of Southern California, 1955. Dissertation: English.

Johnston, June A. Thomas Wolfe as Lover and Critic of America. North Texas State Univ., 1965. Thesis: English.

Jones, Granville H. Walt Whitman, Thomas Wolfe, and Jack Kerouac: Common Origins and Common Aims. Columbia Univ., 1961. Thesis: English.

Kay, Barbara R. Thomas Wolfe: The Exile Motive and the Jews. McGill Univ., 1963. Thesis: English.

Maddock, Lawrence H. The Critical Image of Thomas Wolfe. George Peabody College, 1965. Dissertation: English.

Kennedy, Richard S. A Critical Biography of Thomas Wolfe to His Thirty-Fourth Year. Harvard Univ., 1953. Dissertation: English.

Kilburn, Patrick E. Ulysses in Catawba: A Study of the Influence of James Joyce on Thomas Wolfe. New York Univ., 1954. Dissertation: English.

Kinstley, Barbara J. Thomas Wolfe's Romantic Affinity for Germany. North Texas State Univ., 1966. Thesis: English.

Kleiner, Robert. Thomas Wolfe's Short Stories. Columbia Univ., 1949. Thesis: English.

Kracht, Fritz A. Die Thomas Wolfe--Kritik in den Vereinigten Staaten und Deutschland. Muenchen, 1953. Dissertation: English.

Kytle, Juanita S. Walt Whitman and Thomas Wolfe. Univ. of Oklahoma, 1946. Thesis: English.

LaCapelain, Laurence C. A Form of Formlessness: The Study of a Primary Structuring Device in Thomas Wolfe's *Look Homeward, Angel*. Assumption (Canada), 1962. Thesis: English.

Lancaster, Lyle L.V. Development of Thomas Wolfe's Socio-Political Consciousness as Reflected in His Writings. Texas Christian Univ., 1969. Thesis: English.

Lantos, Carl. Thomas Wolfe: The Struggle for Maturity. Univ. of Texas (Austin), 1948. Thesis: English.

Larrass, Horst. Thomas Wolfe--Zur Problematik des Buergerlichen Dichters im Zeitalter D. Imperialismus. Greifswald, 1961. Dissertation: English.

LaSalle, Claude W. II. Thomas Wolfe: The Dramatic Apprenticeship. Univ. of Pennsylvania, 1964. Dissertation: English.

Lawler, John J. A Study of some of the Relations between the Periodical and Book Publications of Thomas Wolfe. Univ. of North Carolina, 1949. Thesis: English.

Lawler, Joseph H. The Silent Sea of *Look Homeward, Angel*. Columbia Univ., 1957. Thesis: English.

Lawrence, Oliver C. Thomas Wolfe: From Individual to Man-Swarm. Univ. of Washington, 1961. Dissertation: English.

Lehnstul, A.B. A Critical Comment on the Works of Thomas Wolfe. Ohio State Univ., 1942. Thesis: English.

Leslie, Bruce H. Thomas Wolfe in the Early and the Late Manner. Columbia Univ., 1951. Thesis: English.
Linder, Wolfgang. Die epische Struktur des Romanwerkes von Thomas Wolfe. Bonn, 1951. Dissertation: English.
Liner, Harold T. Violence in the Works of Thomas Wolfe. Univ. of Georgia, 1969. Thesis: English.
Lucas, Alec. Thomas Wolfe's Letters to his Mother and his Novels Compared. Queen's (Canada), 1945. Thesis: English.
Maddock, Lawrence H. The Critical Image of Thomas Wolfe. George Peabody College, 1965. Dissertation: English.
Magee, Annie T. The Theory and Techniques of Thomas Wolfe. Southwest Texas State Univ., 1951. Thesis: English.
Mahoney, Hilda F. Thomas Wolfe and the Southern Rhetorical Tradition. Univ. of Tennessee, 1959. Thesis: English.
Malmfeldt, James P. A Study of Thomas Wolfe's Use of Time Symbolism in His Major Novels and Short Stories. Brown Univ., 1964. Thesis: English.
Marley, Lena S. A Study of the Structure of the Narrative in "Proteus: The City." Univ. of North Carolina (Chapel Hill), 1966. Thesis: English.
Maxwell, Allen. Thomas Wolfe: Dichtung und Wahrheit. Southern Methodist Univ., 1940. Thesis: English.
Maxwell, Bert H. Thomas Wolfe's *You Can't Go Home Again*. A Critical Study. Univ. of Texas (Austin), 1954. Thesis: English.
McClellan, Robert W. The Literary Reputation of Thomas Wolfe. Columbia Univ., 1961. Thesis: English.
McCormick, John O. The Novels of Thomas Wolfe: A Comparative Study. Yale Univ., 1948. Dissertation: English.
McCrary, Martha P. Critical Reception of Thomas Wolfe, 1929-1951. Duke Univ., 1951. Thesis: English.
McDonnell, John V. Thomas Wolfe: The Search for Cosmic Consciousness. Brown Univ., 1965. Thesis: English.
McDonald, Walter R. The Concept of Time in Thomas Wolfe's Fiction. Texas Tech Univ., 1957. Thesis: English.
McLelland, Reginald F. The Theme of Alienation in the Novels of Thomas Wolfe. Univ. of Georgia, 1966. Thesis: English.
McNeil, C.C. Epic Qualities in Thomas Wolfe's *Look Homeward, Angel*. Brigham Young Univ., 1960. Thesis: English.
McNeil, Linda M. Escape into Life: The Novels of Thomas Wolfe. Baylor Univ., 1960. Thesis: English.
Michael, Marion C. Thomas Wolfe's Conception of the South. Univ. of Virginia, 1955. Thesis: English.
Miller, John C. Thomas Wolfe as a Novelist. Univ. of Virginia, 1947. Thesis: English.
Min, Hisook L. Thomas Wolfe: The Development of His Themes in Relation to His Conflicts. East Texas State Univ., 1969. Thesis: English.
Mirshak, Robert C. Characteristics of Wolfe's "Morike Lieder." Iowa State Teachers College, 1966. Thesis: English.
Moake, Frank B. An Evaluation of the Criticism of Thomas Wolfe. Southern Illinois Univ. (Carbondale), 1949. Thesis: English.
Moore, Rachel. Thomas Wolfe: The Question of Autobiographical Fiction. Louisiana State Univ., 1963. Thesis: English.

Murnan, Betty L. Thomas Wolfe: Characterization in *Look Homeward, Angel*, and *The Web and the Rock* (First Half). State Univ. of Iowa, 1950. Thesis: English.

Newman, Carol M., Jr. The Symbols of Thomas Wolfe. Univ. of Virginia, 1946. Thesis: English.

O'Dell, Carl A. An Analysis of Certain Poetical Devices in the Prose of Thomas Wolfe. East Tennessee State Univ., 1957. Thesis: English.

Oertel, Ferdinand. Die Europa-Erfahrung Thomas Wolfes. Koln, 1954. Dissertation: English.

Oliver, Virginia H. The Theme of Alienation in the Writing of Thomas Wolfe. McNeese State Univ., 1965. Thesis: English.

Paine, Donald F. Thomas Wolfe: A Study of His Literary Reputation. Univ. of Tennessee, 1963. Thesis: English.

Perreault, John H. Thomas Wolfe: The Growth of an Artist and a Man. Villanova Univ., 1965. Thesis: English.

Pfister, Karin. Zeit und Wirklichkeit bei Thomas Wolfe. Marburg, 1953. Dissertation: English.

Phelps, Phil R. The Train as a Symbol in the Novels of Thomas Wolfe. Univ. of Tennessee, 1966. Thesis: English.

Pleasant, John R. Thomas Wolfe and the Agrarians. Louisiana State Univ., 1965. Thesis: English.

Pledger, Maisie L. Thomas Wolfe's Treatment of Death. Sam Houston State College, 1964. Thesis: English.

Plunkett, James T. The Quest for a Father-God in the Fiction of Thomas Wolfe. Univ. of Minnesota, 1969. Dissertation: English.

Powell, Harold V. Thomas Wolfe and His Art. State Univ. of Iowa, 1950. Thesis: English.

Powell, Walter A. Thomas Wolfe's Short Novels as Related to his Long Fiction. Univ. of South Carolina, 1967. Dissertation: English.

Preslar, Robert W. Thomas Wolfe as Novelist-Satirist: An Evaluation. Univ. of Maryland, 1967. Thesis: English.

Randolph, Ernest C. Women in the Life and Works of Thomas Wolfe. North Texas State Univ., 1968. Thesis: English.

Raper, Julius R. The Uses of Fire and Food Imagery in *Look Homeward, Angel*. Duke Univ., 1962. Thesis: English.

Reader, Willie D. Thomas Wolfe's Autobiographical Approach. Univ. of Texas (Austin), 1960. Thesis: English.

Rebok, Chester T., Jr. Love in the *Confessio Amantis*; Pepys' Dramatic Criticism; and Wolfe's *Mannerhouse*. Pennsylvania State Univ., 1962. Thesis: English.

Reeves, Georges M. Thomas Wolfe et l'Europe. Paris, 1953. Dissertation: English.

Reeves, Walter P., Jr. The Negro in the Works of Thomas Wolfe. Duke Univ., 1957. Thesis: English.

_____. Race and Nationality in the Works of Thomas Wolfe. Duke Univ., 1963. Dissertation: English.

Robinson, Walter R. Thomas Wolfe: His Mother and Eliza Gant. Virginia Polytechnic Institute, 1969. Thesis: English.

Rogers, Elizabeth J. An Analysis of Thomas Wolfe's *Look Homeward, Angel* and *Of Time and the River*. Ohio State Univ., 1944. Thesis: English.

Roschwalb, Jerold. The Quest of an American Faust: A Study of
Thomas Wolfe. Columbia Univ., 1960. Thesis: English.
Ross, Sue F. A Study of Terry's Edition of *Thomas Wolfe's Letters
to His Mother* with Emphasis on Dating Errors. Univ. of North
Carolina (Chapel Hill), 1965. Thesis: English.
Rubin, Larry J. Image and Theme in the Tetralogy of Thomas Wolfe.
Emory Univ., 1956. Dissertation: English.
Rubin, Louis D., Jr. The Weather of His Youth: A Study of the
Form of Autobiographical Fiction in the Work of Thomas Wolfe.
Johns Hopkins Univ., 1954. Dissertation: English.
Sage, Howard. The Form of *Look Homeward, Angel*. Lehigh Univ.,
1965. Thesis: English.
Sauer, Oskar. Thomas Wolfe and Europe. Washington Univ. (St.
Louis), 1951. Thesis: English.
Schiller, William D. Emotion as an Element of Characterization in
Four Major Works of Thomas Wolfe. Texas A & M Univ., 1970.
Thesis: English.
Shufford, Catherine B. Thomas Wolfe and Walt Whitman. North Texas
State Univ., 1941. Thesis: English.
Schulte, Wolfgang. Die Romantischen und Realistischen Elemente
im Werk Thomas Wolfes. Kiel, 1956. Dissertation: English.
Schwartz, Norman. The Technique of Thomas Wolfe in Characterization.
Columbia Univ., 1949. Thesis: English.
Sehon, Elizabeth B. The Optimism of Thomas Wolfe. Baylor Univ.,
1951. Thesis: English.
Seib, Kenneth A. The Shifting Winds: A Study of the Critical
Reaction toward the Works of Thomas Wolfe. Columbia Univ.,
1961. Thesis: English.
Semasko, Boris P. Thomas Wolfe as Playwright. Columbia Univ.,
1950. Thesis: English.
Shealy, Ann. Thomas Wolfe: A Critical Study of His Views of the
American Scene. Univ. of South Carolina, 1947. Thesis:
English.
Sheffield, Jewell F. Female Characters in Thomas Wolfe's Four
Major Novels: *Look Homeward, Angel*; *Of Time and the River*;
The Web and The Rock; and *You Can't Go Home Again*. Texas
A & M Univ., 1968. Thesis: English.
Shott, Gloria R. A Study of the Techniques of Adapting Thomas
Wolfe for the Stage. East Texas State Univ., 1965. Thesis:
Speech.
Shuford, Charlotte. Thomas Wolfe's Attitudes toward the South.
Vanderbilt Univ., 1966. Thesis: English.
Sievers, Margaret W. The Development of Thomas Wolfe's Reputation.
Western State College of Colorado, 1949. Thesis: English.
Simons, Helen T. The Pessimism of Thomas Wolfe. Univ. of
Pittsburgh, 1947. Thesis: English.
Skaggs, Calvin L. Formal Education in Thomas Wolfe's Life and
Works. Duke Univ., 1959. Thesis: English.
Skipp, Francis E. Thomas Wolfe and His Scribner's Editors.
Duke Univ., 1962. Dissertation: English.
Smith, Eleanor G.M. Wolfe's Unfinished Symphony: A Study of
Form in the Novels of Thomas Wolfe. Univ. of Wisconsin, 1948.
Dissertation: English.

Smith, Granville B. The Symbolism of Thomas Wolfe. Pennsylvania State Univ., 1954. Thesis: English.

Smitherman, Betty J. Thomas Wolfe's Imagery. Univ. of Texas (Austin), 1953. Thesis: English.

Sprowles, Harry D., Jr. The Search for Thomas Wolfe: With Particular Stress upon the Meaning of the Amatory Theme. Univ. of Pennsylvania, 1956. Dissertation: English.

Stanzel, Franz. Das Amerikabild Thomas Wolfes (1900-1938). Graz, 1950. Dissertation: English.

Stone, Patricia H. The Short Novels of Thomas Wolfe. Univ. of Colorado, 1967. Thesis: English.

Stover, Arnold R. Thomas Wolfe: His Conception of Art and Its Relation to His Writing. Univ. of Western Ontario, 1960. Thesis: English.

Strange, Sallie M. Two Literary Landmarks: *Look Homeward, Angel* and *The Catcher in the Rye*. Southern Methodist Univ., 1964. Thesis: English.

Strozier, Robert I. Thomas Wolfe and Death. Florida State Univ., 1960. Thesis: English.

_____. The Anatomy of Thomas Wolfe: A Study of the Question of Unity in the Gant-Webber Saga. Florida State Univ., 1965. Dissertation: English.

Suberman, Jack. The Idealism of Thomas Wolfe. Univ. of Florida, 1947. Thesis: English.

Sutliff, Harriet J. Thomas Wolfe, American Legend. Colorado College, 1942. Thesis: English.

Tannenbaum, Irving. Thomas Wolfe: The Conflicts of the Artist. Columbia Univ., 1951. Thesis: English.

Taylor, Douglas C. The Relation between the Poetic Concept and Autobiographical Memory in the Works of Thomas Wolfe. College of the Pacific, 1949. Thesis: English.

Taylor, P.M. Thomas Wolfe, American. Boston Univ., 1942. Thesis: English.

Vause, Edward A. Thomas Wolfe's Narrative Method. Univ. of North Carolina (Chapel Hill), 1949. Thesis: English.

Vickers, James E. Theme and Form in *Of Time and the River*. Univ. of North Carolina (Chapel Hill), 1967. Thesis: English.

Voigt, Walter. Die Bildersprache Thomas Wolfes mit besonderer Berucksichtigung der Metaphorik des Amerikanischen Englisch. Tubingen, 1952. Dissertation: English.

Volpe, Edmund L. Thomas Wolfe as Revealed Through His Satire. Columbia Univ., 1948. Thesis: English.

Ward, William T. The Imagery of Wolfe's *Look Homeward, Angel*. Eastern Kentucky Univ., 1969. Thesis: English.

Ware, Ruth W. Thomas Wolfe: Playwright. Trinity Univ. (Texas), 1968. Thesis: English.

Watts, J.M. Thomas Wolfe: A Consideration of the Balance of Fear and Courage in the Eugene Gant Novels. Univ. of Georgia, 1962. Thesis: English.

Weiss, Paul. Thomas Wolfe: Far-wanderer; a Biographical Essay. Columbia Univ., 1941. Thesis: English.

Wilemon, Billi M.S. Thomas Wolfe and His Editors. Texas Christian Univ., 1964. Thesis: English.

Wilkinson, Billy R. The Thomas Wolfe Collection of the University of North Carolina Library. Univ. of North Carolina (Chapel Hill), 1960. Thesis: English.

Wiltgen, Martin C. Existentialism in the Novels of Thomas Wolfe. Iowa State Teachers College, 1966. Thesis: English.

Winger, William. Thomas Wolfe: God's Lonely Man. Columbia Univ., 1951. Thesis: English.

Woodham, Martha d'A. Critical Opinion of Thomas Wolfe: 1930-1950. Univ. of South Carolina, 1953. Thesis: English.

Woodruff, Lloyd B. A Study of the Structure in the Novels of Thomas Wolfe. Univ. of Southern California, 1948. Thesis: English.

Yonge, Kay N. The Interwoven Themes of Thomas Wolfe. Hardin-Simmons Univ., 1964. Thesis: English.

Zettell, Martin F. The Theme of Travel in the Novels of Thomas Wolfe. Columbia Univ., 1957. Thesis: English.

RICHARD WRIGHT (1908-1960)

Bratz, Gordon T. Art and Experience: The Short Stories of Richard Wright. Univ. of Massachusetts, 1969. Thesis: English.

Brignano, Russell C. Richard Wright: The Major Themes, Ideas, and Attitudes in His Works. Univ. of Wisconsin, 1966. Dissertation: English.

Coleman, Virginia B. Art and Propaganda in the Works of Richard Wright. West Virginia State College, 1941. Thesis: English.

Crosse, Charis E.R. The Novels of Richard Wright: A Study of Major Reactions. Univ. of Maryland, 1964. Thesis: English.

Dillard, M.M. A Survey of the Literary Career of Richard Wright. Ohio Univ., 1945. Thesis: English.

Gonis, Christine O. The Failure of the American Dream: A Study of the Work of Richard Wright, 1934-1945. Duke Univ., 1960. Thesis: English.

Gray, Yohma. An American Metaphor: The Novels of Richard Wright. Yale Univ., 1967. Dissertation: English.

Harold, Beulah V. The Literary Career of Richard Wright. Iowa State Teachers College, 1953. Thesis: English.

Harris, Cassie M. Protest in the Work of Richard Wright prior to 1956. Univ. of Wichita, 1957. Thesis: English.

Jacobs, Connie B. Of Irony in the Fiction of Richard Wright. North Carolina College (Durham), 1969. Thesis: English.

Jordan, Edward S. The Long Loneliness of Richard Wright. San Francisco State College, 1963. Thesis: English.

Kinnamon, Keneth. The Emergence of Richard Wright: A Literary, Biographical, and Social Study. Harvard Univ., 1966. Dissertation: English.

Madigan, Lee W. Richard Wright and His Novels of Protest. Montreal, 1961. Thesis: English.

Margolies, Edward L. A Critical Analysis of the Works of Richard Wright. New York Univ., 1964. Dissertation: English.

Moore, David. Richard Wright and James Baldwin: A Comparison. Univ. of California (Riverside), 1966. Thesis: History.

Newlon, Neil B. *Lawd Today*: An Adaptation of the Novel by Richard Wright. Fresno State College, 1964. Thesis: Speech.

Peters, Ada. Richard Wright: A Study in Fear and Frustration.
    Columbia Univ., 1952. Thesis: English.
Reilly, John M. Insight and Protest in the Works of Richard Wright.
    Washington Univ. (St. Louis), 1967. Dissertation: English.
Story, Suzanne. Human Action and Responsibility in Theodore
    Dreiser's *An American Tragedy* and Richard Wright's *Native Son*.
    Univ. of Texas (Austin), 1965. Thesis: English.
Wilson, Shirley F. An Examination of Richard Wright's *Uncle Tom's
    Children*: Five Long Stories. Univ. of North Carolina (Chapel
    Hill), 1966. Thesis: English.

WILLIAM L. YANCEY (1814-1863)

Draughon, Ralph B., Jr. William Lowndes Yancey: From Unionist to
    Seccessionist, 1814-1852. Univ. of North Carolina (Chapel
    Hill), 1968. Dissertation: History.
Monzell, Thomas I. William L. Yancey, Conspirator: 1850-1861.
    Univ. of Maryland, 1968. Thesis: History.

FRANK YERBY (1916-   )

Hill, William W., Jr. Behind the Magnolia Mask: Frank Yerby as
    Critic of the South. Auburn Univ., 1968. Thesis: English.
Vails, Lavolia. The Literary Reputation of Yerby, 1946-1961.
    North Carolina College (Durham), 1963. Thesis: English.
Yancy, Sandy, Jr. Frank Yerby's Formula for Writing Historical
    Novels. North Carolina College (Durham), 1963. Thesis:
    English.

MARTHA YOUNG (1868-   )

Martin, Nancy B. An Analytical Study of the Writings of Martha
    Young. George Peabody College, 1926. Thesis: English.

STARK YOUNG (1881-1963)

Bledsoe, Charles A. A Critical Study of Stark Young's Fiction.
    Vanderbilt Univ., 1956. Thesis: English.
Davis, Hazel B. Stark Young: His Versatility. West Texas State
    Univ., 1948. Thesis: English.
Drexler, Malcolm B. Stark Young's Ideas on Theatre Practice.
    Univ. of Illinois, 1964. Dissertation: Theater.
Ferguson, Oliver W. Stark Young and the Southern Tradition.
    Vanderbilt Univ., 1948. Thesis: English.
Green, Mary E. An Analysis of the Dramatic Criticisms of Stark
    Young. Louisiana State Univ., 1941. Thesis: Speech.
Johnson, Willie S. Stark Young: These Constant Things.
    Mississippi State Univ., 1956. Thesis: English.
Link, James O. The Central Premise in Stark Young's Theories of
    Art and of Criticism. Cornell Univ., 1968. Dissertation:
    Theater.
Lumianski, Robert M. Stark Young and His Dramatic Criticism.
    Michigan State Univ., 1955. Dissertation: English.

Miller, John M. Stark Young's Principles of Theater Art.
    Tulane Univ., 1962. Dissertation: Speech and Theater.
McAlexander, Hubert H. Tradition in the Novels of Stark Young.
    Univ. of Mississippi, 1966. Thesis: English.
Phut, Joseph L., Jr. Stark Young: A Critical Study. Columbia
    Univ., 1961. Thesis: English.
Ruehlen, Petroula. The Old South in the Novels of Stark Young.
    Louisiana State Univ., 1964. Thesis: English.
Thurman, Bedford. Stark Young: A Bibliography of His Writing
    with a Selective Index to His Criticism of the Arts. Cornell
    Univ., 1954. Dissertation: Speech and Theater.
Weaver, Bruce J. A Comparative Study of the Critical Theories of
    George Jean Nathan and Stark Young. Kansas State College
    (Pittsburgh), 1966. Thesis: English.
Williams, D.T. An Analysis of the Dramatic Criticism of Stark
    Young as Published in *The New Republic*, 1921-1932. Bowling
    Green State Univ., 1962. Thesis: Speech.
Zaworski, Kathleen. Stark Young's Theory of Directing. Baylor
    Univ., 1966. Thesis: Speech.

PART II
CULTURAL, HISTORICAL,
AND SOCIAL BACKGROUNDS OF SOUTHERN LITERATURE

GENERAL

Abbott, Martin L. The Freedman's Bureau in South Carolina, 1865-
1872. Emory Univ., 1954. Dissertation: History.
Abernathy, Frances D. The Building of Johnson County (Texas), and
the Settlement of the Communities of the Eastern Portion of
the County. Univ. of Texas (Austin), 1936. Thesis: History.
Adkins, Thurman J. Yellowstone: Biography of a Steamboat.
Trinity Univ. (Texas), 1969. Thesis: History.
Akins, Billy L. Georgians and the War of 1812. Georgia Southern
College, 1968. Thesis: History.
Alexander, Charles C. Crusade for Conformity: The Ku Klux Klan
in Texas, 1920-1927. Univ. of Texas (Austin), 1959. Thesis:
History.
_____. Invisible Empire in the Southwest: The Ku Klux Klan in
Texas, Louisiana, Oklahoma, and Arkansas, 1920-1930. Univ.
of Texas (Austin), 1962. Dissertation: History.
Alexander, Gladys. Social Life in Texas, 1821-1836. East Texas
State Univ., 1942. Thesis: History. [Chapter four discusses
the beginning and influence of the early educational activities,
newspapers, and religious activities in the cultural develop-
ment of the early Texans]
Allen, Carlos R., Jr. Travel and Communication in the Early
Colonial Period, 1607-1720. Univ. of California (Berkeley),
1956. Dissertation: History.
Ames, Susie M. Studies of the Virginia Eastern Shore in the
Seventeenth Century. Columbia Univ., 1940. Dissertation:
History.
Amlund, Curtis A. The Theory and Practice of Federalism in the
Governmental Organization of the Confederate States of
America. Univ. of Minnesota, 1959. Dissertation: Political
Science.
Andresen, Karl A. The Theory of State Interposition to Control
Federal Action: A Study of the Kentucky and Virginia
Resolutions of 1798, of Calhoun's Doctrine of Nullification,
and the Contemporary Inter-Position Resolutions of some
Southern States. Univ. of Minnesota, 1960. Dissertation:
Political Science.
Atkinson, Bertha. The History of Bell County, Texas. Univ. of
Texas (Austin), 1929. Thesis: History. [Brief mention of
newspapers and of Carnegie Library]
Attig, C.J. Western Flavor in the Lower South, 1815-1850. Univ.
of Chicago, 1935. Thesis: History. [Historical discussion
of the influence of the West on the South]
Auerbach, M.M. Conservatism and Its Contemporary American
Advocates. Columbia Univ., 1958. Dissertation: Political
Science. [Discusses Southern agrarians]
Auten, M.L. A History of Erath County (Texas). Hardin-Simmons
Univ., 1951. Thesis: History. [Social as well as economic
and political development]

Autrey, Max L. The Shaftesbury-Mandeville Debate and Its Influence in America. Wayne State Univ., 1965. Dissertation: English. [Includes Jefferson]

Ayres, Shirley E. Albemarle County, Virginia, 1744-1770: An Economic, Political, and Social Analysis. Univ. of Virginia, 1968. Thesis: History.

Babb, Winston C. French Refugees from Saint Domingue to the Southern United States: 1791-1810. Univ. of Virginia, 1954. Dissertation: History. [Background of Louisiana Creole culture]

Bacon, Hollis P. II. A Historical Geography of Antebellum Nashville. George Peabody College, 1955. Dissertation: Geography.

Baiamonte, John V. New Immigrants in the South: A Study of the Italians of Tangipahoa Parish, Louisiana. Southeastern Louisiana Univ., 1969. Thesis: History.

Bailey, Kenneth P. The Ohio Company of Virginia. Univ. of California (Los Angeles), 1938. Dissertation: History.

Baltimore, Lester B. Southern Nationalists and Southern Nationalism, 1850-1870. Univ. of Missouri, 1968. Dissertation: History. [Includes J.D.B. DeBow, George Fitzhugh, Edward A. Pollard, Robert Barnwell Rhett, Edmund Ruffin, and W.G. Simms]

Barfoot, Jessie L. A History of McCulloch County, Texas. Univ. of Texas (Austin), 1937. Thesis: History.

Baskin, Darryl B. The Pluralist Vision in American Political Thought: Adams, Madison, and Calhoun on Community, Citizenship, and the Public Interest. Univ. of California (Berkeley), 1966. Dissertation: Political Science.

Basset, Mary G. Reading Interests of Negro Children in Two Southern Cities. George Peabody College, 1931. Thesis: English.

Beam, Harold A. A History of Collin County, Texas. Univ. of Texas (Austin), 1951. Thesis: History.

Beard, Elizabeth L. Idealogies of Negro Leaders in the 1940's. Univ. of California (Riverside), 1965. Thesis: History.

Beasley, Edward, Jr. A Study of the Manumission of Negro Slaves to 1832. Kansas State Teacher's College, 1964. Thesis: Social Science.

Beck, Don E. The Rhetoric of Conflict and Compromise: A Study in Civil War Causation. Univ. of Oklahoma, 1966. Dissertation: Speech. [Based on interrelated disciplines of history, political science, rhetorical theory, and the behavioral sciences]

Benjamin, Gilbert G. The Germans in Texas. Yale Univ., 1907. Dissertation: History. [Deals with schools, newspapers, singing societies, literature, and religion]

Benjamin, Rommel. The Nonwhite Population of Atlanta, Georgia: 1940 to 1950. Atlanta Univ., 1961. Thesis: Library Science.

Berkeley, Francis L., Jr. The Berkeleys of Barn Elms, Planters of Colonial Virginia and a Calendar of the Berkeley Papers, 1653-1767. Univ. of Virginia, 1940. Thesis: History.

Berwick, Keith B. Moderates in Crisis: The Trials of Leadership in Revolutionary Virginia. Univ. of Chicago, 1959. Dissertation: History.

Bierman, Mary M. A History of Victoria, Texas, 1824-1900. Univ. of Texas (Austin), 1948. Thesis: History. [Discussion of early newspapers and editors]

Biesele, Rudolph L. The History of the German Settlements in Texas, 1831-1861. Univ. of Texas (Austin), 1928. Dissertation: History. [Discussion of newspapers and of literary and dramatic societies]

Biggers, John T. The Negro Woman in American Life and Education: A Mural Presentation. Pennsylvania State Univ., 1954. Dissertation: Education.

Binder, Frederick M. The Color Problem in Early National America as Viewed by John Adams, Jefferson and Jackson. Columbia Univ., 1962. Dissertation: History.

Bishop, Wallace P. The Struggle for International Copyright in the United States. Boston Univ., 1959. Dissertation: History. [Discusses Southern politicians who opposed international copyright]

Bitner, Julia G. The History of Tom Green County, Texas. Univ. of Texas (Austin), 1931. Thesis: History. [Brief mention of founding of newspaper and of presentations of a dramatic club]

Blackard, Morris. The History of Titus County, Texas, 1929-1964. Univ. of Texas (Austin), 1964. Thesis: History.

Blackwelder, Ruth. An Intellectual and Cultural History of Orange County, North Carolina, 1752-1868. Univ. of North Carolina (Chapel Hill), 1943. Dissertation: History.

Blanton, Silas W., Jr. Virginia in the 1920's: An Economic and Social Profile. Univ. of Virginia, 1969. Dissertation: History.

Block, Robert H. Southern Opinion of Woodrow Wilson's Foreign Policies, 1913-1917. Duke Univ., 1968. Dissertation: History.

Blount, Lora. A Short History of Fisher County (Texas). Hardin-Simmons Univ., 1947. Thesis: History.

Boaz, Sallie R. A History of Amarillo, Texas. Univ. of Texas (Austin), 1950. Thesis: History.

Boethel, Paul C. The History of LaVaca County (Texas). Univ. of Texas (Austin), 1932. Thesis: History. [Brief comment on newspapers in English and in other languages]

Boje, John R. The Political Influence of the Whig Party in Georgia, 1834-1848. Georgia Southern College, 1969. Thesis: History.

Boles, John B. The Religious Mind of the Old South: The Era of the Great Revival, 1787-1805. Univ. of Virginia, 1969. Dissertation: History.

Bolton, George A. The Southern Attitude toward the Tariff, 1860: Literary and Political Aspects. Bowling Green State Univ., 1970. Thesis: American Studies.

Boon, Effie M. The History of Angelina County (Texas). Univ. of Texas (Austin), 1937. Thesis: History. [One Indian legend recounted; newspapers discussed]

[201]

Boswell, Grover C. History of the Bar Lo Ranch of the Eastern
    Panhandle of Texas. Hardin-Simmons Univ., 1933. Thesis:
    History.
Boudreaux, Julianna L. A History of Philanthropy in New Orleans,
    1835-1862. Tulane Univ., 1961. Dissertation: History.
Bowden, Lois. Mike Fink: The Last of the Keelboatmen. Columbia
    Univ., 1928. Thesis: English.
Bowes, Frederick P. The Intellectual Life of Early Charleston
    (South Carolina). Princeton Univ., 1941. Dissertation:
    History.
Bowman, Robert L. Negro Politics in Four Southern Counties. Univ.
    of North Carolina (Chapel Hill), 1963. Dissertation:
    English.
Bradford, Giles E. A History of Mitchell County, Texas. Univ. of
    Texas (Austin), 1937. Thesis: History. [Brief mention of
    newspapers; appendix on cowmen's talk]
Branscum, Virginia M. Some Aspects of the Life of Women in
    Eastern New Mexico and the Texas Panhandle-Plains Area from
    1875-1905. Univ. of Texas (Austin), 1952. Thesis: English.
Bray, Eula. A Survey of the Reading Material in Lawrence County
    [Tennessee] Homes. George Peabody College, 1931. Thesis:
    English.
Breese, Donald H. Politics in the Lower South during Presidential
    Reconstruction, April to November, 1865. Univ. of California
    (Los Angeles), 1964. Dissertation: History.
Brewer, James P. Printing: Its History and Progress in the
    Schools of Tennessee. Univ. of Tennessee, 1934. Thesis:
    Journalism.
Bridges, Jim L. The History of Fort Bend County (Texas). Univ.
    of Texas (Austin). Date Unknown. Thesis: History.
Bright, Margaret D. The Social Development of Houston, Texas,
    1836-1860. Univ. of Texas (Austin), 1940. Thesis: History.
Britt, Lutie. The Mores of the Texas Cowboy. Columbia Univ.,
    1922. Thesis: Sociology. [Songs, dress, conflicts, etc. of
    the cowboy]
Brittain, Joseph M. Negro Suffrage and Politics in Alabama Since
    1870. Indiana Univ., 1958. Dissertation: History.
Broderick, Irwin L. The Spirit of Independence in Virginia,
    1775-1776. Roosevelt Univ., 1968. Thesis: History.
Brophy, William J. Origins of the Southern Conservative Revolt,
    1932-1940. North Texas State Univ., 1963. Thesis: History.
Brown, Donald N. Southern Attitudes toward Negro Voting During
    the Bourbon Period, 1877-1890. Univ. of Oklahoma, 1960.
    Dissertation: History.
Brown, Sally V. A Study of the Reception of the Books Published
    by the University of North Carolina Press from 1922 through
    1952 as Evidenced in Reviews. Univ. of North Carolina
    (Chapel Hill), 1961. Thesis: Library Science.
Brownwell, Blaine A. The Urban Mind in the South: The Growth
    of Urban Consciousness in Southern Cities, 1920-1927.
    Univ. of North Carolina (Chapel Hill), 1969. Dissertation:
    History.
Buckley, Frank. Trends in American Primitivism. Univ. of
    Minnesota, 1939. Dissertation: History. [Includes William
    Byrd]

Buckner, Dellos U. Study of the Lower Rio Grande Valley as a
Culture Area. Univ. of Texas (Austin), 1929. Thesis:
Sociology. [Some discussion of Mexican folk dances and religio-
dramatic dances]
Buckner, John W. The History of Crossett, Arkansas. Northeast
Louisiana Univ., 1969. Thesis: History.
Buni, Andrew. The Negro in Virginia Politics, 1902-1950. Univ.
of Virginia, 1965. Dissertation: History.
Burgess, Roger A. The History of Crosby County, Texas. Univ.
of Texas (Austin), 1927. Thesis: History.
Burns, Kerry O. Ouachita Parish Southern Baptists. Northeast
Louisiana Univ., 1970. Thesis: History.
Buser, John E. After Half a Generation: The South in the 1880's.
Univ. of Texas (Austin), 1968. Dissertation: History.
[Includes political efforts of Jefferson Davis and discusses
Thomas Nelson Page and others who romanticized the Old South;
mentions C. Vann Woodward's *The Strange Career of Jim Crow*]
Butter, Robert R. A History of Kaufman County, Texas. Univ. of
Texas (Austin), 1940. Thesis: History. [Some discussion
of newspapers]
Butterfield, William H. Intellectual Development in Virginia and
Massachusetts Bay to 1849. Univ. of Oklahoma, 1935.
[Discussion of early Virginia writings]
Campbell, Elizabeth A. Land Settlements in the South after the
Civil War. Univ. of California (Riverside), 1959. Thesis:
History.
Canby, Courtlandt. The Intellectual History of Virginia in the
Eighteenth Century. Harvard Univ., 1940. Dissertation:
American Civilization.
Cantrell, Clyde H. The Reading Habits of Antebellum Southerners.
Univ. of Illinois, 1960. Dissertation: Library Science.
Carpenter, Eleanor B. The Culture of Louisville as Affected by
and Reflected in Motion Pictures. Univ. of Louisville, 1941.
Thesis: History.
Carpenter, Louie W. The Stephen Foster Memorial 1931-1969: A
Socio-Cultural Force in a Rural Community. Florida State
Univ., 1969. Dissertation: Music.
Carrow, Catherine I. The Amusements of Texas from 1880-1890.
Univ. of Texas (Austin), 1943. Thesis: History.
[Discussion of cowboy songs, of 'poems' in a young lady's
autograph album, of various square-dance calls, of songs for
play-party games, of amateur theatricals and of plays
presented in various opera houses]
Cassles, Anne E. A History of Hunt County (Texas). Univ. of Texas
(Austin), 1935. Thesis: History. [Brief discussion of
newspapers and of plays presented in opera house]
Cave, Alfred A. The Jacksonian Movement in American Historio-
graphy. Univ. of Florida, 1961. Dissertation: History.
Cawelti, John G. A History of Self-Made Manhood: The Ideal of
the Self-Made Man in Nineteenth Century America. Univ. of
Iowa, 1960. Dissertation: American Studies. [Discusses
Mark Twain]

Cezeaux, Louise C. Social Life in the Republic of Texas, 1836-
1845. Univ. of Texas (Austin), 1933. Thesis: History.
[Brief discussion of folk amusements and of theatrical groups]

Chandler, B. The Abolitionist's Picture of the South. Univ. of
Chicago, 1937. Thesis: History.

Chappell, Ben A. The Southern Unity Movement. North Texas State
Univ., 1956. Thesis: History.

Charles, Reid S. The 1960 Welfare Crisis in Louisiana. Wichita
State Univ., 1970. Thesis: Political Science.

Charlton, Huey E. Stability of the Negro Family in a Southern
Community. Temple Univ., 1958. Dissertation: Psychology.
[South Carolina Community]

Cheape, Kathleen S.H. Confederate Book Publishing with Emphasis
on Richmond, Virginia. Univ. of North Carolina (Chapel
Hill), 1960. Thesis: Library Science.

Choate, J.E., Jr. The Myth of the American Cowboy. Vanderbilt
Univ., 1954. Dissertation: English. [Mentions Twain]

Clare, Carol J. The Woman Suffrage in Virginia: Its Nature,
Rationale, and Tactics. Univ. of Virginia, 1968. Thesis:
History.

Clayton, Bruce L. Southern Critics of the New South, 1890-1914.
Duke Univ., 1966. Dissertation: History. [John Spencer
Bassett, professor of history at Trinity College, 1894-1906;
William Garrott Brown, (Alabama); Edgar Gardener Murphy,
(Alabama clergyman); Walter Hines Page; and William P. Trent.
Also includes John C. Kilgo, Edwin Mims, William P. Few,
James W. Garner, John E. White, Burr J. Ramage, Carl Holliday,
John B. Henneman, Andrew Sledd, Samuel C. Mitchell, and
Clarence H. Poe. Periodicals included are *Sewanee Review* and
South Atlantic Quarterly]

Cocanougher, Sue J. Social History of Wise County, Texas, between
1880 and 1910. Texas Woman's Univ., 1969. Thesis: History.

Coffin, Hugh. Slavery Defended: A Southern View. Univ. of
California (Riverside), 1964. Thesis: English.

Coker, Charles F.W. The North Carolina English Records Project,
1922-1930: An Historical Appraisal, with a Summary of
Preceding and Succeeding Efforts. Univ. of North Carolina
(Chapel Hill), 1969. Thesis: Library Science.

Compton, Bobby D. Baptist Manuals in America: A Study of Baptist
Policy and Practice. Southern Baptist Theological Seminary,
1968. Dissertation: Religion. [Charleston-based]

Connelly, Thomas L. Experiment in Redemption: The Confederate
Invasion of Kentucky in 1862. Rice Univ., 1961. Thesis:
History.

_____. Metal, Fire and Forge: The Army of Tennessee, 1861-1862.
Rice Univ., 1963. Dissertation: History.

Constantine, James R. The African Slave Trade: A Study of
Eighteenth Century Propaganda and Public Controversy.
Indiana Univ. (Bloomington), 1953. Dissertation: History.
[Discusses slave trade as background for Harriet Beecher Stowe]

Cook, Dale E. The Invisible Empire and the Johnson Act: A Study
of the Ku Klux Klan's Role in the 1824 Immigration Act. Univ.
of California (Riverside), 1961. Thesis: History.

Cook, Phillip C.   Antebellum Bienville Parish.   Louisiana
    Polytechnic Inst., 1965.   Thesis: History.
Cooke, John W.   Some Aspects of the Concept of the Free Individual
    in the United States, 1800-1860.   Vanderbilt Univ., 1967.
    Dissertation: History.   [Includes nineteen Southerners]
Coover, Edwin R.   The Migration of Southern Leadership in the
    Twentieth Century.   Univ. of Virginia, 1966.   Thesis:
    History.
CorSette, Sandra I.   Matthew Carey and the American Museum:
    Reflections of American Nationalism.   Southern Methodist Univ.,
    1969.   Thesis: History.   [George Washington, Thomas Jefferson,
    Daniel Boone; periodical articles about the South cited in
    Appendix]
Cowan, Faye P.   A Cultural and Literary Study of the Abbeville Area
    of South Carolina.   Clemson Univ., 1968.   Thesis: English.
Cox, Harold E.   Federalism and Anti-Federalism in Virginia--1787:
    A Study of Political and Economic Motivations.   Univ. of
    Virginia, 1958.   Dissertation: History.
Crabb, Alfred.   The Nashville Literary Societies, 1825-1860.
    George Peabody College, 1941.   Thesis: English.
Crampton, Richard H.   The Break of the Old Northwest and the South.
    Univ. of Virginia, 1967.   Thesis: History.
Cranfill, Leslie W.   The Early History of Denison, Texas.   Hardin-
    Simmons Univ., 1951.   Thesis: History.
Cristol, Geraldine P.   A History of the Dallas Museum of Fine Arts.
    Southern Methodist Univ., 1970.   Thesis: History.
Culley, John J.   Muted Trumpets: Four Efforts to Better Southern
    Race Relations, 1900-1919.   Univ. of Virginia, 1967.
    Dissertation: History.
Cullop, Charles P.   Confederate Propaganda in Europe, 1861-1865.
    Univ. of Virginia, 1962.   Dissertation: History.
Cupp, Ora L.   The Bolling Halls, a Planter Family of Georgia and
    Alabama, 1792-1860.   Univ. of Texas (Austin), 1949.
    Thesis: History.
Curtis, Sara K.   A History of Gillespie County, Texas.   Univ. of
    Texas (Austin), 1943.   Thesis: History.
Dabney, Edgar R.   The Settlement of New Braunfels (Texas).   Univ.
    of Texas (Austin), 1927.   Thesis: History.
Dabney, William M.   Jefferson's Albemarle: History of Albemarle
    County, Virginia, 1727-1819.   Univ. of Virginia, 1951.
    Dissertation: History.
Dalton, Alford P.   Elizabethan Leftovers in Allen County, Ky.
    Western Kentucky Univ., 1936.   Thesis: English.
Daniel, Vivian.   The Territorial Development of Arkansas, 1791-1836.
    Univ. of Texas (Austin), 1929.   Thesis: History.   [Includes a
    discussion of *Arkansas Gazette* and its founder]
Daniels, Ophelia C.   The Formative Years of Johnson City, Tennessee,
    1885-1890.   Tennessee A. & I. Univ., 1948.   Thesis: History.
    [Author discusses the literature, theater, and culture of
    Johnson City]
Davenport, Francis G.   Cultural Life in Nashville on the Eve of the
    Civil War.   Vanderbilt Univ., 1936.   Dissertation: History.
    [Discusses interest in drama, opera, classical music, and
    minstrels]

Davenport, F.G., Jr. The Myth of Southern History--20th Century Variations. Univ. of Minnesota, 1967. Dissertation: History.

Davidson, Katherine H. Anglicanism in the Valley of Virginia. Univ. of Virginia, 1953. Thesis: History.

Davie, Flora A. The Early History of Houston, Texas, 1836-1845. Univ. of Texas (Austin), 1940. Thesis: History. [Considerable discussion of the theater]

Davis, John M. The Image of Lincoln in the South: From Secession to Lincoln Centennial Year (1860-1909). Rice Univ., 1967. Dissertation: History. [From newspapers, magazines, histories, *belles lettres*, published letters, etc.]

Davis, William D. Popular Southern Religion: A Contrast with American Values. Univ. of North Carolina (Chapel Hill), 1968. Thesis: Sociology.

de Hart, Flora B. A History of the West Brothers: Thomas, Francis, John, and Nathaniel in Colonial Virginia, 1608-1659. Univ. of Virginia, 1958. Thesis: History.

de Hart, Sheppard A. A Colonial History of Prince George County, Virginia. Univ. of Virginia, 1957. Thesis: History.

Delano, Donald B. Changes in Goals and Tactics of the Negro Leadership since 1954. Univ. of California (Riverside), 1964. Thesis: Political Science.

DeRosier, Arthur H. The Removal of the Chocktaw Indians from Mississippi. Univ. of South Carolina, 1959. Dissertation: History.

DesChamps, Margaret B. The Presbyterian Church in the South Atlantic States, 1801-1861. Emory Univ., 1952. Dissertation: History.

Dickey, Raymond D. The Confederate Command Problem in the Trans-Mississippi West, 1861-1862. North Texas State Univ., 1960. Thesis: History.

Dickson, John B. History of Gregg County, Texas. Univ. of Texas (Austin), 1957. Thesis: History.

Dinsmare, Linda. Headquarters in the Saddle: Confederate Guerrillas in the Civil War. Univ. of California (Riverside), 1965. Thesis: History.

Dixon, Frederick K. A History of Gonzales County (Texas) in the Nineteenth Century. Univ. of Texas (Austin), 1964. Thesis: History.

Donohue, Jack V. Washington on the Brazos (Texas). Univ. of Texas (Austin), 1935. Thesis: History. [History that includes brief mention of newspapers]

Dorough, Charles D. Religion in the Old South: A Pattern of Behavior and Thought. Univ. of Texas (Austin), 1946. Dissertation: English.

Doyle, Elisabeth J. Civilian Life in Occupied New Orleans, 1862-1865. Louisiana State Univ., 1955. Dissertation: History. [Sources: newspapers, memoirs, biographies, official records]

Drake, Richard B. The American Missionary Association and the Southern Negro, 1861-1888. Emory Univ., 1957. Dissertation: History.

Dreyer, Edward C. A Study of the Patterns of Political Communication in the South. Univ. of North Carolina (Chapel Hill),
1968. Dissertation: Political Science.

Dugas, Vera L. A Social and Economic History of Texas in the
Civil War and Reconstruction Periods. Univ. of Texas (Austin),
1963. Dissertation: History.

Dunn, Robert W. The History of Loving County, Texas. Univ. of
Texas (Austin), 1948. Thesis: History.

Eager, Gerald. Fantastic Painting in America. Univ. of Minnesota,
1969. Dissertation: Fine Arts. [Includes Washington
Allston]

Eagle, Delbert P. Aspects of the Kentucky Frontier. Univ. of
Kentucky, 1938. Thesis: History.

Eatherley, Billy J. The Changing Economic Status of the Mississippi
Negro: 1950-1960. Southern Methodist Univ., 1964.
Dissertation: Economics.

Eaton, William C. Freedom of Thought in the Antebellum South.
Harvard Univ., 1929. Dissertation: English.

Eaves, Charles D. Post City: A Study in Colonization on the
Texas Plains. Univ. of Texas (Austin), 1943. Dissertation:
History. [Discussion of newspaper and of editorial attitude
required by founder of Post City]

Eilers, Kathryn B. A History of Mason County, Texas. Univ. of
Texas (Austin), 1939. Thesis: History.

Eisinger, Chester. The Freehold Concept in American Letters,
1607-1800. Univ. of Michigan, 1946. Dissertation: English.

Elkind, Frederick A. Family and Self-Esteem among Southern Urban
Negro Adolescents. State Univ. of New York (Binghamton),
1970. Thesis: Sociology.

Ellenburg, Martha A. Carpetbagger Policies during Reconstruction
in Arkansas. North Texas State Univ., 1963. Thesis:
History.

Ellis, Mary H. Social Conditions in Texas about 1850. Univ. of
Texas (Austin), 1927. Thesis: History.

Ellis, William E. The Kentucky Evolution Controversy. Eastern
Kentucky Univ., 1967. Thesis: History.

Ellsworth, Lois C. San Antonio during the Civil War. Univ. of
Texas (Austin), 1938. Thesis: History. [Some discussion
of libraries, booksellers, and book advertisements]

Engerrand, George C. The So-called Wends of Germany and Their
Colonies in Texas and in Australia. Univ. of Texas (Austin),
1935. Dissertation: History. [Discussion of Wendish
language in Texas and mention of newspapers]

Ensminger, Ruth. The Continuing Frontier in Arkansas. Southern
Methodist Univ., 1950. Thesis: History. [Mentions Albert
Pike and Sam Houston]

Eoff, Vallie. A History of Erath County, Texas. Univ. of Texas
(Austin), 1937. Thesis: History. [Discussion of literary
and dramatic clubs, of library, of newspapers. Short list
of plays given during 1890's at one opera house]

Ewing, George W. A Study of the Frontier Preacher in Texas. Univ. of Texas (Austin), 1952. Thesis: English.

Faughn, Attie. A Reading-Survey in Benton, Kentucky. George Peabody College, 1937. Thesis: English.

Feldstein, Stanley. The Slave's View of Slavery. New York Univ., 1969. Dissertation: History.

Fennell, Romey, Jr. The Negro in Texas Politics, 1865-1874. North Texas State Univ., 1963. Thesis: History.

Fenner, Mary C. Economic and Social Life of Augusta, Georgia, 1865-1872. Univ. of Texas (Austin), 1939. Thesis: History. [Includes a discussion of Paul H. Hayne, A.B. Longstreet, James Ryder Randall, Fr. Abram J. Ryan, of theaters, and of kinds of plays presented]

Ferguson, Willie L. A Reading Survey of Negro Homes in Beaumont, Texas. George Peabody College, 1932. Thesis: English.

Fiedler, Winnie B.M. A History of Mineral Wells, Texas. Univ. of Texas (Austin), 1953. Thesis: History.

Finger, Joel L. Virginia Fugitives of the 1850's. Univ. of Virginia, 1969. Thesis: History.

Finnie, Gordon E. The Antislavery Movement in the South, 1787-1836: Its Rise and Decline and Its Contribution to Abolitionism in the West. Duke Univ., 1962. Dissertation: Religion.

Fishwick, Marshall W. Virginia, 1902-1941: A Cultural History. Yale Univ., 1949. Dissertation: American Studies.

Flannery, Emerson L. Migration of Talent out of and into Alabama and Florida. Kent State Univ., 1961. Thesis: Sociology and Anthropology.

Fleming, William F. The Keebles: A Half Century of Southern Family Life. Univ. of Texas (Austin), 1951. Thesis: History.

Floyd, Willie M. Thurber, Texas, An Abandoned Coal Town. Southern Methodist Univ., 1939. Thesis: Geography. [Brief mention of newspaper and opera house]

Fogartie, Ruth A.D. Spanish-name People in Texas with Special Emphasis on Those Who Are Students in Texas Colleges and Universities. Univ. of Texas (Austin), 1948. Thesis: English.

Fornell, Earl W. Island City: The Story of Galveston on the Eve of Secession, 1850-1860. Rice Univ., 1956. Dissertation: History.

Franklin, Nancy D. The History of Mexia, Texas. Southern Methodist Univ., 1966. Thesis: History.

Freeman, Donald M. Religion and Southern Politics: The Political Behavior of Southern White Protestants. Univ. of North Carolina (Chapel Hill), 1964. Dissertation: Political Science.

Frick, Bertha M. A History of Printing in Virginia, 1750-1783, with a List of Virginia Imprints for That Period. Columbia Univ., 1933. Thesis: Library Science.

Friedman, Lawrence J. In Search of Uncle Tom: Racial Attitudes of the Southern Leadership, 1865-1920. Univ. of California (Los Angeles), 1967. Dissertation: History. [Centers on ideas of six men: William Brownlow, G.W. Cable, T.N. Page, Tom Watson, Henry Watterson, and Woodrow Wilson]

Frier, William L. The Relationship between Spain and the Confederacy during the American Civil War. Univ. of Texas (Austin), 1958. Thesis: Spanish.

Fry, Gladys-Marie. The Night Riders: A Study in the Social Control of the Negro. Indiana Univ. (Bloomington), 1967. Dissertation: Folklore. [Includes examination of some literature]

Fry, Tillie B.M. A History of Llano County, Texas. Univ. of Texas (Austin), 1943. Thesis: History. [Brief mention of newspapers and of library founded by Culture Club]

Fuller, Wayne E. R.F.D.: A History of the Farmer's Mail. Univ. of California (Berkeley), 1954. Dissertation: History.

Fullinwilder, S.P. The Emancipation of Negro Thought, 1890-1930. Univ. of Wisconsin, 1966. Dissertation: History. [Mentions Booker T. Washington and analyzes literary Negro American movement in 1920's]

Futch, Ovid L. History of Andersonville Prison. Emory Univ., 1959. Dissertation: History.

Gaines, Frances P. The Southern Plantation: A Study in the Development and the Accuracy of a Tradition. Columbia Univ., 1924. Dissertation: English.

Gaines, Francis P., Jr. The Virginia Constitutional Convention of 1850-51: A Study in Sectionalism. Univ. of Virginia, 1950. Dissertation: History.

Gaither, James M. A Return to the Village: A Study of Santa Fe and Taos, New Mexico, as Cultural Centers, 1900-1934. Univ. of Minnesota, 1957. Dissertation: English.

Gaston, Paul M. The Concept of the New South, 1865-1900. Univ. of North Carolina (Chapel Hill), 1953. Thesis: History.

_____. The New South Creed, 1865-1900. Univ. of North Carolina (Chapel Hill), 1961. Dissertation: History.

Geeder, Katherine G. Contribution of the Negro to American Culture. Univ. of Wichita, 1946. Thesis: Education. [Includes George Horton, James Weldon Johnson, Carter G. Woodson]

Genovese, Eugene D. The Limits of Agrarian Reform in the Slave South. Columbia Univ., 1959. Dissertation: History.

Gentry, Mary J. Thurber: The Life and Death of a Texas Town. Univ. of Texas (Austin), 1946. Thesis: History.

Gibson, Dorothy K. Social Life in San Antonio, 1855-1860. Univ. of Texas (Austin), 1937. Thesis: History. [Discussion of literary societies, reading rooms, a proposed literary magazine, theatrical clubs and performances]

Gilchrist, Dorothy. The Virginia Springs: Mirror of Antebellum Society. Univ. of Virginia, 1943. Thesis: History.

Gilliam, Thomas J. The Montgomery Bus Boycott of 1955-1956. Auburn Univ., 1968. Thesis: History.

Gillis, Everett A. Cultural and Literary Value of Baptist Preaching in Early Texas. Texas Christian Univ., 1939. Thesis: English.

Glascock, Harriet B. Lexington: A Cultural Center in the Eighteenth Century West. Univ. of Kentucky, 1928. Thesis: History.

Gnatz, William R. The Negro and the Populist Movement in the South. Univ. of Chicago, 1961. Thesis: History.

Goldman, Pauline S. Letters from Three Members of Terry's Texas Rangers, 1861 to 1865. Univ. of Texas (Austin), 1930. Thesis: History.

Gordon, Dudley M. The History of Cleburne (Texas). Univ. of Texas (Austin), 1929. Thesis: History. [One chapter on newspapers]

Graf, Sr. Mary L., O.S.U. Negro Suffrage in the South, 1870-1900. Marquette Univ., 1951. Thesis: History.

Graham, Julian B. A History of the Years of Agrarian Unrest, 1865-1896, Prepared for High School Use (Parts I and II). New York Univ., 1956. Dissertation: History.

Grant, Ben O. The Early History of Shackelford County (Texas): A Thesis. Hardin-Simmons Univ., 1936. Thesis: History.

Gray, Robert. Southern Powderkeg: Study of the Creek and Cherokee Nations, 1763-1796. Case Western Reserve Univ., 1950. Thesis: History.

Gray, Sarah S. The German-American Community of Fredericksburg, Texas, and Its Assimilation. Univ. of Texas (Austin), 1929. Thesis: Sociology. [Some discussion of reading tastes with reference to newspapers and magazines]

Greenwood, Walter B. Mike Fink, An American Legend. Columbia Univ., 1935. Thesis: English.

Griffin, James D. Savannah, Georgia, during The Civil War. Univ. of Georgia, 1963. Dissertation: History.

Griffin, William A. Antebellum Elizabeth City (N.C.). East Carolina Univ., 1969. Thesis: History.

Griffith, Elwe. A Survey of Books and Magazines Found in Alexandria, Tennessee. George Peabody College, 1927. Thesis: English.

Griffith, Lucille B. The Virginia House of Burgesses, 1750-1844. Brown Univ., 1957. Dissertation: History.

Grindereng, Robert O. Political and Military Events that Saved Kentucky for the Union, 1861-1862. Miami Univ. (Ohio), 1956. Thesis: History.

Grossbach, Barry L. The Scopes Trial: A Turning Point in American Thought? Indiana Univ. (Bloomington), 1964. Dissertation: English.

Guinn, Ernest E. A History of Cleburne, Texas. Univ. of Texas (Austin), 1950. Thesis: History.

Haenel, Olga B.M. A Social History of Baytown, Texas, 1912-1956. Univ. of Texas (Austin), 1956. Thesis: History.

Hair, William I. The Agrarian Protest in Louisiana, 1877-1900. Louisiana State Univ., 1962. Dissertation: History. [Considers this a period of unequalled biracial class consciousness in Louisiana]

Hale, Charles. Political Leadership in Texas during Reconstruction. Lamar Univ., 1965. Thesis: History.

Hale, Myron Q. American Conservatism: Conventionalism, Historicism, Functionalism. Columbia Univ., 1958. Dissertation: Political Science. [Included John C. Calhoun]

Hall, Hines H. The Montgomery Race Conference of 1900: Focal Point of Racial Attitudes at the Turn of the Century. Auburn Univ., 1965. Thesis: History.

Hall, V.S. A Cultural and Recreational History of Corpus Christi, Texas. Univ. of Texas (Austin), 1959. Thesis: History.

Hamilton, Charles G. Mississippi Politics in the Progressive Era, 1904-1920. Vanderbilt Univ., 1958. Dissertation: History.

Hammond, Barbara F. Confederate Government and Mexico: Diplomatic Relations, 1861-1865. North Texas State Univ., 1956. Thesis: History.

Handy, Mary O. A History of Fort Sam Houston. Univ. of Texas (Austin), 1949. Thesis: History.

Hanna, Margaret. Drain of Talent out of Georgia and South Carolina. Kent State Univ., 1957. Thesis: Sociology and Anthropology.

Hannum, Sharon E. Confederate Cavaliers: The Myth in War and Defeat. Rice Univ., 1965. Dissertation: History.

Harkness, Donald R. Crosscurrents: American Anti-Democracy from Jackson to the Civil War (1829-1860). Univ. of Minnesota, 1955. Dissertation: Political Science. [Includes Southern leaders]

Harper, John H. Rousseau's Alabama Raid. Auburn Univ., 1965. Thesis: History.

Harr, John L. The Antebellum Southwest, 1815-1861. Univ. of Chicago, 1941. Dissertation: History.

Harrell, Kenneth E. The Ku Klux Klan in Louisiana, 1920-1930. Louisiana State Univ., 1966. Dissertation: History.

Harris, George E. The Drain of Talent out of Ohio and Kentucky. Kent State Univ., 1956. Thesis: Sociology.

Harry, Jewel H. A History of Chambers County (Texas). Univ. of Texas (Austin), 1940. Thesis: History.

Haskins, Ralph W. The Cotton Factor, 1800-1860: A Study in Southern Economic and Social History. Univ. of California (Berkeley), 1950. Dissertation: History.

Hatch, James R. Life and Labor in Antebellum Claiborne Parish (Louisiana). Louisiana Polytechnic Inst., 1968. Thesis: History.

Hazelwood, Claudia C.G. Forty Years as a Pageant: A Study of the Life of Zelpha Ellen Calhoun. Univ. of Texas (Austin), 1947. Thesis: History. [Partly fictionized account of a woman who migrated to Texas; cowboy dance calls, titles of some books brought to Texas]

Heitz, Flora. A Comprehensive Survey of Cultural Movements in Louisville (Kentucky) during the Nineteenth Century. Univ. of Louisville, 1937. Thesis: History.

Held, Ray E. Spanish Florida in American Historiography, 1821-1921. Univ. of Florida, 1955. Dissertation: History.

Helm, Susan F. Cultural Development of Tennessee, 1865-1900. George Peabody College, 1937. Thesis: History.

Henderson, Adele. Smith County, Texas: Its Background and History in Antebellum Days. Univ. of Texas (Austin), 1926. Thesis: History.

Henderson, Harold P. The 1946 Gubernatorial Election in Georgia. Georgia Southern College, 1967. Thesis: History.

Hendricks, George D. The Bad Men of the West. Univ. of Texas
(Austin), 1938. Thesis: English. [The West treated here
extended from Kentucky to California and doubled back to
Oklahoma; the time is the latter half of the nineteenth century.
Sources of material include books, newspaper clippings, magazine
articles, materials of historical societies and legal documents
containing testimony of witnesses.]

Hickin, Patricia E.P. Antislavery in Virginia, 1831-1861. Univ.
of Virginia, 1968. Dissertation: History. [Includes antislavery stand of *Richmond Whig*]

Hieronymus, Frank L. For Now and Forever: The Chaplains of the
Confederate States Army. Univ. of California (Los Angeles),
1964. Dissertation: History.

Hill, Marilynn W. A History of the Jewish Involvement in the Dallas
[Texas] Community. Southern Methodist Univ., 1967. Thesis:
History. [Considerable cultural information]

Holden, William C., translator. Fray Vicente Santa María:
Historical Account of the Colony of Nuevo Santander and Coast
of the Seno Mexicano, with Introduction and Annotations. Univ.
of Texas (Austin), 1924. Thesis: History. [Indians in area
which is now Texas: some analysis of their languages and some
quotations of their poems and speeches]

_____. Frontier Problems and Movements in West Texas, 1846-1900.
Univ. of Texas (Austin), 1927. Dissertation: History.
[Discussion of square dances and folk humor and of dramatic
clubs and the little theater movement]

Holmes, Oliver W. Stagecoach and Mail From Colonial Days to 1820.
Columbia Univ., 1956. Dissertation: History.

Hoole, William S. The Literary and Cultural Background of
Charleston [S.C.], 1830-1860. Duke Univ., 1934. Dissertation: English.

Hopkins, Jerry B. Mordecai F. Ham: Prohibition and Sensational
Evangelism in Kentucky, 1914-1915. Eastern Kentucky Univ.,
1969. Thesis: History.

Horton, Finas W. A History of Ector County, Texas. Univ. of
Texas (Austin), 1950. Thesis: History.

Howard, Anne. North Carolina's Opposition to the Anti-Evolution
Crusade: 1920-1927. Univ. of California (Riverside), 1967.
Thesis: History.

Hughes, Daisy L. The Use of American History in Motion Pictures.
Univ. of Texas (Austin), 1937. Thesis: History. [Includes
"Daniel Boone," "So Red the Rose," and "Under Southern Stars"]

Hughes, Delos D. The Influence of Ideas on Political Action:
The Agrarian Idea in American Politics. Univ. of North
Carolina (Chapel Hill), 1964. Dissertation: Political
Science. [Includes Jefferson]

Hurst, Lora R. The Effect of Military Operations upon Civilian
Life in Winchester, Virginia, during the Civil War. Kent
State Univ., 1953. Thesis: History.

Hynds, Ernest C., Jr. Antebellum Athens and Clarke County, Georgia.
Univ. of Georgia, 1961. Dissertation: History.

Irby, James A. Confederate Austin [Texas], 1861-1865. Univ. of
Texas (Austin), 1953. Thesis: History.
Jabbs, Theodore H. The Lost Cause: Some Southern Opinion between
1865 and 1900 about Why the Confederacy Lost the Civil War.
Univ. of North Carolina (Chapel Hill), 1967. Thesis: History.
[John Esten Cooke, William Falconer, and T.N. Page; also
discusses writings of several Confederate officers]
Jackson, Kenneth T. The Decline of the Ku Klux Klan, 1924-1932.
Univ. of Chicago, 1963. Thesis: History.
_____. The Ku Klux Klan in the City, 1915-1930. Univ. of Chicago,
1966. Dissertation: History.
James, Dorris C. Antebellum Natchez. Univ. of Texas, 1964.
Dissertation: History.
Jaros, Carol W. The Drain of Eminent Persons out of Louisiana and
Mississippi. Kent State Univ., 1960. Thesis: Sociology and
Anthropology.
Jeffery, Gretchen M. Little Rock Crisis. North Texas State Univ.,
1965. Thesis: History.
Jenkins, John A. To Find A Land: The Modern South and the Agrarian
Tradition. Indiana Univ., 1965. Dissertation: History.
[Includes literature of 1920's and 1930's]
Johns, John E. Florida in the Confederacy. Univ. of North Carolina
(Chapel Hill), 1959. Dissertation: History.
Johnson, LeRoy. The Evolution Controversy during the 1920's.
New York Univ., 1954. Dissertation: History.
Jones, Bobby F. A Cultural Middle Passage: Slave Marriage and
Family in the Antebellum South. Univ. of North Carolina
(Chapel Hill), 1965. Dissertation: History.
Jones, Horace P. Southern Opinion on the Crimean War. Univ. of
Mississippi, 1969. Dissertation: History.
Jones, Newton B. Charlottesville and Albemarle County, Virginia,
1819-1860. Univ. of Virginia, 1950. Dissertation: History.
Jones, Selena H. Southern Indians. Jacksonville State Univ.,
1964. Thesis: History.
Jordon, Edith M. History of Parker County (Texas). Univ. of
Texas (Austin), 1935. Thesis: History. [Brief mention of
newspaper; story of Cynthia Ann Parker]
Jordan, H.G. Farm Life in Webster Parish, Louisiana, 1870-1873,
as Reflected in the Diary of Samuel Worth Jones. Louisiana
Polytechnic Inst., 1968. Thesis: History.
Jordan, Winthrop D. White over Black: The Attitudes of the
American Colonists Toward the Negro, to 1784. Brown Univ.,
1960. Dissertation: History.
Juricek, John T. Indian Policy in Proprietary South Carolina:
1670-1693. Univ. of Chicago, 1962. Thesis: History.
Karon, Bertram P. A Comparative Study of the Personality Structures
and Problems of Northern and Southern Negroes in Terms of the
Effects of Differential Caste Sanctions. Princeton Univ.,
1957. Dissertation: Sociology.
Keith, Ruby. Early History of Dallas (Texas). Univ. of Texas
(Austin), 1930. Thesis: History. [Brief account of first
newspaper]
Kennicott, Patrick C. Negro Antislavery Speakers in America.
Florida State Univ., 1967. Dissertation: History. [84
speakers, a few from the South]

Kienitz, John F. The Generation of the 1850's, 1860's, and 1870's in the Fine Arts of the United States in Relation to Parallel Phases of American Culture. Univ. of Wisconsin, 1938. Dissertation: Fine Arts. [Includes discussion of J.B. Cabell, Kate Chopin, Olive Dargan, Ellen Glasgow, Lafcadio Hearn, H.L. Mencken, O. Henry, and T.N. Page]

Kimbrough, William C. A History of Clay County (Texas). Hardin-Simmons Univ., 1942. Thesis: History.

Kirkpatrick, Arthur R. Missouri, The Twelfth Confederate State. Univ. of Missouri, 1954. Dissertation: History. [Its ordeals as a border state]

Kmen, Henry A. Singing and Dancing in New Orleans: A Social History of the Birth and Growth of Balls and Opera, 1791-1841. Tulane Univ., 1961. Dissertation: History.

Knipmeyer, William B. Settlement Succession in Eastern French Louisiana. Louisiana State Univ., 1956. Dissertation: Geography.

Knox, J.W. Democratic Schism in Texas, 1952-1957: Emergence of National Liberalism in the South. North Texas State Univ., 1959. Thesis: History.

Koen, J.C. A Social and Economic History of Palo Pinto County (Texas). Hardin-Simmons Univ., 1949. Thesis: History.

Konrad, William R. The Diminishing Influence of German Culture in New Orleans Life since 1865. Tulane Univ., 1940. Thesis: German.

Koyama, Yukinori. The Ku Klux Klan in South Carolina during Reconstruction. Roosevelt Univ., 1970. Thesis: History.

Krapp, Ruth L. The Virginia Frontier from 1700 to 1776. Univ. of Cincinnati, 1923. Thesis: History.

Kupersanin, Michael. The Drain of Talent out of Texas and Arkansas. Kent State Univ., 1959. Thesis: Sociology.

Lacey, Mary F. Intellectual Activities of Vicksburg prior to 1860. [School unknown], 1938. Thesis: History. [Educational facilities, newspapers, books and libraries, writers and publications, organizations, lectures, entertainment, and fine arts]

Lacy, Eric R., Sr. Sectionalism in East Tennessee, 1796-1861. Univ. of Georgia, 1963. Dissertation: History.

Laing, James T. The Drain of Talent out of the Virginias. Kent State Univ., 1956. Thesis: Sociology and Anthropology.

Lake, Donald M. The Southern Baptist View of the Church: An Analysis of the Ecclesiology of the Churches Affiliated with the Southern Baptist Convention Based on Selected Literature between 1925 and 1963. Univ. of Iowa, 1967. Dissertation: Religion.

Landers, E.M. A Short History of Taylor County (Texas). Hardin-Simmons Univ., 1929. Thesis: History. [Reviews frontier background of this Texas County in 1870's with attention to the development of schools, churches, and newspapers]

Lane, John D. The Charleston Club. Univ. of Virginia, 1924. Thesis: English.

Lapp, Rudolph M. The Southern Poor White, 1830-1860. Univ. of California (Berkeley), 1950. Thesis: History.

_____. The Antebellum Poor Whites of the South Atlantic States. Univ. of California (Berkeley), 1957. Dissertation: History.

Larson, Allan L. Southern Demagogues: A Study in Charismatic Leadership. Northwestern Univ., 1964. Dissertation: Political Science. [Includes Theodore Bilbo, Huey Long, and Eugene Talmadge]

Lawlor, Virginia G. Historical Background of Cultural Forces in Wilson Country, Tenn. Vanderbilt Univ., 1961. Thesis: English.

Lawson, Elmer. The History of the North Carolina Literary Fund, 1776-1868. Univ. of North Carolina (Chapel Hill), 1956. Dissertation: Education.

Leach, Joseph. The Establishment of the Texas Tradition: The Origins of a Sectional Character Type before 1860. Yale Univ., 1948. Dissertation: American Studies.

Leard, Robert B. Civil War Attempts at Negro Colonization. Univ. of California (Berkeley), 1949. Thesis: History.

Ledbetter, Billy D. Confederate Texas: A Political Study. North Texas State Univ., 1969. Thesis: History.

Lee, Charles R., Jr. The Confederate Constitutions. Univ. of North Carolina (Chapel Hill), 1961. Dissertation: History. [Issues and problems of framing and adoption]

Leftwich, Rodney L. Arts and Crafts of the Cherokee. Bradley Univ., 1952. Dissertation: Education.

Lengert, Margaret E. The History of Milan County [Texas]. Univ. of Texas (Austin), 1949. Thesis: History.

Lewis, Grace L. A History of Real County, Texas. Univ. of Texas (Austin), 1956. Thesis: History.

Lewis, Virginia E. Fifty Years of Politics in Memphis, 1900-1950. New York Univ., 1955. Dissertation: Political Science.

Lightfoot, Billy B. The History of Comanche County, Texas, to 1920. Univ. of Texas (Austin), 1949. Thesis: History.

Liles, Vernen. Pioneering on the Plains: The History of Martin County, Texas. Univ. of Texas (Austin), 1953. Thesis: History.

Lines, Stiles B. Slaves and Churchmen: The Work of the Episcopal Church among Southern Negroes, 1830-1860. Columbia Univ., 1960. Dissertation: Religion.

Livermore, Shaw, Jr. The Twilight of Federalism. Univ. of Wisconsin, 1958. Dissertation: History. [Includes Jefferson]

Loewen, James W. The Mississippi Chinese. Harvard Univ., 1967. Dissertation: Sociology.

Long, Melvin D., Jr. Alabama in the Formation of the Confederacy. Univ. of Florida, 1959. Dissertation: History.

Long, Stanton C. Early Nineteenth Century El Paso [Texas]. Univ. of Texas (Austin), 1953. Thesis: History.

Longton, William H. Some Aspects of Intellectual Activity in Antebellum South Carolina, 1830-1860: An Introductory Study. Univ. of North Carolina (Chapel Hill), 1969. Dissertation: History.

Mackenzie, Kenneth M. American Methodism and Imperialism (1865-1900). New York Univ., 1957. Dissertation: History. [Mentions new unity between North and South "as fulfillment of a Divine Mission" to Methodists]

[215]

Mahan, Terrance L. Virginia Reaction to British Policy, 1763-1776. Univ. of Wisconsin, 1960, Dissertation: History.

Malone, Billy C. An Early History of Austin, Texas. Univ. of Texas (Austin), 1958. Thesis: History.

Malone, Henry T. A Social History of the Eastern Cherokee Indians from the Revolution to the Removal. Emory Univ., 1952. Dissertation: History.

Mangrum, Claude T. The Drain of Talent out of North Carolina and Tennessee. Kent State Univ., 1958. Thesis: Sociology and Anthropology.

Manthei, William E. Charleston, South Carolina: Economic and Social Life, 1855-1865. Lamar Univ., 1964. Thesis: History.

Marshall, Elmer G. The History of Brazos County, Texas. Univ. of Texas (Austin), 1937. Thesis: History. [Several pages of Negro field songs]

Martin, James L. History of Goliad (Texas) from 1836 to 1880. Univ. of Texas (Austin), 1937. Thesis: History.

Martone, William E. Leaders in America: 1789-1865. State Univ. of New York (Brockport), 1961. Thesis: Education. [Includes Andrew Jackson, Thomas Jefferson, James Madison, and George Washington]

Mattingly, Caroline. The American Gentleman in Theory and Practice. Univ. of Washington, 1939. Dissertation: English. [Chapter IV discusses the Southern gentleman]

Mauldin, William D. History of Dallas County, Texas. Univ. of Texas (Austin), 1938. Thesis: History.

Mayfield, Selby N. Reading Interests in New Orleans, 1848-1942. Tulane Univ., 1942. Thesis: Education.

McClure, Charles B. A History of Randall County and the T Anchor Ranch. Univ. of Texas (Austin), 1930. Thesis: History. [Includes unpublished poems and stories by Judge L. Gough]

McCowen, George S., Jr. The British Occupation of Charles Town, 1780-1782. Emory Univ., 1966. Dissertation: History. [Sources include *South Carolina and American General Gazette* and *Royal South Carolina Gazette*]

McDaniel, Curtis E. Educational and Social Interests of the Grange in Texas, 1873-1905. Univ. of Texas (Austin), 1938. Thesis: History. [Discussion of Grange newspaper and Grange libraries which included any interesting literature]

McDonald, Mary L. The History of Lubbock County, Texas. Univ. of Texas (Austin), 1942. Thesis: History.

McDonald, Timothy G. Southern Democratic Congressmen and the First World War, August 1914-April 1917: The Public Record of Their Support for or Opposition to Wilson's Policies. Univ. of Washington, 1962. Dissertation: History. [Based on *Congressional Record* and New York *Times*]

McEachern, Hugh A. Cowboy Heroes and the Western Myth. Univ. of North Carolina (Chapel Hill), 1964. Thesis: English.

McFarland, Daniel M. Rip Van Winkle: Political Evolution in North Carolina, 1815-1835. Univ. of Pennsylvania, 1954. Dissertation: History.

McKinney, Mary E. The Southwestern Town. Univ. of Texas (Austin), 1952. Thesis: History.

Menn, Joseph K. The Large Slaveholders of the Deep South, 1860. Univ. of Texas (Austin), 1964. Dissertation: History.

Merseburger, Marion. A Political History of Houston, Texas, during the Reconstruction Period as Recorded by the Press: 1868-1873. Rice Univ., 1950. Thesis: History.

Meyer, Duane G. The Scottish Highlanders in North Carolina, 1733-1776. State Univ. of Iowa, 1956. Dissertation: History.

Mitchell, Bernard E. A History of Printing in Colonial Virginia. College of William and Mary, 1929. Thesis: English.

Mitchell, Ernest G. History of Coleman County (Texas). Univ. of Texas (Austin), 1949. Thesis: History.

Miles, James C. Fort Worth and World War I. Southern Methodist Univ., 1946. Thesis: History.

Miles, Jim T. Importance of Charleston in Southern History, 1670-1860. North Texas State Univ., 1940. Thesis: History.

Minton, Eli D. Constitutional Reform during the Radical Reconstruction of the South Atlantic States. North Texas State Univ., 1958. Thesis: History.

Mobley, Edward D. An Inventory of Cultural Activities in Selected Georgia Cities. Florida State Univ., 1967. Dissertation: Fine Arts.

Moellering, Arwerd M. A History of Guadalupe County, Texas. Univ. of Texas (Austin), 1938. Thesis: History.

Mondy, Robert W. A History of Lincoln Parish, Louisiana. Univ. of Texas (Austin), 1934. Thesis: History.

Moore, Carl C., Jr. The Story of Southern Unity: A Survey of the Political Communications Pattern and the Unifying of the Confederate People. State Univ. of New York (Brockport), 1962. Thesis: Education.

Moore, Robert J. Historians' Interpretations of the Reconstruction Period in American History. Boston Univ., 1961. Dissertation: History.

Moorer, Virginia C.H. The Free Negro in Texas, 1845-1860. Lamar Univ., 1969. Thesis: History.

Morrow, Ralph E. The Methodist Episcopal Church, The South and Reconstruction, 1865-1880. Indiana Univ., 1954. Dissertation: History.

Morse, Leonard F. History of Mobile (Alabama), 1820-1860. Northwestern Univ., 1930. Thesis: History. [Includes discussion of Octavia Walton Levert and Augusta Evans Wilson]

Moseley, Clement C. The Political Influence of the Ku Klux Klan in Georgia, 1815-1925. Georgia Southern College, 1965. Thesis: History.

Mullin, Gerald W., Jr. Patterns of Slave Behavior in Eighteenth Century Virginia. Univ. of California (Berkeley), 1968. Dissertation: History.

Murray, Robert K. Sherman: Slavery and the South. Ohio State Univ., 1947. Thesis: English.

Mysliwiec, Chester P. A History of Karnes County, Texas. Univ. of Texas (Austin), 1952. Thesis: History.

Nadelhaft, Jerome J. The Revolutionary Era in South Carolina, 1775-1788. Univ. of Wisconsin, 1965. Dissertation: History.

Nau, John F. The German People of New Orleans, 1850-1900. Univ. of South Carolina, 1954. Dissertation: History. [Includes theater and other aspects of cultural background]

[217]

Neelley, Robert L. Wichita Falls (Texas) from Frontier Settlement to City. Southern Methodist Univ., 1964. Thesis: History.

Nelson, Mary L. Benevolent Aspects of the "Peculiar Institution" in Mississippi. Mississippi State Univ., 1965. Thesis: History.

Neumann, Ronald. Cowboy Violence From Texas to Kansas, 1865-1885. Univ. of California (Riverside), 1966. Thesis: History.

Neyland, Leedell W. The Negro in Louisiana since 1900: An Economic and Social Study. New York Univ., 1959. Dissertation: History.

Nichols, David A. Music, Culture, and the Revolution in Eighteenth Century Virginia. Roosevelt Univ., 1970. Thesis: History.

Niehans, Earl F. The Irish in New Orleans, 1803-1862. Tulane Univ., 1961. Dissertation: History.

Nolen, Claude H. Aftermath of Slavery: Southern Attitudes toward Negroes, 1865-1900. Univ. of Texas (Austin), 1963. Dissertation: History.

Norred, Charlotte E. Regionalism vs. Metropolitanism in 1929: A Study in Critical Attitudes. Vanderbilt Univ., 1939. Thesis: English. [Discusses literary pages of the Nashville *Tennessean*, edited by Donald Davidson]

Norton, Donnie, Jr. The Non-Slaveholding People of the Antebellum South, 1830-1860. Southern Methodist Univ., 1942. Thesis: History. [Chapter 4 deals with literary culture]

Norton, Herman A. The Organization and Function of the Confederate Military Chaplaincy, 1861-1865. Vanderbilt Univ., 1956. Dissertation: History.

O'Donnell, James H. III. The Southern Indians in the War of Independence, 1775-1783. Duke Univ., 1963. Dissertation: History.

O'Glee, John C. The Confederate Naval Department and Its Operation in New Orleans. North Texas State Univ., 1960. Thesis: History.

Ortiz, Carmelita L. English Influence on the Spanish of Tampa. Univ. of Florida, 1947. Thesis: Spanish.

Osborne, Fred Y. A Study of Social and Religious Activities in Dallas County (Texas), 1841-1861. Southern Methodist Univ., 1947. Thesis: History. [Music, dramatics, oratory]

Osburn, John D. A History of the Present Red River County, Texas, Area through 1845. Southern Methodist Univ., 1954. Thesis: History.

Osdell, John G., Jr. Cotton Mills, Labor, and the Southern Mind: 1880-1930. Tulane Univ., 1966. Dissertation: History.

Osterweis, Rollin G. Patterns of Romanticism in the Antebellum South. Yale Univ., 1946. Dissertation: History. [Discusses antebellum Southern reading taste]

Owens, Lawrence W. A Survey of Books, Magazines and Papers in Mize, Mississippi. George Peabody College, 1932. Thesis: English.

Owens, Raymond E. Preaching in a Revivalist Tradition: The Influence of Revivalism on Southern Baptist Preaching, 1845-1877. Union Theological Seminary (N.Y.), 1967. Dissertation: English.

Palmer, Paul C. Racial Segregation during Reconstruction: The Evolution of Laws and Practices in Southern States. North Texas State Univ., 1958. Thesis: History.

Papis, Helena C. The Southerner of the Nineteenth Century: How Did He Really See Himself? Univ. of California (Riverside), 1966. Thesis: History.

Partin, James G. A History of Nacogdoches and Nacogdoches County, Texas, to 1877. Univ. of Texas (Austin), 1968. Thesis: History.

Paul, Charles L. Colonial Beaufort: The History of a North Carolina Town. East Carolina Univ., 1965. Thesis: History.

Pearce, Bessie M. Texas through Women's Eyes, 1823-1860. Univ. of Texas, 1965. Dissertation: English. [Harriet A. Ames, Amelia E. Barr, Mrs. William Leslie Eubank, Augusta Evans Wilson, Mrs. Dilve Rose Harris, Mary Austin Holley, Mrs. M.C. Houston, Mary A. Maverick, Mary Crownover Rabb, Elise Tvede Wearenskjold; sources are reminiscences, autobiographies, diaries, and a few novels]

Peavy, Josephine C. A History of Newton County, Texas. Univ. of Texas (Austin), 1942. Thesis: History.

Peltier, James C. Confederate Natchez, 1861-1863. Louisiana State Univ., 1948. Thesis: History.

Pendle, Frank E.J. Southern Populism and Tenancy. Kent State Univ., 1969. Thesis: History.

Pendley, Berry H. Savannah, Georgia, during Reconstruction, 1865-1869. West Georgia College, 1969. Thesis: History.

Perkins, William C. A History of Wheeler County, Texas. Univ. of Texas, 1938. Thesis: History. [Some discussion of newspapers]

Perman, Michael. Southern Politics and American Reunion, 1865-1868. Univ. of Chicago, 1969. Dissertation: History.

Pfaff, Daniel W. The Supreme Court, Civil Rights, and Press Freedom: Another Look at the Negro Revolution. Pennsylvania State Univ., 1968. Thesis: Journalism.

Phillips, Edward H. The Lower Shenandoah Valley during the Civil War: The Impact of War upon the Civilian Population and upon Civil Institutions. Univ. of North Carolina (Chapel Hill), 1958. Dissertation: History.

Phillips, Jenny E.D. Two Decades of Discord: An Examination of the Southern Defense of Slavery, 1850-1860, 1950-1960. Louisiana Polytechnic Inst., 1960. Thesis: History. [Compares arguments of 1850-60 to those of 1950-60]

Phipps, Joe K. The Romanticized Cowboy as a National Hero. Univ. of Texas (Austin), 1950. Thesis: English.

Platzker, Dorris A. Public Vistas, Private Visions: Aspects of the Modern American Political Imagination. Yale Univ., 1966. Dissertation: English. [Closing section deals with works of Robert Penn Warren--novels, poems, essays]

Pool, William C. The History of Bosque County (Texas). Univ. of Texas (Austin), 1946. Thesis: History.

Porter, Joseph M. The Kentucky Jockey Club: Political Involvement in the Twenties. Eastern Kentucky Univ., 1969. Thesis: History.

Porterfield, Robert G., Jr. The Early History of Abilene (Texas) up to 1920. Hardin-Simmons Univ., 1969. Thesis: History.

Portre-Bobinski, Germaine. French Civilization and Culture in Natchitoches (Louisiana). George Peabody College, 1941. Dissertation: History.

Posey, James B. A History of Cherokee County (Texas). Univ. of Texas (Austin), 1928. Thesis: History.

Prestwood, Charles M. Social Ideas of Methodist Ministers in Alabama since Unification. Boston Univ., 1960. Dissertation: Religion.

Preyer, Norris W. The Congressional Fight over the Admission of Kentucky, Tennessee, Louisiana, and Alabama into the Union. Univ. of Virginia, 1950. Thesis: History.

Proctor, Emerson. Georgia Baptists: Organization and Division, 1772-1840. Georgia Southern College, 1969. Thesis: History.

Prouse, Frances D. A History of Gray County, Texas. Univ. of Texas (Austin), 1957. Thesis: History.

Pulley, Raymond H. Old Virginia Restored: An Interpretation of the Progressive Impulse. Univ. of Virginia, 1966. Dissertation: History.

Rankin, Dan F. The Role of the Negro Office Holders in the Reconstruction of the Southwest. North Texas State Univ., 1954. Thesis: History.

Rastegar, Carol C. The Sambo Image: Myth or Reality. Univ. of California (Los Angeles), 1968. Thesis: History. [An examination of the "plantation myth" in history]

Rawson, Donald M. Party Politics in Mississippi, 1850-1860. Vanderbilt Univ., 1964. Dissertation: History.

Reagan, Hugh D. The Presidential Campaign of 1928 in Alabama. Univ. of Texas, 1961. Dissertation: History.

Real, Matilda M. A History of Kerr County, Texas. Univ. of Texas (Austin), 1942. Thesis: History. [Discussion of literary societies, newspapers, and public library]

Reese, James V. A History of Hill County, Texas to 1873. Univ. of Texas (Austin), 1961. Thesis: History.

Refsell, Oliver M. The Massies of Virginia: A Documentary History of a Planter Family. Univ. of Texas (Austin), 1959. Dissertation: History.

Reinders, Robert C. A Social History of New Orleans, 1850-1860. Univ. of Texas (Austin), 1957. Dissertation: History. [Includes press, opera, and education]

Reitveld, Ronald D. The Moral Issue of Slavery in American Politics, 1854-1860. Univ. of Illinois, 1967. Dissertation: History.

Rice, Arnold S. The Southern Wing of the Ku Klux Klan in American Politics, 1915-1928. Indiana Univ. (Bloomington), 1959. Dissertation: History.

Richardson, James T. Social Changes in Hunt County (Texas) for the Decade 1920 to 1930. Univ. of Texas (Austin), 1933. Thesis: Sociology. [Some discussion of little theaters and of Greenville Public Library; statistical report on reading of newspapers and magazines]

Richardson, Joe M. The Negro in the Reconstruction of Florida. Florida State Univ., 1963. Dissertation: History.

Ringold, May S. The Role of the State Legislatures in the Confederacy. Emory Univ., 1956. Dissertation: History.

Risjord, Normal K. The Old Republicans: Southern Conservatives in Congress, 1806-1824. Univ. of Virginia, 1960. Dissertation: History.

Robbins, John B. Confederate Nationalism: Politics and Government in the Confederate South, 1861-1865. Rice Univ., 1964. Dissertation: History.

Robinson, Avis P. Social Conditions of Slavery as Taken from Slave Narratives. Howard Univ., 1938. Thesis: English. [Biographies written by ex-slaves and writers to whom such biographies were dictated form a part of the source material for this thesis]

Robinson, Clayton R. The Impact of the City of Rural Immigrants to Memphis, 1880-1940. Univ. of Minnesota, 1967. Dissertation: English. [Part is a discussion of influence of cultural patterns on Southern writers, including William Faulkner]

Rochelle, John R. Port Arthur (Texas): A History of Its Port to 1963. Lamar Univ., 1969. Thesis: History.

Roeder, Robert E. New Orleans Merchants--1790 to 1837. Harvard Univ., 1959. Dissertation: History.

Roethler, Michael D. Negro Slavery among the Cherokee Indians, 1540-1866. Fordham Univ., 1964. Dissertation: History.

Rogers, Albert A. Family Life in Eighteenth Century Virginia. Univ. of Virginia, 1940. Dissertation: History.

Rogers, William W. Agrarianism in Alabama, 1865-1896. Univ. of North Carolina (Chapel Hill), 1959. Dissertation: History.

Rogin, Michael P. McCarthyism and Agrarian Radicalism. Univ. of Chicago, 1962. Dissertation: Political Science.

Rosenberger, Daniel G. An Examination of the Perpetuation of Southern United States Institutions in British Honduras by a Colony of Ex-Confederates. New York Univ., 1958. Dissertation: Education.

Rowell, Elsie. The Social and Cultural Contributions of the Germans in Louisville (Kentucky) from 1848-1855. Univ. of Kentucky, 1941. Thesis: History.

Ryland, Florence. Some Aspects of Virginia Life as Revealed in Letters and Diaries, 1861-1865. Columbia Univ., 1932. Thesis: History.

St. Romain, Lillian S. A History of Lott (Texas) and Its Vicinity. Univ. of Texas (Austin), 1941. Thesis: History. [Scattered accounts of newspapers; mention of book clubs]

Sartin, John R. History of Copiah County (Mississippi) to 1900. Mississippi College, 1959. Thesis: History.

Saunders, Robert M. The Idealogy of Southern Populists, 1892-1895. Univ. of Virginia, 1967. Dissertation: History.

Schlaefer, Mary B.V. An Account of the Operations of the Book Store and Publishing Business of W.J. Duffie. Univ. of South Carolina, 1943. Thesis: English.

Schnell, Kempes Y. Court Cases Involving Slavery: A Study of the Application of Anti-Slavery Thought to Judicial Argument. Univ. of Michigan, 1955. Dissertation: History.

Schoppe, Lillian G. The History of Bee County, Texas. Univ. of Texas (Austin), 1939. Thesis: History.

Schuyler, L.R. The Liberty of the Press in the American Colonies. New York Univ., 1904. Dissertation: History.

Schwettman, Martin W. The Discovery and Early Development of the Big Lake Oil Field (Texas). Univ. of Texas (Austin), 1941. Thesis: History. [Some oil field legends included]

Scott, Zelma M. The History of Coryell County (Texas) to 1920. Univ. of Texas (Austin), 1946. Thesis: History. [Some discussion of newspapers and of theatrical presentations]

Sergeant, George W. Early History of Tarrant County. Univ. of Texas (Austin), 1953. Thesis: History.

Sheehan, Bernard W. Civilization and the American Indian in the Thought of the Jeffersonian Era. Univ. of Virginia, 1965. Dissertation: History. [Includes Jefferson and John Filson]

Sibley, Marilyn M. Travelers in Texas, 1761-1860. Rice Univ., 1965. Dissertation: History.

Smith, Florence E. The Populist Movement and Its Influence in North Carolina. Univ. of Chicago, 1929. Dissertation: History.

Smith, Glenn C. Pamphleteers and the American Revolution in Virginia, 1752-1776. Univ. of Virginia, 1941. Dissertation: History. [Thomas Jefferson, John Randolph]

Smith, James D. Virginia during Reconstruction, 1854-1870: A Political, Economic and Social Study. Univ. of Virginia, 1960. Dissertation: History.

Smith, Joe O. Reading Material in Homes of Hamilton County, Tennessee, High School Students. George Peabody College, 1930. Thesis: English.

Smith, Leonard G. A History of Runnels County, Texas, 1683-1960. Trinity Univ. (Texas), 1963. Thesis: History.

Smith, Robert. Cultural Activities in Ten Florida Cities. Florida State Univ., 1963. Dissertation: Music. [Art, dance, dramatic art, and music based on 1960 census]

Smith, Robert F. Confederate Attempts to Influence Public Opinion in Arkansas, 1861-1865. Univ. of Arkansas, 1953. Thesis: History.

Smyer, Joe P. A History of McMullen County, Texas. Univ. of Texas (Austin), 1952. Thesis: History.

Sonderegger, Richard P. The Southern Frontier from the Founding of Georgia to the End of King George's War. Univ. of Michigan, 1964. Dissertation: History.

Sonne, Niels H. Liberal Kentucky, 1780-1828. Columbia Univ., 1939. Dissertation: Philosophy.

Southwell, Sam B. A Social and Literary History of Austin from 1881 to 1896. Univ. of Texas (Austin), 1949. Thesis: English.

Spain, Rufus B. Attitudes and Reactions of Southern Baptists to Certain Problems of Society, 1865-1900. Vanderbilt Univ., 1961. Dissertation: History.

Spiers, Patricia L. The Woman Suffrage Movement in New Orleans. Southeastern Louisiana Univ., 1965. Thesis: History.

Stasney, Mollie E. The Czechs in Texas. Univ. of Texas (Austin),
    1938. Thesis: History. [Discussion of dramatic societies,
    newspapers and writers, language, etc.]
Stavinsky, Leonard P. The Negro Artisan in the South Atlantic
    States, 1800-1860: A Study of Status and Economic Opportunity
    with Special Reference to Charleston (S.C.). Columbia Univ.,
    1958. Dissertation: History.
Stephens, Alonzo T. An Account of the Attempts at Establishing
    a Religious Hegemony in Colonial North Carolina, 1663-1773.
    Univ. of Pittsburgh, 1955. Dissertation: History.
Stewart, Martha M. Amusements in the Old South. Southern Methodist
    Univ., 1939. Thesis: History.
Storey, John W. The Negro in Southern Baptist Thought, 1865-1900.
    Univ. of Kentucky, 1968. Dissertation: History.
Straka, Gerald M. The Influence of Thomas Carlyle on the Old South.
    Univ. of Virginia, 1954. Thesis: History.
Strickland, Rex W. History of Fannin County (Texas), 1836-43.
    Southern Methodist Univ., 1929. Thesis: History.
Suhler, Samuel A. Significant Questions Relating to the History
    of Austin, Texas, to 1906. Univ. of Texas (Austin), 1966.
    Dissertation: History.
Sumerline, Oliver W. The History of Bastrop, Texas (1851-1935).
    Univ. of Texas (Austin), 1963. Thesis: History. [Based
    on the files of the Colorado *Reveille* and the Bastrop
    Advertiser]
Sutton, Robert P. The Virginia Constitutional Convention of 1829-
    30: A Profile Analysis of Late-Jeffersonian Virginia. Univ.
    of Virginia, 1967. Dissertation: History.
Swanson, Donald L. The Atlanta Campaign. North Texas State Univ.,
    1961. Thesis: History.
Sweat, Edward F. The Free Negro in Antebellum Georgia. Indiana
    Univ., 1957. Dissertation: History.
Swim, Sammil E. The Church and the Segregation Crisis in the South.
    North Texas State Univ., 1960. Thesis: History.
Swinney, Everette. Suppressing the Ku Klux Klan: The Enforcement
    of the Reconstruction Amendments, 1820-1874. Univ. of Texas
    (Austin), 1966. Dissertation: History.
Sykes, Marion P. A Profile of Colonial Halifax County, North
    Carolina. East Carolina Univ., 1964. Thesis: History.
Taylor, Hubert V. Slavery and the Deliberations of the Presbyterian
    General Assembly, 1833-1838. Northwestern Univ., 1964.
    Dissertation: Speech. [Includes Southern arguments]
Tennis, LeGrand. Frenchmen in Colonial Virginia. Univ. of Virginia,
    1941. Dissertation: English.
Tewell, Fred. A Study of the Channels of Communication Used by One
    Hundred Negroes in Baton Rouge, Louisiana. Louisiana State
    Univ., 1956. Dissertation: Speech.
Thomas, Emory M. The Confederate State of Richmond: A Biography
    of the Capital. Rice Univ., 1966. Dissertation: History.
Thomas, James D., Jr. County Government and Administration in
    Alabama. Ohio State Univ., 1958. Dissertation: Political
    Science.

Thomasson, Eula B. Cultural Factors in the History of York County (S.C.). Winthrop College, 1937. Thesis: History.

Thompson, James H. A Nineteenth Century History of Cameron County, Texas. Univ. of Texas (Austin), 1965. Thesis: History.

Thorton, M.L. Public Printing in North Carolina from 1749 to 1815. Univ. of North Carolina (Chapel Hill), 1943. Thesis: History.

Tolson, Marjorie C. Gonzales, Birthplace of Texas Independence, 1825-1865. Univ. of Texas (Austin), 1966. Thesis: History.

Totaro, Elvera M. Ku Klux Klan: A Study of Southern Reaction to Racial Reconstruction, 1865-1871. Univ. of California (Riverside), 1957. Thesis: History.

Traynor, Martin J. Runaway Slaves in Colonial America, South Carolina, 1750-1776. Roosevelt Univ., 1970. Thesis: History.

Tregle, Joseph G., Jr. Louisiana in the Age of Jackson: A Study in Ego-Politics. Univ. of Pennsylvania, 1954. Dissertation: History.

Tricamo, John E. Tennessee Politics, 1845-1861. Columbia Univ., 1965. Dissertation: History.

Tucker, Mary L. The Negro in the Populist Movement in Alabama. Atlanta Univ., 1957. Thesis: History.

Tull, James E. A Study of Southern Baptist Landmarkism in the Light of Historical Baptist Ecclesiology. Columbia Univ., 1960. Dissertation: Religion.

Turner, Festus E. A History of Buffalo Gap (Texas). Hardin-Simmons Univ., 1951. Thesis: History.

Turner, Wallace B. Kentucky in a Decade of Change, 1850-1860. Univ. of Kentucky, 1954. Dissertation: History.

Vannerson, James T. American Pro-Slavery Arguments, 1840 to 1860. Texas Tech Univ., 1932. Thesis: History.

Vail, Marvin T. History of Grand Prairie (Texas), 1846-1941. Southern Methodist Univ., 1953. Thesis: History.

Van Schaik, Jan J. The Distribution of Books in the United States. Columbia Univ., 1941. Thesis: Business. [Brief information on the South]

Walden, H.N. History of Union County, North Carolina. Appalachian State Univ., 1963. Thesis: History.

Walker, Peter F. Citadel: Vicksburg and Its People, 1860-1865. Vanderbilt Univ., 1958. Dissertation: History.

Wall, Betty J. Confederate Prisons. North Texas State Univ., 1954. Thesis: History.

Wander, Philip C. The Image of the Negro in Three Movements: Abolitionist, Colonizationist, and Pro-Slavery. Univ. of Pittsburgh, 1968. Dissertation: Speech. [Includes *DeBow's Review*, *Southern Literary Messenger*, and *Southern Quarterly Review*]

Watson, Judge. The Economic and Cultural Development of Eastern Kentucky from 1900 to the Present. Indiana Univ. (Bloomington), 1963. Dissertation: History.

Weaver, Estella H. Difficulties in Negro Freedman Adjustment in the South, 1865-1877. Bowling Green State Univ., 1943. Thesis: History.

Weaver, Richard M. The Confederate South, 1865-1910: A Study in the Survival of a Mind and a Culture. Louisiana State Univ., 1943. Dissertation: English.

Webb, Walter P. The Great Plains (Texas). Univ. of Texas (Austin), 1932. Dissertation: History.

Weiss, A.S. The Poor Whites of the Old South (1850-1860). Brooklyn College, 1939. Thesis: History.

West, John O. To Die Like a Man: The "Good" Outlaw Tradition in the American Southwest. Univ. of Texas (Austin), 1964. Dissertation: English.

Weyand, Leonie L. Early History of Fayette County (Texas), 1822-1865. Univ. of Texas (Austin), 1932. Thesis: History. [Considerable emphasis on newspapers]

Whitaker, Hugh S. A New Day: The Effects of Negro Enfranchisement in Selected Mississippi Counties. Florida State Univ., 1965. Dissertation: Political Science.

White, Howard A. The Freedman's Bureau in Louisiana. Tulane Univ., 1956. Dissertation: History.

White, Theodore L. Social and Economic Conditions in Richmond, Virginia, April, 1861, to April, 1865. Univ. of Texas (Austin), 1936. Thesis: History. [Brief discussion of theaters and theatrical performances]

Whitten, Dolphus. A History of Hempstead County, Arkansas. Univ. of Texas (Austin), 1940. Thesis: History.

Wilcox, Louis A. The Early History of Bryan, Texas. Univ. of Texas (Austin), 1952. Thesis: History.

Wild, Philip F. South Carolina Politics: 1815-1833. Univ. of Pennsylvania, 1949. Dissertation: History. [Includes John C. Calhoun]

Williams, Amelia. A Critical Study of the Siege of the Alamo and of the Personnel of Its Defenders. Univ. of Texas (Austin), 1931. Dissertation: History. [Biographical sketches of leaders at Alamo]

Williams, Clanton W. History of Montgomery, Alabama, 1817-1846. Vanderbilt Univ., 1938. Dissertation: History.

Williams, David A. Political Alignments in Colonial Virginia, 1698-1750. Northwestern Univ., 1959. Dissertation: History.

Williams, Ernest R., Jr. The Florida Parish Ellises and Louisiana Politics, 1820-1918. Univ. of Southern Mississippi, 1969. Dissertation: History. [Includes Ezekiel John Ellis and Tom Ellis, who established New Orleans *Democrat* in 1785]

Williams, Jack K. Crime and Punishment in South Carolina, 1790-1860. Emory Univ., 1953. Dissertation: History.

Willson, Helen M. The Development of the Southerner's Concept of the Yankee. Univ. of California (Berkeley), 1948. Thesis: History.

Wilson, Logan. A Sociological Study of Huntsville, Texas. Univ. of Texas (Austin), 1927. Thesis: Sociology. [Brief discussion of newspapers and of little theater]

Winfrey, Dorman H. A History of Rush County, Texas. Univ. of Texas (Austin), 1951. Thesis: History.

Winter, William E. South Carolina State Government Views. Univ. of Missouri, 1955. Dissertation: Journalism. [Culled from newspapers]

[225]

Winters, John D. The Civil War in Louisiana. Louisiana State
     Univ., 1966. Dissertation: History.
Wood, Forrest G. Race Demagoguery during the Civil War and
     Reconstruction. Univ. of California (Berkeley), 1965.
     Dissertation: History.
Wright, Martin. Log Culture in Hill Louisiana. Louisiana State
     Univ., 1956. Dissertation: Geography.
Wright, Pearl M. Religious Fiestas in San Antonio. St. Mary's
     Univ. (San Antonio), 1946. Thesis: History.
Wright, Willard E. Churches in the Confederacy. Emory Univ.,
     1958. Dissertation: History.
Wulf, Helen H. Some Aspects of Desegregation in Dallas, Texas,
     1956-1957. Southern Methodist Univ., 1958. Thesis: Sociology.
     [As reported in four Dallas newspapers]
Yandle, Carolyn D.V. A Delicate Crusade: The Association of
     Southern Women for the Prevention of Lynching. Univ. of
     Virginia, 1969. Thesis: History.
Young, Mary E. Redskins, Ruffleshirts and Rednecks: Indian
     Allotments in Alabama and Mississippi, 1830-1860. Cornell
     Univ., 1955. Dissertation: History.
Zurfluh, Hattie E. The Spanish Heritage in Texas. Baylor Univ.,
     1933. Thesis: History. [In language, literature, and folk
     culture]

BALLADS, FOLKLORE, MUSIC,
AND THE FOLK TRADITION

Akin, Katherine O. Song and Prose of the Cattle Trails. Univ. of
     Texas (Austin), 1948. Thesis: English.
Abrahams, Roger D. Negro Folklore from South Philadelphia, A
     Collection and Analysis. Univ. of Pennsylvania, 1961.
     Dissertation: Folklore. [Most of people interviewed were
     born and reared in South.]
Anderson, Geneva. A Collection of Ballads and Songs from East
     Tennessee. Univ. of North Carolina (Chapel Hill), 1932.
     Thesis: English.
Anderson, Margaret B. The Treatment of Some of the Bible Stories
     in Negro Spirituals. Columbia Univ., 1930. Thesis: English.
     [Based largely on collections by Guy Johnson, James Weldon
     Johnson, and Howard W. Odum]
Anderson, Roy G. The Oral Interpretation of Southwestern Folklore.
     Baylor Univ., 1958. Thesis: Speech.
Angell, Ruth S. Background of Some Texas Cowboy Songs. Columbia
     Univ., 1938. Thesis: English.
Armour, Eugene. The Melodic and Rhythmic Characteristics of the
     Music of the Traditional Ballad Variants Found in the Southern
     Appalachians. New York Univ., 1961. Dissertation: Music.
Arnold, Charles A. The Folklore, Manners, and Customs of the
     Mexicans in San Antonio, Texas. Univ. of Texas (Austin),
     1928. Thesis: Sociology.
Aycock, Etholine G. Americanisms in the Traditional Ballads of
     the Eastern United States. Univ. of Missouri, 1940. Thesis:
     English. [Includes several Southern states]

Bailey, Frederick. The Historical Ballad: Its Tradition in
Britain and America. Univ. of Tennessee, 1963. Thesis:
English. [Includes ballads of the South]

Bales, Mary V. Negro Folk Songs in Texas: Their Definition and
Origin. Texas Christian Univ., 1927. Thesis: English.

Ballard, Lou E. Folktales from Spring Hill, Pigeon Creek, and
Happy Hollow, Alabama. Auburn Univ., 1957. Thesis: English.

Bandy, Lewis D. Folklore of Macon County, Tennessee. George
Peabody College, 1940. Thesis: English.

Barker, Addison R. Folklore in *Blum's Almanac*, 1844-1950. Univ.
of North Carolina (Chapel Hill), 1950. Thesis: English.

Barks, Susan K. Death and A Lady: Echoes of a Mortal Conversation
in English and American Folk Songs Tradition. Univ. of North
Carolina (Chapel Hill), 1967. Thesis: English.

Barnard, Herwanna B. The Comanche and His Literature, with an
Anthology of His Myths, Legends, Folktales, Oratory, Poetry
and Songs. Univ. of Oklahoma, 1941. Thesis: English.

Baskerville, David R. Jazz Influence on Art Music to Mid-Century.
Univ. of California (Los Angeles), 1956. Dissertation:
Music.

Baughman, Ernest W. A Comparative Study of the Folktales of
England and North America. Indiana Univ. (Bloomington), 1953.
Dissertation: English. [709 types; 1051 motifs]

Beard, Anne W. The Personal Folksong Collection of Bascom Lamar
Lunsford. Miami Univ. (Ohio), 1959. Thesis: English. [A
study of the variants in the 315 items of folksong recorded
in 1935 by Bascom Lamar Lunsford for the Columbia University
Library. Mr. Lunsford learned the songs in Western North
Carolina and had a life-long interest in Appalachian Mountain
songs.]

Benson, Norman A. The Itinerant Dancing and Music Masters of
Eighteenth Century America. Univ. of Minnesota, 1963.
Dissertation: Music. [Includes Williamsburg and Charleston]

Binion, Harriett S. Negro Folk Tales for Children. Univ. of
Oklahoma, 1933. Thesis: Education. [Chiefly of Texas]

Bluestein, Eugene. The Background and Sources of an American
Folksong Tradition. Univ. of Minnesota, 1960. Dissertation:
Folklore. [Includes Negro spirituals]

Bogomolny, Michael. A Sociological Interpretation of the Negro
Folk Song. Ohio State Univ., 1929. Thesis: English.

Boswell, George W. Reciprocal Influences of Text and Tune in the
Southern Traditional Ballad. George Peabody College, 1951.
Dissertation: English.

Botkin, Benjamin A. The American Play-Party Song, with a Collection of Oklahoma Texts and Tunes. Univ. of Nebraska, 1931.
Dissertation: English.

Boynton, Madge B. An Evaluation of the Slave Songs as a Historical
Source. Texas Woman's Univ., 1970. Thesis: History.

Brewer, John M. Negro Preacher Tales from the Texas "Brazos
Bottoms." Indiana Univ., 1949. Thesis: English.

Brooks, John L. Paul Bunyan: American Folk Hero. Southern
Methodist Univ., 1927. Thesis: English.

Broucek, Jack W. Eighteenth Century Music in Savannah, Georgia.
Florida State Univ., 1963. Dissertation: Music. [A view of
"music and related cultural conditions"]

Browne, Earl W. Variant Forms of English and Scottish Popular
    Ballads in America. Univ. of Southern California, 1961.
    Dissertation: English. [Mentions folksong "Edward" which
    has version from the Southern Highlands and the Ozarks]
Browne, Ray B. Alabama Folk Songs. Univ. of California (Los
    Angeles), 1956. Dissertation: English.
Buckley, Bruce R. Ballads and Folksongs in Scioto County, Ohio.
    Miami Univ. (Ohio), 1952. Thesis: English. [Many of the
    singers of the ballads were residents of Scioto County and
    originally came from Kentucky, where most of the ballads were
    learned]
Buermann, Theodore B. A History of the North Carolina Folklore
    Society. Univ. of North Carolina (Chapel Hill), 1963.
    Thesis: English.
Buford, Mary E. Folk Songs of Florida and Texas. Southern
    Methodist Univ., 1941. Thesis: English.
Burleson, Nell P. The Evolution of Southern Appalachian Culture
    as Evidenced in Folklore. East Tennessee State Univ., 1963.
    Thesis: English.
Bynum, James L. The Gospel Singing Conventions of Rusk County,
    Texas. Southern Methodist Univ., 1953. Thesis: Sociology.
Cannon, Martin A. Cowboy Song Adaptations. Texas Tech Univ.,
    1966. Thesis: English.
Cameron, Vivian K. Folk Beliefs Pertaining to Health of Southern
    Negro. Northwestern Univ., 1930. Thesis: Sociology.
Campa, Arthur L. Spanish Folk-Poetry in New Mexico. Columbia
    Univ., 1946. Dissertation: Romance Languages.
Campbell, Marie. The Folk Life of a Kentucky Mountain Community.
    George Peabody College, 1937. Thesis: English.
Campbell, Marie. Olden Tales from Across the Ocean Waters: A
    Collection of Seventy-Eight European Folktales Recorded from
    the Oral Tradition of Six Eastern Kentucky Narrators. Indiana
    Univ. (Bloomington), 1956. Dissertation: Folklore.
Carlisle, Irene J. Fifty Ballads and Songs from Northwest
    Arkansas. Univ. of Arkansas, 1952. Thesis: English.
Cavendish, Thomas H. Folk Music in Selected Twentieth Century
    American Opera. Florida State Univ., 1966. Dissertation:
    Music. [Includes a study of Foss's Jumping Frog of Calaveras
    County]
Chamberlain, William W. Folk Music in the Kentucky Barrens.
    Stanford Univ., 1940. Thesis: English.
Chandler, G.W., Jr. The History and Present Status of Folk-Song
    Scholarship in the South. Univ. of North Carolina (Chapel
    Hill), 1936. Thesis: English.
Charles, Norman. Values in Twentieth Century American Popular
    Songs. Univ. of Pennsylvania, 1958. Dissertation: English.
    [Discussion of regionalism in songs]
Cheek, Curtis L. The Singing School and Shaped-Note Tradition:
    Residuals in Twentieth-Century American Hymnody. Univ. of
    Southern California, 1968. Dissertation: Music. [Section
    on Southern hymnody includes Ananias Davisson's Kentucky
    Harmony (1816)]
Childs, Alice M. Some Ballads and Folk Songs from the South. Univ.
    of Missouri, 1922. Thesis: English.

Clarke, Joe E.L. Communal Origins of Songs Among the Negroes. Washington Univ. (St. Louis), 1926. Thesis: English.

Claudel, Calvin A. A Study of Louisiana French Folktales in Avoyelles Parish. Univ. of North Carolina (Chapel Hill), 1948. Dissertation: Romance Languages.

Clements, Caroline. Old English and Scottish Ballads in the Southern Appalachian Mountains. Columbia Univ., 1925. Thesis: English.

Cobb, Buell E., Jr. The Sacred Harp: An Overview of a Tradition. Auburn Univ., 1969. Thesis: English.

Cobb, L.M. Traditional Ballads and Songs of Eastern North Carolina. Univ. of North Carolina (Chapel Hill), 1927. Thesis: English.

Cox, J.H. Folk Songs of the South. Harvard Univ., 1924. Dissertation: English.

Crabtree, Lillian G. Songs and Ballads Sung in Overton County, Tennessee: A Collection. George Peabody College, 1936. Thesis: English.

Crawford, Barbara. Ballad Characteristic in Modern Popular Country Music. East Tennessee State Univ., 1969. Thesis: English.

Crawford, Portia N. A Study of Negro Folk Songs from Greensboro, North Carolina, and Surrounding Towns. Univ. of North Carolina (Chapel Hill), 1965. Thesis: Music.

Crews, Emma K. A History of Music in Knoxville, Tennessee, 1791 to 1910. Florida State Univ., 1961. Dissertation: Music.

Dahlenburg, William J. Music in the Culture of Miami: 1920-1966. Florida State Univ., 1967. Dissertation: Music.

Daniell, Martha L. Sixteen Play-Party Songs from Randolph County, West Virginia. Ohio State Univ., 1943. Thesis: Music.

Davis, Ouida P. A Study of the Terminology of American Country Dances. Univ. of Texas (Austin), 1940. Thesis: Education. [Reference to variations occurring in particular Southern states: Texas and Tennessee, for example]

Davis, Ronald L. A History of Resident Opera in the American West. Univ. of Texas (Austin), 1961. Dissertation: Music.

Dean, Jeannette G. Daniel Boone, an American Folk Hero. Columbia Univ., 1917. Thesis: English.

Dixon, Christa. Wesen and Wandel Gerstlicher Volkslieder, Negro Spirituals. Bonn, 1965. Dissertation: American Literature.

Doran, Edwina B. Folklore in White County, Tennessee. George Peabody College, 1969. Dissertation: Folklore.

Dowell, Paul W. The Devil in Southern Folklore. Univ. of Georgia, 1966. Thesis: English.

Doyle, John G. The Piano Music of Louis Moreau Gottschalk (1829-1869). New York Univ., 1960. Dissertation: Music. [Louisiana Creole folk music as one of his sources]

Dugat, Jean. Legendary American Folk Heroes. Southwest Texas State Univ., 1950. Thesis: English.

Duncan, Ruby. Ballads and Folk Songs Collected in Northern Hamilton County (Tennessee). Univ. of Tennessee, 1939. Thesis: English.

Dunlap, John M. The Outlaw in Southern Folksong. Univ. of North Carolina (Chapel Hill), 1950. Thesis: English.

Eastridge, Nancy E. A Study of Folklore in Adair County, Kentucky. George Peabody College, 1939. Thesis: English.

Edmiston, W.C. A Study of Provincialisms: From Northern Todd County, Kentucky. George Peabody College, 1940. Thesis: English.

Engler, Leo F. The German Folk Song in Comal County, Texas. Univ. of Texas (Austin), 1952. Thesis: German.

Eskew, Harry L. Shape-Note Hymnody in the Shenandoah Valley, 1816-1860. Tulane Univ., 1966. Dissertation: Music. [Discusses folk hymns and books which played a major role in the culture of the period]

Etheridge, Jane. Stephen Foster and the American Folk Ballad. Southern Methodist Univ., 1934. Thesis: English. [Chapter 3 discusses his contribution to literature and his conception of the South]

Fentress, Elza E. Superstitions of Grayson County. Western Kentucky Univ., 1934. Thesis: English. [Kentucky folklore and superstitions]

Ferris, William R., Jr. Black Folklore from The Mississippi Delta. Univ. of Pennsylvania, 1969. Dissertation: Folklore.

Fisher, Miles M. The Evolution of Slave Songs of the United States. Univ. of Chicago, 1948. Dissertation: Divinity.

Fitch, Margaret. The Cowboy in Verse and Song. New Mexico Highlands Univ., 1932. Thesis: English. [Background, cowboy poets and collectors, different types of poetry]

Flesher, Mary. Folk Songs in the Texas Public School Program. East Texas State Univ., 1940. Thesis: Education. [Discusses "amalgamated American folk-songs coupled with those created on this continent"]

Foreman, Ronald C., Jr. Jazz and Race Records, 1920-32: Their Origins and Their Significance for the Record Industry and Society. Univ. of Illinois, 1968. Dissertation: Mass Communications.

Fott, Solie. The Youth Education Activities of the Nashville Symphony Association. George Peabody College, 1958. Dissertation: Music.

Fowler, William E. Stories and Legends of Maury County, Tennessee. George Peabody College, 1937. Thesis: English.

Gamble, Margaret E. The Heritage and Folk Music of Cades Cove, Tennessee. Univ. of Southern California, 1948. Thesis: Music.

Gannaway, Mary A. The Singing Games of the Cumberland Mountains in Tennessee. George Peabody College, 1935. Thesis: English.

Garrison, Theodore. Forty-Five Folk Songs Collected from Searcy County, Arkansas. Univ. of Arkansas, 1944. Thesis: English.

Gates, Florence M. A Study of the Living Conditions in Southern Appalachia as Revealed through the Mountain Ballads. Kansas State Teachers College, 1948. Thesis: English.

George, Robert A. Greek-American Folk Beliefs and Narratives: Survivals and Living Tradition. Indiana Univ. (Bloomington), 1964. Dissertation: Folklore. [Includes six American communities, among them Tarpon Springs, Florida; Savannah, Georgia; and Wichita Falls, Texas]

Glassie, Henry H. III. Pattern in the Material Folk Culture of the Eastern United States. Univ. of Pennsylvania, 1969. Dissertation: Folklore. [Includes South]
_____. Southern Mountain Houses: A Study in American Folk Culture. State Univ. College of N.Y. (Oneonta), 1965. Thesis: English.
Gonzales, Maria d.R. The Spanish Folklore of Webb and Zapata Counties [Texas]. Univ. of Texas (Austin), 1952. Thesis: Spanish.
Goodwyn, Frank. An Interpretation of the Hispanic Folk Hero, Pedro Urdemales. Univ. of Texas (Austin), 1945. Dissertation: Spanish. [Discusses Texas folklore]
Gower, Lemuel H. Traditional Scottish Ballads in the United States. Vanderbilt Univ., 1957. Dissertation: English. [Discusses some Scottish ballads collected in South and Southern ballads traceable to Scotland]
Graves, Gloria R. Superstition in Southside Virginia. Virginia State College, 1957. Thesis: English.
Green, Archie. Recorded American Coal Mining Songs. Univ. of Pennsylvania, 1969. Dissertation: Folklore. [Includes Tennessee and Kentucky]
Green, William F. An Edited Collection of Beech Mountain Folksongs. East Tennessee State Univ., 1968. Thesis: English.
Greene, Maude. Folklore of Shelby County, Tennessee. George Peabody College, 1940. Thesis: English.
Greenway, John. American Folksongs of Social and Economic Protest. Univ. of Pennsylvania, 1951. Dissertation: English.
Greer, Nancy A. Legends and Stories of Franklin, Tennessee. George Peabody College, 1930. Thesis: English.
Guerra, Fermina. Mexican and Spanish Folklore and Incidents in Southwest Texas. Univ. of Texas (Austin), 1941. Thesis: Spanish. [Many folk stories, prose and verse; appendix gives music and words of some folk songs]
Hall, Dorothy C. Comparative Study of the Popular Ballad of England and America. Univ. of Idaho, 1923. Thesis: English. [A comparison of Campbell, O.D. and Sharp, Cecil J., *English Folk Songs from the Southern Appalachians* and Sargent, Helen C. and Kittredge, G.L., *English and Scottish Popular Ballads*]
Hammond, Stella S. Contribution of the American Indian and Negro to the Folk Music of America. Wayne State Univ., 1936. Thesis: Music.
Hansen, Chadwick C. The Ages of Jazz: A Study of Jazz in Its Cultural Context. Univ. of Minnesota, 1956. Dissertation: Music.
Hanson, Henry E. French Influences on the Folk Songs of Louisiana. Stanford Univ., 1938. Thesis: Education.
Hanson, Virginia. Alabama: In Legend and Lore. Birmingham-Southern College, 1937. Thesis: English.
Harrison, Shirley M. The Grand Opera House (Third Varieties Theatre) of New Orleans, Louisiana, 1871 to 1906: A History and Analysis. Louisiana State Univ., 1965. Dissertation: Theater.
Hawkins, Ulista A. Themes in Civil War Songs. George Peabody College, 1929. Thesis: English.

[231]

Haun, Mildred. Cocke County Ballads and Songs. Vanderbilt Univ.,
1937. Thesis: English. [Collection of 206 ballads and
songs handed down in the Haun family of Cocke County,
Tennessee]
Heaps, Porter W. Songs of the Civil War. Northwestern Univ.,
1932. Thesis: History. [Discusses Southern war songs]
Henderson, Eleanor E. An Ozark Songbook. Univ. of Arkansas, 1950.
Thesis: Music.
Hiester, Miriam W. Los Paisanos: Folklore of the Texas-Mexicans
of the Lower Rio Grande Valley. Univ. of Texas (Austin),
1954. Thesis: English.
Holcombe, Julia I. Southern Mountain Folk Songs for American
Schools. Univ. of Rochester, 1941. Thesis: Music Education.
Hopkins, Bessie C. Life and Lore of the Old Natchez Region.
George Peabody College, 1957. Dissertation: Folklore.
Hughen, Lewis D. A Study of the Folk Hero in America. Florida
State Univ., 1954. Thesis: English.
Hudson, A.P. Folk Songs of Mississippi and Their Background: A
Study, with Texts. Univ. of North Carolina (Chapel Hill),
1930. Dissertation: English.
Irvis, K.L. Negro in the Civil War: Songs Ballads. New York
State Univ., 1939. Thesis: English.
Jarreau, Lafayette. Creole Folklore of Pointe Coupée Parish.
Louisiana State Univ., 1931. Thesis: Romance Languages.
Johnson, Ellen L., ed. The Unpublished Mountain Folk Songs
Collected by Dorothy Scarborough. Baylor Univ., 1941. Thesis:
English. [Collected in Virginia, North Carolina, and some
allied mountain regions of South Carolina, Tennessee and
Georgia]
Johnson, Mary E. Stories and Legends of Donelson, Tennessee.
George Peabody College, 1938. Thesis: English.
Jones, Alice M. The Negro Folk Sermons: A Study in the
Sociology of Folk Culture. Fisk Univ., 1942. Thesis:
Sociology and Anthropology.
Jones, Bessie W. A Descriptive and Analytical Study of the
American Negro Folktale. George Peabody College, 1967.
Dissertation: English. [B.A. Botkin, and Langston Hughes]
King, Patricia O. Early Folklore of Galveston Island and the
Texas Gulf Coast. Univ. of Tulsa, 1968. Thesis: English.
Kinscella, Haxel G. Songs of the American Negro and Their
Influence upon Composed Music. Columbia Univ., 1934. Thesis:
Music. [A study of the influence of many Negro spirituals]
Koon, William H. Folk Songs of Watauga [North Carolina]. Univ.
of Georgia, 1967. Thesis: English.
LaHaye, Marie. French Folk Material from St. Landry Parish.
Louisiana State Univ., 1946. Thesis: English.
Lavergne, Remi. A Phonetic Transcription of the Creole Negro's
Medical Treatments, Superstitions, and Folklore in the
Parish of Pointe Coupée. Louisiana State Univ., 1931.
Thesis: Romance Languages.
Laws, George M., Jr. Native American Balladry: A Descriptive
Study and a Bibliographical Syllabus of the Ballads Sung in
the United States. Univ. of Pennsylvania, 1949. Dissertation:
English.

Lopue, Sylvian R. Arcadian Folklore of the "La Cote Francaise."
    Louisiana State Univ., 1932. Thesis: Romance Languages.
Lowrey, Ruth A. A Study of the Changes Resulting from the Oral
    Transmission of the English and Scottish Ballads in America.
    Vanderbilt Univ., 1929. Thesis: English.
Mahan, Katherine H. History of Music in Columbus, Georgia, 1828-
    1928. Florida State Univ., 1967. Dissertation: Music.
Malone, Billy C. A History of Commercial Country Music in the
    United States, 1920-1964. Univ. of Texas (Austin), 1965.
    Dissertation: Folklore. [Roots in "folk culture of the
    rural South"]
Mason, Robert. Folksongs and Folk Tales of Cannon County,
    Tennessee. George Peabody College, 1939. Thesis: English.
Maxwell, Ida E. A Study of the Legends and Stories of Arkansas
    Indians. George Peabody College, 1933. Thesis: English.
Maynard, Loren L. Understanding the Cowboy and His Music. Wayne
    State Univ., 1936. Thesis: Music.
McHargue, Robert M. Studies in the Popular Music of the American
    Frontiers. Univ. of California (Berkeley), 1940. Thesis:
    History.
McMillan, Fay C. Major Themes in Southern Negro Folklore. East
    Tennessee State Univ., 1961. Thesis: English.
McNeese, Florette. American Folk Games. Univ. of Oklahoma, 1916.
    Thesis: English.
McNeil, Norman L. *Corridos de Asuntos Vulgares*, Corresponding to
    the *Romances Vulgares* of the Spanish. Univ. of Texas (Austin),
    1944. Thesis: Spanish. [Ballads collected in the Southern
    part of Texas and the Northern part of Mexico: outlaw ballads,
    "place" ballads, cowboy ballads, ballads of the past, contem-
    porary ballads, and miscellaneous ballads]
_____. The British Ballad West of the Appalachian
    Mountains. Univ. of Texas (Austin), 1956. Dissertation:
    English.
McPheeters, Dean W. A Comparative Study of Some Spanish Songs
    and Ballads Collected in Tampa, Florida. Univ. of Florida,
    1941. Thesis: Spanish.
Merritt, Nancy G. Negro Spirituals in American Collections (A
    Handbook for Students Studying Negro Spirituals). Howard
    Univ., 1942. Thesis: English. [A comprehensive record of
    Negro spirituals and a contrast between Southern white and
    Southern Negro spirituals]
Metcalfe, H.E. American Hymnology. Univ. of Maryland, 1935.
    Thesis: English. [Includes discussion of Francis Scott Key]
Miller, Edna L. A Study of Folklore in Watauga County, N.C.
    George Peabody College, 1938. Thesis: English.
Montell, William L. Supernatural Tales Collected from Negroes
    and Whites in Monroe and Cumberland Counties, Kentucky.
    Indiana Univ. (Bloomington), 1963. Thesis: Folklore.
_____. A Folk History of the Coe Ridge Negro Colony. Indiana
    Univ. (Bloomington), 1964. Dissertation: Folklore.
    [Cumberland County, Kentucky]
Moore, Ethel P. An Experiment in Collecting and Classifying the
    Folk Songs Sung in Oklahoma. Univ. of Oklahoma, 1926.
    Thesis: English.

Morris, Alton C. Folksongs of Florida and Their Cultural Back-
    ground. Univ. of North Carolina (Chapel Hill), 1941. Disser-
    tation: English.
Morris, Ophelia E. Some Characteristics of Negro American Secular
    Folk Songs. Fisk Univ., 1948. Thesis: English.
Moser, Dorothea J. Instrumental Folk Music of the Southern
    Appalachians: A Study of Traditional Fiddle Tunes. Univ. of
    North Carolina (Chapel Hill), 1963. Thesis: English.
Mullen, Patrick B. The Function of Folk Belief Among Texas
    Coastal Fishermen. Univ. of Texas (Austin), 1968. Disser-
    tation: Folklore.
Newberry, Elizabeth. Civil War Anecdotes and Legends of
    Chattanooga. George Peabody College, 1928. Thesis: English.
Newsom, Stella W. A Collection of Mississippi Folklore. Univ. of
    Mississippi, 1931. Thesis: English.
Nickerson, Camille L. Africo-Creole Music in Louisiana: The
    Plantation Songs Created by the Creole Negroes of Louisiana.
    Oberlin College, 1932. Thesis: Music. [The supplement to
    this thesis contains "seven Creole songs collected and
    harmonized."]
Ogilvie, Daniel M. Psychodynamics of Fantasized Flight: A Study
    of People and Folk Tales. Harvard Univ., 1967. Dissertation:
    Social Psychology. [Includes the Creek Indians]
Owens, Bess A. Some Unpublished Folk Songs of the Cumberlands.
    George Peabody College, 1930. Thesis: English.
_____. A Study of the Folk Songs of the Cumberlands. George
    Peabody College, 1942. Dissertation: English.
Owens, William A. The Play-Party in Texas. Southern Methodist
    Univ., 1933. Thesis: English.
_____. Texas Folk Songs. Univ. of Iowa, 1941. Dissertation:
    English.
Paredes, Americo. Ballads of the Lower Border. Univ. of Texas
    (Austin), 1953. Thesis: English. [Mexican and American
    ballads and songs]
Patterson, Cecil L. A Different Drum: The Image of the Negro in
    the Nineteenth Century Popular Song Books. Univ. of
    Pennsylvania, 1961. Dissertation: English.
Patton, Leila E. The Spirituals of the American Negro. Columbia
    Univ., 1938. Thesis: Education.
Pazdral, Olga J. Czech Folklore in Texas. Univ. of Texas (Austin),
    1942. Thesis: English.
Perez, Soledad. Mexican Folklore in Austin. Univ. of Texas
    (Austin), 1949. Thesis: English.
Perry, Henry W. A Sampling of the Folklore of Carter County,
    Tennessee. George Peabody College, 1938. Thesis: English.
Petitjean, Irene M. "Cajun" Folk Songs of Southwest Louisiana.
    Columbia Univ., 1930. Thesis: Romance Languages.
Phillips, Juanita S. The Spanish Folklore of Texas: No. 1,
    Cameron County. Univ. of Texas (Austin), 1950. Thesis:
    Spanish.
Pittard, Homer P. Legends and Stories of Civil War Rutherford
    County, Tennessee. George Peabody College, 1940. Thesis:
    English.

Pitts, DeJuana M. A Study of the Musical Interest and Activities of Thirty-Three Prominent Citizens in Caldwell Parish [La.]. Northeast Louisiana Univ., 1964. Thesis: Music-Education.

Pollan, Loy. Provenience of Certain Cowboy Ballads. Univ. of Oklahoma, 1939. Thesis: English. [Cowboy ballads in Oklahoma, Texas, and elsewhere]

Provence, Jean W.H. Oklahoma Ballad. Columbia Univ., 1948. Thesis: English.

Puckett, Newbell N. Folk Beliefs of the Southern Negro. Yale Univ., 1925. Dissertation: Sociology.

Pyke, Launcelot A. III. Jazz, 1920 to 1927: An Analytical Study (Volumes I and II). State Univ. of Iowa, 1962. Dissertation: Music.

Randall, James C. Medical Folk Beliefs in a Southern Rural Community. Atlanta Univ., 1954. Thesis: Sociology.

Rice, William C. A Century of Methodist Music: 1850-1950. State Univ. of Iowa, 1953. Dissertation: Music. [Includes Southern division of Methodist Episcopal Church, its hymn music and literature]

Roberts, Hilda. Louisiana Superstitions. Univ. of Iowa, 1923. Thesis: English.

Roberts, Leonard W. Eastern Kentucky Folktales: A Collection and a Study. Univ. of Kentucky, 1954. Dissertation: English.

Robinson, Carolyn A. Child Ballads in Eastern Kentucky. Vanderbilt Univ., 1966. Thesis: English.

Rogers, Elizia G. Stories and Legends of Marshall County, North of Duck River. George Peabody College, 1936. Thesis: English.

Rohrbough, Cleora D. Dramatizable Events in the Folk Life of Early Texas. Univ. of Texas (Austin), 1941. Thesis: English.

Rorhbough, Edward G. James Bowie and the Bowie Knife in Fact and Fancy. Univ. of Texas (Austin), 1938. Thesis: English. [The author has traced the Bowie knife legend showing how the legends grew from the few certain facts. In addition the writer has attempted to show how novelists and writers of historic fiction have dealt with Bowie.]

Rouse, Chrystine M. Folklore of Alabama. Univ. of Pittsburgh, 1936. Thesis: English.

Russell, Clyde. Folk Interpretation of Social Values as Found in Folk Songs and Ballads. Univ. of North Carolina (Chapel Hill), 1926. Thesis: Sociology. [Deals in part with folk songs and ballads of the Southern mountaineer]

Russell, Julia B. Legends of an Oklahoma Lottery Town. George Peabody College, 1937. Thesis: English.

Saucier, C.L. Louisiana Folk Tales and Songs in French Dialect with Linguistic Notes. George Peabody College, 1923. Thesis: French.

Schmoll, Joseph B. An Analytical Study of the Principal Instrumental Composition of Wallingford Reigger. Northwestern Univ., 1954. Dissertation: Music. [Composer born in Albany, Ga.]

Sewell, Helen H. Folktales from a Georgia Family: An Annotated Field Collection. Indiana Univ. (Bloomington), 1963. Thesis: Folklore.

Shockett, Bernard I. A Stylistic Study of the Blues as Recorded
    by Jazz Instrumentalists, 1917-1931. New York Univ., 1964.
    Dissertation: Music. [Includes an index]
Slappey, George H. Some Additions to the Study of Negro Folk
    Songs. Oglethorpe Univ., 1928. Thesis: English.
Smetzer, Barbara. An Annotated Collection of Negro Folktales
    from Harrett County, North Carolina. Indiana Univ.
    (Bloomington), 1963. Thesis: Folklore.
Smith, Blanche B. Legends and Old Tales of San Antonio and
    Vicinity. Southwest Texas State Univ., 1943. Thesis:
    History.
Smith, Hugh L., Jr. The Literary Manifestation of a Liberal
    Romanticism in American Jazz. Univ. of New Mexico, 1955.
    Dissertation: English. [Includes discussion of G.W. Cable,
    Lafcadio Hearn, and Mark Twain; discusses Creole songs,
    Negro work songs, and Negro spirituals]
Steckert, Ellen J. Two Voices of Tradition: The Influence of
    Personality and Collecting Environment upon the Songs of
    Two Traditional Folksingers. Univ. of Pennsylvania, 1965.
    Dissertation: Folklore. [Includes materials from Kentucky
    mountains]
Steely, Mercedes. The Folk Songs of Ebenezer Community. Univ. of
    North Carolina (Chapel Hill), 1936. Thesis: English.
Stewart, Mary A. Legends of Mississippi Indians in Poetry and
    Prose. George Peabody College, 1931. Thesis: English.
Stoutamire, Albert L. A History of Music in Richmond, Virginia
    from 1742-1865. Florida State Univ., 1960. Dissertation:
    Music. [Sources: magazines, newspapers, histories,
    biographies; intended as a supplement to literature about
    Richmond]
Tackett, Betty O. Folklore of the Mississippi River and the
    Natchez Trace. Mississippi College, 1965. Thesis: English.
Taylor, Sarah M. A Preliminary Survey of Folklore in Alabama.
    Univ. of Alabama, 1925. Thesis: English.
Thompson, Elizabeth A.J. The Origin and the Contribution that
    Negro Spirituals Have Made in the Area of Folk Music.
    Alabama State Univ. (Montgomery), 1947. Thesis: Education.
Tinsley, Vallie. Some Negro Songs Heard on the Hills of
    Louisiana. Louisiana State Univ., 1928. Thesis: Music.
Trantham, Carrie P. An Investigation of the Unpublished Negro
    Folk Songs of Dorothy Scarborough. Baylor Univ., 1941.
    Thesis: English. [Pertaining to Louisiana, Texas, and
    other Southern states]
Trappey, Adam S.H. Creole Folklore in Phonetic Transcription.
    Louisiana State Univ., 1916. Thesis: English.
Turner, Frederick W. III. Badmen, Black and White: The Continuity
    of American Folk Traditions. Univ. of Pennsylvania, 1965.
    Dissertation: Folklore. [Includes South]
Venable, Tom C. The Study of Folklore in American Education.
    Western Kentucky Univ., 1947. Thesis: Education. [Guy B.
    Johnson, James Weldon Johnson, John Jacob Niles, Howard W.
    Odum]
Wagner, Irene. A Survey of the Folklore of Louisiana with Special
    Reference to Its Distinctive Qualities. Univ. of Kansas, 1933.
    Thesis: English.

Walker, Emma J.   The Contemporary Texas: An Examination of Major
      Additions to the Mythical Texan in the Twentieth Century.
      Univ. of Texas (Austin), 1966.   Dissertation: Folklore.
Warren, Helen F.   Study of the Folk Literature of Nash County,
      North Carolina.   New York State Univ., 1934.   Thesis:
      Education.
Watson, Laura S. (Mrs. Charles Poole).   Negro Folklore of the
      Carolinas.   Stetson Univ., 1937.   Thesis: English.
Weldon, Fred O.   Negro Folk Heroes.   Univ. of Texas (Austin),
      1958.   Thesis: English.
West, Paul M.   Myths and Legends of the Indian Tribes of
      Mississippi.   George Peabody College, 1930.   Thesis: English.
West, Roy A.   Songs of the Mountaineers.   George Peabody College,
      1922.   Thesis: English.
White, Lillian O.   Folksongs of the American Negro and Their Value
      Today.   Univ. of Idaho, 1925.   Thesis: English.   [Discusses
      folksongs of the Southern Negro]
Whitfield, Irene T.   Louisiana French Folk Songs.   Louisiana
      State Univ., 1935.   Thesis: Romance Languages.
Williams, Charlotte F.   American Issues (1865-1900) as Expressed
      in the Songs of the People.   Columbia Univ., 1942.   Thesis:
      History.   [Texas cowboy songs, Southern farmer songs,
      spirituals, and Civil War songs]
Williams, Coral.   Legends and Stories of White County, Tennessee.
      George Peabody College, 1931.   Thesis: English.
Williams, Cratis D.   Ballads and Songs.   Univ. of Kentucky, 1937.
      Thesis: English.   [Lawrence County, Kentucky, ballads]
Williams, Grier M.   A History of Music in Jacksonville, Florida,
      from 1822 to 1922.   Florida State Univ., 1961.   Dissertation:
      Music.
Williams, Thelma A.   Origin and Analysis of Negro Folk Song.
      Wayne State Univ., 1938.   Thesis: Music.   [Analysis of
      intervals, rhythms and structure of slave and other Southern
      folk songs.   Traces idiom to African racial traits]
Willis, Ninevah J.   A Study of the Folklore of a Mountainous
      Section of Southwestern Virginia.   Radford College, 1955.
      Thesis: Education.   [Tales, legends, superstitions, folk
      songs, and folk ways, especially of Carroll County]
Wilson, Gypsy V.   Folklore in Southeastern Kentucky.   George
      Peabody College, 1937.   Thesis: English.
Woods, Genevieve.   The Sacred Harp Singers: A Study of Persistence
      of a Rural Social Institution.   Southern Methodist Univ.,
      1937.   Thesis: Sociology.
Work, John W.   The Folk Songs of the American Negro.   Columbia
      Univ., 1931.   Thesis: Education.   [Contains material
      relevant to the origins of Southern folk songs and tales
      associated with them; analyses of themes and forms of
      spirituals; the origin of the "blues"]
Worthington, Paul C.   Nine Rare Traditional Ballads from Virginia.
      Univ. of Virginia, 1957.   Thesis: English.
Wragg, Eleanor N.   The American Civil War Era as Reflected in the
      Religious Songs of the Age.   Boston Univ., 1935.   Thesis:
      Music.   [Discusses Sidney Lanier and Henry Timrod]

Wright, Maud. Folk Music of Arkansas. Louisiana State Univ.,
    1937. Thesis: Music.
Wyatt, Emma O. Negro Folklore from Alabama. Univ. of Iowa, 1943.
    Thesis: English.
Zander, Marjorie T. The Brass Band Funeral and Related Negro
    Burial Customs. Univ. of North Carolina (Chapel Hill), 1962.
    Thesis: Folklore.

EDUCATION

Abbot, Billy M. A History of the Arden Club of Southern Methodist
    University from 1915 to 1942. Southern Methodist Univ.,
    1951. Thesis: Speech.
Acker, Will H., Jr. History of Theatrical Activities at Lon Morris
    College, Jacksonville, Texas. Southern Methodist Univ.,
    1955. Thesis: Speech.
Amyett, Paddy W. A History of Literary Societies at Baylor
    University. Baylor Univ., 1963. Thesis: History.
Anderson, Justin V.G. The Decline of the Academy in Texas.
    Southern Methodist Univ., 1928. Thesis: Education.
Bacote, C.A. Higher Education in Virginia between 1830 and 1860.
    Univ. of Chicago, 1929. Thesis: History.
Baxter, Madeline E. Negro Education as Viewed in *The Outlook*
    (1893-1935). Univ. of North Carolina (Chapel Hill), 1951.
    Thesis: Education.
Beall, Noble Y. The Northern Baptists and the Higher Education of
    Southern Negroes during 1865-75. Emory Univ., 1944. Thesis:
    Religious Education.
Blair, John E. The Founding of Southern Methodist University.
    Southern Methodist Univ., 1926. Thesis: Education.
Bond, James A. Negro Education in Kentucky. Univ. of Cincinnati,
    1930. Thesis: Education.
Booker, Andrew B. History of the Academies of Augusta County,
    Virginia. Univ. of Virginia, 1949. Thesis: Education.
Bowles, Elizabeth A. The University of North Carolina at
    Greensboro, 1892-1931. Univ. of North Carolina (Chapel
    Hill), 1965. Dissertation: Education.
Bramlett, A.L. Popular Education in North Carolina from 1815 to
    1860. Univ. of Chicago, 1917. Thesis: History.
Britt, Samuel S., Jr. A History of Stonewall Jackson College,
    1868-1930. Univ. of Virginia, 1949. Thesis: Education.
Broce, Thomas E. An Analysis of Gifts and Grants by Ten Major
    Philanthropic Foundations to Institutions of Higher Education
    in the South, 1959-1963. Univ. of North Carolina (Chapel
    Hill), 1965. Thesis: Education.
Brockman, Aubrey S. The History of Randolph-Macon Academy. Univ.
    of Virginia, 1944. Thesis: Education.
Burger, Sallie M. The Church and Independent Schools of the
    Southern Highlands: A Program of Secondary Studies. New
    York Univ., 1925. Thesis: Education.
Burrows, Edward F. The Literary Education of Negroes in Ante-
    bellum Virginia, North Carolina, South Carolina, and Georgia
    with Special Reference to Regulatory and Prohibitive Laws.
    Duke Univ., 1941. Thesis: History.

Carlson, Alden L. A History of Martha Washington College. Univ. of Virginia, 1948. Thesis: Education.

Chaffin, Nora C. Trinity College, 1839-1892: The Beginnings of Duke University. Duke Univ., 1943. Thesis: History.

Chalmers, William E. A Study of the Gainesville Junior College. Southern Methodist Univ., 1951. Thesis: Education.

Clarke, Charles M. Philanthropic Foundations and Teacher Education in the South, 1867-1948. Univ. of North Carolina (Chapel Hill), 1948. Dissertation: English.

Come, Donald R. The Influence of Princeton on Higher Education in the South before 1825. Duke Univ., 1943. Thesis: History.

Copeland, Otis B. Organization and Administration of Agricultural College Editorial Programs in Three Southeastern States. Univ. of Wisconsin, 1958. Dissertation: Journalism. [Tennessee, Georgia, North Carolina]

Craig, John D. Southern Methodist University under the Leadership of Dr. Charles C. Selecman (1923-1925). Southern Methodist Univ., 1965. Thesis: History.

Crow, Mary E.J. Critical Analysis of the Texas Interscholastic League Literary Contest. Southern Methodist Univ., 1952. Thesis: Education.

Cross, Livingston. Past Development and Present Status of the Alabama Educational Television Network. Univ. of Alabama, 1958. Dissertation: Education.

Davis, Drewise. Current trends in Texas High School Yearbooks. Southern Methodist Univ., 1948. Thesis: Education.

Davis, Frank B. The Literary Societies of Selected State Universities of the Lower South. Louisiana State Univ., 1949. Dissertation: English.

Day, Robert W. Legal and Historical Development of Public Education in Alabama, 1901-1942. Univ. of North Carolina (Chapel Hill), 1951. Dissertation: Education.

De Boer, J.J. The Influence of Reconstruction on Education in Alabama. Univ. of Chicago, 1927. Thesis: Education.

Denton, William H. The Impact of Populism upon the Southern Educational Awakening. Univ. of North Carolina (Chapel Hill), 1965. Dissertation: Education.

Drennen, Jean C. A Speech Improvement Program for Schools in Knox County Tennessee. Univ. of Tennessee, 1966. Thesis: English.

Durham, James G. A History of Berea College. Univ. of Kentucky, 1942. Thesis: Education.

Edmund, Gertrude M. The Higher Education of Women in the United States up to 1870. New York Univ., 1919. Dissertation: Education.

Edson, Cyrus M. The Present Status of Dramatic Arts in Eighty-Five North Carolina High Schools. Univ. of North Carolina (Chapel Hill), 1949. Thesis: Education.

Edwards, Austin, Jr. History of the Kentucky State Industrial College for Negroes. Indiana State Univ. (Bloomington), 1936. Thesis: Education.

Edwards, Dorothy L. A History of Transylvania College from 1865 to 1940. Univ. of Kentucky, 1939. Thesis: Education.

Eley, Douglas C. Secondary Education in Norfolk County [Virginia], 1691-1951. Univ. of Virginia, 1951. Thesis: Education.

Engram, Irby D. A History of Andrew College [Cuthbert, Georgia]. Emory Univ., 1939. Thesis: History.

Foerster, Alma P. The State University in the Old South: A Study of Social and Intellectual Influences in State University Education. Duke Univ., 1939. Dissertation: History.

Funke, Francis J. Spanish Literature in the Secondary Schools in the Southeast: Theory and Practice. Florida State Univ., 1964. Dissertation: English.

Gambrell, Herbert D. The Early Baylor University: 1841-1861. Southern Methodist Univ., 1924. Thesis: History.

Gates, Ruby. The Slave Plantation as an Educational Institution: The Whites--Slave Owners, Overseers, and Middle Class. Univ. of Texas (Austin), 1943. Thesis: Education. [Discussion of the theater, of reading, of libraries, etc.]

Glazener, S.M. The History of Franklin College, Pilot Point, Denton County, Texas. Southern Methodist Univ., 1932. Thesis: Education.

Goode, James M. The Confederate University: The Forgotten Institution of the American Civil War. Univ. of Virginia, 1966. Thesis: History.

Greenberg, Howard. The American College during the Revolutionary Era and the Early National Period: A Survey. Brooklyn College, 1964. Thesis: History.

Haynes, William H. History of Bethal College, Russellville, Kentucky. Univ. of Kentucky, 1941. Thesis: Education.

Healey, May-Ballara B. The Origin and History of Dallas College through the Clough Administration, 1915-1949. Southern Methodist Univ., 1950. Thesis: Education.

Hembree, Sillous G. A History of Union College. Univ. of Kentucky, 1938. Thesis: Education.

Higgins, Sr. Martin M., O.S.U. The Catholic Church's Contribution to Negro Education in the United States. St. John's Univ. (Cleveland), 1944. Thesis: Education.

Hornsby, Virginia R. The Higher Education of Virginians in Colonial Days. College of William and Mary, 1936. Thesis: History.

Houser, J.H. The History of Wesley College, Greenville, Texas. Southern Methodist Univ., 1939. Thesis: Education.

Howard, Boyd D. The Origins of Higher Education in the State of Kentucky. Univ. of Cincinnati, 1940. Dissertation: Education.

Hoyle, Hughes B. The Early History of Queens College to 1872. Univ. of North Carolina (Chapel Hill), 1963. Dissertation: Education. [A woman's college in Charlotte, N.C.,; founded in 1857]

Hudspeth, Junia E. A History of the North Texas Agricultural College. Southern Methodist Univ., 1935. Thesis: Education.

Hunter, Katrina. A History of Marion College, Marion, Virginia (1873-1967). East Tennessee State Univ., 1969. Thesis: Education.

Ingram, Margaret H. Development of Higher Education for White Women in North Carolina Prior to 1875. Univ. of North Carolina (Chapel Hill), 1961. Dissertation: Education.

Jennings, Fairie E. Educational Ideals of the Old South from 1760 to 1860. Southern Methodist Univ., 1941. Thesis: Education. [The Old South as represented in the works of such writers as Joseph Glover Baldwin, William H. Caruthers, John Esten Cooke, Ellen Glasgow, Longstreet, T.N. Page, E.A. Poe, W.G. Simms, T.S. Stribling, and William Tappan Thompson]

Jones, Cloyde C. A History of Sue Bennett College. Univ. of Kentucky, 1940. Thesis: Education.

Jones, Wilfred. The History of Randolph-Macon Academy, Front Royal, Virginia. Univ. of Virginia, 1952. Thesis: Education.

Kelly, Isaac P. Art Education in North Carolina. George Peabody College, 1966. Dissertation: Fine Arts.

King, Edith. The Development of Music Education in the Dallas Public Schools. Southern Methodist Univ., 1946. Thesis: Education.

Klages, Alfred D. A History of Texas Lutheran College, 1851-1951. Univ. of Texas (Austin), 1951. Thesis: History.

Lanier, Roy H. Church Related Colleges for Negroes in Texas. Hardin-Simmons Univ., 1950. Thesis: Education.

Long, Emma R. Education in American Literature from 1860 to 1875. Southern Methodist Univ., 1931. Thesis: Education. [As reflected in *DeBow's Review* and in *Southern Magazine*]

Mahan, Jack H. Texas Music Educators Association, 1920-1949. Southern Methodist Univ., 1949. Thesis: Education. [Emphasis on musical programs for youth]

Mason, Mrs. Frank M. The Beginnings of Texas Christian University. Texas Christian Univ., 1930. Thesis: Education.

Mathews, Alice E. Pre-College Education in the Southern Colonies. Univ. of California (Berkeley), 1968. Dissertation: History.

McBride, Otis. The Teaching of English in the Southern Antebellum Academy. George Peabody College, 1941. Dissertation: Education.

McCain, Clara E. Schools of Baylor University in Dallas. Southern Methodist Univ., 1946. Thesis: Education.

McCracken, Jewel. The Teaching of Humanities in Programs of General Education in Southern Association Colleges. George Peabody College, 1957. Dissertation: English.

McMahon, Aileen. A History of Grayson College. Southern Methodist Univ., 1940. Thesis: Education. [Located in Whitewright, Texas]

Measells, Dewitt T., Jr. History of the Expansion of the University of Mississippi, 1848-1947. Univ. of Mississippi, 1947. Thesis: History.

Miler, Emily O. The History of Colonial Education in South Carolina. Columbia Univ., 1912. Thesis: History.

Miller, William R. A History of the Development of Education in the Southwest, but More Specially in Texas, from the Time of the Earliest Settlement to the Period of Reconstruction. New York Univ., 1902. Dissertation: Pedagogy.

Mitchell, Yetta G. The History of Trinity University. Southern Methodist Univ., 1936. Thesis: Education.

Montgomery, James R. The University of Tennessee, 1887-1919. Columbia Univ., 1961. Dissertation: History.

[241]

Newton, James H. History of Paris Junior College, Paris, Texas. Southern Methodist Univ., 1935. Thesis: Education.

Norman, Eroree. The Education of Girls and Young Women in the South from 1800-1865. Southern Methodist Univ., 1940. Thesis: Education.

Ogilvie, Charles F. Academic Freedom in the Colleges of Three Major Southern Denominations, 1865-1965. Univ. of South Carolina, 1966. Dissertation: History. [Methodist Church, South; Presbyterian Church of the United States; Southern Baptist Convention]

Ogle, Boyd. Creative Writing in Selected Schools of Florida. Univ. of Florida, 1951. Thesis: Education.

O'Neall, Katherine. The Education of the Southern Highlander. New York Univ., 1929. Thesis: Education.

Parks, Serena R. Textbooks Published in North Carolina during the Civil War. Univ. of North Carolina (Chapel Hill), 1962. Thesis: Education.

Patrick, George W. Manual Labor Schools in the South. A Documentary History. Univ. of North Carolina (Chapel Hill), 1948. Thesis: Education.

Patrick, Thomas L. Southern Criticism of Northern Educational Influence, 1820-1860. Univ. of North Carolina (Chapel Hill), 1950. Dissertation: Education.

Petit, Judith L. The Founding of Southern Methodist University, 1910-1916. Southern Methodist Univ., 1965. Thesis: History.

Pevey, Wayne. A History of the Department of Drama (The University of Texas). Univ. of Texas (Austin), 1965. Dissertation: Speech and Drama.

Pirkle, William B. A Study of the State Scholarship Aid Program for Negroes in Georgia, 1944-1955. Auburn Univ., 1956. Dissertation: Education.

Porter, Earl W. A History of Trinity College, 1892-1924: Foundations of Duke University. Duke Univ., 1961. Dissertation: History.

Posey, E.B., Jr. The History of Negro Education in Nolan County, Texas. Hardin-Simmons Univ., 1952. Thesis: Education.

Powell, Mae M. The History of Texas Christian University from 1895-1939. Southern Methodist Univ., 1939. Thesis: Education.

Pryor, William H. An Evaluation of the Aural Abilities of Instrumental Music Education Majors in Four Louisiana State Colleges. Northeast Louisiana Univ., 1968. Thesis: Music Education.

Rees, Willa F. A History of Wesleyan Female College from 1836 to 1874. Emory Univ., 1935. Thesis: Religious Education.

Richardson, Eloise G. The Place of Religion on the Southern Methodist University Campus. Southern Methodist Univ., 1951. Thesis: Religious Education.

Sanford, Paul L. The Origins and Development of Higher Education for Negroes in South Carolina to 1920. Univ. of New Mexico, 1965. Dissertation: History.

Schulz, Janice E. The Effectiveness of Northern Aid to Negro Education in the South, 1862-1880. Miami Univ. (Ohio), 1959. Thesis: Teaching History.

Segner, Kenyon B. A History of the Community College Movement in North Carolina, 1927-1963. Univ. of North Carolina (Chapel Hill), 1963. Dissertation: Education.

Sellars, James B. The History of Negro Education in Alabama. Univ. of Chicago, 1925. Thesis: Education.

Sheppard, Lydia D. The History of Shorter College. Emory Univ., 1941. Thesis: Education. [In Georgia]

Shrivanek, John M. The Education of the Czechs in Texas. Univ. of Texas (Austin), 1946. Thesis: Education. [Includes biographies of prominent Czechs]

Skinner, Sara T. A Study of the American Short Story as Presented in Textbooks Used at Newnan Georgia High School Since 1910. Auburn Univ., 1966. Thesis: English.

Smith, Cluster Q. Senior Colleges and Universities in Texas, 1906 to 1936. Southern Methodist Univ., 1939. Thesis: Education.

Smith, Earle R. A History of the East Alabama Male College. Auburn Univ., 1932. Thesis: Education. [Early name of Auburn University]

Smith, J.W. A Survey of the Development and the Needs of the North Texas State Teacher's College, Denton, Texas. Southern Methodist Univ., 1925. Thesis: Education.

Smith, Willard W. The Relations of College and State in Colonial America. Columbia Univ., 1950. Dissertation: History. [Includes College of William and Mary]

Smith, Mildred P. Early History of Higher Education for Women in the Seaboard South. Duke Univ., 1932. Thesis: Education.

Spruill, Albert W. Consequences Encountered by Negro Teachers in the Process of Desegregation of Schools in Four Southern States. Cornell Univ., 1958. Dissertation: Sociology.

Stoekel, Althea L. Politics and Administration in the American Colonial Colleges. Univ. of Illinois, 1958. Dissertation: History. [Includes College of William and Mary]

Strother, Martha D. The History of Lon Morris College. Southern Methodist Univ., 1941. Thesis: Education. [Jacksonville, Texas]

Tietjen, Charles H. A Survey of Negro Education in Orange County, North Carolina. Univ. of North Carolina (Chapel Hill), 1948. Thesis: Education.

Vaughn, William P. The Sectional Conflict in Southern Public Education: 1865-1876. Ohio State Univ., 1961. Dissertation: History.

Wade, Louise H. The History of the Development and Growth of the Speech and Drama Department at Grambling College. Northeast Louisiana Univ., 1971. Thesis: Speech. [In Louisiana]

Wake, Orville W. A History of Lynchburg College, 1903-1953. Univ. of Virginia, 1957. Dissertation: Education.

Wayland, Frances S. The Educational Efforts of the Methodist Church in Texas during the Reconstruction Period. Southern Methodist Univ., 1942. Thesis: History. [Discussion of several Texas Colleges]

Webb, Russell F. History of Early Colleges of Callahan County, Texas. Hardin-Simmons Univ., 1949. Thesis: Education.

[243]

West, Carole T. The Informal Education of Southern Children as
    Revealed in the Literature of the Period 1830-1860. Univ.
    of North Carolina (Chapel Hill), 1969. Dissertation:
    Education.
Wheeler, Guy H., Jr. The History of Education in Texas during the
    Reconstruction Period. North Texas State Univ., 1953. Thesis:
    History.
Wilson, Ellen G. Higher Education in the Old South, Its Contri-
    bution to the Nation. New York Univ., 1928. Thesis:
    Education.
Wilson, George P., Jr. A History of Speech Education at the
    University of Virginia, 1825-1953. Columbia Univ., 1958.
    Dissertation: Speech. [Jefferson's plans; traits of
    Southern culture, society, and oratory]
Wing, Lucy F. Northern Educators in the Colleges of the Lower
    South, 1800-1850. Columbia Univ., 1943. Thesis: History.
Winter, Roberta P. A Plan for a Coordinated Speech and Drama
    Program for the University Center in Georgia. New York Univ.,
    1954. Dissertation: Education.
Witherington, H.C. A History of State Higher Education in Tennessee.
    Univ. of Chicago, 1931. Dissertation: English.
Woodward, Mrs. Mary T. History of Texas Presbyterian College,
    Milford, Texas. Southern Methodist Univ., 1945. Thesis:
    Education.
Yarborough, Legrand I. A History of the Early Teaching of Agri-
    culture in South Carolina. Univ. of Florida, 1956. Disser-
    tation: Education.

HISTORY OF THEATER

Andrews, Jack E. Community Theatre in Virginia: A Summary of
    Activity and Methods, 1953-54. Univ. of Virginia, 1954.
    Thesis: Speech and Drama.
Archer, Leonard C. The National Association for the Advancement
    of Colored People and the American Theatre: A Study of
    Relationships and Influence. Ohio State Univ., 1959. Disser-
    tation: Speech and Drama.
Arnold, Coleman. A History of the Lexington Theater from 1887 to
    1900. Univ. of Kentucky, 1956. Dissertation: Speech and
    Drama. [Lexington, Kentucky]
Ashby, Clifford C. Realistic Acting and the Advent of the Group
    in America: 1889-1922. Stanford Univ., 1963. Dissertation:
    Theater. [Discusses Minnie Maddern Fisk]
Bailey, Frances M. A History of the Stage in Mobile, Alabama,
    1824-1850. Univ. of Iowa, 1934. Thesis: Dramatic Art.
Barton, Henry. A History of the Dallas Opera House, with a Day
    Book for the Seasons, 1901- 02 to 1910- 11. Southern
    Methodist Univ., 1935. Thesis: English.
Beckham, John L. Dion Boucicault in New Orleans, 1841-1865.
    Tulane Univ., 1954. Thesis: English.
Becton, Emma B. The Little Theatre Movement in Four Universities.
    George Peabody College, 1931. Thesis: English.
Bender, Lorelle C. The French Opera House of New Orleans, 1859-
    1890. Louisiana State Univ., 1940. Thesis: English.

Bonsteel, Abbie B. The Carolina Playmakers. Mercer Univ., 1930.
Thesis: English.

Boyce, Monique D. The First Forty Years of the Augusta, Georgia,
Theatre. Univ. of Georgia, 1957. Thesis: English.

Bradford, Clinton W. The Non-Professional Theatre in Louisiana.
Louisiana State Univ., 1952. Dissertation: Speech and
Drama.

Bradford, Thomazine B. Educational Value of the Little Theatre.
Texas Christian Univ., 1931. Thesis: English. [Discusses
over twenty Texas little theaters]

Brady, Donald V. History of El Paso Theatre: 1881 to 1905.
Tulane Univ., 1965. Dissertation: Speech and Theater.
[Emphasizes history of Myar Opera House in El Paso, Texas]

Brian, George C. The Non-professional Theatre in Louisiana,
1900-1925. Louisiana State Univ., 1965. Dissertation:
Theater.

Bristow, Eugene K. "Look Out for Saturday Night": A Social
History of Professional Variety Theater in Memphis, Tennessee,
1859-1880. State Univ. of Iowa, 1956. Dissertation: Speech
and Theater.

Brodnax, Margaret O. The Theater in Fort Worth, 1901-1962.
Texas Christian Univ., 1959. Thesis: English.

Brown, Edward D. History of the Shreveport Little Theatre,
Shreveport, Louisiana, 1922 to 1956. Univ. of Denver, 1958.
Dissertation: Speech and Drama.

Brown, Mozelle. The Little Theater Movement: A Survey of the
Activities in Alabama. Auburn Univ., 1937. Thesis: English.

Cashin, Lillian E. The Relation between the Public and the
Theater. Fisk Univ., 1917. Thesis: English. [Includes
section on drama at Negro universities: Atlanta, Fisk, and
Talladega]

Chiles, Ruth. The Birmingham Theatres, 1886-1900. Birmingham-
Southern College, 1936. Thesis: English. [Birmingham,
Alabama]

Clarke, Mitchell. The Early Theatre in Kentucky. Western
Kentucky Univ., 1947. Thesis: English.

Clay, Lucille N. The Lexington Theatre from 1800 to 1840. Univ.
of Kentucky, 1930. Thesis: English. [Lexington, Kentucky]

Cory, Joyce B. The Dallas Theater Center: A History. Trinity
Univ. (Texas), 1968. Thesis: Drama.

Coulson, James P. The Development of the American National
Theatre Concept. Univ. of Kansas, 1965. Dissertation:
Speech and Drama.

Coyne, Bernard A. A History of Arena Stage, Washington, D.C.
Tulane Univ., 1964. Dissertation: Speech and Drama.

Crum, Mabel T. The History of the Lexington Theater from the
Beginning to 1860. Univ. of Kentucky, 1956. Dissertation:
English. [Lexington, Kentucky]

Culp, Ralph B. Drama and Theater as a Source of Colonial American
Attitudes Toward Independence, 1758-1776. Cornell Univ.,
1962. Dissertation: Theater. [Lists and comments on plays
performed in Williamsburg, Virginia, Annapolis, Maryland; and
Charleston, S.C.]

Curtis, Mary J. The Early Charleston Stage: 1703-1798. Indiana Univ. (Bloomington), 1968. Dissertation: Theater.

Davidson, Frank C. The Rise, Development, Decline and Influence of the American Minstrel Show. New York Univ., 1952. Dissertation: Speech and Drama. [Argues that without the large Negro population in the South, it is unlikely that the Minstrel show would have been born]

Davis, Jackson. A History of Professional Theater in Dallas, Texas 1920-1930. Louisiana State Univ., 1962. Dissertation: Theater.

Dietz, Mary M. A History of the Theater in Louisville. Univ. of Louisville (Kentucky), 1921. Thesis: English.

Dormon, James H. Development of Professional Theatrical Activity in the South, 1815-1845. Univ. of North Carolina (Chapel Hill), 1959. Thesis: History.

Dormon, James H., Jr. The Theater in the Antebellum South, 1815-1861. Univ. of North Carolina (Chapel Hill), 1966. Dissertation: History.

Duggar, Mary M. The Theatre in Mobile [Ala.], 1822-1860. Univ. of Alabama, 1941. Thesis: Speech.

Estes, Maxie C. A Century of Theatre Activity in the Capital City of Florida: An Historical Study of Theatrical Entertainment in Tallahassee, Florida, from 1857-1957. Florida State Univ., 1962. Dissertation: Speech and Theater.

Faulkner, Seldon. The New Memphis Theater of Memphis, Tennessee, from 1859-1880. State Univ. of Iowa, 1957. Dissertation: Theater.

Fife, Iline. The Theatre during the Confederacy. Louisiana State Univ., 1949. Dissertation: Fine Arts.

Free, Joseph M. Studies in American Theatre History: The Theatre of Southwestern Mississippi to 1840. Univ. of Iowa, 1941. Dissertation: English.

Gafford, Lucile. Material Conditions in the Theatres of New Orleans before the Civil War. Univ. of Chicago, 1925. Thesis: English.

_____. History of the St. Charles Theatre 1835-43. Univ. of Chicago, 1930. Dissertation: English. [St. Charles Theatre of New Orleans]

Gober, Ruth B. The Professional Theatre in Oklahoma City, 1889-1941. Northwestern Univ., 1941. Thesis: Speech.

Golden, Joseph. The Position and Character of Theater-in-the-Round in the United States. Univ. of Illinois, 1954. Dissertation: Theater. [Includes Carousel Theater at University of Tennessee]

Green, Russell E. Legal and Moral Restrictions in the Colonial American Theatre. Univ. of South Carolina, 1950. Thesis: English.

Hadley, Richard H. The Theatre in Lynchburg, Virginia, from Its Beginnings in 1822 to the Outbreak of the Civil War. Univ. of Michigan, 1947. Dissertation: Dramatic Art.

Hammack, Henry E. A History of the Dallas Little Theatre, 1920-1943. Tulane Univ., 1967. Dissertation: Theater.

Hanley, Kathryn T. The Amateur Theatre in New Orleans before 1835. Tulane Univ., 1940. Thesis: English.

[246]

Head, Sadie F.E. A Historical Study of the Tulane and Crescent
    Theatres of New Orleans, Louisiana: 1897-1937. Louisiana
    State Univ., 1963. Dissertation: Speech and Drama.
Hemmingson, Nadine E. A History of the Opposition to the American
    Theatre up to 1774. Northwestern Univ., 1927. Thesis:
    Journalism. [One chapter concerns Maryland and Virginia]
Henderson, Jerry E. A History of the Ryman Auditorium in
    Nashville, Tennessee: 1892-1920. Louisiana State Univ.,
    1962. Dissertation: Speech and Drama.
Hervey, Hubert C. A History of the Community Little Theater of
    Texas: Emphasizing the Dallas Little Theater as Representative.
    Univ. of Texas (Austin), 1930. Thesis: English.
Hester, Wyoline. The Savannah Stage. Auburn Univ., 1930.
    Thesis: English. [Savannah, Georgia]
Hill, West T. A Study of the Macauley's Theatre in Louisville,
    Kentucky, 1873-1880. State Univ. of Iowa, 1954. Disser-
    tation: History.
Hostetler, Paul S. James H. Caldwell: Theatre Manager.
    Louisiana State Univ., 1964. Dissertation: Theater.
    [Principally in New Orleans, but also Natchez, Nashville,
    and Huntsville]
Hyams, Frances I. A Brief History of the American Theater, with
    Especial Reference to the Eighteenth Century, Supplemented
    by Collections toward a Bibliography before 1800. Radcliffe
    College, 1916. Dissertation: English.
Johnson, M.M. Margo Jones' Dallas Theatre, Inc., 1945-49. North
    Texas State Univ., 1967. Thesis: Speech and Drama.
Jones, Jane E. History of the Stage in Louisville, Kentucky, from
    Its Beginning to 1845. Univ. of Iowa, 1932. Thesis:
    Dramatic Arts.
Jones, Marian P. Some Notes for a History of the Chattanooga
    Theater, 1877-1888. Duke Univ., 1942. Thesis: English.
Karem, Fred J. The Little Theatre Movement in Louisville. Univ.
    of Louisville, 1938. Thesis: English.
Keller, Helen B. The History of the Theater in Columbus, Georgia,
    from 1828 to 1865. Univ. of Georgia, 1957. Thesis: English.
Kennedy, Lucile B. A History of the Dallas Opera House (A Record
    of the Plays and Their Reception), with a Day Book for
    Seasons, 1911-1912 through 1921. Southern Methodist Univ.,
    1940. Thesis: English.
Kennedy, Mary A. The Theater Movement in Washington, 1800-1835.
    Catholic Univ., 1933. Thesis: English.
Ketchum, Barbara. Actors in the Charleston Theatre, 1837-1861.
    Univ. of Texas (Austin), 1942. Thesis: English.
King, Clyde R. A History of the Theatre in Texas, 1722-1900.
    Baylor Univ., 1962. Dissertation: English.
Kumli, Helen K. Movements in the Modern Theater in Great Britain
    and America. Birmingham-Southern College, 1937. Thesis:
    English. [North Carolina Playmakers]
Land, Robert H. Theatre in Colonial Virginia. Univ. of Virginia,
    1936. Thesis: History.
_____. The Theater in Colonial Virginia. Univ. of Virginia,
    1942. Dissertation: History.

Lane, Doris A. A History of the Fort Worth Theater from 1880-1888. Texas Christian Univ., 1948. Thesis: English.

Langley, William O. The Theatre in Columbus, Georgia, from 1828-1878. Auburn Univ., 1937. Thesis: English.

Langworthy, Helen. The Theatre in the Frontier Cities of Lexington, Kentucky, and Cincinnati, Ohio 1797-1835. State Univ. of Iowa, 1952. Dissertation: Speech and Drama.

Latshaw, Sylvia L. Status of the Acted Drama in the Colleges and Universities of the United States. Univ. of North Carolina (Chapel Hill), 1921. Thesis: Education. [The Carolina Playmakers, the University of Louisville Players, and other Southern college groups]

Little, Paul J. Reactions to the Theatre: Virginia, Massachusetts, and Pennsylvania, 1665-1793. Syracuse Univ., 1969. Dissertation: Theater.

Lominac, Harry G. The Carolina Dramatic Association: Its History, 1922-1962. Univ. of North Carolina (Chapel Hill), 1962. Thesis: English.

Lyle, Beverly B. A Detailed Survey of the New Orleans Theatre from 1800 to 1825 (English Productions). Louisiana State Univ., 1938. Thesis: Speech.

Maguire, Agatha C.F. The American Theater before the Revolution. Boston Univ., 1936. Thesis: English. [The Southern theater--especially of Virginia, Maryland, and South Carolina--before the Revolution]

Maiden, Lewis S. A Chronicle of the Theater in Nashville, Tennessee, 1876-1900. Vanderbilt Univ., 1955. Dissertation: English.

Maloff, Saul. The Theory and Practice of the New Theatre Movement. State Univ. of Iowa, 1952. Dissertation: English. [Discusses Paul Green]

McBryde, Donald M. The Design and Equipment Specifications of a Theatre Building for the University of Mississippi. Univ. of Denver, 1964. Dissertation: Speech and Drama.

McDowell, Sara-Jean. The Carolina Playmakers, Its History--1918-1950. Univ. of North Carolina (Chapel Hill), 1962. Thesis: Dramatic Art.

McNamara, Brooks B. The Development of the American Playhouse in The Eighteenth Century. Tulane Univ., 1965. Dissertation: Theater. [Includes Williamsburg and Richmond, Virginia]

Manser, Ruth B. The Influence of the American Actress on the Development of the American Theater from 1835 to 1895. New York Univ., 1937. Dissertation: English. [Mary Anderson, Mrs. Leslie Carter, Minnie Madderen Fiske]

Meek, Beryl. A Record of the Theatre in Lexington, Kentucky, from 1799-1850. Univ. of Iowa, 1930. Thesis: Dramatic Art.

Metten, Charles L. The Development in America of Theories of Directing as Found in American Writing, 1914-1930. State Univ. of Iowa, 1960. Dissertation: Theater. [Includes Minnie Maddern Fiske and Stark Young]

Moehlenbrock, Arthur H. The German Drama on the New Orleans Stage. Univ. of Iowa, 1941. Dissertation: German.

Moore, Harris P. II. The Theater in Fort Worth, 1902-1903. Texas Christian Univ., 1963. Thesis: English.

Moore, Kemper M. The Theater as It Reflects the Problems of the
South: A Study of the American Theater from 1919 to 1947
insofar as It Has Reflected the Social and Economic Problems
of the Southeastern Region of the United States. New York
Univ., 1950. Dissertation: English.

Morris, Marjorie R. A Proposed Reconstruction of the Elizabethan
Globe Theater in Odessa, Texas. North Texas State Univ.,
1950. Thesis: English.

Morrow, Anne M.H. A History of Drama at Auburn University from
1913 to 1965. Auburn Univ., 1966. Thesis: Speech.

Morrow, Marguerite H. A History of the English Stage in New
Orleans from 1817-1837. Univ. of Iowa, 1933. Thesis:
Dramatic Art.

Murray, Jean O. The Aims of the Little Theater in American
Colleges and Universities. Ohio Univ., 1939. Thesis:
Dramatic Arts. [Includes Louisiana State University,
University of North Carolina, Rollins College]

O'Steen, Arthur M. A List of Theatrical Performances in Durham,
North Carolina, from 1913 Through 1923. Duke Univ., 1954.
Thesis: English.

Palmer, Richard H. The Outdoor Theatre Movement in the United
States from 1900 to 1920. Univ. of Iowa, 1965. Disser-
tation: Theater. [One of major sources is papers of
Charles D. Coburn at The University of Georgia Library]

Parrott, Frederick J. The Mid-Nineteenth Century American Theater,
1840-1860: A Survey of Theatre Production, Comment, and
Opinion. Cornell Univ., 1948. Dissertation: Fine Arts.
[Brief discussion of theatre production in South during
this period]

Payne, Newcomb L., Jr. The Theater in Fort Worth: 1900-1901.
Texas Christian Univ., 1956. Thesis: English.

Perkins, Johnnie A. Dramatic Productions in New Orleans from
1817 to 1861. Louisiana State Univ., 1929. Thesis: English.

Pettit, Paul B. The Showboat Theater: The Development of the
Showboat on the Mississippi River and on the Eastern Water-
ways. Cornell Univ., 1943. Thesis: Humanities.

Phelps, LaVerne P. A History of the Little Theater Movement in
Amarillo from 1888 to 1946. West Texas State Univ., 1946.
Thesis: Speech.

Potts, Helen J. A Study of the Little Theatre of Dallas [Texas]:
1920-1943. Southern Methodist Univ., 1968. Thesis:
History.

Quinby, George H. Academic Theaters in the U.S., 1930-1943. Yale
Univ., 1946. Thesis: Fine Arts. [Discussion includes
theaters in Florida, Georgia, Louisiana, and Texas]

Rabke, Barbara. Theater in San Antonio [Texas], 1886-1891.
Trinity Univ. (Texas), 1964. Thesis: Drama.

Rankin, Hugh F. The Colonial Theatre: Its History and Operations.
Univ. of North Carolina (Chapel Hill), 1960. Dissertation:
History. [Includes Virginia and South Carolina]

Ritter, Charles C. The Theatre in Memphis, Tennessee, from Its
Beginning to 1859. Univ. of Iowa, 1956. Dissertation:
English.

Roden, Sally A. History of the St. Charles Theatre of New Orleans Under the Management of David Bidwell, 1880-1888. North Texas State Univ., 1969. Thesis: Speech and Drama.

Roppolo, Joseph P. A History of the American Stage in New Orleans, 1842-1845. Tulane Univ., 1948. Thesis: English.

_____. A History of the English Language Theatre in New Orleans, 1845-1861. Tulane Univ., 1950. Dissertation: English.

Rotter, Charles C. The Theatre in Memphis, Tennessee, from Its Beginnings to 1859 (Parts One-Five). State Univ. of Iowa, 1956. Dissertation: Theater.

Sandle, Floyd L. A History of the Development of the Educational Theatre in Negro Colleges and Universities from 1911 to 1959. Louisiana State Univ., 1959. Dissertation: Theater. [Mainly Southern schools; discusses the Southern Association of Dramatic and Speech Arts]

Shaffer, Virginia M. The Theatre in Baltimore (from Its Beginnings to 1786). Johns Hopkins Univ., 1926. Thesis: English.

Shapard, William. Margo Jones and Her Theatre in Dallas: 1945-1959. Southern Methodist Univ., 1960. Thesis: Speech and Theater.

Shiffler, Harrold C. The Opposition of the Presbyterian Church in the United States of America to the Theatre in America, 1750-1891. State Univ. of Iowa, 1953. Dissertation: Theater. [Includes Richmond theaters]

Shockley, Martin S. A History of the Theater in Richmond, Virginia, 1819-1838. Univ. of North Carolina (Chapel Hill), 1938. Dissertation: English.

Smith, Elden T. Four Representative Little Theatres. Case Western Reserve Univ., 1947. Dissertation: Dramatic Arts. [Discusses *Le Petit Theatre du Vieux Carré* and the Little Theater of Dallas]

Smither, Nelle K. A History of the English Theater at New Orleans, 1806-1842. Univ. of Pennsylvania, 1942. Dissertation: English.

Sparks, Andrew H. A History of the Theatre in Savannah, 1800-1836. Univ. of Georgia, 1940. Thesis: English.

Sterling, Wallace. The Front St. Theatre of Memphis: The Emergence of a Resident Professional Theatre in the Mid-South. Southern Illinois Univ. (Carbondale), 1966. Dissertation: Theater.

Stevens, Eva. The History of the Theatre in Nashville, Tennessee, 1871-1875. Vanderbilt Univ., 1935. Thesis: English.

Stone, Delza H. Drama in San Antonio, 1889-1894. St. Mary's Univ. (San Antonio), 1944. Thesis: English.

Strait, Bruce C. Dramatic Censorship in the United States, 1900-1950. Univ. of North Carolina (Chapel Hill), 1952. Thesis: Drama. [Includes some discussion of censorship of Southern plays]

Strickland, Francis C. A History of the Little Theatre Movement in America. Northwestern Univ., 1926. Thesis: Speech. [Includes discussion of Carolina Playmakers and Dallas Little Theatre]

Summers, Wayne E. A History of Playmakers, Incorporated, the Community Theater at Sans Souci Forest, Covington, Louisiana, 1955-1970. Northeast Louisiana Univ., 1970. Thesis: Speech.

Tedford, Harold C. A Study of Theatrical Entertainments in
Northwest Arkansas from Their Beginning Through 1889.
Louisiana State Univ., 1965. Dissertation: Theater.
Temple, Lura. The Dallas Little Theatre: A History (1920-1927).
Southern Methodist Univ., 1927. Thesis: English.
Treser, Robert M. Houston's Alley Theatre. Tulane Univ., 1967.
Dissertation: Theater.
Turner, Vivian D. The Stage in New Orleans after 1837. Univ. of
Iowa, 1929. Thesis: Dramatic Art.
Turnipseed, La Margaret. The Antebellum Theatre in Montgomery
Alabama: 1840-1860. Auburn Univ., 1948. Thesis: English.
Walsh, Charles R. Shakespeare on the Colonial Stage. Fordham
Univ., 1948. Dissertation: English.
Ward, Willie P. English and American Plays in New Orleans. Univ.
of Texas (Austin), 1940. Thesis: English.
Warner, Frank L. A History of the Tulane University Theatre,
1937-1967. Tulane Univ., 1968. Dissertation: Theater.
Williams, Anne S.C. Theatre Promotion in North Carolina. Univ. of
North Carolina (Chapel Hill), 1952. Thesis: Drama.
Wilmeth, Don B. A History of the Margo Jones Theatre. Univ. of
Illinois, 1964. Dissertation: Theater. [Theater in Dallas,
Texas]
Woodruff, Joe H. History of the Theatrical Activity at South-
western State College, Weatherford, Oklahoma. Southern
Methodist Univ., 1952. Thesis: Speech.
Wooten, Denham L. Annals of the Stage in Little Rock, Arkansas,
1834-1890. Columbia Univ., 1935. Thesis: English.
Yerby, Frank G. The Little Theater in the Negro College. Fisk
Univ., 1938. Thesis: English. [Discussion includes
numerous Southern colleges and universities]
Yocum, Jack H. A History of the Theatre in Houston, 1936-1954.
Univ. of Wisconsin, 1955. Dissertation: Speech and Drama.

LIBRARIES AND LYCEUMS

Anders, Mary E. The Development of Public Library Service in the
Southeastern United States, 1895-1950. Columbia Univ.,
1958. Dissertation: Library Science.
Beaver, Frances E. A Survey of Texas Libraries. Univ. of Texas
(Austin), 1943. Thesis: Education. [A history as well as
a survey]
Carr, Louise D. The Reverend Willie Lee Buffington's Life and
Contribution to the Development of Rural Libraries in the
South. Atlanta Univ., 1958. Thesis: Library Science.
Gay, Birdie S. The Presentation of Books by and about American
Negroes in the Central Library of the Atlanta Public Library
System. Atlanta Univ., 1960. Thesis: Library Science.
Goudeau, John M. Early Libraries in Louisiana: A Study of the
Creole Influence [with] Volume II: Source Materials.
Western Reserve Univ., 1965. Dissertation: Library Science.
[From earliest to about 1900]
Hamilton, Mary. The Lyceum in New Orleans, 1840-1860. Louisiana
State Univ., 1948. Thesis: Speech.

Hayes, Cecil B. The American Lyceum: Its History and Contribution to the Advancement of Education. Stanford Univ., 1930. Thesis: Education. [Discusses Georgia and District of Columbia]

Hembree, Myrtle. The Growth and Development of Libraries in the Elementary Schools of Texas. Southern Methodist Univ., 1937. Thesis: Education.

Hendrix, Julia S. A Survey of Public Library Facilities in South Carolina. Univ. of South Carolina, 1925. Thesis: English.

Houlette, William D. Plantation and Parish Libraries in the Old South. Univ. of Iowa, 1933. Dissertation: History.

Hulbert, James A. A Survey of the Services of the Atlanta University Library. Univ. of Columbia, 1938. Thesis: Library Service.

Jarrell, Louise. The Austin Lyceum, 1839-1841. Univ. of Texas (Austin), 1941. Thesis: English.

Jones, Houston G. The Public Archives of North Carolina, 1663-1903. Duke Univ., 1965. Dissertation: History.

Krenitsky, Michael V. A Study of Junior College Libraries in Texas. Southern Methodist Univ., 1954. Thesis: Education.

Little, Sadie P. The Need for Libraries in South Carolina and the Remedy. Univ. of South Carolina, 1925. Thesis: English.

MacLear, Martha. The American Lyceum Movement and Mechanics Institutes. Columbia Univ., 1910. Thesis: Education.

Maestri, Helen L. A History of the New Orleans Commercial Library Society, 1831-1852. Tulane Univ., 1943. Thesis: English.

Manint, Helen A. A History of the New Orleans Public Library and the Howard Memorial Library. Tulane Univ., 1942. Thesis: History.

Napier, Suzan. The History of the Everette De Golyer Book Collection. Southern Methodist Univ., 1967. Thesis: History. [Dallas, Texas, the De Golyer-Western Library, is not at Southern Methodist University]

Patterson, John M. Private Libraries in Virginia in the Eighteenth Century. Univ. of Virginia, 1936. Thesis: English.

Petersen, Vesta. The American Colonial Library Movement. Columbia Univ., 1932. Thesis: History. [The South Carolina Library Society, private libraries in Virginia, the founding of the College of William and Mary, etc.]

Powell, Benjamin E. The Development of Libraries in Southern State Universities to 1920. Univ. of Chicago, 1947. Dissertation: Library Science.

Robinson, Riva. The American Lyceum (1865-1885). Columbia Univ., 1933. Thesis: History.

Rouse, Roscoe, Jr. A History of the Baylor University Library, 1845-1919. Univ. of Michigan, 1962. Dissertation: Library Science.

Scott, Ellen. The History and Influence of the Old Library of Transylvania University. Univ. of Kentucky, 1929. Thesis: English.

Shafer, Henry B. College Libraries in the United States from 1790-1830. Columbia Univ., 1927. Thesis: History.

Shores, Louis. Origins of the American College Library, 1638-
1800. George Peabody College, 1934. Dissertation: English.
Spain, Frances L. Libraries of South Carolina: Their Origins
and Early History, 1700-1830. Univ. of Chicago, 1945.
Dissertation: Library Science.
Stephenson, Harriet S.K. History of the Louisiana State Library,
Formerly Louisiana Library Commission. Louisiana State Univ.,
1957. Dissertation: Library Science.
Stoddard, Paul W. The Place of the Lyceum in American Life.
Columbia Univ., 1929. Thesis: Education. [Country lyceums
in Georgia are mentioned]
Tamblyn, Eldon W. Censorship and North Carolina Public Libraries.
Univ. of North Carolina (Chapel Hill), 1964. Thesis: Library
Science.
Thurber, Evangeline. The Library of the Land-Grant College, 1862-
1900: A Preliminary Study. Columbia Univ., 1928. Thesis:
Library Science.
Townsend, H.E. A History of the Louisiana Chatauqua. Louisiana
State Univ., 1929. Thesis: Education.
White, K.C.R. The Lyceum in America. Harvard Univ., 1918.
Dissertation: English.
Young, Catherine. The History of the Texas State Library. Univ.
of Texas (Austin), 1932. Thesis: Education.

ONOMASTIC STUDIES

Bass, Mary F. A Study of Place Names of Clarke County, Mississippi.
Univ. of Alabama, 1942. Thesis: English.
Berry, Nora. Place Names of Natchitoches Parish [Louisiana].
Louisiana State Univ., 1935. Thesis: English.
Bloodworth, Bertha E. Florida Place Names. Univ. of Florida,
1959. Dissertation: Linguistics.
Brackett, Walter L. Place Names of Five Northeast Counties of
Oklahoma. Univ. of Tulsa, 1944. Thesis: English.
Clover, Margaret G. The Place Names of Atascosa County, Texas.
Univ. of Texas (Austin), 1952. Thesis: English.
Coumes, John V. A Study of Some Place Names in Tangipahoa Parish,
Louisiana. Auburn Univ., 1968. Thesis: English.
Douglass, Lillian. Place Names of East Feliciana Parish
[Louisiana]. Louisiana State Univ., 1932. Thesis: English.
Dulin, Ruth C. Geographical Place Names in the Lomax Ballads.
Hardin-Simmons Univ., 1952. Thesis: English.
Ford, Zillah. The Pronunciation of Spanish Place Names in the
Southwestern United States. Univ. of Oklahoma, 1947.
Thesis: English. [Primarily Texas]
Foscue, Virginia O. The Place Names of Sumter County, Alabama.
Univ. of Alabama, 1959. Thesis: English.
Garrett, Patrick P. A Study of Place Names in Lincoln Parish,
Louisiana. Auburn Univ., 1963. Thesis: English.
Godley, Margaret W. Georgia County Place Names. Emory Univ.,
1935. Thesis: English.
Gordon, James W., Jr. French Place Names in Virginia. Univ. of
Virginia, 1933. Thesis: French.
Hagood, Thomas N. Place Name Patterns in Jefferson County,
Alabama. Birmingham-Southern College, 1960. Thesis: English.

Kenny, Hamill T. The Origin and Meaning of the Indian Place
    Names of Maryland. Univ. of Maryland, 1951. Dissertation:
    English.
Lindsey, Bertha D. A Study of Some Place Names in Calhoun County,
    Alabama. Auburn Univ., 1962. Thesis: English.
Lorio, Elaine C. The Place Names of Pointe Coupée Parish
    [Louisiana]. Louisiana State Univ., 1932. Thesis: English.
McDonald, Fred L. A Study of Place Names in Lowndes County,
    Georgia. Auburn Univ., 1961. Thesis: English.
McJimsey, George D. Topographic Terms in Virginia. Columbia
    Univ., 1941. Dissertation: English.
McMullen, Edwin W. English Topographic Terms in Florida, 1563-
    1874. Columbia Univ., 1950. Dissertation: English.
Mockler, William E. The Surnames of Trans-Allegheny Virginia:
    1750-1800. Ohio State Univ., 1955. Dissertation: Linguistics.
Oliphant, M.C.S. Some French Names in Charleston District, South
    Carolina. Univ. of North Carolina (Chapel Hill), 1940.
    Thesis: Romance Languages.
Ordoubadian, Reza. Rutherford County: A Study in Onomastics.
    Auburn Univ., 1968. Dissertation: Linguistics. [Place
    names in Tennessee]
Patterson, Lucy A.H. A Study of Some Place Names of Southeastern
    Lee County, Alabama. Auburn Univ., 1963. Thesis: English.
Reynolds, Jack A. Louisiana Place Names of Romance Origin.
    Louisiana State Univ., 1942. Dissertation: English.
Richmond, Winthrop E. Place Names in the English and Scottish
    Popular Ballads and Their American Variants. Ohio State
    Univ., 1947. Dissertation: English. [References to North
    Carolina and Virginia ballads]
Seale, Lea L. Indian Place Names in Mississippi. Louisiana State
    Univ., 1939. Dissertation: English.
Smith, Jack A. A Study of Place Names in Forrest County, Missis-
    sippi. Auburn Univ., 1969. Dissertation: Linguistics.
Turner, Sara A. Place Names of Webster Parish: A Linguistic
    Historical Study. Louisiana State Univ., 1935. Thesis:
    English.
Wilson, Raymond G. Place Names of Six Northeast Counties of
    Oklahoma. Univ. of Tulsa, 1940. Thesis: English.

SOUTHERN LANGUAGE, SPEECH,
ORATORY, AND DIALECT

Albright, Theresa. The Vocabulary of the Younger Generation in
    the Richmond Area of Virginia. Univ. of Maryland, 1969.
    Thesis: English.
Anshen, Frank S. Speech Variation Among Negroes in a Small
    Southern Community. New York Univ., 1969. Dissertation:
    Linguistics. [Hillsborough, North Carolina]
Avis, Walter S. The Mid-Back Vowels in the English of the Eastern
    United States. Univ. of Michigan, 1956. Dissertation:
    Linguistics.
Babcock, Clarence M. A Study of the Social Significance of the
    Language of the American Frontier. Univ. of Denver, 1946.
    Thesis: English.

Babin, Lawrence J. A Glossary of the French Spoken on Grand
    Isle [Louisiana]. Louisiana State Univ., 1937. Thesis:
    Romance Languages.
Baird, Scott J. Employment Interview Speech: A Social Dialect
    in Austin, Texas. Univ. of Texas (Austin), 1969. Disser-
    tation: Linguistics.
Barrett, Madie W. A Phonology of Southeast Alabama Speech. Univ.
    of North Carolina (Chapel Hill), 1948. Dissertation:
    Comparative Linguistics.
Beaupre, Walter J. The Influence of Speech from Three Dialect
    Areas in the United States on Personality Rating of Judges
    from Four Speech Regions. Columbia Univ., 1962. Disser-
    tation: Speech. [Includes Winston-Salem, N.C.]
Beckham, A.S. Characteristics and Decline of Negro Dialects. Ohio
    State Univ., 1917. Thesis: English.
Bentley, Harold W. A Dictionary of Spanish Terms in English with
    Special Reference to the American Southwest. Columbia Univ.,
    1932. Dissertation: English.
Bernard, Lorene M. A Study of Louisiana French in Lafayette
    Parish. Louisiana State Univ., 1933. Thesis: Romance
    Languages.
Bever, Ronald D. An Analysis of Speaking in the American Restora-
    tion Movement, 1820-1849. Northwestern Univ., 1968. Disser-
    tation: Speech. [Kentucky]
Bienvenu, Charles J. The Negro-French Dialect of the Saint Martin
    Parish. Louisiana State Univ., 1933. Thesis: Romance
    Languages.
Bierschwale, Margaret. English of the Texas Range. Columbia
    Univ., 1920. Thesis: English.
Bond, George F. A Study of an Appalachian Dialect. Univ. of
    Florida, 1929. Thesis: English. [Dialect of the Broad
    River Valley section of North Carolina]
Bourgeois, Eugene O. Creole Dialect. Louisiana State Univ.,
    1927. Thesis: Romance Languages.
Bowman, Blanche S. Study of a Dialect Employed by the People of
    the Kentucky Mountains and Presented through a Group of
    Original Short Stories. Kansas State Univ., 1940. Thesis:
    English.
Bowman, Hazel L. Background Materials for the Study of Florida
    Speech. Univ. of Florida, 1948. Thesis: English.
Bowman, Myrtle E. A Comparative Study of the Vocabularies of
    White and Colored Children. Baylor Univ., 1936. Thesis:
    English.
Boyette, Dora S. Variant Pronunciation from Rockingham County,
    North Carolina, 1829-1860. Univ. of North Carolina (Chapel
    Hill), 1951. Thesis: English.
Braun, Alfred S. Advocates of Reform: Patterns of Rhetoric in
    Selected Educational Reform Movements. Stanford Univ., 1966.
    Dissertation: Speech. [Includes Jabez L.M. Curry]
Briggs, Delores G. Deviations from Standard English in Papers of
    Selected Alabama Negro High School Students. Univ. of
    Alabama, 1968. Dissertation: Linguistics.

Briggs, Olin D. A Study of Deviations from Standard English in
    Papers of Negro Freshmen at an Alabama College. Univ. of
    Alabama, 1968. Dissertation: Linguistics. [Gadsden State
    Junior College]
Broaddus, James W. The Folk Vocabulary of Estill County, Kentucky.
    Univ. of Kentucky, 1958. Thesis: English.
Broussard, Mamie J. The Creole and French of Lafayette, Louisiana:
    A Comparative Study. Atlanta Univ., 1945. Thesis: French.
    [A Study of the French influences on the City of Lafayette
    with regard to its history, language, and customs]
Butler, Melvin A. A Vocabulary Study of Negroes in Austin, Texas.
    Univ. of Texas (Austin), 1962. Thesis: English.
_____. Lexical Usage of Negroes in Northeast Louisiana. Univ.
    of Michigan, 1968. Dissertation: Linguistics.
Cabaza, Berta. The Spanish Language in Texas. No. 2: Cameron
    and Willacy Counties. Univ. of Texas (Austin), 1950. Thesis:
    Spanish.
Caffee, Nathaniel M. A Phonological Study of the Speech of a
    Homogeneous Group in Charlottesville, Virginia. Univ. of
    Virginia, 1935. Dissertation: English.
Campbell, Ellen. A Study of Words Mispronounced in the High
    Schools of West Texas. Texas Tech Univ., 1934. Thesis:
    English.
Carson, William P. Literary Dialect of the Southern Highlander.
    Columbia Univ., 1926. Dissertation: English.
Cerda, Gilbert O. The Spanish Language in Texas. No. 1: Val
    Verde, Edwards, and Kinney Counties. Univ. of Texas (Austin),
    1950. Thesis: Spanish.
Chalk, Sarah C. A Vocabulary Study of Dallas County, Texas. Univ.
    of Texas (Austin), 1958. Thesis: English.
Chaudoir, Charles C. A Study of the Grammar of the Avoyelles
    French Dialect. Louisiana State Univ., 1938. Thesis:
    Romance Languages.
Coco, Eunice R. Etymological Glossary of Variants from Standard
    French in Avoyelles Parish. Louisiana State Univ., 1933.
    Thesis: Romance Languages.
Coleman, Wilma. Mountain Dialects in North Georgia. Univ. of
    Georgia, 1936. Thesis: English.
Conwell, Marilyn J. Lafayette French Phonology: A Descriptive,
    Comparative, and Historical Study of a Louisiana French
    Dialect. Univ. of Pittsburgh, 1961. Dissertation:
    Linguistics.
Cornett, John M. A Descriptive Study of Speaking in the 1968
    Florida Democratic Senatorial Primary Campaign. Florida
    State Univ., 1969. Dissertation: Speech. [LeRoy Collins
    and Earl Faircloth]
Counts, William M. The Contents of the Episcopal Addresses of
    American Methodism, 1812-1960. Southern Methodist Univ.,
    1963. Thesis: History.
Criswell, Elijah. Lewis and Clark: Linguistic Pioneers. Univ.
    of Missouri, 1937. Dissertation: English.
Crow, Porter. Standardization of American Speech: Reflected by
    One Texas Family of Five Generations. Southern Methodist
    Univ., 1950. Thesis: Speech.

Dabbs, Phyllis S.   A Descriptive-Analytical Study of Ethical
    Standards in Contemporary American Public Address.   Univ. of
    Southern California, 1961.   Dissertation: Speech.   [Includes
    radio speeches of Huey Long]
Daigle, Anna T.   Folklore and Etymological Glossary of the
    Variants from Standard French in Jefferson Davis Parish,
    Louisiana.   Louisiana State Univ., 1935.   Thesis: Romance
    Languages.
Dearden, Elizabeth J.   A Word Geography of the South Atlantic
    States.   Brown Univ., 1941.   Thesis: English.
_____.   Dialect Areas of the South Atlantic States as Determined
    by Variations in Vocabulary.   Brown Univ., 1943.   Disser-
    tation: English.
DeBlanc, Bertrand F.   A Glossary of Variants from Standard French
    Found in St. Martin Parish, Louisiana.   Louisiana State Univ.,
    1935.   Thesis: Romance Languages.
Dendy, W.E.   A Study in Negro Dialect.   Oglethorpe Univ., 1927.
    Thesis: English.
Denison, Ronald H.   A Rhetorical Analysis of Speeches by Segre-
    gationists in the Deep South.   Purdue Univ., 1961.   Disser-
    tation: Speech.
Dick, Robert C.   Rhetoric of the Negro Antebellum Protest Movement.
    Stanford Univ., 1969.   Dissertation: Speech.
Diehl, George W.   The Rise and Development of Southern Oratory.
    Univ. of Richmond, 1917.   Thesis: History.   [Nathaniel Bacon,
    John C. Calhoun, Henry Clay, Jefferson Davis, Robert Young
    Hayne, Patrick Henry, Benjamin H. Hill, Richard Henry Lee,
    William Pinckney, John Randolph, William Wirt, William
    Lowndes Yancey]
Dodd, Celeste V.   The Speech of a San Antonio American Family: A
    Study in Texas Pronunciation.   Univ. of Texas (Austin), 1938.
    Thesis: English.
Dugas, Alice M.   A Glossary of Variants from Standard French Used
    in St. Martin Parish.   Louisiana State Univ., 1935.   Thesis:
    English.
Duke, Francis J.   A Phonetic Study of Italo-American Speech in
    Richmond, Virginia.   Univ. of Virginia, 1938.   Dissertation:
    Italian.
Durand, Sidney J.   A Phonetic Study of the Creole Dialect.
    Louisiana State Univ., 1930.   Thesis: Romance Languages.
Edwards, A.M.   The Speech of Joshua of a Few Dialectical
    Peculiarities of North Central Texas.   Univ. of Oklahoma,
    1904.   Thesis: English.
Ellingsworth, Huber W.   Southern Reconciliation Orators in the
    North, 1868-1899.   Florida State Univ., 1955.   Dissertation:
    Speech.
Enzor, Edwin H., Jr.   The Preaching of James M'Gready; Frontier
    Revivalist.   Louisiana State Univ., 1964.   Dissertation:
    Speech.   [ca. 1800 in Kentucky]
Everidge, Dorothy J.   An Evaluation of Ministerial Speech Training
    in Meeting the Speech Needs of Ministers in the Fort Worth-
    Dallas Area.   North Texas State Univ., 1964.   Thesis: Speech
    and Drama.

[257]

Faneuf, Mildred A. Dialect Study of Auburn, Lee County, Alabama, Made as a Preliminary Investigation for the Preparation of Work Sheets for the Linguistic Atlas. Auburn Univ., 1939. Thesis: English.

Faras, Maria J. The Spanish Language in Texas. No. 3: Duval, Webb, and Zapata Counties. Univ. of Texas (Austin), 1951. Thesis: Spanish.

Faries, Clyde J. The Rhetoric of Private John Allen. Univ. of Missouri, 1965. Dissertation: Speech. [Mississippi Congressman, 1885-1901]

Farrison, William E. The Phonology of the Illiterate Negro Dialect of Guilford County, North Carolina. Ohio State Univ., 1936. Dissertation: English.

Fisher, Hilda B. A Study of the Speech of Jackson, Louisiana, at Three Age Levels. Louisiana State Univ., 1938. Thesis: Speech.

Fluke, Dorotha L. A Descriptive Study of the Speech of Dutchtown, Louisiana, at Three Age Levels. Louisiana State Univ., 1938. Thesis: Speech.

Foley, Lawrence M. A Phonological and Lexical Study of the Speech of Tuscaloosa County, Alabama. Univ. of Alabama, 1969. Dissertation: Linguistics.

Folk, Mary L. A Word Atlas of North Louisiana. Louisiana State Univ., 1961. Dissertation: Linguistics.

Forrester, Christine D. A Word Geography of Kentucky. Univ. of Kentucky, 1953. Thesis: English.

Foscue, Virginia O. Background and Preliminary Survey of the Linguistic Geography of Alabama. Univ. of Wisconsin, 1966. Dissertation: Linguistics.

Foushee, Isabella L. A Vocabulary Study of Brunswick and New Hanover Counties, North Carolina. East Carolina Univ., 1968. Thesis: English.

Fowler, Carl M. Demonstrations of Chaucerian Influence on Southern Language. West Texas State Univ., 1966. Thesis: English. [Mark Twain, Hamlin Garland, J.C. Harris, Paul Lawrence Dunbar, Dubose Heyward, Elizabeth Madox Roberts, Marjorie Kinnan Rawlings, and William Faulkner]

Gibson, Frances M. The Speech of the Vicksburg-Natchez Area of Mississippi. Univ. of Oklahoma, 1946. Thesis: English.

Gillespie, Elizabeth. The Dialect of the Mississippi Negro in Literature. Univ. of Mississippi, 1939. Thesis: English.

Goff, John H. Ballads and Dialects of the Southern Mountaineers. Oglethorpe, [date unknown]. Thesis: English.

Goodman, Morris F. A Comparative Study of Creole French. Columbia Univ., 1961. Dissertation: Linguistics.

Granier, Ervin L. A Glossary of the French Spoken in St. John Parish. Louisiana State Univ., 1939. Thesis: Romance Languages.

Graves, Richard L. Language Differences Among Upper- and Lower-Class Negro and White Eighth Graders in East Central Alabama. Florida State Univ., 1967. Dissertation: Linguistics.

[258]

Green, Elizabeth. Dialect study of Mobile, Mobile County, Alabama, Made as a Preliminary Investigation for the Preparation of Work sheets of the Linguistic Atlas. Auburn Univ., 1944. Thesis: English.

Guest, Charles B. A Survey of the Dialect of the Lee County, Alabama, Negro. Auburn Univ., 1932. Thesis: English.

Guilbeau, John. A Glossary of Variants from Standard-French in Lafourche Parish. Louisiana State Univ., 1936. Thesis: Romance Languages.

_____. The French Spoken in Lafourche Parish, Louisiana. Univ. of North Carolina (Chapel Hill), 1950. Dissertation: Romance Languages.

Hale, Lulu C. A Study of English Pronunciation in Kentucky. Univ. of Kentucky, 1930. Thesis: Education.

Hall, Joe D. A Dialect Study of Langdale, Chambers County, Alabama, Made as a Preliminary Investigation for the Preparation of Work sheets for the Linguistic Atlas. Auburn Univ., 1941. Thesis: English.

Hall, Joseph S. The Phonetics of Great Smoky Mountain Speech. Columbia Univ., 1942. Dissertation: Speech.

Hall, Leila M. Phonology and Orthography of *The Austin Papers*: A Study of the Origins of Texas Pronunciation. Univ. of Texas (Austin), 1938. Thesis: English. [A study of linguistic tendencies contributing to the building up of the colloquial speech of Texas]

Hamilton, Ruth S. A Study of Deviations from Standard Southern Speech as Shown by Louisiana State University Freshmen Born in Louisiana. Louisiana State Univ., 1942. Thesis: Speech.

Hardy, Zelma B. A Vocabulary Study of Kerr County, Texas. Univ. of Texas (Austin), 1950. Thesis: English.

Harris, Alberta. Southern Mountain Dialect. Louisiana State Univ., 1948. Thesis: Speech.

Haynes, Randolph A. A Vocabulary Study of Travis County, Texas. Univ. of Texas (Austin), 1954. Thesis: English.

Heard, Betty R. A Phonological Analysis of the Speech of Hays County, Texas. Louisiana State Univ., 1969. Dissertation: Linguistics.

Hefling, Woodford A. Characteristic Features of New Mexico English between 1805 and 1890. Univ. of Chicago, 1941. Dissertation: English.

Hestand, Jo. Typical Borrowings of English Words in the Newspapers of the Mexican Border. Texas Tech Univ., 1931. Thesis: English. [Discusses fusion of American and Mexican Languages along the border]

Hickman, Frances M. The French Speech of Jefferson Parish. Louisiana State Univ., 1940. Thesis: Romance Languages.

Hillbruner, Anthony. The Concept of Equality in the Speeches of Selected Speakers between the Revolutionary War and the Civil War. Northwestern Univ., 1953. Dissertation: Speech. [Includes Thomas Jefferson, Henry Clay, John C. Calhoun]

Hoff, Patricia J. A Dialect Study of Faulkner County, Arkansas. Louisiana State Univ., 1968. Dissertation: English.

Hoijer, Harry. Tonkawa: An Indian Language of Texas. Univ. of
    Chicago, 1931. Dissertation: Anthropology.
Holland, DeWitte T. A Rhetorical Analysis of the Preaching of
    George W. Truett. Northwestern Univ., 1956. Dissertation:
    Speech. [1867-1944; pastor, First Baptist Church, Dallas]
Howren, Robert R. The Speech of Louisville, Kentucky. Indiana
    Univ., 1958. Dissertation: Linguistics.
Huber, Paul. A Study of the Rhetorical Theories of John A.
    Broadus. Univ. of Michigan, 1956. Dissertation: Speech.
    [Southern Baptist minister; taught homiletics]
Hunt, Hazel E. A Study of the Speech of Haynesville, Louisiana,
    at Three Age Levels. Louisiana State Univ., 1938. Thesis:
    Speech.
Hunter, Edwin R. The American Colloquial Idiom, 1830-1860.
    Univ. of Chicago, 1925. Dissertation: English. [Includes
    study of works of Joseph G. Baldwin, William A. Caruthers,
    David Crockett, J.P. Kennedy, A.B. Longstreet, W.G. Simms,
    William T. Thompson, and Thomas Bangs Thorpe]
Hurst, Harry M. A Glossary of the French Spoken in St. Charles
    Parish. Louisiana State Univ., 1937. Thesis: Romance
    Languages.
Huson, Vonita E. A Survey of Speech Patterns and Characteristics
    of Selected Residents of Lincoln Parish in Louisiana.
    Louisiana Polytechnic Inst., 1968. Thesis: Speech.
Idol, Harriett R. A Strobophotographic Study of Southern
    Intonation. Louisiana State Univ., 1937. Dissertation:
    English.
Jaffe, Hilda. The Speech of the Central Coast of North Carolina:
    The Carteret County Version of the Banks "Brogue." Michigan
    State Univ., 1966. Dissertation: Linguistics.
Jeansonne, Samuel L. A Glossary of Words that Vary from Standard-
    French in Avoyelles Parish. Louisiana State Univ., 1938.
    Thesis: Romance Languages.
Johansen, Kjell M. A Vocabulary Study of Gillespie and Kendall
    Counties. Univ. of Texas (Austin), 1962. Thesis: English.
Jones, Phyllis R. A Glossary of the Speech of Virginia North of
    the James River. Brown Univ., 1944. Thesis: English.
Jones, Ruth E. A Comparison of British and American Stress and
    Intonation in Informal Speech. Fisk Univ., 1942. Thesis:
    English. [Includes transcriptions of a story entitled
    "The Shirker" illustrating pronunciation of persons from
    seven localities which include Nashville, Tennessee, Charleston,
    South Carolina, and Augusta, Georgia]
Kearney, Kevin E. Speaking in Florida on the Issues of Presidential
    Reconstruction 1865-1867: A Rhetoric of Reunion. Univ. of
    Florida, 1960. Dissertation: Speech.
Kelly, Rex R. Vocabulary as Used on the Mexican Border. Baylor
    Univ., 1938. Thesis: Spanish. [Texas-Mexican border
    Spanish]
King, Andrew A. The Metaphor in Civil Rights Oratory: The
    Rhetoric of Accommodation. Univ. of Minnesota, 1968.
    Dissertation: Speech. [Examines three orators: Frederick
    Douglass, Booker T. Washington, and Martin Luther King, Jr.]

Klipple, Florence C. A Study of the Speech of Spicewood, Texas.
    Univ. of Texas (Austin), 1944. Thesis: English.
Kriger, Albert. A Study of the Speech of Clinton, Louisiana, at
    Three Age Levels. Louisiana State Univ., 1942. Thesis:
    Speech.
Kroll, H.H. A Comparative Study of Upper and Lower Southern Folk
    Speech. George Peabody College, 1925. Thesis: English.
La Ban, Frank K. Phonological Study of the Speech of the Conchs,
    Early Inhabitants of the Florida Keys, at Three Age Levels.
    Louisiana State Univ., 1965. Dissertation: Linguistics.
Ladd, Mary P. A Vocabulary Study of Early Texas English. Univ.
    of Texas (Austin), 1942. Thesis: English.
Leach, Frank C. The Phonology of Mexican Border Spanish. Univ.
    of Rochester, 1938. Thesis: Romance Languages. [Spanish
    of Mexicans in Texas]
LeCompte, Nolan P., Jr. A Word Atlas of La Fourche Parish and
    Grand Isle, Louisiana. Louisiana State Univ., 1967. Disser-
    tation: Linguistics.
Lewis, Jessie B. North Carolina English as Reflected in Old
    Documents. Univ. of North Carolina (Chapel Hill), 1939.
    Thesis: English.
Lucke, Jessie R. A Study of the Virginia Dialect and Its Origin
    in English. Univ. of Virginia, 1949. Dissertation: English.
MacCurdy, Raymond R., Jr. The Spanish Dialect in St. Bernard
    Parish, Louisiana. Univ. of North Carolina (Chapel Hill),
    1948. Dissertation: Romance Literature.
Martin, Elizabeth K. Lexicon of the Texas Oil Fields. East Texas
    State Univ., 1969. Dissertation: Linguistics.
McBride, John S. Hill Speech in Southwestern Tennessee. Columbia
    Univ., 1936. Thesis: English.
McConnell, Joseph M. Southern Oratory from 1829 to 1860. Univ.
    of Virginia, 1907. Dissertation: English.
McCord, Stanley J. A Historical and Linguistic Study of The
    German Settlement at Roberts Cove, Louisiana. Louisiana
    State Univ., 1969. Dissertation: Linguistics.
McIver, Zadie R. Linguistic Borrowings from the Spanish as
    Reflected in Writing of the Southwest. Univ. of Texas
    (Austin), 1939. Thesis: English.
McMillan, James B. Phonology of the Standard English of East
    Central Alabama. Univ. of Chicago, 1946. Dissertation:
    English.
Meredith, Frederick D. A Study of 30 Selected American Public
    Addresses on the Subject of Public School Integration, 1954-
    1958. Kent State Univ., 1960. Thesis: Speech. [Many
    speeches by Southerners]
Merritt, Juanita F. A Study of the Pronunciation of West Texas
    Students in Hardin-Simmons University. Louisiana State Univ.,
    1943. Thesis: Speech.
Miles, Marie A. The Language of Lubbock County: A Contribution
    toward a Texas Speech Survey. Univ. of Texas (Austin),
    1939. Thesis: English. [Lubbock, Texas]

Mitchell, Henry H. The Genius of Negro Preaching: A Linguistic and Stylistic Examination of the Homiletical Twin Brother to the American Negro Spiritual, with Some Possible Implications of the Result for American Protestant "White" Churches. Fresno State College, 1965. Thesis: English.

Mitchell, S.L. Spanish of the Southwestern Part of the United States, with Particular Reference to English Influence. Univ. of Colorado, 1926. Thesis: Romance Languages.

Montgomery, Erin. A Glossary of Variants from Standard French in Vermilion Parish, Louisiana. Louisiana State Univ., 1946. Thesis: Romance Languages.

Nail, William A. The Phonology of the Speech of Crawford, Texas. Univ. of Texas (Austin), 1948. Thesis: English.

Nelson, Agnes D. A Study of the English Speech of the Hungarians of Albany, Livingston Parish, Louisiana. Louisiana State Univ., 1956. Dissertation: Speech.

Nies, Frederick J. The Phonology of the Globe Primitive Baptist Church Minutes, 1797-1911. Univ. of North Carolina (Chapel Hill), 1952. Thesis: English.

Nixon, Cynthia D. Negro Speech in Haynesville, Ruston, and Baton Rouge, Louisiana. Louisiana State Univ., 1945. Thesis: Speech.

Norman, Arthur M.Z. A Southeast Texas Dialect Study. Univ. of Texas (Austin), 1955. Dissertation: English.

Olivier, Louise. A Glossary of Variants from Standard-French in St. Landry Parish. Louisiana State Univ., 1937. Thesis: Romance Languages.

Olien, Michael D. A Study of North Carolina Negro Speech: Its Phonological Characteristics. Univ. of North Carolina (Chapel Hill), 1962. Thesis: Sociology.

Pardoe, T.E. A Historical and Phonetic Study of Negro Dialect. Louisiana State Univ., 1937. Dissertation: Speech.

Parks, Thomas I. A Linguistic Study of the Choctaw Language in Mississippi. Northeast Louisiana Univ., 1965. Thesis: English.

Parr, Una M. A Glossary of the Variants from Standard French in Terrebonne Parish. Louisiana State Univ., 1940. Thesis: Romance Languages.

Pearson, Zula H. Figurative Language in the Speech of Texans. Northwestern Univ., 1937. Thesis: Speech.

Pence, James W. A History and Evaluation of Student Public Speaking in the Literary Societies of the University of Virginia, 1825-1900. Univ. of Virginia, 1951. Thesis: Speech.

Perret, Michael J. A Study of the Syntax and Morphology of the Verb of the Creole Dialect. Louisiana State Univ., 1933. Thesis: Romance Languages.

Perritt, Margaret F. A Study of the Usage of the "r" Phoneme by Freshman Speech Students at Louisiana State University. Louisiana State Univ., 1942. Thesis: Speech.

Perry, Louise S. A Study of the Pronoun *hit* in Grassy Branch, North Carolina. Louisiana State Univ., 1940. Thesis: Speech.

Phillips, Hosea. A Glossary of the Variants from Standard French Used in Evangeline Parish. Louisiana State Univ., 1935. Thesis: Romance Languages.

Pirkle, Nina B. Variants from Standard French Common to the Dialects of Lafayette Parish and Canada. Louisiana State Univ., 1935. Thesis: English.

Plank, Grace G. Pronunciation in American Speech. Univ. of Rochester, 1930. Thesis: English. [One chapter on Negro dialect]

Polk, Lee R. An Analysis of Argumentation in the Virginia Slavery Debate of 1832. Purdue Univ., 1967. Dissertation: Speech.

Preston, Elaine L. Lexical Variations in the Speech of Mid-South Carolina. Samford Univ., 1969. Thesis: Linguistics.

Prince, Evelyn C. Anomalous Speech in Louisiana. Louisiana State Univ., 1932. Thesis: Romance Languages.

Rash, Coralee. Dialect Study of Kinston, Coffee County, Alabama, Made as a Preliminary Investigation for the Preparation of Work Sheets for the Linguistic Atlas. Auburn Univ., 1941. Thesis: English.

Reinecke, John E. Marginal Languages: A Sociological Survey of the Creole Languages and Trade Jargons. Yale Univ., 1967. Dissertation: Linguistics.

Reynolds, Jack A. The Pronunciation of English in Southern Louisiana. Louisiana State Univ., 1934. Thesis: English.

Reynolds, William M. Deliberative Speaking in Antebellum South Carolina: The Idiom of a Culture. Univ. of Florida, 1960. Dissertation: Speech. [Based on 500 speeches]

Rizzo, Sr. Mary J. The Speech of New Orleans, Louisiana, at Three Age Levels. Louisiana State Univ., 1945. Thesis: Speech.

Robert, Jane G. An Analysis of a Corpus of English Spoken by Negroes in South Central Louisiana. Louisiana State Univ., 1967. Thesis: English.

Rodgers, Catherine. Dialect Study of Camp Hill, Tallapoosa County, Alabama, Made as a Preliminary Investigation for the Preparation of Work Sheets for the Linguistic Atlas. Auburn Univ., 1940. Thesis: English.

Salden, Dan R. An Analysis of Selected Propaganda Speeches in the Southern Confederacy, 1861-1865. Univ. of Akron, 1963. Thesis: Speech.

Sanders, I.S. Some Phases of Negro English. Univ. of Chicago, 1926. Thesis: English. [Includes Southern Negro English]

Satterfield, Cecile. Dialect Studies of Marbury School District, Autauga County, Alabama, Made as a Preliminary Investigation for the Preparation of Work Sheets for the Linguistic Atlas. Auburn Univ., 1939. Thesis: English.

Sawyer, Janet B.M. A Dialect Study of San Antonio, Texas: A Bilingual Community. Univ. of Texas (Austin), 1957. Dissertation: Linguistics.

Searles, Charlotte L. A Study of the Speech of Minden, Louisiana, at Three Age Levels. Louisiana State Univ., 1938. Thesis: Speech.

Sherman, J.E. An Objective Study of the Nasalization of Diphthongs in the Speech of Natives of Alabama. Univ. of Alabama, 1942. Thesis: Speech.

Shewmake, Edwin F. The English Language in Virginia. Univ. of Virginia, 1920. Dissertation: English.

Smith, Harley. A Recording of English Sounds at Three Age Levels in Ville Platte, Louisiana. Louisiana State Univ., 1936. Thesis: Speech.

Smith, Jack A. A Survey of Localisms Used by the Native English-speaking Key Wester. Auburn Univ., 1962. Thesis: English.

Smith, Robert W. A Rhetorical Analysis of the Populist Movement in North Carolina, 1892-1896. Univ. of Wisconsin, 1957. Dissertation: Speech.

Stanley, Oma. The Speech of East Texas. Columbia Univ., 1937. Dissertation: English.

Steetle, Ralph W. A Study of the Speech of Lake Charles, Louisiana, at Three Age Levels. Louisiana State Univ., 1938. Thesis: Speech.

Stephenson, Edward A. Early North Carolina Pronunciation. Univ. of North Carolina (Chapel Hill), 1958. Dissertation: Linguistics.

Stokes, George M. A Study of the Pronunciation of Texas Towns. Baylor Univ., 1947. Thesis: Speech.

Tarpley, Fred A. A Word Atlas of Northeast Texas. Louisiana State Univ., 1960. Dissertation: Linguistics. [Shows language closely related to that of South and South-midland areas of Kurath's atlas]

Tedford, Thomas L. An Investigation of Public Address as Taught by the Baptist Training Union of the Southern Baptist Convention. Louisiana State Univ., 1958. Dissertation: Speech.

Thompson, Marion C. A Study of Yeoman Speech of Leon County, Florida, and Nearby Areas: A Contribution to a Dialect Dictionary. Florida State Univ., 1951. Thesis: English.

Todd, Julia M. A Phonological Analysis of the Speech of Aged Citizens of Claiborne County, Mississippi. Louisiana State Univ., 1965. Dissertation: Speech.

Tozer, G. The Ozark Dialect. Univ. of Kansas, 1932. Thesis: English.

Trahan, Lucie M. Etymological Glossary of the Variants from Standard-French in Assumption Parish. Louisiana State Univ., 1936. Thesis: Romance Languages.

Trappey, Maud. The French Speech of Iberia Parish. Louisiana State Univ., 1940. Thesis: Romance Languages.

Ulrey, Evan A. The Preaching of Barton Warren Stone. Louisiana State Univ., 1955. Dissertation: Speech. [Frontier preacher ca. 1800 in South, later moved West]

Van Riper, William R. The Loss of Post-Vocalic R in the Eastern United States. Univ. of Michigan, 1958. Dissertation: Linguistics. [Includes Mid- and South-Atlantic states]

Viator, Audrey B. A Glossary of Neologisms, Loan-words, and Variants from Standard-French in the Parish of St. John the Baptist. Louisiana State Univ., 1935. Thesis: Romance Languages.

Wacker, Marilynn A.Z. A Study of the Speech of a Group of
    Freshmen in the University of San Antonio. Univ. of Texas
    (Austin), 1942. Thesis: English.
Walker, Saunders E. A Dictionary of the Folk Speech of the East
    Alabama Negro. Case Western Reserve Univ., 1956. Disser-
    tation: English.
Ward, Madie B. The Treatment of *R* in Southeast Alabama Speech.
    Univ. of North Carolina (Chapel Hill), 1946. Thesis:
    Comparative Linguistics.
Weeks, Abigail E. The Speech of the Kentucky Mountaineer as I
    Know It. Columbia Univ., 1921. Thesis: Education.
White, Larry A. A Rhetorical Survey of the 1963-1964 Democratic
    Gubernatorial Primaries in Louisiana. Louisiana Polytechnic
    Inst., 1964. Thesis: Speech.
Williams, Elizabeth J. The Grammar of Plantation Overseer's
    Letters, Rockingham County, 1829-1860. Univ. of North
    Carolina (Chapel Hill), 1953. Thesis: English.
Williams, Ray R. Representative Antebellum Oratory in South
    Carolina. Univ. of South Carolina, 1924. Thesis: English.
Williamson, Juanita V. A Phonological and Morphological Study
    of the Speech of the Negro of Memphis, Tennessee. Univ. of
    Michigan, 1961. Dissertation: Linguistics.
Wise, Harry S. A Phonetic Study of the Southern American (aI)
    Phoneme. Louisiana State Univ., 1937. Thesis: Speech.
Yauger, James T. A Rhetorical Study of Selected Radio Speeches
    of Governor W. Lee O'Daniel of Texas in Behalf of Social
    Security Legislation, 1939-1941. Louisiana State Univ.,
    1968. Dissertation: Speech.
Yeomans, Gordon A. A Rhetorical Study of the Cotton Advocacy of
    James Thomas Heflin, 1904-1920. Louisiana State Univ., 1966.
    Dissertation: Speech. [Alabama representative]

SOUTHERN CULTURE THROUGH OTHERS' EYES

Anderson, Emmett H. Appraisal of American Life by French Travelers,
    1860-1914. Univ. of Virginia, 1954. Dissertation: English.
    [Includes travels in the South]
Bartholomae, Edgar W., Translator. A Translation of H. Ehrenberg's
    Fahrten und Schicksale eines Deutschen in Texas, with
    Introduction and Notes. Univ. of Texas (Austin), 1925.
    Thesis: German. [The translator calls Ehrenberg's book "a
    creditable contribution to the literature of Texas of that
    period"]
Cochrane, William G. Freedom without Equality: A Study of Northern
    Opinion of the Negro Issue, 1861-1870. Univ. of Minnesota,
    1957. Dissertation: History. [Information as provided
    primarily by newspapers]
Cronholm, Christie. Die Nordamerikanische Sklavenfrage im
    Deutschen Schrifttum des 19. Jahrhunderts. Freie Universität
    (West Berlin), 1959. Dissertation: English.
Doty, Dorothy S. The Southerner as Seen by the Northern Novelists,
    1865-1900. Columbia Univ., 1950. Thesis: English.
Doughty, Doris F. Views of Northern Travelers on Social Conditions
    in the South, 1850-1866. Lamar Univ., 1966. Thesis: History.

Dugdale, Mattie W. Travelers' Views of Louisiana before 1860.
Univ. of Texas (Austin), 1938. Thesis: History. [Discussion
of floating theaters, theaters in New Orleans, slave dances,
and plantation life as reflected in plantation names, slave
names, libraries, etc.]

Elrod, G.W. Tennessee, 1796-1860: As Seen through the Accounts
of Travelers. George Peabody College, 1940. Thesis:
English.

Floan, Howard R. The South in Northern Eyes, 1831-1861: A Study
of Antebellum Attitudes toward the South among the Major
Northern Men of Letters Who Were Actively Writing on the
Eve of the Civil War. Columbia Univ., 1959. [Includes
Bryant, Emerson, Longfellow, Lowell, Melville, Thoreau,
Whitman, and Whittier]

Green, Alan W.C. Legacy of Illusion: The Image of the Negro in
the Pre-Civil War North, 1787-1857. Claremont Graduate
School, 1968. Dissertation: History. [Discusses attitudes
toward South and stereotypes that carry over into fiction]

Hall, Doris B. The Southern Poor White in the Writings of John
William De Forest and Other Northern Writers, 1860-1880.
Univ. of North Carolina (Chapel Hill), 1962. Thesis:
English.

Harris, Anne B. The South as Seen by Travelers, 1865-1880.
Univ. of North Carolina (Chapel Hill), 1967. Dissertation:
History.

Haynes, Roger G. Anthony Trollope's Observations of America.
Southern Methodist Univ., 1948. Thesis: English. [Includes
description of cultural activities in several Southern
cities]

Hilliard, Billie B. British Authors in America from Paine to
Arnold. Southern Methodist Univ., 1934. Thesis: English.
[Five authors who traveled in and gave their opinions of
the South: Matthew Arnold, James Bryce, Harriett Martineau,
William M. Thackeray, and Anthony Trollope]

Hornsby, Alton. Southern Negroes, 1877-1929: The Outsider's
View. Univ. of Texas (Austin), 1970. Dissertation:
History.

Kolb, Alfred. Frederich Gerstacker and the American Frontier.
Syracuse Univ., 1966. Dissertation: English. [A German
whose three visits to America included Tennessee, Arkansas,
and the lower Mississippi River area]

Landa, Bjarne E. The American Scene in Friedrich Gerstacher's
Works of Fiction. Univ. of Minnesota, 1952. Dissertation:
English.

Logue, Hanchey, Jr. How William Cullen Bryant Misread the Mind
of the South. Auburn Univ., 1968. Thesis: English.

Meyer, Audrey M. Mary Ashley Townsend: Biographical and Critical
Study. Tulane Univ., 1938. Thesis: English. [Townsend
lived from 1837-1901; though not Southern, some of her
writings are about the South]

Pemberton, Luola S. Thomas Hughes in Rugby, Tennessee. George
Peabody College, 1947. Thesis: English. [British author
(1822-1896) who founded a cooperative colony at Rugby,
Tennessee, while on a visit to the U.S.]

Ryan, Lee W. French Travelers in America between 1775 and 1800 with Special Reference to the Southern States. Univ. of Virginia, 1934. Dissertation: Romance Languages.

Santerre, Eloise. *Reunion*: A Translation of Dr. Savardan's *Un Naufrage au Texas* with an Introduction to *Reunion* and a Biographical Dictionary of the Settlers. Southern Methodist Univ., 1936. Thesis: English.

Schmidt, Charles F. A Translation of Viktor Bracht's *Texas im Jahre 1848*. Univ. of Texas (Austin), 1927. Dissertation: History. [Many pages of excerpts from letters and some discussion of newspapers and language]

Seat, William R. III. Harriet Martineau in America. Indiana Univ. (Bloomington), 1957. Dissertation: English. [Includes a discussion of her travels in the South]

Shain, Charles E. A British Image of America: A Survey of America and the Americans as They Appeared in the English Novel, 1830-1890. Princeton Univ., 1949. Dissertation: English. [Includes descriptions of Confederate States and slavery]

Simon, Walter A. Henry O. Tanner: A Study of the Development of An American Negro Artist: 1859-1937. New York Univ., 1961. Dissertation: Fine Arts. [Born in Pittsburg, Tanner lived from 1859-1937; part of this dissertation concerns Tanner's experiences in the South]

Smith, Beatrice M. Impressions of Virginia from Contemporary Accounts, 1697-1776. Univ. of Virginia, 1968. Thesis: History.

Strauss, Grace. Northern Opinion of the South, 1880-1900, as Revealed in the Magazines. Columbia Univ., 1939. Thesis: History. [As expressed in *The Atlantic Monthly*, *Catholic World*, *Harper's*, and *Scribner's*]

Thomas, Margaret M. Tours in the Deep South: Alabama as Recorded by Travelers, 1819-1860. Univ. of North Carolina (Chapel Hill), 1949. Thesis: Education.

Traber, Michael. The Treatment of the Little Rock, Arkansas, School Integration Incident in the Daily Press of the Union of South Africa, West Nigeria and Ghana from September 1 to October 31, 1957. New York Univ., 1960. Dissertation: Journalism.

Warsh, Louis P. The Evolution of Anti-Southern Concepts in the North, 1830-1860. Univ. of California (Berkeley), 1930. Thesis: History.

Wells, Ila A. A Survey of the Negro Problem in the United States as Seen by British Travelers to America, 1800-1861. Northern Illinois Univ., 1969. Dissertation: English. [Includes life on plantations in the South]

Whitener, Catherine V. Walt Whitman and the South. Duke Univ., 1940. Thesis: English.

PART III
LITERATURE

STUDIES THAT INCLUDE THE SOUTH

Abbott, Hazel B. And What of the Indian? His Literature and His
    Treatment in Our Dramatic Literature. Columbia Univ., 1924.
    Thesis: English. [Includes G.W.P. Curtis]
Ackerley, Virginia. Imagist Poets and Poetry. Columbia Univ.,
    1928. Thesis: English. [Includes John Gould Fletcher]
Adams, Sr. Mary B., S.S.F. The Development of Race Pride in
    American Negro Poetry. Xavier Univ. (New Orleans), 1942.
    Thesis: English. [Includes Joseph S. Cotter, Jr.,
    Frances W. Harper, George Horton, and Albery A. Whitman]
Adams, Robert J. Some Types and Backgrounds in Contemporary
    American Literature. Temple Univ., 1928. Thesis: English.
    [Includes O. Henry, Elizabeth Robins, Francis H. Smith, and
    Wilbur D. Steel]
Adkisson, Mary E. The American Civil War as Presented in Longer
    Fiction. Univ. of Illinois, 1940. Thesis: English.
    [Includes James Lane Allen, Joseph A. Altsheler, Mary Raymond
    Andrews, G.W. Cable, John Esten Cooke, Thomas Dixon, Clifford
    Dowdey, John Fox, Jr., Helen H. Gardener, Ellen Glasgow,
    Caroline Gordon, J.C. Harris, Mary Johnston, Sara Beaumont
    Kennedy, Sidney Lanier, Lafayette McLaws, Margaret Mitchell,
    T.N. Page and Augusta Evans Wilson]
Agee, William H. The Initiation Theme in Selected Modern American
    Novels of Adolescence. Florida State Univ., 1966. Disser-
    tation: English. [Includes Truman Capote and Carson
    McCullers]
Aiken, Mary P. The Child as a Character in American Short Fiction
    of the 1930's. Univ. of North Carolina (Chapel Hill), 1953.
    Thesis: English. [Includes William Faulkner, Caroline
    Gordon, Sara Haardt, Margaret Weymouth Jackson, E.A. Poe,
    Katherine Anne Porter, James Still, and Leane Zugsmith]
Akins, Thomas W. The Mississippi River in Literature. Southern
    Methodist Univ., 1936. Thesis: English.
Alalouf, Carol E. A Character Study of Teachers as They Appear
    in American Fiction since 1900. Univ. of New Mexico, 1966.
    Thesis: English. [Includes Thomas Wolfe and Richard Wright]
Albright, Daniel. An Account of the Discussion of Narrative
    Technique, from Poe up to James. Univ. of Chicago, 1956.
    Dissertation: English.
Alexander, Ida G. Personality in the American Sonnet. Ohio Univ.,
    1930. Thesis: English. [Includes Washington Allston,
    Paul H. Hayne, Henry A. Sampson, W.G. Simms, John Banister
    Tabb, and Henry Timrod]
Allen, Edna L. Literary Fads and Fashions in America of the
    1840's. Univ. of Texas (Austin), 1924. Thesis: English.
    [Includes E.A. Poe]
Allen, Gay W. A History of the Prosody of the Chief American
    Poets. Univ. of Wisconsin, 1934. Dissertation: English.

Allen, Helen B. The Minister of the Gospel in Negro American
Fiction. Fisk Univ., 1937. Thesis: English. [Includes
Zora Neale Hurston]

Allen, Mozelle S. Farm Life in Early American Fiction. Univ.
of Texas (Austin), 1930. Thesis: English. [Includes
William A. Caruthers, J.P. Kennedy, A.B. Longstreet, E.A. Poe,
W.G. Simms, and Nathaniel B. Tucker]

Ammirati, Theresa P. Wright, Baldwin, and Ellison: A Comparative
Study of the Negro Novel. Lehigh Univ., 1966. Thesis:
English.

Anderson, Carl. The Swedish Reception of Sinclair Lewis and His
Contemporaries. Univ. of Pennsylvania, 1954. Dissertation:
English. [Includes comments on Ellen Glasgow and Mark Twain]

Anderson, Dorothy A. The Background of Natural History Writing in
America before Thoreau. Columbia Univ., 1925. Thesis:
English. [Includes James Audubon, William Byrd, and Thomas
Jefferson]

Anderson, Frank W., Jr. American Literary Political Satire,
1812-1850. Univ. of North Carolina (Chapel Hill), 1951.
Dissertation: English. [Includes David Crockett, J.P.
Kennedy, A.B. Longstreet, and Nathaniel B. Tucker]

Anderson, Jeanette H. A Study of Social Protest of Contemporary
Negro Poets. Virginia State College, 1943. Thesis: English.
[Includes James Weldon Johnson and Richard Wright]

Anderson, Kay E. A Study of Theme in Autobiographical Works of
Claude Brown, Dick Gregory, Malcolm X, and Richard Wright,
with Emphasis on the Autobiographical Writings of James
Baldwin. Whittier College, 1971. Thesis: English.

Anderson, Shirley L. The Interpretation of Important Features of
American Life from 1814 to 1860 in the Historical Novel.
Univ. of Illinois, 1943. Thesis: English. [Includes
Moncure Daniel Conway, J.C. Harris, and Richard M. Johnston]

Anderson, Vivienne. A Critical Study of the Pulitzer Prize
Poetry, 1928-1938. Temple Univ., 1939. Thesis: Education.
[Includes George Dillon]

Andrews, Mary L. Modern Poetic Drama in America (1900-1942).
New York Univ., 1943. Dissertation: English. [Includes
Roark Bradford, Mary Johnston, and Cale Young Rice]

Angotti, Vincent L. American Dramatic Criticism, 1800-1830.
Univ. of Kansas, 1967. Dissertation: Theater. [Mentions
Poe by comparison and includes a chapter on the state of
the American theater in general during the period]

Archer, Leonard C. Negro Life as a Folk Basis in Contemporary
American Drama. Toronto, 1939. Thesis: English.

Ard, Jo-Anne. Three Picaresque Novels of the Twentieth Century.
Auburn Univ., 1971. Thesis: English. [Includes *Huckleberry
Finn* as background]

Arnold, Dovie M. American Indians in Fiction. Austin College
(Texas), 1938. Thesis: English. [Includes W.G. Simms and
John Smith]

Arnold, Ruby E. The Negro Woman as Portrayed in the American
Novel. Sam Houston State Univ., 1950. Thesis: English.

Atkinson, W.H., Jr. Satire in the Recent American Novel, 1913-1922. Univ. of North Carolina (Chapel Hill), 1923. Thesis: English. [Includes J.B. Cabell and T.S. Stribling]

Babcock, Havilah. Some Aspects of the Literary Influence of the Civil War. Univ. of South Carolina, 1929. Dissertation: English. [Includes Charles E. Craddock, J.C. Harris, Paul H. Hayne, Lafcadio Hearn, Richard Malcolm Johnston, Sidney Lanier, Hugh S. Legaré, A.B. Longstreet, O. Henry, T.N. Page, E.A. Poe, and Charles H. Smith]

Bailey, Florence M. The Interpretation of the American Civil War in American Fiction. Univ. of Louisville, 1939. Thesis: English. [Includes William Mumford Baker, Jeremiah Clemens, H.H. Crozier, William Faulkner, Lucy Virginia Smith French, Ellen Glasgow, Caroline Gordon, Mary Jane Holmes, Mary Johnston, Emily Lafayette McLaws, Margaret Mitchell, T.N. Page, Evely Scott (Mrs. John Metcalfe), Allen Tate, Augusta Jane Evans Wilson, and Stark Young]

Bailey, James O. Scientific Fiction in English: 1817-1914. A Study of Trends and Forms. Univ. of North Carolina (Chapel Hill), 1948. Dissertation: English. [Includes E.A. Poe]

Bain, Vada. The Distribution of Present-day Short Story Writers over the United States. Texas Tech Univ., 1940. Thesis: English. [Considerable attention given to the South and to Southern writers]

Baker, James R. Studies in the Realistic Novel. Univ. of Denver, 1954. Dissertation: English. [Includes William Faulkner]

Baker, Ruth T. The Philosophy of the New Negro as Reflected in the Writings of James Weldon Johnson, Claude McKay, Langston Hughes, and Countee Cullen. Virginia State College, 1941. Thesis: English.

Baker, Susan. The Crowned Knot of Fire: A Study of the Influence of Medieval Symbolism on Modern Poetry. Univ. of Minnesota, 1966. Dissertation: English. [Includes Allen Tate]

Baker, William D., Jr. The Influence of Mesmerism in Nineteenth Century American Literature. Northwestern Univ., 1950. Dissertation: English. [Includes E.A. Poe]

Ball, Rachel. A Study of Some American Religious Problem Novels. Southern Methodist Univ., 1930. Thesis: English. [Includes James Lane Allen and T.S. Stribling]

Ballinger, Sara E. The Reception of the American Novel in German Periodicals, 1945-1957. Indiana Univ. (Bloomington), 1959. Dissertation: English. [Includes Erskine Caldwell, William Faulkner, Mark Twain, and Thomas Wolfe]

Barbour, Dorothy H. Negro Poetry in American Literature. Ohio Univ., 1943. Thesis: English. [Includes Frances W. Harper, George Moses Horton, James W. Johnson, and Albery A. Whitman]

Barclay, Lillian E. The Coyote in American Literature. Univ. of Texas (Austin), 1937. Thesis: English. [Presents a collection of informational matter, tales, narratives, and poems of the Americas]

Barer, Bertram. A Rhetorical Analysis of the American Presentational Social Theatre of the Thirties. Univ. of Minnesota, 1960. Dissertation: Theater. [Includes Paul Green]

Barksdale, Marjorie. A Survey of American Best Sellers from 1926 to 1936 with the Purpose of Determining the Psychology of Their Popularity. Univ. of Texas (Austin), 1937. Thesis: English.

Barnes, Nora P. A Study of Persistent Quaker Elements of American Thought as Revealed in the Works of Certain American Writers. Kansas State Teachers College, 1932. Thesis: English. [Includes William Byrd, Thomas Jefferson, and Sidney Lanier]

Barnett, Linda A. The American Businessman in the Fiction of the "Guilded Age." Univ. of Massachusetts, 1966. Thesis: English. [Includes Mark Twain]

Barrancos, Susana C. Notes on American Literature. Univ. of Miami (Coral Gables), 1955. Thesis: English. [Includes William Faulkner, Elizabeth M. Roberts, and Tennessee Williams]

Bartlett, Marion R. The Contemporary Short Story in America. Columbia Univ., 1925. Thesis: English. [Includes G.W. Cable, Kate Chopin, Charles E. Craddock, W.A. Dromgoole, J.C. Harris, O. Henry, T.N. Page, and E.A. Poe]

Barz, Hermine. The Development of the Poetry of the Negro in North America. Mainz, 1951. Dissertation: English.

Bassford, Jean A. The Social Concerns of American Postwar Poetry. Univ. of Southern California, 1940. Thesis: English. [Includes Richard Wright]

Bates, Mary D. Columbia's Bards: A Study of American Verse from 1783 through 1799. Brown Univ., 1954. Dissertation: English. [Extensive examination of poets, including those who are Southern or who wrote about the South]

Bates, Robert H. A Study of the Literature of the Mountains and of Mountain Climbing Written in English. Univ. of Pennsylvania, 1947. Dissertation: English. [Includes Mark Twain]

Baumbach, Jonathan. The Theme of Guilt and Redemption in the Post-Second World War American Novel. Stanford Univ., 1961. Dissertation: English. [Includes Ralph Ellison, Flannery O'Connor, William Styron, and Robert Penn Warren]

Baumser, Ruth. The Dominant Themes in the Major American Novels between 1919 and 1929. Columbia Univ., 1947. Thesis: English. [Includes J.B. Cabell, William Faulkner, and Thomas Wolfe]

Baylis, John F. The Theme of Humanity in the Fiction of Selected Negro American Writers, 1920-1965. Indiana State Univ., 1967. Thesis: English.

Beck, Betty S. The Fallible Narrator in Nineteenth Century American Fiction. Univ. of Oklahoma, 1963. Dissertation: English. [Includes J.P. Kennedy, E.A. Poe, W.G. Simms, and Mark Twain]

Beja, Morris. Evanescent Moments: The Epiphany in the Modern Novel. Cornell Univ., 1963. Dissertation: English. [Includes William Faulkner and Thomas Wolfe]

Belcher, Fannin S., Jr. The Place of the Negro in the Evolution of the American Theatre, 1767 to 1940. Yale Univ., 1945. Dissertation: English. [Includes Paul Green]

Bell, Bennie V. Short Stories by Negro Authors: A Study of Subject Matter. Fisk Univ., 1934. Thesis: English. [Includes Charles W. Chesnutt, Zora Neale Hurston, and Jean Toomer]

Bell, H.M. The Development of Dialect in the American Short
    Story. Ohio State Univ., 1925. Thesis: English. [Includes
    G.W. Cable, Kate Chopin, J.C. Harris, T.N. Page, and Charles
    Alphonso Smith]
Bender, Clifford A. The Labor Problem in the American Novel.
    Univ. of Minnesota, 1923. Thesis: English.
Bertram, Ray M. The Novel of America's Past: A Study of Five
    American Novelists, 1925-1950. Univ. of Michigan, 1954.
    Dissertation: English. [Includes James Boyd]
Bethel, Charles C. Specific Types of Heroines in American Fiction
    since 1900. Southern Methodist Univ., 1952. Thesis:
    English. [Includes Erskine Caldwell, William Faulkner,
    Ellen Glasgow, Margaret Mitchell, Thomas Wolfe, and Frank
    Yerby]
Betts, William W., Jr. The Fortunes of Faust in American
    Literature. Pennsylvania State Univ., 1954. Dissertation:
    English. [Chapter 2, "Faust in the Old South," mentions
    J.P. Kennedy, Sidney Lanier, E.A. Poe, W.G. Simms, Henry
    Timrod, and Mark Twain]
Bickham, Robert S. The Origins and Importance of the Initiation
    Story in Twentieth Century British and American Fiction.
    Univ. of Minnesota, 1961. Dissertation: English. [Includes
    Mark Twain]
Billingsley, William F. The Influence of Marxism on Contemporary
    American Literature. Ohio State Univ., 1936. Thesis:
    English. [Includes Grace Lumpkin]
Billups, Edgar P. Some Principles for the Representation of Negro
    Dialect in Fiction. Emory Univ., 1922. Thesis: English.
    [Includes G.W. Cable, Octavus Roy Cohen, Harrison Dickson,
    J.C. Harris, John Trotwood Moore, and T.N. Page]
Blackburn, Clara B. Influences on American Expressionistic Drama.
    Ohio State Univ., 1937. Dissertation: English. [Includes
    Paul Green]
Blagg, Mary E. India in English and American Prose Fiction since
    Kipling. Texas Woman's Univ., 1943. Thesis: English.
    [Includes Harry Hervey]
Blaine, Harold A. The Frontiersman in American Prose Fiction,
    1800-1860. Case Western Reserve Univ., 1936. Dissertation:
    English. [Includes John Esten Cooke, David Crockett, and
    W.G. Simms]
Blair, Walter. Two Phases of American Humor. Univ. of Chicago,
    1931. Dissertation: English.
Blake, Fay M. The Strike in the American Novel. Univ. of
    California (Los Angeles), 1970. Dissertation: English.
    [Includes Erskine Caldwell]
Blickenstaff, Mildred E. Literary Life in America, 1885-1900.
    Univ. of Southern California, 1944. Thesis: English.
    [Includes O. Henry]
Blue, Ila J. A Study of Literary Criticism by Some Negro Writers,
    1910-1950. Univ. of Michigan, 1960. Dissertation: Education.
    [Includes Gwendolyn Bennett, William Braithewaite, Benjamin
    Brawley, Ralph Ellison, Nick Ford, Richard Wright, and
    Frank Yerby]

Bluefarb, Samuel. The Escape Motif in the Modern American Novel: Mark Twain to Carson McCullers. Univ. of New Mexico, 1967. Dissertation: English.

Blum, Morgan. The Traditionist Postwar Poetry. Louisiana State Univ., 1936. Thesis: English. [Includes Donald Davidson, John Crowe Ransom, Allen Tate, and Robert Penn Warren]

Bond, Frederick W. The Direct and Indirect Contribution Which the American Negro Has Made to Drama and the Legitimate Stage, with the Underlying Conditions Responsible. New York Univ., 1939. Dissertation: English. [Includes Paul Green, DuBose Heyward, and Willis Richardson]

Bone, Robert A. A History of the Negro Novel from the Civil War to World War II. Yale Univ., 1955. Dissertation: English.

Bonn, Marion J. The American Novelists of the Twenties: Their Exile and Return. Pennsylvania State Univ., 1955. Dissertation: English. [Includes William Faulkner and Thomas Wolfe]

Borrowdale, Howard O. The Antiwar Propaganda Novel. Univ. of Southern California, 1940. Thesis: Comparative Literature. [Includes Margaret Mitchell]

Bowman, John S. The Proletarian Novel in America. Pennsylvania State Univ., 1939. Dissertation: English. [Includes Olive Dargan, Grace Lumpkin, and Leane Zugsmith]

Boyd, William P. The Beginnings of the Short Story in America. Univ. of Texas (Austin), 1936. Thesis: English. [Includes E.A. Poe]

Bradford, Robert W. Journey into Nature: American Nature Writing, 1773-1860. Syracuse Univ., 1957. Dissertation: English. [Includes James Audubon, William Bartram, and William Byrd]

Braly, Earl B. The Reputation of David Hume in America. Univ. of Texas (Austin), 1955. Dissertation: English. [Includes Thomas Jefferson and his opinion of Hume's work as philosophy and literature]

Brame, J.R. The Origin of the Virginia Plantation in American Literature. Western Kentucky Univ., 1934. Thesis: English. [Includes J.P. Kennedy]

Bray, Mila M. The Negro's Contribution to the American Theatre. Northwestern Univ., 1929. Thesis: Speech. [Includes Paul Green, Dorothy and DuBose Heyward, and Jean Toomer]

Breland, Hazel L. The Negro in the Field of American Drama. Univ. of Virginia, 1929. Thesis: English. [Includes Georgia Douglas Johnson, Willis Richardson, and Jean Toomer]

Brickey, Helen. The Changing Interpretation of the Jew in Certain Typical Novels for the Period 1817 to 1914. Kansas State Teachers College, 1935. Thesis: English. [Includes T.N. Page]

Bright, Clara M. A Study of the Short Story. Tulane Univ., 1904. Thesis: English. [Includes E.A. Poe]

Brink, Florence R. Literary Travelers in Louisiana between 1803 and 1860. Louisiana State Univ., 1930. Thesis: English.

Britt, David D. The Image of the White Man in the Fiction of Langston Hughes, Richard Wright, James Baldwin, and Ralph Ellison. Emory Univ., 1968. Dissertation: English.

Brodsky, Sylvia. The John Brown Legend in American Literature. Columbia Univ., 1943. Thesis: English. [Includes Thomas Dixon]

Brosin, Isadore G. Certain Trends in the Critical Analysis of American Literature since the World War, 1919-40. Univ. of Southern California, 1942. Thesis: English. [Includes H.L. Mencken]

Broussard, Louis. The Modern Allegorical Play in America. New York Univ., 1963. Dissertation: Speech and Drama. [Includes Tennessee Williams' *Camino Real*]

Brown, Deming B. American Authors in Soviet Russia: 1917-1941. Columbia Univ., 1951. Dissertation: Literature and Linguistics. [Includes O. Henry and Mark Twain]

Brown, Esther E. The French Revolution and the American Man of Letters. Univ. of Missouri, 1948. Dissertation: English. [Includes Thomas Jefferson]

Brown, Samuel A., Jr. *The American Review*, 1933-37. Vanderbilt Univ., 1946. Thesis: English. [Discusses the Agrarian movement in relation to *The American Review*]

Brown, Sterling A. Negro Life and Character in American Literature. Harvard Univ., 1933. Dissertation: English.

Brown, William R. American Soldier Poets of the Second World War. Univ. of Michigan, 1965. Dissertation: English. [Includes Randall Jarrell]

Browne, Robert M. Theories of Convention in Contemporary American Criticism. Catholic Univ., 1956. Dissertation: English. [Includes Cleanth Brooks, John Crowe Ransom, and Allen Tate]

Bruce, Charles T. Major Literary Concepts of the Soldier as Illustrated in Certain American War Novels. Texas Tech Univ., 1960. Dissertation: English. [Includes J.P. Kennedy's *Horse-Shoe Robinson*]

Bryant, Loy Y. The Pocahontas Theme in American Literature. Univ. of North Carolina (Chapel Hill), 1935. Thesis: English. [Includes Virginia Carter Castleman, John Esten Cooke, G.W.P. Curtis, John Gould Fletcher, James Barron Hope, and Mary Johnston]

Bucks, Dorothy S. The American Drama of Ideas from 1890 to 1929. Northwestern Univ., 1944. Dissertation: English. [Includes Laurence Stallings]

Bullock, Penelope L. The Treatment of the Mulatto in American Fiction from 1826 to 1902. Atlanta Univ., 1944. Thesis: English. [Includes William Wells Brown, G.W. Cable, Charles W. Chesnutt, Thomas Dixon, and Frances W. Harper]

Burke, Marianne T. The Black Knight: The Negro as the Hero in the Twentieth Century American Novel. Univ. of Tennessee, 1944. Thesis: English. [Includes more than 75 writers, among whom are Arna Bontemps, Roark Bradford, James Saxon Childers, William Faulkner, George Wylie Henderson, DuBose Heyward, Zora Neale Hurston, James Weldon Johnson, Emmett Kennedy, Stella George Stern Perry, Julia Peterkin, Lyle Saxon, T.S. Stribling, Octave Thanet, W.E. Turpin, Walter White, Clement Wood, and Richard Wright]

Burke, Sally M. Mine of a Thousand Legends. Baylor Univ., 1937. Thesis: English. [San Saba gold mine legends traced through poetry, fiction, ballads, etc., including that of J. Frank Dobie, John C. Duval, Eugene P. Lyle, and Charles Webber]

Burke, William M. American Playwrights' Treatment of War, 1914-1949. Univ. of Pennsylvania, 1949. Dissertation: American Studies. [Includes Paul Green's *Johnny Johnson* and Lillian Hellman's *The Searching Wind* and *Watch on the Rhine*]

Burnes, Bert D. The Detective as a Hero in Fiction. Univ. of Texas (Austin), 1941. Thesis: English. [Includes E.A. Poe and S.S. Van Dine]

Burnes, E.M. The Negro in American Fiction. Univ. of Mississippi, 1949. Thesis: English. [Includes G.W. Cable, J.C. Harris, and Mark Twain]

Burns, Stuart L. The Novel of Adolescence in America: 1940-1963. Univ. of Wisconsin, 1964. Dissertation: English. [Includes Flannery O'Connor]

Burtch, Lillian W. A Character Study of the Physician in American Literature. Kansas State Teachers College, 1934. Thesis: English. [Includes James Lane Allen's *The Doctor's Christmas Eve*, G.W. Cable's *Dr. Sevier*, and T.N. Page's *Red Rock*]

Burton, Lula F. Proletariat of the Reconstruction Era in American Fiction, 1865-1900. Atlanta Univ., 1934. Thesis: English.

Burton, Luthera H. Seven American Humorists: Selections Edited with an Introduction. Univ. of Maine, 1934. Thesis: English. [Includes A.B. Longstreet]

Busacca, Basil. On the Limits of Criticism: An Essay in Location. Univ. of Wisconsin, 1950. Dissertation: English. [Includes John Crowe Ransom]

Busfield, Roger M., Jr. From Idea to Dialogue: An Analysis of the Playwriting Process as Derived from the Non-Dramatic Writings of a Selected Group of Successful Dramatists, 1899-1950. Florida State Univ., 1954. Dissertation: English. [Includes Lillian Hellman]

Buxbaum, Melvin H. The Bad Boy in American Fiction through *Huckleberry Finn*. Roosevelt Univ., 1960. Thesis: English.

Byers, Kansas. The Arthurian Legend in American Literature. Univ. of North Carolina (Chapel Hill), 1924. Thesis: English. [Includes James Lane Allen, Madison Cawein, Armistead Churchill Gordon, Paul H. Hayne, Sidney Lanier, Francis Orray Ticknor, and Stark Young]

Byers, N.E.K. American Contributions to Recent Literature for Children. Purdue Univ., 1931. Thesis: English. [Includes J.C. Harris and James Weldon Johnson]

Byrd, James W. The Portrayal of White Character by Negro Novelists, 1900-1950. George Peabody College, 1955. Dissertation: English.

Cady, Anna. The Development of American Literary Biography. Ohio Univ., 1936. Thesis: Education. [Includes Hugh A. Garland, W.G. Simms, and Parson Weems]

Cady, Edwin H. The Concept of the Gentleman in Representative American Authors. Univ. of Wisconsin, 1943. Dissertation: English. [Includes Thomas Jefferson]

Callaway, Marian H.   A Comparative Study of the Development of
    Skills in Plot Construction by a Group of Living American
    Dramatists.   Univ. of Iowa, 1941.   Dissertation: Speech.
    [Includes Paul Green]
Campbell, Fuller R., Jr.   A Correlation of Plot Structures and
    Character Types in Protest Plays of the 1930's about Negroes.
    Univ. of South Carolina, 1969.   Thesis: English.
Campbell, Julius G.   A Study of Some Problems of Negro Race
    Relations in American Novels, 1940-1950.   Univ. of South
    Carolina, 1954.   Thesis: English.   [Includes Erskine
    Caldwell, William Faulkner, Lillian Smith, and Richard Wright]
Campbell, Warren C.   The Historical Development of the Sonnet Form,
    with Special Reference to England and America.   Boston Univ.,
    1931.   Thesis: English.   [Includes Paul H. Hayne]
Cannon, Gladys M.   The Modern Short Story.   Oglethorpe Univ., 1934.
    Thesis: English.
Carlock, Mary S.   I Celebrate Myself, and Sing Myself: Character-
    Types in Early American Autobiographies, 1840-1870.   Columbia
    Univ., 1958.   Dissertation: English.   [Covers wide range of
    autobiographies, with the following Southern autobiographies
    included: Belle Boyd, *Belle Boyd in Camp and Prison*; John
    Brooks, *The Life and Times of the Rev. John Brooks, In Which
    are Contained a History of the Great Revival in Tennessee,
    With Many Incidents of Thrilling Interest*; Theodore Clapp,
    *Autobiographical Sketches and Recollections During a Thirty-
    Five Years' Residence in New Orleans*; Thomas Douglas,
    *Autobiography of Thomas Douglas, Late Judge of the Supreme
    Court of Florida*; Zella Fitz-James, *The Female Bandit of the
    South-West, or the Horrible, Mysterious, and Awful Disclosures
    in the Life of the Creole Murderess, Zella Fitz-James,
    Paramour and Accomplice of Green H. Long, The Treble
    Murderer, for the Space of Six Years*; James Jenkins,
    *Experiences, Labours, and Sufferings of Rev. James Jenkins
    of the South Carolina Conference*; Alfred M. Lorrain, *The
    Helm, The Sword, and The Cross: A Life Narrative*; Annie
    Nelles, *The Life of a Book Agent.   An Autobiography*;
    Winfield Scott, *Memoirs of Lieut.-General Scott*; Joseph
    Travis, *Autobiography of the Rev. Joseph Travis, a Member of
    the Memphis Annual Conference, Embracing a Succinct History
    of the Methodist Episcopal Church, South, Particularly in
    Part of Western Virginia, the Carolinas, Georgia, Alabama,
    and Mississippi.   With Short Memoirs of Local Preachers, and
    An Address to His Friends*; [William Capers] William M.
    Wightman, *Life of William Capers, One of the Bishops of the
    Methodist Church, South; Including an Autobiography*; Daniel
    Drake, *Pioneer Life in Kentucky.   A Series of Reminiscential
    Letters from Daniel Drake to His Children*]
Carlson, Eric W.   An Attempt to Define the Function of Modern
    Poetry.   Boston Univ., 1936.   Thesis: English.   [Includes
    John Gould Fletcher]
_____.   The Expanding Range of Poetic Function in American
    Democracy.   Boston Univ., 1947.   Dissertation: English.
    [Includes Sidney Lanier and E.A. Poe]

Carman, Travers D., Jr. The American Novel in the Twentieth
Century. Boston Univ., 1933. Thesis: English. [Includes
J.B. Cabell, Ellen Glasgow, and Elizabeth M. Roberts]
Carmichael, Herbert K. The Best Representative Short Plays in the
United States: 1900-1940. Univ. of Minnesota, 1943. Disser-
tation: Speech and Drama. [Includes Paul Green]
Carothers, Robert L. The Theme of Frustration in the American
Drama of the Thirties. Kent State Univ., 1966. Thesis:
English. [Includes Jack Kirkland's adaptation of Erskine
Caldwell's *Tobacco Road*]
Carpenter, Thomas P. The Material of Abnormal Psychology in Some
Contemporary English and American Novels. Stanford Univ.,
1947. Dissertation: English. [Includes Ellen Glasgow]
Carriger, Thomas P. The Religious and Ethical Aspects of Recent
Negro Poetry. Duke Univ., 1935. Thesis: Divinity.
Carroll, Mary C. Expressions of Racial Consciousness in Negro
Poetry: A Study with Particular Reference to Negro Poets
prior to 1880. Columbia Univ., 1931. Thesis: English.
[Includes Frances W. Harper, George Moses Horton, and Albery A.
Whitman]
Carter, A.D., Jr. The Protestant Minister as Pictured in Recent
American Fiction. East Tennessee State Univ., 1961. Thesis:
English. [Includes Erskine Caldwell and Thomas Wolfe]
Cary, Joseph B., Jr. The Theory and Practice of the Vague: A
Study in a Mode of Nineteenth Century Lyric Poetry. New York
Univ., 1962. Dissertation: English. [Includes E.A. Poe]
Casey, Lucian T. The Negro in the American Novel. Niagara Univ.,
1942. Thesis: English. [Includes G.W. Cable, W.J. Cash,
and Ellen Glasgow]
Castles, William H., Jr. The Backwoods in Three Early American
Novels: *Modern Chivalry*, *Nick of the Woods*, and *Horse-Shoe
Robinson*. Univ. of South Carolina, 1950. Thesis: English.
Catel, Jean. Destructive Images in Some Modern American Poets.
Univ. of Minnesota, 1919. Thesis: English.
Cawelti, John G. A History of Self-Made Manhood: The Ideal of
the Self-Made Man in Nineteenth Century America. State Univ.
of Iowa, 1960. Dissertation: English. [Includes Mark
Twain]
Cederstrom, Moyle F. American Factual Voyage Narratives, 1815 to
1860. Univ. of Washington, 1932. Dissertation: English.
[Includes Francis L. Hawks and E.A. Poe]
Cella, Charles R. Two Reactions against the Stereotype of the Old-
Fashioned Girl in American Novels, 1890-1920. Univ. of
Kentucky, 1968. Dissertation: English. [Includes Mary
Johnston's *Hagar*]
Chace, Eleanor F. The Development of Negro Poetry in the
Twentieth Century. Boston Univ., 1940. Thesis: English.
[Includes Sterling A. Brown, Georgia Douglas Johnson, and
James Weldon Johnson]
Chamberlayne, John H. Essay on American Literature. Univ. of
Virginia, 1957. Thesis: English.
Chambers, Robert W. The Influence of Magazine Journalists on
the Rise of Realism in America, 1870-1890. Univ. of Texas
(Austin), 1964. Dissertation: English. [Includes Mark
Twain as editor of *Galaxy*]

Chandler, Samuel C. A Study of the Moral Confession (1918-
1939) as Portrayed in the Pulitzer Prize Plays. Brigham
Young Univ., 1950. Thesis: English. [Includes Paul
Green's *In Abraham's Bosom*]
Charvat, William. The Origins of American Critical Thought,
1810-1835. Univ. of Pennsylvania, 1934. Dissertation:
English. [Includes Washington Allston, J.P. Kennedy, Hugh S.
Legaré, Albert Pike, and E.A. Poe]
Childers, Helen W. American Novels about Adolescence, 1917-1953.
George Peabody College, 1958. Dissertation: English.
[Includes William Faulkner]
Choate, Julian E., Jr. The Myth of the American Cowboy: A Study
of the Cattleman's Frontier in History and Fiction. Vander-
bilt Univ., 1954. Dissertation: English.
Christianson, Victor C. The Theories of Certain Recent American
Literary Critics. Univ. of Washington, 1926. Thesis:
English. [Includes H.L. Mencken]
Ciancio, Ralph A. The Grotesque in Modern American Fiction: An
Existential Theory. Univ. of Pittsburgh, 1964. Disser-
tation: English. [Includes John Barth, Truman Capote,
William Faulkner, Carson McCullers, Flannery O'Connor, and
Eudora Welty]
Clareson, Thomas D. The Emergence of American Science Fiction,
1880-1915: A Study of the Impact of Science upon American
Romanticism. Univ. of Pennsylvania, 1956. Dissertation:
English. [Includes E.A. Poe briefly]
Clark, Edith L. The Negro In Fiction: A Historical and Critical
Sketch. Univ. of Texas (Austin), 1902. Thesis: English.
[Includes Virginia Frazier Boyle, J.C. Harris, T.N. Page,
and Ruth McEnery Stuart]
Clark, Graves G. The Development of the Surprise Ending in the
American Short Story from Washington Irving through O. Henry.
Columbia Univ., 1931. Thesis: English.
Clark, James J. The Theme of Success in American Literature, 1914-
1929. New York Univ., 1958. Dissertation: English.
[Includes Ellen Glasgow]
Clarke, Gordon W. The Changing Conception of the Businessman in
the American Novel, 1865-1940. Univ. of Illinois, 1949.
Dissertation: English. [Includes Mark Twain's *The Gilded
Age*]
Clauss, Sr. Anne R. Digression as Narrative Technique in
Contemporary Fiction. Univ. of Wisconsin, 1970. Disser-
tation: English. [Includes John Barth]
Clecak, Pete E. Marxism and American Literary Criticism.
Stanford Univ., 1965. Dissertation: English. [Includes
Cleanth Brooks, John Crowe Ranson, and Robert Penn Warren]
Cobb, Ima W. A Study of Negro Dialects in American Poetry. Univ.
of Southern California, 1941. Thesis: English. [Includes
Hervey Allen, Sterling A. Brown, J.C. Harris, DuBose Heyward,
James Weldon Johnson, Sidney Lanier, T.N. Page, and Irwin
Russell]
Cobb, Thomas S. Social Attitudes in 1932 Fiction. Columbia Univ.,
1934. Thesis: Social Science. [Includes Ellen Glasgow and
Julia Peterkin]

Coffin, Helen T. American Negro Prose since the World War: A Social Study. Univ. of Texas (Austin), 1932. Thesis: Sociology. [Includes Arna Bontemps, W.E.B. DuBois, and Jean Toomer]

Cole, Charles W. The Beginnings of Literary Nationalism in America, 1775-1800. George Washington Univ., 1939. Dissertation: English.

Cole, Lila L. A Critical Evaluation of the Treatment of the Negro in Fiction Written for Children. Howard Univ., 1946. Thesis: Education. [Includes Arna Bontemps, Sterling A. Brown, Octavus Roy Cohen, and F.P. Gaines]

Cole, Nina E. Art in Contemporary American Biography. Univ. of Texas (Austin), 1940. Thesis: English. [Includes Douglas Southall Freeman's *Robert E. Lee*]

Coley, James W. The Schoolmaster in Some Works of American Literature. Univ. of North Carolina (Chapel Hill), 1953. Thesis: Education. [Includes A.B. Longstreet's *Georgia Scenes*]

Collins, John D. American Drama in Antislavery Agitation, 1792-1861. State Univ. of Iowa, 1963. Dissertation: Theater. [Includes plays which deal with aspects of Southern thought on slavery and attitudes toward Negroes]

Collins, Robert G. Four Critical Interpretations in the Modern Novel. Univ. of Denver, 1961. Dissertation: English. [Includes *Light in August*]

Colwell, Charles C. The Judgment of Literature. Emory Univ., 1958. Dissertation: English. [Includes criteria from Cleanth Brooks]

Condit, L.D. The Patriotic Lyric in the Literature of North and South America. Ohio State Univ., 1925. Thesis: English. [Includes Francis Scott Key, Sidney Lanier, Theodore O'Hara, Albert Pike, and James Randall]

Conkle, Ellsworth P. Dramatic Usage of Historical Material in the American Civil War Plays. Univ. of Nebraska, 1923. Thesis: English. [Includes Thomas Dixon and Edward Peple]

Conner, Frederick W. Cosmic Optimism: A Study of the Interpretation of Evolution by American Poets from Emerson to Robinson. Univ. of Pennsylvania, 1944. Dissertation: English. [Includes Madison Cawein, Sidney Lanier, and E.A. Poe]

Conway, Viola C. Portrayal of the Protestant Clergy in American Novels. Univ. of Rhode Island, 1965. Thesis: English. [Includes *Light in August*]

Cook, Florence L. American History as a Source in the Early American Prose Fiction (1800-1830). Columbia Univ., 1934. Thesis: English. [Includes G.W.P. Curtis and Thomas Jefferson]

Coplan, Ruth E. A Study of Predominant Themes in Selected Best-Selling American Fiction, 1850-1915. Univ. of Pennsylvania, 1966. Dissertation: English. [Includes anti-slavery themes]

Covington, Mary F. *The Atlantic* and *Harper's* in Relation to Southern Literature, 1865-1900. Duke Univ., 1939. Thesis: English.

Cowgill, Lenna A. Battle Poetry of the Civil War: An Annotated
    Study. George Peabody College, 1930. Thesis: English.
Crain, Harold C. Characterization in the Plays of Modern
    Dramatists: Techniques and Practices. Univ. of Iowa, 1947.
    Dissertation: Speech and Drama. [Includes Paul Green]
Crane, Fred A. The Noble Savage in America, 1815-1860: Concepts
    of the Indian, with Special Reference to the Writers of the
    Northeast. Yale Univ., 1952. Dissertation: History.
    [Includes W.G. Simms]
Crider, Bess M. The Poets Laureate of the American States. Univ.
    of Maryland, 1927. Thesis: English. [Includes C.T. Davis,
    Arkansas; Violet McDougal, Oklahoma; John T. Cotton Noe,
    Kentucky; and Frank L. Stanton, Georgia]
Critoph, Gerald E. The American Literary Reaction to World War I.
    Univ. of Pennsylvania, 1957. Dissertation: English.
    [Includes James Lane Allen, J.B. Cabell, Olive Tilford
    Dargan, Thomas Dixon, William Faulkner, John Gould Fletcher,
    Ellen Glasgow, Lafcadio Hearn, H.L. Mencken, Alexander Percy,
    Katherine Anne Porter, Lizette Woodworth Reese, Cale Young
    Rice, and Thomas Wolfe]
Cronkhite, George F. Literature as a Livelihood: The Attitude of
    Certain American Writers toward Literature as a Profession
    from 1820 to the Civil War. Harvard Univ., 1948. Disser-
    tation: English. [Includes John Esten Cooke, Paul H. Hayne,
    E.A. Poe, W.G. Simms, Mrs. E.D.E.N. Southworth, and Henry
    Timrod]
Cronyn, George W. The Frontier in American Literature prior to
    the Civil War. Columbia Univ., 1917. Thesis: English.
Crowell, Alfred A. Citations of American Literature in *The
    Edinburgh Review* from 1802 to 1859. Univ. of Oklahoma, 1934.
    Thesis: English. [Includes E.A. Poe]
Cummings, Frank A. The Civil War in Historical Fiction, 1928-1938.
    Univ. of Vermont, 1939. Thesis: English. [Includes Roark
    Bradford, Gwen Bristow, James Boyd, Clifford Dowdey, H.J.
    Eckenrode, William Faulkner, Caroline Gordon, DuBose Heyward,
    Margaret Mitchell, T.S. Stribling, and Stark Young]
Curtis, Cecil. *Scribner's Monthly Magazine* and the Development of
    Southern Literature. Univ. of North Carolina (Chapel Hill),
    1947. Thesis: English.
Curvin, Jonathan W. The Realistic Tradition in American Art and
    Drama. Cornell Univ., 1941. Dissertation: Speech and
    Drama. [Includes E.A. Poe and W.G. Simms]
Cusker, Thomas J. Revolt of the Titans: The Civil War Era as
    Seen through the Works of James R. Lowell, David R. Locke,
    and Charles H. Smith. Seton Hall Univ., 1961. Thesis:
    English.
Danforth, Mildred E. Examples of the Reaction of American Drama to
    Major War Crises in Our History. Univ. of North Carolina
    (Chapel Hill), 1949. Thesis: Dramatic Art. [Chapter on
    the Civil War]
Darlington, Marion. A Study of the Poetry of the Indians of North
    America and Its Influence on Modern American Poetry. Columbia
    Univ., 1943. Thesis: English. [Includes John Gould
    Fletcher]

Daugherty, George H., Jr. North American Indian Literature. Univ. of Chicago, 1925. Dissertation: English. [Includes Caddo, Cherokee, Creek, and Osage]

Davenport, John S. The Ode in American Literature. Univ. of North Carolina (Chapel Hill), 1934. Dissertation: English. [Includes Madison Cawein, Thomas H. Chivers, Paul H. Hayne, Edwin Clifford Holland, James Barron Hope, Sidney Lanier, and E.A. Poe]

Davies, Douglas D. The Possibilities of the Hero in Three Contemporary Novels. San Francisco State College, 1966. Thesis: English. [Includes Walker Percy]

Davis, David B. Attitudes towards Homicide in American Fiction, 1798-1860: A Study in Intellectual History. Harvard Univ., 1956. Dissertation: American Studies. [South represented in a discussion of lynching and dueling]

Davis, Elma G. The Development of Sectionalism in American Poetry. Univ. of Arkansas, 1930. Thesis: English. [Includes Madison Cawein, Paul H. Hayne, Annie C. Ketchum, Sidney Lanier, J.W. Palmer, James Ryder Randall, Father Abram J. Ryan, Henry Timrod, J.R. Thompson, and W.H. Thompson]

Dawson, Harry H. Dream and Reality in Modern American Fiction. Univ. of Virginia, 1964. Thesis: English. [Brief analysis of Faulkner's *The Bear*]

Dawson, Mary E. The Idea of Tragedy in the Contemporary American Theatre. Univ. of Iowa, 1944. Dissertation: English. [Includes Paul Green and Lillian Hellman]

Deal, Bernice M. A Course of Study in American Literature for Slow Learners. Grade 11. College of the Holy Names, 1965. Thesis: English. [Brief comment, with study questions, on Thomas Jefferson, Harper Lee, E.A. Poe, and Mark Twain]

Dean, Ernest P. The American Political Novel, 1870-1910. Univ. of Rochester, 1937. Thesis: History. [Includes T.N. Page]

DeClark, William E. The Relationship between Periodical Fiction and the Rise of Realism in the United States: A Study of *Scribner's Magazine*, 1887-1939. New York Univ., 1951. Dissertation: Education. [Includes discussion of Thomas Wolfe]

Del Porto, Joseph A. A Study of American Anti-Slavery Journals. Michigan State Univ., 1953. Dissertation: English. [Includes Southern opinion]

Depew, Ollie. Vers Libre. Univ. of Kentucky, 1923. Thesis: English. [Includes Sidney Lanier and E.A. Poe]

DeRoche, Louis. The Novel of the Civil War. Univ. of Georgia, 1936. Thesis: English. [Includes John Esten Cooke, Ellen Glasgow, T.N. Page, and Stark Young]

Deubach, Vila. American Industry in the Short Story since the Civil War. Univ. of Colorado, 1944. Dissertation: English.

Deutschberger, Paul. Man and Movements in Modern Literature. Columbia Univ., 1941. Thesis: Comparative Literature. [Includes John Gould Fletcher and Thomas Wolfe]

Devin, Lola M. Birds in American Prose. Univ. of Texas (Austin), 1929. 'Thesis: English. [Prose writers of the colonial and revolutionary periods including J.P. Kennedy, John Smith, and George Washington]

Devine, Lorraine A. Problems of the American Farmer in Fiction
(1890-1939). Univ. of Colorado, 1946. Thesis: English.
[Includes Erskine Caldwell, Ellen Glasgow, Paul Green, and
Elizabeth M. Roberts]
Dew, Deborah S. Expressionism in the American Theater, 1922-1936.
Yale Univ., 1968. Dissertation: English. [Includes
detailed analysis of Paul Green's *Johnny Johnson*]
Dickinson, Elizabeth. The Work of the Negro Dramatist in America.
An Evaluation. Univ. of Wyoming, 1964. Thesis: English.
Dierolf, Claude E. The Pageant Drama and American Pageantry.
Univ. of Pennsylvania, 1953. Dissertation: English.
[Emphasis on Paul Green, but also includes Frederick H. Koch]
Diffey, C.T. Out of That Generous Land: A Study of the Scope of
the Novel Based on American Practice from Cooper to Faulkner.
Bristol, 1964. Dissertation: English.
Dilday, Grace O. The Influence of Industrialism in Modern American
Poetry. Louisiana State Univ., 1939. Thesis: English.
[Includes Sidney Lanier]
Dixon, Bessie L. The Negro Character in American Drama. Howard
Univ., 1936. Thesis: English. [Includes Paul Green, J.C.
Harris, DuBose Heyward, and Irwin Russell]
Dodge, Robert K. The Influence of Machines and Technology on
American Literature of the Late Nineteenth and Early Twentieth
Centuries. Univ. of Texas (Austin), 1967. Dissertation:
English. [Includes Mark Twain]
Doherty, Mary J. The American Comic Travel Book. Univ. of Texas
(Austin), 1958. Thesis: English. [Includes David
Crockett's *Exploits and Adventures in Texas*]
Dolan, Paul J. Tradition in Modern Literary Criticism. New York
Univ., 1966. Dissertation: English. [Includes Cleanth
Brooks and criticism of the Agrarians]
Doner, Dean B. The Burdening of Narrative. State Univ. of Iowa,
1953. Dissertation: English. [Includes *You Can't Go Home
Again*]
Donigan, Marilyn R. The Novel as Social Criticism: An Essay on
Five Narratives on the Theme of Class. Univ. of Texas
(Austin), 1953. Thesis: English. [Includes Robert Penn
Warren and Richard Wright]
Donn, Robert S. The Theme of Loneliness among Women in Recent
Drama. Brooklyn College, 1952. Thesis: English. [Includes
Carson McCullers and Tennessee Williams]
Dorsey, Virginia F. Pro-Slavery Thought in the Fiction of the
1850's. Johns Hopkins Univ., 1961. Thesis: History.
Dougherty, Robert G. A Critical Survey of the Novels of Richard
Wright, Ralph Ellison, and James Baldwin. East Texas State
Univ., 1968. Thesis: English.
DuBois, Mary L. A Study of a Decade of the O. Henry Memorial
Award Prize Stories. East Texas State Univ., 1951. Thesis:
English.
DuBreuil, Alice J. The Novel of Democracy in America: A Contri-
bution to the Study of the Progress of Democratic Ideas in
the American Novel. Johns Hopkins Univ., 1922. Dissertation:
English. [Includes Joseph A. Altsheler, William A. Caruthers,
John Esten Cooke, Thomas Dixon, Ellen Glasgow, Henry Sydnor
Harrison, J.P. Kennedy, T.N. Page, and W.G. Simms]

Duffey, Bernard I. The Place of Poetry: Theories of Poetic Function in the Formalist Literary Criticism of England and the United States, 1908 to the Present. Ohio State Univ., 1947. Dissertation: English. [Includes John Crowe Ransom and Allen Tate]

Dumond, Helen M. The Gothic Romance in America. Columbia Univ., 1918. Thesis: English. [Includes E.A. Poe]

Dunbar, Vida H. Trends in American Fiction as Reflected in Best Sellers since 1900. Univ. of Texas (Austin), 1941. Thesis: English. [Includes Margaret Mitchell]

Duncan, Joseph E. The Relationship of Seventeenth Century and Twentieth Century Metaphysical Poetry. Univ. of Louisville, 1946. Thesis: English. [Includes Cleanth Brooks, John Crowe Ransom, Allen Tate, and Robert Penn Warren]

Dunlap, George A. The City in the American Novel, 1789-1900. Univ. of Pennsylvania, 1934. Dissertation: English. [Includes William A. Caruthers and Ellen Glasgow]

Durden, Francis C. Negro Women in Poetry from Phyllis Wheatley to Margaret Walker. Atlanta Univ., 1947. Thesis: English. [Includes Sterling A. Brown, Frances W. Harper, Georgia Douglas Johnson, James Weldon Johnson, Anne Spencer, Jean Toomer, and Margaret Walker]

Dusenberry, Robert B. Attitude toward Religion in Representative Novels of the American Frontier, 1820-1890. Univ. of Washington, 1951. Dissertation: English. [Includes W.G. Simms and Mark Twain]

Dusenburg, Winifred L. The Theme of Loneliness in Modern American Drama. Univ. of Florida, 1956. Dissertation: English. [Includes Carson McCullers, Elmer Rice, Tennessee Williams, and Thomas Wolfe]

Ealy, Ruth R. The Sonnet in America. Univ. of Pittsburgh, 1924. Thesis: English. [One section on the sonnet in the South]

Earle, Osborne. The Reputation and Influence of William Godwin in America. Harvard Univ., 1938. Dissertation: English. [Includes Godwin's influence on E.A. Poe and W.G. Simms]

Early, Minnie L. The Negro as a Character in Recent American Fiction. North Texas State Univ., 1936. Thesis: English. [Includes Roark Bradford and Erskine Caldwell]

Eaton, Richard B., Jr. A History of American Prosody from Its Beginnings to 1880. Univ. of North Carolina (Chapel Hill), 1967. Dissertation: English. [Includes theories of Thomas Jefferson, Sidney Lanier, and E.A. Poe]

Eby, Edwin H. American Romantic Criticism, 1815 to 1860. Univ. of Washington, 1927. Dissertation: English. [Includes Hugh S. Legaré and E.A. Poe]

Echols, William G. The Theology of the American Poets. Birmingham-Southern College, 1924. Thesis: Religion. [Includes Sidney Lanier and E.A. Poe]

Eckman, Frederick W. The Language of American Poetry, 1900-1910. Ohio State Univ., 1954. Dissertation: English. [Includes Madison Cawein, Sidney Lanier, George E. Woodberry, and Lizette Woodworth Reese]

Edlen, Annie. The One-Act Play in America: Techniques of Construction. Univ. of Southern California, 1944. Thesis: Speech. [Includes Paul Green]

Edmondson, Elsie F.L. The Writer as Hero in Important American
Fiction since Howells. Univ. of Michigan, 1954. Disser-
tation: English. [Includes J.B. Cabell]
Edyvean, Alfred R. A Critical Appraisal of American Dramas
(1935-1949) in the Light of the Christian View of Man.
Northwestern Univ., 1952. Dissertation: English. [Includes
Paul Green's *Johnny Johnson*, Lillian Hellman's *Watch on the
Rhine*, and Tennessee Williams' *A Streetcar Named Desire*]
Ehrlich, Heyward B. A Study of Literary Activity in New York City
during the 1840-Decade. New York Univ., 1963. Disser-
tation: English. [Includes E.A. Poe]
Elfenbein, Josef A. American Drama (1782-1812) as an Index to
Socio-Political Thought. New York Univ., 1951. Disser-
tation: Drama. [149 plays considered, including a history
of the American drama to 1812]
Ellington, Mary D. Plays by Negro Authors with Special Emphasis
upon the Period from 1916-1934. Fisk Univ., 1934. Thesis:
English. [Includes Joseph S. Cotter, Jr., W.E.B. DuBois,
Randolph Edmons, Georgia Douglas Johnson, Willis Richardson,
and Jean Toomer]
Elliston, Stephen F. Dramatic and Narrative Art: Studies of
Dramatizations on the New York Stage, 1919-1958. Univ. of
Illinois, 1959. Dissertation: English. [Includes Erskine
Caldwell's *Tobacco Road* and Carson McCullers' *The Member of
the Wedding*]
Emmons, Winfred S. The Materials and Methods of American Horror
Fiction in the Nineteenth Century. Louisiana State Univ.,
1952. Dissertation: English. [Includes E.A. Poe]
Engdahl, Bonnie T. Paradise in the New World: A Study of the
Image of the Garden in the Literature of Colonial America.
Univ. of California, 1967. Dissertation: English. [Presents
idea of the South as aristocratic, grand]
Erskine, Lucile. Outline History of Criticism (with Reference to
Poe's Theory of Aesthetics). Washington Univ. (St. Louis),
1907. Thesis: English.
Evans, Edwin B. The Social Aspects of Modern American Poetry: A
Sociological Interpretation of Poetry. New York Univ., 1928.
Dissertation: Education. [Includes Madison Cawein, John
Gould Fletcher, and Sidney Lanier]
Ezell, Lonnie B. Industrialism in American Poetry. Univ. of Texas
(Austin), 1930. Thesis: English. [Includes Sidney Lanier
and E.A. Poe]
Ezor, Edwin L. The Image of the Teacher in the American Academic
Novel, 1900-1960. New York Univ., 1969. Dissertation:
English.
Falb, Lewis W. The Critical Reception of the American Drama in
France, 1945-1960. Yale Univ., 1967. Dissertation: English.
[Includes Tennessee Williams]
Farrell, Alfred. The Negro Novel in America, 1920-1946. Ohio
State Univ., 1946. Dissertation: English.
Farrell, Harold A. Theme and Variation: A Critical Evaluation of
the Negro Novel, 1919-1947. Ohio State Univ., 1949. Disser-
tation: English.

Fein, Richard J. The Major American Poetry of World War II. A Critical Study. New York Univ., 1960. Dissertation: English. [Includes Randall Jarrell]

Ferguson, Phyllis M. Women Dramatists in the American Theatre, 1901-1940. Univ. of Pittsburgh, 1957. Dissertation: English. [Includes Lillian Hellman]

Ferrell, Wilfred A. Portrait of the Politician in the American Novel: 1870-1910. Univ. of Texas (Austin), 1959. Dissertation: English. [Includes Ellen Glasgow and Mark Twain]

Fertig, Goldie M. The Treatment of Adolescence in Contemporary American Literature. Univ. of Louisville, 1942. Thesis: English. [Includes *Look Homeward, Angel*]

Fiegenbaum, Martha T. Local Color as Observed in Certain American Authors. Univ. of Nebraska, 1929. Thesis: English. [Includes James Lane Allen, G.W. Cable, Kate Chopin, and T.N. Page]

Fink, Kenneth E. Relationship of Journalism and Literature in America as Shown by the Lives and Works of American Men of Letters. Univ. of Texas (Austin), 1931. Thesis: Journalism. [Includes J.C. Harris, Lafcadio Hearn, O. Henry, T.N. Page, and E.A. Poe]

Finlinson, Vance J. An Analysis of the Modern Political Novel: Its Place and Function in Politics. Brigham Young Univ., 1968. Thesis: Political Science. [Includes William Faulkner, Mark Twain, and Robert Penn Warren]

Firestone, Paul A. The "Educational Value and Power" of the Pulitzer Prize Plays. Columbia Univ., 1968. Dissertation: English. [Includes Tennessee Williams]

Fiske, John C. American Classics in Soviet Criticism. Harvard Univ., 1954. Dissertation: English. [Includes E.A. Poe]

Fitch, Noel R. An American Bookshop in Paris: The Influence of Sylvia Beach's Shakespeare and Company on American Literature. Washington State Univ., 1969. Dissertation: English. [Includes Katherine Anne Porter and Allen Tate]

Fleming, Harold S., Jr. From Social Protests to Introspection (A Study of Six Important Novels by Negro Authors). Columbia Univ., 1954. Thesis: English. [Includes Ralph Ellison and Richard Wright]

Fletcher, M.S. The Relative Emphasis of Authors in Histories of American Literature. George Peabody College, 1930. Thesis: English.

Flores, Vetal. A Comparative Analysis of Poetry and the Poet According to Selected American Authors. Hardin-Simmons Univ., 1953. Thesis: English. [Includes E.A. Poe]

Flory, Claude R. Economic Criticism in American Fiction, 1792-1900. Univ. of Pennsylvania, 1935. Dissertation: English. [Includes G.W. Cable, J.P. Kennedy, and T.N. Page]

Floyd, Virginia I.H. An Analytical Study of the Role of *Hubris* in the Spiritual Environment of American Drama from 1945-1961. Northwestern Univ., 1967. Dissertation: Theater. [Discusses 220 plays, some by Southern writers]

Forbes, Mary E. Contemporary Negro Essayists: An Analysis of Style. Fisk Univ., 1940. Thesis: English. [Includes Benjamin G. Brawley, W.E.B. DuBois, James Weldon Johnson, Kelley Miller, William Pickens, and Booker T. Washington]

Ford, Edwin H. The Newspaper Mind in American Literature.
Columbia Univ., 1928. Thesis: Journalism. [Includes
H.L. Mencken and O. Henry]
Ford, Nick A. The Negro Author's Use of Propaganda in Imaginative
Literature. Univ. of Iowa, 1946. Dissertation: English.
[Includes Arna Bontemps, Sterling A. Brown, W.E.B. DuBois,
Randolph Edmonds, Zora Neale Hurston, James Weldon Johnson,
George Lee, Willis Richardson, Walter Edward Turpin,
Margaret Walker, Walter White, and Richard Wright]
Foster, Edith M. American Life and Characters as Represented in
Original Native Drama from 1870 to 1890. Univ. of Colorado,
1945. Thesis: English and Speech. [Includes Henry C.
DeMille]
Foster, Edward F. A Study of Grim Humor in the Works of Poe,
Melville, and Twain. Vanderbilt Univ., 1957. Dissertation:
English.
Foster, Estelle L. Biographies by American Negro Authors: A
Study of Subject Matter. Fisk Univ., 1935. Thesis: English.
[Includes James Brawley, William Wells Brown, Charles W.
Chesnutt, D. Webster Davis, W.E.B. DuBois, Josiah Henson,
James Weldon Johnson, Elizabeth Keckley, Jermain W. Loguen,
Robert Russa Moton, William Pickens, and Booker T. Washington]
Foster, John B. China and the Chinese in American Literature,
1850-1950. Univ. of Illinois, 1953. Dissertation: English.
[Includes John Gould Fletcher]
Foster, Richard J. Modern Critics and Romantic Sensibility: A
Study of the Romanticism of the New Criticism. Syracuse
Univ., 1957. Dissertation: English. [Includes Allen Tate]
Foster, Ruel E. Freudian Influences in the American Autobiograph-
ical Novel. Vanderbilt Univ., 1941. Dissertation: English.
[Includes Thomas Wolfe]
Fowler, Herbert E. Criticism of Education in Twentieth Century
American Novels. New York Univ., 1932. Dissertation:
Education. [Includes Charles Wertenbaker, Thomas Wolfe, and
Stark Young]
Fox, Velda M. The Development of the Pocahontas Story in American
Literature, 1607-1927. Univ. of Iowa, 1927. Thesis: English.
[Based on historical and fictional writing]
Franchere, Hoyt C. A Study of Tragedy and the Tragic Character in
the Recent American Novel. Univ. of Washington, 1950.
Dissertation: English. [Includes *Light in August*]
Frank, Mortimer H. Music in American Literary History: A Survey
of the Significance of Music in the Writings of Eight American
Literary Figures. New York Univ., 1968. Dissertation:
English. [Includes Sidney Lanier, E.A. Poe, and Mark Twain]
Franke, Helen L. Early American Travel Literature. Univ. of
Texas (Austin), 1931. Thesis: English. [Covers the period
from John Smith's *True Relation* to Parson Weems' *Letters*]
Franklin, Frances M. The Negro Character in Novels about the
Civil War and Reconstruction Periods, 1936-1944. Atlanta
Univ., 1946. Thesis: English. [Includes Gwen Bristow,
Clifford Dowdey, Caroline Gordon, J.P. Kennedy, Margaret
Mitchell, Lella Warren, and Stark Young]

Frazar, Lois. Imagism. Univ. of Kentucky, 1934. Thesis: English. [Includes John Gould Fletcher and E.A. Poe]

Frazier, Paul B. A Preliminary Study of the Negro in American Drama. Univ. of Kentucky, 1939. Thesis: English. [Includes Paul Green]

Free, William J. *The Columbian Magazine* and Its Contribution to American Literary Nationalism. Univ. of North Carolina (Chapel Hill), 1962. Dissertation: English. [Specifically mentions writings of Thomas Jefferson]

Freeland, Leona L. A Study of Typical Situations in American Civil War Drama. Northwestern Univ., 1933. Thesis: Speech.

Friedsam, Wilma M. The Contemporary Poetry of the States West of the Mississippi. Baylor Univ., 1927. Thesis: English. [Includes Stanley E. Babb, Karle Wilson Baker, George Band, Faye Bishop, Arna Bontemps, Jedge Rector Burton, William L. Cettendon, William R. Clark, Grace N. Crowell, Irene Mary Davidson, Patricia Drake, Glenn W. Dresback, Jan I. Fortune, Hilton R. Greer, Clyde W. Hill, Judd M. Lewis, Terese Lindsey, Robert L. Lowe, Whitney Montgomery, Ernest Powell, Charles J. Quirck, John Syolander, Isaac Wade, and Jewel Wurtzbough]

Fuller, Landon E. The Supernatural Element in American Prose Fiction. Univ. of Virginia, 1926. Thesis: English. [Includes E.A. Poe]

Gaffney, Wilbur G. An Enquiry into the Value of American Negro Poetry. Univ. of Nebraska, 1928. Thesis: English. [Includes Sterling A. Brown and James Weldon Johnson]

Gallagher, Sr. Mary F. Contributions of the Negro to Contemporary American Poetry. Fordham Univ., 1933. Thesis: English. [Includes James Weldon Johnson and Albery A. Whitman]

Gapen, Clara M. Children in American Poetry from 1800-1860. Columbia Univ., 1925. Thesis: English. [Includes George Henry Miles and E.A. Poe]

Garcia, Daniel P. Theories of Catharsis in Modern Literary Criticism: In Influences of Psychoanalysis, Anthropology, and the New Criticism. Univ. of Oregon, 1962. Dissertation: English. [Includes John Crowe Ransom]

Gardner, Laura A. The Comic Stage Politician as Portrayed in Selected American Plays, 1870-1956. Kent State Univ., 1960. Thesis: Speech. [Includes Southern politician]

Garson, Helen S. The Fallen Women in American Naturalistic Fiction: From Crane to Faulkner. Univ. of Maryland, 1967. Dissertation: English.

Garton, Christiana. The Portrayal of the Negro Character in the American Drama and Novel. Univ. of Colorado, 1942. Thesis: English. [Includes Paul Green, Dorothy and DuBose Heyward, Julia Peterkin, and T.S. Stribling]

Garvey, Margaret. The Loyalist Prose Writers of the American Revolution. Columbia Univ., 1946. Thesis: English. [Jonathan Boucher]

Gearhart, Sally M. Some Modern American Concepts of Tragic Drama as Revealed by the Critical Writings of Twentieth Century American Playwrights. Bowling Green State Univ., 1953. Thesis: Speech. [Includes Paul Green and Tennessee Williams]

Geier, Woodrow A. Images of Man in Five American Dramatists: A Theological Critique. Vanderbilt Univ., 1959. Dissertation: Religion. [Includes Paul Green and Tennessee Williams]

George, Marie. Comparison of Modern Fiction with the Earlier Canons of Criticism. Texas Tech Univ., 1941. Thesis: English. [Includes Thomas Wolfe]

Georgi, Charlotte. Twenty-five Years of Pulitzer Prize Novels, 1918-1943: A Content Analysis. Univ. of North Carolina (Chapel Hill), 1956. Thesis: Library Science. [Includes Ellen Glasgow, Caroline Miller, Margaret Mitchell, Julia Peterkin, and T.S. Stribling]

Geppert, Eunice C. Conflicting Tendencies in the Development of Form in the Short Story. Univ. of Texas (Austin), 1946. Thesis: English. [Includes Erskine Caldwell, William Faulkner, E.A. Poe, and Katherine Anne Porter]

Gerber, John C. American Literary Criticism in the Forties. Univ. of Pittsburgh, 1932. Thesis: English. [Includes E.A. Poe]

Gerlach, John C. The Kingdom of God and Nineteenth Century American Fiction. Arizona State Univ., 1969. Dissertation: English. [Includes Mark Twain]

Gibbons, Eleanor H. Some Outstanding Characteristics in the Development of American Fiction since the Civil War. Pennsylvania State Univ., 1920. Thesis: English. [Includes G.W. Cable, Charles E. Craddock, J.C. Harris, and T.N. Page]

Gilbert, Prentiss B. Historical Development of the Short Story. Univ. of Rochester, 1916. Thesis: English. [Includes E.A. Poe]

Gill, Eloise W. The Changing Attitude toward the Indian in American Literature. Louisiana State Univ., 1935. Thesis: English. [Includes W.G. Simms]

Gill, John M. Bernard Devoto and Literary Anticriticism: Theory and Experience. New York Univ., 1964. Dissertation: English. [Includes William Faulkner, Mark Twain, and Thomas Wolfe]

Gillett, Rupert W. Characterization in the Contemporary Short Story. Univ. of Texas (Austin), 1921. Thesis: English. [Includes James Lane Allen, G.W. Cable, Irvin S. Cobb, John Fox, Jr., J.C. Harris, O. Henry, and T.N. Page]

Gilliam, Theodore E. The Negro Image in Representative American Dramas. Tulane Univ., 1967. Dissertation: Speech and Theater. [Includes William Faulkner's *Requiem for a Nun* and plays by Paul Green]

Gillis, Everett A. American Prosody in the Eighteen Nineties with Special Reference to Magazine Verse. Univ. of Texas (Austin), 1948. Dissertation: English. [Substantial portions given to Madison Cawein and Lizette Woodworth Reese]

Gittlen, Arthur J. Political and Social Thought Contained in the Jewish-American Novel (1867-1927). Michigan State Univ., 1969. Dissertation: English. [Includes "Southern rural novel"]

Gladding, Corinne J. The Significance of the Religious Figure in American Drama of 1919-1929. Columbia Univ., 1931. Thesis: English. [Includes Paul Green]

Glahn, George A. Natural Eloquence and the Democratic Gospel: The Idea of an American Rhetoric from the Second Awakening to Cooper's *Natty Bumppo*. Univ. of North Carolina (Chapel Hill), 1969. Dissertation: English. [Includes Peter Cartwright]

Gloster, Hugh M. American Negro Fiction from Charles W. Chesnutt to Richard Wright. New York Univ., 1943. Dissertation: English.

Gober, Ruth B. The American Novelist Interprets the Student of Higher Education. Univ. of Oklahoma, 1956. Dissertation: Education. [Includes Thomas Wolfe]

Gobrecht, Eleanor A. A Descriptive Study of the Value Commitments of the Principal Characters in Four Recent American Plays: *Picnic*, *Cat on a Hot Tin Roof*, *Long Day's Journey into Night*, and *Look Homeward, Angel*. Univ. of Southern California, 1963. Dissertation: Speech and Drama.

Goede, William J. Tradition in the American Negro Novel. Univ. of California (Riverside), 1967. Dissertation: English. [Includes Arna Bontemps, Ralph Ellison, Chester Himes, Langston Hughes, Claude McKay, Jean Toomer, and Richard Wright]

Goldstein, Samuel. The Technique of Time in Fiction. Boston Univ., 1937. Thesis: English. [Includes E.A. Poe]

Goldstone, Richard H. The Pariah in Modern American and British Literature: An Illustration of a Method for Teachers of Literature. Columbia Univ., 1960. Dissertation: English. [Includes G.W. Cable and William Faulkner]

Gosling, Thomas W. Negro in American Fiction. Univ. of Cincinnati, 1911. Dissertation: English. [Includes James Lane Allen, George W. Bagby, Joseph Glover Baldwin, Nancy Huston Banks, Frances G. Baylor, Robert Beverley, Marguerite Bouvet, Benjamin G. Brawley, William G. Brown, G.W. Cable, W.A. Caruthers, Charles W. Chesnutt, Kate Chopin, John Esten Cooke, Mary Evelyn Moore Davis, Thomas Dixon, Mrs. M.H. Eastman, John Fox, Jr., Will N. Harben, J.C. Harris, Joseph H. Ingraham, Mary Johnston, R.M. Johnston, A.B. Longstreet, Howard W. Odum, Opie Read, Anne Newport Royall, Molly E. Seawell, W.G. Simms, Ruth McEnery Stuart, Marion Harland, Lucy M. Thurston, Nathaniel B. Tucker, St. George Tucker, Catherine A. Warfield, Booker T. Washington, George A. Wauchope, and C.H. Wiley]

Graff, Gerard E. The Dramatic Theory of Poetry. Stanford Univ., 1964. Dissertation: English. [Includes Cleanth Brooks]

Graham, Louise. The Development of Historical Plays in America. Univ. of South Carolina, 1931. Thesis: English. [Includes Lula Vollmer]

Graham, Philip E. Birds in American Poetry. Univ. of Texas (Austin), 1924. Thesis: English. [Includes Madison Cawein, Paul H. Hayne, Sidney Lanier, Cale Young Rice, Fr. Abram J. Ryan, W.G. Simms, J.B. Tabb, and Francis O. Ticknor]

Grahame, Roberta M. A Study of the Cross-Section Novel Written in English since 1915. Univ. of Minnesota, 1940. Dissertation: English. [Includes Julia Peterkin]

Granger, Bruce I. Political Satire in the American Revolution (1763-1783). Cornell Univ., 1947. Dissertation: English.

Graves, Allen W. Difficult Contemporary Short Stories: William Faulkner, Katherine Anne Porter, Dylan Thomas, Eudora Welty, and Virginia Woolf. Univ. of Washington, 1954. Dissertation: English.

Gray, Gordon W. A Selective Guide to the American Regional Novel. Columbia Univ., 1948. Dissertation: English.

Greatwood, Y'Vonne L. The Civil War in American Fiction: A Consideration of the Four Waves which Treat the War between the States. Canisius College, 1941. Thesis: English. [Includes Mary Johnston, Margaret Mitchell, and Evelyn Scott]

Green, Adwin W. The American War Novel. Univ. of Virginia, 1927. Thesis: English. [Includes John Esten Cooke, Charles E. Craddock, Thomas Dixon, J.C. Harris, and W.G. Simms]

Greenaway, Minnie. Modern Trends in the American Short Story. New York Univ., 1934. Thesis: English. [Includes Erskine Caldwell, William Faulkner, O. Henry, William March, and Wilbur D. Steele]

Greer, Kathleen C. The Development of the Heroine in the American Novel from 1850 to 1900. North Texas State Univ., 1948. Thesis: English. [Includes James Lane Allen, Frances H. Burnett, G.W. Cable, DuBose Heyward, T.N. Page, Julia Peterkin, and T.S. Stribling]

Gregoric, Michael T. Principles and Practice in Modern Dramatic Criticism. Cornell Univ., 1961. Dissertation: Speech and Drama. [Includes Stark Young]

Griffin, Max L. The Relations with the South of Six Major Northern Writers, 1830-1861. Univ. of North Carolina (Chapel Hill), 1943. Dissertation: English.

Griffith, Malcolm A. The Grotesque in American Fiction. Ohio State Univ., 1966. Dissertation: English. [Includes William Faulkner and Mark Twain]

Grigsby, Gordon K. The Modern Long Poem: Studies in Thematic Form. Univ. of Wisconsin, 1960. Dissertation: English. [Includes Tennessee Williams]

Grimes, Geoffrey A. The Use of the Persona by Four American Humorists. Texas Tech Univ., 1969. Thesis: English. [Includes Mark Twain]

Grissom, Ruby M. Contribution of the Negro to American Literature. Southwest Texas State Univ., 1940. Thesis: English. [Includes Arna Bontemps, James Weldon Johnson, Booker T. Washington, and Richard Wright]

Grove, James L. Visions and Revisions: A Study of the Obtuse Narrator in American Fiction from Brockden Brown to Faulkner. Harvard Univ., 1968. Dissertation: English.

Guest, Charles B. The Position of Women as Considered by Representative American Authors since 1800. Univ. of Wisconsin, 1943. Dissertation: English. [Includes J.B. Cabell, Sidney Lanier, H.L. Mencken, E.A. Poe, and W.G. Simms]

Guilds, Mildred A. Representative Boys in American Literature. Univ. of South Carolina, 1937. Thesis: English. [Includes Frances Hodgson Burnett, John Fox, Jr., O. Henry, T.N. Page, and Alice Hegan Rice]

Gunn, D.W. The American and British Author in Mexico, 1911-1914. Univ. of North Carolina (Chapel Hill), 1968. Dissertation: English. [Includes Katherine Anne Porter and Tennessee Williams]

Hackenberg, George R. The Clergyman in American Novels since the First World War. Univ. of Pittsburgh, 1948. Thesis: English. [Includes Erskine Caldwell and Ellen Glasgow]

Hadley, Marie P. The Critical Spirit in Modern American Literature Reflected by Critics and Novelists. Ohio State Univ., 1935. Thesis: English. [Includes H.L. Mencken]

Hagood, Monroe J. The Early Demand for a Native American Literature, from the Revolution to 1825. Univ. of North Carolina (Chapel Hill), 1932. Thesis: English. [Discusses *The Portico, a Repository of Science and Literature* and *The Western Review and Miscellaneous Magazine*]

Hakac, John R. The Juvenile Hero as a Literary Device in Selected American Novels. Univ. of Texas (Austin), 1963. Dissertation: English. [Includes *Huckleberry Finn*]

Hall, Ernest J. The Satirical Element in the American Novel. Univ. of Pennsylvania, 1922. Dissertation: English. [Includes J.P. Kennedy and Nathaniel B. Tucker]

Halline, Allan G. Main Currents of Thought in American Drama. Univ. of Wisconsin, 1936. Dissertation: English. [Includes Paul Green]

Haman, James B. The Growth of the Use of Negro Dialect in American Verse and Short Story to 1900. Duke Univ., 1939. Thesis: English. [A study of the use of Negro dialect in American poetry and short stories from about 1721 to 1900]

Hamilton, John B. The American Physician as Novelist. Univ. of North Carolina (Chapel Hill), 1951. Dissertation: English. [One chapter on Alfred Mercier]

Hamilton, Marie P. Race Consciousness in American Negro Poetry. Univ. of Arizona, 1926. Thesis: English. [Includes James Weldon Johnson]

Hardman, Marion P. Terror in American Prose Fiction to 1835. Univ. of Minnesota, 1939. Dissertation: English. [Includes *Rob of the Bowl, Swallow Barn,* and *Horse-Shoe Robinson*]

Hare, Mabel. Criticism Aroused by Pulitzer Prize Fiction Awards. West Texas State Univ., 1949. Thesis: English. [Ellen Glasgow, Margaret Mitchell, Julia Peterkin, T.S. Stribling, and Robert Penn Warren]

Harker, Virginia W. American Poetry from 1875 to 1880 and from 1895 to 1900. Univ. of Colorado, 1945. Thesis: English. [Includes Paul H. Hayne and Sidney Lanier]

Harms, Roger D. The Development of the Anti-Hero in the American Novel: 1833-1962. Kansas State Teachers College, 1965. Thesis: English. [Includes *Barren Ground* and *Huckleberry Finn*]

Harris, Ida H. The Modern American Short Story. Univ. of
    Alabama, 1924. Thesis: English. [Includes O. Henry,
    E.A. Poe, Wilbur D. Steele, and Thyra Samter Winslow]
Harris, John W., Jr. The Glorification of American Types in
    American Literature from 1775 to 1825. Univ. of North
    Carolina (Chapel Hill), 1928. Dissertation: English.
Harris, Victor I. Thackeray in America. Univ. of Virginia,
    1932. Thesis: English. [Discusses Thackeray in the South]
Harrison, James G. American Newspaper Journalism as Described in
    American Novels of the Nineteenth Century. Univ. of North
    Carolina (Chapel Hill), 1945. Dissertation: English.
    [Includes John Esten Cooke, John Fox, Jr., and J.P. Kennedy]
Harrison, Mary K. The Negro in American Fiction, 1800-1864.
    Columbia Univ., 1925. Thesis: English. [Includes Mary H.
    Eastman (Mrs. Seth Eastman) and J.P. Kennedy]
Hart, George. Rhetorical Techniques in the American Proletarian
    Short Story. Pennsylvania State Univ., 1939. Thesis:
    English. [Includes Erskine Caldwell]
Hart, Robert C. Writers on Writing: The Opinions of Six Modern
    American Novelists on the Craft of Fiction. Northwestern
    Univ., 1954. Dissertation: English. [Includes Thomas Wolfe]
Hartley, Lois T. Pocahontas Plays, 1808-1855. Pennsylvania State
    Univ., 1945. Thesis: English. [Includes G.W.P. Curtis]
Hartung, Jean B. An Investigation of the Literature Concerning
    the Spanish Missions of California and the Southwest. Univ.
    of Denver, 1944. Thesis: English. [A survey of literature
    connected with the Spanish missions in Arizona, California,
    New Mexico, and Texas]
Haselton, Stephen J. The Fairest Meed: Biography in America
    before 1865. Columbia Univ., 1959. Dissertation: English.
Hassig, Nancy. Colonial Fiction in America. Southern Methodist
    Univ., 1934. Thesis: English. [Includes John Esten Cooke,
    Mary Johnston, and W.G. Simms]
Havens, Daniel F. The Development of a Native Tradition in Early
    American Social Comedy, 1787-1845. Univ. of Michigan, 1965.
    Dissertation: English. [Includes R.M. Bird, William Dunlap,
    and Royall Tyler]
Hawkins, Maude M. Religious Aspects of Modern American Fiction.
    Univ. of South Carolina, 1932. Thesis: English. [Includes
    Elizabeth M. Roberts]
Hawkins, Sylvia V. Representative Negroes in American Poetry.
    Temple Univ., 1935. Thesis: Education. [Includes Joseph S.
    Cotter, Jr., Frances W. Harper, John W. Holloway, George
    Moses Horton, Georgia Douglas Johnson, James Weldon Johnson,
    and Anne Spencer]
Hayes, Harriet. The Appeal of the Literary Profession in the Cases
    of Two Generations of American Authors: A Study in Auto-
    biography. Stanford Univ., 1917. Thesis: English. [Includes
    Sidney Lanier]
Haynes, Alice M. The Bad Negro in Contemporary Novels by Negro
    Authors. Fisk Univ., 1942. Thesis: English. [Includes
    Clayton Adams, Arna Bontemps, Charles W. Chesnutt, George W.
    Henderson, Zora Neale Hurston, George Lee, Walter E. Turpin,
    and Richard Wright]

Hays, Eugene W. The Role of the Intruder in Contemporary Drama.
John Carroll Univ., 1968. Thesis: English. [Includes
Tennessee Williams]

Hazard, Lucy L. The Frontier in American Literature. Univ. of
California (Berkeley), 1925. Dissertation: English.
[Includes William Byrd, David Crockett, and W.G. Simms]

Hedgcock, Ernest D. Tradition in American Literature. Univ. of
Texas (Austin), 1936. Thesis: English.

Heiser, Merrill F. Representative Early American Satirists. Univ.
of Wisconsin, 1948. Dissertation: English. [Includes
E.A. Poe]

Henderson, Harry B. The American Historical Novel from Cooper to
Crane. Yale Univ., 1968. Dissertation: English. [Includes
Mary Twain's *Connecticut Yankee*]

Hendon, Telfair. A Critical Survey of Poetry by American Negroes.
Univ. of New Mexico, 1931. Thesis: English. [Includes
James Weldon Johnson and Jean Toomer]

Henry, Grace S.C. Peace and War as Viewed in Ten Selected Dramas
of the Modern American Theater. Hardin-Simmons Univ., 1950.
Thesis: English. [Includes Paul Green's *Johnny Johnson* and
Lawrence Stallings' *What Price Glory?*]

Henry, William C. The Supernatural as a Significant Motif in
Modern American Drama. Florida State Univ., 1950. Thesis:
English. [Includes Stark Young]

Herron, Ima H. The American Small Town: A Literary Study (from
1850 through the Modern Revolt). Southern Methodist Univ.,
1926. Thesis: English.

Herrscher, Walter J. Some Ideas in Modern American Nature Writing.
Univ. of Wisconsin, 1969. Dissertation: English. [Includes
Joseph Wood Krutch]

Hevener, Fillmer, Jr. An Investigation of the Contemporary Negroe's
Aspirations as Revealed through His Poetry. Madison College,
1957. Thesis: English. [Includes annotated bibliography]

Hewitt, Francis S. Pessimism in the Modern American Novel.
Rutgers Univ., 1936. Thesis: English. [Includes J.B.
Cabell, William Faulkner, and Thomas Wolfe]

Heyman, Charlotte. The Sonnet in American Literature. Univ. of
Texas (Austin), 1928. Thesis: English.

Hicklin, Fannie E.F. The American Negro Playwright, 1920-1964.
Univ. of Wisconsin, 1965. Dissertation: Speech and Drama.
[Includes DuBose Heyward]

Higgins, Catherine C. Woman's Place in a Changing Social Order
Reflected in the Best Selling Novels of 1910 and 1930.
Temple Univ., 1938. Thesis: Education. [Includes
Fannie C. Macaulay and T.N. Page]

Higgins, Kathryn L. Aframerican Fiction. East Texas State Univ.,
1940. Thesis: English. [Includes Arna Bontemps, Charles W.
Chesnutt, W.E.B. DuBois, George W. Henderson, Zora Neale
Hurston, Jean Toomer, Walter Edward Turpin, Walter White, and
Richard Wright]

Higgins, Sheila M. Twentieth Century Negro Poets. Western
Kentucky Univ., 1936. Thesis: English. [Includes Sterling A.
Brown, Joseph S. Cotter, Jr., James Weldon Johnson, and Jean
Toomer]

Higgs, Robert J. The Unheroic Hero: A Study of the Athlete in
  Twentieth Century American Literature. Univ. of Tennessee,
  1967. Dissertation: English. [Includes William Faulkner,
  Robert Penn Warren, Tennessee Williams, and Thomas Wolfe]
Hilburn, Thelma. The Negro as a Tragic Character in American
  Drama. Texas Christian Univ., 1935. Thesis: English.
  [Includes William Wells Brown, Joseph S. Cotter, Jr., Paul
  Green, DuBose Heyward, James D. McCabe, Willis Richardson,
  and Eulalie Spence]
Hilfer, Anthony C. The Revolt from the Village in American Liter-
  ature, 1915-1930. Univ. of North Carolina (Chapel Hill),
  1963. Dissertation: English. [Includes T.S. Stribling,
  Mark Twain, and Thomas Wolfe]
Hill, Douglas B., Jr. Studies in the Development of First-Person
  Narrative in American Literature to 1850. Columbia Univ.,
  1969. Dissertation: English. [Includes E.A. Poe]
Hill, Gladys B. The Treatment of the Civil War in American Fiction
  before 1900. Ohio Wesleyan Univ., 1944. Thesis: English.
Hiller, Gretchen L. A Comparative Study of Five Novels of the
  Civil War. Pennsylvania State Univ., 1940. Thesis: English.
  [Includes James Boyd and Ellen Glasgow]
Hilliard, Frances P. The Mississippi in Literature from 1803 to
  Mark Twain. Duke Univ., 1937. Thesis: English. [Includes
  Joseph H. Ingraham, W.G. Simms, Frederick W. Thomas, T.B.
  Thorpe, and Nathaniel B. Tucker]
Hines, Edgar A., Sr. America's Literary Physicians. Wofford
  College, 1933. Thesis: English. [Includes Edward C.L.
  Adams, George W. Bagby, James Turner Barclay, William A.
  Caruthers, Thomas H. Chivers, Samuel H. Dickson, William
  Alexander Hammond, William H. Holcombe, Arthur Lee, Alfred
  Mercier, John Kearsley Mitchell, Merrill Moore, John
  Williamson Palmer, Samuel M. Peck, David Ramsay, John Shaw,
  Francis Orray Ticknor, and Tobias Watkins]
Hinz, John P. Restless Heir: The Boy in American Fiction.
  Columbia Univ., 1959. Dissertation: English. [Includes
  David Crockett and Mark Twain, among others]
Hipkiss, Robert A. The Values of Expatriation for the Major
  American Novelists, 1914-1941. Univ. of California (Los
  Angeles), 1966. Dissertation: English. [Includes Thomas
  Wolfe]
Hitt, Ralph E. Controversial Poetry of the Civil War Period,
  1830-1878. Vanderbilt Univ., 1955. Dissertation: English.
  [Chapter entitled "Poetry of the South" deals with John Esten
  Cooke, William Grayson, Paul H. Hayne, Sidney Lanier,
  T.N. Page, Catherine Poyas, Innes Randolph, August Requier,
  Fr. Abram J. Ryan, Frank Ticknor, and Henry Timrod]
Hoar, Victor H., Jr. The Confidence Man in American Literature.
  Univ. of Illinois, 1965. Dissertation: English. [Includes
  William Faulkner and Mark Twain]
Hobart, Mabel E.K. The Revival of the Historical Novel in America
  between 1892-1908. Univ. of Illinois, 1928. Thesis:
  English. [Includes James Lane Allen, G.W. Cable, John Fox,
  Jr., Ellen Glasgow, Mary Johnston, and T.N. Page]

Hockey, Dorothy C. The Good and the Beautiful: A Study of Best-
Selling Novels in America, 1895-1920. Case Western Reserve
Univ., 1947. Dissertation: English. [Includes James Lane
Allen's *The Choir Invisible, The Reign of Law*; Maria Thompson
Daviess' *The Melting of Molly*; Thomas Dixon's *The Clansman*;
John Fox's *The Little Shepherd of Kingdom Come, The Trail of
the Lonesome Pine*; Ellen Glasgow's *The Deliverance, The Wheel
of Life*; Henry S. Harrison's *Queed, V.V.'s Eyes*; Mary
Johnston's *Audrey, Lewis Rand, Sir Mortimer, To Have and to
Hold*; Eleanor M. Lane's *Katrine*; T.N. Page's *Gordon Keith,
Red Rock*; Alice Hegan Rice's *Lovely Mary, Sandy, Mrs. Wiggs
of the Cabbage Patch*; Hallie Erminie Rives' *Satan Sanderson*;
Francis H. Smith's *Caleb West, Tom Grogan*; Louis J. Vance's
The Brass Bowl]

Hodges, Cecilia B. Minorities in Contemporary Drama: A Study of
Dramatic Propaganda. Columbia Univ., 1948. Thesis: English.
[Includes Paul Green, Willis Richardson, Jean Toomer, and
Richard Wright]

Hollenbach, John W. A Study of Economic Individualism in the
American Novel from 1865-1888. Univ. of Wisconsin, 1941.
Dissertation: English. [Includes Mark Twain]

Holloway, Rufus E. The Feeling for Nature in American Poetry.
Univ. of Texas (Austin), 1912. Thesis: English. [Includes
E.A. Poe]

Holmes, Jerry D. An Ancient Structure: A Study of the Influence
of Medieval Drama on Selected Contemporary English and
American Plays. Univ. of Mississippi, 1969. Dissertation:
English. [Includes *Camino Real*]

Holt, Charles C. Short Fiction in American Periodicals: 1775-
1800. Auburn Univ., 1965. Dissertation: English.

Holt, Frances E. The Negro Character in the American Drama from
1917 to 1934. Fisk Univ., 1934. Thesis: English.
[Includes Joseph S. Cotter, Jr., Randolph Edmons, Paul Green,
Zora Neale Hurston, Georgia Douglas Johnson, Willis
Richardson, and Jean Toomer]

Hopcraft, Margaret L. Attitudes toward the Indian as Found in
American Literature, 1700-1800. Univ. of New Mexico, 1943.
Thesis: English. [Includes William Byrd, Thomas Jefferson,
James Monroe, and George Washington]

Hopson, James O. The Negro in Contemporary American Fiction.
Univ. of Pittsburgh, 1934. Thesis: English. [Includes
Roark Bradford, DuBose Heyward, Howard Odum, Julia Peterkin,
T.S. Stribling, and Clement Wood]

Howard, James K. The American Proletarian Novel. Univ. of Texas
(Austin), 1939. Thesis: English. [Includes Erskine
Caldwell, Thomas Wolfe, and Richard Wright]

Howell, Gretchen. The Influence of the MacDowell Colony on
American Literature. East Texas State Univ., 1939. Thesis:
English. [Includes John Gould Fletcher, DuBose Heyward, and
Julia Peterkin]

Howell, John M. The Waste Land Tradition in the American Novel.
Tulane Univ., 1963. Dissertation: English. [Includes
The Sound and the Fury]

Hruby, Norbert J. Successful American Plays, 1919-1929: Patterns
and Their Implications. Loyola Univ. (Chicago), 1951.
Dissertation: English. [Includes Dorothy and DuBose
Heyward]

Hubbell, William K. The Role of Children's Books as Socializing
Agents. Univ. of North Carolina (Chapel Hill), 1952. Thesis:
Sociology. [The South is the locale for many of the books
discussed.]

Huddleston, Eugene L. Topographical Poetry in America, 1783-1812.
Michigan State Univ., 1965. Dissertation: English.
[Includes John Blair Lynn of South Carolina]

Hudnut, Ruth A. The Status of Women as Reflected in the Modern
Novel. Univ. of Maryland, 1927. Thesis: English. [Includes
Ellen Glasgow]

Hudson, Lura T. *The North American Review* and *Atlantic Monthly*:
Their Places in the History of American Literature. Stetson
Univ., 1927. Thesis: English. [Includes Walter Hines Page]

Hughes, Bettye S. A Study of the Historical Novel. East Texas
State Univ., 1951. Thesis: English. [Includes James Boyd,
Mary Johnston, Laura Krey, and Margaret Mitchell]

Hull, Kenneth G. Prejudice as Depicted by Four Novelists:
Richard Wright, Sinclair Lewis, Lillian Smith, and Ann Petry.
Fort Hays Kansas State College, 1966. Thesis: English.

Hunter, Kenneth M. Some Recent Tendencies in American Literary
Criticism. Univ. of Idaho, 1923. Thesis: English.
[Includes H.L. Mencken]

Hunter, Mary D. Idealism in American Literature. Univ. of South
Carolina, 1923. Thesis: English. [Includes E.A. Poe]

Hurley, Leonard B. The American Novel, 1830-1850: Its Reflection
of Contemporary Religious Conditions, with a Bibliography of
Fiction. Univ. of North Carolina (Chapel Hill), 1932.
Dissertation: English. [Includes bibliography of works
published 1830-1850, including Southern authors]

Hux, Samuel H. American Myth and Existential Vision: The
Indigenous Existentialism of Mailer, Bellow, Styron, and
Ellison. Univ. of Connecticut, 1965. Dissertation:
English.

Hyde, Frederic G. American Literature and The Spanish-American
War: A Study of the Work of Twain, Norris, Fox, and R.H.
Davis. Univ. of Pennsylvania, 1963. Dissertation: English.

Hyland, Sr. Mary d.C. The Fictional Treatment of Women in the
Cow Country. Univ. of Texas (Austin), 1947. Thesis:
English.

Ingham, Alix A. The Nature of Hubris in Modern American Tragedy.
Univ. of Virginia, 1962. Thesis: English. [Includes *The
Bear*, *Absalom, Absalom!*, *The Sound and the Fury*, and *Light
in August*]

Inglis, Reney B. The Realistic Treatment of the Boy in American
Fiction since 1865. Univ. of Minnesota, 1923. Thesis:
English.

Ingram, Forrest L. Representative Twentieth Century Short Story
Cycles: Studies in a Literary Genre. Univ. of Southern
California, 1967. Dissertation: English. [Includes
The Unvanquished and *Sartoris*]

[297]

Inman, Sarah E. Chaucer in America. Univ. of North Carolina
    (Chapel Hill), 1940. Thesis: English. [Publications by
    Sidney Lanier, J.C. Harris, and others]
Irvine, Donald V. The Best-Selling Novel in America, 1900-1910.
    Univ. of Kentucky, 1942. Thesis: English. [Includes
    James Boyd, Charles E. Craddock, John Fox, Jr., Mary Johnston,
    Margaret Mitchell, and Alice Hegan Rice]
Ives, Chauncey B. The Materials of American Negro Fiction: Injury
    and Reaction in Novels by Negroes, 1943-1952. Univ. of North
    Carolina (Chapel Hill), 1953. Thesis: English.
_____. Development in the Fictional Themes of Negro Authors.
    Univ. of North Carolina (Chapel Hill), 1957. Dissertation:
    English. [Includes more than 60 novels, some Southern,
    covering a period of more than 100 years]
Jablonski, Sr. M.G. The Relevance of Four Major Extrinsic
    Criteria to an Intrinsic Evaluation of Poetry. Duquesne
    Univ., 1960. Thesis: English. [Includes Cleanth Brooks,
    John Crowe Ransom, and Robert Penn Warren]
Jackson, Augusta V. Renascence of Negro Literature, 1922 to
    1929. Atlanta Univ., 1936. Thesis: English. [Includes
    Arna Bontemps, Charles W. Chesnutt, W.E.B. DuBois, Georgia
    Douglas Johnson, and James Weldon Johnson]
Jackson, George B. Of Irony in Negro Fiction: A Critical Study.
    Univ. of Michigan, 1953. Dissertation: English. [Includes
    Walter White's *The Fire in the Flint*]
Jackson, Margaret Y. An Investigation of Biographies and Auto-
    biographies of American Slaves Published between 1840 and
    1860: Based upon the Cornell Special Slavery Collection.
    Cornell Univ., 1954. Dissertation: English.
Jackson, Mattye A. The Civil War in American Fiction. Univ. of
    Tulsa, 1942. Thesis: English. [Includes G.W. Cable,
    Thomas Dixon, Clifford Dowdey, William Faulkner, John Fox,
    Jr., Ellen Glasgow, Mary Johnston, Margaret Mitchell, T.N.
    Page, T.S. Stribling, Allen Tate, and Stark Young]
Jacobs, Edith C. Political and Economic Commentary in American
    Musicals of the 1930's. Univ. of North Carolina (Chapel
    Hill), 1961. Thesis: Drama. [Includes Paul Green's
    Johnny Johnson]
Jacobs, J.S. The Historicity of the Contemporary Civil War Novel.
    Brigham Young Univ., 1939. Thesis: English. [Includes
    Gwen Bristow, Clifford Dowdey, William Faulkner, Caroline
    Gordon, DuBose Heyward, Laura Krey, Andrew Lytle, Margaret
    Mitchell, Evelyn Scott, and Stark Young]
Jacobson, Margery E. The American Stage Negro from 1850 to 1870.
    Brown Univ., 1946. Thesis: English.
James, Stuart B. Race Relations in Literature and Sociology.
    Univ. of Washington, 1960. Dissertation: English. [Includes
    William Faulkner, Eudora Welty, and Richard Wright]
Jauney, Alice M. A Study of Recent Negro Poetry. George Peabody
    College, 1926. Thesis: English.
Jenkins, Lucile. The Development of Folk Drama in America.
    Northwestern Univ., 1929. Thesis: Speech. [Includes Paul
    Green, Dorothy and DuBose Heyward, Hatcher Hughes, and Lula
    Vollmer]

Johnson, Beulah V.   The Treatment of the Negro Woman as a Major
    Character in American Novels 1900-1950. New York Univ., 1955.
    Dissertation: English. [Discusses attempts to romanticize
    the restoration of white supremacy in the South]
Johnson, Charles D.   A Study of Three Novels, One by Each of
    Three Authors (Nathaniel Beverley Tucker, Harriet Beecher
    Stowe, and William Alexander Caruthers) with Respect to the
    Social and Political Thought of the Pre-Civil War Period,
    1820-1860. Madison College, 1956. Thesis: English.
    [Deals with *The Partisan Leader, Uncle Tom's Cabin,* and
    The Kentuckian in New York]
Johnson, Ellwood G.   Some Versions of Individualism in American
    Literature and Thought. Univ. of Washington, 1969.
    Dissertation: English. [Includes *The Mysterious Stranger*]
Johnson, Ivon H.   The American Negro as Portrayed in Prose Liter-
    ature by American Authors from 1900 to 1932. Univ. of
    Southern California, 1938. Thesis: English. [Includes
    Roark Bradford, Irvin S. Cobb, Octavus Roy Cohen, Thomas
    Dixon, Paul Green, J.C. Harris, DuBose Heyward, Howard W.
    Odum, T.N. Page, Julia Peterkin, T.S. Stribling, Jean Toomer,
    and Clement Wood]
Johnson, Jean O.   The American Political Novel in the Nineteenth
    Century. Boston Univ., 1958. Dissertation: English.
    [Includes Nathaniel B. Tucker and Mark Twain]
Johnson, Jerrilou H.   Social Protest Written by Black American
    Poets prior to 1900. Roosevelt Univ., 1970. Thesis:
    English. [Includes Joseph Cotter, Sr., George Moses
    Horton, James Weldon Johnson, George McLlelan, Daniel
    Payne, and Alberry A. Whitman]
Johnson, Oakley C.   Literary Allusion and Reference in Contemporary
    American Literature. Univ. of Michigan, 1928. Dissertation:
    English. [Includes J.B. Cabell and E.A. Poe]
Johnson, Robert E.   The American Political Novel: 1792-1950.
    A Survey. Univ. of California (Los Angeles), 1956. Disser-
    tation: English. [Includes discussions of "Tariff and
    Nullification," "The Southern View of Slavery," and
    "Southern Commentary: Racism and Fascism"; also includes a
    discussion of works that concern Huey Long and a discussion
    of Mark Twain]
Johnson, William R. III.   The Influence of the "Deep South" on
    the Life and Work of F. Scott Fitzgerald. Univ. of Virginia,
    1966. Thesis: English.
Johnston, E.E.   Disillusionment in Contemporary American Poetry.
    Florida State Univ., 1937. Thesis: English.
Jones, Arthur E., Jr.   A Study of Literary Criticism in America,
    1742-1820. Syracuse Univ., 1948. Dissertation: English.
Jones, Edward.   The Negro in American Poetry, 1900-1930. East
    Texas State Univ., 1938. Thesis: English. [Includes Arna
    Bontemps, Benjamin Brawley, Joseph Seaman Cotter, Jr.,
    Waring Cuney, Frank Horne, and Georgia Douglas Johnson]
Jones, E.M.   Dramatic Treatment of Race Prejudice. Ohio State
    Univ., 1929. Thesis: English. [Includes Paul Green and
    Dorothy and DuBose Heyward]

Jones, George E., Jr. The American Indian in The American Novel (1875-1950). New York Univ., 1958. Dissertation: English.

Jones, Lucy T. A Comparative Study of the American Indian in Prose Fiction from *Edgar Huntley* to *Ramona*. Univ. of Virginia, 1925. Thesis: English. [Includes R.M. Bird and W.G. Simms]

Jones, Sr. Mary H. The Concept of God in the Poetry of the American Negro. Xavier Univ. (New Orleans), 1943. Thesis: English. [Includes James Weldon Johnson]

Jones, Octavia R. A Study of Contemporary Negro Literature. Ohio State Univ., 1929. Thesis: English. [Includes Lewis Alexander, George Leonard Allen, Arna Bontemps, Sterling A. Brown, Joseph S. Cotter, Sr., Clarissa Scott Delany, Blanch Taylor Dickinson, DuBose Heyward, Georgia Douglas Johnson, James Weldon Johnson, James Edward McCall, Anne Spencer, and Jean Toomer]

Jones, Robert C. The Attack on Pretension: America, 1850-1900. Univ. of Texas (Austin), 1958. Dissertation: English. [Includes Joseph G. Baldwin, David Crockett, G.W.P. Curtis, A.B. Longstreet, William T. Thompson, and Thomas B. Thorpe]

Kalin, Berkley. Social Criticism in Twentieth Century American Poetry. St. Louis Univ., 1967. Dissertation: English. [Includes John Crowe Ransom and Allen Tate]

Kamarck, Edward L. Regional Playwriting. Cornell Univ., 1947. Thesis: English.

Kane, Patricia L. Legal Fictions: The Lawyer in the American Novel. Univ. of Minnesota, 1961. Dissertation: English. [Includes William Faulkner, Thomas Jefferson, and Mark Twain]

Kaplan, Robert B. An Analysis of Contemporary Poetic Structure, 1930-1955. Univ. of Southern California, 1963. Dissertation: English. [Includes John Crowe Ransom, Allen Tate, and Robert Penn Warren]

Karlson, Robert E. American Short Story Criticism, 1885-1919. George Washington Univ., 1969. Dissertation: English. [Poe as viewed in 1885 by Brander Matthews]

Kauth, Priscilla J. Hemingway, Steinbeck, Warren, Faulkner: The Sense of the Past. Stetson Univ., 1962. Thesis: English.

Keaton, Eloise R. Religious Themes in Modern Drama (1890-1940). Univ. of Tennessee, 1946. Thesis: English. [Paul Green's *The Lord's Will*]

Keim, Miriam E. The American Novel of 1931-1933 as Depression Literature. Temple Univ., 1939. Thesis: Education. [Includes J.B. Cabell, Erskine Caldwell, William Faulkner, Ellen Glasgow, DuBose Heyward, Mary Johnston, Grace Lumpkin, Caroline Miller, Julia Peterkin, Elizabeth M. Roberts, Evelyn Scott, T.S. Stribling, and Thomas Wolfe]

Kelley, Abner W. Music and Literature in The American Romantic Movement: A Study of the Knowledge of, Use Of, and Ideas Relating to the Art of Music in Emerson, Hawthorne, Longfellow, Poe, Thoreau, Lowell, Whitman, and Lanier. Univ. of North Carolina (Chapel Hill), 1929. Dissertation: English.

Kellog, Thelma L. Early American Social Satire before 1800,
    with Especial Reference to Social Satire in the Early
    American Almanac. Radcliffe College, 1929. Dissertation:
    English.
Kelly, H.F. Literary Continuity from *Huckleberry Finn* to *Catcher
    in the Rye*. Duquesne Univ., 1962. Thesis: English.
Kennedy, Ellen C. Images of the City in the American Novel from
    1885 to the Present. Univ. of North Carolina (Chapel Hill),
    1969. Thesis: History. [Includes Thomas Wolfe]
Kerr, Elizabeth M. The Twentieth Century Sequence Novel. Univ.
    of Minnesota, 1942. Dissertation: English.
Kerr, Howard H. Spiritualism in American Literature, 1851-1886.
    Univ. of California (Los Angeles), 1968. Dissertation:
    English. [Includes *Huckleberry Finn* and *Life on the
    Mississippi*]
Kerrane, Kevin J. Aristotle's *Poetics* in Modern Literary Criticism.
    Univ. of North Carolina (Chapel Hill), 1968. Dissertation:
    English. [Chapter VII, on the new critics, emphasizes John
    Crowe Ransom]
Ketels, Arthur O. The American Drama of the Twenties. A
    Critical Re-evaluation. Northwestern Univ., 1960. Disser-
    tation: Speech and Drama. [Includes Paul Green]
Keyes, Daniel. The Writer as a Character in Modern American
    Fiction: Henry James to Thomas Wolfe. Brooklyn College,
    1961. Thesis: English.
Kibel, Alvin C. After Such Knowledge: Modern Criticism and Its
    Ideology. Columbia Univ., 1963. Dissertation: English.
    [Includes John Crowe Ransom and Allen Tate]
Kicklen, Fannie E.F. The American Negro Playwright, 1920-1964.
    Univ. of Wisconsin, 1965. Dissertation: Theater.
Kimball, William J. The Civil War in American Novels: 1920-1939.
    Pennsylvania State Univ., 1957. Dissertation: English.
    [Includes Hervey Allen, William Faulkner, Caroline Gordon,
    Andrew Lytle, Margaret Mitchell, Allen Tate, and Stark
    Young]
Kincheloe, H.G. British Periodical Criticism of American Litera-
    ture, 1851-1870. Duke Univ., 1948. Dissertation: English.
    [Includes E.A. Poe]
King, Esther F. The Objective and Subjective Approaches to the
    Problem of Earning a Livelihood as Revealed in Contemporary
    American Fiction: A Study of the Influence of Certain Socio-
    economic Factors upon Family Life in the U.S. Fisk Univ.,
    1942. Thesis: English. [Includes Erskine Caldwell,
    William Faulkner, and Richard Wright]
King, Rosa M. The Most Modern American Short Stories. Oglethorpe
    Univ., 1931. Thesis: ENglish.
King, Thelma F. The Awakening of National Consciousness in
    American Literature. Boston Univ., 1938. Thesis: English.
    [Includes Thomas Jefferson and Parson Weems]
King, Velma N. Negro Attitudes in Negro Novels. Atlanta Univ.,
    1938. Thesis: English. [Includes Arna Bontemps, Charles W.
    Chesnutt, W.E.B. DuBois, and Zora Neale Hurston]

Kinsey, Juanita. Successful Plays on Broadway from 1920 to 1930. Texas Christian Univ., 1931. Thesis: English. [Includes Paul Green, DuBose Heyward, William Hurlburt, Channing Pollock, and Lula Vollmer]

Kirchner, Jeanne S. Attitudes on the Modern Family Found in Recent American Fiction. Univ. of Southern California, 1940. Thesis: Sociology. [Includes Barry Benefield, Ellen Glasgow, Marjorie Kinnan Rawlings, and Lyle Saxon]

Kitch, John C. Dark Laughter: A Study of the Pessimistic Tradition in American Humor. Northwestern Univ., 1964. Dissertation: English. [Includes Joseph Glover Baldwin, William Faulkner, Johnson Jones Hooper, H.L. Mencken, and Mark Twain]

Klein, Marcus N. The Novel in America in the 1950's: An Introduction to a Thematic Study. Columbia Univ., 1962. Dissertation: English. [Includes Ralph Ellison]

Klein, Ralph A. The American Military Heroes and the Heroines of the Revolutionary War, the War of 1812, and the Civil War: An Analysis of Character Based on Representative American Plays Written between the Years 1774 and 1907. Univ. of Denver, 1967. Dissertation: English. [Includes Andrew Jackson and George Washington]

Klotman, Phyllis R. The Running Man as Metaphor in Contemporary Negro Literature. Case Western Reserve Univ., 1969. Dissertation: English. [Includes Ralph Ellison and Richard Wright, with brief mention of Mark Twain]

Klotz, Marvin. The Imitation of War, 1800-1900: Realism in the American War Novel. New York Univ., 1959. Dissertation: English. [Includes John Esten Cooke and T.N. Page]

Knutson, Wayne S. A Definition of Modern Tragedy. Univ. of Denver, 1956. Dissertation: English. [Includes William Faulkner, Paul Green, Robert Penn Warren, and Tennessee Williams]

Kolker, Sr. M.D. Spanish Legends in English and American Literature: 1800-1860. Catholic Univ., 1953. Dissertation: English. [Includes W.G. Simms]

Kolodny, Annette. The Pastoral Impulse in American Writing, 1590-1850: A Psychological Approach. Univ. of California (Berkeley), 1969. Dissertation: English. [Includes James Audubon, Robert Beverly, William Byrd, and W.G. Simms]

Kontos, Peter G. The Influence of Marxism on Novels of Social Protest: 1930-1939. Kent State Univ., 1965. Thesis: History. [Includes Grace Lumpkin's *To Make My Bread* and Mary Heaton Vorse's *Strike*]

Koppenhoefer, Hazel L. Twentieth Century Thought in American Sonnets. Univ. of Cincinnati, 1938. Thesis: English. [Includes Madison Cawein, Merrill Moore, David Morton, Lizette Woodworth Reese, and John Van Alstyn Weaver]

Kramer, Aaron. The Prophetic Tradition in American Poetry, 1835-1900. New York Univ., 1966. Dissertation: English. [Includes the theme of the fugitive slave law and mentions Poe]

Kramer, Maurice I. The Fable of Endurance: A Study of the American Novel between Hawthorne and Howells. Harvard Univ., 1958. Dissertation: English. [Includes Rebecca Harding Davis]

Krieger, Murray. Towards a Contemporary Apology for Poetry. Ohio State Univ., 1952. Dissertation: English. [Includes John Crowe Ransom and Allen Tate]

Labrenz, Ernest T. A Critical Analysis of the Negative Attitudes in Plays Exclusive of Musical Comedies Which Won the Pulitzer Prize between 1948 and 1957. Univ. of Southern California, 1962. Dissertation: English. [Includes *Cat on a Hot Tin Roof* and *A Streetcar Named Desire*]

Lack, Marion. The Agrarian Revolt in American Fiction, 1865-1900. Columbia Univ., 1946. Thesis: History. [Includes James Lane Allen, G.W. Cable, and Sarah Barnwell Elliott]

LaGrone, Robert A. The Inadequacy of American Teacher Fiction. Univ. of Texas (El Paso), 1967. Thesis: English. [Includes Harper Lee, Jesse Stuart, and Mark Twain]

Lamelin, Robert E. Antebellum Books of Travel and Description as Social and Cultural Indexes, 1830-1861. Univ. of Maryland, 1967. Dissertation: English.

Lange, Letitia R. American Juvenile Literature, 1830-1880. Emory Univ., 1958. Thesis: English. [Includes Sidney Lanier and Mark Twain]

Lange, Marva. The Treatment of the Negro in Modern American Drama from 1900-1950. Fort Hays Kansas State College, 1951. Thesis: English.

Larkin, Sr. Aloysia M. The New Image of the Negro In American Fiction: The Search for Identity. St. Bonaventure Univ., 1968. Thesis: English. [Includes Ralph Ellison]

Laufe, Abe. The Long-Running Plays on the New York Stage, 1918-1950: A Literary Evaluation. Univ. of Pittsburgh, 1952. Dissertation: English. [Includes Tennessee Williams]

Lawler, John J. Comment on Art and Literature from the Personal Writings of a Group of Well Traveled, Early American Writers and Artists: A Critical Collation. Florida State Univ., 1960. Dissertation: English. [Includes Washington Allston]

Lawrence, Elwood P. The Immigrant in American Fiction, 1890-1920. Case Western Reserve Univ., 1943. Dissertation: English. [Includes Thomas Dixon and Alice French]

Lawrence, Martha. Objectivity, Its Function and Growth in the Development of the Novel. Austin College, 1934. Thesis: English. [Includes Erskine Caldwell and Julia Peterkin]

Lawson, Hilda J. The Negro in American Drama. Univ. of Illinois, 1939. Dissertation: English. [Includes Joseph S. Cotter, Jr., Randolph Edmonds, Paul Green, DuBose Heyward, and Willis Richardson]

Lay, Donald M. The Doctor in American Literature. Univ. of Southern California, 1943. Thesis: English. [Includes Margaret Mitchell and Rosalie Slaughter Morton]

Leaska, Mitchell A. The Rhetoric of Multiple Points of View in Selected Contemporary Novels. New York Univ., 1968. Dissertation: English. [Includes *Absalom, Absalom!*]

LeClair, Thomas E. The Grail Myth in Five Contemporary Novels: *The Winter of Our Discontent, Invisible Man, Morte D'Urban, Other Voices, Other Rooms, The Natural*. Univ. of Vermont, 1967. Thesis: English.

Lee, Robert C. Portrayal of the College in Modern American
    Novels, 1932-1942. George Peabody College, 1944. Disser-
    tation: Education. [Includes Marion Boyd, James Saxon
    Childers, and T.S. Stribling]
Lees, Charles L. An Introductory Study of the American People
    of the Eighteenth Century through Their Drama and Theatrical
    History. Univ. of Wisconsin, 1934. Dissertation: English.
Lefkowith, Ada O. A Critical Study of the Pulitzer Prize Novels.
    Temple Univ., 1934. Thesis: Education. [Includes Julia
    Peterkin and T.S. Stribling]
Lehan, Richard. Existentialism and the Modern American Novel.
    Univ. of Wisconsin, 1959. Dissertation: English. [Includes
    Ralph Ellison, William Faulkner, and Richard Wright]
Leighton, Wallace R. Black Humor: A Comic Vision of the World.
    Kansas State Teachers College, 1966. Thesis: English.
    [Includes John Barth and William Faulkner]
Leisy, Ernest E. The American Historical Novel before 1860.
    Univ. of Illinois, 1923. Dissertation: English. [Includes
    R.M. Bird, William A. Caruthers, John Esten Cooke, J.P.
    Kennedy, and W.G. Simms]
Leland, Lowell P. Theories of Fiction in America: 1789-1870.
    Ohio State Univ., 1941. Dissertation: English. [Includes
    John Esten Cooke, J.P. Kennedy, and W.G. Simms]
Lehnart, Charmenz S. The Influence of Music on American Poetry.
    Univ. of Illinois, 1952. Dissertation: English and
    Linguistics. [Based on Sidney Lanier's *The Science of English
    Verse*; includes E.A. Poe]
Leonard, Ella. Short Stories as Interpreters of America.
    Oglethorpe Univ., 1928. Thesis: English.
Leslie, Emily J. Escape Literature, American and British, in
    Prose Fiction since 1890. Univ. of Southern California,
    1940. Thesis: English. [Includes J.B. Cabell]
Levine, Darwin S. A Brief Survey of the Activities of Jews in
    American Literature. Columbia Univ., 1928. Thesis:
    Education. [Includes Abraham de Lyon, Georgia; Michael
    Israel and John Levy, Virginia; and Moses Elias Levy,
    Florida]
Levine, Paul R. The Intemperate Zone: The Climate of Contemporary
    American Fiction. Harvard Univ., 1967. Dissertation:
    American Civilization. [Includes Truman Capote, Carson
    McCullers, and Flannery O'Connor]
Levine, Samuel H. Changing Concepts of Palestine in American
    Literature to 1867. New York Univ., 1953. Dissertation:
    English. [Includes Mark Twain]
Levy, David W. Attitudes in Antislavery Fiction: 1836-1864.
    Univ. of Chicago, 1961. Thesis: History.
Lewin, David. The Literary Expatriate as a Social Critic of
    America. New York Univ., 1963. Dissertation: English.
    [Includes Lafcadio Hearn]
Lewis, Adelene E. The Concept of Freedom in the Negro American
    Novel, 1865-1941. Fisk Univ., 1943. Thesis: English.
    [Includes Arna Bontemps, William Wells Brown, Charles W.
    Chesnutt, W.E.B. DuBois, George W. Henderson, Zora Neale
    Hurston, James Weldon Johnson, Walter E. Turpin, Walter F.
    White, and Richard Wright]

Lewis, Bertram A. Four American Negro Poets. Univ. of Nebraska, 1937. Thesis: English. [Includes James Weldon Johnson]
Lewis, Harrison D., Jr. The Beginning and Development of Negro Characterization in American Drama. Depaul Univ., 1948. Thesis: English.
Lewis, Juanity A.O. The Changing Tide: An Analysis of the Growth of Negro Poetry in America from 1746 to 1961. Univ. of Tulsa, 1961. Thesis: English.
Lieberman, Elias. The American Short Story. New York Univ., 1911. Dissertation: English.
Liedel, Donald E. The Antislavery Novel. Univ. of Michigan, 1961. Dissertation: History.
Linnehan, Edward G. We Wear the Mask: Life and Character of the Negro in American Drama. Univ. of Pennsylvania, 1949. Dissertation: American Studies. [Includes Paul Green, DuBose Heyward, and Richard Wright]
Linson, Cora B.R. Education in American Poetry and Fiction: 1800-1870. Univ. of Texas (Austin), 1939. Thesis: Education. [Includes William A. Caruthers, J.P. Kennedy, and A.B. Longstreet]
Lippincott, Elmira R. Local Color in the Short Story. Temple Univ., 1927. Thesis: Education. [Includes James Lane Allen, G.W. Cable, Charles E. Craddock, J.C. Harris, O. Henry, and T.N. Page]
Lively, Robert A. The Novelist as Historian of the Civil War: A Survey and Evaluation. Univ. of North Carolina (Chapel Hill), 1950. Dissertation: History. [Examines 512 novels in the Richard H. Wilmer Collection of Civil War Novels at the University of North Carolina at Chapel Hill]
Lloyd-Jones, Richard. Major Variations in the Sonnet since 1919. Univ. of North Carolina (Chapel Hill), 1950. Thesis: English. [Includes a discussion of Merrill Moore and mentions several other Southern poets]
Lockhart, Malcolm W. The Negro in American Drama. Louisiana State Univ., 1932. Thesis: English. [Includes Paul Green, DuBose Heyward, Georgia Douglas Johnson, and Willis Richardson]
Loeffler, Donald L. An Analysis of the Treatment of the Homosexual Character in Dramas Produced in the New York Theatre from 1950 to 1968. Bowling Green State Univ., 1969. Dissertation: Speech. [Includes plays of Lillian Hellman and Tennessee Williams]
Loftus, Sr. M.C. The Democratic Movement in Modern American Poetry, 1912-1925. Fordham Univ., 1936. Dissertation: English. [Includes John Gould Fletcher]
Logan, Mary A. The Negro in American Fiction of Economic Protest, 1932-1940. Howard Univ., 1944. Thesis: English. [Includes Fielding Burke, Erskine Caldwell, Grace Lumpkin, and Richard Wright]
Logan, Susan H. Concepts of Love in the Novel with an Emphasis on the Twentieth Century American Novel. Florida State Univ., 1966. Dissertation: English. [Emphasizes Carson McCullers' *Ballad of the Sad Cafe* as the norm and includes works of William Faulkner and Thomas Wolfe]

Logan, Winford B. An Investigation of the Theme of the Negation of Life in American Drama from World War II to 1958. Ohio State Univ., 1961. Dissertation: Theater. [Includes Tennessee Williams]

Loggins, Vernon. The Negro Author: His Development in America. Columbia Univ., 1931. Dissertation: English.

Lopushansky, Joseph. A Study of the Sonnet in American Literature. Univ. of Illinois, 1929. Thesis: English. [Includes Sidney Lanier and E.A. Poe]

Losey, Charles J. Early American Humour from Its Beginnings to Mark Twain. Montreal, 1961. Thesis: English.

Loshe, Lillie D. The Early American Novel (1789-1830). Columbia Univ., 1907. Dissertation: English.

Lovenstein, Louis. Poetry and Novels by American Negro Writers. Univ. of Virginia, 1928. Thesis: English. [Includes Frances W. Harper, George M. Horton, and James Weldon Johnson]

Lowenburg, Sara. The Spiritual Element in Modern American Poetry. Temple Univ., 1933. Thesis: Education. [Includes John Gould Fletcher, James Weldon Johnson, Aline Kilmer, Lizette Woodworth Reese, Elizabeth M. Roberts, and Irwin Russell]

Lubell, Albert J. Social Reform in Representative American Fiction, 1870-1903. Columbia Univ., 1942. Thesis: English. [Includes G.W. Cable, Ellen Glasgow, and T.N. Page]

Lucas, John S. Rhythms of Negro Music and Negro Poetry. Univ. of Minnesota, 1944. Thesis: English.

Lucas, Portia M. Ethno-Centrism in the Poetry and Fiction of Contemporary Negro Authors: A Critical Analysis. Fisk Univ., 1939. Thesis: English. [Includes Arna Bontemps, Joseph S. Cotter, Jr., W.E.B. DuBois, Zora Neale Hurston, James Weldon Johnson, Walter White, and Richard Wright]

Lucker, Dorothy F. The American Interest in European Democracy: A Study of the Literary Reaction to the Revolutions of 1848. Univ. of Texas (Austin), 1942. Dissertation: English. [Includes Thomas Jefferson and W.G. Simms]

Lyons, John O. The Novel of Academic Life in America. Univ. of Florida, 1960. Dissertation: English. [Includes Thomas Wolfe]

Macomber, Adar M. The Spirit of the Soil as Reflected in Some Modern Fiction. Kansas State Teachers College, 1932. Thesis: English. [Includes Ellen Glasgow and Elizabeth M. Roberts]

Madden, Roby Z. American Antislavery Fiction, 1850-1865. Howard Univ., 1941. Thesis: English. [Includes William Wells Brown, Frances W. Harper, and Margaret Bayard Smith]

Maddocks, Gladys L. Ideas of Life after Death in the Modern Short Story. Univ. of Texas (Austin), 1939. Thesis: English. [Includes Roark Bradford, J. Frank Dobie, William Faulkner, Ellen Glasgow, and O. Henry]

Maddox, Notley S. Phases of Literary Nationalism in America, 1855-1900. Ohio State Univ., 1940. Dissertation: English. [Includes G.W. Cable and Mary N. Murfree]

Madison, Arthur L. The Scapegoat Story in the American Novel.
Univ. of Oklahoma, 1966. Dissertation: English. [Includes
Mark Twain's *Joan of Arc*]

Magee, Carolyn J. Negro Drama in America. Boston Univ., 1937.
Thesis: English. [Includes Randolph Edmonds, Paul Green,
Dorothy and DuBose Heyward, Georgia Douglas Johnson, Willis
Richardson, and Eulalie Spence]

Makwrath, Paul A., Jr. A Study of Henry Adams's *Democracy*.
Univ. of Virginia, 1968. Thesis: English.

Manfull, Helen A. The New Realism (A Study of American Dramatic
Realism from 1918-1929). Univ. of Minnesota, 1961. Disser-
tation: Speech and Drama. [Mentions dramatic criticism of
Stark Young]

Manning, Charles. American Literary Culture, 1865-1886, by
Selected Critics. Univ. of North Carolina (Chapel Hill),
1950. Thesis: English.

Mantz, Harold E. French Criticism of American Literature before
1850. Columbia Univ., 1917. Dissertation: Romance
Languages. [Includes Poe]

Mapes, Eleanor M. The Indian in American Poetry, 1840-1860.
Univ. of Texas (Austin), 1940. Thesis: English. [Includes
A.B. Meek and W.G. Simms]

Marable, William I. The American Historical Novel since 1870.
Univ. of Virginia, 1925. Thesis: English. [Includes
Thomas Dixon and Mary Johnston]

Marchand, William M. The Changing Role of the Medical Doctor in
Selected Plays in American Drama. Univ. of Minnesota, 1966.
Dissertation: Theater. [Includes Paul Green, Lillian
Hellman, and Tennessee Williams]

Mariott, Alice C. Contributions of the Negro Creative Artist to
American Literature. Kansas State Teachers College, 1944.
Thesis: English. [Includes Arna Bontemps, Roark Bradford,
Charles W. Chesnutt, Frances W. Harper, DuBose Heyward,
Zora Neale Hurston, James Weldon Johnson, Booker T.
Washington, Walter White, and Richard Wright]

Marker, Forrest M., Jr. The Sonnet in American Literature: 1827-
1887. Vanderbilt Univ., 1937. Thesis: English. [Includes
Paul H. Hayne, E.A. Poe, W.G. Simms, and Henry Timrod]

Markham, Edith L. Poetry Written for the Opening Exercises and
the Fourth of July Celebration at the 1876 Centennial
Exhibition in Philadelphia. Univ. of North Carolina (Chapel
Hill), 1950. Thesis: English. [Includes Sidney Lanier's
"The Centennial Meditation of Columbia"]

Marmur, Justine. The Anti-War Novel in America (1918-1928).
Columbia Univ., 1948. Thesis: English. [Includes William
Faulkner, Henry Sydnor Harrison, and Elizabeth Robins]

Marovitz, Sanford E. Frontier Conflicts: Villains, Outlaws, and
Indians in Selected "Western" Fiction: 1799-1860. Duke
Univ., 1968. Dissertation: English. [Includes Alfred W.
Arrington, R.M. Bird, Jeremiah Clemens, W.G. Simms, and
Charles Webber]

Martin, Lynne E. The Negro Character in Drama Depicted by the
Negro Playwright, 1960-1965. Pennsylvania State Univ., 1966.
Thesis: Theater.

Martin, Marco. Some Aspects of the Development of Poetic Drama in America. Univ. of Cincinnati, 1941. Thesis: English. [Includes Olive T. Dargan, Hortense Flexner, Cale Young Rice, and Stark Young]

Martin, Terence J. The Emergence of the Novel in America: A Study in the Cultural History of an Art Form. Ohio State Univ., 1954. Dissertation: English. [Includes Thomas Jefferson and Parson Weems]

Martincich, Robert. Analogy and Criticism: The Development and Demonstration of a Critical Premise. San Francisco State College, 1957. Thesis: English. [Includes *The Sound and the Fury*]

Mason, Juan P. A Resource Unit of Negro Poetry for Use In Secondary School Literature Courses. Univ. of Texas (Austin), 1947. Thesis: Education. [Includes Sterling A. Brown, Joseph S. Cotter, Sr., Joseph S. Cotter, Jr., Frances W. Harper, George Moses Horton, Georgia Douglas Johnson, James Weldon Johnson, and Jean Toomer]

Mathews, Ruth E. The Pioneer Women in Certain American Novels of the Twentieth Century. Univ. of Kentucky, 1933. Thesis: English. [Includes Elizabeth M. Roberts]

Mathis, Cynthia H. The Concept of Feminine Beauty in Novels by Negroes. Fisk Univ., 1937. Thesis: English. [Includes Arna Bontemps, Charles W. Chesnutt, W.E.B. DuBois, Frances W. Harper, G.W. Henderson, Zora Neale Hurston, James Weldon Johnson, Yorke Jones, Jean Toomer, and Walter White]

Maxwell, Robert H. War Hysteria in American Poetry, 1850-1870. Vanderbilt Univ., 1932. Thesis: English. [Confederate song writers, Confederate women poets, and other Southern poets]

May, Fannie. The Sea in American Poetry. Univ. of Texas (Austin), 1928. Thesis: English. [Includes Sidney Lanier and E.A. Poe]

Mayberry, George B. Industrialism and the Industrial Worker in the American Novel, 1814-1890. Harvard Univ., 1942. Dissertation: American Civilization. [Includes Thomas Stewart Denison and Alice French]

Mays, Benjamin E. The Development of the Idea of God in Contemporary Negro Literature. Univ. of Chicago, 1935. Dissertation: Religion. [Includes Benjamin Brawley, Charles W. Chesnutt, W.E.B. DuBois, Franklin Frazier, John W. Holloway, Georgia Douglas Johnson, James Weldon Johnson, Kelley Miller, Robert Russa Moton, Booker T. Washington, and Walter White]

Mays, Katherine B. The Social Note in Modern American Poetry as Shown by the Major Poets, Both White and Colored, from 1900-1940. Florida State Univ., 1945. Thesis: English. [Includes James Weldon Johnson]

McAndrew, Sr. Mary H. A Comparative Study of Some Themes Treated by American Soldiers in the Verse of the Civil War and in That of the World War. Univ. of Notre Dame, 1935. Thesis: English. [Includes H. Lynden Flash, Paul H. Hayne, Sidney Lanier, James Ryder Randall, Fr. Abram J. Ryan, Francis O. Ticknor, Henry Timrod, and John R. Thompson]

McCalman, Marjorie C. An Inquiry into the Musical Aspects of the Literature of Poe, Lanier, Whitman. Univ. of Tulsa, 1956. Thesis: English.

McCausland, Harriet R.-L. The Soldier in Modern English and
American Drama as an Expression of the Spirit of the Times.
Stanford Univ., 1927. Thesis: English. [Includes Florence
Converse, Hubert C. Heffner, Lula Vollmer, Rita Wellman,
and Stark Young]
McCloskey, John C. The Effect of the War of 1812 upon the Rise
of National American Literature with Special Reference to
The Portico. Univ. of Iowa, 1928. Thesis: English.
McCormack, Mary B. Negro Drama. Marquette Univ., 1933. Thesis:
Speech. [Includes Octavus Roy Cohen, Paul Green, DuBose
Heyward, Georgia Douglas Johnson, Willis Richardson, and
Eulalie Spence]
McCracken, Fern. The Rise of New Poetry. Pennsylvania State
Univ., 1945. Thesis: English. [Includes Lizette
Woodworth Reese]
McCutcheon, M.L. The Influence of Locality on the American Short
Story. Ohio State Univ., 1916. Thesis: English. [Includes
G.W. Cable, Charles E. Craddock, and T.N. Page]
McDaniel, Susie T. Orientalism in American Poetry up to 1900.
Univ. of Texas (Austin), 1928. Thesis: English. [Includes
Madison Cawein, E.A. Poe, John Banister Tabb, and Henry
Timrod]
McFarlane, Catherine N. The Gothic Element in American Literature.
Univ. of Mississippi, 1931. Thesis: English. [Includes
Sidney Lanier, E.A. Poe, and W.G. Simms]
McGraw, Rex T., Jr. The Role of the Villain in Civil War Melo-
dramas. Indiana Univ. (Bloomington), 1966. Dissertation:
Theater. [Covers period 1861-1914; most of the villains
depicted are Southerners]
McGuire, R.Q.V. Modern Development of the Sonnet in America. New
York Univ., 1935. Thesis: English. [Includes Lizette
Woodworth Reese]
McKenzie, Barbara A. Isolation: A Thematic Study in the American
Novel since 1920. Univ. of Miami (Coral Gables), 1958.
Thesis: English. [Includes Truman Capote, William Faulkner,
Carson McCullers, and Thomas Wolfe]
_____. Region and World: The Achievement of American Women
Writers of Fiction since 1930. Florida State Univ., 1963.
Dissertation: English. [Includes Caroline Gordon,
Shirley A. Grau, Shirley A. Jackson, Carson McCullers,
Flannery O'Connor, Eudora Welty, and Katherine Ann Porter]
McLeran, Paul D. The Presentation of the Negro in American Drama.
Florida State Univ., 1953. Thesis: English.
McMillan, Eldene N. The Influence of Early American Childhood on
Children's Literature. Trinity Univ. (Texas), 1952. Thesis:
Education.
McNeer, Marietta W. The Boy as a Character in American Fiction
by Standard Authors from Cooper to Mark Twain. Univ. of
North Carolina (Chapel Hill), 1934. Thesis: English.
[Includes John Esten Cooke, J.P. Kennedy, E.A. Poe, and
W.G. Simms]
Meador, Arabelle. A Study of Certain Christian Themes in Selected
Contemporary Poems. East Tennessee State Univ., 1959.
Thesis: English. [Includes John Crowe Ransom]

Melito, The Reverend Ignatius M., C.M. Themes of Adolescence:
Studies in the American Fiction of Adolescence. Univ. of
Denver, 1965. Dissertation: English. [Includes Thomas
Wolfe and Mark Twain]

Meredith, Jessie A. Education in the American Novel and Non-
Professional Periodicals from 1890-1905. Southern Methodist
Univ., 1935. Thesis: Education. [Includes the Southern
Negro]

Meriwether, Frank T. The Development of Character Types in
American Humor before 1860. Louisiana State Univ., 1949.
Thesis: English. [Includes Joseph Glover Baldwin, William
Byrd, G.W. Harris, Johnson Jones Hooper, A.B. Longstreet,
William T. Thompson, and Thomas B. Thorpe]

Metzger, Adelia C. Some Aspects of American Negro Poetry. Univ.
of Illinois, 1934. Thesis: English. [Includes Waverly
Turner Carmichael and James Weldon Johnson]

Miller, M.L. Original Federal Theatre Protest Plays, 1936-1939:
New Deal Contributions to the American Drama of Social
Concern. Univ. of California (Los Angeles), 1968. Disser-
tation: English. [Includes Paul Green]

Mills, Fanny H. Nature Coloring in the American Novel with
Emphasis upon Its Use in the Works of Craddock, Allen,
Howells, Glasgow, Cather and Ostenso. Univ. of Virginia,
1928. Thesis: English.

Miner, Earl R. The Japanese Influence on English and American
Literature, 1850-1950. Univ. of Minnesota, 1955. Dissertation: English. [Includes Lafcadio Hearn]

Miner, Louie. Our Rude Forefathers: American Political Verse,
1783-1788. Columbia Univ., 1936. Dissertation: English.

Minkwitz, Berneta A. The Gothic Element in American Literature.
Univ. of Texas (Austin), 1926. Thesis: English. [Includes
E.A. Poe]

Minter, David L. The Interpreted Design: A Study in American
Prose. Yale Univ., 1965. Dissertation: English. [Includes
William Faulkner]

Mizell, Phoebe G. Education in American Literature of the 1830's.
Southern Methodist Univ., 1928. Thesis: Education.
[Includes E.A. Poe]

Modisette, Eldon L. Changing Political Thought in the American
Drama, 1919-1951. Univ. of Minnesota, 1954. Dissertation:
Political Science. [Includes John Howard Lawson]

Modlin, Charles E. Political Satire in America, 1789-1801. Univ.
of Tennessee, 1969. Dissertation: English. [Includes
St. George Tucker; also includes Jefferson as the subject
of satire]

Moe, Christian H. From History to Drama: A Study of the Influence
of the Pageant, the Outdoor Epic Drama, and the Historical
Stage Play upon the Dramatization of Three American Historical
Figures. Cornell Univ., 1958. Dissertation: Theater.
[Includes Paul Green; historical figures are Thomas
Jefferson, Abraham Lincoln, and George Washington]

Monsell, Helen A. A Study of Girlhood in American Fiction from
1850 to 1860. Columbia Univ., 1922. Thesis: English.
[Includes John Esten Cooke, W.G. Simms, Mrs. E.D.E.N.
Southworth, and Augusta Jane Evans Wilson]

Montes, Marcia M.S. Education as Reflected in American Fiction, 1865-1900. Univ. of Texas (Austin), 1943. Thesis: Education. [Includes G.W. Cable, J.G. Holland, Richard M. Johnston, and T.N. Page]

Moody, Richard. Romanticism in American Drama and the Theatre from the Beginning to 1900. Cornell Univ., 1942. Dissertation: English. [Includes a discussion of Southern romanticism and of plays about the Civil War; also includes W.G. Simms]

Moore, Ethel K. American Short Stories of the Depression Decade. Texas College A & I, 1947. Thesis: English. [Includes Erskine Caldwell and William Faulkner]

Moore, Irene. The Tradition of the College in the American Novel, 1895-1937. Univ. of Texas (Austin), 1940. Thesis: Education. [Includes James Lane Allen, James Boyd, and Thomas Wolfe]

Moore, Letricia J.B. The Novelist's Interpretation of American Education. Univ. of Texas (Austin), 1958. Thesis: Education. [Includes Hariette Arnow and Randall Jarrell]

Moore, Rayburn S. Southern Writers and Northern Literary Magazines, 1865-1890. Duke Univ., 1956. Dissertation: English.

Moore, William L. The Literature of the American Negro prior to 1865: An Anthology and a History. New York Univ., 1942. Dissertation: English.

Morgan, N.V. Periods of Significant Achievement in the Poetic Drama of America. Texas Tech Univ., 1941. Thesis: English. [Includes Paul Green]

Moriarty, Jane V. The American Novel in France. Univ. of Wisconsin, 1953. Dissertation: English. [Includes William Faulkner and Mark Twain]

Morris, Ann R. A Study of Rhythm in the Novel. Florida State Univ., 1961. Dissertation: Philosophy. [Includes William Faulkner and Thomas Wolfe]

Morris, Mason T. In Pursuit of Self: A Study of the Process of Initiation in Four Novels. Univ. of Louisville, 1969. Thesis: English. [Includes James Agee, Truman Capote, and Flannery O'Connor]

Morris, Wesley A. The Rediscovery of Historicism in Contemporary American Literary Theory. Univ. of Iowa, 1968. Dissertation: English. [Includes John Crowe Ransom]

Morrison, Claudia C. Depth Psychology in American Literary Criticism, 1900-1926. Univ. of North Carolina (Chapel Hill), 1964. Dissertation: English. [Includes E.A. Poe and Mark Twain as subjects of criticism]

Morse, Dorothea B. Study of Juvenile Writings of Eight American Authors of the Second Half of the Nineteenth Century. Univ. of Illinois, 1952. Dissertation: English. [Includes Mark Twain]

Morton, Lois G. Illustrations in Recent Novels of Negro Life. Fisk Univ., 1938. Thesis: English. [Includes Arna Bontemps, Roark Bradford, Octavus Roy Cohen, Harry Stillwell Edwards, DuBose Heyward, Zora Neale Hurston, Howard W. Odum, Archibald Rutledge, and T.S. Stribling]

Most, Ralph C. Civil War Fiction from 1890 to the Present Day. Univ. of Pennsylvania, 1942. Dissertation: English.

Mueller, Walter E. Protestant Ministers in Modern American Novels, 1927-1958: The Search for a Role. Univ. of Nebraska, 1961. Dissertation: English.

Mumma, Anne E. The Short Story: A Study of Trends as Revealed in Anthologies Published from 1925 to 1939. Ohio Univ., 1941. Thesis: English. [Includes E.A. Poe and Wilbur D. Steele]

Mürbe, Hans. The American Image of Germany as Found in Nineteenth Century Travel Books. Ohio State Univ., 1964. Dissertation: English. [Mark Twain mentioned briefly]

Murdaugh, James E.D. Political Thought in the Early American Essay. Univ. of Virginia, 1925. Dissertation: English. [Includes Thomas Jefferson]

Murray, Marion R. *Scribner's-Century*: A Force in American Literature. Southern Methodist Univ., 1925. Thesis: English. [Chapter 2 discusses relationship of *Scribner's* with Southern writers]

Myers, Nettie E. Development of the Gothic Romance. Univ. of Illinois, 1909. Thesis: English. [Includes E.A. Poe]

Myers, Ralph G. The Small Town in the American Novel, 1870-1920. Univ. of Virginia, 1934. Thesis: English. [Includes James Lane Allen, Ellen Glasgow, R.M. Johnston, Mary Johnston, and Francis H. Smith]

Myers, Randolph L. Development of the Negro Novelist. Atlanta Univ., 1941. Thesis: English. [Includes William Wells Brown, Charles W. Chesnutt, W.E.B. DuBois, J.C. Harris, Jean Toomer, and Richard Wright]

Myrbo, Calvin L. An Analysis of the Character of the Clergyman in Novels for Adolescents. Univ. of Minnesota, 1964. Dissertation: English. [In two volumes; includes William Faulkner]

Nannes, Casper H. Politics in the American Drama, as Revealed by Plays Produced on the New York Stage, 1890-1945. Univ. of Pennsylvania, 1948. Dissertation: English. [Includes Hamilton Basso, Lillian Hellman, and Robert Penn Warren]

Napiecinski, Thomas H. The Dramatization of the American Serious Novel, 1926-1952. Univ. of Wisconsin, 1959. Dissertation: Theater. [Includes Erskine Caldwell, Truman Capote, and Richard Wright]

Nash, Winifred H. The Inter-Relations of Music and Poetry. Boston Univ., 1931. Dissertation: English. [Includes John Gould Fletcher, Sidney Lanier, and E.A. Poe]

Neil, Tecora W. The Message of the New Negro Poet. Univ. of Dayton, 1948. Thesis: English. [Includes Jean Toomer]

Nelson, John H. The Negro Character in American Literature. Cornell Univ., 1923. Dissertation: English.

Nelson, Lawrence E. Vocabularies of Nineteenth and Twentieth Century American Prose Writers: A Comparative Study. Stanford Univ., 1931. Dissertation: English. [Includes H.L. Mencken, E.A. Poe, and W.G. Simms]

Nelson, Linnette L. Recurrent Motif as an Element of Form in Modern Free Verse. Univ. of Minnesota, 1926. Thesis: English.

Nichol, John W. American Literature and Social Crisis, 1837-1842.
   Ohio State Univ., 1953. Dissertation: English. [Includes
   discussion of E.A. Poe's contempt for democratic society]
Nichols, Charles H. A Study of the Slave Narrative. Brown
   Univ., 1949. Dissertation: English.
Nilon, Charles H. Some Aspects of the Treatment of Negro
   Character by Five Representative American Novelists: Cooper,
   Melville, Tourgée, Glasgow, Faulkner. Univ. of Wisconsin,
   1952. Dissertation: English.
Nirenberg, Morton I. The Reception of American Literature in
   German Periodicals, 1820-1850. Johns Hopkins Univ., 1967.
   Dissertation: English. [Portions of text in German;
   includes James Audubon, Robert M. Bird, and W.G. Simms]
Nix, Theo B. Negro Contributors to American Literature: A Hand-
   book on Colored Writers. Kansas State Univ., 1941. Thesis:
   English. [Includes Arna Bontemps, Benjamin G. Brawley,
   Sterling A. Brown, Charles W. Chesnutt, W.E.B. DuBois,
   Rudolph Fisher, E. Franklin Frazier, Zora Neale Hurston,
   Georgia Douglas Johnson, James Weldon Johnson, William
   Pickens, Jean Toomer, Walter E. Turpin, Walter White,
   Carter G. Woodson, and Richard Wright]
Norris, Carolyn B. The Image of the Physician in Modern American
   Literature. Univ. of Maryland, 1969. Dissertation: English.
   [Includes William Faulkner, Ellen Glasgow, Carson McCullers,
   Katherine Anne Porter, Robert Penn Warren, and Tennessee
   Williams]
Nye, Gertrude E. The Negro in American Drama. Univ. of New
   Hampshire, 1940. Thesis: English. [Includes DuBose
   Heyward and Julia Peterkin]
Obenchain, Louise F. Some Aspects of the Modern Psychological
   Novel. Birmingham-Southern College, 1929. Thesis: English.
   [Includes Ellen Glasgow]
Oberg, Arthur K. Contemporary Verse and Poetic Drama. Harvard
   Univ., 1966. Dissertation: English. [Includes Tennessee
   Williams]
Oberle, Catherine L. The Antiwar Drama on the American Profess-
   ional Stage from World War I to World War II. Univ. of
   Southern California, 1945. Thesis: English. [Includes
   Paul Green, Channing Pollock, and Laurence Stallings]
O'Connor, John W. The Negro in American Fiction since 1870.
   Univ. of Missouri, 1929. Thesis: English. [Includes
   Octavus Roy Cohen, Thomas Dixon, W.E.B. DuBois, J.C. Harris,
   T.S. Stribling, Walter White, and Clement Wood]
O'Connor, William V. Sense and Sensibility in Modern Poetry.
   Columbia Univ., 1948. Dissertation: English. [Includes
   Donald Davidson, John Gould Fletcher, E.A. Poe, John Crowe
   Ransom, Allen Tate, and Robert Penn Warren]
Oettinger, Elmer R. The Characterization of the Businessman in
   American Drama. Univ. of North Carolina (Chapel Hill),
   1966. Dissertation: English. [Includes Lillian Hellman
   and Tennessee Williams]
Old, James E. *Harper's Magazine*: A Criterion of American Literary
   Taste, 1850-1892. Southern Methodist Univ., 1928.
   Thesis: English. [Discusses policy of *Harper's* with regard
   to Southern writers after the Civil War]

Olderman, Raymond M. Beyond the Waste Land: A Study of the
American Novel in the Nineteen-Sixties. Indiana Univ.
(Bloomington), 1969. Dissertation: English. [Includes
John Barth; mentions tradition of William Styron and Ralph
Ellison]

Oppewall, Peter. The Critical Reception of American Fiction in
the Netherlands, 1900-1953. Univ. of Michigan, 1961.
Dissertation: English. [Includes William Faulkner]

Ossive, Cora A. A Study of American Poetry with a View to Its
Philosophy. George Washington Univ., 1915. Thesis: English.
[Includes Sidney Lanier and E.A. Poe]

Otis, William B. American Verse, 1625-1807: A History. New York
Univ., 1908. Dissertation: English.

Oxendine, Pearl M. An Evaluation of Negro Historians during the
Period of the Road to Reunion. Howard Univ., 1947. Thesis:
History. [Includes William Wells Brown and Booker T.
Washington]

Palmer, Anna S. The Present Tendencies of American Fiction. Univ.
of Illinois, 1895. Thesis: English. [Includes James Lane
Allen, Charles E. Craddock, J.C. Harris, and T.N. Page]

Palmer, Raymond R. The Negro as Subject in American Fiction,
1939-1949. Washington Univ. (St. Louis), 1949. Thesis:
English.

Parkin, James E. Jean Lafitte in History, Legend and Literature.
Southern Methodist Univ., 1951. Thesis: English. [As
portrayed in American novels]

Pasko, Michael. Existentialism and Three American Novels.
Southern Illinois Univ. (Carbondale), 1954. Thesis: English.
[Includes Richard Wright]

Patterson, Samuel W. The Spirit of the American Revolution as
Revealed in the Poetry of the Period: A Study of American
Patriotic Verse from 1760 to 1783. New York Univ., 1913.
Dissertation: English.

Pennington, Loren E. The Origins of English Promotional Literature for America, 1553-1625. Univ. of Michigan, 1962.
Dissertation: History. [Discusses promotional literature;
mentions English settlement of Florida]

Peper, Juergen. Bewusstseinslagen des Erzachlte Wirklichkeit--
Dargestellt am Amerikanischen Romanen des 19 und 20
Jahrhunderts, Insbesondere am Werk William Faulkners. Frei
Universität (Berlin), 1966. Dissertation: English.

Peteler, Patricia. The Social and Symbolic Drama of the English
Language Theatre, 1929-1949. Univ. of Utah, 1961. Dissertation: Drama. [Includes Tennessee Williams]

Philbrick, Norman D. Democracy and Social Comedy in America from
1800 to 1833. Cornell Univ., 1949. Dissertation: English.
[Includes discussion of Southern attitude toward the theater]

Phillips, Kathryn C. A Comparison of the Technique of the
Elizabethan and the Modern Short Story. Pennsylvania State
Univ., 1944. Thesis: English. [Includes William Faulkner]

Pinkett, Lilly L. Folk Elements in American Drama from 1870 to
1936. Howard Univ., 1939. Thesis: English. [Includes
Paul Green, DuBose Heyward, Hatcher Hughes, Lynn Riggs, and
Lula Vollmer]

Pinson, Leah F.   The Outstanding Contributions of Women to
    American Literature during the Nineteenth Century.   Temple
    Univ., 1935.   Thesis: Education.   [Includes Margaret Junkin
    Preston]
Piper, James K.   The Novel of Stories: Form and Content in Four
    Collections of Related Short Stories.   San Francisco State
    College, 1965.   Thesis: English.   [Includes *Go Down, Moses*]
Pitts, Ella S.   The Industrial Problem in American Novels after
    1860.   Southern Methodist Univ., 1930.   Thesis: English.
    [Includes Francis H. Smith]
Poag, Thomas E.   The Negro in Drama and the Theater.   Cornell
    Univ., 1944.   Dissertation: Speech and Drama.   [Includes
    William Wells Brown, Randolph Edmonds, Paul Green, and
    Dorothy and DuBose Heyward]
Pollak, Georgiana H.   The Influence of Music on American Poetry.
    New York Univ., 1950.   Dissertation: English.
Pomeranz, Regina E.   The Search for Self in the Adolescent
    Protagonist in the Contemporary American Novel: A Method
    of Approach for the College Teacher of Literature.   Columbia
    Univ., 1966.   Dissertation: English.   [Includes Carson
    McCullers]
Porcello, Patricia L.   The Railroad in American Literature:
    Poetry, Folk Song, and the Novel.   Univ. of Michigan, 1968.
    Dissertation: English.   [Traces railroad from South to
    West; includes discussion of *Look Homeward, Angel* and
    Of Time and the River]
Porterfield, Neil B.   Criticism of Material Success in the American
    Novel.   Univ. of the Pacific, 1967.   Thesis: English.
    [Includes Mark Twain]
Powell, Frank W.   The Sonnet in American Magazines before 1860.
    Univ. of Virginia, 1932.   Dissertation: English.
Powell, Lilla H.   Literary Culture in the United States, 1830-
    1860.   Texas Woman's Univ., 1932.   Thesis: History.
Powell, Nancy H.   The Sociology of Some of the Modern Novels.
    Univ. of South Carolina, 1914.   Thesis: English.   [Includes
    Mary Johnston and T.N. Page]
Powers, William J.   The Narrative Concept and American Conscious-
    ness.   Univ. of Illinois, 1966.   Dissertation: English.
    [Touches briefly on Jefferson's vision of individual
    potential]
Prevost, Maurice E.   The Negro in Literature and Life.   Xavier
    Univ. (New Orleans), 1940.   Thesis: English.   [Includes
    Roark Bradford, Paul Green, DuBose Heyward, Georgia Douglas
    Johnson, T.N. Page, and Willis Richardson]
Price, Sue W.   Romantic Elements in Certain Early American Prose
    Fiction Writers.   Baylor Univ., 1925.   Thesis: English.
    [Includes E.A. Poe]
Pridgeon, Charles T.   Insanity in American Fiction from Charles
    Brockden Brown to Oliver Wendell Holmes.   Duke Univ., 1969.
    Dissertation: English.   [Includes Robert M. Bird, E.A. Poe,
    and W.G. Simms]
Provost, Louisa M.   Treatment of Native Historical Material by
    American Dramatists, 1763-1925.   Univ. of Idaho, 1932.
    Thesis: English.

Quinn, Sr. Mary B. Metamorphosis in Modern American Poetry. Univ.
of Wisconsin, 1952. Dissertation: English. [Includes
Randall Jarrell]
Rackin, Phyllis R.F. Poetry without Paradox: The Limitations of
the New Criticism of the Lyric. Univ. of Illinois, 1962.
Dissertation: English. [Includes Cleanth Brooks]
Raichle, Donald R. The Image of the Constitution in American
History: A Study in Historical Writing from David Ramsay to
John Fiske. Columbia Univ., 1956. Dissertation: History.
[Includes David Ramsay and George Tucker]
Rainsberry, Frederick B. The Irony of Objectivity in the New
Criticism. Michigan State Univ., 1952. Dissertation:
English. [Includes Cleanth Brooks, John Crowe Ransom, and
Allen Tate]
Raiziss, Sonia. The Metaphysical Mode: Some Modern American
Poets and Their Seventeenth Century Heritage. Univ. of
Pennsylvania, 1944. Dissertation: English. [Includes
Donald Davidson, John Gould Fletcher, Merrill Moore, John
Crowe Ransom, Laura Riding, and Allen Tate]
Raspillaire, Jeanne H. The Use of the Oral Idiom in the Modern
American Novel. Ohio State Univ., 1941. Thesis: English.
[Includes William Faulkner]
Reardon, John D. Verse Drama in America from 1765 to the Civil
War: The End of a Tradition. Univ. of Kansas, 1957.
Dissertation: English. [Includes W.G. Simms]
Reddick, La Bertha. The Element of Protest in the Poetry of the
Negro. Fisk Univ., 1940. Thesis: English.
Redding, J.S. The Trends and Developments in Negro Creative
Literature. Brown Univ., 1932. Thesis: English.
Reed, Joanda O. The Bifurcation of the Short Story. Mississippi
State Univ., 1962. Thesis: English. [Includes Truman
Capote, William Faulkner, Carson McCullers, O. Henry,
Katherine Anne Porter, Robert Penn Warren, and Eudora Welty]
Reid, Barney F. A Study on the Rise of Devotional Literature
among American Negroes. Univ. of Cincinnati, 1932. Thesis:
English. [One chapter on the Negro slave spirituals]
Reninger, H.W. The Theory and Practice of the American Novel,
1867-1903. Univ. of Michigan, 1938. Dissertation: English.
[Includes W.G. Simms]
Reynolds, Jerry D. Attitude Change by the Stimulus of the Oral
Interpretation of Poetic Literature. Ohio State Univ.,
1966. Dissertation: Speech. [Includes the poetry of
Truman Capote and Langston Hughes]
Rhode, Robert D. The Functions of Setting in the American Short
Story of Local Color, 1865-1900. Univ. of Texas (Austin),
1940. Dissertation: English. [Includes James Lane Allen,
G.W. Cable, Charles E. Craddock, and T.N. Page]
Rhodes, Marjorie A. Isolation and Identity in Four Negro Novels.
Univ. of Houston, 1968. Thesis: English. [Includes Ralph
Ellison and Richard Wright]
Rice, Joseph A. Flash of Darkness: Black Humor in the Contem-
porary Novel. Florida State Univ., 1967. Dissertation:
English.

Richardson, Caroline F. Some Comments on the Prevalence of
Psychology and Analysis in the Modern Novel. Tulane Univ.,
1906. Thesis: English. [Includes James Lane Allen]
Richardson, M.M. Treatment of Christianity by Contemporary
Poets. Univ. of Texas (Austin), 1921. Thesis: English.
[Includes Madison Cawein and Stark Young]
Roberts, George R. Social Protest in Contemporary American
Poetry. Temple Univ., 1925. Thesis: Education. [Includes
Sarah N. Cleghorn and Lizette Woodworth Reese]
Robertson, Elsie M. Education in American Literature from 1875 to
1890. Southern Methodist Univ., 1931. Thesis: Education.
[Includes Sidney Lanier]
Robertson, Martin B. The Historical Element in the American Novel.
Pennsylvania State Univ., 1920. Thesis: English. [Includes
James Lane Allen, G.W. Cable, John Esten Cooke, Charles E.
Craddock, J.C. Harris, Sidney Lanier, T.N. Page, and W.G.
Simms]
Robinson, Francis C. The Wealthy Class in the American Novel,
1870-1930. Stanford, 1952. Dissertation: English.
[Includes Ellen Glasgow]
Robinson, Nathaniel E. A Study of American Literature, 1760-1860.
George Washington Univ., 1902. Thesis: English. [Includes
J.P. Kennedy, E.A. Poe, and W.G. Simms]
Robison, Z.C.H. The Color Problem as It Finds Expression in
Modern American Negro Literature. Univ. of Utah, 1941.
Thesis: English. [Includes Arna Bontemps, Sterling A.
Brown, Joseph Seaman Cotter, Jr., Georgia Douglas Johnson,
James Weldon Johnson, Robert Russa Moton, Walter White,
and Richard Wright]
Robson, Leila C. The Development of Social Protest in American
Literature since 1890. Univ. of Oregon, 1941. Thesis:
General Studies. [Includes Leane Zugsmith]
Rock, Mildred E. Attitudes of Certain Novelists and Short Story
Writers toward Character Delineation. Univ. of Southern
California, 1941. Thesis: English. [Includes Ellen
Glasgow]
Roehr, Janis T. Black Novels of the Thirties. Univ. of Wyoming,
1970. Thesis: English.
Rogers, Albert A. The Small Town in American Literature: A
Study of the Small Town in America as Illustrated Particularly
by the Stories of Sherwood Anderson. Auburn Univ., 1931.
Thesis: English Education. [Includes discussion of Ellen
Glasgow and Mark Twain]
Rogers, Arra C. The Civil War in American Fiction. Southern
Methodist Univ., 1934. Thesis: English. [Includes John
Esten Cooke, Ellen Glasgow, and Mary Johnston]
Rogers, Judy R. The Modern Bildungsroman: An Individual versus
His Society. Univ. of North Carolina (Chapel Hill), 1966.
Thesis: English. [Includes *Look Homeward, Angel*]
Rogers, Mary E. The Reconstruction Period as Treated in American
Fiction. Southern Methodist Univ., 1938. Thesis: English.
[Includes Thomas Dixon, Margaret Mitchell, T.N. Page, and
Stark Young]

Roller, Bert. Children in American Poetry, 1610-1900. George
Peabody College, 1930. Dissertation: English. [Includes
George Alsop, Madison Cawein, Ebernezer Cook(e), John Esten
Cooke, John Cotton, Richard Dabney, J.C. Harris, Paul H.
Hayne, Sidney Lanier, W.G. Simms, John Smith, John
Bannister Tabb, Henry Timrod, St. George Tucker, and Mark
Twain]

Root, Frank B. Modern Literary Style. Austin College, 1935.
Thesis: English. [Includes J.B. Cabell and H.L. Mencken]

Root, Robert W. The Religious Ideas of Some Major Early Writers
of America. Syracuse Univ., 1959. Dissertation: History.
[Includes Thomas Jefferson]

Rosenthal, Bernard. Nature's Slighting Hand: The Idea of Nature
in American Writing, 1820-1860. Univ. of Illinois, 1968.
Dissertation: English. [Includes E.A. Poe]

Ross, Eugene G. The American Novel of Fantasy. Univ. of Virginia,
1949. Dissertation: English. [Includes George W. Bagby,
J.B. Cabell, Roark Bradford, J.C. Harris, Julia Peterkin,
E.A. Poe, and Nathaniel B. Tucker]

Ross, Maude C. Moral Values of the American Woman as Presented
in Three Major American Authors. Univ. of Texas (Austin),
1964. Dissertation: English. [Includes William Faulkner]

Rubin, Joseph J. The American Women Dramatists of the Twentieth
Century. Pennsylvania State Univ., 1933. Thesis: English.
[Includes Lula Vollmer]

Ruddick, Edna A. The Social Value of the American Short Story.
Columbia Univ., 1918. Thesis: Sociology. [Includes
J.C. Harris and E.A. Poe]

Rude, Roland V. A Consideration of Jung's Concept of the Self
as an Aid to the Understanding of Character in Prose Fiction.
Northwestern Univ., 1960. Dissertation: Theater. [Includes
Erskine Caldwell]

Ruhmann, Lucy B. The Negro in the American Short Story, 1930-1940.
Univ. of Texas (Austin), 1941. Thesis: English.

Rundle, Marjorie A. The Concept of the Lady in the American Novel,
1850-1900. Univ. of Cincinnati, 1956. Dissertation: English.
[Southerners as "loyal defenders of the traditional lady"]

Runyan, Harry. The Backgrounds and Origins of Realism in the
American Novel, 1850-1880. Univ. of Wisconsin, 1949.
Dissertation: English. [Includes Mark Twain]

Russell, Helen. Social Satire as Depicted by American Women
Playwrights. Univ. of Denver, 1958. Dissertation: Theater.
[Includes Lillian Hellman, Carson McCullers, and Lillian
Smith]

Russell, Jason A. The Indian in American Literature, 1775-1875.
Cornell Univ., 1932. Dissertation: English. [Includes
W.G. Simms]

Russell, Rebecca P. Sectionalism in American Poetry. Univ. of
Texas (Austin), 1924. Thesis: English. [A survey of
Civil War poetry that attempts to determine "the extent to
which sectionalism pervaded the verse of each contending
section"]

Rydene, Alma P. A Study in the History of American Dramatics up
to 1820. Columbia Univ., 1914. Thesis: English. [Includes
William Crafts and John Blake White]

Sadler, George M. Emerson and the South. Duke Univ., 1934.
Thesis: English.
St. John, William E. The Conception of the Novel as Presented by
the Leading English and American Novelists since 1800.
Univ. of Southern California, 1936. Dissertation: English.
[Includes J.B. Cabell]
Sandvos, Annis. Flight from Aristotle: The Development of the
Tragedy of the Common Man. Columbia Univ., 1951. Disser-
tation: English. [Includes Tennessee Williams]
Sauer, N.J. American Indian Words in the Literature of the West
and Southwest. Texas Tech Univ., 1939. Thesis: English.
Savage, George M. Regionalism in the American Drama. Univ. of
Washington, 1935. Dissertation: English. [Includes Paul
Green, Lynn Riggs, and Lula Vollmer]
Sawey, Orlan L. The Cowboy Autobiography. Univ. of Texas (Austin),
1953. Dissertation: English.
Scanlon, Sr. Stella M., S.M. The Development of the American
Historical Novel, 1821-1914. Villanova Univ., 1940. Thesis:
English. [Includes G.W. Cable, Ellen Glasgow, and Mary
Johnston]
Scheide, Mabel C. The American Historical Novel from 1895 to
1905. Southern Methodist Univ., 1930. Thesis: English.
Schirone, Charles N. The Spirit of Aristocracy as Reflected in
the American Novel of the 1830's. New York Univ., 1955.
Dissertation: English. [Includes William A. Caruthers,
J.P. Kennedy, and Nathaniel B. Tucker]
Schmidt, M.C. American Sketch Books from Irving to Longfellow.
Univ. of Minnesota, 1931. Thesis: English.
Schmitz, Neil. Politics and the New Man in Nineteenth Century
American Fiction. Stanford Univ., 1967. Dissertation:
English. [Discusses J.P. Kennedy's *Quodibet*]
Schrader, Neil H. The Civil War in American Novels. Univ. of
Cincinnati, 1948. Thesis: English. [Includes G.W. Cable,
John Esten Cooke, Mary Johnston, Sidney Lanier, Molly Elliot
Seawell, James Street, Octave Thanet, and Mary Spear
Tiernan]
Schupbach, Deanna J. Ideality and Reality: A Study of Reactions
to the Gilded Age. Univ. of Texas (Austin), 1963. Thesis:
English. [Reactions in literature; includes Mark Twain]
Schuster, Richard. The Civil War in American Fiction. Columbia
Univ., 1961. Dissertation: English. [Discusses Civil
War novel to 1880; includes William M. Baker, John Esten
Cooke, and T.N. Page]
Schwartz, Sr. M.F., O.S.F. School Life in American Prose.
Niagara Univ., 1945. Dissertation: English. [Includes
W.E.B. DuBois, John Fox, Jr., Marjorie Kinnan Rawlings,
Lyle Saxon, Lillian Smith, James Street, Allen Tate, and
Leane Zugsmith]
Scott, Marion G. The Aspects of Modern Negro Poetry: An
Interpretation of Its Lyrical, Religious, Evocative, and
Racial Qualities. Ohio State Univ., 1933. Thesis: English.
[Arna Bontemps, Sterling A. Brown, Charles S. Johnson,
James Weldon Johnson, and Jean Toomer]

Sedgwick, William E. The Problem of American Literature as Seen by Contemporary Critics, 1815-1830. Harvard Univ., 1934. Dissertation: English.

See, Katharine A. The Christmas Story in American Literature. Univ. of Louisville, 1943. Thesis: English. [Includes James Lane Allen, Charles E. Craddock, John Fox, Jr., T.N. Page, and Ruth McEnery Stuart]

Sensabaugh, George F. The Element of Wonder in American Romanticism. Univ. of North Carolina (Chapel Hill), 1930. Thesis: English. [Includes E.A. Poe]

Seydow, John J. The Objective Aesthetic in American Literature, 1828-1838. Ohio Univ., 1968. Dissertation: English. [Includes Robert M. Bird and E.A. Poe]

Shackelford, Louis B. Aesthetic Criticism of Literature in Contemporary America. Univ. of Kentucky, 1927. Thesis: English. [Includes E.A. Poe]

Shaffer, Arthur H. The Shaping of a National Tradition: Historical Writing in America, 1783-1820. Univ. of California (Los Angeles), 1966. Dissertation: History. [Includes Thomas Jefferson, David Ramsay, William Stith, Hugh Williamson, and William Wirt]

Shankle, George E. Poetry of American Farm Life. George Peabody College, 1926. Dissertation: English. [Includes J.C. Harris, Sidney Lanier, T.N. Page, Irwin Russell, and Henry T. Stanton]

Shannon, Florine F. Women in American Fiction from 1920 until 1941. Univ. of Tulsa, 1942. Thesis: English. [Includes Ellen Glasgow, DuBose Heyward, Margaret Mitchell, Julia Peterkin, and Thomas Wolfe]

Shapiro, Stephan A. The Ambivalent Animal: Man in the Contemporary British and American Novel. Univ. of Washington, 1965. Dissertation: English. [Includes John Barth]

Sharma, Mohan L. The Functional Preface in American Fiction. Ohio State Univ., 1965. Dissertation: English. [Includes A.W. Tourgée and Mark Twain]

Shearon, B.F. Negro-White Conflicts in Twentieth Century American Drama. Univ. of Louisville, 1966. Thesis: English.

Shepherd, Douglas A. The Dilemma of the Artist in American Fiction. Southern Illinois Univ. (Carbondale), 1957. Thesis: English. [Includes Thomas Wolfe]

Sherman, Alfonso. The Diversity of Treatment of the Negro Character in American Drama prior to 1860. Indiana Univ., 1964. Dissertation: Theater.

Sherr, Paul C. Political Satire in the American Musical Theatre of the 1930's. Univ. of Pennsylvania, 1965. Dissertation: English. [Includes Paul Green's *Johnny Johnson*]

Shirk, Samuel. The Characterization of George Washington in American Plays since 1875. Univ. of Pennsylvania, 1948. Dissertation: English.

Shockley, Frederick A. Reconstruction as Seen through the American Historical Novel, 1865-1898. Emory Univ., 1961. Thesis: History. [Includes A.W. Tourgée, Charles E. Craddock, and James M. Thompson]

Shuck, Emerson C. Clergymen in Representative American Novels, 1830-1930: A Study in Attitudes toward Religion. Univ. of Wisconsin, 1943. Dissertation: English. [Includes Ellen Glasgow, A.B. Longstreet, and W.G. Simms]

Silverman, Kenneth E. Colonial American Poetry: An Anthology. Columbia Univ., 1964. Dissertation: English. [Chapter 6 deals with Southern poetry]

Simoni, John P. Art Critics and Criticism in Nineteenth Century America. Ohio State Univ., 1952. Dissertation: Fine Arts. [Includes Washington Allston, along with many other Southerners]

Simpson, Charmaine E. The Supernatural Element in Recent Literature. Univ. of Oklahoma, 1920. Thesis: English. [Includes E.A. Poe]

Simms, Billie J. The Poet Laureates of the States of the United States. West Texas State Univ., 1950. Thesis: English. [Chapter 3 deals with the poet laureates of the South]

Skinner, Donald T. The Civil War as a Subject for American Drama, 1861-1947. Northwestern Univ., 1948. Dissertation: Speech.

Skinner, Ruth J. American Letters to Children. Univ. of North Carolina (Chapel Hill), 1941. Thesis: English. [Includes G.W. Cable, J.C. Harris, Robert E. Lee, and Walter Hines Page]

Slicer, George W. Superstition and Religion in American Negro Drama, 1913-40. Ohio State Univ., 1944. Thesis: English. [Includes Randolph Edmonds, Paul Green, and Willis Richardson]

Slicheinska, Freida M. The Literary Life of the Negro: A Study in American Literature. Niagara Univ., 1946. Thesis: English. [Includes William S. Braithewaite, Sterling A. Brown, William Wells Brown, Charles W. Chesnutt, Joseph Cotter, Jr., William DuBois, Frances W. Harper, James Weldon Johnson, Jean Toomer, Booker T. Washington, Walter White, and Richard Wright]

Slonaker, Ethel H. Pulitzer Prize Plays, 1918-1940: An Index to Commentary and Criticism with Interpretative Data. Univ. of North Carolina (Chapel Hill), 1967. Thesis: Library Science. [Includes Paul Green]

Smalley, Merla K. A Study of the Development of American Humor. Kansas State Teachers College, 1952. Thesis: English. [Includes David Crockett and Mark Twain]

Smalley, Webster L.C. The Characterization of the Male Protagonist in Serious American Drama from 1920 to 1940. Stanford Univ., 1960. Dissertation: Theater. [Includes Laurence Stallings]

Smith, David E. John Bunyan in America: A Critical Inquiry. Univ. of Minnesota, 1962. Dissertation: English. [Includes a discussion of Bunyan's influence on *Innocents Abroad*]

Smith, Elizabeth. Arguments for and against Slavery as Presented in American Fiction up to 1860. Columbia Univ., 1917. Thesis: English. [Includes Mary H. Eastman, J.P. Kennedy, and Nathaniel B. Tucker]

Smith, Eula M. Imagery in Representative Contemporary Negro Poets. Xavier Univ. (New Orleans), 1941. Thesis: English. [Includes James Weldon Johnson]

Smith, F.L. Man and Minister in Recent American Fiction. Univ.
of Pennsylvania, 1968. Dissertation: English. [Includes
Erskine Caldwell, William Faulkner, and Richard Wright]
Smith, Frank R. American Short Fiction in the 1940's: An Analysis
of Annually Anthologized Short Stories. Univ. of Texas
(Austin), 1956. Thesis: English. [Includes William Faulkner
and Peter Taylor]
Smith, Helena M. Negro Characterization in the American Novel:
A Historical Survey of Work by White Authors. Pennsylvania
State Univ., 1959. Dissertation: English. [Includes
G.W. Cable, Erskine Caldwell, William Faulkner, T.N. Page,
W.G. Simms, A.W. Tourgée, and Mark Twain]
Smith, Herbert F. The Editorial Influence of Richard Watson
Gilder, 1870-1909. Rutgers Univ., 1961. Dissertation:
English. [Editor for G.W. Cable, J.C. Harris, Sidney Lanier,
T.N. Page, and Mark Twain]
Smith, Hubert W. Some American Fiction Writers and Their Reviewers:
A Study of the Reviews and Reviewers in Connection with Eight
Representative Fiction Writers, 1918-1941. Univ. of
Pennsylvania, 1949. Dissertation: English. [Includes Ellen
Glasgow]
Smith, Lorraine O. Anti-Romanticism in American Literature. Univ.
of Rochester, 1941. Thesis: English. [Includes J.B. Cabell
and Ellen Glasgow]
Smith, Mamie E. Literary Fads and Fashions in America of the
1830's. Univ. of Texas (Austin), 1926. Thesis: English.
[Includes E.A. Poe]
Smith, Marjorie G. The Modern Novel of the Soil. Boston Univ.,
1947. Thesis: English. [Includes Ellen Glasgow, Caroline
Miller, and Elizabeth Madox Roberts]
Smith, Patrick J. Typology and Peripety in Four Catholic Novels.
Univ. of California (Davis), 1967. Dissertation: English.
[Includes Caroline Gordon and Flannery O'Connor]
Smith, Rebecca W. The Civil War and Its Aftermath in American
Fiction, 1861-1899, with a Dictionary Catalogue and Indexes.
Univ. of Chicago, 1932. Dissertation: English. [Includes
Sherwood Bonner, G.W. Cable, Jeremiah Clemens, John Esten
Cooke, Thomas Cooper DeLeon, J.C. Harris, Sidney Lanier,
and Charles Henry Smith]
Smith, Robert A. Contemporary Negro Poets: A Critical Study,
with Comprehensive Bibliographies. New York Univ., 1937.
Thesis: English. [Includes James Weldon Johnson]
Smith, Ross D. A Survey of Native American Serious Drama from
1900 to 1918. Univ. of Utah, 1952. Dissertation: English.
[Includes Thomas Dixon's *The Clansman*]
Smithline, Arnold. Natural Religion and American Literature. New
York Univ., 1962. Dissertation: English. [Includes
Thomas Jefferson]
Sniderman, Stephen L. The "Composite" in Twentieth Century
American Literature. Univ. of Wisconsin, 1969. Disser-
tation: English. [Includes *Go Down, Moses*]
South, Elizabeth G. The Struggle over Slavery and Its Reflection
in American Fiction of the 1850's. Univ. of Illinois, 1943.
Thesis: English. [Includes Mary Eastman, E.A. Pollard, and
Calvin H. Wiley]

Speck, Ernest B. American Short Story, 1930-1940: A Study in Form
and Content. Univ. of Texas (Austin), 1959. Dissertation:
English. [Includes Erskine Caldwell, William March,
O. Henry, Katherine Anne Porter, and Eudora Welty]
Spicehandler, Daniel. The American War Novel. Columbia Univ.,
1960. Dissertation: English. [Mentions Laurence
Stallings]
Sprague, Juanita R. The Best Selling Novel in America from 1890-
1900. Univ. of Kentucky, 1942. Thesis: English. [Includes
James Lane Allen, John Fox, Jr., and William Faulkner]
Springer, Anne M. The American Novel in Germany: A Study of the
Critical Reception of Eight American Novelists between the
Two World Wars. Univ. of Pennsylvania, 1959. Dissertation:
English. [Includes William Faulkner]
Springer, Mary L. The Goncourt and Pulitzer Prize Novels: A
Comparative Study. Univ. of Southern California, 1939.
Thesis: Comparative Literature. [Includes Caroline Miller,
Margaret Mitchell, Julia Peterkin, and T.S. Stribling]
Stahr, William E. The Demand for an American Literature and Its
Context, 1825-1835. George Washington Univ., 1965. Disser-
tation: English. [Includes J.P. Kennedy, Francis Scott
Key, Hugh S. Legaré, and W.G. Simms]
Stanford, Rayney B. The Tradition of Heroism and the Modern
Novel. Columbia Univ., 1965. Dissertation: English.
[Includes William Faulkner]
Starke, Catherine J. Negro Stock Characters; Archetypes, and
Individuals in American Literature: A Study for College
Teachers. Columbia Univ., 1963. Dissertation: English.
Starling, Marion W. The Slave Narrative: Its Place in American
Literary History. New York Univ., 1946. Dissertation:
English.
Staub, August W. The Subjective Perspective: Aspects of Point of
View in Modern Drama. Louisiana State Univ., 1960.
Dissertation: Theater. [Relates discussion to stream of
consciousness in William Faulkner]
Steadman, Mark S., Jr. American Humor: 1920-1955. Florida State
Univ., 1963. Dissertation: English. [Includes Roark
Bradford and Irving S. Cobb]
Stedtfeld, Wolfgang. Aspects of the New Criticism. Freiburg,
1956. Dissertation: English.
Steene, Kerstin B. The American Drama and the Swedish Theater,
1920-1958. Univ. of Washington, 1960. Dissertaton: Speech
and Drama. [Includes *The Glass Menagerie*; deals primarily
with plays that develop the racial issue of the South and
that were produced in Sweden during World War II]
Steinberg, Abraham H. Jewish Characters in the American Novel
to 1900. New York Univ., 1956. Dissertation: English.
[Includes Joseph Holt Ingraham and Mrs. E.D.E.N. Southworth]
Steiner, David E. The American Military: Theme and Figure in
New York Stage Plays from 1919 to 1941. Univ. of Oregon,
1969. Dissertation: Theater. [Includes *What Price Glory?*]
Steinmetz, Marion L. A History of American Poetry (1860-1869).
Brown Univ., 1957. Dissertation: English. [Argues that
Southern poets justified slavery and felt the Civil War to
be holy]

Sterner, Lewis G. The Sonnet in American Literature. Univ. of
    Pennsylvania, 1930. Dissertation: English. [Includes
    T.H. Chivers, Paul H. Hayne, Sidney Lanier, William A.
    Percy, E.A. Poe, John Crowe Ransom, Lizette Woodworth Reese,
    and W.G. Simms]
Stevens, George. Philosophic Trend of American Negro Poetry.
    Xavier Univ. (New Orleans), 1939. Thesis: English.
    [Includes Sterling A. Brown and James Weldon Johnson]
Stiff, Anna L. An Analysis of Similarity in Tone in the Poetry
    of Ransom, Jarrell, and Lowell. Midwestern Univ., 1965.
    Thesis: English.
Stimson, Frederick S. Spanish Themes in Early American Literature:
    In Novels, Drama, and Verse, 1770-1830. Univ. of Michigan,
    1953. Dissertation: English. [Includes Thomas Digges,
    Thomas Jefferson, and W.G. Simms]
Stineback, David C. Social Change and Nostalgia in Ten American
    Novels. Yale Univ., 1969. Dissertation: English.
    [Includes *The Hamlet*]
Stone, Edith O. Democratic Values in Modern Narrative Poems.
    Univ. of Michigan, 1960. Dissertation: English. [Includes
    Brother to Dragons]
Stone, Sadie. The Negro in Literature. Univ. of Kansas, 1911.
    Thesis: English. [Includes W.E.B. DuBois, Frances W.
    Harper, George M. Horton, Kelley Miller, and Booker T.
    Washington]
Stout, Belle M. Interest in Science in Early American Writers
    with Special Reference to Jefferson. Univ. of Iowa, 1928.
    Thesis: English.
Street, Natalie M. Life after Death in Sixteen Twentieth Century
    Plays. Univ. of Southern California, 1947. Thesis:
    English.
Stubberfield, Charles F. A Freight of Faith and Hope: A Study
    of the Quest in the American Novel. Univ. of Denver, 1967.
    Dissertation: English. [Includes William Faulkner and
    Mark Twain]
Stuckey, William J. A Critical History of the Pulitzer Prize
    Novels, 1917-1947. Washington Univ. (St. Louis), 1959.
    Dissertation: English. [Includes *All the King's Men*]
Suderman, Elmer F. Religion in the American Novel: 1870-1900.
    Univ. of Kansas, 1961. Dissertation: English. [Discusses
    150 novels, plus periodicals and nonfiction dealing with
    religion; includes James Lane Allen, Charles E. Craddock,
    Ellen Glasgow, and Mark Twain]
Sullivan, Barbara W. A Gallery of Grotesques: The Alienation
    Theme in the Works of Hawthorne, Twain, Anderson, Faulkner,
    and Wolfe. Univ. of Georgia, 1968. Dissertation: English.
Sullivan, J.B. Changes in the Short Story from 1925 to 1935.
    Texas Tech Univ., 1936. Thesis: English. [Includes
    William Faulkner and Thomas Wolfe]
Summers, Marcia P. The Use of Subordinate Characters as Dramatized
    Narrators in Twentieth Century Novels. Univ. of Illinois,
    1969. Dissertation: English. [Includes *All the King's Men*
    and *Absalom, Absalom!*]

Suss, Irving D. The Drama of Social Protest, 1928-1938. Columbia
      Univ., 1948. Thesis: English. [Includes Paul Green]
Swartwood, Joan. The Pulitzer Prize Novel: 1918-1955. Univ. of
      Florida, 1956. Thesis: English. [Includes William Faulkner]
Sweet, Israel: Prose Literature of the Colonial Almanacs (1763-
      1767). Columbia Univ., 1946. Thesis: English. [Includes
      South Carolina, 1764; *South Carolina and Georgia Almanac*,
      1767]
Sykes, Lillian E. The American Woman's Struggle for Independence
      as Reflected in the Lines of the Heroines of Popular American
      Novels since 1789. Fisk Univ., Data Unknown. Thesis:
      English. [Includes Kate Chopin]
Talmage, Mabel B. The Epic in American Literature. Univ. of
      North Carolina (Chapel Hill), 1943. Thesis: English.
      [Includes Thomas H. Chivers, William Crafts, Walter Malone;
      discusses epics published in the *Southern Literary Messenger*]
Tandy, Jennette R. The Crackerbox Philosophers. Columbia Univ.,
      1925. Dissertation: English. [Includes David Crockett,
      A.B. Longstreet, Thomas B. Thorpe, Johnson Jones Hooper,
      William T. Thompson, and Charles Henry Smith]
Tanner, P.A. The Uses of Wonder and Naivety in American Literature,
      with Special Reference to Mark Twain and the Development of
      the Vernacular Child Narrator. Cambridge Univ. (Kings), 1965.
      Dissertation: English.
Taylor, Alma F. Identity as a Theme in the Novels of Richard
      Wright, Ralph Ellison, and James Baldwin. Univ. of Montevallo,
      1969. Thesis: English-Education.
Taylor, Walter F. Economic Unrest in American Fiction, 1880-1901.
      Univ. of North Carolina (Chapel Hill), 1930. Dissertation:
      English. [Includes Florence Converse, Thomas S. Denison,
      and Ellen Glasgow]
Templeton, Joan. Expressionism in British and American Drama.
      Univ. of Oregon, 1966. Dissertation: English. [Includes
      Camino Real]
Thomas, Caroline E. The Problem of Race Relationships as Reflected
      in the Novels by Negro Authors. Univ. of Florida, 1948.
      Thesis: English. [Includes Arna Bontemps, Charles W.
      Chesnutt, Frances W. Harper, George W. Henderson, Zora Neale
      Hurston, James W. Johnson, George Lee, Walter E. Turpin,
      Richard Wright, and Frank Yerby]
Thomas, Nellie K. American Winners of the Nobel Prize in
      Literature. East Texas State Univ., 1969. Thesis: English.
      [Includes William Faulkner]
Thompson, John. The Cult of Preciosity: A Survey of Ultra-
      Sophisticated Writers in American Literature. Vanderbilt
      Univ., 1932. Thesis: English. [Includes William Byrd,
      Lafcadio Hearn, Frances Newman, and E.A. Poe]
Thompson, Nancye M. An Evaluation of Trends in Children's
      Literature since 1930. Auburn Univ., 1940. Thesis: English.
      [Mentions many Southern writers]
Thomson, Susan. The Christ Figure: A Focus of the Search for
      Meaning in American Literature. Florida State Univ., 1969.
      Thesis: English. [Includes William Faulkner]

Thomson, Woodruff C. The Spanish-American War in American
    Literature. Univ. of Utah, 1962. Dissertation: English.
    [Includes Mark Twain]
Thorn, E.P. The Influence of Naturalism on the Contemporary
    American Novel. Brooklyn College, 1956. Thesis: English.
    [Includes William Faulkner by brief mention]
Tierney, Sr. Jane F. An Investigation of the Contributions to the
    Art of the Short Story Made by Four Contemporary Women:
    Elizabeth Bowen, Mary Lavin, Katherine Anne Porter, and
    Eudora Welty. Canisius College, 1956. Thesis: English.
Tiller, Lessie. Gullar in American Literature. Univ. of South
    Carolina, 1923. Thesis: English. [Traces the origin of
    the Gullah dialect and its establishment in the South;
    discusses Sherwood Bonner, Howard Gillman, A.E. Gonzales,
    J.C. Harris, Charles Colcock Jones, E.A. Poe, and Malvina S.
    Waring]
Tillery, Inez. The Development of the Yankee Character in American
    Drama. Univ. of Alabama, 1939. Thesis: English. [Includes
    N.H. Bannister and Cornelius A. Logan]
Tillson, M.W. The Frontiersman in American Drama: An Analytical
    Study of the Characters and Plays Reflecting the Phenomenon
    of Westerward Expansion. Univ. of Denver, 1951. Disser-
    tation: English.
Timpe, Eugene F. The Reception of American Literature in Germany,
    1861-1871. Univ. of Southern California, 1961. Disser-
    tation: English. [Includes Mark Twain]
Tips, Bessie B. Bad Boys in American Literature. Columbia Univ.,
    1920. Thesis: English. [Includes Francis Robert Goulding
    and O. Henry]
Tipton, Lois. Symbolism in American Literature. Univ. of Texas
    (Austin), 1936. Thesis: English. [Includes E.A. Poe]
Todd, Harold. The Protestant Minister in American Fiction.
    Southern Illinois Univ. (Carbondale), 1950. Thesis: English.
    [Includes T.S. Stribling]
TraBue, Ann M. An Analysis of Guidance Procedure Reflected in
    Student-Teacher Relationships Portrayed in Selected Popular
    Fiction. Univ. of North Carolina (Chapel Hill), 1962.
    Dissertation: Education. [Includes both fiction and drama
    written by Southerners]
Tracy, Thomas J. The American Attitude toward American Literature
    during the Years 1800-1812. St. John's Univ. (N.Y.), 1941.
    Dissertation: English.
Traylor, Edna M. Evolution of the American Short Story as
    Indicated in Current Magazines from 1785-1925. North
    Western Univ., 1926. Thesis: Journalism. [Includes
    James Lane Allen, J.C. Harris, Richard M. Johnston, Charles E.
    Craddock, and T.N. Page]
Trensky, Anne T. The Cult of the Child in Minor American Fiction
    of the Nineteenth Century. City Univ. of New York (Brockport),
    1969. Dissertation: English. [Designates movement as
    reaching climax in *Huckleberry Finn*]
Triplett, Eva B. A Study of War Drama from 1915 to 1941. Univ.
    of Pittsburgh, 1945. Thesis: English. [Includes Paul
    Green, Lillian Hellman, and Laurence Stallings]

Troesch, Helen D. The Negro in Dramatic Literature. Case Western
    Reserve Univ., 1940. Dissertation: English. [Includes
    Dorothy and DuBose Heyward]
Turner, Clarena S. The Decade of Social Protest in the American
    Drama, 1929-1939. Southern Methodist Univ., 1950. Thesis:
    English. [Includes Paul Green, Lillian Hellman, and
    Tennessee Williams]
Turner, Cora E. Parent-Child Conflict in Selected American Dramas,
    1919-1939. Univ. of Florida, 1946. Thesis: English.
    [Includes Ann Preston Bridgers and Lillian Hellman]
Turner, John M., Jr. The Response of Major American Writers to
    Darwinism, 1859-1910. Harvard Univ., 1956. Dissertation:
    English. [Includes Sidney Lanier and Mark Twain]
Turner, J.W. Relative Importance of American Writings through
    Emphasis in Literary Histories. George Peabody College,
    1935. Thesis: English.
Turner, Vashti D. The Negro in Literature by the Negro. Miami
    Univ. (Ohio), 1944. Thesis: English. [Includes W.E.B.
    DuBois, E. Franklin Frazier, Zora Neale Hurston, James Weldon
    Johnson, Jean Toomer, Carter G. Woodson, and Richard Wright]
Turner, Willis L. City Low-Life on the American State to 1900.
    Univ. of Illinois, 1956. Dissertation: Theater. ["From
    time of Robert Montgomery Bird to time of Edward Harrigan"]
Tyner, Raymond E. English Criticism of American Literature,
    1850-1900. Univ. of Georgia, 1948. Thesis: English.
    [Includes G.W. Cable and E.A. Poe]
Ulbrich, Armand H. The Trend toward Religion in the Modern
    American Novel, 1925 to 1951. Univ. of Michigan, 1952.
    Dissertation: English. [Includes William Faulkner and
    Ellen Glasgow]
Umphlett, Wiley L. The Essential Encounter: The Myth of the
    Sporting Hero in American Fiction. Florida State Univ.,
    1967. Dissertation: English. [Includes William Faulkner
    and Caroline Gordon]
Valencia, Willa F. The Picaresque Tradition in the Contemporary
    English and American Novel. Univ. of Illinois, 1968.
    Dissertation: English. [Includes John Barth, Mark Twain,
    and Thomas Wolfe]
Valgemae, Mardi. Expressionism in American Drama. Univ. of
    California (Los Angeles), 1964. Dissertation: English.
    [Includes *Tread the Green Grass*, *Johnny Johnson*, and
    Camino Real]
Van Benschoten, Virginia K. The Influence of Scientific and
    Socio-Scientific Ideologies on Some Examples of the Modern
    American Popular Novel. Univ. of Michigan, 1960. Disser-
    tation: English. [Includes Mary Johnston]
Van Deusen, L.M., Jr. J.E. Spingarn and American Criticism.
    Univ. of Pennsylvania, 1953. Dissertation: English.
    [Includes John Crowe Ransom and Allen Tate]
Van Tassel, David D. Recording America's Past: American
    Historical Writing, 1607-1889. Univ. of Wisconsin, 1956.
    Dissertation: History. [Discusses histories of the colonies,
    early biographies of George Washington, and Thomas
    Jefferson's writings]

Varner, John G. Sarah Helen Whitman, Seeress of Providence.
Univ. of Virginia, 1941. Dissertation: English. [Extensive
treatment of Poe]
Vaughan, William E. Some Types of the Short Story. Columbia
Univ., 1911. Thesis: English. [Includes E.A. Poe]
Veal, Martha A. Modern Trends in the American Short Story Growing
out of the Impressionistic School. Univ. of Oklahoma, 1937.
Thesis: English. [Includes Erskine Caldwell, William
Faulkner, O. Henry, and E.A. Poe]
Veatch, Grace D. The History of American Literature, 1869-1873.
Univ. of Wisconsin, 1928. Thesis: History. [One chapter
on Southern literature]
Veltman, Willard G. Deism in American Literature. Southern
Methodist Univ., 1963. Thesis: English. [Includes Thomas
Jefferson]
Veizer, John K. Racial Prejudice as a Theme in Modern Drama.
Univ. of Virginia, 1967. Thesis: English.
Vincent, James E. Freedom and Responsibility: An Introductory
Essay on Existential Themes in American Drama. Univ. of
Wisconsin, 1962. Dissertation: Theater. [Includes *Camino
Real*]
Virden, James M. The Rebirth Motif in the Novels of Three Major
Negro Writers. Univ. of Maryland, 1963. Thesis: English.
[Includes Richard Wright]
Vitelli, James R. The Resurrection of the Puritan: A Study of an
American Literary Symbol. Univ. of Pennsylvania, 1955.
Dissertation: American Studies. [Deals with several critics,
H.L. Mencken included]
Vivian, Dalton W. The Civil War on the Stage. Trinity Univ.
(Texas), 1957. Thesis: Drama.
Voight, Gilbert P. The Religious and Ethical Elements in the
Major American Poets. Univ. of South Carolina, 1925.
Dissertation: English. [Includes Sidney Lanier and E.A. Poe]
Vollmer, Clement. The American Novel in Germany, 1871-1913.
Univ. of Pennsylvania, 1915. Dissertation: German.
[Includes G.W. Cable, Lafcadio Hearn, and Mark Twain]
Von Szeliski, John J. Pessimism and the Tragic Vision: A Study
of Tragedy in the Modern American Theatre. Univ. of
Minnesota, 1962. Dissertation: Theater. [Includes
Tennessee Williams]
Von Tornow, Georgiana J. The Heroine in American Drama and Theatre
down to the Civil War: And Her Relation to "Life" and the
Novels of the Times. Cornell Univ., 1945. Dissertation:
English.
Voorhees, Lillian W. The American Negro and the Drama: The
Contribution of the American Negro to Dramatic Art. Facts
Interpreted in Terms of potentialities for the Negro and for
the Drama. Columbia Univ., 1925. Thesis: English.
[Includes W.E.B. DuBois and Willis Richardson]
Wadlington, Warwick P. The Theme of the Confidence Game in
Certain Major American Writers. Tulane Univ., 1967. Disser-
tation: English. [Includes Ralph Ellison and Mark Twain]

Waite, Norman O. The Attitude of Recent American Novelists
toward the Land. Southern Methodist Univ., 1950. Thesis:
English. [Includes Ellen Glasgow; also discusses Louis
Bromfield's and Rose Wilder Lane's views of the South]
Walker, Grace E. Novels by Negro Authors: A Study of Subject
Matter. Fisk Univ., 1933. Thesis: English. [Includes
Arna Bontemps, William Wells Brown, Charles W. Chesnutt,
W.E.B. DuBois, Frances W. Harper, James Weldon Johnson,
Yorke Jones, and Walter White]
Walker, Martha E. Pulitzer Prize-Winning Novels, 1944-1960: A
Content Analysis. Univ. of North Carolina (Chapel Hill), 1963.
Thesis: Library Science. [Includes James Agee, William
Faulkner, and Robert Penn Warren]
Walker, Robert G. Censure of Majority Rule as a Theme in American
Literature, 1787-1853. Univ. of Michigan, 1943. Disser-
tation: English. [Includes William A. Caruthers, Donald
Davidson, James Ewell Heath, Thomas Jefferson, J.P. Kennedy,
James Madison, and E.A. Poe]
Walker, Virginia R.H. Well Known American Fiction Writers with
Reportorial and/or Editorial Background. East Texas State
Univ., 1965. Thesis: Journalism. [Includes O. Henry,
E.A. Poe, and Marjorie Kinnan Rawlings]
Walls, Aileen S. Cultural Image of the United States: North
American Novelists and Spanish American Reviewers. Univ.
of Illinois, 1962. Dissertation: English. [Includes
Erskine Caldwell and William Faulkner]
Ward, Frances L. An Examination of the Boy's Loss of Innocence
in American Fiction. Texas A & M Univ., 1970. Thesis:
English. [Includes William Faulkner, Harper Lee, and
Mark Twain]
Ward, Robert J. Europe in American Fiction: The Vogue of the
Historical Romance, 1890-1910. Univ. of Missouri, 1967.
Dissertation: English. [Includes Caroline Lee Hentz and
Mrs. E.D.E.N. Southworth]
Wasserman, Maurice M. The American Indian as Seen by the
Seventeenth Century Chroniclers. Univ. of Pennsylvania,
1954. Dissertation: English. [Includes John Smith and
Robert Beverly]
Watts, Carol J. The Social and Political Aspects of the Pro-
letarian Literary Movement, 1929-1935. Southern Methodist
Univ., 1967. Thesis: History. [Includes Erskine Caldwell
and Mary Heaton Vorse]
Watts, Latona M. Pulitzer Prize Dramas, 1919-1929. East Texas
State Univ., 1938. Thesis: English. [Traces American
authors represented and attempts to discover the type of
dramas ranked as the best for each season]
Watts, Maud M. A Study of Family Disorganization as Treated in
American Fiction between 1920 and 1930. Univ. of Texas
(Austin), 1932. Thesis: Sociology. [Includes Ellen
Glasgow]
Weathers, Winston W. The Broken Word: The Theme of Communication
Failure in Twentieth Century Literature. Univ. of Oklahoma,
1964. Dissertation: English. [Includes Tennessee Williams]

Webb, James W. Biography in American Literature. Univ. of North
   Carolina (Chapel Hill), 1958. Dissertation: English.
   [Includes W.G. Simms and Parson Weems]
Weber, John S. The American War Novel Dealing with the
   Revolutionary and Civil Wars. Univ. of Wisconsin, 1947.
   Dissertation: English. [Includes James Boyd, Clifford
   Dowdey, Ellen Glasgow, Sidney Lanier, Margaret Mitchell,
   Evelyn Scott, and W.G. Simms]
Webster, Claudia R.C. Aspects of Religious Thought Found in
   Modern Drama. Southern Methodist Univ., 1940. Thesis:
   Comparative Literature. [Includes Hatcher Hughes]
Weeks, Francis W. Some Aspects of Pseudo-Sciences in Nineteenth
   Century American Literature. Columbia Univ., 1939. Thesis:
   English. [Includes E.A. Poe]
Weeks, Lewis E. American and British Periodical Criticism of
   Certain Nineteenth Century American Authors, 1840-1860.
   Boston Univ., 1961. Dissertation: English. [Includes
   E.A. Poe and Mrs. E.D.E.N. Southworth]
Wegelin, Christof A. The Concept of Europe in American Fiction
   from Irving to Hawthorne. Johns Hopkins Univ., 1947.
   Dissertation: English. [Includes E.A. Poe and W.G. Simms]
Weigant, Leo A. The Manners Tradition and Regional Fiction in
   Nineteenth Century America. Duke Univ., 1969. Dissertation:
   English. [Includes Robert M. Bird, J.P. Kennedy, and
   Mark Twain]
Weingart, Seymour L. The Form and Meaning of the Impressionist
   Novel. Univ. of California (Davis), 1964. Dissertation:
   English. [Sees William Faulkner as the apogee]
Weissbuch, Theodore N. Literary and Historical Attitudes toward
   Reconstruction Following the Civil War. Univ. of Iowa, 1964.
   Dissertation: English. [Includes G.W. Cable, Sidney Lanier,
   T.N. Page, and A.W. Tourgée]
Welker, Vida G. Melodrama in the United States during the Last
   Half of the Nineteenth Century. Kansas State Teachers College,
   1937. Thesis: English. [Includes Hatcher Hughes and
   James D. McCabe, Jr.]
Welsh, John W. The Development of the American Novel. Northwestern
   Univ., 1902. Thesis: English. [Includes E.A. Poe]
Wenstrand, Thomas E. An Analysis of Style: The Application of
   Sector Analysis to Examples of American Prose Fiction.
   Columbia Univ., 1967. Dissertation: English. [Includes
   William Faulkner and Robert Penn Warren]
Werner, Dorothy L. The Idea of Union in American Verse (1776-1876).
   Univ. of Pennsylvania, 1931. Dissertation: English.
   [Discusses Paul H. Hayne, Sidney Lanier, and a few Southern
   magazines]
West, Alfred T. The Development and Influence of the Folk Interest
   in Contemporary Drama. Univ. of Alabama, 1933. Thesis:
   English. [Emphasis on Frederick H. Koch and the Carolina
   Playmakers; includes discussion of Paul Green, Hatcher Hughes,
   Laurence Stallings, Lula Vollmer, and Thomas Wolfe]
West, B.J. Attitudes toward American Women as Reflected in
   American Literature between the Two World Wars. Univ. of
   Denver, 1954. Dissertation: English. [Includes Erskine
   Caldwell and William Faulkner]

West, Harry C. Nine Native American Humorists: A Study of
    Imagery. Duke Univ., 1966. Thesis: English. [Includes
    G.W. Harris, Johnson Jones Hooper, and A.B. Longstreet]
Wheeler, Effie J. Narrative Art in the Prose Fiction of the
    Eighteenth Century American Magazines. Univ. of Michigan,
    1942. Dissertation: English. [Includes *North Carolina
    Magazine, or Universal Intelligencer*, Newbern, N.C.; *South
    Carolina Weekly Museum*, Charleston; and *Weekly Museum*,
    Baltimore]
Wheeler, Joseph T. Literary Culture in Colonial America, 1700-
    1776. Brown Univ., 1939. Dissertation: History.
Wheeler, Sanford G. Plays on American Civil War Themes. Cornell
    Univ., 1942. Thesis: English.
Whisnant, Emeline G. Social Protest in the Poems of American
    Negroes. East Tennessee State Univ., 1951. Thesis: English.
White, James A. The Era of Good Intentions: A Survey of American
    Catholics' Writing between the Years 1880 and 1915. Univ.
    of Notre Dame, 1957. Dissertation: History. [Mentions
    J.C. Harris]
White, Robert L. Some Passionate Pilgrims: The Image of Italy in
    American Romanticism. Univ. of Minnesota, 1959. Dissertation:
    English. [Includes Washington Allston]
Whiteside, Constance H. The Negro in American Literature. Ohio
    State Univ., 1930. Thesis: English. [Includes Charles W.
    Chesnutt, J.C. Harris, and James Weldon Johnson]
Whitley, George T. The Development of the American Short Story.
    Univ. of North Carolina (Chapel Hill), 1909. Thesis:
    English. [Includes E.A. Poe]
Whitney, Blair. American Poetic Drama: 1900-1966. Univ. of
    Illinois, 1967. Dissertation: English. [Includes Tennessee
    Williams]
Weiss, Frank J. The Progress of the Technical and Artistic Sides
    of English Mystery Fiction. Ohio State Univ., 1930. Thesis:
    English. [Includes E.A. Poe]
Wilbanks, Evelyn R. American Novels about Doctors, 1870-1955.
    Duke Univ., 1956. Thesis: English. [Includes G.W. Cable
    and William Faulkner]
Wild, Henry D. Democratic Idealism in American Literature from
    Penn to Whitman. Univ. of Chicago, 1924. Dissertation:
    English. [Includes James Audubon, John Filson, and Thomas
    Jefferson]
Wiley, Charles G. A Study of the American Woman as She Is
    Presented in the American Drama of the Nineteen-Twenties.
    Univ. of New Mexico, 1957. Dissertation: English. [Includes
    Paul Green and DuBose Heyward]
Wiley, E.C. A Study of the Noble Savage Myth in Characterizations
    of the Negro in Selected American Literary Works. Univ. of
    Arkansas, 1964. Dissertation: English. [Includes Erskine
    Caldwell, William Faulkner, J.C. Harris, Carson McCullers,
    and Richard Wright]
Wilkerson, Helen C. The Trend and Movement of the Modern Drama
    during the Five Year Period 1925-1930. Louisiana State Univ.,
    1930. Thesis: English. [Includes Paul Green, Dorothy and
    DuBose Heyward, and Laurence Stallings]

[331]

Willeford, Charles R. The Immobilized Man: A New Hero in Modern
    Fiction. Univ. of Miami (Coral Gables), 1964. Thesis:
    English. [Includes Truman Capote, Carson McCullers, and
    Thomas Wolfe]
Willer, William H. Native Themes in American Short Prose Fiction,
    1770-1835. Univ. of Minnesota, 1944. Dissertation: English.
Williams, E.V. Religion and the Church as Motifs in American
    Fiction. Vanderbilt Univ., 1930. Thesis: English. [Includes
    Cora Harris]
Williams, Joseph. Conditions Assigned by Providence: Proslavery
    Sentiment in American Fiction before the Civil War. Harvard
    Univ., 1964. Dissertation: English.
Williams, Philip E. The Biblical View of History: Hawthorne,
    Mark Twain, Faulkner, and Eliot. Univ. of Pennsylvania,
    1964. Dissertation: English.
Williamson, Jerry M. The Transitional Period between Romanticism
    and Realism in the American Arts. Florida State Univ., 1963.
    Dissertation: Fine Arts. [Includes G.W. Cable, J.C. Harris,
    and Mark Twain]
Willingham, John R. Social Problems in American Drama from 1930
    to 1940. North Texas State Univ., 1948. Thesis: English.
    [Includes Erskine Caldwell, Paul Green, and Lillian Hellman]
Willoughby, Pearl V. The Achievements of Modern Dramaturgy,
    British and American. Univ. of Virginia, 1923. Disser-
    tation: English. [Includes a brief discussion of Stark
    Young's *The Twilight Saint*]
Wilsey, Mildred. Nature in American Literature before 1700.
    Columbia Univ., 1927. Thesis: English. [Includes travel
    in the South, its topography, and its natural beauty]
Wilson, Benjamin H. Quiet Realism: Women Writers in the William
    Dean Howells Tradition. Univ. of North Carolina, 1965.
    Dissertation: English. [Includes Ellen Glasgow]
Wilson, David S. The Streaks of the Tulip: The Literary Aspects
    of Eighteenth Century American Natural Philosophy. Univ. of
    Minnesota, 1968. Dissertation: English. [Includes Mark
    Catesby's *Natural History of Carolina (1731-1743)*; emphasizes
    English view of America]
Wilson, Robert N. The American Poet: A Role Investigation.
    Harvard Univ., 1952. Dissertation: Sociology. [Includes
    Randall Jarrell and Merrill Moore]
Winstead, Gloria. Hemingway, Wolfe, Faulkner: The Theme of
    Initiation. Mississippi College, 1963. Thesis: English.
Winters, Arthur Y. A Study of the Post-Romantic Reaction in
    Lyrical Verse, and Incidentally in Certain Other Forms.
    Stanford Univ., 1935. Dissertation: English. [Includes
    Allen Tate]
Witham, William T. The Forge of Life: Problems of Adolescents
    in American Novels, 1920-1958. Univ. of Illinois, 1961.
    Dissertation: English.
Wolfe, Sr. St. Patrick Mary. The New Criticism and Morality: A
    Study of the Problem as Presented by Richards, Winters, Brooks,
    and Tate. St. Michael's College, 1953. Thesis: English.
Wolfinger, Roy J. The Humorous Short Story in American Literature.
    Univ. of Oklahoma, 1916. Thesis: English. [Includes Joseph
    Glover Baldwin, J.C. Harris, A.B. Longstreet, and O. Henry]

Woloch, Nancy S. The Self-Image of Antebellum Reformers: A
    Study of Nineteenth Century American Autobiography. Indiana
    Univ. (Bloomington), 1968. Dissertation: History.
    [Includes Moncure Conway]
Wood, Helen E. Progress towards the Realization of a National
    Drama as Seen in the Pulitzer Prize Plays. Boston Univ.,
    1939. Thesis: English. [Includes Paul Green]
Woodward, Barbara C. Theories of Meaning in Poetry, 1915-1940:
    A Critical History. Univ. of Michigan, 1946. Dissertation:
    English. [Includes Cleanth Brooks, John Gould Fletcher,
    John Crowe Ransom, Allen Tate, and Robert Penn Warren]
Woolridge, Nancy B. The Negro Preacher in American Fiction before
    1900. Univ. of Chicago, 1942. Dissertation: English.
    [Includes James Lane Allen, Robert M. Bird, Kate Chopin,
    Jeremiah Clemens, Henry Stillwell Edwards, Armistead C.
    Gordon, J.C. Harris, Caroline Lee Hentz, J.P. Kennedy,
    Mrs. E.D.E.N. Southworth, Ruth McEnery Stuart, and Thomas
    Bangs Thorpe]
Wouters, Alfrédie. America in Literature, 1920-1940. Cornell
    Univ., 1950. Dissertation: English.
Wyatt, Robert D. The Aesthetics of Doubt: Three Studies in
    Ironic Narrative. Univ. of Oregon, 1969. Dissertation:
    English. [Includes E.A. Poe briefly]
Yarbrough, Eunice K. Education in American Literature in the
    1840's. Southern Methodist Univ., 1929. Thesis: Education.
    [Includes E.A. Poe]
Yarbrough, Jerry W. The Preacher as Certain American Writers Saw
    Him from 1840 to 1900. Univ. of Texas (Austin), 1962.
    Thesis: English. [Includes Johnson Jones Hooper and Mark
    Twain; emphasizes the "religious climate of the South and
    West"]
Yarnall, John N. Romance a la mode, 1896-1906. Univ. of
    Pittsburgh, 1941. Dissertation: English. [Includes J.B.
    Cabell, G.W. Cable, Thomas Dixon, and Ellen Glasgow]
Yates, Naomi S. A Survey of the Development of the Poetry of the
    American Negro. Univ. of Maryland, 1935. Thesis: English.
    [Includes Arna Bontemps and James Weldon Johnson]
Yellin, Jean F. The Negro in Pre-Civil War Literature. Univ. of
    Illinois, 1969. Dissertation: English. [Includes William
    Wells Brown, Ellen Crafts, William Crafts, Frederick
    Douglass, Thomas Jefferson, J.P. Kennedy, and George Tucker]
Yevish, Irving A. The Education of the Literary Artist in Modern
    Novels of College and University Life. Columbia Univ.,
    1965. Dissertation: English. [Includes Look Homeward, Angel]
Young, Phyllis D. Manhattan Life in the Novel: 1920-1940.
    Southern Methodist Univ., 1948. Thesis: English. [Includes
    Arna Bontemps and Thomas Wolfe]
Zietlow, Edward R. Wright to Hansberry: The Evolution of Outlook
    in Four Negro Writers. Univ. of Washington, 1967. Disser-
    tation: English. [Also discusses Ralph Ellison]
Zuther, Gerhard H.W. Problems in Translation: Modern American
    Dramas in German. Indiana Univ. (Bloomington), 1959. Disser-
    tation: English. [Includes Tennessee Williams]

STUDIES RESTRICTED TO
SOUTHERN LITERARY TOPICS AND
SOUTHERN WRITERS[1]

Ackerman, Hugh. The Novel's Place in History: A Study of Florida
     Fiction. Univ. of Florida, 1955. Thesis: History.
Alexander, A.G. Louisiana Writers, 1875-1900. George Peabody
     College, 1931. Thesis: English.
Amacher, Anne W. Myths and Consequences: Allen Tate's and Some
     Other Vanderbilt Traditionalists' Images of Class and Race
     in the Old South. New York Univ., 1956. Dissertation:
     American Civilization. [Undertakes to examine the extent to
     which some images of the Old South in the writings of Allen
     Tate, Andrew Lytle, and some other Vanderbilt Agrarians may
     lend support to anti-liberal or undemocratic attitudes on
     class and race. Involves a study of Tate's writings, as well
     as major (and many minor) works of Andrew Lytle, Donald
     Davidson, Frank L. Owsley, John Crowe Ransom, and Robert
     Penn Warren up through 1955. Emphasizes nonfiction, but also
     treats relevant fiction and poetry]
Amour, Joella G. Literary History of Hempstead County [Texas].
     East Texas State Univ., 1949. Thesis: English.
Anderson, John Q. Trends of Thought in Southern Writings,
     1607-1750. Louisiana State Univ., 1948. Thesis: English.
     [George Alsop, John Archdale, Thomas Ashe, Robert Beverley,
     Edward Bland, John Buckell, William Byrd, W. Crashaw, Thomas
     Glover, John Hammond, William Hilton, Robert Horne, Hugh
     Jones, George Percy, John Pory, Richard Rich, George Sandys,
     John Smith, and William Stith]
Anderson, Mary C. The Huguenot in the South Carolina Novel.
     Univ. of South Carolina, 1967. Dissertation: English.
     [Gwen Bristow, Katherine Drayton, Ambrose Elliott Gonzales,
     DuBose Heyward, Thornwell Jacobs, Mary Elizabeth Moragné,
     Herbert Ravenel Sass, Gertrude Matthews Shelby, Mayrant
     Simons, W.G. Simms, Annie Raymond Stillman, and Samuel
     Gaillard Stoney]
Anfuso, Marian. The Interpretation of the Georgia Cracker in the
     Works of Augustus Baldwin Longstreet, Richard Malcolm Johnston,
     and Joel Chandler Harris. St. John's Univ. (N.Y.), 1951.
     Thesis: English.
Arbour, Marjorie. The Outstanding Writers of Louisiana. Louisiana
     State Univ., 1925. Thesis: English. [Lucy Bakewell
     Audubon, G.W. Cable, Thomas Wharton Collins, Mary Evelyn
     Moore Davis, Dorothy Dix, Alcee Fortier, Charles Gayarré,
     Lafcadio Hearn, Grace King, Fannie Heaslip Lea, Alfred
     Mercier, O. Henry, Stella Perry, Julien Pydras, Henry Rightor,
     Adrienne Rouquette, Lyle Saxon, Ruth McEnery Stuart, and
     Mary Ashley Townsend]
Armour, Robert A. The Literature of Anti-Methodism in Eighteenth
     Century Virginia. Univ. of Georgia, 1968. Dissertation:
     English.

---

[1]These include theses and dissertations restricted to but
dealing with two or more Southern writers.

Armour, Florence T. The Civil War Themes of Six Southern Poets.
    George Peabody College, 1929. Thesis: English.
Armstead, T.J. The Social Realism of Langston Hughes and
    Sterling Brown. Boston Univ., 1946. Thesis: English.
Armstrong, Richard A. Yoknapatawpha and the Natchez Trace: A
    Study of Regional Influences on William Faulkner and Eudora
    Welty. Columbia Univ., 1955. Thesis: English.
Atwell, Priscilla A. Freedom and Diversity: Continuity in the
    Political Tradition of Thomas Jefferson and John C. Calhoun.
    Univ. of California (Los Angeles), 1967. Dissertation:
    History.
Autrey, Sybil L. The Creole in Fact and Fiction. Univ. of Texas
    (Austin), 1953. Thesis: English.
Baily, Edith. David Crockett and Augustus Baldwin Longstreet as
    Pioneers in the Democratic Literature of America. Louisiana
    State Univ., 1936. Thesis: English.
Bainum, Mary I. A Collection of Legends and Writings about
    St. Augustine, Florida. George Peabody College, 1931.
    Thesis: English.
Ball, Donald L. The Eastern Shore of Maryland Literature. Univ.
    of Delaware, 1951. Thesis: English.
Bamberg, Robert D. Plantation and Frontier: A View of Southern
    Fiction. Cornell Univ., 1961. Dissertation: English.
    [William Faulkner, Ellen Glasgow, Caroline Gordon,
    J.P. Kennedy, W.G. Simms, T.S. Stribling, Allen Tate,
    Robert Penn Warren, and Stark Young]
Bankston, Lilian E. The Louisiana Plantation as Seen Through
    Literature. Louisiana State Univ., 1934. Thesis: English.
Barrett, Leonora. The Texas Cowboy in Literature. Univ. of
    Texas (Austin), 1930. Thesis: English.
Barsun, Helen. "Los Pastores," A Remnant of Medieval Drama in
    San Antonio. St. Mary's Univ. (San Antonio), 1943. Thesis:
    English.
Bartley, Glenda H. The Development of Literature as Social History
    in the South. North Texas State Univ., 1955. Thesis:
    History.
Barton, Mary A. The Growth of Realism in the Southern Novel Since
    the Civil War to 1928. Univ. of Virginia, 1928. Thesis:
    English.
Bass, Robert D. The Plays and Playwrights of South Carolina.
    Univ. of South Carolina, 1927. Thesis: English.
Baugh, Harvey F. III.   The Placement of the Creoles of Louisiana
    in American Literature through the Novels and Short Stories
    of George Washington Cable, Kate Chopin, and Grace Elizabeth
    King. Univ. of Virginia, 1930. Thesis: English.
Beeson, Katherine S. The Old South as Portrayed in the Short
    Story. George Peabody College, 1925. Thesis: English.
Beale, Robert C., Jr. The Development of Short Story in the
    South. Univ. of Virginia, 1910. Dissertation: English.
    [Joseph G. Baldwin, Sherwood Bonner, G.W. Cable, Kate Chopin,
    Caroline Gilman, Johnson J. Hooper, A.B. Longstreet, Grace
    King, T.N. Page, E.A. Poe, W.G. Simms, W.T. Thompson, and
    T.B. Thorpe]

Beasley, William M. The New South and Five Southern Novelists
(1920-1950). Vanderbilt Univ., 1957. Dissertation: History.
[Erskine Caldwell, William Faulkner, Ellen Glasgow, William
March, and T.S. Stribling]

Beavis, Catherine J. A Literary History of Lamar County [Texas].
East Texas State Univ., 1941. Thesis: English.

Bennett, Frank D. The Southern Character as Presented by American
Playwrights from 1923-1947. Univ. of Florida, 1950. Thesis:
Speech.

Binder, Frederick M. The Color Problem in Early National America
as Viewed by John Adams, Jefferson, and Jackson. Columbia
Univ., 1962. Dissertation: History. [Discusses both the
Negro and the Indian]

Black, Regina H. A Comparison of the Creoles of George Washington
Cable and Kate Chopin. Univ. of Wyoming, 1952. Thesis:
English.

Blackshear, Emmett C. Three Louisiana Plays: A Commentary.
Louisiana State Univ., 1935. Thesis: Speech. [*The Cajun*
by Ada Jack Carver, *C'est le Sang Qui Parle* by Jack Reynolds,
and *The Teche Comes* by John E. Uhler]

Blankenstein, Mark E. The Southern Tradition in Minor Mississippi
Writers since 1920. Univ. of Illinois, 1965. Dissertation:
English. [William Attaway, Louis Cochran, Hubert Creekmore,
Louise Crump, Broden Deal, Ellen Douglas, John Faulkner,
Shelby Foote, Alice W. Graham, Edward Kimbrough, George Lee,
Walter Lowrey, James R. Peery, Thomas Hal Phillips, Clark
Porteous, Robert Rylee, Elizabeth Spencer, Richard Wright,
and Jefferson Young]

Bogey, Anna Mae. A Literary Survey of the State of Arkansas.
East Texas State Univ., 1943. Thesis: English.

Boggs, John C. Voices out of Dixie: The Contemporary Renascence
of Southern Literature. Columbia Univ., 1957. Thesis:
English.

Bohannon, Alice H. The Influence of Environmental Growth on
Texas Verse. Univ. of Missouri, 1941. Thesis: English.
[Alfred W. Arrington, Karle Wilson Baker, Fannie Baker
Darden, Molly M. Davis, Hilton Ross Greer, Margaret Houston,
Mirabeau B. Lamar, John A. Lomax, Whitney Montgomery,
R.M. Potter, and Stark Young]

Bond, Lizzie M. The Place of the Tenant Farmer in Southern
Literature. Southern Methodist Univ., 1943. Thesis:
English. [Erskine Caldwell, John Faulkner, Ellen Glasgow,
Paul Green, Lyle Saxon, and T.S. Stribling]

Bonds, Georgia A. Basic Themes in the Poetry of Ransom, Warren,
and Tate. Louisiana State Univ., 1940. Thesis: English.

Bonn, Franklyn G., Jr. The Idea of Political Party in the Thought
of Thomas Jefferson and James Madison. Univ. of Minnesota,
1964. Dissertation: Political Science.

Bonner, Mattie L. Robert E. Lee as Portrayed in Southern Fiction.
Univ. of Georgia, 1941. Thesis: English. [John Esten Cooke,
Surrey of Eagles' Nest; Thomas Dixon, *The Man in Gray*;
Clifford Dowdey, *Bugles Blow No More*; John Fox, Jr., *The
Little Shepherd of Kingdom Come*; Ellen Glasgow, *The Battle
Ground*; Mary Johnston, *The Long Roll*; T.N. Page, *The Burial
of the Guns*; Herbert Ravenel Sass, *Look Back to Glory*; Lella
Warren, *Foundation Stone*; and Stark Young, *So Red the Rose*]

Bosse, Mary E. Literary Spartanburg [S.C.], 1900-1925. Univ. of
   South Carolina, 1926. Thesis: English.
Bowman, Mamie I. The Negro in the Work of Three Contemporary
   Louisiana Writers. George Peabody College, 1931. Thesis:
   English.
Boyd, Jimmye T. The Early Kentucky Frontier as Represented in
   Novels by Robert Montgomery Bird, James Lane Allen, Winston
   Churchill, and Elizabeth Madox Roberts. Texas Christian
   Univ., 1962. Thesis: English.
Braack, Gerhard. Myth and Metaphysics in the Critical Prose of
   John Crowe Ransom and Allen Tate. Vanderbilt Univ., 1965.
   Thesis: English.
Bradbury, John M. The Fugitive Critics: A Critical History.
   Univ. of Iowa, 1948. Dissertation: English.
Bradshaw, Sidney E. On Southern Poetry Prior to 1860. Univ. of
   Virginia, 1900. Dissertation: English. [Study of about
   fifty poets who flourished before the Civil War]
Bradsher, Enolia. The Transfer of Louisiana from France to Spain
   in Louisiana Drama. Louisiana State Univ., 1935. Thesis:
   English. [Louis Placide-Canonge, *France et Espagne* (in
   French); Thomas Wharton Collens, *The Martyr Patriots*; and
   Auguste Lussan, *Les Martyrs de la Louisiane* (in French)]
Brechbiel, Grace R. A Definition and Illustration of the Modern
   Gothic Literary Genre Based on the Selected Works of Truman
   Capote, Carson McCullers and Flannery O'Connor. Millersville
   State College, 1967. Thesis: English.
Brewer, Pat B. Females, Fiction and the Negro Image: Attitudes
   Toward the Negro as Reflected in the Work of Southern Female
   Writers of Fiction. Vanderbilt Univ., 1969. Thesis: English.
   [Ellen Glasgow, Caroline Gordon, Carson McCullers, Katherine
   Anne Porter, Elizabeth Madox Roberts, and Eudora Welty]
Brice, Ashbel G. Novels Dealing with the South, 1865-1900. Duke
   Univ., 1939. Dissertation: English.
Bridges, Thomas W., Jr. New Orleans: A Literary History.
   Vanderbilt Univ., 1931. Thesis: English.
Brooks, John J.B. A Survey of Negro Literature in Georgia. Univ.
   of Georgia, 1934. Thesis: English. [Caroline Bagley,
   Edward Randolph Carter, Miles Mark Fisher, Thomas Jefferson
   Flanagan, Judea C. Jackson Harris, William H. Heard, John
   Wesley Holloway, Georgia Douglas Johnson, Charles Henry
   Phillips, John Wesley Wood, Richard Robert Wright, Sr., and
   Richard Wright]
Brown, Dorothy W. The Negro Problem in the Fiction of Thomas
   Nelson Page, Joel Chandler Harris, and George Washington
   Cable: 1880-1900. Texas Christian Univ., 1950. Thesis:
   English.
Brown, Ruth B. Arkansas as a Literary Background. Southern
   Methodist Univ., 1927. Thesis: English. [Authors who have
   used Arkansas as a literary background]
Brown, Sara M. The Plantation Negro in Southern Literature:
   Symbol for the Perpetuation of a Tradition. Univ. of
   Cincinnati, 1948. Thesis: English. [James Lane Allen,
   Sherwood Bonner, G.W. Cable, Kate Chopin, Harry Stillwell
   Edwards, Ellen Glasgow, Armistead C. Gordon, J.C. Harris,
   Mary Johnston, J.P. Kennedy, Grace E. King, Margaret

Mitchell, T.N. Page, William A. Percy, Irwin Russell,
W.G. Simms, Francis Hopkinson Smith, and Howard Weeden]

Browne, Margaret A. Southern Reactions to *Uncle Tom's Cabin*.
Duke Univ., 1946. Thesis: History. [Sources for this study
are magazines, newspapers, published diaries, travel books,
and fiction. Mary H. Eastman, Caroline Lee Hentz, and
Mrs. Henry R. Schoolcraft, among others, are included in the
discussion]

Browning, Sr. M.C. A Concordance to the Poetry of Fr. Tabb, and
a Comparative Study of the Vocabulary of Poe and Tabb.
Catholic Univ., 1946. Thesis: English.

Buchanan, Jane B. Violence in Two Keys: Gothicism in the Works
of Carson McCullers and William Faulkner. Univ. of Akron,
1967. Thesis: English.

Budge, Glee I. The South as Reflected in Certain Selected
Representative Novels Published between 1830 and 1935.
Kansas State Teachers College, 1938. Thesis: English.
[G.W. Cable, John Esten Cooke, Charles E. Craddock, Thomas
Dixon, William Faulkner, Ellen Glasgow, DuBose Heyward,
Mary Johnston, J.P. Kennedy, T.N. Page, Julia Peterkin,
Elizabeth Madox Roberts, and T.S. Stribling]

Burckhalter, Elizabeth. The Negro in Eastern South Carolina
Fiction. Univ. of Virginia, 1927. Thesis: English.
[DuBose Heyward, Julia Peterkin, and W.G. Simms]

Bush, Robert B. Louisiana Prose Fiction, 1870-1900. State Univ.
of Iowa, 1957. Dissertation: English. [G.W. Cable, Grace
King, Lafcadio Hearn, Kate Chopin, and Ruth McEnery Stuart]

Cain, Belva. Social Attitudes of the Pioneers as They Are
Reflected in the Literature of the Southwest. West Texas
State Univ., 1939. Thesis: English. [Edwin Lanham,
O. Henry, and Dorothy Scarborough]

Callahan, Sr. M.G. The Literature of Travel in Texas, 1803-1846:
An Analysis of Ideas and Attitudes. Univ. of Texas (Austin),
1945. Dissertation: English.

Callan, Mamie A. The Spanish Influence on Life and Literature of
Texas. East Texas State Univ., 1957. Thesis: English.

Cambron, Roga. Five Texas Novelists. East Texas State Univ.,
1941. Thesis: English. [J. Frank Dobie, Donald Joseph,
Norma Patterson, Dorothy Scarborough, and John William
Thomason]

Carageorge, Ted. An Evaluation of Hoke Smith and Thomas E. Watson
as Georgia Reformers. Univ. of Georgia, 1963. Dissertation:
History.

Cardwell, Frances L. A Comparison of the Old and the New Negro in
Southern Literature. Univ. of South Carolina, 1937. Thesis:
English.

Carnley, J.A., Jr. Alabama Writers Born Since 1850. Auburn Univ.,
1933. Thesis: English. [Includes a chapter each on John
William Abercrombe, Charles Minnigerode Beckwith, Eugene
DuBose Bondurant, William Garrott Brown, Thomas Clanton
Calloway, Oliver Cromwell Carmichael, Katherine Hopkins
Chapman, Kate Upson Clark, Charles Wallace Collins, Bolling
Hall Crenshaw, William Watson Davis, George Hutcheson Denny,
James Edgar Dillard, Horace Mellard DuBose, Joel Campbell
Dubose, Benjamin Minge Duggar, John Frederick Duggar, Mary

McNeil Fenollosa, Walter Lynwood Fleming, Martha Sawyer
Gielow, Philip Thomas Hale, Peter Joseph Hamilton, Gerrard
Harris, Belle Richardson Harrison, Mary Johnston, Helen Adams
Keller, Cincinnatus Decatur Killebrew, Robert Loveman, Anne
Bozeman Lyon, Thomas Chalmers McCorvey, Kate Slaughter
McKinney, John Matthews Manly, Patrick Hues Mell, Jr.,
Wightman Fletcher Melton, Emerson R. Miller, Andrew Philip
Montague, Albert Burton Moore, John Trotwood More, Ella
Lowery Moseley, Robert Russa Moton, Edgar Gardiner Murphy,
Herman Clarence Nixon, Charles J. O'Malley, Clarence Owsley,
Marie Bankhead Owen, Thomas McAdory Owen, Leonidas Warren
Payne, Jr., Samuel Minturn Peck, Maia Pettus, Amélie Rives,
Thaddeus Luther Rose, Charles Hunter Ross, William Berney
Saffold, John Richard Sampey, William Oscar Scroggs, Hudson
Strode, Mifflin Wyatt Swartz, Hannis Taylor, Julia Strudwick
Tutwiler, Jehu Wellington Vandiver, John Henry Wallace, Jr.,
Lollie Belle Wylie, Booker Taliaferro Washington, and Martha
Young]

Carson, Mary B. Reconstruction as Viewed through the Southern Novel.
Univ. of Georgia, 1937. Thesis: English. [Thomas Dixon,
J.C. Harris, Margaret Mitchell, and T.N. Page]

Cater, Althea. Social Attitudes in Five Contemporary Southern
Novelists: Erskine Caldwell, William Faulkner, Ellen
Glasgow, Caroline Gordon, and T.S. Stribling. Univ. of
Michigan, 1945. Dissertation: English.

Caulfield, Ruby V.A. The French Literature of Louisiana. Columbia
Univ., 1929. Dissertation: English.

Chisman, Margaret S. Literature and the Drama in Memphis,
Tennessee, to 1860. Duke Univ., 1942. Thesis: English.

Christie, Annie M. Literary Criticism in the Old South. Columbia
Univ., 1919. Thesis: English.

Cioffari, Philip E. Major Themes in Southern Fiction Since World
War II. New York Univ., 1967. Dissertation: English.
[Truman Capote, William Humphrey, Carson McCullers, Flannery
O'Connor, William Styron, and Robert Penn Warren]

Clagett, Frank M. Tradition and Regionalism in the Works of
John Crowe Ransom and Allen Tate. Univ. of Maryland, 1956.
Thesis: English.

Clapp, Nell W. New Orleans in American Fiction. Univ. of South
Carolina, 1931. Thesis: English.

Clapp, Theodasia. American Folk Drama of the South. Boston Univ.,
1934. Thesis: English. [Paul Green, Dorothy and DuBose
Heyward, Hatcher Hughes, and Lula Vollmer]

Clark, Frances E. The New South in Contemporary Fiction (1920-
1940). Howard Univ., 1946. Thesis: English. [Erskine
Caldwell, Ellen Glasgow, Paul Green, Grace Lumpkin, Elizabeth
Madox Roberts, Lyle Saxon, Dorothy Scarborough, T.S.
Stribling, Walter White, and Stark Young]

Clary, Mary T. Political Pamphleteers of Pre-Revolutionary
Virginia, 1750-1775. Univ. of Richmond, 1944. Thesis:
English. [Richard Bland, John Camm, Landon Carter, Thomas
Jefferson, Arthur Lee, Robert Carter Nicholas, John Randolph,
and Peyton Randolph]

Coale, Samuel C. The Role of the South in the Fiction of William Faulkner, Carson McCullers, Flannery O'Connor and William Styron. Brown Univ., 1970. Dissertation: American Civilization.

Coldwell, Frances. A Study of the Conscious Poetry of the Cattle Culture of the Southwest with a Selected Anthology. Univ. of Texas (Austin), 1951. Thesis: English.

Coleman, Wade H., Jr. Verse Writing in Alabama. Univ. of Alabama, 1927. Thesis: English. [Discussion of over seventy Alabama verse writers]

Collins, Carvel E. The Literary Tradition of the Southern Mountaineer, 1824-1900. Univ. of Chicago, 1944. Dissertation: English.

Contoski, Victor J. The Southern Aristocratic Lover: Symbol of National Unity, 1865-1885. Univ. of Wisconsin, 1969. Dissertation: English. [G.W. Cable, William A. Caruthers, John Esten Cook, Sara Josepha Hale, Caroline Lee Hentz, J.P. Kennedy, Mrs. E.D.E.N. Southworth, and Albion W. Tourgée]

Cook, Virginia L. Southerners Discover the South: The Depression and the Non-Fictional Literature of Self-Discovery. Univ. of Virginia, 1968. Thesis: History.

Cowan, Louise S. The Fugitives: A Critical History. Vanderbilt Univ., 1953. Dissertation: English.

Cowell, M. The War of the Revolution in the South as Depicted in Historical Fiction. Univ. of Toledo, 1939. Thesis: English. [John Esten Cooke, John Fox, Jr., and W.G. Simms]

Cox, George W. The Negro and the Writers of the Southern Short Story. Univ. of South Carolina, 1918. Thesis: English.

Cox, H.M., Jr. The Charleston Poetic Renascence, 1920-1930. Univ. of Pennsylvania, 1958. Dissertation: English. [Discusses Poetry Society of South Carolina, calling "Poetry South," by Hervey Allen and DuBose Heyward, the "general manifesto of this regional renascence"; other writers discussed are Helen Von Kolnitz Heyer, Josephine Pinckney, Beatrice Witte Ravenal, Katherhine D.M. Simons, and Granville P. Smith]

Craig, Marjorie. Survivals of the Chivalric Tournament in Southern Life and Literature. Univ. of North Carolina (Chapel Hill), 1935. Thesis: English.

Crawford, Marcia. Versions of Southern Womanhood in the Writings of Tennessee Williams and William Faulkner. Louisiana State Univ., 1957. Thesis: English.

Crews, J.C. The Treatment of Social Problems in Recent Southern Literature. Baylor Univ., 1944. Thesis: Sociology. [Erskine Caldwell, Donald Davidson, William Faulkner, Paul Green, George Milburn, John Crowe Ransom, Marjorie Kinnan Rawlings, Jesse Stuart, Allen Tate, Thomas Wolfe, and Richard Wright]

Croft, Joseph E. "Faulknerian" Themes in James Lane Allen. Suggestions for a Re-Examination of the Southern Literary Renaissance. Univ. of Virginia, 1964. Thesis: English.

Crowell, Lloyd T., Jr. The Agrarian Criticism of the New South. Vanderbilt Univ., 1953. Thesis: English.

Cunningham, Emma R. The Attitude in Recent Southern Fiction Toward
     the Negro: Tennessee. Atlanta Univ., 1946. Thesis: English.
     [John Porter Fort, Caroline Gordon, and T.S. Stribling]
Curtis, Jeanne C. Interpreters of the Charleston Country [South
     Carolina]. Univ. of Missouri, 1939. Thesis: English.
     [Ambrose Elliott Gonzales, Paul H. Hayne, DuBose Heyward,
     Julia Peterkin, W.G. Simms, and Henry Timrod]
Daniel, Mary M. A Literary History of Dallas County [Texas]. East
     Texas State Univ., 1950. Thesis: English.
Darwin, Patsy E. The Theory of the Creative Personality and Its
     Application to Three Georgia Women Journalists--Lollie Belle
     Wylie, Emily Woodward, and Margaret Mitchell. Univ. of
     Georgia, 1965. Thesis: English. [One chapter on Margaret
     Mitchell's *Gone With the Wind*]
Davenport, F.G., Jr. The Myth of Southern History--Twentieth
     Century Variations. Univ. of Minnesota, 1967. Dissertation:
     English. [Discusses five works: *Leopard's Spots*, *I'll Take
     My Stand*, *Absalom, Absalom!*, *All the King's Men*, and
     Brother to Dragons]
Davis, Maggie R. The Literary South, 1888-1893. George Peabody
     College, 1935. Thesis: English.
Day, James M. The Writing and Literature of the Texas Mier
     Expedition, 1842-1844. Baylor Univ., 1967. Dissertation:
     English. [John Alexander, Rufus Alexander, Thomas W. Bell,
     Israel Canfield, Willis Copeland, George B. Erath, James
     Glassrock, Thomas Jefferson Green, John Christopher Columbus
     Hill, George Lord, Joseph D. McCutchan, William Preston
     Stapp, George Washington Trahern, William A.A. Wallace;
     also discusses *Texas Monument*, the newspaper of the expedition]
De Carion, Flavia J. Some Florida Proverbs and Their Literary
     Background. Univ. of Florida, 1948. Thesis: English.
Dew, Joanna. The Slavery Problem in Southern Fiction Prior to
     1860. Duke Univ., 1941. Thesis: History. [Summarizes
     the treatment of Negro slavery in Southern novels and
     humorous sketches written before 1860]
Dillard, Irene. A History of Literature in South Carolina. Univ.
     of North Carolina (Chapel Hill), 1924. Dissertation:
     English.
Dillon, Sr. Mary I., S.S.N.D. The Influence of the South on
     American Fiction, 1870-1921. Fordham Univ., 1922. Disser-
     tation: English.
Dober, Virginia D. Analysis of the Social Life and Customs of
     the Southern Appalachians as Reflected in Selected Children's
     Books. Univ. of North Carolina (Chapel Hill), 1956. Thesis:
     Library Science.
Dodson, Leslie W. The Mississippi Sharecropper in Fact and Fiction.
     Mississippi State Univ., 1952. Thesis: History.
Don Carolos, Louisa C. Writers of Tennessee. Univ. of Kansas,
     1926. Thesis: English.
Donley, Beatrice L. Mississippi: The Matrix of Creative Writers:
     An Investigation of Causes. Mississippi College, 1964.
     Thesis: English.
Douglas, Elaine E. The Treatment of the Negro in the Novels of
     Louisiana, 1920-1940. Atlanta Univ., 1940. Thesis: English.
     [Hamilton Basso, Barry Benefield, Roark Bradford, Elma

Godchaux, Grace Elizabeth King, Edwin P. O'Donnell, and
Lyle Saxon]

Douglas, Robert, Jr. The Native Drama of the Carolina Playmakers.
Georgetown Univ., 1933. Thesis: Literature.

Dring, Lovilla R. Literary Backgrounds of the Santa Fe Trail.
Univ. of New Mexico, 1934. Thesis: English. [Philip
St. George Cooke and James O. Pattie]

Duck, George F. The Modern Southern Short Story: Its Suitability
for the Senior High School English Curriculum. Auburn Univ.,
1965. Thesis: Education.

Duehring, Frederica E. A Study of the Memoirs Published between
1865 and 1915 Concerning Civilian Life in Virginia. Duke
Univ., 1939. Thesis: History. [Myrta Lockett Avary,
Letitia M. Burwell, John Herbert Claiborne, T.C. DeLeon,
Thomas Dixon, John Goode, Belle Boyd Hardinge, Constance
Cary Harrison, William E. Hatcher, Alexander Hunter,
Jeremiah Bell Jeter, J.B. Jones, Judith W. Brockenbrough
McGuire, Richard McIlwaine, John E. Massey, Beverley B.
Munford, Charles T. O'Ferrall, Duval Porter, Sarah Agnes
Pryor, Mrs. Sallie A. Brock Putnam, William L. Royall, and
Mary Virginia Terhune]

Dunn, Velmarae. A Study of the Louisiana Acadians as They Are
Reflected in the Fiction of Louisiana. Univ. of Oklahoma,
1937. Thesis: English. [G.W. Cable]

Duvall, Severn P.C., Jr. The Legend of the South and Southern
Historical Fiction, 1820-1861. Princeton Univ., 1955.
Dissertation: English. [William A. Caruthers, J.P.
Kennedy, and W.G. Simms]

Dyson, Jean M. A Comparative Study of the Characters in Cat on
a Hot Tin Roof and Absalom, Absalom! Virginia State College,
1968. Thesis: English.

Edwards, Dorothy E. The Dialect of the Southern Highlander as
Recorded in North Carolina Novels. Univ. of Rochester,
1935. Thesis: English. [Olive Dargan, Paul Green, and
DuBose Heyward]

Edwards, Thomas D. A Critical Study of the Literature Portraying
the Mountain Folk of Eastern Kentucky and Tennessee. Univ.
of Southern California, 1939. Thesis: English.

Elliot, Mary A. The Southern Fugitives: Their Opposition to the
Mid-Western School of Whitmanesque Poetry. Univ. of
Maryland, 1962. Thesis: English.

England, Kenneth. The Decline of the Southern Gentleman Character
as He is Illustrated in Certain Novels by Present-Day
Southern Novelists. Vanderbilt Univ., 1957. Dissertation:
English. [J.B. Cabell, William Faulkner, Ellen Glasgow,
Robert Penn Warren, and Stark Young]

English, Julia B. The Southern Aristocrat in Contemporary Fiction
about the Civil War. Howard Univ., 1939. Thesis: English.
[William Faulkner, Caroline Gordon, DuBose Heyward, Margaret
Mitchell, T.S. Stribling, and Stark Young]

Evans, George P. Literary Taste in Virginia from 1825 to 1860.
Univ. of Chicago, 1923. Thesis: English.

Fagan, Joe P. The Spirit of Home in the Literature of the Lower
South. Univ. of Missouri, 1917. Thesis: English. [Harry
Stillwell Edwards, Will N. Harben, Corra Harris, J.C. Harris,

Henry Rootes Jackson, Richard M. Johnston, Sidney Lanier,
A.B. Longstreet, and Irwin Russell]

Fagg, Max W. A Literary History of Collin County [Texas]. East
Texas State Univ., 1952. Thesis: English.

Faulk, John H., Jr. Ten Negro Sermons. Univ. of Texas (Austin),
1940. Thesis: English. [By Texas Negroes]

Faust, Katherine E. The Renaissance of Poetry in South Carolina.
Univ. of South Carolina, 1925. Thesis: English.

Ficklin, Kroes. An Anthology of the Civil War Soldier-Poets of
the South (three volumes). George Washington Univ., 1930.
Thesis: English.

Finley, Katherine P. Mississippi Drama from 1870 to 1916: An
Exploration. Tulane Univ., 1964. Thesis: English.

Firmin, Suzanne. The Faulkners and the Southern Code of Honor.
Tulane Univ., 1961. Thesis: English.

Fletcher, Baylis J. A Study of Local Color in the Short Stories
of the South. Univ. of Texas (Austin), 1928. Thesis:
English.

Fletcher, Marie. The Southern Heroine in the Fiction of Repre-
sentative Southern Women Writers, 1850-1960. Louisiana State
Univ., 1962. Dissertation: English. [Kate Chopin, Charles E.
Craddock, Eliza Dupuy, Caroline Gordon, Shirley Ann Grau,
Caroline Lee Hentz, Mary Jane Holmes, Grace King, Katherine
Anne Porter, Elizabeth M. Roberts, Mrs. E.D.E.N. Southworth,
Eudora Welty, and Augusta Evans Wilson]

Flournoy, Fitzgerald. Distinctive Characteristics of Southern
Poetry. Washington and Lee Univ., 1922. Thesis: English.
[Includes John Henry Boner, Madison Cawein, Marguerite E.
Easter, Harry Stillwell Edwards, Stephen Foster, Paul H.
Hayne, William Hamilton Hayne, Sidney Lanier, Walter Malone,
Gordon McCabe, Samuel Minturn Peck, Edward Coote Pinkney,
E.A. Poe, Cale Young Rice, W.G. Simms, Frank L. Stanton,
John Bannister Tabb, Henry Timrod, James Morris Thompson,
and Richard Henry Wilde]

Fones, Bernice W. The Development of Texas Literature. Idaho
State Univ., 1959. Thesis: Education.

Fountain, Alvin M. Charleston, South Carolina, as a Literary
Center before the Civil War. Columbia Univ., 1930. Thesis:
English.

Fowler, Bill F. The Treatment of Religion in the Humor of the
Old Southwest. Univ. of Texas (Austin), 1966. Thesis:
English.

Francis, Mattie B.C. Poetry in Texas: Yesterday and Today.
Southwest Texas State Univ., 1957. Thesis: English.

Fraser, Nellie F. A Survey of Mississippi Fiction from 1920
through 1941. George Peabody College, 1942. Thesis:
English.

Freedman, Aviva. The Critic as Artist: A Study of the Critical
and Creative Work of John Ransom, Allen Tate and Robert Penn
Warren. Montreal, 1968. Dissertation: English.

Freeman, Bernice. Georgia Short Stories, Chiefly Contemporary.
Columbia Teachers College, 1952. Dissertation: English.

Freund, Sr. M.A., S.S.N.D. Metrical Theories of Poe and Lanier:
A Comparative Study. Loyola Univ. (Chicago), 1937. Thesis:
English.

Gallier, William H. The Social Ideas of the Southern Agrarians.
    Univ. of North Carolina (Chapel Hill), 1963. Thesis:
    History. [Concentrates on Donald Davidson, John Crowe
    Ransom, Allen Tate, and Robert Penn Warren]
Gamble, Lottie P. A History of the Literature of Alabama to
    1870 with Bibliography. Univ. of Alabama, 1937. Thesis:
    English.
Garner, Leona C. A Study of Local Color with Emphasis on Selected
    Works of Three Georgia Authors. Univ. of Georgia, 1965.
    Thesis: English.
Garrett, Hattie C. Louisiana Romance in Literature. Louisiana,
    1929. Thesis: English. [Roark Bradford, G.W. Cable, Kate
    Chopin, Lafcadio Hearn, Grace King, Desiree Martin, Julia
    Peterkin, and Opie Read]
Garrett, Martha L. Short Stories and Novelettes Written in French
    by Louisiana Authors. Louisiana State Univ., 1939. Thesis:
    Romance Languages. [Fernand Armant, Eugene Berjot, Louis-
    Placide Canonge, Edward Dessommes, Louise Augustin Fortier,
    Sidonie De la Houssaye, Alfred Mercier, and François
    Tujague]
Gatlin, Jesse C., Jr. A Comparison of the Returned Veteran Theme
    in William Gilmore Simms' *Woodcraft* and William Faulkner's
    Soldier's Pay. Univ. of North Carolina (Chapel Hill), 1957.
    Thesis: English.
Gerbetz, Elizabeth S. The Small Southern Town in Modern Fiction.
    East Texas State Univ., 1952. Thesis: English.
Gerke, Sr. M.A. New Orleans in Southern Fiction. Univ. of Notre
    Dame, 1935. Thesis: English. [G.W. Cable, Kate Chopin,
    Grace King, and Ruth McEnery Stuart]
Gilbert, Robert B. Attitudes Toward the Negro in Southern Social
    Studies and Novels: 1932-1952. Vanderbilt Univ., 1953.
    Dissertation: English. [Erskine Caldwell, Brainard Cheney,
    William Faulkner, Ellen Glasgow, Carson McCullers, and T.S.
    Stribling]
Girod, John G. "The Redneck": A Study of the Use of the Huey
    Long Story in Five American Novels. Louisiana State Univ.,
    1958. Thesis: English.
Givens, Bessie. A Literary History of Mississippi. Vanderbilt
    Univ., 1932. Thesis: English. [Joseph Baldwin, Sherwood
    Bonner, Joseph Cobb, Joseph Holt Ingraham, and Irwin
    Russell]
Goforth, Juanita. Evolution of the Negro Character in Fiction by
    Six Representative Southern White Writers: Kennedy, Simms,
    Page, Harris, Caldwell, Faulkner. East Tennessee State Univ.,
    1965. Thesis: English.
Gooch, Margaret M. Point of View and the Frontier Spirit in the
    Old Southwestern Tales of Baldwin, Longstreet, Hooper, and
    G.W. Harris. Univ. of North Carolina (Chapel Hill), 1968.
    Dissertation: English.
Goode, Mary L. The Creole: A Type in Literature. Univ. of
    South Carolina, 1922. Thesis: English.
Goodin, Gayle. The Protagonist in the Modern Georgia Novel.
    Univ. of Mississippi, 1966. Thesis: English. [Agnes
    Cochran Bramlett, Erskine Caldwell, Carson McCullers,
    Margaret Mitchell, and Flannery O'Connor]

Gordon, Armistead C., Jr. Virginian Writers of Fugitive Verse.
Univ. of Virginia, 1921. Dissertation: English. [Discusses
over fifty poets]

Gossett, Louise Y. Violence in Recent Southern Fiction. Duke
Univ., 1961. Dissertation: English. [Includes Erskine
Cadlwell, Truman Capote, William Faulkner, Shirley Ann Grau,
William Goyen, Carson McCullers, Flannery O'Connor, William
Styron, Peter Taylor, Robert Penn Warren, Eudora Welty,
Tennessee Williams, and Thomas Wolfe]

Govier, Robert A. German Poetry Written in New Braunfels, Texas.
Univ. of Texas (Austin), 1962. Thesis: German.

Gower, Herschel. Agrarianism and Religion. Vanderbilt Univ.,
1952. Thesis: English. [Concentrates on Donald Davidson,
Andrew Lytle, Frank L. Owsley, John Crowe Ransom, and
Allen Tate]

Grammor, Norma R. Writings by Women in Texas Before 1865. Texas
Christian Univ., 1937. Thesis: English. [Mary Austin
Holley, Mathilda Houston, Cora Montgomery, Melinda Rankin,
Augusta Evans Wilson, and Terese Griffin Viele]

Gray, Virginia G. The Southern Lady of the Forties. Univ. of
Wisconsin, 1925. Thesis: History. [As depicted in fiction
written by Southern women in the 1840's: Maria Jane
McIntosh, Mary Milward, Mrs. E.D.E.N. Southworth, and Susan
Walker]

Green, Homer. Plot Elements of the Southern Proletarian Novel of
the 1930's. Univ. of Mississippi, 1948. Thesis: English.

Gregory, Mary J. A Literary History of Camp County [Texas]. East
Texas State Univ., 1949. Thesis: English.

Griffin, Constance F. A Literary History of Rains County [Texas].
East Texas State Univ., 1952. Thesis: English.

Grise, George. The People of Kentucky as Pictured by American
Novelists. George Peabody College, 1950. Dissertation:
English.

Grubb, Sandra S. A Study of the Relationships in the Fiction of
Carson McCullers and Truman Capote. Kansas State Univ.,
1963. Thesis: Education.

Hager, Esther C. Interpreters of the Mississippi: A Study in
American Regionalism. Univ. of Missouri, 1932. Thesis:
English. [Roark Bradford, Ben Lucien Burman, G.W. Cable,
John Gould Fletcher, Grace Elizabeth King, W.G. Simms, and
Ruth McEnery Stuart]

Hagler, Dorse H. The Agrarian Theme in Southern History to 1860.
Univ. of Missouri, 1968. Dissertation: History. [J.D.
DeBow, George Fitzhugh, Thomas Jefferson, W.G. Simms, and
Edmund Ruflin]

Haley, Margaret C. Texas as a Background in Literature. Southern
Methodist Univ., 1925. Thesis: English. [A study of Texas
backgrounds in literature, especially in fiction, to discover
just how Texas life, history, and legend have been employed
by American writers]

Hall, Lillie M. The Kentucky Mountaineer as a Character in
Fiction. Univ. of South Carolina, 1928. Thesis: English.

Hall, Louise H. Literary Battle Between George W. Cable and Grace
King. Univ. of Kansas, 1927. Thesis: English.

Hall, Nell. The History of Harriet A. Ames during the Early Days of Texas. East Texas State Univ., 1941. Thesis: English. [Annotation of a manuscript concerned with Ames' life in early Texas]

Hall, Wade H. A Study of Southern Humor: 1865-1913. Univ. of Illinois, 1961. Dissertation: English. [Charles E. Craddock, Anne Virginia Culbertson, Harry Stillwell Edwards, J.C. Harris, John Trotwood Moore, and Ruth McEnery Stuart]

Hamer, Marcelle L. Anecdotal Elements in Southwestern Literature. Univ. of Texas (Austin), 1939. Thesis: English.

Haniford, C.M. The Treatment of the Creoles in the Fiction of George Washington Cable, Grace Elizabeth King, and Kate Chopin. Univ. of North Carolina (Chapel Hill), 1945. Thesis: English.

Harrington, Catherine S. Southern Fiction and the Quest for Identity. Univ. of Washington, 1963. Dissertation: English. [William Faulkner, Katherine Anne Porter, Peter Taylor, Robert Penn Warren, and Eudora Welty]

Harris, Isabella D. The Southern Mountaineer in American Fiction, 1824-1910. Duke Univ., 1948. Dissertation: English. [Charles E. Craddock, John Fox, Jr., Will N. Harben, and George Tucker]

Harrison, Louis H. The Influence of George Washington Harris in the Writings of Mark Twain. Univ. of Texas (Austin), 1963. Thesis: English.

Harrison, Marion C. Social Types in Southern Prose Fiction. Univ. of Virginia, 1921. Dissertation: English. [John Esten Cooke, Charles E. Craddock, Ellen Glasgow, Will N. Harben, T.N. Page, E.A. Poe, and W.G. Simms]

Hart, Bertha S. Introduction to Georgia Literature. Mercer Univ., 1927. Thesis: English.

Haskell, Ann S. The Representation of Gullah-Influenced Dialect in Twentieth Century South Carolina Prose: 1922-30. Univ. of Pennsylvania, 1964. Dissertation: Linguistics. [E.L.C. Adams, Ambrose Gonzales, Julia Peterkin, Gertrude Shelby, Samuel Stoney, and Marcellus S. Whaley]

Haskett, Deanie B. An Anthology of North Carolina Poetry. East Carolina Univ., 1933. Thesis: English.

Hathaway, Marlene C. They Take Their Stand: Five Themes in Modern Southern Fiction. Univ. of Akron, 1965. Thesis: English.

Hayes, Ada H. Texas Humor, 1830-1900. Southern Methodist Univ., 1940. Thesis: English. [John Duval, Samuel Hammett, J. Armory Knox, O. Henry, and Alex E. Sweet]

Haywood, Violet G. The Southern Gentleman in Negro American Fiction. Fisk Univ., 1937. Thesis: English. [Arna Bontemps, William Wells Brown, Charles W. Chesnutt, W.E.B. DuBois, Zora Neale Hurston, James Weldon Johnson, and Walter White]

Heatley, Katherine S. Contemporary Women Poets of Texas. North Texas State Univ., 1942. Thesis: English. [Karle Wilson Baker,. Grace Noll Crowell, Margaret Houston, Vaida Stewart Montgomery, Berta Hart Nance, Lexie Dean Robertson, and Fay McCormick Yauger]

Hebron, Mary D. Sir Walter Scott in New Orleans, 1833-1850.
Tulane Univ., 1940. Thesis: English.

Henderson, Dora M. The Attitudes of Recent Mississippi Novelists
toward Negroes, 1920 to 1946. Atlanta Univ., 1947. Thesis:
English. [John Faulkner, William Faulkner, Edward Kimbrough,
James Street, Alice Walworth, and Stark Young]

Hendrix, Lucille D. The Nashville Agrarians. East Texas State
Univ., 1955. Thesis: English. [Concentrates on Donald
Davidson, John Gould Fletcher, Henry B. Kline, Lyle Hicks
Lanier, Andrew Lytle, Herman Clarence Nixon, Frank L. Owsley,
John Crowe Ransom, Allen Tate, John D. Wade, Robert Penn
Warren, and Stark Young]

Hess, Bertha R. Backwoods Humor of the South. Auburn Univ., 1933.
Thesis: English. [Period emphasized is 1850-1860; authors
include Joseph Glover Baldwin, Charles M. Bird, Ernest
Brackenridge, William Byrd, Maristan Chapman, Charles E.
Craddock, David Crockett, Joel Campbell Dubose, Lucy Furman,
Philip Henry Gosse, G.W. Harris, Lucy Lockwood Hazard,
J.J. Hooper, Richard M. Johnston, J.P. Kennedy, Edmund J.
Kirk, A.B. Longstreet, Fritz L. Longstreet, S.A. Link,
E.T. Mason, Franklin J. Meine, Edwin Mims, Marie Bankhead
Owen, Constance Rourke, W.G. Simms, and Mark Twain]

Hestir, Bluford B. The Urges to a Texas Literature, 1526-1716.
Univ. of Texas (Austin), 1947. Thesis: English.

Herrington, Linwood E. Southern Literary Criticism of Four
Nineteenth Century English Novelists. Univ. of Georgia,
1937. Thesis: English. [Criticism of Bulwer-Lytton, Dickens,
Disraeli, and Thackeray which appeared primarily in the
Southern Literary Messenger]

Hicks, Helena. Recent Literature on Legendary Louisiana. Southern
Methodist Univ., 1952. Thesis: English.

Hierth, Harrison E. Ellen Glasgow's Ideal of The Lady with Some
Contrasts in Sidney Lanier, George Washington Cable, and
Mark Twain. Univ. of Wisconsin, 1956. Dissertation:
English.

Hinton, M.M. Southern Regional Drama, 1918-1933: A Study of the
Local and Universal Aspects of the Southern Mountain and
Farm Plays. Smith College, 1934. Thesis: English.

Hirsch, Leota K. The Literary Milieu in the Seventeenth Century
South. Univ. of Minnesota, 1967. Dissertation: English.

Holbrook, Nancy L.N. Violence and Order in the Short Stories of
Eudora Welty, Flannery O'Connor, and Peter Taylor. Vanderbilt
Univ., 1961. Thesis: English.

Holland, Sallie W. South Carolina Life Prior to 1850 as Portrayed
in Fiction. Columbia Univ., 1926. Thesis: English.
[A.B. Longstreet and W.G. Simms]

Hollins, Mary P. A Comparative Study of the Humor of Mark Twain
and Will Rogers. East Texas State Univ., 1950. Thesis:
English.

Hopkins, Anne P. Virginia Life in Fiction, 1861-1865. Duke
Univ., 1939. Thesis: English. [John Esten Cooke,
Clifford Dowdey, Ellen Glasgow, Mrs. Burton Harrison, Mary
Johnston, and T.N. Page]

Horne, Eunice A. Early Florida in Historical Fiction. Univ. of
Florida, 1947. Thesis: English. [Harris Dickson, George
Fort Gibbs, Lafayette McLaws, and W.G. Simms]

Howard, William. Three Nineteenth Century Georgia Humorists: A
Comparative Study of the Writings of Augustus Baldwin
Longstreet, William Tappan Thompson, and Richard Malcolm
Johnston. Auburn Univ., 1950. Thesis: English.

Hoyt, Lucy R. Poetry and Fiction in South Carolina since 1890.
Univ. of South Carolina, 1923. Thesis: English.

Hubbell, Jay B. Virginia Life in Fiction. Columbia Univ., 1922.
Dissertation: English.

Huddleston, Josephine A. The Small Town in Southern Fiction.
Univ. of Georgia, 1942. Thesis: English. [Joseph G.
Baldwin, G.W. Cable, Irvin S. Cobb, Ellis M. Coulter,
Charles E. Craddock, Ellen Glasgow, J.C. Harris, Thornwell
Jacobs, Richard M. Johnston, J.P. Kennedy, T.W. Lane,
A.B. Longstreet, T.N. Page, Elizabeth Madox Roberts,
W.G. Simms, Mary N. Stanard, and T.S. Stribling]

Hudson, Florence. Two Interpreters of the Creole Country: A
Comparison of the Materials and Methods of George Washington
Cable and Grace Elizabeth King. Univ. of Missouri, 1947.
Thesis: English.

Hughey, Annie C. The Treatment of the Negro in South Carolina
Fiction. Univ. of South Carolina, 1933. Thesis: English.

Inteso, Maxine M. The Development of the Legendary Texan in Fact
and Fiction. East Texas State Univ., 1967. Thesis: English.

Irvine, Kate T. The Beauchamp Tragedy in American Fiction. Univ.
of Kentucky, 1932. Thesis: English. [Emphasizes W.G. Simms]

Jablonsky, Roberta N. The Kentucky Tragedy in 19th Century
American Fictive Literature. The City College of New York,
1966. Thesis: English.

Jacobi, Gertrude F. Minor Poets of South Carolina. Univ. of
Florida, 1937. Thesis: English. [Discusses or mentions
111 South Carolina poets of the eighteenth, nineteenth and
twentieth centuries]

Jennings, Buford. Contemporary Alabama Writers. Auburn Univ.,
1931. Thesis: English. [Arthur Kellog Akers, Rufus Olin
Ansley, Frank Willis Barnett, Albert Richmond Bond, Peter
Alexander Brannon, Bozeman Bulger, James Saxon Childers,
Octavus Roy Cohen, Mary Chase Cornelius, Erwin Craighead,
Richard Henry Crossfield, Mercy Bradshaw Darnall, Francois
Ludgere Diard, Frances Ruffin Durham, Scottie McKenzie
Frasier, Franklin Potts Glass, James Hope Glennon, John
Temple Graves II, Frances Nimmo Green, Grover Cleveland Hall,
May Harris, Annie May Burton Hollingsworth, Robert Macon
Hunter, Morgan Davis Jones, Walter Burgwyn Jones, Joseph M.
Kalin, Lawrence Lee, Alice Alison Lyde, Maud McKnight Lindsay,
John Emery McLean, Mildred Ann Martin, Pitt Lamar Matthews,
Sarah Powell Haardt Mencken, Nellie Kimball Murdoch, Frank
Lawrence Owsley, Kate Speake Penney, George Petrie, Lucille
Gill Price, Louise Crenshaw Ray, Margaret Ellen Henry Ruffin,
Martha Lyman Shillito, Brockenbrough Fitzhugh Smith, Edgar
Valentine Smith, Mary Eleanor Stewart, Oliver Day Street,
T.S. Stribling, Annie Southern Tardy, Willie Hughes Tarpley,
Howell Herbert Vines, Clement Richardson Wood]

Johnson, Alice V. A Critical Analysis of Negro Character in the
American Novel of the South, 1935-1940. Xavier Univ. (New
Orleans), 1943. Thesis: English. [Includes Roark
Bradford, Gwen Bristow, Elma Godchaux, DuBose Heyward,
Margaret Mitchell, Julia Peterkin, Lyle Saxon, and Stark
Young]
Johnson, Verna F. Texas Verse prior to 1880. Univ. of Texas
(Austin), 1936. Thesis: English.
Johnston, Mary L. The State of Literary Culture in Georgia before
1860. Mercer Univ., 1927. Thesis: English.
Jones, Dorothy W. Indebtedness of the Southern Novel to the
Waverley Novels. Southern Methodist Univ., 1939. Thesis:
English. [John Esten Cooke, Caroline Gordon, Mary Johnston,
J.P. Kennedy, Margaret Mitchell, T.N. Page, Francis Hopkinson
Smith, and Stark Young]
Jones, Frances E. The Background of the Louisiana Short Story.
Louisiana State Univ., 1936. Thesis: English. [Roark
Bradford, G.W. Cable, Ada Jack Carver, Kate Chopin, Mary
Evelyn Davis, Lavinia Egan, Alcée Fortier, Elma Godchaux,
Edith Ogden Harrison, Lafcadio Hearn, Grace King, Addie
McGrath Lee, Bartlett Napier, Col. James W. Nicholson,
E.P. O'Donnell, Lyle Saxon, Ruth McEnery Stuart, and Andrews
Wilkinson]
Jones, Lee C. Antebellum Humor in the Old Southwest (1830-1867)
as the Beginning of American Literary Realism and the
Humorous Era Which Produced Mark Twain. Brigham Young Univ.,
1963. Thesis: English.
Jones, Lewis P. Carolinians and Cubans: The Elliots and
Gonzales, Their Work and Their Writings. Univ. of North
Carolina (Chapel Hill), 1952. Dissertation: English.
[William Elliott and Ambrose Gonzales]
Jones, Sue B. Study of the Characters in the Stories of Middle
Georgia Writers. George Peabody College, 1933. Thesis:
English.
Julian, Grace L. Southern Novels, 1850-1855. A Study in Culture.
Tulane Univ., 1942. Thesis: English. [Caroline Lee Hentz
and Mrs. E.D.E.N. Southworth]
Jungling, Mathilde K. A Literary Sketch of Natchez, Mississippi.
Louisiana State Univ., 1939. Thesis: English.
Justice, Donald R. The Fugitive-Agrarian "Myth." Univ. of North
Carolina (Chapel Hill), 1947. Thesis: English.
Justus, James H. The Kentucky Tragedy in Simms and Warren: A
Study in Changing Milieux. Univ. of Tennessee, 1953. Thesis:
English.
Kane, Hope F. Colonial Promotion and Promotion Literature of
Carolina, 1660-1700. Brown Univ., 1930. Dissertation:
History.
Karanikas, Alexander. John Crowe Ransom and Allen Tate: A Study
of the Southern Agrarian Theory of Literature. Northwestern
Univ., 1953. Dissertation: English.
Kasten, Agnes M. Texas Travel Literature, 1830-1860. Univ. of
Texas (Austin), 1954. Thesis: English.

Kelleher, Sr. Mary A. A Survey of Virginia Poetry, 1607-1870. Fordham Univ., 1933. Thesis: English. [John Esten Cooke, Philip Pendleton Cooke, James Barron Hope, William Gordon McCabe, Margaret Junkin Preston, and John Reuben Thompson]

Kenney, Reginald A. Robert Burns and the Old South. College of William and Mary, 1935. Thesis: English.

Kerlin, Charles M., Jr. Life in Motion: Genteel and Vernacular Attitudes in the Works of the Southwestern American Humorists, Mark Twain and William Faulkner. Univ. of Colorado, 1968. Dissertation: English. [Includes, in addition to Faulkner and Twain, A.B. Longstreet, Joseph Glover Baldwin, Johnson J. Hooper, Thomas Bangs Thorpe, and G.W. Harris]

Kern, Mary K. The Poets of the Shenandoah Valley in the Nineteenth Century. Duke Univ., 1949. Thesis: English.

Key, Louise. Literary Productions in Alabama since the Civil War. Univ. of Alabama, 1924. Thesis: English.

Keye, Richard E., Jr. The Growth of Nationalistic Ideas in Southern Literature in the Last Quarter of the Nineteenth Century. Univ. of Mississippi, 1940. Thesis: English.

King, James K. George Washington Cable and Thomas Nelson Page: Two Literary Approaches to the New South. Univ. of Wisconsin, 1964. Dissertation: English. [A contrast of liberal and conservative attitudes toward Southern problems]

Knight, Donald R. Religion as a Subject of Southwestern Humor. Univ. of Tennessee, 1968. Thesis: English.

Knoth, Sibyl C. Civil War Poems by Confederate Women. George Peabody College, 1929. Thesis: English.

Lagysin, Carol A. A Comparative Analysis of the Lives and Writings of James Branch Cabell and Ellen Glasgow. Whittier College, 1970. Thesis: English.

LaMance, Ella B.P. The Poet Laureate Movement in Texas. Univ. of Texas (Austin), 1946. Thesis: English.

Lamb, Sara C. The Literary South: 1894-1900. George Peabody College, 1935. Thesis: English.

Lame, Gloria J. A Critical Analysis of Selected Plays of "The Shepherd of the Hills Country." Bowling Green State Univ., 1959. Thesis: Speech.

Lane, Donna D. A Comparative Study of the South as Represented in the Fiction of Stark Young and William Faulkner. Univ. of Mississippi, 1968. Thesis: English.

Lane, Helyn. The Creoles in American Literature. Birmingham-Southern College, 1937. Thesis: English. [G.W. Cable, Kate Chopin, Lafcadio Hearn, Grace King, and Lyle Saxon]

Lang, Herbert H. Nineteenth Century Historians of the Gulf States. Univ. of Texas (Austin), 1954. Dissertation: History. [Includes John Francis Hamtramck Claiborne, Charles Gayarré, John Wesley Monette, Albert James Pickett, and Henderson K. Yoakum]

Lanier, Emilio A. The Southern Gentleman in American Literature. Harvard Univ., 1932. Dissertation: English.

Lasswell, Margaret W. The Theme of Love and Separation in the Short Story Collections of Carson McCullers, Flannery O'Connor, and Eudora Welty. Our Lady of the Lake College, 1968. Thesis: English.

Lawson, Lewis A. The Grotesque in Recent Southern Fiction. Univ.
of Wisconsin, 1964. Dissertation: English. [William
Faulkner, Flannery O'Connor and E.A. Poe]

Leach, Joseph. The Establishment of the Texas Tradition: A
Part of the History of Fictional Treatments of the West.
Yale Univ., 1946. Dissertation: English.

Leichtling, Barry H. Place in Contemporary Southern Literature.
Univ. of California (Riverside), 1964. Thesis: English.

Leininger, Mary E. The Regionalist Movement in the Cumberlands.
Ohio State Univ., 1942. Thesis: English. [James Still,
Jesse Stuart, and Jean Thomas]

Lemay, J.A.L. A Literary History of Colonial Maryland. Univ. of
Pennsylvania, 1964. Dissertation: English. [Numerous
writers discussed]

Leonard, Nancy H. Regionalism in Contemporary Alabama Poetry.
George Peabody College, 1941. Thesis: English.

Lerner, Gerda. Abolitionists from South Carolina: A Life of
Sarah and Angelina Grimké. Columbia Univ., 1966. Disser-
tation: History. [Sara Grimké (1792-1873) wrote *The
Equality of The Sexes and the Condition of Women*; Angelina
Grimké (1805-1879) wrote *Appeal to the Christian Women of
the Southern States*]

Lewis, Ruth F. The Southern Mountaineer in Fiction. Univ. of
Virginia, 1929. Thesis: English. [Charles E. Craddock,
John Fox, Jr., DuBose Heyward, Rose W. Lane, Elizabeth
Madox Roberts, and T.S. Stribling]

Little, Caroline L. Tennessee: A Setting for Prose Fiction.
George Peabody College, 1929. Thesis: English.

Logan, Josephine M. Some Views of Slavery from the Writings of
Virginia Authors, 1824-1865. Univ. of Richmond, 1956.
Thesis: History.

Lovelace, Robert E. The Deep South as Seen in Stribling and
Faulkner. Washington Univ. (St. Louis), 1939. Thesis:
English.

Lowe, Virginia S. Southern Romanticism: Antebellum Mississippi
as Depicted by Mississippi Romantic Novelists. Mississippi
State Univ., 1968. Thesis: History.

Lumpkin, Ben G. Southern Life as Reflected in the Short Story
from 1850 to 1890. Univ. of Mississippi, 1935. Thesis:
English.

_____. Diversity in the Characters Portrayed in Southern
Regional Short Stories of the Nineteenth Century. Univ. of
North Carolina (Chapel Hill), 1944. Dissertation: English.

Lunsford, Juanita. The Louisiana Creole in Literature. Louisiana
State Univ., 1939. Thesis: English. [G.W. Cable, Kate
Chopin, Lafcadio Hearn, and Grace King]

Lyons, Helene G. The Grotesque World of Carson McCullers and
Tennessee Williams. Univ. of Maine, 1967. Thesis: English.

Magruder, Augustin F. Literary Criticism in the South (1834-1842).
Stanford Univ., 1925. Thesis: English. [J.P. Kennedy]

Maiden, Emory V., Jr. A Comparison of the Negro Dialect Poetry of
Irwin Russell and Thomas Nelson Page. Univ. of Virginia,
1969. Thesis: English.

Manley, Nora B. Techniques of Local Colorists of Louisiana. East
Texas State Univ., 1953. Thesis: English.

Mardaugh, Nell W. East Texas in Contemporary Fiction. East Texas State Univ., 1959. Thesis: English.

Marshall, Donald R. The Southern Quest for Identity--A Cycle: Isolation, Identity and the Past. Brigham Young Univ., 1964. Thesis: English. [Truman Capote, William Faulkner, Shirley Ann Grau, Carson McCullers, Flannery O'Connor, Katherine Anne Porter, and Eudora Welty]

Martin, Charles B. The Survivals of Medieval Religious Drama in New Mexico. Univ. of Missouri, 1959. Dissertation: Speech and Drama.

Masey, Edith. The Lyric in Contemporary Southern Poetry. George Peabody College, 1925. Thesis: English.

Mason, Walter S., Jr. The People of Florida as Portrayed in American Fiction. George Peabody College, 1948. Dissertation: English.

McCalib, Paul T. Moore and Stuart: Rival Editors in Early Texas (1837-1862). Univ. of Texas (Austin), 1948. Thesis: Journalism. [Francis Moore, 1808-1864; Hamilton Stuart, 1813-1894]

McCaskey, Nancy J. Southwestern Humor: British and American Prose Styles. Univ. of North Carolina (Chapel Hill), 1969. Thesis: English.

McGinity, Sue S. The Image of the Spanish-American Woman in Recent Southwestern Fiction. East Texas State Univ., 1968. Dissertation: English.

McGlothlin, Mary L. The Literary Tradition of the Southern Lady. Vanderbilt Univ., 1932. Thesis: English. [Tradition of the glamorous Southern lady of antebellum days, as depicted in magazine stories and articles of the post-bellum period]

McGlynn, William E. A Study into the Causes of the Lack of Poetry in the South. Niagara Univ., 1938. Thesis: English. [Thomas Holley Chivers, Sidney Lanier, E.A. Poe, Fr. Abram Ryan, and Henry Timrod]

McIlwaine, Ardrey S. The Beauchamp Tragedy in American Drama. Univ. of Chicago, 1927. Thesis: English. [Thomas Holley Chivers and E.A. Poe]

_____. The Southern Poor-White: A Literary History. Univ. of Chicago, 1939. Dissertation: English. [Includes James Lane Allen, Robert M. Bird, William Byrd, G.W. Cable, Erskine Caldwell, William A. Caruthers, Kate Chopin, Irvin S. Cobb, David Crockett, Mary E.M. Davis, Harry S. Edwards, William Faulkner, Alice French, Ellen Glasgow, Paul Green, Will N. Harben, J.C. Harris, Johnson Jones Hooper, Mary Johnston, J.P. Kennedy, Sidney Lanier, A.B. Longstreet, T.N. Page, Walter H. Page, Marjorie Kinnan Rawlings, Opie Pope Read, Elizabeth Madox Roberts, Dorothy Scarborough, W.G. Simms, Charles H. Smith, T.S. Stribling, Maurice Thompson, Thomas B. Thorpe, Albion Tourgée, John Uhler, and Henry Watterson]

McJilton, Eloise C. Appreciations, Attitudes, Concepts, and Ideals Found in the Literature of the Southwest for Children of the Upper Elementary Grades. Univ. of Texas (Austin), 1944. Thesis: Education. [Arkansas, Oklahoma, and Texas]

McKinney, Rheable M. The Treatment of the Negro in the Fiction of
    South Carolina, 1920 to 1940. Atlanta Univ., 1940. Thesis:
    English. [Ambrose Elliot Gonzales, DuBose Heyward, and
    Julia Peterkin]
McLaurin, Nancy D. A Study of the Southern Frontier in Prose
    Fiction prior to 1860. Univ. of South Carolina, 1958.
    Dissertation: English. [Includes Joseph Glover Baldwin,
    William A. Caruthers, John Esten Cooke, David Crockett,
    J.J. Hooper, Joseph H. Ingraham, G.W. Harris, Caroline Lee
    Hentz, J.P. Kennedy, Henry C. Lewis, A.B. Longstreet,
    E.A. Poe, Thomas B. Thorpe, and W.G. Simms]
McLeod, John A. The Southern Highlands in Prose Fiction. Univ.
    of North Carolina (Chapel Hill), 1930. Thesis: English.
    [Includes Joseph Alexander Altsheler, Frances Courtenay
    Baylor, R.M. Bird, Sherwood Bonner, William A. Caruthers,
    John Esten Cooke, Charles E. Craddock, Thomas Dixon, Harry
    Stillwell Edwards, John Fox, Jr., Will N. Harben, Corra
    Harris, Mary Johnston, J.P. Kennedy, E.A. Poe, W.G. Simms,
    and T.S. Stribling]
Mead, Mildred F. Indians of Texas in Legend and Poetry. Sam
    Houston State Univ., 1941. Thesis: English.
Mebane, Mary E. Existential Themes in Ellison's *Invisible Man*
    and Wright's *The Outsider*. Univ. of North Carolina (Chapel
    Hill), 1961. Thesis: English.
Megibben, Katherine. Early Kentucky Historians, 1784-1824. Univ.
    of Kentucky, 1931. Thesis: History. [John Filson,
    Alexander Fitzroy, Gilbert Imlay, William Littell, Humphrey
    Marshall, and Harry Toulmin]
Meredith, Claire. The Decline of the Southern Aristocratic
    Tradition in American Drama: Paul Green, Lillian Hellman,
    Tennessee Williams, and Joshua Logan. Columbia Univ.,
    1962. Thesis: English.
Meriwether, Frank T. The Rogue in the Humor of the Old Southwest.
    Louisiana State Univ., 1953. Dissertation: English.
Meyer, Sr. M.C., C.S.A. New Poetry of the American South: A
    Study of Its Art, Its Tradition, and Its Critical Ideas.
    Loyola Univ. (Chicago), 1943. Thesis: English. [John
    Peale Bishop, Donald Davidson, John Crowe Ransom, Allen
    Tate, and Robert Penn Warren]
Middleton, Sarah. Kentucky Life as It Is Represented in Kentucky
    Novels. Univ. of Virginia, 1930. Thesis: English. [James
    Lane Allen, Nancy Huston Banks, Charles N. Buck, Irvin S.
    Cobb, Sally R. Ford, Lucy Furman, and Elizabeth M. Roberts]
Mikules, Leonard. The Road to William Faulkner: A Reading of
    Southern Fiction. Univ. of California (Los Angeles), 1958.
    Dissertation: English.
Miles, Guy S. Literary Beginnings in Nashville, 1815 to 1825.
    Vanderbilt Univ., 1941. Dissertation: English.
Miller, Anna K. The Life of the Ozarks Seen through the Literature
    of the Region. Miami Univ. (Ohio), 1940. Thesis: English.
    [Charlie Mae Simon and Charles Morrow Wilson]
Miller, Lou E.W. Florida in Fiction. Florida State Univ., 1939.
    Thesis: English. [Will Allen Dromgoole, Harry Stillwell
    Edwards, Zora Neale Hurston, Rose Wilder Lane, Marjorie
    Kinnan Rawlings, and W.G. Simms]

Miller, Temple. The Dirt Farmer in Texas Fiction. Texas Christian
Univ., 1961. Thesis: English.

Miller, Theodore C. Some Representative Figures of the Southern
Gentleman in American Fiction, 1865-1915. New York Univ.,
1969. Dissertation: English. [Albion W. Tourgée, and
Mark Twain]

Milliner, Gladys W. The Sense of Guilt and Isolation in Faulkner
and Warren. Tulane Univ., 1965. Thesis: English.

Mills, Gordon H. Myth and Ontology in the Thought of John Crowe
Ransom and Allen Tate. Univ. of Michigan, 1946. Dissertation:
English.

Mills, Jesse C. Treatment of the Proletariat in Southern Novels,
1929-1939. Univ. of Tennessee, 1949. Thesis: English.

Moon, Annie L. Birmingham's Literary Overture. Birmingham-
Southern College, 1937. Thesis: English. [Jack Bethea,
James Saxon Childers, Octavus Roy Cohen, Edgar Valentine
Smith, and Howell Vines]

Moore, Eva L. Two Virginia Regionalists: A Comparison of the
Materials and Methods of Thomas Nelson Page and Ellen Glasgow.
Univ. of Missouri, 1931. Thesis: English.

Moore, Opal. The Development of the Negro Character in Louisiana
Fiction. Louisiana State Univ., 1942. Thesis: English.
[Hamilton Basso, Arna Bontemps, Roark Bradford, G.W. Cable,
Kate Chopin, Mary Evelyn Moore Davis, Dorothy Dix, Zora
Neale Hurston, Robert E. Kennedy, Grace King, Eldred Kurtz
Means, Lyle Saxon, Ruth McEnery Stuart, Jeannette Ritchie
Walworth, and Andrews Wilkerson]

Moreland, Mary E. A Comparison of Cable's and Twain's Treatment of
the Negro Question in *The Grandissimes* and *Pudd'nhead Wilson*.
Columbia Univ., 1962. Thesis: English.

Morgan, Paul. The Treatment of the Indian in Southwestern Literature since 1915: A Study in Primitivism. Univ. of Texas
(Austin), 1954. Dissertation: English.

Morris, Cincinnatus. On Southern Literature. Univ. of Virginia,
1856. Thesis: [?] [No copy known to be extant. The
title is listed in the Public Day Program for June 17, 1856.]

Morrison, Robert H. The Literature and Legends of the Great Dismal
Swamp. Univ. of North Carolina (Chapel Hill), 1947.
Thesis: English.

Morriss, Berniece H.A. Literary History of Fannin County [Texas].
East Texas State Univ., 1952. Thesis: English.

Moses, Henry C. III. History as Voice and Metaphor: A Study of
Tate, Warren, and Faulkner. Cornell Univ., 1968. Dissertation: English.

Mullane, Eileen M. (Sister M. Rose Genevieve, O.P.). Two Creole
Women. St. John's Univ. (N.Y.), 1953. Thesis: English.
[Kate Chopin and Grace King]

Mullen, Emmie D. A Southern Journal of 1838: Its Historical,
Social, and Literary Backgrounds. Univ. of Tennessee, 1946.
Thesis: English. [Based on the journal written by Mary
Elizabeth Maragne of Abbeville district, South Carolina]

Murdaugh, Nell W. East Texas in Contemporary Fiction. East Texas
State University, 1959. Thesis: English. [Dillon Anderson,
Oren Arnold, Karle Wilson Baker, John Barry Benefield,
Sigman Byrd, Mary Stuart Chamberlain, Madison Cooper, Ruth

Cross, Horton Foote, Jewel Gibson, William Goyen, William
Humphrey, Donald Joseph, Mary King, Elithe Hamilton Kirkland,
Laura Krey, William A. Owens, George Sessions Perry, Evelyn
Pierce, Dorothy Scarborough, John W. Thomason, Jr., David
Westheimer, Elizabeth Lee Wheaton, and John W. Wilson]

Musgrove, Janice A. Children's Writers of the South in the
Nineteenth Century: Harris, Page, Bennett and Others.
Duke Univ., 1949. Thesis: English.

Nelson, Sophia P. The Negro in Georgia Fiction from 1920 to
1940. Atlanta Univ., 1940. Thesis: English. [Erskine
Caldwell, Harry S. Edwards, J.C. Harris, and Margaret
Mitchell]

Nicholls, Andrew. The Southern Poor White as Pictured by Some
Contemporary Authors. Southwest Texas State Univ., 1952.
Thesis: English.

Niedecken, Patsy C. A Comparison of One Presentation of Southern
Plantation Life in *Swallow Barn* and *So Red the Rose*. Hardin-
Simmons Univ., 1969. Thesis: English.

New, Ina C. The Kentucky Tragedy as a Literary Source. Louisiana
State Univ., 1957. Thesis: English.

Newman, Anne E. Contemporary Southern Literature. Univ. of
Alabama, 1926. Thesis: English. [Includes Karle Wilson
Baker, Herschell Brickell, J.B. Cabell, Madison Cawein,
Irvin S. Cobb, Octavus Roy Cohen, Joseph Wood Krutch, Olive
Tilford Dargan, Lucy Furman, Ellen Glasgow, Paul Green,
Corra Harris, DuBose Heyward, Hatcher Hughes, James Weldon
Johnson, Mary Johnston, Aline Kilmer, Robert Loveman,
Walter Malone, Virginia Taylor McCormick, John McLure, John
Trotwood Moore, David Morton, Frances Newman, O. Henry,
William A. Percy, Julia Peterkin, John Crowe Ransom,
Lizette Woodworth Reese, Cale Young Rice, Elizabeth Madox
Roberts, Laurence Stribling, Charles Hanson Towne, Lula
Vollmer, Clement Wood, Martha Young, and Stark Young]

Newton, Craig A. Southern Writers of National History 1785-1816.
Case Western Reserve Univ., 1964. Dissertation: History.

Olenick, Monte. Albion W. Tourgée, George W. Cable and Charles W.
Chesnutt on the Negro and the South: 1865-1905. Brooklyn
College, 1958. Thesis: English.

Owen, Mary C. The Rise of the Nineteenth Century Southerner as
Portrayed in Biographies. George Peabody College, 1942.
Dissertation: English.

Park, Ulna F. The Early Literature of East Tennessee: A Study of
Literary Publications and Their Backgrounds from the Beginning
to 1840. Univ. of Tennessee, 1954. Thesis: English.

Patrick, Walton R. Literature in the Louisiana Plantation Home
Prior to 1861: A Study in Literary Culture. Louisiana
State Univ., 1937. Dissertation: English.

Peacock, Bernon. Georgia Writers on Broadway, 1945-1965. Univ.
of Georgia, 1966. Thesis: Journalism. [Roark Bradford,
Erskine Caldwell, Lonnie Coleman, Mac Hyman, Nunnally Johnson,
Carson McCullers, Johnny Mercer, Lillian Smith, Calder
Willingham, and Donald Windham]

Peale, Marjorie E. Charleston as a Literary Center, 1920-1933.
Duke Univ., 1941. Thesis: English.

Pendergrass, Jo Anna J. Charleston, South Carolina, as an Antebellum Literary Center. Southern Methodist Univ., 1928. Thesis: English.

Penrod, John H. Character Types and Humorous Devices in the Old Southwest Yarns. George Peabody College, 1952. Dissertation: English.

Pilkington, William T., Jr. My Blood's Country: Studies in Southwestern Literature. Texas Christian Univ., 1969. Dissertation: English.

Pirkle, Golden A. Atlanta Verse. Oglethorpe Univ., 1931. Thesis: English.

Poe, John W. An Emerging Moral Consciousness in Southern Literature in Twain, Faulkner, Warren, and McCullers. Kansas State Teachers College, 1964. Thesis: English.

Polhemus, G.W. Literary Romanticism in the Old South: 1830-1860. Univ. of Mississippi, 1951. Thesis: English. [William A. Caruthers, J.P. Kennedy, W.G. Simms, and Nathaniel B. Tucker]

Pollard, Ella T. The Gullah Negroes in Regional Literature. Oklahoma State Univ., 1936. Thesis: English. [J.C. Harris, DuBose Heyward, and W.G. Simms]

Porter, Estelle R. "They are a curious and most native stock" (The Southern Mountaineer in the Short Story). Winthrop College, 1945. Thesis: English.

Preis, Richard I. The Kentucky Tragedy in Prose Fiction. Univ. of Kansas, 1953. Thesis: English.

Price, Francis I. (Mrs. Webster Street). Literary Culture in Colonial Virginia, an Inquiry into the Intellectual Status of the Colony, Based Particularly upon a Study of Colonial Libraries. Stanford Univ., 1923. Thesis: English.

Pryor, William L. An Examination of the Southern Milieu in Representative Plays by Southern Dramatists, 1923-1956. Florida State Univ., 1959. Dissertation: English. [George Abbott, Ann Preston Bridgers, Paul Green, Lillian Hellman, Dorothy and DuBose Heyward, Hatcher Hughes, Jack Kirkland, Joshua Logan, Carson McCullers, Paul Peters, George Sklar, Lula Vollmer, and Tennessee Williams]

Purcell, James S., Jr. Literary Culture in North Carolina before 1820. Duke Univ., 1950. Thesis: English.

Purcell, James S. The Southern Poor White in Fiction. Duke Univ., 1938. Thesis: English. [Erskine Caldwell, William Faulkner, Ellen Glasgow, Paul Green, Will N. Harben, DuBose Heyward, Mary Johnston, Margaret Mitchell, Marjorie Kinnan Rawlings, Amélie Rives, Elizabeth Madox Roberts, W.G. Simms, T.S. Stribling, and Thomas B. Thorpe]

Ramey, Medford G. The Growth of Realism in the Southern Novel from the Civil War to 1930. Washington and Lee Univ., 1930. Thesis: English. [James Lane Allen, J.B. Cabell, John Esten Cooke, Charles E. Craddock, William Faulkner, Ellen Glasgow, DuBose Heyward, Mary Johnston, Frances Newman, T.N. Page, Julia Peterkin, and Elizabeth Madox Roberts]

Randall, Helen L. Thomas Nelson Page and Ellen Glasgow as Interpreters of Southern Women. Univ. of Iowa, 1933. Thesis: English.

Rasco, Ann. A Study of Recent Central Texas Fiction. Univ. of
Texas (Austin), 1953. Thesis: English.
Raunick, Selma M. Was haben die Deutschen einwanderer und deren
nachkommen in Texas auf dem gebiet der dicht-kunst geleistet?
Univ. of Texas (Austin), 1922. Thesis: German. [Collection
of poems written by German Texans, with introduction and with
biographical sketches of authors]
Rechnitz, Robert M. Perception, Identity, and the Grotesque: A
Study of Three Southern Writers. Univ. of Colorado, 1967.
Dissertation: English. [Carson McCullers, Flannery
O'Connor, and Eudora Welty]
Reeves, Miriam G. Social and Economic Problems in Southern
Poetry, 1607-1900. Wofford College, 1940. Thesis: English.
[William Byrd, Madison Cawein, Paul H. Hayne, Thomas
Jefferson, Francis Scott Key, Sidney Lanier, Charles Lynch,
James R. Randall, Irwin Russell, Fr. Abram Ryan, W.G. Simms,
Francis O. Ticknor, and Henry Timrod]
Rehn, Dorothy. San Antonio and the Missions in the Literature of
the Southwest. Univ. of Texas (Austin), 1938. Thesis:
English. [A portrayal of San Antonio as the city appears
in the literature of the Southwest]
Reid, Emily J. Local Color in Louisiana Fiction. Columbia Univ.,
1923. Thesis: English.
Renshaw, Edyth. Recent Indigenous Drama of North Carolina.
Southern Methodist Univ., 1928. Thesis: English. [Paul
Green and Hatcher Hughes]
Rettig, Ethel. The Place of Literature of the Southwest in the
American Literature Program of Texas High Schools. Univ. of
Texas (Austin), 1948. Thesis: Education. [Critical
discussion of many examples of literature of the Southwest]
Rhea, Carolina M. Sketches and Legends of Upper East Tennessee.
George Peabody College, 1932. Thesis: English.
Riley, John A. The Use of Violence in Selected Southern Short
Stories of the Twentieth Century. Univ. of South Carolina,
1958. Thesis: English.
Rion, Mary. Civilization of the Frontier: Literary Activity in
Kentucky before 1830. Johns Hopkins Univ., 1957. Disser-
tation: English.
Risien, J.L. The Preservation of the Vanished Caste in Southern
Literature. Trinity Univ. (Texas), 1955. Thesis: English.
Robertson, Thomas L., Jr. The Unfolding Magnolia: A Literary
History of Mississippi until 1876. Vanderbilt Univ., 1960.
Dissertation: English. [Joseph G. Baldwin, Newton
Berryhill, Sherwood Bonner, J.F.H. Claiborne, James Beckham
Cobb, Sarah Ann Dorsey, Eliza Ann Dupuy, John Saunders Holt,
Joseph Holt Ingraham, Henry Clay Lewis, "Pearl Rivers," and
Irwin Russell]
Rock, Virginia J. The Making and Meaning of *I'll Take My Stand*:
A Study in Utopian-Conservatism, 1925-1939. Univ. of
Minnesota, 1961. Dissertation: English.
Roddy, Kathryne. Literary History of Grayson County. East Texas
State Univ., 1952. Thesis: English.
Roller, Bert A. Tennessee in Poetry and Song. George Peabody
College, 1923. Thesis: English.

Rollins, Hyder E. The Short Story in the South: A Critical and
Historical Sketch. 1912. Thesis: English.
Romig, Winston E. The Development of Romanticism in the Drama of
the South. Pennsylvania State Univ., 1932. Thesis: English.
[William DeMille, Charles Gayarré, Paul Green, James Ewell
Heath, Hatcher Hughes, George H. Miles, Robert Munford,
W.G. Simms, and Lula Vollmer]
Rousseve, Charles B. The Negro in Louisiana: Aspects of His
History and His Literature. Xavier Univ. (New Orleans), 1935.
Thesis: English. [Includes Joseph Beaumont, Hippolyte
Castra, Joseph Chaumette, Rodolphe L. Desdunes, Adolphe
Duhart, Louisa R. Lamotte, Armand Lanusse, Mirtil-Ferdinand
Liotan, Eugene V. Macarty, Lucien Mansion, P.B.S. Pinchback,
Joanni Questy, Victor Ernest Rillieux, Joseph-Colastin
Rousseau, Michel Saint-Pierre, Michel Séligny, Victor Sejour,
and Camille Theiry]
Rowlison, Mariena. Kentucky Schools in Fiction. Western Kentucky
Univ., 1944. Thesis: Education. [Includes James Lane Allen,
Charles N. Buck, Irvin S. Cobb, John Fox, Jr., Lucy Furman,
Alice Hegan Rice, Jesse Stuart, Rachel McBrayer Varble (Mrs.
Pinckney Varble, III), and Robert Penn Warren]
Roy, Beryl M. Southern Novels, 1855-1860. A Study in Culture.
Tulane Univ., 1942. Thesis: English. [Includes Isabel
Drysdale, J.P. Kennedy, Anne Royall, and George Tucker]
Ruane, Martin. Comparative Study of the Lives, Careers, and Works
of Ellen Glasgow and Mary Johnston. St. John's Univ. (N.Y.),
1961. Thesis: English.
Rubin, Steven J. Richard Wright and Ralph Ellison: Black
Existential Attitudes. Univ. of Michigan, 1969. Disser-
tation: English.
Ruby, Carrie L. Attitudes Toward Latin Americans as Revealed in
Southwestern Literature. Univ. of Texas (Austin), 1953.
Thesis: English.
Rudolph, Earl L. Confederate Broadside Verse. Harvard Univ.,
1947. Dissertation: English.
Russell, Mary F. Loneliness, Violence and Love in the Fiction of
Eudora Welty, Flannery O'Connor and Carson McCullers. Univ.
of Massachusetts, 1965. Thesis: English.
St. John, James I. Literary Contributions of Colonial Charleston,
South Carolina (1670-1780). Univ. of South Carolina, 1969.
Thesis: English.
Salmon, Charlotte S. The Black Waxy in Literature: The Culture of
the Texas Black Land as Interpreted in Its Fiction. Southern
Methodist Univ., 1935. Thesis: English.
Sandmel, F.F. The Conception and the Creation: A Critical
Evaluation of the Work of the Carolina Playmakers. Univ. of
North Carolina (Chapel Hill), 1941. Thesis: Dramatic Art.
Santmyer, Sue P. The "Nashville Agrarians" as Critics of American
Society. Vanderbilt Univ., 1951. Thesis: English.
Saucier, Earl N. The Literary South: 1867-1877. George Peabody
College, 1929. Thesis: English.
Schamber, Margaret A. Mississippi Prose Literature from 1860-1900.
George Peabody College, 1930. Thesis: English.

Schumpert, Mary F. A Survey of Mississippi Fiction and Verse
    since 1900. Univ. of Mississippi, 1931. Thesis: English.
Scott, Elizabeth. A Study of the Chronicles of Indian Captivity
    in the Southwest. Univ. of Texas (Austin), 1946. Thesis:
    English.
Sewell, Annie M. A Literary History of Montgomery, Alabama.
    Auburn Univ., 1935. Thesis: English.
Shaw, Harry L., Jr. The Georgia Cracker as a Type in American
    Literature. Univ. of South Carolina, 1927. Thesis: English.
Shay, George H. The Views of Prominent Southern Literary Men
    Regarding Slavery (1830-1860). Rutgers Univ., 1931. Thesis:
    History. [Williams A. Caruthers, William J. Grayson, Hinton
    Rowan Helper, J.P. Kennedy, W.G. Simms, and Nathaniel B.
    Tucker]
Sheets, Nat M. A Study of the Poetry of the Fugitives. Louisiana
    State Univ., 1934. Thesis: English.
Shell, Lorraine. The Literary South: 1900-1905. George Peabody
    College, 1938. Thesis: English.
Shelton, Edna E. Poets and Poetry in North Carolina since 1870.
    Univ. of South Carolina, 1922. Thesis: English.
Sherlock, Vivian. Sociological Trends in Five Novels of the
    South. Florida State Univ., 1948. Thesis: English.
    [Includes Hamilton Basso, Fielding Burke, Erskine Caldwell,
    William Faulkner, Ellen Glasgow, Grace Lumpkin, Julia Peterkin,
    Marjorie K. Rawlings, Elizabeth M. Roberts, Evelyn D. Scott,
    Lillian Smith, T.S. Stribling, and Richard Wright]
Shields, Harvey G. The Nashville Agrarians During the 1930's.
    Tulane Univ., 1962. Thesis: History.
Shover, Martha. Some Great Georgia Writers. Oglethorpe Univ.,
    1927. Thesis: English.
Sides, Sudie D. Women and Slaves: An Interpretation Based on
    the Writings of Southern Women. Univ. of North Carolina
    (Chapel Hill), 1969. Dissertation: History. [Mary Boykin
    Chesnut, Sarah Morgan Dawson, Constance Cary Harrison, Sarah
    Agnes Pryor, and Kate Stone]
Siedlecki, Peter A. Fool's Gold in the Main-Stream of American
    Literature: The Popular Position of Poe and Twain. Niagara
    Univ., 1966. Thesis: English.
Skaggs, Merrill A.M. The Plain-Folk Tradition in Southern Local
    Color Fiction. Duke Univ., 1966. Dissertation: English.
Smith, Ursula L. A Literary History of Montgomery County,
    Tennessee. Austin Peay State Univ., 1954. Thesis: English.
Smith, Ann M. The Development of the Temple Drake Type of Heroine
    in the Fiction of Selected Southern Novelists of the
    Twentieth Century. Trinity Univ. (Texas), 1965. Thesis:
    English.
Smith, Dorothy E. Attitudes toward the Civil War and the Recon-
    struction Period by Southern Novelists. Univ. of Southern
    California, 1939. Thesis: English. [James Lane Allen,
    James Boyd, G.W. Cable, John Esten Cooke, Thomas Dixon, Ellen
    Glasgow, DuBose Heyward, Margaret Mitchell, T.N. Page,
    Francis H. Smith, T.S. Stribling, and Stark Young]

Smith, Irene D. The Louisiana Creole in Fiction. Tulane Univ.,
1926. Thesis: English. [G.W. Cable, Kate Chopin, Mary
Evelyn Moore Davis, Sarah Anne Dorsey, Alcée Fortier,
Charles Gayarré, Lafcadio Hearn, Alfred Mercier, and James
Wilkinson]

Smith, Wilburn P. Local Color Found in Stories Dealing with
Georgia Prior to 1911. Emory Univ., 1923. Thesis: English.
[J.C. Harris, Corra May Harris, Richard Malcolm Johnston, and
Augustus Baldwin Longstreet]

Smith, Winnie D. Reasons for the Late Development of Poetry in
Texas. Sul Ross State Univ., 1941. Thesis: English.

Smith, Anna G. Fifty Years of Southern Writing, 1900-1950. Univ.
of North Carolina (Chapel Hill), 1948. Dissertation:
Sociology. [Catalog of Southern writing since 1900]

Snapp, Alma F. Local Color in the Southern Short Story from 1835
to 1892. Birmingham-Southern College, 1931. Thesis: English.
[James Lane Allen, Joseph G. Baldwin, G.W. Cable, Charles E.
Craddock, J.C. Harris, A.B. Longstreet, and T.N. Page]

Speer, Mary T. Four Women Writers of the Southwest: Mary Hunter
Austin, Dorothy Scarborough, Katherine Anne Porter, Loula
Grace Erdman. Univ. of Texas (El Paso), 1959. Thesis:
English.

Steele, Frank P. Modern Tennessee Poetry: A Critical Anthology.
Univ. of Tennessee, 1968. Dissertation: English. [Includes
Donald Davidson, Randall Jarrell, Stephen Mooney, Merrill
Moore, Paul Ramsey, John Crowe Ransom, and George Scarborough]

Stembridge, Helen. Types in American Literature: The Negro and
the "Cracker" as Portrayed by Four Middle Georgia Writers:
Augustus B. Longstreet, Richard Malcolm Johnston, Joel
Chandler Harris, Harry Stillwell Edwards. Columbia Univ.,
1929. Thesis: Education.

Stephenson, Velma J. The Southern Mountaineer in Fact and in
Fiction. Ohio State Univ., 1934. Thesis: English. [James
Boyd, Fielding Burke, Charles E. Craddock, John Fox, Jr.,
Lucy Furman, Samuel Emmett Gowan, DuBose Heyward, Caroline
Miller, Louise S. Murdock, Elizabeth M. Roberts, and T.S.
Stribling]

Stewart, John L. The Fugitive-Agrarian Writers: A History and a
Criticism. Ohio State Univ., 1948. Dissertation: English.
[Donald Davidson, Merrill Moore, John Crowe Ransom, Allen
Tate, and Robert Penn Warren]

Stiff, James E. The Spanish Element in Southwestern Fiction.
Southern Methodist Univ., 1928. Thesis: English. [O. Henry]

Stilley, Hugh M. William Faulkner and George Washington Harris;
Frontier Humour in the Snopes Trilogy. Univ. of British
Columbia, 1965. Thesis: English.

Stitt, Peter A. The Poetry of Agrarianism: A Study of Donald
Davidson, John Crowe Ransom, Allen Tate and Robert Penn
Warren. Univ. of North Carolina (Chapel Hill), 1969.
Dissertation: English.

Stocking, Fred H. Poetry as Knowledge: The Critical Theory of
John Crowe Ransom and Allen Tate. Univ. of Michigan, 1946.
Dissertation: English.

Stone, Marion. The Kentucky Novel. Univ. of Kansas, 1916.
    Thesis: English. [James Lane Allen, Joseph Altsheler,
    Nancy Huston Banks, Charles Neville Buck, John Fox, Jr.,
    Abbie Carter Goodloe, Eliza Calvert Hall, Creddo Fitch
    Harris, Roe R. Hobbs, Eleanor Talbot Kinkhead, Edwin Carlisle
    Litsey, Fannie Caldwell Macaulay, George Madden Martin,
    Abbie Meguire Roach, Harrison Robertson, and Elizabeth
    Robins]
Straw, Ethel M. A Study of Some Contemporary Male Novelists of
    the South. Ohio State Univ., 1933. Thesis: English.
    [Jack Bethea, James Boyd, Charles N. Buck, J.B. Cabell,
    Thomas Dixon, William Faulkner, DuBose Heyward, and T.S.
    Stribling]
Sturdivant, Pina S. A Topical and Analytical Index to *The Trail
    Drivers of Texas*. Univ. of Texas (Austin), 1965. Thesis:
    English.
Tabor, Carole A.S. The Role of the Kentucky Tragedy in Four
    American Novels. Texas Christian Univ., 1966. Thesis:
    English.
Talbot, Willie L. The Development of the Negro Character in the
    Southern Novel, 1824-1900. Louisiana State Univ., 1938.
    Thesis: English. [G.W. Cable, Thomas Dixon, Mary H.
    Eastman, Caroline H. Gilman, J.H. Ingraham, Belle Kearney,
    J.P. Kennedy, A.B. Longstreet, E.A. Meriwether, T.N. Page,
    Margaret J. Preston, Francis H. Smith, T.B. Thorpe, George
    Tucker, and Nathaniel B. Tucker]
Tapia, Ignatius. American Literature in Louisiana. New Mexico
    Highlands Univ., 1930. Thesis: English. [G.W. Cable,
    Charles P. Dimitry, Charles Gayarré, Lafcadio Hearn, Grace
    King, and Ruth McEnery Stuart]
Tate, Sandra P. A Study of Family Relationships in Works by
    Three Southern Writers. Emory Univ., 1970. Dissertation:
    English. [Carson McCullers, Katherine Porter, and Eudora
    Welty]
Taylor, Frances B. Nature in the Poetry of the South. Univ. of
    Texas (Austin), 1918. Thesis: English. [Paul H. Hayne
    and Sidney Lanier]
Taylor, Ruth. Tennessee Writers from 1890-1920. George Peabody
    College, 1937. Thesis: English.
Thomas, Percy L. The Literary South: 1877-1887. George Peabody
    College, 1930. Thesis: English.
Thomson, Lucille M. Southern Novels, 1845-1850: A Study in
    Culture. Tulane Univ., 1949. Thesis: English.
Tidwell, James N. The Literary Representation of the Phonology
    of the Southern Dialect. Ohio State Univ., 1948. Disser-
    tation: English. [Charles W. Chesnutt, Charles E. Craddock,
    J.C. Harris, Richard Malcolm Johnston, A.B. Longstreet,
    T.N. Page, and W.G. Simms]
Tinker, Edward L. Les Ecrits de langue francaise en Louisiana
    au XIX siecle: Essais biographiques et bibliographiques.
    Paris, 1933. Dissertation: English.
Tinkler, Mary E.C. Stories of North Alabama. Univ. of Florida,
    1957. Thesis: English.

Tobolowsky, Sarah. The Background of Texas Poetry. Southern
Methodist Univ., 1938. Thesis: English. [Karle Wilson
Baker, William E. Bard, Grace Noll Crowell, Hilton Ross
Greer, Margaret Houston, Whitney Montgomery, and Patrick D.
Moreland]

Townes, Alys. The Tall Tale in the South. Louisiana State Univ.,
1938. Thesis: English. [David Crockett and A.B. Longstreet]

Trahern, Joseph B., Jr. The George Washington Cable-Charles
Waddell Chesnutt Correspondence. Vanderbilt Univ., 1959.
Thesis: English.

Tribble, Joseph L. The Kentucky Tragedy and American Fiction.
Harvard Univ., 1968. Dissertation: English.

Trotter, Eva V. Writers of the Southern Plains (1800-1875).
Univ. of Oklahoma, 1946. Thesis: History. [Deals primarily
with historians, but some other writers are treated, among
whom are Hilton Ross Greer and John Rollin Ridge]

Uhler, John E. The Delphian Club: A Contribution to the Literary
History of Baltimore in the Early Nineteenth Century. Johns
Hopkins Univ., 1924. Thesis: English.

Utterback, Elizabeth. History of the Development of Drama in the
South. George Peabody College, 1930. Thesis: English.

_____. A Study of Critical Method for Teachers: A Regional
Approach to the Plays of Five Southern Dramatists. Columbia
Univ., 1945. Dissertation: English.

Vandiver, Oscar. Georgia Prose Writers: 1860-1870. George Peabody
College, 1932. Thesis: English.

Vorpahl, Ben M. Such Stuff as Dreams are Made On: History, Myth
and the Comic Vision of Mark Twain and William Faulkner. Univ.
of Wisconsin, 1966. Dissertation: English.

Wade, Emma H. Southern Women Novelists: 1800-1900. George
Peabody College, 1933. Thesis: English.

Wages, Jack D. Southern Colonial Elegiac Verse. Univ. of
Tennessee, 1968. Dissertation: English. [Covers wide range
of elegiac verse published in Southern gazettes and elsewhere]

Waldrip, Myrtle L. A Study of Georgia's Literature and Writers
between the Ends of the World Wars. Univ. of Georgia, 1967.
Thesis: Journalism.

Walhout, Clarence P. Religion in the Thought and Fiction of Three
Antebellum Southerners: Kennedy, Caruthers, and Simms.
Northwestern Univ., 1964. Dissertation: English.

Walker, Lennie M. The Beginnings of Texas Fiction. Univ. of Texas
(Austin), 1935. Thesis: English. [A first-hand study of
the earliest Texas writers of fiction and their work from
1819-1955 and with attention given to the little known authors
rather than to the better known]

Walker, Lola C. The Literature of the Ozarks. Southern Methodist
Univ., 1936. Thesis: English. [Shows the extent and nature
of the influence of the Ozarks upon both fiction and non-
fiction]

Walsh, Anastasia. Charleston in Fiction. Duke Univ., 1941.
Thesis: English. [DuBose Heyward, Thornwell Jacobs, Susan P.
King (Mrs. C.C. Bowen), Josephine Pinckney, Herbert Ravenel
Sass, W.G. Simms, and Annie L. Sloan]

Walsh, Emmet. Literary Taste and Culture in Early Washington, D.C.
    Catholic Univ., 1940. Dissertation: English.
Warren, Minnie. Writers of the Eastern Shore: A Biographical
    and Critical Compilation. Univ. of Maryland, 1940. Thesis:
    English. [The Maryland "Eastern Shore"]
Watson, Charles S. Early Dramatic Writing in the South: Virginia
    and South Carolina Plays, 1798-1830. Vanderbilt Univ., 1966.
    Dissertation: English. [Includes Stephen Carpenter,
    G.W.P. Custis, Joseph Doddridge, Isaac Harby, William Ioor,
    Robert Munford, W.G. Simms, and John Black White]
Watt, Gerry S. Dialect Variants in Florida Fiction. Univ. of
    Miami (Coral Gables), 1949. Thesis: English.
Watt, Reed L. Kentucky Themes Used as a Basis for Literature.
    George Peabody College, 1924. Thesis: English.
Watts, Mary E. Two William Faulkners: A Study in Contrasts.
    Univ. of Texas (Austin), 1941. Thesis: English.
Weller, Grace H. Kentucky (1770-1865) in American Fiction. Duke
    Univ., 1940. Thesis: English. [Includes James Lane Allen,
    Nancy Huston Banks, William A. Caruthers, Thomas Dixon,
    Timothy Flint, John Fox, Jr., Sallie J. Hancock, Mary Jane
    Holmes, Eva Wilder McGlasson, Clark McMeekin, James Duncan
    Nourse, Elizabeth M. Roberts, and W.G. Simms]
Wetmore, Thomas H. The Literary and Cultural Development of
    Antebellum Wilmington, North Carolina. Duke Univ., 1941.
    Thesis: English.
Whalen, Sharon I.R. Tradition in Works of John Crowe Ransom and
    Allen Tate. Miami Univ. (Ohio), 1965. Thesis: English.
Whitehead, Kenneth. A Comparative Study of Characterization in
    the Short Stories of Erskine Caldwell and Flannery O'Connor.
    East Tennessee State Univ., 1962. Thesis: English.
Whittaker, John W., Jr. The Nashville Fugitives, 1922-1935: A
    Critical Study. Fisk Univ., 1937. Thesis: English.
Whittington, Joseph R. The Regional Novel of the South: The
    Definition of Innocence. Univ. of Oklahoma, 1963. Disser-
    tation: English. [William Faulkner, Shelby Foote, Caroline
    Gordon, Andrew Lytle, William March, Ovid William Pierce,
    Robert Penn Warren, and Eudora Welty; special emphasis on
    The Sound and the Fury]
Wierwill, Jonathan P. A Comparison of the Value Notions of God,
    Love, and Person in the Writings of Martin Luther King, Jr.
    and Thomas Merton. Bowling Green State Univ., 1970. Thesis:
    American Studies.
Wikie, Rosemary S.H. Huey P. Long Figures in Fiction. East Texas
    State Univ., 1969. Thesis: English.
Wilcox, Jim J. A Study of the Interpretative Ability of English
    Students and English Teachers as Revealed in a Survey of
    Certain Lyric Poetry of the South. Kansas State Teachers
    College, 1938. Thesis: English.
Williams, Clyde V. A Study of Some Relations of Fugitives to
    Agrarians. Mississippi State Univ., 1961. Thesis: English.
Williams, Cratis D. The Southern Mountaineer in Fact and Fiction.
    New York Univ., 1961. Dissertation: English. [Harriette
    Arnow, Sarah Barnwell, Charles E. Craddock, William Elliott,
    John Fox, Jr., Lucy Furman, Will N. Harben, Maria Louise
    Pool, James Still, and Jesse Stuart]

Williamson, Juanita V. The Treatment of the Negro in the Fiction of North Carolina, 1920-1940. Atlanta Univ., 1940. Thesis: English. [Thomas Dixon, Paul Green, J.P. Kennedy, and Thomas Wolfe]

Wilson, James W. Primitivism and Progress in the Fiction of George S. Perry and Fred Gipson. North Texas State Univ., 1968. Thesis: English.

Wilson, Velez H. Truman Capote: Echoes of Edgar Allan Poe. Tulane Univ., 1968. Thesis: English.

Wolinski, Mabel J. A Study of the Relationship of White and Negro Characters in the Works of William Faulkner and Ellen Glasgow. Florida State Univ., 1960. Thesis: English.

Wood, Eunice W. A Literary History of Cass County, Texas. East Texas State Univ., 1950. Thesis: English.

Wood, Marjorie E. William Faulkner and Eudora Welty: A Comparative Study. Northern Illinois Univ. (Carbondale), 1967. Thesis: English.

Wormley, Margaret J. The Negro in Southern Fiction, 1920-1940. Boston Univ., 1948. Dissertation: English.

Wright, Mary F. The Historical Development of Oklahoma Literature. Univ. of Oklahoma, 1945. Thesis: History.

Wyche, Charlyne S. A Survey of the Southern Legend in the Recent Southern Novel. McNeese State Univ., 1969. Thesis: English.

Yates, Frances T. Browning Interest in Texas. Texas Christian Univ., 1941. Thesis: English.

Yates, Irene. The Literary Utilization of Folklore in the Works of Contemporary South Carolina Writers. Univ. of Virginia, 1939. Thesis: English. [E.C.L. Adams, Ambrose E. Gonzales, Julia Peterkin, Samuel Stoney]

BIBLIOGRAPHIES AND CHECKLISTS

Bain, Drucilla G. American Regional Literature for Children. Miami Univ. (Ohio), 1947. Thesis: English-Education. [Much of this thesis is a list and summary of regional books for children listed by states]

Ballentine, Nelle. A Bibliographical Checklist of Knoxville and Memphis Imprints, 1867-1876, with an Introductory Essay on the Knoxville and Memphis Press. Univ. of Tennessee, 1957. Thesis: English.

Bourgeois, Clotilde J. A Critical Bibliography of Material on Louisiana and Other Publications by Louisianians in the French Language in the Louisiana State University Library. Louisiana State Univ., 1927. Thesis: Romance Languages.

Brooks, Jessie M. North Carolina Fiction, 1795-1861: A Checklist. Duke Univ., 1942. Thesis: English.

Brown, Dorothy O. Civil War Songs in the Harris Collection of American Poetry and Plays at Brown University. Brown Univ., 1959. Thesis: Music.

Cardwell, Guy A., Jr. Charleston Periodicals, 1795-1860: A Study in Literary Influences, with a Descriptive Check-list of Seventy-five Magazines. Univ. of North Carolina (Chapel Hill), 1936. Dissertation: English.

Castañeda, Carlos E. A Report on the Spanish Archives, San Antonio,
Texas. Univ. of Texas (Austin), 1923. Thesis: History.
[List of mission records as well as legal records and
official correspondence]

Chidamian, Claude. The Programmatic Use of English and American
Literature in Symphonic, Operatic, and Larger Choral Forms:
An Abbreviated List. Univ. of Southern California, 1944.
Thesis: English. [Includes G.W. Cable, J.C. Harris, DuBose
Heyward, and Sidney Lanier]

Collins, Karen L.S. Guide to Diaries in the University of Texas
Archives Produced before 1906. Univ. of Texas (Austin),
1967. Thesis: History.

Crocker, William J. An Annotated Bibliography of Current Tall
Tales. Florida State Univ., 1966. Thesis: English.

Cross, Douglas. An Annotated Bibliography of Historical Fiction
Dealing with the Commonwealth of Virginia. East Tennessee
State Univ., 1970. Thesis: Library Science.

Davis, Sheldon E. Character and Development of Educational
Periodicals in the United States during the Nineteenth
Century. Univ. of Virginia, 1936. Dissertation: English.
[Exhaustive bibliography of educational periodicals,
including Southern, in existence prior to 1915]

Dietrich, Rosalia K.T. American Literature in Poland: A Pre-
liminary Check List, 1790-1940, with A Critical Introduction
Concerning the Reputation of Barlow, Franklin and Irving.
Columbia Univ., 1965. Dissertation: English. [Includes
William Faulkner, E.A. Poe, and Mark Twain]

Durden, George D. Southern Novels, 1775-1850: A Bibliography.
Duke Univ., 1941. Thesis: English.

Durrance, Eura L. An Annotated Bibliography of Florida in Prose
Literature Since 1840. Univ. of Wyoming, 1949. Thesis:
English.

Duty, Elaine. An Annotated Bibliography of Books by Southwest
Virginia Authors. East Tennessee State Univ., 1968. Thesis:
Library Science.

Eddy, Henrie M. A Study of Bibliographic Guides Available for
the Formation of a Collection of Florida History and Literature, with a Special Study of the *Guide to Historical
Literature* as a Means of Selecting Regional Material.
Columbia Univ., 1934. Thesis: Library Science.

Edwards, Hugh L. An Annotated Bibliography of Southwestern
Historical Literature Contained in the Library of the East
Texas State Teachers College. East Texas State Univ., 1945.
Thesis: History.

Ellinger, Esther P. Southern War Poetry of the Civil War. Univ.
of Pennsylvania, 1918. Dissertation: English. [A
bibliography with a short preface]

Elliott, William Y. Local Color in Southern Literature: A
Bibliography. Univ. of Alabama, 1929. Thesis: English.

Ellison, Rhoda C. Early Alabama Publications: A Study in
Literary Interests, with a Checklist of Alabama Imprints,
1807-1870. Univ. of North Carolina (Chapel Hill), 1945.
Dissertation: English.

Farris, Lester C. A Bibliography of Works on the Literature of the Southern States. Columbia Univ., 1917. Thesis: English.

Feldman, Ruth E. A Checklist of Atlanta Newspapers, 1846-1948. Emory Univ., 1948. Thesis: Journalism.

Floyd, Mrs. Escar B. (Jennie W.). An Annotated Bibliography on Texas from American Periodicals before 1900. Southern Methodist Univ., 1933. Thesis: English.

Fuller, Juanita B. An Annotated Bibliography of Biographies and Autobiographies of Negroes, 1839-1961. Atlanta Univ., 1963. Thesis: Library Science.

George, Zelma W. A Guide to Negro Music. An Annotated Bibliography of Negro Folk Music, and Art Music by Negro Composers or Based on Negro Thematic Material. New York Univ., 1953. Dissertation: Music.

Glenn, Eleanor V.T. Calendar of the Roquette Material in the Archdiocesan Archives of New Orleans. Tulane Univ., 1942. Thesis: French.

Goodwin, Frank. A Study of Personal and Social Organization. Univ. of Pennsylvania, 1943. Dissertation: Sociology. [Contains annotated bibliography of 32 novels in which the action takes place entirely, or largely, on the eastern shore of Maryland, some by Southern writers]

Gove, Philip B. The Imaginary Voyage in Prose Fiction; A History of Its Criticism and a Guide for Its Study, with an Annotated Check List of 215 Imaginary Voyages from 1700-1800. Columbia Univ., 1941. Dissertation: English.

Griffin, Max L. A Bibliography of New Orleans Magazines. Tulane Univ., 1931. Thesis: English.

Hart, James A. American Poetry of the First World War (1914 to 1920): A Survey and Checklist. Duke Univ., 1965. Dissertation: English.

Hartin, John S. The Southeastern United States in the Novel Through 1950: A Bibliographic Review. Univ. of Michigan, 1956. Dissertation: Library Science.

Haywood, Charles. Bibliography of the American Folklore and Folk Song. Columbia Univ., 1951. Dissertation: English.

Healey, Margaret M. The Short Story in Louisiana during the Local Color Period, 1869-99. Univ. of Chicago, 1935. Thesis: English. [Catalog of more than 200 stories by the following authors: George Augustin, James Augustin, Napier Bartlett, Sherwood Bonner, G.W. Cable, Kate Chopin, Matt Crim, Mary E.M. Davis, John Dimitry, Mary T. Earle, Harry S. Edwards, Martha Field, B.B. Garrison, Fearn Gray, James A. Harrison, Lafcadio Hearn, H.C. Joor, Margaretta W. Kernan, Grace King, A.M. Lee, Rixford Lincoln, Caroline Marsdale, Clara Marshall, Justin McCarthy, Regina Murphy, Delphine Points, Marie Louise Points, Maria Louise Pool, Mary Belle Poole, Annie Porter, Cecil Rey, Mrs. C.C. Scott, Ruth M. Stuart, M. Agnes Thompson, and Marie B. Williams]

Henline, Ruth. Travel Literature of Colonists in America, 1754-1783: An Annotated Bibliography with an Introduction and an Author Index. Northwestern Univ., 1947. Dissertation: English.

Hinson, Kathrine W. North Carolina Writers of Literary Prose
    from 1900 to 1940: Biographies and Bibliographies. East
    Carolina Univ., 1942. Thesis: English. [Includes James
    Boyd, Katherine Newlin Burt, Maxwell Struthers Burt,
    Jonathan Daniels, Josephus Daniels, Charlotte Hilton Green,
    Bernice Kelly Harris, Phillips Russell, and Thomas Wolfe]
Hooker, Billie J.S. An Annotated Bibliography of Biographies and
    Autobiographies of Negroes, 1962-1966. Atlanta Univ., 1967.
    Thesis: Library Science.
Horton, O.E., Jr. A Descriptive Bibliography of Historical and
    Imaginative Writings in Georgia. Vanderbilt Univ., 1933.
    Dissertation: English.
Hosch, Katharine K. An Analysis of Some Critics and Historians
    of Georgia Literature: A Bibliographical Study. Univ. of
    Georgia, 1938. Thesis: History.
Howland, Paul L. Annotated Bibliography of Popular Sociological
    Literature. Kansas State Teachers College, 1943. Thesis:
    English. [Includes Olive Tilford Dargan and Richard Wright]
Hyde, Grace V. A Bibliographical Checklist of Nashville Imprints,
    1867-1876, with an Introductory Essay on Nashville Liter-
    ature and Publishers of the Reconstruction Era. Univ. of
    Tennessee, 1953. Thesis: English.
Johnson, James G. Southern Fiction Prior to 1860: An Attempt
    at a First-hand Bibliography. Univ. of Virginia, 1909.
    Dissertation: English.
Jones, Laura B.W. Louisiana Pamphlets, 1860-1877: An Annotated
    Bibliography. Louisiana State Univ., 1940. Thesis:
    Library Science.
Kennerly, Sarah L. Confederate Juvenile Imprints: Children's
    Books and Periodicals Published in the Confederate States
    of America, 1861-1865. Univ. of Michigan, 1957. Disser-
    tation: Library Science.
Kielman, Chester V. The University of Texas Archives: An
    Analytical Guide to the Historical Manuscripts in the
    University of Texas Archives. Univ. of Texas (Austin), 1968.
    Dissertation: History.
Kinken, Ann D. The Southern Pamphlet Collection: An Evaluation
    and Chronological Checklist of the South Carolina Portion,
    1820-1900. Univ. of North Carolina (Chapel Hill), 1963.
    Thesis: Library Science.
Kraus, Joe W. Book Collections of Five Colonial College Libraries:
    A Subject Analysis. Univ. of Illinois, 1960. Dissertation:
    Library Science. [Includes College of William and Mary]
Lackey, Elizabeth R. The A. Amos Crane Collection of Miscellaneous
    Periodicals Located in the University of North Carolina
    Library, Chapel Hill. Univ. of North Carolina (Chapel Hill),
    1964. Thesis: Library Science.
Lanyon, Elizabeth V. An Annotated Bibliography of the Short
    Story. Kansas State College (Pittsburg), 1932. Thesis:
    English.
Lewis, Benjamin M. A History and Bibliography of American
    Magazines, 1800-1810. Univ. of Michigan, 1956. Dissertation:
    Library Science.

Lipsman, Malcolm H. A Bibliography of Published Drama of the
Southeastern Part of the United States of America, Written
between 1916 and 1946. Columbia Univ., 1947. Thesis:
English.
Longmire, R. Dictionary Catalogue of the Short Stories of
Arkansas, Missouri, and Iowa from 1869 to 1900. Univ. of
Chicago, 1932. Thesis: English.
Lowe, Edna H. Mississippi Bibliography. Univ. of Mississippi,
1928. Thesis: History. [Lists books, pmaphlets, magazine
. and newspaper articles]
Martin, Carolyn P. The North Carolina Collection in the University
of North Carolina Library. Univ. of North Carolina (Chapel
Hill), 1961. Thesis: Library Science.
McClanahan, Mary E. A Descriptive Bibliography of Tennessee
Authors with Biographical Notes. Vanderbilt Univ., 1932.
Thesis: English. [Fiction and poetry only, prior to 1917]
McInnes, Rose Y. An Annotated Bibliography of the Negro in the
United States, 1928-1938. Fisk Univ., 1944. Thesis:
English.
McLean, Frank. Periodicals Published in the South Before 1880.
Univ. of Virginia, 1928. Dissertation: English. [Checklist
with brief annotations]
McLendon, Althea L. A Finding List of Play-Party Games. Univ.
of Florida, 1944. Thesis: English. [Attempts to gather
into one inclusive list all the play-party songs found in
regional collections]
Meats, Stephen E. A Bibliography of Contributions by South
Carolinians to the New York *Spirit of the Times* and to
Porter's *Spirit of the Times*. Univ. of South Carolina, 1969.
Thesis: English.
Michael, Luevenia V. Utopian Thought in American Negro Literature.
Fisk Univ., 1957. Thesis: English. [A bibliography that
includes sections on spirituals, poetry, novels, and short
stories]
Millirons, Martha W. A Bibliographical Checklist of Tennessee
Imprints in Small Towns, 1867-1876, with an Introductory
Essay on an Inquiry into Reconstruction Publications of
Village Tennessee, 1867-1876. Univ. of Tennessee, 1965.
Thesis: English.
Millspaugh, Kathryn G. Notes on Early Nashville Newspapers,
1797-1850. Vanderbilt Univ., 1936. Thesis: History.
[A complete check list of the files of each paper to be found
in the principal newspaper depositories of Nashville follows
the notes on each paper]
Minick, A.R. A History of Printing in Maryland, 1791-1800, with
a Bibliography of Works Printed in the State during the
Period. Columbia Univ., 1948. Thesis: Library Service.
Miscally, Mildred L. An Historical and Annotated Compilation of
Current Georgia Newspapers, with a Tracing of Trends in the
Modern Press. Univ. of Georgia, 1946. Thesis: Journalism.
Mitchell, Elanor D. A Bibliographical Checklist of Tennessee
Imprints, 1861-1877, with an Introductory Essay on the Civil
War Press in Tennessee. Univ. of Tennessee, 1950. Thesis:
English.

Molenaer, Harriet. Folk Tales in Texas, A Preliminary Checklist. Univ. of Texas (Austin), 1956. Thesis: English.

Newman, Carol M. A Catalogue of Virginia Authors and Books, with a Preface on Virginia Literature. Univ. of Virginia, 1903. Dissertation: English.

Pollard, William R. An Analysis and Evaluation with a Chronological Checklist of the Georgia Section of the Southern Pamphlet Collection, 1820-1919. Univ. of North Carolina (Chapel Hill), 1965. Thesis: Library Science.

Porter, Dorothy B. Afro-American Writings Published before 1835, with an Alphabetical List (tentative) of Imprints Written by American Negroes, 1760-1835. Columbia Univ., 1932. Thesis: Library Service. [Benjamin Banneker's and George Moses Horton's almanacs]

Ray, Frank J. Tennessee Writers: A Bibliographical Index. Univ. of Tennessee, 1929. Thesis: English.

Rhyme, Betty J. An Index to Criticisms of Selected American Novels, 1900-1950. Univ. of North Carolina (Chapel Hill), 1961. Thesis: Library Science. [Includes Erskine Caldwell, Truman Capote, William Faulkner, Ellen Glasgow, Carson McCullers, Robert Penn Warren, and Thomas Wolfe]

Roberts, Francis W. American Literary Bibliography. Univ. of Texas (Austin), 1949. Thesis: English. [Includes William Faulkner and Mark Twain]

Robinson, Frank L. The Edgar Lee Masters Collection at the University of Texas at Austin: A Critical, Bibliographical, and Textual Study. Univ. of Texas (Austin), 1969. Dissertation: English.

Robinson, Mary K. An Annotated Bibliography of the Negro in the United States, 1939-43. Fisk Univ., 1944. Thesis: English.

Rose, Lisle A. A Descriptive Catalogue of Economic and Politico-Economic Fiction in the United States, 1902-1909. Univ. of Chicago, 1930. Dissertation: English. [Includes Thomas Dixon and James Weldon Johnson]

Saunders, Harold R. English Books Written by Floridians, Residents and Visitors. Univ. of Florida, 1929. Thesis: English. [Author bibliography of Florida writers]

Scott, Olivia B. A Classified Sociological Source Bibliography of Periodical and Manuscript Materials on the Negro in Atlanta, Georgia. Atlanta Univ., 1948. Thesis: Sociology. [Lists much material of interest to the literary historian]

Smiley, Clara P. A Summary and Bibliography of the Criticism of the American Short Story, 1929-1950. Univ. of Kansas, 1950. Thesis: English. [Includes William Faulkner, Katherine Anne Porter, and Jesse Stuart]

Smith, Loren E. The Library List of 1783: Being A Catalogue of Books, Composed and Arranged by James Madison, and Others, and Recommended for the Use of Congress on January 24, 1783, with Notes and an Introduction. Claremont Graduate School, 1969. Dissertation: History. [Besides Madison, Jefferson also contributed]

Smither, Nelle K. Library of Humorous American Works: A Bibliographical Study. Columbia Univ., 1936. Thesis: English. [Contains information relevant to the South and Southwest]

Spann, Marcella J. An Analytical and Descriptive Catalogue of the Manuscripts and Letters in the Louis Zukofsky Collection at the University of Texas (Austin). Univ. of Texas (Austin), 1969. Dissertation: English.

Spivey, Herman E. A Critical Bibliography for the Years 1917 to 1922 of Representative American Authors. Univ. of North Carolina (Chapel Hill), 1929. Thesis: English. [Includes references to Robert M. Bird, J.C. Harris, Paul H. Hayne, Lafcadio Hearn, Sidney Lanier, O. Henry, and E.A. Poe]

Stephens, Andrew J. A Calendar of the Writings of Sam Houston in the Various Collections in Austin [Texas]. Univ. of Texas (Austin), 1927. Thesis: History.

Taylor, Doris N. Short Stories of the Southwest. Univ. of Oklahoma, 1939. Thesis: English. [Extensive bibliography]

Thiessen, N.T. An Annotated Bibliography of American Historical Fiction. Kansas State Teachers College, 1937. Thesis: English. [Includes James Lane Allen, Roack Bradford, Thomas Dixon, Ellen Glasgow, DuBose Heyward, T.N. Page, and Elizabeth Madox Roberts]

Thompson, Ralph. American Literary Annuals and Gift Books, 1825-1865. Columbia Univ., 1936. Dissertation: English.

Van Camp, Eliza L. Bibliography of Masters' Theses Accepted by English Departments in Texas. Sam Houston State Univ., 1939. Thesis: English. [With annotations]

Walker, Martha W. An Annotated Bibliography of the William Faulkner Section of the Shaw Collection of Contemporary Authors in the Univ. of Tulsa's McFarlin Library. Univ. of Tulsa, 1965. Thesis: English.

Walker, William S., Jr. An Annotated Bibliography of the Short Story. Kansas State College (Pittsburg), 1932. Thesis: Languages and Literature. [Includes Irvin S. Cobb]

Wallenberg, Mrs. Harry. A Bibliography of Texas Poetry. Texas Christian Univ., 1927. Thesis: English.

Waller, James W. The Southern Pamphlet Collection: Virginia Section; an Analysis and Evaluation, with a Chronological Checklist, 1820-1879. Univ. of North Carolina (Chapel Hill), 1968. Thesis: Library Science.

Washburn, Alice. A Descriptive Catalogue of Confederate Music in the Duke University Collection. Duke Univ., 1937. Thesis: History.

Wilkinson, Billy R. The Thomas Wolfe Collection of the University of North Carolina Library. Univ. of North Carolina (Chapel Hill), 1960. Thesis: Library Science.

Wilson, Esther L. An Annotated Bibliography of the Short Story. Kansas State College (Pittsburg), 1933. Thesis: English. [Annotation of several hundred short stories]

Winstandley, Grace V. Five Rare Kentucky Books: An Historical and Bibliographical Study of the First Works Produced before 1812 in Different Types of Writing. Columbia Univ., 1942. Thesis: Library Service.

Wolfe, Dorothy E. An Annotated Bibliography of the Short Story.
    Kansas State College (Pittsburg), 1932. Thesis: English.
Wright, Eugene P. A Descriptive Catalogue of the Joanna Southcott
    Collection at the University of Texas. Univ. of Texas
    (Austin), 1966. Dissertation: English.

COMPARATIVE STUDIES

Adams, Eugenia I. Poe's Relation to the French Symbolists. Univ.
    of Texas (Austin), 1939. Thesis: English.
Alexander, Jean. Poe and Baudelaire: A Study of Comparative
    Literature. Univ. of Chicago, 1918. Thesis: English.
Allen, Mozelle S. Poe's Debt to Gautier, to Pascal, and to
    Voltaire. Univ. of Texas (Austin), 1941. Dissertation:
    English.
Anderson, Don M. Edgar Allan Poe's Influence upon Baudelaire's
    Style. State Univ. of Iowa, 1955. Dissertation: English.
Anderson, Lorine. A Century of Dandyism: From Poe and
    Baudelaire to Wallace Stevens. Columbia Univ., 1954.
    Thesis: English.
Ater, Leroy E., Jr. An Examination of Three Major Novels in
    World Literature in the Light of Critical Precepts Derived
    From Tolstoy's *What Is Art?* Univ. of Southern California,
    1964. [Includes *Huckleberry Finn*]
Atkinson, James B. Moral Implications in the Poetry of Edgar
    Allan Poe and Arthur Rimbaud. Columbia Univ., 1961.
    Thesis: English.
Ayres, William W., Jr. The Lyre in the Sky: A Study of Possible
    Celtic Influences in Selected Poems of Edgar Allan Poe.
    Tulane Univ., 1969. Thesis: English.
Bailey, Dale S. Slavery in the Novels of Brazil and the United
    States: A Comparison. Indiana Univ. (Bloomington), 1961.
    Dissertation: English. [Arna Bontemps, Roark Bradford,
    G.W. Cable, Thomas Dixon, and Caroline Gordon]
Barfott, Anne. Social Opportunism in Balzac and Faulkner.
    Univ. of Southern Mississippi, 1967. Thesis: English.
Barthelme, Marilyn M. L'Influence d'Edgar Allan Poe sur la vie
    la pensée et l'oeuvre de Stéphane Mallarimé. Rice Univ.,
    1955. Thesis: French.
Belanger, Joseph R. (Brother Joseph Emilian, F.M.S.). The French
    Element in Edgar Allan Poe's Dupin Trilogy. St. John's
    Univ. (N.Y.), 1955. Thesis: English.
Belli, Angela. The Use of Greek Mythological Themes and Characters
    in Twentieth Century Drama: Four Approaches. New York Univ.,
    1965. Dissertation: English. [Includes Tennessee Williams'
    Orpheus Descending]
Berets, Ralph A. The Irrational Narrator in Virginia Woolf's
    The Waves, William Faulkner's *The Sound and the Fury*, and
    Gunter Grass's *The Tin Drum*. Univ. of Michigan, 1969.
    Dissertation: English.
Brownlee, May. Edgar Allan Poe and Charles Baudelaire. Columbia
    Univ., 1912. Thesis: English.
Burton, Jack L. Charles Baudelaire, Traducteur d'Edgar Allan Poe.
    Occidental College, 1967. Thesis: English.

Cambiaire, Célestin P. The Influence of Edgar Allan Poe in France. Univ. of Iowa, 1925. Dissertation: English.

Carter, Norma F. The Faust Legend in Marlowe, Goethe, Wolfe, and Mann. East Tennessee State Univ., 1968. Thesis: English.

Castillion, Pauline S. The French Language and Literature in the Prose Works of Edgar Allan Poe. Texas Christian Univ., 1965. Thesis: English.

Chipman, Doris. The attitude of Hawthorne toward Science Compared with the Attitudes of Rousseau, Wordsworth, Goethe, and Poe. Fort Hays Kansas State College, 1958. Thesis: Comparative Literature.

Christen, Elizabeth L. The Presentation of Consciousness in As I Lay Dying by William Faulkner and L'Emploi du Temps by Michael Butor. Purdue Univ., 1967. Thesis: English.

Clark, Kathleen. The Problem of Incest in Three Selected Modern Dramas: Henrik Ibsen's Ghosts, Eugene O'Neill's Desire Under the Elms, and Tennessee Williams' A Streetcar Named Desire. North Carolina College (Durham), 1964. Thesis: English.

Cobb, Palmer. The Influence of E.T.A. Hoffman on the Tales of Edgar Allan Poe. Columbia Univ., 1908. Dissertation: German.

Collins, Sr. M. Carol A., S.S.N.D. William Faulkner, Julien Green and the Freudian Personality. John Carroll Univ., 1962. Thesis: English.

Colonnell, Robert. Fyodor Dostoyevsky and Thomas Wolfe: A Comparison. East Tennessee State Univ., 1970. Thesis: English.

Crane, Joshua. A Comparison of G.B. Shaw's Saint Joan and Lillian Hellman's Adaptation of The Lark by Jean Anouilh. Univ. of Florida, 1961. Thesis: English.

Dawson, William M. The Female Characters of August Strindberg, Eugene O'Neill and Tennessee Williams. Univ. of Wisconsin, 1964. Dissertation: Speech and Drama.

Day, Marjery F. Literary Kinship of Edgar Allan Poe and August Strindberg. Univ. of Kansas, 1926. Thesis: English.

Delakas, Daniel L. Thomas Wolfe et les romanciers français. Paris, 1950. Dissertation: English.

Donaghy, Joyce. A Search for Human Significance: Flannery O'Connor and Pierre Teilhard de Chardin. Georgia State Univ., 1969. Thesis: English.

Dowden, Wilfred S. Some Influences of E.T.A. Hoffman upon Edgar Allan Poe. Vanderbilt Univ., 1940. Thesis: German.

Ehilich, Mary D.S. Faulkner's Fondness for Modern French Technique. Univ. of South Carolina, 1953. Thesis: English.

Englekirk, John E. Edgar Allan Poe in Hispanic Literature. Columbia Univ., 1934. Dissertation: Romance Languages.

Feathers, Sherrell N. Hell Hath No Fury: Feminine Characterization in Selected Plays of Euripides and Tennessee Williams. East Tennessee State Univ., 1964. Thesis: English.

Fernández, Roberta A. The Stream-of-Consciousness Technique: A Comparative Study. Univ. of Texas (Austin), 1966. Thesis: Spanish. [William Faulkner]

Fleming, Isabelle R. Chekhovian Influence and Parallels in the
    Works of Tennessee Williams and Arthur Miller. Columbia
    Univ., 1954. Thesis: English.
Fraker, Charles F. The Development of Modernism in Spanish-
    American Poetry. Harvard Univ., 1931. Dissertation:
    Modern Languages. [Includes E.A. Poe]
Friedrich, Peter O. The Literature of the Air: Themes and
    Imagery in the Works of Faulkner, Saint-Exupery, and Gaiser.
    Harvard Univ., 1968. Dissertation: Comparative Literature.
Fuller, Louise F. Poe and Puckler-Muskau: "The Domain of
    Annheim" and *The Tour of a German Prince*. Univ. of
    Tennessee, 1966. Thesis: English.
Gegerias, Mary. Michel Butor and William Faulkner: Some
    Structures and Techniques. Columbia Univ., 1968. Disser-
    tation: English.
Gilman, Madeline. *Faerie Queen*; An Auden poem; and Twain and
    Kafka. Pennsylvania State Univ., 1965. Thesis: English.
Gomeau, Harold O. Heroines of August Strindberg and Tennessee
    Williams: A Study in Anti-feminism. Columbia Univ., 1953.
    Thesis: English.
Gould, Loyal N. A Comparison of the German and American Agrarian
    Novels. Univ. of North Carolina (Chapel Hill), 1953.
    Thesis: Comparative Literature. [Includes Thomas Dixon's
    The Clansman and Ellen Glasgow's *Barren Ground*]
Grava, Arnolds. L'Aspect métaphysique du mal dans l'oeuvre
    littéraire de Charles Baudelaire et d'Edgar Allan Poe. Univ.
    of Nebraska, 1954. Dissertation: English.
Gravely, William H., Jr. The Lunar Voyage in Literature from
    Lucian to Poe. Univ. of Virginia, 1934. Thesis: English.
Halloran, Sr. M.T., O.P. The Superiority of the Technique of
    Edgar Allan Poe over that of James Sheridan LeFanu in the
    Treatment of the Weird. Catholic Univ., 1934. Thesis:
    English.
Hansard, J.D. Poe and Chekhov. Oglethorpe Univ., 1934. Thesis:
    English.
Hardwick, Diana L. A Study of Parallels between Christ Symbols
    in William Faulkner and Fyodor Dostoyevsky. Brown Univ.,
    1957. Thesis: English.
Harkey, Joseph H. *Don Quixote* and American Fiction through Mark
    Twain. Univ. of Tennessee, 1969. Dissertation: English.
Harris, Stephen L.R. "The Ecstacy and the Horror": A Review of
    the Poe-Baudelaire Affinity. Cornell Univ., 1961. Thesis:
    English.
Haskel, Peggy I. William Faulkner and Ivan Bunin: Their Worlds.
    Univ. of Texas (Austin), 1952. Thesis: English.
Hilton, Susan W. "Old Beauty and New Truth": The Continuation
    of the Major Themes of Henrik Ibsen in the Plays of Tennessee
    Williams. Stetson Univ., 1966. Thesis: English.
Hodges, Elizabeth L. The Bible as Novel: A Comparative Study of
    Two Modernized Versions of Biblical Stories, Zola's *La
    Faute de L'Abbe Mouret* and Faulkner's *A Fable*. Univ. of
    Georgia, 1969. Dissertation: Comparative Literature.
Hoffman, Roberta M. Tragedy: From Athens to Yoknapatawpha.
    Columbia Univ., 1961. Thesis: English.

Hosillos, Lucila V. William Faulkner and Nick Joaquin: An Approach through Dialectics. Indiana Univ. (Bloomington), 1962. Thesis: Comparative Literature.

Hudson, Susie M. A Comparative Study of the Growth in Artistic Purpose: Miguel Cervantes, Henry Fielding and Mark Twain. West Texas State Univ., 1963. Thesis: English.

Hulme, Francis P. A History of Music-Imagery in European Literature with Special Emphasis on Nineteenth and Twentieth Century English, American, and French Literature. Univ. of Minnesota, 1947. Dissertation: English. [Sidney Lanier and E.A. Poe]

Ikui, Haruko. Poems by John Gould Fletcher Compared with Japanese Poetry Haiku. Iowa State Teachers College, 1965. Thesis: English.

Jaeger, Robert O. The Influence of Edgar Allan Poe on the Leading "Modernista" Writers of Latin America. Washington Univ. (St. Louis), 1947. Thesis: English.

Kahn, Ernst. Edgar Allan Poe und Charles Baudelaire: Ein Vergleich ihrer Weltanschauung und Kunstlehre. Heidelberg, 1921. Dissertation: English.

King, Emily B. The Elements of Rousseauism in the Work of Sidney Lanier. Duke Univ., 1935. Thesis: French.

Kitzinger, Angela M. Lafcadio Hearn and French Literature. Univ. of Southern California, 1958. Dissertation: English.

Kominars, Sheppard B. Encounter with Satan: A Study of Dostoyevski, Mann, and Faulkner. Columbia Univ., 1959. Thesis: English.

Lemonnier, Léon. Les Traducteurs d'Edgar Poe en France de 1845 à 1875: Charles Baudelaire. Paris, 1928. Dissertation: English.

Long, Madeleine J. Sartrean Themes in Contemporary American Literature. Columbia Univ., 1967. Dissertation: English-Education. [Includes Ralph Ellison's *Invisible Man*]

Lowery, Marilyn M. The Philosophy of Kant as Seen in the Poetry of John Crowe Ransom. Univ. of Southern California, 1956. Thesis: English.

Lubka, Bernice. A Comparative Study in the Aesthetics of Paul Valery and Edgar Allan Poe. Columbia Univ., 1948. Thesis: French.

Managano, Kathryn F. A Comparative Thematic Study in the Major Novels of Faulkner and Dostoevsky. Arizona State Univ., 1966. Thesis: English.

Marquardt, Helen L. E.A. Poe and Friedrich Gerstaecker: A Comparison. Pennsylvania State Univ., 1933. Thesis: English.

McCormick, John O. Thomas Wolfe, Andre Malraux, Hermann Hesse: A Study in Creative Vitality. Harvard Univ., 1951. Dissertation: English.

McWilliams, David D. The Influence of William Faulkner on Michel Butor [Portions of Text in French]. Univ. of Oregon, 1969. Dissertation: English.

Messac, G.R. Influences francaises dans L'oeuvre d'Edgar Poe. Paris, 1929. Dissertation: English.

Middlebrook, Mary E. An Analysis of the Influence of Edgar
    Allan Poe upon Charles Baudelaire. Baylor Univ., 1941.
    Thesis: English.
Morokoff, Gene E. Jean-Paul Sartre and the Modern American
    Novel. Univ. of North Carolina (Chapel Hill), 1951. Thesis:
    Comparative Literature. [Includes William Faulkner and
    Erskine Caldwell]
Newberry, Elizabeth. A Comparison of the Short Stories of Poe and
    Maupassant. Univ. of Tennessee, 1934. Thesis: French.
Newton, Margaret E. The Texas Cowboy and Argentine Gaucho in
    Literature, as Found in Andy Adams' Novels, Badger Clark's
    Poetry, Ricardo Güiraldes' *Don Segundo Sombra* and José
    Hernández's *Martín Fierro*. Univ. of Texas (Austin), 1942.
    Thesis: English.
Oppel, Ilse. Edgar Allan Poe und Charles Baudelaire. Vienna,
    1950. Dissertation: English.
Patterson, Arthur S. L'Influence d'Edgar Poe sur Charles
    Baudelaire. Grenoble, 1903. Dissertation: English.
Penick, Edwin A., Jr. A Theological Critique of the Interpretation
    of Man in the Fiction and Drama of William Faulkner, Ernest
    Hemingway, Jean-Paul Sartre, and Albert Camus. Yale Univ.,
    1954. Dissertation: Religion.
Plant, John F. Charles Baudelaire et la Pensée littéraire
    d'Edgar Allan Poe. Univ. of British Columbia, 1967. Thesis:
    English.
Pochmann, Henry A. The Influence of the German Tale on the Short
    Stories of Irving, Hawthorne, and Poe. Univ. of North
    Carolina (Chapel Hill), 1928. Dissertation: English.
Preston, Fannie R. A Comparative Study of the Works of Edgar
    Allan Poe and Gustavo Adolfo Becquer. Univ. of Texas
    (Austin), 1920. Thesis: Spanish.
Quinn, Patrick F. The French Face of Edgar Poe. Columbia Univ.,
    1953. Dissertation: English.
Ray, Ruth M. Sources of the French Quotations in Poe's Works.
    Columbia Univ., 1924. Thesis: English.
Reifield, Beatrice. Three Studies in English: *Sir Gawain and the
    Green Knight*; Eliot's *The Cocktail Party*; Baudelaire and Poe.
    Pennsylvania State Univ., 1968. Thesis: English.
Resnick, Seymour. The Influence of Edgar Allan Poe on José
    Asuncion Silva. New York Univ., 1943. Thesis: English.
Richards, Lewis A. The Literary Styles of Jean-Paul Sartre and
    William Faulkner: An Analysis, Comparison, and Contrast.
    Univ. of Southern California, 1963. Dissertation: English.
Ritter, Jesse P., Jr. Fearful Comedy: The Fiction of Joseph
    Heller, Gunter Grass, and the Social Surrealist Genre. Univ.
    of Arkansas, 1967. Dissertation: English. [Relates movement
    to Ralph Ellison and William Faulkner]
Rogers, Rodney O. *A Tramp Abroad*, *A Connecticut Yankee*, and Taine's
    L'Ancien Regime: An Instance of Source Adaptation in Mark
    Twain's Writing. Univ. of Virginia, 1967. Thesis: English.
Ross, Crystal R. Le Conteur américain O. Henry et l'art de
    Maupassant. Strasbourg, 1925. Dissertation: English.
Rundel, Judith A. Proust, Faulkner and Durrell: Modes of
    Fictional Relativity. John Carroll Univ., 1963. Thesis:
    English.

Scarborough, Charles W., Jr. The Influence of Hawthorne and Poe on the Work of Julien Green. Univ. of Maryland, 1969. Thesis: English.

Schinzel, Elisabeth. Natur und Natursymbolik bei Poe, Baudelaire und den franzosischen Symbolisten. Bonn, 1931. Dissertation: English.

Searle, William M. The Saint and the Skeptics: Joan of Arc in the Works of Mark Twain, Anatole France, and Bernard Shaw. Univ. of California (Berkeley), 1968. Dissertation: English.

Seylaz, Louis. Edgar Poe et les premiers symbolistes français. Lausanne, 1923. Dissertation: English.

Sheerin, William V. The Nature of the Influence of Edgar Allan Poe on French poetry. Fordham Univ., 1933. Thesis: English.

Simon, John K. The Glance of the Idiot: A Thematic Study of Faulkner and Modern French Fiction. Yale Univ., 1963. Dissertation: English.

Smith, John C. Voltaire and H.L. Mencken, Critics of Society. Univ. of Texas (Austin), 1960. Thesis: French.

Stanton, Edgar E., Jr. Hegel and Thomas Wolfe. Florida State Univ., 1960. Dissertation: English.

Stewart, David H. William Faulkner and Mikhail Sholokhov: A Comparative Study of Two Representatives of the Regional Conscience, Their Affinities and Meanings. Univ. of Michigan, 1958. Dissertation: English.

Stewart, Frances L. Afro-American: A Comparative Study of Langston Hughes, Luis Palés Matos, and Nicolás Guillén. Univ. of Texas (Austin), 1969. Thesis: Spanish.

Stone, Edward. Henry Louis Mencken's Debt to Friedrich Wilhelm Nietzsche. Univ. of Texas (Austin), 1937. Thesis: English.

Tauzin, Mary N. Camus' Adaptation of Faulkner's *Requiem for a Nun*. Univ. of Georgia, 1967. Thesis: English.

Tharp, James B. Poe and Maupassant. Univ. of Illinois, 1924. Thesis: Romance Languages.

Thomas, Jesse J. The Image of Man in the Literary Heroes of Jean-Paul Sartre and Three American Novelists: Saul Bellow, John Barth, and Ken Kesey: A Theological Evaluation. Northwestern Univ., 1967. Dissertation: Religion.

Thomas, Martha L. The Reappearing Character in Faulkner and Balzac. Univ. of Georgia, 1961. Thesis: English.

Treat, Ariss. A Study of the Influence of Edgar Allan Poe on the Critical Thinking of Charles Baudelaire. San Diego State College, 1959. Thesis: English.

Trobaugh, Robert J. The Nature of Man in the Writings of Reinhold Niebuhr and William Faulkner. Vanderbilt Univ., 1966. Dissertation: Religion.

Wächtler, Paul. Edgar Allan Poe und die deutsche Romantik. Liepzig, 1911. Dissertation: English.

Wallace, Mrs. J.H. A Comparison of the Short Stories of Edgar Allan Poe and Guy de Maupassant. Univ. of Oklahoma, 1919. Thesis: English.

Weinstein, Arnold L. The Reconstructive Mode in Fiction: A Study of Faulkner and the French New Novel. Harvard Univ., 1968. Dissertation: Comparative Literature.

Weisstein, Ulrich W. Types of Projection in Romantic Literature:
    E.T.A. Hoffman and Edgar Allan Poe. Indiana Univ., 1953.
    Thesis: English.
White, George L., Jr. Scandinavian Themes in American Fiction.
    Univ. of Pennsylvania, 1935. Dissertation: English.
    [Includes Erskine Caldwell, Lafacadio Hearn, and T.N. Page]
Williams, Hazael S. Baudelaire, Translator of Poe, as Seen in
    the *Histoires Extraordinaires* and the *Nouvelles Histoires
    Extraordinaires*. Southern Methodist Univ., 1934. Thesis:
    English. [Seeks to reveal the type of work Baudelaire did
    in translating Poe's works and to show what it meant to
    Baudelaire to know Poe, the man, as revealed in his works]
Wurfl, George J. Poe's Influence upon Baudelaire. Pennsylvania
    State Univ., 1926. Thesis: English.
Young, R.C. The Unanswered Man (A Comparative Study of John
    Barth, *End of the Road*; Samuel Beckett, *Molloy*; Albert
    Camus, *The Strangers*; Hermann Hesse *Steppenwolf*; and Eugene
    O'Neill, *The Iceman Cometh*). Fairleigh Dickinson Univ.,
    1966. Thesis: English.
Zrimc, Marie-Antoinette U. Creation of Atmosphere in the Novels
    of Hawthorne, Faulkner, and Julien Green. Harvard Univ.,
    1969. Dissertation: Comparative Literature.

NEWSPAPERS AND PERIODICALS

Adams, Raymond W. A Study of the Chief Literary Magazines of the
    South During the Years 1865 to 1880. Univ. of North Carolina
    (Chapel Hill), 1921. Thesis: English.
Adams, Virgil E. A History of the Jackson *Herald*. Univ. of
    Georgia, 1956. Thesis: Journalism.
Agnew, Virginia M. *Russell's Magazine*. Duke Univ., 1937. Thesis:
    English.
Allen, Marjorie A. Patterns of Thought in American Periodical
    Criticism from 1835 to 1840: A Study of Eight Magazines.
    Univ. of Texas (Austin), 1944. Thesis: English. [Includes
    Southern Literary Messenger and *Southern Literary Journal*]
Ames, William E. A History of the *National Intelligencer*,
    1800-1869. Univ. of Minnesota, 1962. Dissertation: History.
    [Based in Washington, D.C., and tied in with Jefferson, whom
    its editors supported. Its managing editors after 1820 were
    Joseph Gales, Jr., from North Carolina, and his brother-in-law
    William Winston Seaton]
Anderson, Sara F.L. A History of Burnet County Newspapers and
    Newspapermen. Univ. of Texas (Austin), 1950. Thesis:
    Journalism. [Burnet County, Texas]
Arp, Marjorie L. The History of Newspapers in Texas from 1865-1876.
    Univ. of Texas (Austin), 1936. Thesis: Journalism.
Arrendell, Odes C. Coverage of the 1968 Democratic and Republican
    Presidential Campaigns by Texas Daily Newspapers: An
    Evaluation Related to Social Responsibility Theory. Univ.
    of Texas (Austin), 1969. Dissertation: Journalism.
Ashley, Frank W. Selected Southern Liberal Editors and the
    States' Rights Movement of 1948. Univ. of South Carolina,
    1959. Dissertation: History. [Includes Jonathan Daniels,

Raleigh *News and Observer*; Virginius Dabney,
Richmond *Times-Dispatch*, and Ralph McGill, Atlanta
Constitution]

Ashley, Perry J. Selection and use of State News by Weekly
Newspapers in Kentucky. Southern Illinois Univ. (Carbondale),
1968. Dissertation: Journalism.

Atchison, Ray M. Southern Literary Magazines, 1865-1887. Duke
Univ., 1956. Dissertation: English. [Surveys eleven states
of Confederacy and four border states]

Autrey, William R. The Negro Press: Southern Style Militancy--
The Atlanta *Independent* and Savannah *Tribune* (1904-1928).
Atlanta Univ., 1963. Thesis: History.

Bagby, Nathe P. Editorial Policies of the Dallas *News*. Univ. of
Texas (Austin), 1930. Thesis: Journalism.

Baker, Thomas H. III. The Memphis *Commercial Appeal*, 1865-1941.
Univ. of Texas (Austin), 1965. Dissertation: History.

Barrow, Robert M. Newspaper Advertising in Colonial America,
1704-1775. Univ. of Virginia, 1967. Dissertation: History.

Barthold, A.J. The French Newspaper Press in America, 1780-1790.
Yale Univ., 1932. Dissertation: Romance Languages. [A
short chapter entitled 'Courier du Vendredi, New Orleans,
1785-1786]

Barton, Eva M. A History of Journalism in Glasgow, Kentucky.
George Peabody College, 1934. Thesis: English.

Beall, O.T., Jr. Literary Criticism in Five American Magazines,
1801-1832. Univ. of Minnesota, 1933. Thesis: English.

Bearden, Elizabeth S. *The Southern Review*. Columbia Univ.,
1925. Thesis: English.

Bentley, Imogene. Texas Literary and Educational Magazines:
Their History and Educational Content. George Peabody
College, 1941. Dissertation: English. [Includes *Corona*,
Dixieland, *Guardian*, *Gulf Messenger*, *Frontier Times*]

Berger, Thomas E. The Beginnings and Early Development of Baptist
Newspapers in Texas, 1855-1900. Univ. of Texas (Austin),
1969. Thesis: Journalism.

Bowen, Frances J. The New Orleans *Double Dealer*: January 1921-
May 1926, A Critical History. Vanderbilt Univ., 1954.
Dissertation: English.

Bowles, Frances P. A Study of the Work of Alabama Writers
Published in the *Spirit of the Times*, 1845-1855. Auburn
Univ., 1956. Thesis: English.

Box, Hazel M. The Image of the Public High School in North
Carolina from 1905 to 1925 as Reflected in Selected Daily
Newspapers. Univ. of North Carolina (Chapel Hill), 1968.
Dissertation: Education. [Includes Greensboro *Daily News*,
The Charlotte *Observer*, *The News and Observer*, The
Fayetteville *Observer*]

Brandis, Martha M. History of the *University of North Carolina
Magazine*, 1844-1948. Univ. of North Carolina (Chapel Hill),
1964. Thesis: Library Science.

Brantley, Raburn L. A Brief History of the Macon *Telegraph*.
Mercer Univ., 1924. Thesis: English. [Macon, Georgia]
_____. Georgia Journalism of the Civil War Period. George
Peabody College, 1928. Dissertation: English.

Burgess, Samuel L. Georgia Journalism, 1951-60. Univ. of
Georgia, 1966. Thesis: Journalism.

Caffery, Doris L. French Literature in Louisiana Country
Newspapers: *Le Meschacébé*, *Le Foyer Créole*, and *L'Intérim*,
1880-1899. Louisiana State Univ., 1944. Thesis: Romance
Languages.

Calhoun, Richard J. Literary Criticism in Southern Periodicals:
1828-1860. Univ. of North Carolina (Chapel Hill), 1959.
Dissertation: English. [*Southern Review*; *Southern Literary
Messenger*; *Southern Literary Journal*; *Magnolia*; *Southern
Quarterly Review*; *Orion*; *DeBow's Review*; *Southern Literary
Gazette*; *Southern and Western Monthly Magazine and Review*;
Russell's Magazine]

Calvert, Julia D.B. A Quantitative Analysis of Two Southern
Journals. Columbia Univ., 1916. Thesis: Sociology.
[Richmond, Virginia, *News-Leader* and *Evening Journal*]

Cantrill, Mary L. A Study of Gothic Fiction in American
Periodicals, 1800-1850. Columbia Univ., 1945. Thesis:
English. [Includes *DeBow's Review*, *Southern Quarterly
Review* (Charleston), and *Southern Rose* (Charleston)]

Carson, Clements. Four Magazine Centers of the Old South.
Vanderbilt Univ., 1933. Thesis: English. [Baltimore,
Charleston, New Orleans, and Richmond]

Carter, Myrtle B. An Analysis of the Feature Stories of the
Houston *Chronicle*, 1902-1932. Univ. of Texas (Austin),
1932. Thesis: Journalism.

Carter, Virginia. Literary Periodicals of the Southwest,
Especially as Shown by a Detailed Study of the *Southwest
Review*. Univ. of Oklahoma, 1933. Thesis: English.

Casey, James R. The Short Stories in the *Southern Review*
(1935-1942). Vanderbilt Univ., 1949. Thesis: English.
[Robert Penn Warren and Cleanth Brooks]

Castles, William H., Jr. The *Virginia Gazette*, 1736-1766: Its
Editors, Editorial Policies, and Literary Content. Univ.
of Tennessee, 1962. Dissertation: English.

Cearley, J.H. A Comparative Study of the Short Story in the
Quality and Popular Magazines. Texas Tech Univ., 1940.
Thesis: English. [Includes *American Mercury*; discusses
Elizabeth M. Roberts, James Still, and Jesse Stuart]

Chambers, Robert W. A Study of the Readability of Staff-written
Copy in the Dallas *Morning News*. Univ. of Texas (Austin),
1948. Thesis: Journalism.

Chenet, Horace S. Le Comte Joseph-Gabriel de Baroncelli-javon,
Journaliste Polémiste de la Nourvelle-Orleans. Tulane Univ.,
1940. Thesis: French.

Chunn, Calvin E. History of News Magazines. Univ. of Missouri,
1950. Dissertation: Journalism. [Includes *Southern
Illustrated News*, 1862-1865]

Cleland, Ann S. The Memphis *Daily Appeal*: Its Desperate Fight
for Southern Independence. Univ. of California (Los Angeles),
1967. Thesis: Journalism.

Cline, John. Thirty-Eight Years of the *South Atlantic Quarterly*:
A Chapter in the Progress of Liberalism in the South. Duke
Univ., 1940. Thesis: English.

Cohen, Henry H. *The South Carolina Gazette*. (1732-1775): Its History and some Aspects of Its Cultural Content. Tulane Univ., 1951. Dissertation: English.

Cole, Richard R. A Journal of Free Voices: The History of *The Texas Observer*. Univ. of Texas (Austin), 1966. Thesis: Journalism.

Comeggs, Robert G. The Agrarian and Rural Tradition as Reflected in National Periodical Literature. Stanford Univ., 1958. Dissertation: English. [Includes 28 magazines, some Southern]

Cook, Elizabeth C. Literary Influences in Colonial Newspapers, 1704-1750. Columbia Univ., 1912. Dissertation: English.

Cooksey, Virginia C. The Columbus [Georgia] *Enquirer*: A Study of Literary Culture as Reflected in One Southern Newspaper. Auburn Univ., 1948. Thesis: English.

Cope, Neil B. A History of the Memphis *Commercial Appeal*. Univ. of Missouri, 1969. Dissertation: Journalism.

Cord, Helen L. American Newspaper and Periodical Literature before 1830. Univ. of Cincinnati, 1920. Thesis: English. [Includes *Maryland Gazette*, *South Carolina Gazette*, *The Virginia Gazette*, *Western Review* and *Miscellaneous Magazine* (Kentucky)]

Corley, Viola F. American Periodical Criticism of French Fiction from 1800 to 1860. Univ. of Texas (Austin), 1925. Thesis: English. [Includes *DeBow's Review*, *Southern Literary Messenger*, and *Southern Quarterly Review*]

Covington, Jess B. A History of the Shreveport *Times*. Univ. of Missouri, 1964. Dissertation: Journalism.

Cowan, Louise S. *The Fugitive*: A Critical History. Vanderbilt Univ., 1953. Thesis: English.

Cowdin, Hugh P. A Study of the Treatment and Its Effects upon the Community of the 1957 Little Rock Integration Crisis by the Two Little Rock Daily Newspapers. Marquette Univ., 1959. Thesis: Journalism.

Crouch, C.V. Life in Tennessee as Reflected in Some Newspapers Prior to 1820. Univ. of Chicago, 1924. Thesis: History. [Tennessee newspapers]

Cunningham, Charles. The Press in St. Landry Parish, 1841-1865: A Study in Louisiana Journalism. Louisiana State Univ., 1935. Thesis: Journalism.

Current-Garcia, Eugene. Criticism and the Problem of Literary Expression in a Democratic Society. Harvard Univ., 1947. Dissertation: English. [Based on *DeBow's Review*, *Southern Literary Messenger*, *Southern Quarterly Review*, and other Southern antebellum magazines]

Cutler, Ronald E. A History and Analysis of Negro Newspapers in Virginia. Univ. of Richmond, 1965. Thesis: History.

da Ponte, Durant H. *The Double-Dealer*, A National Magazine from the South. Tulane Univ., 1941. Thesis: English.

Davis, Norris G. Freedom of the Press in Texas: A Comparative Study of State Legal Controls on Mass News Media. Univ. of Minnesota, 1954. Dissertation: English.

Delaney, Margaret A. Factors of Survival in the Poetry Magazines of the United States. Univ. of Missouri, 1933. Thesis: Journalism.

Demaree, Albert L. The American Agricultural Press, 1819-1860. Columbia Univ., 1941. Dissertation: History.

Dempsey, Ray. The History and Influence of Major Southern Literary Magazines prior to the Civil War. Univ. of Georgia, 1947. Thesis: Journalism. [*DeBow's Review, Augusta Mirror, Niles' Weekly Register, Orion, Russell's Magazine, Southern Ladies' Book, Southern Review*, and *Southern Quarterly Review*]

Dennis, Frank A. West Tennessee Newspapers during the Civil War, 1860-1865. Mississippi State Univ., 1970. Dissertation: History.

Donnald, Morrill B. A Study on Nashville Newspapers, 1850-1875. Vanderbilt Univ., 1937. Thesis: History.

Doty, Lillian V. *DeBow's Review*. Univ. of South Carolina, 1930. Thesis: English.

Doyle, Mildred D. Sentimentalism in American Periodicals, 1741-1800. New York Univ., 1941. Dissertation: English. [Includes Baltimore *Weekly Magazine* and South Carolina *Weekly Museum*]

Duchein, Annette O. Anglo-Saxon Press of New Orleans, 1835-1861. Louisiana State Univ., 1933. Thesis: Journalism.

Durham, Alice M. What is Negro News? A Study of Three Negro Newspapers. Atlanta Univ., 1938. Thesis: Sociology. [Includes Baltimore *Afro-American*]

Dyer, Robert V. The Background and Content of the *Southern Review*. George Peabody College, 1939. Thesis: English.

Eaton, Carlton O. Editorial Attitudes of a Daily Newspaper Concerning Educational Issues. Southern Methodist Univ., 1956. Thesis: Education. [*Morning News* of Dallas, Texas]

Edwards, Rondle E. A Study of the Virginia Constitutional Convention as seen through the Richmond *Times*. Virginia State College, 1960. Thesis: History.

Ellen, John C., Jr. Political Newspapers of the Piedmont Carolinas in the 1850's. Univ. of South Carolina, 1958. Dissertation: History.

Elliott, Robert N. North Carolina Newspapers in the Federal Period, 1789-1800. Univ. of North Carolina (Chapel Hill), 1949. Thesis: History.

_____. The Raleigh *Register*, 1799-1863. Univ. of North Carolina (Chapel Hill), 1953. Dissertation: History.

Ellis, Miriam W. The Development of the Magazine in the Eighteenth Century in America. Boston Univ., 1936. Thesis: English. [Includes *The North Carolina Magazine*]

Eriksson, Eric M. Establishment and Rise of the Washington [D.C.] *Globe*. Univ. of Iowa, 1921. Thesis: Journalism.

Eskridge, Charles S. Selected Newspaper Verse Published in Texas, 1836-1846. Univ. of Texas (Austin), 1965. Thesis: Journalism.

Fairchild, Edith M. The Early American Magazines. Columbia Univ., 1902. Thesis: English. [Includes *South Carolina Weekly Museum and Complete Magazine*]

Fenderson, Lewis H. Development of the Negro Press: 1827-1948. Univ. of Pittsburgh, 1949. Dissertation: English.

Ferry, Robert M. Early Literary Magazines in Kentucky. Western Kentucky Univ., 1934. Thesis: English.

Flanders, Bertram H. Georgia Literary Periodicals to 1865. Duke Univ., 1942. Dissertation: English.

Flewelling, Howard L. Literary Criticism in American Periodicals, 1783-1820. Univ. of Michigan, 1931. Dissertation: English. [Includes *The Monthly Register and Review of the United States*]

Fort, Randolph L. History of the Atlanta *Journal*. Emory Univ., 1930. Thesis: Journalism.

Frantz, Joe B. The Newspapers of the Republic of Texas. Univ. of Texas (Austin), 1940. Thesis: History.

Frazier, Mary G. Texas Newspapers during the Republic (March 2, 1836-February 19, 1846). Univ. of Texas (Austin), 1931. Thesis: Journalism.

Fuller, Landon E. *The United States Magazine and Democratic Review*, 1837-1859: A Study of Its History, Contents, and Significance. Univ. of North Carolina (Chapel Hill), 1948. Dissertation: English. [Among the contributors to this magazine, founded in Washington, were T.H. Chivers, E.A. Poe, and W.A. Simms. The thesis discusses the magazine's coverage of the Poe-Chivers controversy.]

Gallaway, John F. Freedom of Thought in Antebellum Virginia as Revealed in the *Southern Literary Messenger*. Univ. of Georgia, 1931. Thesis: Journalism.

Garwood, Irving. American Periodicals from 1850 to 1860. Univ. of Chicago, 1922. Dissertation: English. [Listings and discussions of many Southern magazines such as *DeBow's Review*, *North Carolina University Magazine*, *Southern Ladies' Magazine*, and *Southern Literary Messenger*]

Gleason, James. Newspapers of the Southwest and the Davis Administration. Lamar Univ., 1965. Thesis: History.

Goldsmith, Adolph O. A Study of the Objectivity of Treatment of Governor Huey P. Long by Six Louisiana Newspapers during Long's First Eleven Months in Office. Univ. of Iowa, 1967. Dissertation: Journalism. [Period from May, 1928 to April, 1929]

Golson, Graham E. The Accuracy of Atlanta Newspapers. Emory Univ., 1938. Thesis: Journalism.

Gossett, Thomas F. A History of the *Southwest Review*: 1915-1942. Southern Methodist Univ., 1948. Thesis: English.

Graham, Harvey L. *The Northern Standard*, 1842-48: A Texas Frontier Newspaper. Univ. of Texas (Austin), 1927. Thesis: History.

Graham, Hugh D. Tennessee Editorial Responses to Change in the Bi-Racial System, 1954-60. Stanford Univ., 1965. Dissertation: History.

Grasty, Margaret E. The History of the Houston *Post*. Univ. of Texas (Austin), 1939. Thesis: Journalism.

Gray, Elizabeth K. The Clemson *News*: A Porject in South Carolina Weekly Journalism. Univ. of Iowa, 1943. Thesis: Journalism.

Greenbaum, Leonard A. The *Hound & Horn*: Episodes in American Literary History, 1927-1934. Univ. of Michigan, 1963. Dissertation: English. [Allen Tate as Regional Editor]

Griffith, Louis T. History of the Georgia Press Association.
    Univ. of Georgia, 1941. Thesis: Journalism.
Groce, George C. Charleston Society in the 1850's as Revealed
    in the Charleston (S.C.) *Courier*. Univ. of Texas (Austin),
    1923. Thesis: Sociology. [Critical analysis of poems
    printed in *Courier*, report on magazines read, on tastes in
    reading as shown by books advertised, and on the theater.]
Groen, Henry J. German Literature in the English-Language News-
    papers of New Orleans before 1880. Louisiana State Univ.,
    1940. Thesis: German.
Hagood, Monroe J. The Beginnings of Literary Nationalism in
    American Magazines, 1770-1827. Univ. of North Carolina
    (Chapel Hill), 1948. Dissertation: English. [Includes
    Niles' Weekly Register, *Southern Literary Gazette*, *Southern
    Review*, *Virginia Evangelical and Literary Review*]
Harding, Jacobina B. A History of the Early Newspapers of San
    Antonio, 1832-1874. Univ. of Texas (Austin), 1951. Thesis:
    History.
Harper, Clifton E. The Country Press of Louisiana, 1860-1910.
    Louisiana State Univ., 1939. Thesis: Journalism.
Harper, Myrtle B. The Country Press of Louisiana, 1794-1860.
    Louisiana State Univ., 1939. Thesis: Journalism.
Harrelson, Otho M. A Survey of the Weekly Newspapers in Arkansas
    from 1929-1932, including a Study of the Effects of the
    Business Depression. Northwestern Univ., 1932. Thesis:
    Journalism.
Hart, John F. The Newspapers and Newspapermen of Hunt and Kaufman
    Counties (Texas). Univ. of Texas (Austin), 1937. Thesis:
    Journalism.
Herbert, Mary A. Louisiana Journalism of the Civil War Period
    (1860-1865). Louisiana State Univ., 1937. Thesis:
    Journalism.
Herron, Dorothy A. Educational Interests as Revealed in the
    Newspaper Advertisements of Virginia and North Carolina
    between 1800 and 1840. Univ. of North Carolina (Chapel Hill),
    1948. Thesis: Education.
High, Thomas O. Albert Taylor Bledsoe's *Review*: A Southern
    Apologia. Vanderbilt Univ., 1942. Thesis: English.
Hinton, Virginia C.C. The Columbus *Enquirer* and Literature,
    1855-1872. Univ. of Georgia, 1967. Dissertation: English.
    [Columbus, Georgia. Includes discussion of G.W. Harris and
    Mark Twain]
Hodge, Llewellyn B. A Descriptive and Critical Analysis of
    Uncle Remus's Magazine. Univ. of Georgia, 1948. Thesis:
    English.
Holland, Cullen J. The Cherokee Indian Newspapers, 1828-1906:
    The Tribal Voice of a People in Transition. Univ. of
    Minnesota, 1956. Dissertation: Journalism. [Newspapers
    published in New Echota (near Calhoun), Georgia]
Horne, McDonald K., Jr. The Consolidated Printing of Weekly
    Newspapers. Univ. of North Carolina (Chapel Hill), 1932.
    Thesis: Economics. [Includes a list of publishers printing
    more than one weekly newspaper in Alabama, Arkansas, Florida,
    Kentucky, Mississippi, South Carolina, Tennessee, Texas, and
    Virginia]

Howard, Carl D. A Study of Medina County Newspapers and News-
    papermen. Univ. of Texas (Austin), 1960. Thesis:
    Journalism. [Medina County, Texas]
Howard, P.L., Jr. Conceptions of Nationalism in the *Northern
    American Review* and the *Southern Literary Messenger* before
    the Civil War. Univ. of Chicago, 1926. Thesis: English.
Howell, Irene M. A Study of the Contents of the *Southern
    Literary Messenger* (1834-1865). Univ. of Illinois, 1935.
    Thesis: English.
Hutto, John H. III. Magazines of South Carolina: 1820-1864.
    Univ. of South Carolina, 1969. Thesis: English.
Hyatt, Lewis P. The Clarksville *Leaf Chronicle*, 1808-1956,
    A History. George Peabody College, 1957. Dissertation:
    History. [Clarksville, Tennessee, newspaper]
Hyder, Gretchen. A Study of the *Taylor-Trotwood Magazine*.
    George Peabody College, 1929. Thesis: English.
Jeffery, Benjamin M. Short Stories in the *American Mercury*:
    1924-1933. Univ. of Texas (Austin), 1950. Thesis:
    English.
Johnson, Aliene. Southern Literary Magazines of the Reconstruction
    Period. A Chapter in the History of American Periodicals;
    Being a Detailed Study of *DeBow's Review*, *The Southern Review*,
    and *The Southern Magazine*, with a Brief Treatment of other
    Literary Magazines of the Reconstruction Period. Duke Univ.,
    1935. Thesis: English.
Jones, Frances E. A History of the *Arkansas Gazette*. George
    Peabody College, 1930. Thesis: English.
Juniger, Mildred. Texas Verse in Texas Newspapers, 1846-1861.
    Univ. of Texas (Austin), 1928. Thesis: English. [A record
    of Texas verse as it appeared in the newspapers of the state
    from Annexation to Secession, in order to determine the
    literary tastes of the people by a study of their poetic
    productions]
Keel, Edna A. A History of the Newspapers of Huntsville, Alabama,
    1812-1939. George Peabody College, 1939. Thesis: English.
Kerr, Willis H. Periodical Literature in America from the
    Revolution to 1815. Columbia Univ., 1902. Thesis: English.
    [Includes *Museum* (Nashville, Tenn.) and *South Carolina
    Weekly Museum and Complete Magazine*]
Key, Howard C. *The Arkansas Gazette*. 1819-1843. Univ. of Texas
    (Austin), 1935. Thesis: History.
Kilgore, Linda E. The Ku Klux Klan and the Press in Texas, 1920-
    1927. Univ. of Texas (Austin), 1964. Thesis: Journalism.
Kincaid, Naomi H. The Abilene *Reporter-News* and Its Contribution
    to the Development of the Abilene Country. Hardin-Simmons
    Univ., 1945. Thesis: Journalism. [Abilene, Texas]
Kleber, Brooks E. The Colonial Newspaper and the Emergence of an
    American Community. Univ. of Pennsylvania, 1957. Disser-
    tation: History. [Discusses press of Charleston, S.C.,
    Williamsburg, Virginia, from date of earliest journals
    until meeting of the First Continental Congress]
Knudson, Jerry W. The Jefferson Years: Response by the Press,
    1801-1809. Univ. of Virginia, 1962. Dissertation: History.
    [Includes Richmond *Enquirer* and Richmond *Recorder*]

Kobre, Sidney. The Development of the Colonial Newspaper.
Columbia Univ., 1944. Dissertation: Sociology.

Koen, Ottis V. Beginnings of Literary Culture in West Texas as
Revealed in the *Taylor County News* from 1885 to 1900.
Columbia Univ., 1933. Thesis: English.

Lander, Frances B. History of Journalism in Hopkinsville,
Kentucky. George Peabody College, 1928. Thesis: English.

Lang, Lawrence C. A Study of Texas Newspaper from 1876 to 1890.
Univ. of Texas (Austin), 1949. Thesis: Journalism.

Lawson, Milton A. The Influence of the Migration upon Negro
Newspapers. Fisk Univ., 1941. Thesis: Sociology and
Anthropology. [Baltimore *Afro-American*, Norfolk *Journal
and Guide*]

Leach, Sr. St. Dorothy. Addisonian Influence in American Periodicals, 1722-1805. St. John's Univ. (N.Y.), 1942. Thesis:
English. [Includes periodicals of Charleston, S.C.]

Lemann, Harriet M. The Literary Aspects of *DeBow's Review*.
Tulane Univ., 1953. Thesis: English.

Linneman, William R. American Life as Reflected in Illustrated
Humor Magazines: 1877-1900. Univ. of Illinois, 1960.
Dissertation: English. [Includes *Texas Siftings* and
The Arkansaw Traveler]

Long, Edgar. *Russell's Magazine* as an Expression of Antebellum
South Carolina Culture. Univ. of South Carolina, 1932.
Dissertation: English.

Luther, Jessie W. America's Literary Periodicals of the 1850's.
Univ. of Wisconsin, 1927. Thesis: History. [Includes
*DeBow's Review, The Southern Lady's Companion, Southern
Literary Messenger, Southern Quarterly Review*]

Lutwack, Leonard I. The Dynamics of Conservative Criticism:
Literary Criticism in American Magazines, 1880-1900. Ohio
State Univ., 1950. Dissertation: English. [Southern
magazines included]

Lyman, Susan E. Colonial Life and Learning as Reflected in
American Almanacs, 1639-1776. Columbia Univ., 1933. Thesis:
History. [Includes George Andrews, *The South Carolina
Almanak and Register* (Charleston, S.C., 1870); John T.N.
Windsor, *The South Carolina Almanak* (1755, 1758); and
Theophilus Wreg, *The Virginia Almanac* (Williamsburg, 1758)]

MacKenzie, Aline F.-F. *DeBow's Commercial Review*: Son Attitude
Envers la Culture Francaise (1846-1860). Tulane Univ.,
1934. Thesis: French.

Madison, Beryl. North Louisiana Life as Revealed in the Monroe
Bulletin, 1880-1884. Louisiana State Univ., 1937. Thesis:
English.

Maranto, Samuel P. A History of Dallas Newspapers. North Texas
State Univ., 1952. Thesis: History.

Marbut, Frederick B. The Washington Newspaper Corps in the
Nineteenth Century. Harvard Univ., 1947. Dissertation:
History.

Marino, Samuel J. The French-Refugee Newspapers and Periodicals
in the United States, 1789-1825. Univ. of Michigan, 1962.
Dissertation: Library Science. [Some based in New Orleans:
Le Moniteur de la Louisiane (1794) and *Le Courier de la
Louisiane*]

Martin, Lillian D. The History of the Galveston *News*. Univ. of Texas (Austin), 1929. Thesis: History. [Galveston, Texas]

Mason, Julian D., Jr. The Critical Reception of American Negro Authors in American Magazines, 1800-1885. Univ. of North Carolina (Chapel Hill), 1962. Dissertation: English. [Some Southern magazines considered; over 150 authors discussed, from 1800-1885]

Masterson, Clara E. A History of Knoxville Journalism. George Peabody College, 1933. Thesis: English. [Knoxville, Tennessee]

Mayfield, Edith E. A History of Journalism in Bowling Green, Ky. George Peabody College, 1926. Thesis: English.

McAdams, Ina M.O. A Study of the Mt. Vernon *Optic-Herald*, 1906-1931, and Its Community. Univ. of Texas (Austin), 1960. Thesis: Journalism. [Mt. Vernon, Texas]

McDonald, Florin L. Book Reviewing in the American Newspaper. Univ. of Missouri, 1927. Dissertation: English. [Includes Baltimore *Evening Sun*, Birmingham *News*, Birmingham *Post*, Charleston *Gazette*, Charlotte *Observer*, Dallas *Morning News*, Ft. Worth *Star-Telegram*, Jacksonville (Florida) *Times-Union*, Louisville *Courier-Journal*, Richmond *Times-Dispatch*, Tampa *Tribune*]

McGill, Allan C. One Hundred Years with a Newspaper, The San Antonio *Express*, 1865-1965. Trinity Univ. (Texas), 1965. Thesis: History. [San Antonio, Texas]

McIntyre, James P. *Russell's Magazine*: A Look at the Antebellum South. Univ. of Texas (Austin), 1964. Thesis: English.

McLean, Francis E.H. Periodicals Published in the South before 1880. Univ. of Virginia, 1928. Dissertation: English. [Includes *DeBow's Review*, *Southern Literary Messenger*, *Southern Magazine*, *Southern Review*]

McRedmond, Evelyn T. Criticism in *The Fugitive*. Auburn Univ., 1970. Thesis: English.

Meacham, Alice. Little Magazines in Twentieth Century America, 1912-1920. Columbia Univ., 1941. Thesis: English. [Includes *The Minaret* (Washington, D.C.), *The Poet and Philosopher* (Tampa, Fla.)]

Merritt, Mary L. A History of the Miami *Herald*. Univ. of Georgia, 1951. Thesis: Journalism. [Miami, Florida]

Mikkelson, Dwight L. *Kentucky Gazette*, 1787-1848: "The Herald of a Noisy World." Univ. of Kentucky, 1963. Dissertation: History. [Editors were Thomas Benning and John and Fielding Bradford; includes also Thomas Smith and his rival newspaper *Lexington Observer and Kentucky Reporter*]

Miles, Virginia. Kentucky Literary Magazines since 1900. Western Kentucky Univ., 1935. Thesis: English.

Miller, William R. Short Story Trends in the *Southern Literary Messenger*. Univ. of Maryland, 1964. Thesis: English.

Mims, Eleanor E. The Editors of the Edgefield *Advertiser*, Oldest Newspaper in South Carolina, 1836-1930. Univ. of South Carolina, 1930. Thesis: English.

Monie, John F. The Trend in the Use of Latin Words and Phrases in New Orleans Newspaper Editorials (1840-1925). Tulane Univ., 1942. Thesis: Education.

Montesi, Albert J. *The Southern Review* (1935-1942): A History
and Evaluation. Pennsylvania State Univ., 1955. Dissertation: English.

Montgomery, Reid H. Libel and South Carolina Newspapers. New
York Univ., 1955. Dissertation: Political Science.
[Begins at 1791]

Moore, Jack B. Native Elements in American Magazine Short
Fiction 1741-1800. Univ. of North Carolina (Chapel Hill),
1963. Dissertation: English. [The Indians, The Negro,
the Unreal, sentimental stories, didactic stories, humorous
stories, Realistic uses of Native materials. Eighty-three
magazines are examined, some Southern]

Moore, L.H. Poetry in *The Sunny South*, 1882. Emory Univ., 1959.
Thesis: English.

Moore, Maurice T. A Quantitative Study of Certain Southern
Journals. Columbia Univ., 1916. Thesis: Sociology.
[*Ledger Dispatch* and *Virginia Pilot*, both of Norfolk,
Virginia]

Morgan, Paul. Literary Trends as Indicated in Texas Newspapers,
1836-1846. Univ. of Texas (Austin), 1926. Thesis: English.
[In this study the author attempts to show evidence of
reading done by the citizens of the Republic and to determine
the extent of their interest in drama]

Morrison, Madge E. From Cattle Town to Agricultural Center--a
West Texas Frontier Newspaper Study, 1885-1900. Northwestern
Univ., 1937. Thesis: Journalism. [A chapter devoted to
the history of Abilene, Texas, before 1885]

Mott, Frank L. American Magazines, 1865-1880. Columbia Univ.,
1928. Dissertation: English.

Myers, Gibbs. Maryland Newspapers in the Eighteenth Century.
Univ. of Maryland, 1931. Thesis: History.

Nalle, Virginia. The History of the Austin [Texas] *Statesman*.
Univ. of Texas (Austin), 1935. Thesis: Journalism.

Nash, Janie K. The First Fifty Years of Texas Journalism.
Columbia Univ., 1929. Thesis: Journalism.

Nesbitt, Robert A. Texas Confederate Newspapers, 1861-65. Univ.
of Texas (Austin), 1936. Thesis: Journalism.

Nesbitt, William W. History of the San Antonio *Express*, 1865-1965.
Univ. of Texas (Austin), 1965. Thesis: Journalism. [San
Antonio, Texas]

Newsome, Parks S. An Historical and Editorial Study of the
Washington (Ga.) *News-Reporter*. Univ. of Georgia, 1966.
Thesis: Journalism.

Niemann, Lillian C. Representative Magazines of the Civil War
and Reconstruction Period. Univ. of Wisconsin, 1922.
Thesis: History. [Includes *DeBow's Review* and *Southern
Literary Messenger*]

Norse, Clifford C. *The Southern Cultivator*, 1843-1861. Florida
State Univ., 1969. Dissertation: History. [Farm journal
published in Augusta, Georgia]

Oliver, Saide M. The History and Development of the Atlanta
Daily World (the nation's only Negro daily newspaper).
Hampton Inst., 1942. Thesis: Education. [Atlanta, Georgia]

O'Neal, Orville W. The Development of Illustration in Newspapers.
Univ. of Texas (Austin), 1930. Thesis: Journalism.
[Some Southern newspapers are cited]

Osbon, Kenneth. The Influence of Colonial Newspapers in Awakening
National Consciousness. Northwestern Univ., 1930. Thesis:
Journalism. [Includes *Maryland Gazette*, *South Carolina
Gazette*, and *Virginia Gazette*]

Overall, John H. A Review and Critical Study of the *Fugitive*.
George Peabody College, 1928. Thesis: English.

Parker, Ralph H. The History of the Dallas *Morning News*. Univ.
of Texas (Austin), 1930. Thesis: History. [Dallas, Texas]

Parten, Ailese. The Dallas *News*. Columbia Univ., 1932. Thesis:
Journalism. [Dallas, Texas]

Pennekamp, A.H.C. The Treatment of the Negro in the Literary
Magazines of the South during the Reconstruction Period from
1865 to 1880. Univ. of North Carolina (Chapel Hill), 1936.
Thesis: English.

Perdue, Robert E. The Negro as Reflected in the Atlanta
Constitution, Atlanta *Intelligencer*, and Atlanta *Daily New Era*
from 1868-1880. Atlanta Univ., 1963. Thesis: History.
[Atlanta, Georgia]

Perkins, Mary K. A Critical Analysis of the Fiction and Poetry in
the *Southern Review*. Sam Houston State Univ., 1962. Thesis:
English.

Pfennig, Hazel T. Periodical Literary Criticism, 1800-1865:
A Study of the Book Reviews from 1800 to the Close of the
Civil War, dealing with the Successive Works of Irving,
Cooper, Bryant, Hawthorne, and Thoreau, Which Appeared in
American Publications within the Lifetime of the Individual
Authors. New York Univ., 1932. Dissertation: English.

Phillips, Stewart G. The Treatment of Literature in *DeBow's
Review*, 1846-1862. Auburn Univ., 1964. Thesis: English.

Pickering, David. *Texas Siftings* and Texas Journalism: 1881-1884.
Univ. of Texas (Austin), 1969. Thesis: Journalism.

Plunkett, Leland W. The History of the *Arkansas Gazette*. Univ.
of Texas (Austin), 1938. Thesis: Journalism.

Pockwinse, Florence B. A History of the *Fugitive* and the
Fugitives. Boston Univ., 1938. Thesis: English.

Price, David G. American Journalism in the Eighteenth Century as
Influenced by English Journalism. Univ. of Maryland, 1934.
Thesis: English. [Includes the *Georgia Gazette*, the
Maryland Gazette, and the *Virginia Gazette*]

Price, Frank J. The Country Press of Louisiana, 1911-1940.
Louisiana State Univ., 1940. Thesis: Journalism.

Pride, Armistead S. A Register and History of Negro Newspapers
in the United States, 1827-1950. Northwestern Univ., 1950.
Dissertation: English.

Prior, Granville T. A History of the Charleston *Mercury*, 1822-
1852. Harvard Univ., 1947. Dissertation: History.

Rabinovitz, Albert L. The Criticism of French Novels in American
Magazines, 1830-1860. Harvard Univ., 1941. Dissertation:
Romance Languages. [Includes *Southern Literary Messenger*,
Southern Quarterly Review, *Russell's Magazine*]

Ragsdale, Robert L. A History of the *Georgia Alumni Record*.
Univ. of Georgia, 1969. Thesis: Journalism.

Ramsey, Edmond F. Analysis of Public School Publicity in Certain Virginia Newspapers. Univ. of North Carolina (Chapel Hill), 1950. Thesis: Education.

Randolph, John. The Newspaper "colyum" in America. Vanderbilt Univ., 1934. Thesis: English. [T.H. Alexander]

Redden, Sr. M.M. The Gothic Fiction in the American Magazines, 1765-1800. Catholic Univ., 1940. Dissertation: English.

Reynolds, Donald E. Southern Newspapers in the Secession Crisis, 1860-1861. Tulane Univ., 1966. Dissertation: History.

Rhodes, Robert N. The Sensational Star: An Analysis of the Development of the *Tyler Star* Newspaper in Tyler, Texas, between 1938 and 1958. Univ. of Texas (Austin), 1970. Thesis: Journalism.

Rice, Elizabeth M. *The Oil and Gas Journal*: A Historical Stylistic Study of a Trade and Industrial Periodical. Univ. of Texas (Austin), 1948. Thesis: English.

Richards, H.G. Literary Criticism in the Old South: A Study of the *Southern Literary Messenger*. Univ. of Chicago, 1922. Thesis: English.

Richardson, Lyon N. A History of Early American Magazines, 1741-1789. Columbia Univ., 1931. Dissertation: English.

Rigler, Frank C. The History of the San Antonio *Express*. Univ. of Texas (Austin), 1932. Thesis: Journalism. [San Antonio, Texas]

Roadman, George H. The Life and Times of the Washington *Reporter*, 1808-1877. Univ. of Pittsburgh, 1957. Dissertation: History.

Robinson, Louise. *The Southern Review*; with a Bibliography of Its Contents. Univ. of Georgia, 1937. Thesis: English.

Rogers, Edward R. Southern Periodicals prior to 1860. Univ. of Virginia, 1902. Dissertation: English. [*DeBow's Review*, *Southern Literary Messenger*, *Southern Quarterly Review*, and *Southern Review*]

Rollins, Walter H. The American Negro Press: Content Analysis of Five Newspapers. Univ. of Minnesota, 1945. Thesis: Journalism. [Includes *Afro-American* (Baltimore, Md.) and Norfolk *Journal and Guide*]

Ross, Andrea L. A History of the Duke University Press and Its Three Humanities Journals: *American Literature*, *The Hispanic American Historical Review*, and *The South Atlantic Quarterly*. Univ. of North Carolina (Chapel Hill), 1967. Thesis: Library Science.

Roy, Addie M. History of *Telegraph and Texas Register*, 1835-1846. Univ. of Texas (Austin), 1931. Thesis: History.

Rozier, John W. A History of the Negro Press in Atlanta. Emory Univ., 1947. Thesis: Journalism.

Ryan, Frank W. *The Southern Quarterly Review*, 1842-1857: A Study in Thought and Opinion in the Old South. Univ. of North Carolina (Chapel Hill), 1956. Dissertation: History.

Sanford, Robert M. The Literary Elements in the Florida Newspapers of the Civil War Period. Univ. of Florida, 1936. Thesis: English.

Schaeffer, Drayton D. Theories Concerning American Fiction Expressed in Leading American Periodicals, 1870-1880. Southern Methodist Univ., 1941. Thesis: English. [G.W. Cable]

Shepard, Ruth W. A History of The New Orleans *Monthly Review*.
    Tulane Univ., 1951. Thesis: English.
Short, Lois. A History of American Women's Magazines of the
    General Type, 1880-1900. Columbia Univ., 1936. Thesis:
    History. [The bibliography lists ladies' magazines in the
    South from 1819-1860]
Semes, Robert L. The Virginia Press Looks at the New Deal, 1933-
    1937. Univ. of Virginia, 1968. Thesis: History.
Simms, Elizabeth L. A Study of the *Flag of the Union*, a
    Tuscaloosa, Alabama, Newspaper, 1833-42: Its Importance
    and Influence. Univ. of Alabama, 1950. Thesis: Journalism.
Singleton, Marvin K. A History of the *American Mercury* under the
    Editorship of Henry Mencken, 1924-1933. Duke Univ., 1960.
    Thesis: English.
Smith, Culver H. The Washington Press in the Jacksonian Period.
    Duke Univ., 1933. Dissertation: History. [Essentially a
    study in propaganda technique, including the relationship
    between printers and politicians]
Smith, Mary D. A Quantitative Study of Certain Southern Journals.
    Columbia Univ., 1916. Thesis: Sociology. [Includes
    Times Dispatch and *Richmond Virginian*, both of Richmond,
    Virginia]
Smith, William I. The *Picayune* as a Record of Literary History of
    the Early Victorian Period, 1837-1847. Tulane Univ., 1938.
    Thesis: English.
Spiers, Mabel A. The Earliest American Magazines. Colonial
    Culture as Reflected in the Magazines of 1741-1746.
    Columbia Univ., 1930. Thesis: English. [Includes *The South
    Carolina Gazette* (Charleston, S.C.), *The Virginia Gazette*
    (Williamsburg, Va.)]
Stewart, Guy H. History and Bibliography of Middle Tennessee
    Newspapers, 1799-1876. Univ. of Illinois, 1957. Disser-
    tation: History.
Stradley, Paul G. Some Phases of Newspaper Criticism of the
    Confederacy in North Carolina, South Carolina and Virginia.
    Duke Univ., 1932. Thesis: History.
Strauss, Gerald H. The *Double-Dealer* (1921-1926): A Little
    Magazine from the South. Columbia Univ., 1957. Thesis:
    English.
Stroupe, Henry S. History of the *Biblical Recorder*, 1835-1907,
    as Recorded in Its Files. Wake Forest Univ., 1937. Thesis:
    History.
_____. The Religious Press in the South Atlantic States, 1802-
    1865. Duke Univ., 1942. Dissertation: History.
Sumerlin, Claude W. A History of Southern Baptist State News-
    papers. Univ. of Missouri, 1968. Dissertation: Journalism.
Sutherland, Sallie B. Newspapers of Nashville, Tennessee, before
    1868. George Peabody College, 1933. Thesis: English.
Talbot, Margaret J. Reprints of German Literature in the German
    Newspapers of New Orleans. Louisiana State Univ., 1940.
    Thesis: German.
Talley, Banks C. A Study of Issues and Trends in Public School
    Education in North Carolina from 1925-1950 as Reflected in
    the *News and Observer* and The Raleigh *Times*. Univ. of

North Carolina (Chapel Hill), 1966. Dissertation: Education.

Terwilliger, William B. A History of Literary Periodicals in Baltimore. Univ. of Maryland, 1941. Dissertation: English.

Thomas, Forney E. Greenville Life as Revealed by the Greenville *Advocate*, 1867-1877. Auburn Univ., 1935. Thesis: History.

Thompson, Dan M. Current Trends in Texas High School Newspapers. Southern Methodist Univ., 1950. Thesis: Education.

Trimble, Carolyn C. A Study of the *Southern Review*, 1935-1942. Columbia Univ., 1949. Thesis: English.

Trippet, Mary M. A History of the *Southwest Review*: Toward an Understanding of Regionalism. Univ. of Illinois, 1966. Dissertation: English.

Turner, Alice L. A Study of the Contents of The *Sewanee Review* with Historical Introduction. George Peabody College, Dissertation: English.

Turner, Elizabeth L. *The Terrell Tribune*, 1916-1966. Univ. of Texas (Austin), 1966. Thesis: Journalism. [Terrell, Texas, newspaper]

Uhler, John E. Literary Taste and Culture in Baltimore: A Study of the Periodical Literature of Baltimore from 1815 to 1833. Johns Hopkins Univ., 1927. Dissertation: English.

Vaughan, Voyle. A History of the Journalism of the South Plains. Texas Tech Univ., 1937. Thesis: History.

Vineyard, Catherine M. *The Arkansas Traveler*. Univ. of Texas (Austin), 1942. Thesis: English.

Vogel, Joe B. History of Caldwell County [Texas] Newspapers. Univ. of Texas (Austin), 1948. Thesis: Journalism.

Wardlaw, Harold C. A Gatekeeper Analysis of Minority and Majority Newspapers: Atlanta *Inquirer*, Atlanta *World*, and Atlanta *Constitution*. Univ. of Georgia, 1969. Thesis: Journalism. [Atlanta, Georgia]

Washington, Alexander W. Growth and Influence of the Negro Press in the United States with Emphasis on the Period since 1921. Ohio State Univ., 1947. Thesis: Journalism. [Atlanta *Daily World*]

Webb, Vina W. A Study of the Negro Magazine: With Special Reference to Its Literary Value. North Carolina College (Durham), 1946. Thesis: English. [Includes *Phylon*, *Southern Workman*, *Southland*, *Stylus*, *Voice of the Negro*]

Webster, Robert L. Publicity Methods in Weekly Newspapers: A Study Based upon Conditions found in Weekly Newspapers of North Carolina. Columbia Univ., 1929. Thesis: Journalism.

Weems, John E. A Study of Newspapers of the Texas Cattle Kingdom, 1866-1885. Univ. of Texas (Austin), 1949. Thesis: Journalism.

Wendt, Lloyd M. A Study of the Colonial Newspaper as a Force in the American Revolution. Northwestern Univ., 1934. Thesis: Journalism. [Studies in the *Cape Fear Mercury*, *Georgia Gazette*, *Maryland Gazette*, *North Carolina Gazette*, *South Carolina Gazette*, *Virginia Gazette*]

Westmoreland, Reginald C. The Dallas *Times-Herald*, 1879-1961. Univ. of Missouri, 1961. Dissertation: Journalism.

Wheeler, Joseph T. The Maryland Press, 1777-1790. Brown Univ.,
    1936. Thesis: History.
Wilkerson, Marcus M. History and Development of the Baton Rouge
    Newspapers. Louisiana State Univ., 1926. Thesis: Journalism.
Williford, Lyde G. Provincial Literary Magazines in America, 1915
    to 1932. Southern Methodist Univ., 1932. Thesis: English.
    [Includes *The Reviewer*, *Sewanee Review*, *Southwest Review*,
    Texas Review, *Virginia Quarterly Review*]
Woodbury, Ruth G. Newspapers and Public Opinion in Civil War
    Memphis. Univ. of Mississippi, 1947. Thesis: History.
Young, Laura N. Southern Literary Magazines, 1865-1887: With
    Special Reference to Literary Criticism. Duke Univ., 1940.
    Thesis: English.

ORIGINAL WORKS WRITTEN
AT SOUTHERN UNIVERSITIES

Adams, Thomas E. Two Stories: "Sled" and "Cloister." Univ. of
    Florida, 1967. Thesis: English.
Babiak, Shirley. *Ring True* (Original Short Stories). Univ. of
    Louisville, 1967. Thesis: English.
Banks, Carolyn. *Worlds, a Collection of Short Stories*. Univ. of
    Maryland, 1969. Thesis: English.
Barthel, Thomas H. *A Saturday at the Lake and Other Stories*.
    Univ. of North Carolina (Greensboro), 1969. Thesis: English.
Baxter, Delmar. *South: A Play*. Univ. of Tennessee, 1963. Thesis:
    English.
Brown, Axson E. *Five Short Stories*. Vanderbilt Univ., 1961.
    Thesis: English.
Buffinton, Robert R. *Kynon: A Short Novel*. Vanderbilt Univ.,
    1958. Thesis: English.
Carter, Melinda. *The Ritual and Other Stories*. Univ. of North
    Carolina (Greensboro), 1969. Thesis: English.
Chieffet, George. *Three Stories*. Univ. of North Carolina
    (Greensboro), 1969. Thesis: English.
Clarkson, Sheelah. *Lady with Unicorn*. Univ. of North Carolina
    (Greensboro), 1969. Thesis: English.
Cobb, William S. *The Stone Soldier and Other Stories*. Vanderbilt
    Univ., 1963. Thesis: English.
Der, Anne W. *Root of Evil, A Story*. Univ. of Florida, 1964.
    Thesis: English.
Dodson, Mayhew W. III. *The Hydra's Blood* (Three Related Stories).
    Univ. of Florida, 1955. Thesis: English.
Douglas, Otis W. *Four Stories*. Auburn Univ., 1968. Thesis:
    English.
Easterly, Helen A. *The Lion in the Garden and Other Stories*.
    Univ. of Florida, 1964. Thesis: English.
Edge, Loretta. *Four Stories* and *Wise Blood*. Univ. of North
    Carolina (Chapel Hill), 1968. Thesis: English. [Four
    original stories: "The Train," "The Peeler," "The Heart
    of the Park," and "Enoch and the Gorilla"]
Flick, Robert G. *The Long Return and Other Stories: A Trilogy*.
    Univ. of Florida, 1954. Thesis: English.

Ford, Jesse H., Jr. *The Thundering Tide* (A Novel). Univ. of Florida, 1955. Thesis: English.

Gibson, Jane F. *Guest at-the Wedding and Other Stories.* Vanderbilt Univ., 1964. Thesis: English.

Glasser, William A. *Short Stories.* Univ. of Florida, 1959. Thesis: English.

Goins, Melinda. *The Crimmons Place and Other Stories.* Univ. of North Carolina (Greensboro), 1969. Thesis: English.

Grey, Robert W. *Wreath of Wax.* Univ. of Virginia, 1969. Thesis: English.

Haley, Michael C. *The Fifth Sunday of the Land and Other Stories.* Univ. of Alabama, 1969. Thesis: English.

Hallam, George W. *The Fortress and Other Stories.* Univ. of Florida, 1954. Thesis: English.

Hannold, Francis H., Jr. *At the End of Adam and Other Stories.* Univ. of Florida, 1964. Thesis: English.

Haubold, Clive E. The Life and Times of Floto, Texas: Three Plays. Univ. of Texas (Austin), 1968. Dissertation: Theater. [Original plays set in Floto]

Himber, Alan B. *Discobolus and Other Stories.* Univ. of Florida, 1964. Thesis: English.

Hopper, William O. *Sons of Eden.* Univ. of Alabama, 1954. Thesis: English.

Hudgins, Jewel E. *The Glass Dome* (Novel). Univ. of Alabama, 1953. Thesis: English.

Koch, Claude F. *The Hour of Nones: A Novel.* Univ. of Florida, 1955. Thesis: English.

Landiss, Thomas H. *Four Short Stories.* Vanderbilt Univ., 1959. Thesis: English.

Leaman, Warren C. *Time of the First Rains and Other Stories.* Vanderbilt Univ., 1951. Thesis: English.

Lebovitz, Richard. *Poems, 1967-1968.* Univ. of North Carolina (Greensboro), 1969. Thesis: English.

Lentz, Perry C. *White and Purple: Four Short Stories.* Vanderbilt Univ., 1967. Thesis: English.

Lewis, Donald A. *Strange Capers* (A Novella). Univ. of Florida, 1958. Thesis: English.

Miller, Clyde J. *The Gentle Season: A Novella.* Univ. of Florida, 1952. Thesis: English.

Miller, Heather R. *Delphi: A Collection of Stories.* Univ. of North Carolina (Greensboro), 1969. Thesis: English.

Mitchell, Grant. *On Long Winter Nights and Other Stories.* Univ. of Florida, 1961. Thesis: English.

Morefield, John D. *The Bear in the Street and Other Stories.* Univ. of Florida, 1964. Thesis: English.

Morgan, Robert. *Zirconia Poems.* Univ. of North Carolina (Greensboro), 1969. Thesis: English.

Parra, Albert. *Edge of the Wind.* Univ. of Florida, 1959. Thesis: English.

Peters, Patricia. *Thinking on Sidewalks.* Univ. of North Carolina (Greensboro), 1969. Thesis: English.

Porter, Richard N. *Into a Far Country: Sections of a Novel.* Vanderbilt Univ., 1958. Thesis: English.

Reiser, Gayla R. *Six Stories for Children Adapted from Animal Folklore of the Southwest*. Texas Christian Univ., 1969. Thesis: English. [Original works]

Rose, Charles. *The Lost Ceremony*. Univ. of Florida, 1954. Thesis: English.

Rountree, Thomas J. *Light on the Land*. Univ. of Alabama, 1952. Thesis: English.

Shreve, Susan R. *Mary Had a Baby*. (A Short Work of Fiction). Univ. of Virginia, 1969. Thesis: English.

Shumsky, Allison D. *The World Between* (Four Short Stories). Univ. of Florida, 1955. Thesis: English.

Snyder, Mary E. *Five Original Short Stories*. Vanderbilt Univ., 1964. Thesis: English.

Stripling, Kathryn. *Windows*. Univ. of North Carolina (Greensboro), 1969. Thesis: English.

Stroud, Oxford S. *The Brown Arm of Current*. Auburn Univ., 1953. Thesis: English.

Taylor, Charles D. *Dimaggio Winter and Other Stories*. Univ. of Florida, 1964. Thesis: English.

Tinkler, John D. *A Liver-and-White Pointer and Other Stories*. Univ. of Florida, 1957. Thesis: English.

von Kleist, Carl E. Three Modern Plays on Classical Themes. Univ. of Texas (Austin), 1969. Dissertation: Theater. [Two are *John Crow* and *Tennessee Boy*]

Waters, John P. *A Far Away Land and Other Stories*. Univ. of Florida, 1962. Thesis: English.

Wells, Glenn L., Jr. *You Can't Cross There*. Univ. of Alabama, 1969. Thesis: English.

Whitehead, James T. *The Growth: Sections of a Novel*. Vanderbilt Univ., 1960. Thesis: English.

ACKNOWLEDGMENTS

In addition to those already acknowledged in the "Introduction," we express our appreciation to the following individuals who assisted us in the preparation of this bibliography. All of these must indeed be considered co-compilers.

Doris Allen, California State College
Frank T. Allen, University of Iowa
Aimee H. Alexander, Eastern Kentucky University
Ruth Alford, University of Delaware
Elizabeth N. Anderson, Dominican College
Charles R. Andrews, Case Western Reserve University
Claire L. Andrews, State University College (Brockport)
Christine I. Andrew, Yale University
Alice Angelo, Saint Joseph College
Jean Aroeste, University of California (L.A.)
Nancy Artz, Oakland University
Robert Balay, Yale University
Joyce Ball, University of Nevada (Reno)
Robert J. Bassett, University of Tennessee
Sarah M. Bauer, Kent State University
Barbara A. Beall, University of Maryland
Thomas C. Bechtle, Fordham University
Susan Beklares, University of Illinois at Urbana-Champaign
Floyd H. Bennett, Sam Houston State University
Leonidas Betts, North Carolina State University
Leona P. Berry, Eastern Michigan University
Barbara Blebush, Sonoma State College
Mary Bires, Saint Louis University

Hugh Black, Southwest Texas State University
Muriel Ballard Bliss, Boston College
Ethel Blumann, College of the Holy Name
Bette Bohler, Northwestern University
Beverly Boyer, University of South Carolina
J. Edward Briggs, SUNY (Binghamton)
Louis Budd, University of North Carolina (Chapel Hill)
Julia Bugge, Emory University
Mary Ann Burns, West Chester State College
Marc T. Campbell, Fort Hays Kansas State College
Robert Canary, University of Wisconsin (Kenosha)
Helen W. Carnine, William Patterson College of New Jersey
Myrtle L. Carpenter, Wisconsin State University
Denise M. Carrenthers, North Texas State University
L. Moffitt Cecil, Texas Christian University
Diane Cranford, University of North Dakota
Myrtle M. Carroll, Florida State University
Helen B. Caver, Jacksonville State University
Mary Beth Chamberlin, Texas Woman's University
Richard Chamberlin, Indiana University of Pennsylvania
March Chambers, University of Rochester
Thomas W. Chandler, Oglethorpe University
Shirley L. Chang, Pennsylvania State University

Terry A. Churchill, University of California (L.A.)
Antoinette Ciolli, Brooklyn College
Georgia Clark, University of Arkansas
Howard Clinton, University of Kansas
Ruth Corrigan, Carnegie-Mellon University
Allan Covici, University of California (Berkeley)
Duane Crawford, University of North Dakota
Harvey Cromwell, Mississippi State College for Women
J. Larley Jameson, Memphis State University
Leola Miller Davis, Southeast Missouri State College
Kee De Boer, Colorado College
John Deardorff, Shippensburg State College
Eunice Dennis, East Texas State University
Elizabeth A. Devine, Marquette University
Eleanor R. Devlin, Ohio State University
Leon J. Divel, Kansas State College of Pittsburg
Ann M. Donnelly, Saint John's University
Joan Downing, Idaho State University
Joseph Drazan, University of Alaska
Herbert W. Drummond, Sacramento State College
Kenneth W. Duckett, Southern Illinois University
Jacqueline Dumser, C.W. Post College
Charles L. Dwyer, Sam Houston State University
S. Dyson, Louisiana Tech University
Hines Edwards, West Georgia College
J. Ehresmann, SUC (Brockport)
Suzanne Fergreson, University of California (Santa Barbara)
Margaret Flores, University of Maryland

Tom E. Francis, The University of Wyoming
Virginia Francis, The University of Florida
Nancy R. Frazier, University of North Carolina (Chapel Hill)
Thomas Frazier, Western Washington State College
Mrs. Paula Frank, Hofstra University
Pauline Franks, The University of Akron
Joyce A. Garber, University of Virginia
Elizabeth A. Gatlin, Hardin-Simmons University
Richard Gercken, University of Montana
Sister Mary Giles, Barry College
Eleanor E. Goehring, University of Tennessee
Sara Lou Goff, University of Nebraska at Omaha
Barbara Goldberg, SUNY (Buffalo)
Arthur Goldsmith, Jr., Austin Peay State University
Sandra Golob, Loyola University (Chicago)
Martha L. Goold, Kent State University
Yvonne E. Greear, The University of Texas at El Paso
Diane Green, Northeast Louisiana University
Louise Green, Villanova University
Alice E. Gregg, Loma Linda University
Mary L. Gregory, Florida State University
B. Gutekunst, Catholic University
Norma Halmes, Brooklyn College
Edith Baker Hampel, Temple University
Blaine H. Hall, Brigham Young University
Pattie B. Hall, University of North Carolina (Chapel Hill)
Linda A. Harmon, University of Massachusetts

[396]

Robert L. Harned, University
of Pennsylvania
Larry E. Harrelson, The
University of Oklahoma
C. Harris, Texas A & M
University
Betty Hartbank, Eastern
Illinois University
Judy B. Harvey, University
of California (Riverside)
Melba S. Harvill, Midwestern
University
Lois Harzfeld, University of
California (Davis)
M. Hellman. Montclair State
College
Ruth V. Hewleth. Tufts
University
John T. Hiers, Valdosta State
College
Pauline L. Higgins, Texas
Woman's University
Lutie Higley, University of
Arizona
Allie A. Hodgin, Appalachian
State University
Mrs. Ruth P. Hoffman, Fitchburg
State College
Harley P. Holden, Harvard
University
B. Hoskin, University of
Santa Clara
J.B. Howell, Mississippi
College
John Howell, Southern Illinois
University (Carbondale)
Elke Hueter, Radford College
Lawrence Huff, Georgia Southern
College
Ann Hulett, Adelphi University
H.E. Hutchinson, The University
of South Florida
Sabina Jacobson, George
Washington University
Olive C. James, CUNY (Flushing)
Betty M. Jarboe, Indiana
University (Bloomington)
Barbara Jones, University of
Kansas
J. Frank Jones, University of
the Pacific
M.A. Joseph, University of
Alabama (Huntsville)
James H. Justus, Indiana
University (Bloomington)

Margaret Kahn, University of
California (Irving)
Alexander Karanikas, University
of Illinois at Chicago
Circle
Margaret J. Keefe, University
of Rhode Island
Charles H. Kemp, Pacific
University
Edith Keys, East Tennessee
State University
Eloise P. Kibbie, Central
Missouri State College
Floreine Kibler, Northeast
Missouri State College
William J. Kimball, Converse
College
Karen Kinney, Columbia
University
Robert Klein, Lorcas College
Darbien G. Klug, South Dakota
State University
W. Klundt, United States
International University
Donald M. Koslow, University
of Massachusetts
Katherine G. Kraft, Harvard
University
S.F. Krauss, Ohio University
Mrs. E.H. Krueger, John Carroll
University
Nobel S. La Fond, Western New
Mexico University
Zanier Lane, University of
New Mexico
Charles A. Lawler, Southern
Illinois University
(Carbondale)
Roger Leachman, University of
Virginia
Frank H. Leayall, Baylor
University
James Lee, North Texas State
University
Max Legel, The University of
South Dakota
Gertrude Lemon, Kansas State
Teachers College
Mary G. Lewis, Stetson
University
Dennis Lien, University of
Minnesota
Jane M. Lopes, Simmons College
Daniel Lorcrie, Brandeis
University

Pattie B. McIntyre, University of North Carolina (Chapel Hill)
Wayne McLaurin, Arkansas State University
Ethel Madden, Seton Hall University
Ronald J. Mahoney, Fresno State College
Susan O. Marcell, University of Virginia
Margaretta Martin, Emory University
Norman Martin, Whitewater University
Norris K. Maxwell, University of New Mexico
Thelma Mielke, Long Island University (Brooklyn Center)
M.R. Middleton, Johns Hopkins University
Cora Miller, University of Portland
Michael M. Miller, North Dakota State University
Edna M. Milliken, Murray State University
F. Hunter Miracle, The University of Tulsa
Ann E. Mitchell, University of Tennessee
Alouisia Moore, Lamar University
Mary Frances Morris, East Carolina University
Ann M. Mumper, Bucknell University
Robert Mulligan, Rutgers University
Edward E. Narkis, University of Louisville
Janet Nelson, Princeton University
O. Gene Norman, Indiana State University
Harold Otness, Southern Oregon College
Myla T. Parsons, Middle Tennessee State University
William Peden, University of Missouri
Claude Petrie, Hunter College

Richard H. Perrine, Rice University
Claire A. Phipps, Chico State College
Mary S. Pierce, University of Redlands
Dorothy E. Pittman, University of Georgia
Marietta Plank, Georgetown University
Henry A. Pockmann, University of Wisconsin
Angela Poulos, Bowling Green State University
Sister Lora Ann Quinonez, Our Lady of the Lake College
Joyce M. Quinsey, Humboldt State College
Pauline L. Ralson, Syracuse University
Barbara Randle, Case Western Reserve University
Will Rebentisch, Edinboro State College
Robert Richardson, University of Denver
Mary E. Riley, Lehigh University
Mary Rivard, St. Michael's College
Frank W. Robert, Joint University Libraries (Nashville)
W.R. Robinson, University of Florida
James E. Rocks, Tulane University
Elizabeth H. Rodgers, University of Montevallo
J. Roihroch, Middlebury College
Joe Ross, University of Alabama in Birmingham
James Rothenberger, University of California (Riverside)
E. Rubacha, Wesleyan University
Virginia Ruskell, West Georgia College
John Saeger, Occidental College
Patricia Salomon, Bowling Green State University
H. Kay Schmidt, The American University
Sam Schrag, Wichita State University
Mabel A. Schulte, Pepperdine College

Elizabeth Schumann, Brown
University
L. Severns, Kearney State
College
John H. Sharpe, Chico State
College
Edith Shaw, Eastern Washington
State College
Eugene P. Sheesh, Columbia
University
Janet E. Sheets, Joint Univer-
sity Libraries
(Nashville)
Gary Shearer, Loma Linda
University
Douglas H. Shepard, SUNY
(Fredonia)
Allen Shepherd, University
of Vermont
Johannah Sherrer, University
of Dayton
Leta C. Showalter, Madison
College
Lewis P. Simpson, Louisiana
State University
Robert B. Sinclair, Miami
University
Mattilee N. Skelton, University
of Missouri (K.C.)
Robert M. Slabey, University
of Notre Dame
Carolyn Smith, Johns Hopkins
University
Roberta K. Smith, The Univer-
sity of Connecticut
Leslie Sorn, Illinois Institute
of Technology
W.J. Sowder, Longwood College
Beverly Sperring, University
of Chicago
Caroline T. Spicer, Cornell
University
Polly Spital, La Verne College
Charles L. Stahl, Northern
Arizona University
Mark Stauter, Duke University
Diane Sternfels, California
State College
Joan Stewart, Mount St. Mary's
College
Jocelyn E. Stevens, North
Carolina Central Univer-
sity
Donald O. Stone, Florida
State University

Margaret Stone, Morehead
State University
Robert B. Stone, University
of New Hampshire
Erica Strasser, Duquesne
University
William A. Sutton, Ball State
University
The Rev. J.P. Talmage, Marquette
University
Mrs. William Tate, University
of Georgia
Henry Taylor, University of
Utah
Howard Teeple, Chicago City
College
Jeainine Thubauville, University
of Wisconsin
Elaine Tieman, McNeese State
University
Mary Louise Tipton, Southern
Methodist University
Warren I. Titus, George Peabody
College
Kate Theurer, University of
Utah
Patricia Todd, Sul Ross State
University
Carolee Tolotti, Boston
University
Alice M. Tonra, Boston Univer-
sity
Ileana Torruellas, University
of Puerto Rico
W. Troust, Wagner College
Timothy Tung, City College of
New York
Margaret Umberger, State
University College
(Oneonta)
Doris Viacova, Iona College
Catherine V. vonSchon, SUNY
(Stony Brook)
Roberta B. Vore, Highlands
University
Ben M. Vorpahl, University of
California (L.A.)
Judith S. Wainwright, University
of San Francisco
Mary Jo Walker, Eastern New
Mexico University
Ruth Walling, Emory University
Leland E. Warren, College of
William and Mary

James W. Webb, University of Mississippi
Kenneth Weeks, Connecticut College
Glenn Whaley, California State Polytechnic University
Emilie C. White, Mississippi State University
Janet F. White, The University of Michigan
Mrs. Paul Whiteley, Millersville State College
Helene Whitson, San Francisco State College
Mrs. Janice Wieckhorst, University of Northern Iowa
Virginia Lee Wilder, Atlanta University

Mrs. Avery Williams, Roosevelt University
Doris Williams, Wayne State University
Charlene Wilson, Whittier College
Henry W. Wingate, Jr., Western Carolina University
Lillian Wingertsalm, St. Bonaventure University
Cynthia Wise, Florida State University
Marion H. Withington, Clemson University
Marvin E. Wiggins, Brigham Young University
Mrs. W. Yates, Iowa State University

We also want to express our appreciation to Mr. Leonard Rawls, a student assistant at The University of Alabama, and to the following student assistants at Auburn University, all of whom worked long hours in recording and editing titles: Katherine Benson, Carolyn Howell, Kalyn H. Johnson, Douglas Logan, Linda McKee, Glenda Parr, Patricia Richardson, Bernie Steele, Brenda W. Thomas, Elizabeth Till, and Carol C. Weems.

For typing of the original manuscript we owe a special thanks to Mrs. Shirley Dixon, Mrs. Bonnie Foster, Mrs. Charlene Johnson, and Mrs. Norma McDougal, all of Texas Tech University.

Finally, in addition, we wish to express our gratitude to Ms. Jan Wilson, whose help in preparing this manuscript was made possible by a grant from the College of Arts and Sciences of The University of Alabama. To Deans Douglas Jones, Robert Garner and George Wolfe we are also indebted.

[400]